American Multiculturalism
and the Anti-Discrimination Regime

Other Books of Interest from St. Augustine's Press

Roger Kimball, *The Fortunes of Permanence: Culture and Anarchy in an Age of Amnesia*

Chilton Williamson, Jr., *The End of Liberalism*

Zbigniew Janowski, *Homo Americanus: The Rise of Totalitarian Democracy in America*

Daniel J. Mahoney, *Recovering Politics, Civilization, and the Soul: Essays on Pierre Manent and Roger Scruton*

David Lowenthal, *Slave State: Rereading Orwell's 1984*

Richard Ferrier, *The Declaration of America: Our Principles in Thought and Action*

Ellis Sandoz, *Give Me Liberty: Studies in Constitutionalism and Philosophy*

Rémi Brague, *Moderately Modern*

Marvin R. O'Connell, *Telling Stories that Matter: Memoirs and Essays*

Josef Pieper, *Traditional Truth, Poetry, Sacrament: For My Mother, on her 70th Birthday*

Anne Drury Hall, *Where the Muses Still Haunt: The Second Reading*

Alexandre Kojève, *The Concept, Time, and Discourse*

Gene Fendt, *Camus' Plague: Myth for Our World*

Roger Scruton, *The Politics of Culture and Other Essays*

Roger Scruton, *The Meaning of Conservatism: Revised 3rd Edition*

Roger Scruton, *An Intelligent Person's Guide to Modern Culture*

Allen Mendenhall, *Shouting Softly: Lines on Law, Literature, and Culture*

Klaus Vondung, *Paths to Salvation: The National Socialist Religion*

Stanley Rosen, *The Language of Love: An Interpretation of Plato's Phaedrus*

Will Morrisey, *Shakespeare's Politic Comedy*

Will Morrissey, *Herman Melville's Ship of State*

Winston Churchill, *The River War*

American Multiculturalism and the Anti-Discrimination Regime

The Challenge to Liberal Pluralism

THOMAS F. POWERS

ST. AUGUSTINE'S PRESS
South Bend, Indiana

Copyright © 2023 by Thomas F. Powers

All rights reserved. No part of this book may be reproduced, stored in a retrieval system, or transmitted, in any form or by any means, electronic, mechanical, photocopying, recording, or otherwise, without the prior permission of St. Augustine's Press.

Manufactured in the United States of America.

1 2 3 4 5 6   28 27 26 25 24 23

Library of Congress Control Number: 2023936523

Paperback ISBN: 978-1-58731-045-4
Ebook ISBN: 978-1-58731-047-8

∞ The paper used in this publication meets the minimum requirements of the American National Standard for Information Sciences – Permanence of Paper for Printed Materials, ANSI Z39.48-1984.

St. Augustine's Press
www.staugustine.net

To my mother, Jo Marie Powers,
and the memory of my father, Thomas F. Powers

We are engaged in a great adventure—as great as that of the last century, when our fathers marched to the western frontier. Our frontier today is of human beings, not of land.
– Lyndon Johnson, "Message on the 1966 Civil Rights Bill"

TABLE OF CONTENTS

Acknowledgements xi

Chapter 1. Introduction 1
Anti-Discrimination Regime? 3
Multiculturalism as Teacher of the Anti-Discrimination Regime 6
Multicultural Education: The Importance of James A. Banks 10
Postmodernism, Handmaiden of the Civil Rights Revolution 13
Remedying the Neglect of Multicultural Education 15
Liberal Pluralism as Touchstone: Is Anti-Discrimination Liberal? 16
A Political Interpretation 20

Part 1. Political History: The Anti-Discrimination Revolution and the Development of American Multicultural Education

Chapter 2. The Failure of Liberalism in the Case of Race and the Necessity of the Anti-Discrimination Revolution 25
The Failure of Liberalism in the Case of Race 26
Early Liberal Limits to Reform 30
The Anti-Discrimination Revolution 32
From Revolution to Regime 36

Chapter 3. Anti-Discrimination Regime, Anti-Discrimination Law 39
Law Lesson 1: Title VII, the Expanding Center of Anti-Discrimination Law 41
Law Lesson 2: Three Ways to Gauge the Scope and Scale of Anti-Discrimination Law 44
The Spirit of Anti-Discrimination Law 48

Penetrating Aims: Regulating Society and Individual Behavior,
    Speech, and Thought 49
Privatized Enforcement, Citizen-Enforcers 53
Corrective Firing and Cancel Culture:
    The Hidden Fist of Anti-Discrimination Law 55
A New Civic Sensibility:
    Blurring the Line Between Civil and Criminal Law 58
Affirmative Action (Or: Disparity-as-Discrimination) 60
A Note on Constitutional Law 63
Anti-Discrimination Politics is Architectonic:
    What Multiculturalism Can Teach Us 65

Chapter 4. A Brief (Political) History of
American Multicultural Education 68
From Cultural Deprivation to Cultural Difference
    to Multiculturalism 71
Multicultural Education as Civil Rights Policy: Federal Efforts 75
Multicultural Education Policy in the States 79
Institutionalizing Civil Rights Reform
    in the Domain of Teacher Education 82
Why Multiculturalism's Political History Matters 84

Part 2. The Idea of Multiculturalism in America

Chapter 5. The "Multicultural Ideology" of James A. Banks 89
Why Banks? 92
"Change the Center" 95
The Fight Against Discrimination: Generalizing the Particular 99
Civic Education as Political Pedagogy 103
The "Psychological Project" 111
Moral Education 116
The Substance of the New Morality 120
Multiculturalism as a Form of Pluralism 128

The Unanswered Question:
    Multiculturalism and the Liberal Tradition 131

Chapter 6. Postmodernist Multiculturalism:
    When Theory and Politics Radicalize One Another **136**

The Merging of Politics and Theory in the late 1980s and early 1990s:
    The "Nietzscheanization of the Left," Continued 141
What Is Postmodernist Multiculturalism? 143
Politics at the Center 148
Defined By Contradiction 151
Radical Theory Unbound 152
Politics Radicalized by Theory and Vice Versa:
    "Critical Rather Than Merely Good Citizens" 154
Everything Exaggerated and Negative 158
The Question Concerning "Moral Technology" 162
"Oppositional Utopia"—or Doubt and Despair? 167
"Naming Whiteness": Postmodernist Multiculturalism's
    Contribution to Civil Rights Discourse 169
Benefits of the Merger—and Costs 176

Part 3. The Challenge to Liberal Pluralism

Chapter 7. The Liberal Pluralist Tradition 185
The Structure of Liberal Pluralism 186
The Outline of Liberal Pluralism in Locke's
    Letter Concerning Toleration 188
The Liberal Pluralist Tradition in America:
    Variations on Essential Themes 194
Limited Government and "Political Liberalism" 202
A Worldly Wise Pluralism? 205

Chapter 8. The New Pluralism and the Old 209
Multiculturalism and Liberal Pluralism Compared 211

Tamed Groups, Politicized Groups 218
Where Multiculturalism and Liberal Pluralism Agree:
      Anti-Assimilation, Diversity, and Epistemology 225
Return of the Political 229

Chapter 9. Politics and Morality: A Task for Political Science 233
Legislating Morality 236
A Spirited Morality 238
A Task for Political Science 242

Chapter 10. The New Morality and the Old 249
Identity versus Liberty 250
Respect versus Toleration 254
Equity and the New Equalities 255
Inclusion and Group Representation 259
Recognition versus Interest 263
A Politics of Justice and Injustice: The Spirit of the New Morality 265
When Injustice Is the Center 268
The New Morality and the Old 272

Chapter 11. The New American Dilemma:
      Anti-Discrimination Regime and Citizen 275
Underestimating the Anti-Discrimination Revolution 276
Moral Reform, Political Unease 279
Anti-Discrimination and the Liberal Tradition 285
Regime and Citizen: The Case for Old-Fashioned Political Science 290

Bibliography 297

Endnotes 376

Index 443

ACKNOWLEDGEMENTS

I am happy to have this occasion to acknowledge my gratitude to several people. In college I had the amazing good fortune to take a year-long freshman great books seminar with Amy and Leon Kass. I also had several other outstanding teachers as an undergraduate and as a graduate student: Allan Bloom, Clifford Orwin, Thomas Pangle, and Nathan Tarcov. I am grateful to them for their instruction and example. Another excellent teacher was in addition my doctoral thesis supervisor, H. Donald Forbes. I learned much from him about political theory and social science and about the subject matter of this book.

I am grateful also for reactions and recommendations concerning this project early on from my University of Toronto professors, to include especially Robert Vipond, and for suggestions from James A. Banks, Nathan Glazer, and Philip Gleason. In the (many) years since this was my dissertation, several people have read and commented upon or otherwise encouraged works that wound up in one form or another in this book, above all Tim Burns. I express my thanks also to Alex Aceto, Gabriel Bartlett, Paul Carrese, John and Eve Grace, Mahindan Kanakaratnam, Steve Kautz, Michael Kochin, Alan Levine, Mark Lutz, Chris Lynch, Dan Magurshak, Daniel Mahoney, Josh Martin, Arthur Milikh, Peter Nichols, Michael and Linda Rabieh, Paul Rasmussen, Nicholas Ravnikar, David Schaefer, Paul Ulrich, Ron Weed, Ken Weinstein, Thomas West, Adam Wolfson, Zabi Yaqeen, and Scott Yenor. Gabriel Bartlett was in addition a helpful and careful guide through the final stage and, at St. Augustine's Press, I thank Katie Godfrey for shepherding the project to completion. At Carthage College I wish also to express my gratitude to Judith Schaumberg.

The dedication acknowledges my great debt to my parents, Thomas F. and Jo Marie Powers, idealistic White Midwestern liberals who, before 1964, integrated two hotels in the South and went on to start a hotel and restaurant management program at HBCU Morris Brown College in Atlanta (the latter with the help of a federal grant they secured).

Finally, I am very happy to thank my wife, Katherine, for her loving assistance, patience, and encouragement.

Chapter 1
INTRODUCTION

Democracy is being reshaped—in the United States and across the globe—by the commitment to fighting discrimination. This revolution was planned by no one and its manifold expansions and disruptions were not foreseen or even imagined by those present at the beginning (for the sake of convenience, let us say in 1964). One need only mention the pressing causes of just the past few years to demonstrate the striking character of the claims that civil rights (anti-discrimination) politics is making upon our world: critical race theory, the 1619 Project, gay marriage, transgender rights, corrective firing, cancel culture, woke capitalism, the Black Lives Matter movement, and heightened attention to "Whiteness" (privilege, supremacy, fragility). How much is at stake—how broad a transformation is under way—is indicated above all by the myriad challenges to the *liberal democratic* tradition in America posed by these and other developments.

We cannot but notice the changes under way, but neither can we claim to understand them very well. The revolution and its many secondary and tertiary effects were not only unplanned but seem today to continue to unfold unpredictably under powerful but not immediately intelligible imperatives. One could say that there is an obvious and simple *idea* here: democracy has awakened to the injustices of discrimination and to the expansive and formidable task of rectifying them. We sense that there is a kind of "successor ideology" at work among us, but we do not name it in the simplest terms available to us (anti-discrimination democracy, anti-discrimination regime) in part because there is no Karl Marx or John Rawls of the anti-discrimination revolution who, by championing and theorizing it, helps us to understand it.[1] Some, like John McWhorter, see here a "new religion," but we cannot seem to name its prophet (2021, 23–60). The Left, very much in the grips of this new spirit of our politics and busy doing its work, is not inclined to stop to reflect on what it is and what it means with anything like detachment. The Right, thrown into disarray by a disruptive democratic force of immense power not only taking aim at conservatives' relatively lackluster commitment to the new order but also now assaulting the whole tradition of American democratic history, liberal constitutionalism, and the Enlightenment, must nevertheless somehow bow to much of what is going on.

This book offers a way to see all at once and to think about the complex whole that is the civil rights revolution. I take on that task, first, by exploring the novel expression of democratic pluralism and civic education inspired by the fight against discrimination that has been articulated by theorists of American *multicultural education* over the course of the past fifty years. A second strategy of the work is to contrast that vision of things with the traditional liberal democratic understanding of politics as it has been expressed in a long line of accounts of liberal *pluralism* (whenever I use the term *liberal*, delineated in more detail below, I always have in mind liberal democracy as a comprehensive concept, and not the common narrower usage indicating "the Left" in contemporary political life). Both these steps require some preliminary justification and I will address them each in turn below. But, in brief, the reason to proceed this way is that contrasting the new and the old as forms of pluralism helpfully sheds light on many things at once. Every account of pluralism is a far-reaching and imaginative complex rendering of many different dimensions of social life. In taking this approach, we will not disregard other aspects of anti-discrimination (its laws in particular are very important and we will consider them), but an examination at the level of pluralism compels us to reckon with the effect that politics has on the categories of our thinking, especially our moral thinking. It is true that every pluralism in a way begins, in its appeal to diversity and not unity, by seeking to *conceal* its essential political core, and this is no less true for multiculturalism than it is for liberal pluralism. But this disadvantage, once corrected by an analysis that puts the political substance of things front and center, must be seen in light of the many advantages associated with the wide-ranging and relatively complex account of social life offered by every pluralism. Contrasting the two democratic pluralisms now vying for predominance in our world reveals much of importance very quickly. Doing so certainly provides us with powerful evidence that the commitment to fighting discrimination operates according to a political and moral logic or spirit that breaks with the liberal democratic tradition in many important ways. Just as important, this approach also allows the anti-discrimination regime to begin to reveal itself to us, as a distinct entity, on its own terms. There is no better way to begin to understand a thing than to distinguish it from a closely kindred class and, in the distinction, to begin to make clearer the nature or form or essential character of each.[2]

In the years since the civil rights revolution, it has become, perhaps paradoxically, very difficult and even dangerous to speak openly and frankly and without reserve about many questions pertaining to civil rights. The danger of entering into this territory (if losing one's job and career and social standing is danger) exists mainly because of the shape the fight against discrimination has taken in the law. Nevertheless, it is still possible to speak openly at a general level about the character of the anti-discrimination regime taken as a whole and about its relation to the liberal tradition or, as in multiculturalism, about the vision of politics and morality and life associated with the new order and the challenges it poses to the old. Today, discussion on that wide and elevated plane of the political and moral order, which the encounter between multiculturalism and liberal pluralism permits, is useful in more ways than one.

Anti-Discrimination Regime?

The commitment to civil rights is today an unquestioned premise of democratic life, an ideal that swept through the United States and indeed through all the liberal democracies of the world in the years following World War II. The suddenness of anti-discrimination policy's rise has been matched by the seeming finality and completeness of its acceptance as a defining element of contemporary politics: to oppose the anti-discrimination regime today is to put oneself outside the circle of effective political life and, indeed, outside polite society. Led at first ably and with great dignity by American Blacks, the anti-discrimination revolution was embraced by other similarly situated groups—women, the disabled, the elderly, religious minorities, gays and lesbians, Christians, transgender persons, and others—in ways that transformed the very self-understanding of members of those groups. But its effect has been even more pervasive, reshaping the hearts and minds of all citizens in the direction of a new account of the promise, and the demands, of democratic politics generally speaking—introducing a more exacting rule of justice, a new standard of how individuals should treat one another.

The commitment to fighting discrimination has also been at the center of a series of unsettling and divisive debates. Heated and polarized battles over second- and third-generation civil rights issues—affirmative action, hate speech regulations, racial profiling, persisting group inequalities, group representation, reparations claims, LGBT rights, and the like—continue to occupy public attention. New terms of claim and counterclaim somehow associated with the politics of anti-discrimination—microaggressions, safe spaces, trigger warnings, deplatforming, virtue signaling, social justice warriors, transexclusionarity, cisnormativity, Antifa, the Alt-Right, the Regressive Left—tax the powers of any but the most committed partisans to keep current. The new muscle of anti-discrimination groups (no longer "interest groups" but now "social movements") has created novel political-social cleavages—party alignments, church schisms. Reflecting the ferment and giving voice to it, new and strange theories fly from the pens of our intellectuals—the politics of identity, the politics of recognition, the politics of inclusion, of difference, of intersectionality, of equity—all employing a terminology that is novel and unsettling but also somehow inescapable and compelling.[3] Especially in the case of women, lesbians, gays, bisexuals, and transgender persons, the claims of these recently energized and now more assertive groups challenge long-standing and deeply held social conventions and moral and religious convictions in unpredictable ways. At the same time, and from a very different direction, some religious conservatives now embrace the anti-discrimination framework on behalf of the Christian majority in hopes of dismantling the "strict" separation of church and state and in order to protect themselves in various culture wars battles with other anti-discrimination constituencies (especially today, LGBT groups). Critics from the Left as well as from the Right hold that the new political program distracts attention from more pressing questions of class conflict and economic justice; that it exalts group-based equality and expands the state at the expense of individual liberty; that it promotes politically correct thought control and stifles freedom of speech; that it advances under a banner of diversity a campaign of egalitarian leveling and conformity; that it bolsters a kind of cultural relativism sapping the foundation of our Enlightenment-era principles; that it heightens group conflict and mistrust on behalf of special interests, undermining civic unity; that it encourages demagogic leadership and a counterproductive politics of victimhood; that it provokes groups to make demands about matters (identity, recognition, respect) that no democratic politics can ever address in a way satisfactory to all; that it fixates public attention on past injustices that cannot be undone, breeding resentment and eroding civic pride in now-tarnished heroes; that it indulges, by valorizing claims of identity, troubling tendencies (self-involved, narcissistic) of the democratic soul. Taken together, such charges (justified or not), and the answers to them, map out a significant territory of our public deliberations, and while no one of these disputes captures the whole truth about the anti-discrimination revolution, all of them are somehow connected to that deep source of our contemporary life. Surely few if any of these developments were foreseen at the outset, now more than half a century ago.

Nothing is more important for understanding the commitment to fighting discrimination than to see this puzzling combination: anti-discrimination politics is surrounded by controversy on every side but is at the same time absolutely unquestioned, held indeed to be the necessary starting point for thinking about the meaning of contemporary democratic life. Any analysis of anti-discrimination that does not somehow come to terms with its destabilizing character will be an exercise in evasion or wishful thinking.

Anti-discrimination politics appears as several different kinds of things that are all nevertheless connected to one another as a unity. It comes to sight first as a *moral* commitment—our sense that racism, sexism, and other forms of discrimination are unjust and that justice demands some significant effort to stand up to them. It is also obviously somehow a representation of the interests or claims or demands of the *groups* commonly thought to be the victims of discrimination in need of protection from it. It is, in addition, and very noticeably, a complex array of new *laws* and government institutions put in place to make the effort on behalf of those groups, and in the name of their moral claims, a reality. It is also a complex set of new *ideas* elaborating not just the new moral and legal requirements of the effort but other terms of social, psychological, and cultural description of the world needed to make sense of this new political commitment. Finally, it is an extensive project of social institution-building undertaken by activist-leaders empowered and inspired by all of the above. Taken together, these disparate elements provide, as the advocates of the fight of discrimination often say, a "lens" through which we are to see anew, perhaps for the first time truly, social life, democracy, and our world. It is this complex combination that justifies our use of the very old term "regime" and it is this that the study of *multiculturalism*, more helpfully than any other dimension of the whole, puts us in a position to see.

Multiculturalism as Teacher of the Anti-Discrimination Regime

The idea that we should try to understand anti-discrimination politics by looking to multicultural education will be controversial. Multicultural education is a subfield of American teacher education, and neither teacher education as an academic field nor the theorists of multicultural education (not even leading theorist James A. Banks, a central figure in this book) have a reputation of the sort that makes such a choice immediately obvious. The rest of this book is the full response to that kind of objection, but, in brief, we may point out now that multicultural education is simultaneously a new civic education and a new form of democratic pluralism. When a country has a new civic education and a new pluralism, these are clear signs visible to all (changes operating in broad daylight) that demand our attention, evidence of a major shift at the center of the political order. And, especially in the United States, when the new civic education and the new pluralism have no important reliance upon their liberal democratic antecedents, we are put on alert that the alteration signaled thereby is fundamental. The formulation of multicultural education writer Sonia Nieto cannot be improved upon: "antiracism, and antidiscrimination in general, is at the very core of a multicultural perspective" (1992, 208). If we take them at their word, multicultural education theorists demonstrate very directly the power of a new political impulse to call into being a complex rethinking of the aspirations and requirements of democratic life.

Other ways to see or to approach anti-discrimination politics as a whole—by way of the history, or the law, or the "groups" of anti-discrimination—are too complicated to be summarized in a simple and helpful way. Moreover, to repeat, there is no well-recognized theory or theorist (or prophet) of the anti-discrimination revolution to whom we might turn. No political participant—no group or movement leader, no legislator or politician—provides us with an account of the whole that does justice to the ambition of the new order or its transformative civic and moral meaning. One could imagine an attempt to summarize anti-discrimination by reference to all of its many laws (I offer a brief characterization and summary in chapter 3). But to do that in a reliable and authoritative way would be hard to manage in a short space. Even if we could do it, the law's formality would not tell us what we most want to know about why and to what end. Moreover, and just as problematic, the law's convoluted shape (statutes, bureaucratic regulations and interpretations, court decisions, constitutional considerations), as well as its contested nature, would render every general interpretation controversial. Academic theories of identity or difference or inclusion or equity (mentioned above) do exist, but these are all *products* of the anti-discrimination regime that do not seek to speak for it, or even about it, in an all-embracing way. These theories are interesting *evidence* of the anti-discrimination revolution (and its effects on democratic intellectuals—I discuss them in chapters 9 and 10) but they are not the kind of helpful comprehensive starting point we need. Too partial, too academic, and at any rate highly radicalized, such theories are far removed from the mainstream of American political life. (One sign of this is that such theories, all of the Left, are commonly quite critical of anti-discrimination law—and in a deeply misleading way because the criticisms are always in the name of nothing other than exaggerated notions of the commitment to fighting discrimination.)[4]

The theorists of multicultural education are valuable to us for this reason: as a result of more or less deliberate reflection, and because of the requirements imposed upon them by their special situation or position, they draw together in one place the full civic, moral, and psychological complexity of the commitment to fighting discrimination. Disciplined by the need to advance their cause on a contested political field (as we will see, multicultural education policy is law), their claims are made always in an appeal to the wider political community. This also means that multicultural education theorists articulate their complex teachings for the most part in the commonsense language of ordinary political life. These theorists (or at least the non-postmodernists among them) are not burdened unduly by intellectual idiosyncrasies (theoretical jargon, epistemological commitments) that might distract us from the straightforward political program they champion. It is hard not to be impressed as well by the scale of their project, which entails rethinking not only American education but also American democratic life and the American identity. Their vision lives up to the claim that what they offer is a new civic education. Multicultural education's *location and purpose* thus compel its advocates to state broadly—indeed, in universal terms that seek to appeal to all citizens—the ends and means of the fight against discrimination. At the same time, separately, the work of multicultural education's theorists provides a helpful case study of social institution-building undertaken in the name of civil rights politics, showing what can be accomplished by dedicated activist-leaders operating within the spirit of the law but also extending its shaping power into new uncharted territories. To some degree, multicultural education will, in all of this, seem to be a kind of extreme or revolutionary stance, especially because so many of its new teachings run counter to the traditional liberal understanding of things. But this is precisely its great contribution, to show that it is only the working-out of the logic of anti-discrimination politics, and not something else, that gives this new aspiration of democratic politics its seemingly radical character.

That the original meaning of the term *multiculturalism* in the United States derives from multicultural education, and that multicultural education was from the first essentially defined by anti-discrimination politics, is a relatively straightforward matter. It is true that the vital positive political meaning of multiculturalism has been obscured to some degree by later reinterpretations of the idea (especially by academics), as well as by various misinterpretations.[5] The story is also complicated by the fact that soon after multicultural education appeared, postmodernist theorists rushed to join in its efforts (about which more below). But the initial appearance of the terms *multicultural* and *multiculturalism* in the United States (in the late 1960s) can be traced with precision to the immediate aftermath of the major victories of the civil rights revolution. It was multicultural education writers and nobody else who first introduced this terminology in American life. (There is no evidence to support the claim of Nathan Glazer and others that multiculturalism in the United States

Introduction

"come[s] to us from our neighbor to the north."⁶) In the United States, multiculturalism has always been essentially a positive way to say antidiscrimination. Multicultural education writers themselves explicitly reject historical connections to the liberal pluralist tradition in America, and they see arguments for liberal "cultural pluralism" in particular (an idea that first emerged a century ago) to be merely "a historical antecedent of multicultural education, not a root of the current movement."⁷ From the very start, the idea of multiculturalism was used to advance civil rights reform efforts in the domain of education. As it developed in the 1970s and 1980s, multicultural education was supported at every step by a web of federal and state civil rights policies. In the late 1980s and early 1990s, by which point multicultural education was well established in the academic world as a subdiscipline in the field of teacher education, the concept of multiculturalism gained wider national attention during the course of contentious debates in New York, California, and other states over the adoption of multicultural education curriculum reforms.⁸

Although this is for me a secondary question (I want to make use of it to help us understand the logic or vision of anti-discrimination politics), one could make a *causal* claim on behalf of multicultural education, which has played some significant role in shaping the practice of American education over the past fifty years. To be sure, among all the laws affecting American education, directives governing teacher education in particular (which is where multicultural education gains its official status and power) are not the best known—Title IX and state and local curriculum content guidelines (especially for American history) are much more visible. But teacher education mandates, laid down in a direct way by state law and enforced through semi-official accreditation standards, do represent an important domain of American education policy. For many decades now, teacher education as an academic discipline, a not unimportant source of educational theorizing in the United States, has put the fight against discrimination at its center, and multicultural education is the center of that center. It is worth noting, for example, that secretaries of education under Presidents Barack Obama and Joe Biden received their doctorates in teacher education and wrote their dissertations on educational racial disparities.⁹

Multicultural Education: The Importance of James A. Banks

The historical record thus provides us with one helpful nonarbitrary starting point for insisting that multiculturalism's most important meaning has something to do with the civil rights revolution. But it is the substance of the vision of anti-discrimination politics we are after, and that is available only through an examination of the thought of multicultural education's theorists. This task in turn is necessarily double, following a basic divide between those under the sway of postmodernist theory and those who are not. It is those whose theorizing is *not* encumbered by the jargon and preoccupations of postmodernism who are our best guides. They came first, and their essential political commitment provides the more fundamental essence to which postmodernist attributes would later be added. We are very fortunate indeed that James A. Banks, the most influential of all multicultural education writers, resisted the temptations of postmodernism that most other writers in his field did not. As a result, Banks offers us much more direct access to the complex logic of civil rights politics, free from the many distracting claims associated with the postmodernist school.

Anyone who thinks that the real challenge to modern democratic politics today comes from postmodernist theory will be disappointed by this book. (I take up postmodernist multiculturalism in chapter 6, but Banks is the true center of my analysis.) It is true that today, generally speaking, Left advocacy of anti-discrimination politics is so bound up with the terminology and commitments of postmodernism that we cannot ignore the latter. This widespread political-theoretical combination has been an established fact characterizing multicultural education, and teacher education more broadly, since the late 1980s. It is also a development now affecting, to some degree, all of modern intellectual life. It is undeniable that, through postmodernism, radical theory has become the handmaiden of the civil rights revolution; wherever one finds anti-discrimination politics today, one is almost certain to find postmodernist thought—and vice versa. No serious attempt to discuss either multiculturalism or anti-discrimination politics can avoid addressing the role of postmodernism.

But it is very important that we not fall into the trap of letting the flash and bang of postmodernism overshadow the more important political development that is the heart of things. We must also resist a common line

Introduction

of thinking, especially among conservative critics of these developments, which assumes that the history of modern *ideas* broadly conceived best explains our current situation. Many would adapt something like the argument of Allan Bloom's *Closing of the American Mind* and apply it (as Bloom did not) in order to understand myriad unsettling phenomena associated with anti-discrimination politics. As though the best way to try to understand political correctness or multiculturalism or identity politics and the like would be to study the thought of Rousseau, Herder, Hegel, Marx, Nietzsche, Freud, Heidegger, and Marcuse.[10] This book shows why that is a deeply misleading way of thinking about these issues. Intellectual history does not explain our woke ways. Time and again, the anti-discrimination revolution compels us to confront instead the shaping power of the *political order* in our lives—and to see in particular how, when ideas become publicly important, they indeed become subordinated to more powerful forces.

Looking, therefore, first and foremost to politics, I privilege our excellent non-postmodernist guide, Banks. That we need to study Banks will not be flattering to those who would prefer, for various reasons (not all of them good), to try their hand at navigating the tortured history of modern intellectual life. But following where he leads us is much more worthwhile if what we want is to understand the civil rights revolution and its general reworking of democratic life. I offer a systematic account of Banks's political and educational thought; then, in later chapters of the book, I rely to a great extent on his vision of things to think through the challenge that multiculturalism and anti-discrimination politics pose to the liberal pluralist tradition. Postmodernist thinkers *do* attack liberalism (to say the least), but their criticisms are heedlessly radical and tend to be formal, abstract, and epistemological; and while they claim to be attuned to "the political," they are amazingly lacking in self-awareness of their own political commitment to the anti-discrimination regime. They are thus not very helpful if what we want is to clarify the relationship between liberalism and anti-discrimination. (Another reason not to focus on postmodernist multiculturalism is that a contrast with the liberal tradition beginning there would skew the overall result by exaggerating the differences between the old and the new to such a degree as to render the comparison less useful and in a way that might seem—politically—suspect.)

In stark contrast, Banks, in what he himself terms a "multicultural ideology," offers and intends to offer a far-reaching and complex delineation of the substance of American democratic education that is rich and worthy of our attention—and one rooted always in a commitment to civil rights reform. His thought never fails to clarify the full meaning of the anti-discrimination revolution and its many implications, and without all the exaggerations and extreme radicalism of the postmodernists. While it is true that James A. Banks is not exactly a household name, studying his work teaches us much more about the source of the new civic outlook arising out of the anti-discrimination revolution than does the work of better-known social and political theorists who have been writing under its influence for the past two or three decades but whose intellectual radicalism and/or theoretical preoccupations get in the way of a proper grasp of the real issues. As a theorist, moreover, fighting on the front lines to advance a real-world political program (with all of the discipline that comes from actual political engagement and its limitations), Banks is impelled always to frame what he is saying on behalf of the civil rights revolution in terms of general appeals to the political community as a whole. This may be contrasted with postmodernist multiculturalists and other academic theorists who, inspired by the new order but not disciplined by it, often make claims that in their radicalism greatly obscure their simple political starting point. Banks, who deliberately avoids postmodernist entanglements, is so useful to us precisely because he may be relied upon to start and end more simply and, if I may say so, more honestly, with the task of advancing the cause of the fight against discrimination.

Advancing a new civic education and a new pluralism, Banks's theory of multicultural education teaches, to begin with, the essential political and moral lessons of the anti-discrimination revolution in a fairly direct way. This is a complex undertaking that employs a variety of pedagogical methods of persuasion and instruction touching many different areas of life. Banks's educational strategies in turn depend upon a sophisticated social or political psychology that clarifies both the harms of discrimination and the work that multicultural education must do to overcome them: challenging and rejecting old identities shaped by discrimination and replacing them with new identities anchored in the commitment to fighting discrimination itself. Similarly, his new exposition of democratic *pluralism* reimagines the social order by way of a new account of the "group"—and then reconceives the connections between the group, the individual, the state, and other groups according to the requirements of anti-discrimination politics. Most important, at its core, multicultural education expresses a new vision of democracy and of the American political self-understanding that culminates in a new and distinctive set of general or universal claims and demands—a new moral logic. The new moral terms in play—identity, inclusion, recognition, respect, equity, and other newly necessary categories—arise naturally out of the attempt to articulate the fight against discrimination. They are employed by Banks and other multicultural education writers inescapably and effortlessly and they were used by them well before debates about the meaning of all these terms became a cottage industry for contemporary social and political theorists. The ambition of Banks's theorizing, which takes on the task of supplying in detail the substantial assumptions and reasoning that can make sense of the imperatives of a profound political and cultural reform, is sustained at every step by his belief in the justice of the civil rights revolution and by his manifest confidence in its hold on American life.

I am not saying that multicultural education as Banks presents it is worth studying because he and its other advocates are the *originators* of a new understanding of American democracy. Certainly the aspirations he expresses have a wider political origin and had presumably been articulated before in one form or another by others: anti-discrimination is the cause of multiculturalism, not the other way around. Instead, to repeat, it is *that*, and *how*, he conveys all at once the broad and complex vision of the new politics that makes him so useful to us. We must adopt the stance of "originalism" when it comes to the study of multiculturalism, precisely because doing so points us back to multicultural education and from there to the civil rights revolution; originalism in this instance is justified on both historical and pedagogical grounds.

Postmodernism, Handmaiden of the Civil Rights Revolution

As I have indicated, compared with the thought of Banks, *postmodernist* multiculturalism is much less useful to us if what we want is to understand anti-discrimination politics on its own terms. Nevertheless, for good or ill, the fates of civil rights and postmodernist theory are today powerfully intertwined. Some effort must be made to think about this union of theory and politics—to consider how they go together and how they do not.

As we shall see, when postmodernist thought and anti-discrimination politics are combined, each works to radicalize the other in a dynamic that makes both of them worse versions of their original selves. I will argue that, between the two, the political partner in this combination is predominant. Postmodernism gains something in the exchange, no doubt, but what in the end is left of its pretensions to theoretical radicalism when it appears in the service of one of the most revered civic authorities of our age? The benefit to multiculturalism, on the *political* side of the ledger, is less immediately obvious—and there certainly is a price to be paid for teaming up with anti-rationalist anti-essentialism. Is the radicalism of postmodernist theory perhaps attractive to anti-discrimination politics because there is something intrinsically radical in the latter that yearns to be unbound with the help of the former?

Our study of Banks, on the one hand, and of the postmodernist multiculturalists, on the other, will provide some useful insights concerning, and corrections to, the discussion of critical race theory and related phenomena that is at the forefront of public debate at the current moment. Generally speaking, we may say that the study of multiculturalism shows that contemporary discussion of critical race theory underestimates what is at issue. Critical race theory is prominent today because its radical ideas are informing workplace diversity training and the teaching of American schoolchildren. Multicultural education has been working, perhaps less visibly but certainly more effectively, to advance very similar lessons as an important part of the education establishment (indeed, often mandated by law) for more than fifty years. Critical race theory is also controversial because, like postmodernist multiculturalism, it wears its theoretical radicalism on its sleeve. But the study of multicultural education teaches us to discount the part played by intellectual history and to focus on the political substance of things instead. As in the case of multicultural education, when we examine the politics of critical race theory we are confronted with the fact that what is new here is nothing other than the aspirations of the civil rights revolution. (I cannot resist pointing out that Robin DiAngelo, author of *White Fragility* and one of the chief sources of vexation for critical race theory's critics at the moment, got her doctorate in education under the supervision of Banks.)[11]

In the attack on critical race theory and related phenomena (conservatives have discovered a vulnerability here and are pressing the point), the common tendency to exaggerate the role of *ideas*, and to overlook the role of anti-discrimination politics, may be explained in a variety of ways. To some degree it may simply reflect a preference for high-sounding explanations of social phenomena that presuppose a degree of sophistication or education. But it may also suggest a certain amount of wishful thinking. By blaming what troubles them on seemingly alien intellectual developments (postmodernism, relativism) or already-vanquished enemies of the past ("cultural Marxism"), today's critics (especially but not only conservatives) permit themselves to characterize these developments as something outside the norm, hard to defend, and politically exposed. Were they to see that what makes them uncomfortable is in fact a certain interpretation of the fight against discrimination, their position would become much more difficult. The study of multicultural education, on the other hand, forces into view a much deeper and vital source of fundamental conflict at the heart of contemporary battles over our shared vision of the democratic future. To repeat, the theorizing of Banks (who explicitly rejects both postmodernism and Marxism) proves that multicultural education, which offers teachings for America that are no less unorthodox than those of critical race theory, has *no important source* other than the civil rights revolution.

Remedying the Neglect of Multicultural Education

Perhaps enough has been said by now to make plausible the claim that the exploration of American multicultural education—in its non-postmodernist and postmodernist variants—can help to illuminate the shape and substance of democratic life today. But American multicultural education has been neglected by contemporary intellectuals, and that means by its natural allies on the Left. This is partly the result of the academic debate over multiculturalism taken up among the professional social and political theorists, where analytical philosophy and postmodernism predominate. In particular, the work of Canadian multiculturalism theorist Will Kymlicka (of the analytical camp) has been enormously influential in academia. In the large debate about multiculturalism among the professoriate that emerged in response to his work, which does not center explicitly on the anti-discrimination revolution, American multicultural education is almost completely ignored and overlooked—or, where it is noticed, it is dismissed as philosophically unsophisticated, morally insufficient, or both.[12] But, as my engagement with Banks will make plain, that is a deeply misguided snobbery that underestimates multicultural education and that absolutely needs to be discarded if we are to learn what it can teach us.

One might say, then, that what is needed to remedy the failings of our social and political *theorists* is the sober realism of political *science*. Certainly a heavy dose of the empirical facts on the ground, and attention to what is really going on in contemporary democratic life, might go some distance toward clarifying an idea the original meaning of which has been to some considerable degree obscured by unjustified neglect. But it turns out that our political scientists are apparently even less interested in American multiculturalism and American multicultural education than are our social and political theorists. Despite the fact that it presents itself as precisely a new civic education, and takes the shape of a new form of democratic pluralism arising out of civil rights politics, American multiculturalism, as rooted in multicultural education, has not been taken seriously by contemporary American political science. This is true even when civic education itself is the focus of attention.[13] We must not permit the inadequacies of our reigning intellectual authorities to stand in the way of the valuable lessons about our situation that multicultural education brings to light.

Liberal Pluralism As Touchstone: Is Anti-Discrimination Liberal?

In setting out to reveal the inner logic and essence of anti-discrimination politics by way of a contrast between multiculturalism and liberal pluralism, I begin by assuming that the liberal democratic tradition is an indispensable touchstone for understanding the dramatic alteration of things that the civil rights revolution has been. Those who would reject an approach that thus starts from liberalism (as unsophisticated or unscientific or polemical) bear the burden of suggesting an alternative way of fixing anti-discrimination politics in the mind's eye that does justice to its great reach and ambition and transformative power. Indeed, precisely because the logic of liberal democratic politics runs so deep in modern life, an approach distinguishing anti-discrimination from it is more necessary than anything else. For if we do *not* disentangle it from liberalism where that is called for, the fight against discrimination will remain concealed to us by the confusion in our minds resulting from our (civic) assumption that ours is one coherent political world, as well as from the powerful tendency of liberalism to dominate our political thinking (precisely while seeming, paradoxically, in the language of freedom, to *depoliticize* it). Once we begin to see anti-discrimination in its differentiation from liberalism, however, we will not be able any longer to unsee it as a distinct entity.

In making liberalism my point of contrast I argue along the lines of a small number of legal scholars who, since the 1990s, have approached anti-discrimination politics in this way—most notably, on the Right, Richard Epstein and, on the Left, Andrew Koppelman.[14] While I, like them, believe that the law and its development provide crucial indications of the changes under way (surveyed in chapter 3), the main evidence I want to focus on is looser and more wide-ranging, and shows in my view more helpfully how the new political order is changing the way we think, introducing new moral categories and new basic terms of social and political description (new "modes and orders"). It is above all because multiculturalism and multicultural education illuminate this dimension of the civil rights revolution that it deserves our attention.

Because multiculturalism is a form of pluralism expressing a new political aspiration, contrasting it with liberal pluralism illuminates a number of things all at the same time. Pluralist formulations have served important functions in the liberal democratic political understanding from the very start. Originating in the logic of *religious* pluralism and spelled out by thinkers like John Locke and some of the American founders, this way of looking at social life has been rearticulated many times in different ways, using different terms, over the past couple centuries. Some of the best known reformulations of the idea include interest group pluralism (set forth famously in *Federalist* 10), Horace Kallen's brief for "cultural pluralism" in the early twentieth century, social science's embrace of the pluralism concept (partly descriptive, partly prescriptive) in the 1950s and 1960s, contemporary academic theories of "values pluralism," and the pluralist efforts of John Rawls's later writings. Differing somewhat in what they emphasize, all of these are members of a close-knit family, expressing through the language of group politics some of the essential assumptions and principles of the liberal democratic political outlook.

Multiculturalism in no way originates in this tradition; indeed to some degree it defines itself against it. (Our comparative political approach solves the striking puzzle that immediately confronts anyone interested in these concepts: how can something called "multiculturalism" not be the same thing as something called "cultural pluralism"?) Any debts that multiculturalism may owe to liberal pluralism are purely formal—a rhetoric of diversity and anti-assimilation (problematic in liberalism and multiculturalism alike) and a tendency to universalism. But, at the level of its positive content or substance—political, pedagogical, moral, psychological—multiculturalism diverges in important ways from the liberal tradition and its logic. "Voluntary associations" are replaced by "ascriptive identity groups"; toleration and liberty are replaced by respect and identity; peaceful competitive cooperation in the "private sphere" is replaced by a new politics of friends and enemies enlisting the power of government and law as a matter of course.

The contrast between anti-discrimination and liberalism, which multiculturalism compels us to confront, becomes explicit in the later chapters of this book and is a central question throughout. It is therefore useful now to say something about what I mean by liberalism. I do not have in mind the usage according to which liberal means progressive/Left, the opposite of conservative/Right, in contemporary political battles. When I refer to liberalism, I always mean that general understanding of politics that is still shared in the United States by *both* the Left and the Right, Democrats and Republicans. According to this wider usage, liberal democracy differs from "democracy" plain and simple in that it imposes constraints on what the majority—the people—may do. Liberalism, as I use the term, refers to the extremely influential modern and contemporary view of political life that begins and ends with some defining notion of individual rights and freedom, as well as some view, therefore, of the importance of "limited" government (the Left and Right admittedly have different views of what that means, but each nevertheless places this idea at the heart of things). Liberalism has been reformulated many times by different theorists, but it is not necessary to rely on any of them in particular; indeed, it is both possible and useful to describe liberalism by reference to an immediately recognizable bundle of ideas and practices that prevail in modern democracies like the United States.[15] My use of the term cannot thus be dismissed as referring narrowly (politically or historically) to what defenders call libertarianism and critics call neoliberalism—or to some rigid notion of "classical" liberalism—all of which might suggest a tendency to advance free market capitalism. Crucially, liberal *pluralism* is agnostic on the debate over government regulation of economic life.

It is true that highlighting the tensions between anti-discrimination and the liberal tradition contradicts the prevailing view of the civil rights revolution. What one may call the standard interpretation, embraced by progressives as well as by conservatives, holds with leading civil rights historian Hugh Davis Graham that, while affirmative action may go beyond liberalism, the 1964 Civil Rights Act as such enshrined only "classic liberalism's core command against discrimination"—a view held not only by historians but also by law professors, social and political theorists, and social and political scientists.[16] Few would disagree with Daniel Patrick Moynihan's assessment at the moment of the civil rights movement's great successes: "The Negro American revolution holds forth the prospect that the American Republic, which at birth was flawed by the institution of slavery, and which throughout its history has been marred by the unequal treatment of Negro citizens, will at last redeem the full promise of the Declaration of Independence" (1967, 47). Historian Arthur Schlesinger and sociologist Nathan Glazer apply the same interpretive framework to the idea of multiculturalism as well, insisting that while there is definitely something new and strange at work here, something at odds with the liberal tradition in particular, whatever it is cannot be that "grand effort, the civil rights revolution."[17]

Are there not perhaps good civic reasons to try to find ways to hold these things together instead of emphasizing their differences? Alternatively, might not an interpretation that emphasizes the many lines of tension between the new and the old, and that characterizes the new as revolutionary, be suspect from a political perspective—as perhaps undertaken with a view to raising an alarm about the one to rouse defenders of the other? One might object, as multiculturalism theorist and advocate Christine Sleeter does, that those who present multicultural education as a "political" stance may seek merely to mask their own politics behind a purportedly "neutral" or "apolitical" perspective (1995a, 87). Such doubts or concerns must not be permitted to halt a political interpretation in this instance. Indeed, elsewhere Sleeter herself writes that "multicultural education has been a highly political change strategy" (1996, 8). I at any rate do not hold that the alternatives to multiculturalism in the United States are somehow neutral or apolitical. Today we have both civic and theoretical reasons to follow where multiculturalism leads us as we try to understand the nature of anti-discrimination politics.

This study may have political implications, but it tries to resist as much as possible the easy slide in all things touching anti-discrimination into political partisanship and factional bias. I therefore do not to frame this examination of the civil rights revolution in terms of a general global judgment for or against. I aim for impartial (which is not the same as "value neutral") judgment, and that means at least some amount of self-criticism is unavoidable (self-refutation being the highest task of political science). I have tried to write a book on these controversial matters that might be read with benefit by both Left and Right. On contemporary political questions I am more or less a conservative, and so for me trying to be impartial has meant having to learn to listen to the Left, never uncritically, with a view to seeing how what those on the Left say about multiculturalism and anti-discrimination reveals some portion of the truth. It is conceivable that this study could contribute to public debate, politically, by reframing the way we think about these topics—by heightening our sense of the untraditional character of the commitment to fighting discrimination as an element of modern democratic politics. But that by itself would not of course settle the question of the relative merits of the old and the new.

A Political Interpretation

This book is divided into three parts. The first part (chapters 2–4) provides an historical survey establishing beyond a reasonable doubt American multiculturalism's deep original connection to civil rights politics. This historical treatment also begins to give some indication of the revolutionary character of the anti-discrimination regime taken as a whole. All three of these chapters show the vitally important role of *law*, but in chapter 3 in particular I offer a general overview of anti-discrimination law to draw attention to aspects of the new order's basic legal workings that challenge the traditional liberal understanding of politics (some of these, like speech restrictions, are obvious; others are not). In addition, chapter 4 examines one instance of activist-led institution-building—in the story of the establishment of multicultural education as an academic discipline. In part 2 (chapters 5 and 6) I explore the *idea* of multiculturalism as it was developed by American multicultural education theorists, non-postmodernist and postmodernist. Although my sympathies here are clearly with our non-postmodernist Banks, and though I believe we learn much more from him, the study of both together illuminates much of the territory of contemporary political and intellectual life. The third part (chapters 7–10) then lays out a deliberate comparison of American multiculturalism and the liberal pluralist tradition with a view to clarifying the meaning and character of anti-discrimination politics in comprehensive terms. In chapters 7 and 8, I undertake that comparison at the level of the old and the new as schemes of "pluralism"; chapters 9 and 10 focus on what we learn by examining the notable differences in their *moral* categories and sensibilities. In the course of this study we will thus make use of many different *kinds* of evidence to assess the nature of anti-discrimination politics, evidence necessary to sustain the claim of its broad transformative power in modern democratic life. By taking together its laws, its political history, its educational program, its ideas, its moral outlook, its activist-leaders and some of the social institutions they have introduced—on the way to and through the study of one key part, multiculturalism—we can see their unity and we can begin to try to come to grips with their general shape and meaning.

Our social and political scientists have not done much to try to say in a general way what the civil rights revolution taken as a whole has meant for democratic politics taken as a whole.[18] This neglect or lack of theoretical interest is mystifying, considering the importance of anti-discrimination in contemporary life, and it speaks volumes about the disposition of contemporary social and political science. My investigation of multiculturalism as one pathway to that important task assumes the centrality of the regime or political order as the most important formative cause of what happens in all other spheres of social or cultural life. What is obvious on the surface—the crude, massive outline of things established (authoritatively) in societies at the level of the regime or political order and reflected most obviously but not exclusively in the law—must be the starting point of social analysis, however naïve or unsophisticated such a stance may seem. Without simply accepting common sense as the last word, this approach to political science begins by taking its bearings precisely by the pressing questions of political life that any informed and thoughtful citizen would be inclined to raise. To be sure, there are not a few social and political scientists who, themselves operating under the influence of the new order, chronicle the extent to which we have or have not succeeded in eradicating racism, sexism, and other forms of discrimination from every area of life (the reports forthcoming are pessimistic, if from the point of view of a somewhat exacting interpretation of the meaning of success). But this is only more evidence of the anti-discrimination revolution's power to shape American (intellectual) life—and further justification for the approach I am taking.

Once we have become prepared to look for them, other kinds of general political evidence—in almost every area of policy, in party alignments, in constitutional law, institutions, political culture, group dynamics—tell a similar tale of the transformative effects of the new order. Then, in turn, we will also be better able to see still other important changes in American life in what liberalism calls the private sphere—in intellectual life and in the categories of our moral outlook (some of which we encounter here), in commerce and the workplace, in the nature and meaning of sexuality and the family, in contemporary religion, and in the arts and literature and popular culture. The disruptive and revolutionary nature of anti-discrimination politics makes it the unwitting and inadvertent teacher of the reemergence of what might be said to be the "natural" political dimension at work in democratic life—citizen-shaping, mind-shaping, culture-shaping, architectonic—out of and against the influence of liberalism.

Everything I have said to this point suggests that, in America, multiculturalism means one thing, one political thing. This conclusion will be developed at length but the basic point is worth making now: contrary to appearances, multiculturalism as an idea does not have anything to do with *diversity* (cultural or otherwise) in any simple sense. The most common meaning of multiculturalism, its literal meaning—a colorful array of cultural possibilities, and so on—*conceals* its only important meaning, a simple, powerful, unified political meaning rooted in the civil rights revolution. Somewhat paradoxically, and perhaps disappointingly, the study of multiculturalism turns out at every step to be a meditation on our *own* culture, or, more precisely, on the new political order that is its formal or general cause.

PART 1.
POLITICAL HISTORY:
THE ANTI-DISCRIMINATION REVOLUTION AND THE DEVELOPMENT OF AMERICAN MULTICULTURAL EDUCATION

Chapter 2
THE FAILURE OF LIBERALISM IN THE CASE OF RACE AND THE NECESSITY OF THE ANTI-DISCRIMINATION REVOLUTION

Multiculturalism is an excellent teacher of the meaning and import of the new commitment to fighting discrimination in America, and especially of the new civic outlook that has taken hold in the hearts of individuals shaped by it. But it is also both useful and necessary to step back first to provide a rough outline of key features of the new legal and political framework set in place by the civil rights revolution that is American multiculturalism's ultimate source. Doing so serves a necessary ground-clearing purpose, providing the general context that gave American multiculturalism its original impetus and shape. This sketch, moreover, will help to awaken us to the broad scope and scale of this new democratic project. To summarize the anti-discrimination revolution all at once is unavoidably to indicate its ambitious aims, its manifold instruments and techniques, and some of its powerful effects—all of which our closer study of multiculturalism will help us to confirm and to explore in greater detail. In attempting such a summary, we cannot help but notice and draw attention to many of the important ways in which the new order breaks with and challenges the liberal tradition. This question confronts us immediately when we consider the birth and rise of anti-discrimination policy, for that story cannot be told without sorting through the decisively important role played by the basic terms of liberal democratic politics. That today anti-discrimination has taken us beyond liberalism is explained to some considerable degree by the original pre-1964 relationship between liberalism and civil rights reform.

The Failure of Liberalism in the Case of Race

The rise of anti-discrimination policy in America is at least to some degree a history of struggle against liberal categories and principles. To be sure, the civil rights struggle was itself inspired by important liberal ideals, but key framing terms of liberal politics were also used, and for a century used more effectively, by defenders of an order of racial hierarchy and discrimination that predominated even after the Civil War and despite the new guarantee of the "equal protection of the laws" that was that struggle's great constitutional achievement in the Fourteenth Amendment. One could well argue that in this case liberal categories and principles were hijacked—distorted and abused—for fundamentally illiberal ends, but for the purpose of understanding anti-discrimination's final result and its relation to liberalism, it is necessary to face the fact that liberalism is to some degree implicated in the unjust treatment of American Blacks from 1865 to 1964.

Liberal democratic theory, the view of politics that begins in notions of individual liberty and rights and culminates in a system of "limited government," an outlook that has long defined American politics and informed its laws, was by itself incapable of dealing with the question of race.[1] The liberal public-private divide seemed to have worked well in other areas to frame group politics in a pluralism of "private" or "voluntary" associations and "interest groups," most notably in the case of religion—a doctrine beginning with individual religious liberty and culminating in the separation of church (private) and state (public). But not only did this view of political life fail to protect the most basic rights of American Blacks, it may even be said to have worked to support the era of racial discrimination that deprived them of those rights. As one prominent American historian put it, "tragically, southern resistance to national consolidation and totalitarian tendencies, combined with a discretely admirable defense of community autonomy, has historically served as a rationale for the defense of . . . racial segregation and manifold injustices."[2]

The failure of the liberal democratic understanding of political life in this respect was indeed double, as marked out by the language of the liberal public-private divide itself. Liberalism promised to protect citizens in the public sector, but left their doings in the private sector a matter of freedom. By thus creating an obstacle to the regulation of private life, liberalism may be said to have protected private discrimination. Is it surprising, then, that its efforts to regulate public discrimination were less than vigorous?

Now, to be sure, looking back from the present day, it is possible to glean in the decade immediately following the Civil War an ambitious anti-discrimination regime that includes both public and private efforts, and one that seemed to provide a significant leadership role for the federal government. Public sphere non-discrimination was made a constitutional principle by the Fourteenth and Fifteenth Amendments. Private sector anti-discrimination was indicated by the reach of the 1866 and 1875 Civil Rights Acts to include the regulation of contracts, private property, and what we call public accommodations (the 1866 Act made constitutional by the Thirteenth Amendment, the 1875 Act by reading section 5 of the Fourteenth Amendment expansively). Forceful federal leadership was made plain by the basic terms of the Fourteenth Amendment and by the Enforcement Acts of 1870 and 1871. Had there been the will to build on such a legal foundation, it is possible to imagine something like the development of contemporary anti-discrimination politics from these beginnings. But, obviously, this was not to be—and, in the stifling of this project at the outset, the terms of liberal democratic politics played a crucial role.

The possibility of a more robust anti-discrimination regime noted here will be important later. Anyone who tries to trace the origins of the *idea* of contemporary anti-discrimination politics to something else—to intellectual history or relativism, or to cultural or social sources, or to the expansion of the welfare-regulatory state—must reckon with this much simpler origin story. The idea of anti-discrimination was a straightforwardly political one born in the 1860s, and it remained a legal-moral aspiration for civil rights reformers until they succeeded in bringing it to life a century later. It might go too far to say that anti-discrimination is *causa sui*, but it is certainly true that at the outset it was an obvious effort to address an obvious need.

But, to repeat, it was a lesser, much more restricted, view of this effort that was insisted upon at the outset, and according to the terms of liberal principle. Unlike today, when statute is supreme in the anti-discrimination effort (rendering constitutional law a relative backwater), in the postbellum years it was the rule of constitutional principle that governed the whole. The guarantees of the Fourteenth and Fifteenth Amendments to equality in the public sphere (guarantees made to individuals as "citizens" that included the "privileges or immunities of citizens," "due process of law," the "equal protection of the laws," and the right to vote) are rather emphatically drawn by reference to the public-private divide, offering by their own explicit terms no clear path to the governing of private sector discrimination. Moreover, in a turn not simply required by these provisions, this public sector guarantee was in 1883 interpreted by the United States Supreme Court, in the *Civil Rights Cases*, as a *limit* to government protection of the rights of American Blacks.[3] The idea that making public sector equality a reality might *require* governmental efforts in the private sector as well, a view that we take for granted today, was emphatically cast aside. When the Reconstructionist Congress's 1875 Civil Rights Act prohibited segregation and discrimination in hotels, restaurants, and other similarly private institutions (the last federal civil rights bill to be passed until 1957), the Supreme Court struck it down as "running the slavery argument into the ground."[4] Justice Bradley stated with brutal clarity the stinginess of the public-private divide logic at work in his articulation of the quintessentially liberal "state action" doctrine that was central in this case: so long as "not sanctioned in some way by the State, or not done under State authority," the "wrongful act of an individual . . . is simply a private wrong."[5]

The first failing of the liberal framework, then, was to underestimate the harm associated with the "private wrongs" of racial discrimination. Discriminatory practices permitted in the private sphere affected every important area of life—from employment (differential rates of pay; arbitrary employment practices; exclusion from professions; segregated industries, labor unions, and workplaces) to common society (segregated housing, hotels, restaurants, transportation, sports arenas, concert halls, theaters, beaches, hospitals, blood banks—even churches and cemeteries).[6] By assuming that "private" prejudices are no concern of the state, American liberal race doctrine ignored certain massive facts of social life, facts of great consequence for those on the receiving end of such "private wrongs."[7]

What happened next exposed a further problem in the liberal perspective on political life. The tyranny of the majority as pertains to Whites and Blacks in America did not in fact halt at a line drawn by "private" persecution or even by an overbearing mass public (which is of course to say collective private) opinion. Once the private prejudices of the White majority were given legal sanction, not surprisingly, they came to inform the framework of the law—the basic terms of the public sector—as well. Thus, the second manifest failing of American liberalism was that it did not live up to its own standard of safeguarding public equality, or equal citizenship, for Blacks. *Unequal* treatment was indeed the law of the land—in voting, in the courtroom, in the criminal law, and in the provision of government services.[8] Not surprisingly, this state of affairs involved a good bit of legal maneuvering. The purported privacy of the contract, a legal shield used to exclude Blacks from private employment and housing, for example, was ignored when it came to contracts in an area of life as intimate as marriage: the public-private divide was no bar to overt state prohibitions of interracial marriage.[9] Outright segregation in the public sphere, ultimately enshrined as constitutional doctrine in 1896 by the Supreme Court in *Plessy v. Ferguson*, extended not only to transportation (at issue in *Plessy*), but also to public education (higher and lower), libraries, public parks, recreation centers, health care, public housing, mental institutions, the military, and prisons.[10]

In "separate but equal," liberal principle was clearly distorted (compulsory separation of the races by law being in no way compatible with equality before the law). Since this is the case, one might try to defend liberalism here by saying that its theoretical terms were not of course by themselves the real source of the problem. But the crucial legal and political preparation for this distortion of liberalism was the basic idea that permitting private discrimination could be thought of as a matter of right, a stance that the quintessentially liberal divide between public and private, and liberalism's vow to erect protective walls between the two, readily lends itself to and may even demand. One student of liberalism (considering the case from the point of view of religion and the situation of Jews in Weimar Germany in particular) states the basic issue with useful clarity.

> Liberalism stands or falls by the distinction between state and society, or by the recognition of a private sphere, protected by the law but impervious to the law, with the understanding that, above all, religion as particular religion belongs to the private sphere. Just as certainly as the liberal state will not "discriminate" against its Jewish citizens, so is it constitutionally unable and even unwilling to prevent "discrimination" against Jews by individuals or groups. To recognize a private sphere in the sense

indicated means to permit private "discrimination," to protect and thus in fact to foster it. The liberal state cannot provide a solution to the Jewish problem, for such a solution would require a legal prohibition against every kind of "discrimination," i.e. the abolition of the private sphere, the destruction of the liberal state. (Strauss 1965, 6; see Strauss 1989, 232)

Taking no position, as a matter of theory, on the private prejudices and prejudiced actions (even if they are "private wrongs," as Justice Bradley put it), was not a neutral stance in practice. As one prominent civil rights attorney put it in 1949, "American law . . . pays a moral price for the discrimination it validates and upholds. The moral cost of discrimination . . . is to be seen resulting from two sources: (1) the cost flows from discrimination which exists because of the law; and (2) the cost flows from discrimination which exists despite the law" (Konvitz 1949, 51). Whether we understand this state of affairs from the point of view of the public or the private side of the divide (the state must not interfere; individuals must be left free to discriminate), this is a blind spot in liberal theory that the forces of race discrimination were able to exploit.

Early Liberal Limits to Reform

Today, under the influence of the new order, it is easy to forget just how powerfully the liberal understanding framed the question of race discrimination prior to the anti-discrimination revolution. The civil rights movement was itself initially cast in these terms. Frederick Douglass states the basic issue by using a once common distinction between social (private) equality on the one hand and political (public) equality on the other, a distinction that anti-discrimination politics has now rendered obsolete: "Now I hold that there is but one way of wisely disposing of the colored race and that is to do them right and justice. It is not only to break the chains of their bondage and accord to them personal liberty, but it is to admit them to the full and complete enjoyment of civil and political Equality. . . . The question is not can there be social equality. That does not exist anywhere."[11] Since the Fourteenth Amendment guarantees only public sector equality, *Brown v. Board of Education*, as important as it was, could not go beyond the limit of formal liberal theory (asserting equality in public education).¹² Even Martin Luther King Jr., in appealing to the Declaration's self-evident truth of the equality of all men, insisted only that "the Negro [be] granted his citizenship rights" (1986, 218).

Likewise, when the cause of civil rights reform was poised for its ultimate victory, the voice of opposition relied on the terms of traditional liberalism. This was the position of George Wallace and Southern members of Congress opposed to the 1964 Civil Rights Act. One held that "its passage would be a power grab that could lead to a totalitarian dictatorship by the Federal Government."¹³ But it was also the position of principled conservatives as well. Urging patience and gradualism, President Eisenhower leaned on the traditional liberal view that "it is difficult through law and through force to change a man's heart" (a view echoed by his Democratic opponent Adlai Stevenson) (Klarman 2004, 324–25). It is little remembered that the Civil Rights Act was the most important question of domestic policy in the 1964 presidential election, Republican Barry Goldwater maintaining that there was "no constitutional basis" for Titles II and VII (regulating the private sector, public accommodations, and employment) and decrying what he saw as an attempt to "legislate morality" that would lead to "the creation of a police state."¹⁴ Robert Bork (later Solicitor General and Supreme Court nominee), who would, like Goldwater, eventually change his position, originally opposed the 1964 Act in traditional liberal terms, deeming it a new form of "McCarthyism": "It is one thing when stubborn people express their racial antipathies in laws which prevent individuals, whether white or Negro, from dealing with those who are willing to deal with them, and quite another to tell them that even as individuals they may not act on their racial preferences in particular areas of life" (1963, 22).

More striking are similar concerns, hesitations, and second thoughts among noted progressives. Civil libertarians and even some civil rights advocates were among the opponents of early private sector anti-discrimination efforts in New York state and, later, of the 1964 Civil Rights Act.¹⁵ Organized labor's initial resistance to desegregation, as voiced by the American Federation of Labor's National Legislative Committee chairman, appealed explicitly to liberal principle as well. "The executive council does not believe, however, that imposition of any policy, no matter how salutary, through compulsory Government control of freely constituted associations of workers, accords with the basic right of freedom of association among the American people."[16] Perhaps most famously, Hannah Arendt defended a right to discriminate in the private sphere according to the dictates of traditional liberal theory: "Discrimination is as indispensable a social right as equality is a political right. The question is not how to abolish discrimination, but how to keep it confined within the social sphere, where it is legitimate, and prevent its trespassing on the political and the personal sphere, where it is destructive" (1959, 51). Such hesitations are reflected in the 1964 Act itself, which has not one but two different (one Democratic, one Republican) constitutional justifications written into the law to reassure the Supreme Court and anyone else who might think that the measure had gone beyond the strictures of traditional liberalism.[17]

Now it is important not to go too far here. While traditional liberalism was constitutionally incapable of seeing and thus reaching abuses suffered by American Blacks in what it deemed the private domain, there is surely nothing in liberalism that intends such treatment of some citizens by others. The particular circumstances of American Blacks—the legacy of policies permitting slavery that were manifestly incompatible with liberalism—is a fact of history for which liberalism cannot be blamed. Indeed, there is much in its universal claim of human equality and its tradition of toleration that cuts against racism, however inadequate it may seem to us from our post-1964 vantage point. Americans also, of course, fought and won a civil war to end slavery at least partly in the name of liberal principle. Moreover, there can be no doubt that it was the promise of liberal equal citizenship that served to provide Black Americans and their leaders with a goal that inspired resistance to the regime of racial discrimination that could reasonably be hoped to have purchase with many Americans, as in the event it did. The standard of public sector equality, though distorted by *Plessy*, was never abandoned, and it helped to support and sustain the view that racial discrimination itself—whether public or private—was dubious and unjust.[18]

The Anti-Discrimination Revolution

Nevertheless, it cannot be surprising that, to overcome racism, eventually political actors began to think that it would not be enough simply to restore the traditional liberal standard of equal citizenship, even by rejecting the hypocrisy of "separate but equal," the great achievement of *Brown*. The full remedy, anti-discrimination policy, like the evil of discrimination itself, could not be limited by the boundary separating public from private. Only an effort to uproot discrimination and prejudice fully and completely and at their source, in the private sphere, could hope to solve the problem of racism in America. The 1964 Civil Rights Act (and not the *Brown* decision a decade earlier) is the crucial turning point: the willingness to take the fight against discrimination into the private sphere (in Title II and Title VII) marked in unmistakable terms a gathering of political will to insist upon a dramatically different settlement of the question of race and race discrimination in America. (One may say that the public-private divide has *never* in fact organized American civil rights politics: prior to 1964 racial discrimination was a reality in the public and private domains; after 1964 the fight against it was likewise total and pervasive.)

The shift from a policy of mere non-discrimination in the public sphere to one of anti-discrimination that extends not only to the public but also to the private sphere may seem at first to be a development of merely technical, legalistic import. But in the context of American liberalism, this shift is crucial and has had far-reaching consequences. Breaking with liberalism's defining terms, anti-discrimination policy has had a radical cast from the very start.

Before sketching the substance of the ambitious legal and political architecture of the anti-discrimination effort it is worth noting other elements of its early history that suggest its revolutionary nature. Major changes of political form do not have to be sudden or dramatic, but when they are, this is a sign that we should not ignore. Earlier efforts of reform had remained within the confines of the liberal public-sector framework of civil rights protections and had done little to affect the regime of racial discrimination. Surely they do not foretell what was to come. Court-mandated desegregation of the (public sector) schools after *Brown* had proved ineffective. By 1960, six years after the Supreme Court's landmark decision, very little had changed in the South (not a single Black pupil attended a desegregated public school in the five states of the deep South prior to the fall of 1960; see Klarman 2004, 349). Lacking widespread cultural or popular support, early governmental efforts were precarious. Attempts by the executive branch alone had been consistently weakened and undermined by Congress during the Roosevelt and Truman administrations. As president, Eisenhower actually inclined in the direction of ending some of the new programs (see Graham 1990, 18). New York State's pioneering State Commission Against Discrimination, launched in 1945, sought to regulate discrimination in the private sphere but the results were mixed and such efforts made little headway outside a handful of other northern states (see Evans Case 2004, 72–77).

When the fundamental political and legal change came it was decisive, controversial, and largely unanticipated. As New York's efforts indicate, private sector anti-discrimination law was not unheard of—the idea had been around since the doomed efforts of the 1866 and 1875 Civil Rights Acts—but its status as national policy was far from assured prior to 1964. Gunnar Myrdal's monumental 1944 work *An American Dilemma* provides a detailed accounting of American race discrimination but one looks in vain in its pages for even a hint that the solution ought to be a campaign like the one eventually undertaken. The same limitation is visible in sociologist Robert MacIver's 1948 sketch of a general theory of group relations in a book subtitled "A Program for the Control of Inter-Group Discrimination in the United States." MacIver advocated relatively ambitious government efforts to counteract discrimination in the public sphere but, even though private sector discrimination might be "vexatious and may cause much rankling and embitterment," he held that "it does not lie within our province" (1948, 16). Commenting on the introduction by the Kennedy administration in 1963 of what later became the 1964 Civil Rights Act, William F. Buckley noted that it "was not even conceived of as recently as a year ago" (Klarman 2004, 435). Martin Luther King Jr. exaggerated only slightly when he said, speaking of the law, that "the bill now pending in Congress is the child of a storm, the product of the most turbulent motion the nation has ever known in peacetime" (1986, 170). While both parties had civil rights planks in their platforms, in 1956 neither Democrats nor Republicans contemplated the possibility of efforts beyond the public sector; and in 1960 only the Democrats—tentatively and cautiously—hinted at the possibility.

Not only was the moment of change unexpected and dramatic, but compulsion was not absent from it. The use of federal troops by Eisenhower at Little Rock and by Kennedy in Mississippi and Alabama (Kennedy also sent five hundred US marshals to Alabama in 1961) did not involve outright violence, but this application of force should not be minimized for that reason. While the Black civil rights movement stressed nonviolence, this was nevertheless an energetic and effective political protest movement exerting a kind of pressure running outside the give-and-take of normal political life. Its efforts also marked a shift away from the gradualist legal strategy and hopes of steady incremental change over the long term that had characterized the reform movement in earlier years. In any event, the violence of White resistance was of course no small part of the drama and led, eventually, to significant efforts of federal law enforcement agencies (the FBI, after much foot-dragging and some active resistance and obstructionism, did eventually become an effective force supporting the new order [see O'Reilly 1989]). The circumstances under which the 1964 Act itself passed also suggest the dramatic nature of the change underway. After a year of intensifying protests, and in the immediate wake of the Kennedy assassination, the energetic exertions of Lyndon Johnson helped to overcome many obstacles (to include the opposition of Southern congressional committee chairs and a "record shattering southern filibuster" in the Senate) that would have otherwise made passing a bill as groundbreaking as the 1964 Act unlikely (Graham 1990, 151).

Historians and political scientists offer competing explanations for how and why the civil rights revolution succeeded when it did. Some emphasize the deft strategizing and morally powerful protests of American Blacks in the South, ably led by a combination of ministers, students, lawyers, and others within that community (with the support of other groups, notably, Jewish Americans). Others emphasize more broadly the upheaval of World War II—Black participation in the war, the horrifying example of the Holocaust, and the hypocrisy of a struggle against racialist Nazism by a country claiming the moral high ground while suppressing racial groups at home. In these explanations, the moral opinion—of Whites as well as Blacks—is properly included among the causes of the reform's success. Still others place the civil rights struggle in a context of "decolonization" efforts elsewhere (characterizing anti-discrimination itself as a form of "domesticated anti-colonialism").[19] A number of political scientists and historians, on the other hand, emphasize the role of foreign policy and the cost of American racism in international relations during a competition on the world stage with communist regimes in the context of the Cold War.[20] However one rates the primacy of these different explanations, they all suggest extraordinary pressures and, taken together, help to make intelligible the extent and suddenness of the change.

Finally, anti-discrimination's transformative power is also signaled by the remarkable fact that political opposition to the reform disappeared almost overnight. This political change had clear winners and losers, and the losers have almost vanished from the public scene. Today no one but the White supremacist fringe would speak of a legitimate area of "private" discrimination against Blacks. Significant opposition to anti-discrimination policy suffered a mortal blow in Goldwater's defeat in 1964, and it died with George Wallace's 1968 Independence Party presidential bid. Today no one calls for repeal of the 1964 Act, and anyone invoking liberal principle to oppose anti-discrimination policy in the private sphere is summarily dismissed by the Right as much as by the Left.[21] The principle and policy of a robust commitment to anti-discrimination is no longer opposed by any politically relevant (elected or electable) actor. This was a fundamental and seemingly irrevocable political decision—like those taken in the Revolutionary and Civil Wars—that cannot be said to characterize even many of the basic accomplishments of the New Deal. The most important explanation for this decisive and more or less total change in the citizen perspective has to do with the relationship between politics and morality—which is extremely important in the case of anti-discrimination—and the power of morality to establish simple and clear lines of opposition: what once was right is now wrong, what once was authoritative is now ignoble.

From Revolution to Regime

To speak of "regime change" in the context of American politics is controversial. Has not the American liberal democratic *constitutional* order remained firm, ruling from on high for more than two centuries, largely unchanged, despite several significant political upheavals? To think in terms of regimes or political orders seems an old-fashioned, premodern, way of looking at things. It also privileges political (and legal) change over social, cultural, intellectual, or economic developments. It certainly contradicts vital assumptions of the liberal democratic mind, some of which carry over into social science. Morally, liberal political theory views "regimes" and their narrow or partial claims as likely illegitimate threats to the decisive and general or universal relationship that it champions, the relationship between individual rights bearers and the state. All rule and nobody rules; certainly no part "deserves" to rule if rule means ruling over others. Rule as such may indeed be said to be immoral, a violation of individual freedom. At the same time, according to liberal social science, democratic politics is a fluid system in which the interests of all—whether understood as individuals or individualistic groups—are aggregated and sorted. Nobody—no regime—"rules" on that view either.

It is a measure of the revolutionary character of American anti-discrimination politics that it compels us to rethink the adequacy of such a view of things. Even on the basis of what we have seen thus far, we can already begin to see the broad challenge to it posed by the civil rights revolution. The commitment to fighting discrimination in the private as well as the public sphere signals not a total but nevertheless an important change in the basic character of the American political order. While breaking with and challenging the liberal framework of politics, anti-discrimination certainly does not aim to *replace* liberalism with some new general account of political life. But if political life in a democracy is to some great extent constituted by who and what "the citizen" is, then anti-discrimination marks an important alteration of things at a fundamental level. America has become, as we say, a more "inclusive" place since the 1960s. In addition, the civil rights revolution also ushers in a new sense of what citizens *deserve* from one another. The movement of Blacks (and women and all of the other newly protected groups) from "second-class citizenship" to full first-class citizenship captures this development in the not unhelpful terms of our commonsense political language.

But the *full* force of the revolution would not be felt for some years. Tracing all the avenues along which the anti-discrimination regime advanced from the end of the 1960s until, say, 2015, when gay marriage became the law of the land, will occupy historians of the future. Multicultural education will be one part of that story and an important one because, unlike law and policy pronouncements, multicultural education thinks and speaks in full, explaining to us what we need to do in the name of the new regime and why. But before turning to that dimension of the new order, to the interpretation of its aspirations or logic or ideas, it will be useful to examine in a general way, and to sketch in rough outlines, the development, after the 1960s, of anti-discrimination law. Surveying that territory will provide other opportunities to be impressed by the tensions between the new world and the old.

Chapter 3
ANTI-DISCRIMINATION REGIME, ANTI-DISCRIMINATION LAW

It is very easy for us to see how and why the anti-discrimination revolution was necessary. Less obvious is how and why that original impulse, which is unquestionable today, has become bound up with so many controversies and disagreements at the heart of our public life. Likewise, it is not simply obvious how and why that necessary reform would in turn become so central to our understanding of the basic meaning of democracy—and would come to be felt so forcefully and pervasively in so many areas of daily life.

One partial answer to those questions is to be had by recourse to the complex legal architecture that is vital to the anti-discrimination effort. It is true that the law, unlike multicultural education, does not explain to us why it is doing what it is doing—or even sometimes what it is doing—but no understanding of civil rights politics can dispense with at least some attempt to come to grips with the laws that have done so much to create its present shape. I admit that a tour of laws will not be a pleasing prospect for most sensible people, and that piling up lists of laws is ultimately an inadequate way to explain or interpret social and political phenomena. But law is too important to the life of the anti-discrimination regime to ignore, and it provides one indispensable (concrete, authoritative, hard to dismiss) starting point for thinking about the contours of this complex general development.

One reason to study the laws undergirding the anti-discrimination effort with some care may be stated now. Nowhere in all our laws will one find the following: "You shall lose your job, and, depending on the kind of work you do, quite possibly your career, if you are shown to be (or in some cases only plausibly accused of being) a racist, sexist, homophobe, or the like." Nor is there any law stating that the same rule applies in particular, and with added vigor, to leaders and managers, informing them that they may lose their livelihoods and status for failing, in addition, to police *other* people's discrimination adequately. There is not even any statute explicitly calling upon corporations, universities, or other important institutions in our society to enforce anti-discrimination norms internally, to teach their lessons, or to fire and banish from their ranks anyone violating their requirements. Such measures, now commonplace in democratic life, seem to be undertaken voluntarily by institutions and by the individuals within them, acting of their own accord—not by government agents acting in some official capacity. But these practices are indeed mandated by the law, somewhat indirectly perhaps but effectively nonetheless, though this is obscured in many ways by the law's complexity and by the fact that most of the law has been developed out of sight, in bureaucratic directives and court decisions. Uncovering the *legal basis* of what we now commonly deem the novel (and, to many, perplexing) "woke" mentality of our central (often nongovernmental) institutions and many of our citizens will for the future be necessary to our very self-understanding, for we are the children of these laws.[1]

In what follows I begin by offering two short "lessons" in the law (I stress their brevity: the first is four paragraphs; the second is three). The first focuses on what I take to be the heart of anti-discrimination law, Title VII of the 1964 Civil Rights Act and its many expansions (plus, very briefly, Title IX of the 1972 Education Amendments). This lesson serves to explain the great penetrating force of anti-discrimination law in our lives. The second surveys in a general way the broad scope and scale of the anti-discrimination effort taken as a whole—areas of life regulated; institutions dedicated to the work; groups championed. We will be rewarded for having done our legalistic homework by being prepared to start to think about the effects of these laws on the nature of democratic life. Their essential features suggest a new spirit of the laws that is very far from anything in the liberal tradition: through the law, the fight against discrimination has been made into an energetic campaign of the regulation of many of the relatively intimate interpersonal relations of citizens, as well as of their speech and thought, implemented not by government but by private citizens, enforced with relatively severe sanctions (above all, the loss of employment), and shaping a new and distinctive civic-moral sensibility. We are more than justified in resorting to the language of the regime to reckon with these developments.

Law Lesson 1:
Title VII, the Expanding Center of Anti-Discrimination Law

Title VII of the 1964 Civil Rights Act, regulating employment discrimination, may be said to occupy the *center* of civil rights law; it thus serves as an indispensable starting point for understanding the whole. The workplace is a crucial site of life in modern democracies, and the laws regulating it in the name of the civil rights revolution serve that effort in a way that is simultaneously pervasive and powerful. Moreover, because Title VII employment discrimination cases have been so heavily litigated, many crucial questions are addressed there first. Legal tests and standards developed by the courts for Title VII are then exported to neighboring domains of anti-discrimination law.[2] One can indeed judge other kinds of anti-discrimination protection by asking whether they measure up to the standards set by Title VII (separate statutory regimes for disability and age discrimination, for example, do not, a complaint of attorneys in those fields).[3] But most important, it is in and through Title VII that the anti-discrimination regime came to devise, eventually, its most powerful and severe modes of *enforcement*.

Most of the significant developments of Title VII have been expansions of the original law, almost all of them developed by the federal civil rights bureaucracy and the courts (and never codified in federal statute); they are therefore hidden from view to a significant degree. Six expansions of Title VII in particular have proven crucial. (I leave aside for now a seventh—disparate impact/affirmative action—one of the earliest and most important expansions of anti-discrimination law, and treat it separately at the end.) The first was granting the EEOC the power to bring Title VII lawsuits against employers on behalf of private individuals (making the EEOC similar to a public prosecutor). This is the only one of these expansions undertaken by Congress in a federal statute, the Equal Employment Opportunity Act of 1972. The second and third important expansions—defining "discrimination" so as to include *stereotypes* and *harassment*—were ideas dreamed up by law professors, embraced by the EEOC, and eventually cemented into the structure of the whole authoritatively by decisions of federal courts and, ultimately, the Supreme Court.[4] Harassment, especially, has always been an expansive concept, extending from the start to words and deeds held to create a "hostile work environment"—later coming to encompass also the "hostile educational environment," the "hostile public accommodations environment" (to include "hostile patron speech"), and, today, emerging notions of the hostile online environment.[5] Taken together, stereotypes and harassment have significantly enlarged our understanding of what constitutes discrimination, a term never defined in Title VII or any other civil rights statute.

A fourth crucial expansion is concealed not only by its legally obscure origins but also by the uninteresting heading under which it appears: employer liability. The result of this shift in the 1990s, combined with the view that discrimination includes stereotypes and harassment, was to extend the responsibility of employers beyond the region of their own policies and official, overt employment actions (hiring and firing, etc.)—to include, eventually, all of the actions (whether work-related or not) of everyone operating anywhere within the sphere of the workplace. No longer does Title VII mean merely that employers embrace non-discriminatory employment practices; now institutions are to take on responsibility for the deeds, words, and even the opinions of those in their employ—regardless of whether those individuals are acting on behalf of the employer or as private individuals engaging in private activities that merely occur in the workplace. Moreover, employers became responsible not only for their own employees (and all of them, not just executives, managers, or supervisors), but also third parties like contractors, vendors, and customers. Owning responsibility for what *might* happen anywhere in the workplace, and in relation to everyone operating in that space, would become the starting point for employers facing discrimination lawsuits and would change the expectations of everyone involved (management, employees, government, the public).[6] A fifth crucial expansion then followed from the fourth. In answering the anxieties of employers now facing a new and massive liability threat (harassment settlements in the millions, toxic reputational harm), the civil rights bureaucracy and the courts reassured them that they could protect themselves at least to some degree by undertaking "preventive and corrective measures." Those measures begin with what we today call diversity training but they include as well, crucially, various *disciplinary* measures—up to and including the firing of employees. The fourth and fifth expansions—heightened liability and the legal path of corrective measures to be taken to avoid its penalties—are spelled out explicitly in EEOC guidance documents appearing as early as 1980 that were eventually accepted as authoritative by the federal courts.[7] The Supreme Court gave its blessing to the new arrangement, somewhat obliquely but clearly enough, when it announced the so-called *Ellerth-Faragher* test in 1998.[8] The sixth expansion of Title VII occurred when America's employment institutions—following the advice of their attorneys and noting with alarm headlines trumpeting famous harassment lawsuits with large settlements—embraced the new regime.[9] Employers would henceforth police a broad and loose understanding of discrimination using a wide array of tools, to include the punishment of violators and what must be called efforts of moral and civic education.[10] What is today called woke capitalism was built upon this legal foundation.

What Title VII did for the workplace, Title IX of the Education Amendments of 1972 did for the domain of education. Because education is also already regulated by Title VII (schools and universities being employers), this additional layer of dedicated regulation, aggressively pursued by the Department of Education (DOE), struck with added force. Indeed, as Shep Melnick's excellent study, *The Transformation of Title IX*, makes clear, where employers under Title VII were to some degree left to sort these things out for themselves, the DOE and its Office of Civil Rights (OCR) led with a heavier hand (with, in effect, "liability standards more demanding than the *Ellerth-Faragher* framework"). "OCR developed a sophisticated, two-part enforcement strategy. Part 1 involved turning each *individual* sexual assault complaint against a school into a well-publicized and costly investigation of the practices of the *entire institution*." These investigations, themselves powerful weapons of enforcement, and backed by the federal funding cut-off threat of Title VI of the 1964 Act, were then implemented using "legally binding compliance agreements." The main result of these compliance agreements was the mandatory creation of new anti-discrimination offices and officers within the universities—"compliance units . . . responsive to OCR." In undertaking all of this the Department of Education's civil rights lawyers did not follow the guidance of Congress or even the courts; they simply made the rules up and imposed them on American colleges and universities. As Melnick reports, no American institution of higher education resisted these efforts to any significant degree.[11] In this way, through a nexus of interrelated laws, the anti-discrimination regime came to command two crucial sites of American life: the workplace and the university.

Law Lesson 2: Three Ways to Gauge the Scope and Scale of Anti-Discrimination Law

When we look to anti-discrimination law taken *as a whole*, it is tempting simply to say that there is no important area of life untouched by its requirements. We are reminded of this in an especially vivid way at the present moment by the Biden administration's launching of a "whole-of-government equity agenda," a "generational commitment," and by the three hundred *new* equity initiatives commenced in its name in April 2022 (involving "90 federal agencies across the federal government, including all Cabinet-led agencies as well as over 50 independent agencies").[12] But the pervasive reach of anti-discrimination law was already in place, as is indicated by other plentiful and obvious evidence. Some anti-discrimination regulations, like Title VII's extension into all areas of employment, have a built-in effect that is already pervasive. Similarly, Title III of the 1964 Act prohibited segregation and discrimination in all government facilities and in the provision of government services. Title II of the 1964 Act, which, like Title VII, extends the law into the private sector, covers one specific domain: "public accommodations." But this of course expands the reach of the law into several different kinds of social gathering spaces simultaneously: "any inn, hotel, motel"; "any restaurant, cafeteria, lunchroom, lunch counter, soda fountain"; "any retail establishments"; "any gasoline station"; "any motion picture house, theater, concert hall, sports arena, stadium or other place of exhibition or entertainment."[13] The 1964 Act's Title VI federal funding cut-off power likewise licenses government to extend its reach into many different areas of life, public and private, all at once. One need not agree with historian Hugh Davis Graham that Title VI was "the sleeper that in time would become by far the most powerful weapon of them all," indeed, more powerful than "all the other titles in the landmark civil rights bill combined" (I would insist on the supreme importance, eventually, of Title VII), in order to note its wide-ranging effect

(Graham 1990, 82–83). There are, in addition, other major anti-discrimination statutes designed to deal with specific domains of life. Of particular concern to us are the many federal laws prohibiting discrimination in the field of education (some of which we have already mentioned and which we will survey in more detail in chapter 4). Measures targeting discrimination in housing, and laws related to them governing real estate development, lending, banking, and insurance, were also important from the first. Still other narrower policies launched by many different federal agencies spread the reach of anti-discrimination law to every nook and cranny of modern life. Dedicated government policies fight environmental racism; promote the health of women and racial minorities; support minority business owners; advance the interests of racial minority farmers; harness the power of the police (both to protect against violence against women or victims of hate crimes and to police the police itself in its dealings with minorities); and advance the interests of minority veterans.[14] Crucially important, what we commonly call the cultural domain of life is mapped over a number of times by anti-discrimination laws regulating the mass media (print, radio, and television), advertising, the film industry, as well as internet content and even internet search algorithms. Official policy now also ensures that an appropriate anti-discrimination lens is applied in the management of our national parks and historical monuments and in the work of historical preservation.[15] Other policies mandate efforts on behalf of anti-discrimination groups in the arts, in the humanities, and in the sciences.[16] The Biden administration's 2022 equity initiative adds several more of these focused efforts—advancing, for example, "equity enterprise," "transportation equity," "inclusive innovation," "minority broadband initiatives," "climate change equity," "domestic violent extremism equity," and "property appraisal and valuation equity."[17]

Another crude but useful measure of the anti-discrimination regime's wide embrace may be taken by reference to the array of dedicated *institutions* created to enforce its laws and promote its ends. Were all the agencies of the federal anti-discrimination effort massed together into one "U.S. Department of Anti-Discrimination," it would be a sizeable entity. Ibram Kendi's call for a "Department of Anti-racism" has made him notorious, but in fact his imagination understates what already exists (Kendi 2019b). At the top, legal leadership, as well as some loose coordination of anti-discrimination efforts throughout the federal bureaucracy, is provided by the

Civil Rights Division of the Department of Justice (DOJ). Two prominent independent commissions, the Civil Rights Commission and the Equal Employment Opportunity Commission (EEOC), are wholly devoted to the cause. Through the EEOC (massive and very influential in the development of the law), the federal government oversees anti-discrimination enforcement in the private workplace (reviewing complaints; launching investigations; bringing lawsuits), while the DOJ does the same for the workplace of state and local government. Then there are four *layers* of anti-discrimination offices that may be found at every level of the federal government, in every one of its institutions. All major federal government agencies have an Office of Civil Rights (OCR) (or Office of Equal Employment Opportunity, or the like) to police discrimination within the institutions of government itself. These OCR's also, in some cases, take on other important specific civil rights enforcement tasks—in the field of education, for example—connected to the work of the institutions in which they reside. Another layer of bureaucracy has only very recently been called into being (on February 16, 2023) by a Biden administration executive order creating "Agency Equity Teams" in every important agency of the federal government ("my Administration has embedded a focus on equity into the fabric of Federal policymaking and service delivery").[18] We do not yet know how these Agency Equity Teams and the older OCR's will interact, but if the role of the OCR is any guide, we can expect the former to take on substantial duties. OCR's are sometimes very powerful institutions in their own right. OCR's take on various regulatory tasks and in so doing wield the Title VI federal funding cut-off threat (potentially applicable to a range of public and private entities under their jurisdiction). The efforts of these offices are coordinated through the DOJ's Civil Rights Division. The OCR's of the Departments of Education and Labor, in particular, are well-known for aggressively advocating an expansive vision of anti-discrimination policy in their areas of responsibility. The third layer, another agency wholly given over to anti-discrimination enforcement across the span of federal institutions, is the "little known but influential" Office of Federal Contract Compliance Programs (OFCCP) in the Department of Labor (launched by a famous 1965 executive order [No. 11246] and never authorized by any federal statute [Melnick 2018, 35]). This office uses "the awesome power of the federal purse" to demand adherence to a variety of anti-discrimination rules, to include affirmative action plans, for any private business seeking a federal contract from any government institution.[19] Fourth, all major federal agencies have an Office of Small and Disadvantaged Business Utilization (OSDBU) to encourage and monitor government support for minority and women-owned private sector businesses (coordinated through a Federal OSDBU Directors Interagency Council). Through agency OCR's, Agency Equity Teams, and OSDBU's, and through the efforts of the OFCCP, there are now four sets of civil rights institutions watching over everything the federal government does and, in places, guiding its activities. There are also, last but not least, many other federal offices that take on more targeted anti-discrimination tasks. Central to our investigation of multicultural education, desegregating and reforming American public education was of course vital to the civil rights revolution, these various efforts being led by the Department of Education's (DOE) OCR and extended in a variety of other educational reforms that the law has supported or mandated (most famously, Title IX). But other smaller DOE programs and offices, like the Minority Science and Engineering Improvement Program, the Women's Educational Equity Program, and the Office of Special Education and Rehabilitation Services, also make or have made a contribution. A variety of additional smaller dedicated offices administer a number of specific, narrower civil rights initiatives that are, or have been, housed in the Departments of Agriculture, Commerce, Housing and Urban Development, Health and Human Services, Justice, Labor, State, Treasury, and Veterans Affairs.[20] The Biden administration's recent efforts add at least another seven new offices, as well as several high-profile individual "Equity" or "Diversity" officers, to this list.[21]

Finally, the breadth of the anti-discrimination effort is suggested in the more or less immediate expansion of the law to cover a wide array of different kinds of *groups* ("protected classes"). Less revealing, this is perhaps the most common way to summarize anti-discrimination law all at once. Anti-discrimination policy, originally designed to deal with one specific case—the extraordinary situation of Black Americans—was quickly extended to a diverse array of other groups that could make a persuasive claim for protection. From the outset, racial and ethnic groups, religious groups, and women and men were all included among Title VII's list of protected classes. Other federal statutes soon extended the anti-discrimination regime to others: the elderly in 1967; language minorities in 1968; the disabled in 1973; pregnant women in 1978. In 2008, persons who have been genetically coded were added to the list.[22] Today it is lesbians, gays, bisexuals, and transgender persons who press most visibly for full inclusion under the anti-discrimination legal umbrella. Other protected categories of discrimination's victims have been included to different degrees in different contexts. Writing in 1989, one political scientist counted some thirty different kinds of discrimination prohibited at least to some degree by American laws, to include discrimination on the basis of financial status and receipt of public assistance, criminal record, and drug or alcohol dependency—and many more have been added since then (Knopff 1989, 65n12). Even supposedly "privileged" groups—like Whites claiming reverse discrimination and reverse harassment and members of the Christian majority declaiming anti-religious bias—now adopt the mantle of discrimination victim as a matter of course.

The Spirit of Anti-Discrimination Law

Seeing all at once these laws and institutions, and some of their immediate effects, puts us in a position to understand better a range of perplexing and unsettling contemporary developments that we try to express under somewhat vague (but not wrong) headings like political correctness, identity politics, woke ideology, cancel culture, and the like. Taking the liberal tradition as our point of departure, we may say that anti-discrimination law has achieved an amazing inversion of liberalism's basic terms, retaining the appearances of the distinction between public and private, state and society, but now in order to enlist the private sector to bring about a forceful, effective, and wide-ranging regulation of every area of life, public and private, in the name of an extraordinarily ambitious, explicitly civic or political, and ultimately moral, project. Anyone who begins from the basic logic of liberalism will be struck by four characteristic features of life under this regime, four aspects or consequences of the law that we do not always attribute to the law because the role of law is often hidden by its very terms. First is the great penetrating reach of the law's aims, extending to many dimensions of life we deem private. Second is the law's reliance upon novel forms of nongovernmental—in a way, privatized—enforcement. Third are new and distinctive forms of coercive power employed by anti-discrimination law in a punitive mode—what we call "cancellation," for example, but also, above all, what I term corrective firing. Fourth is the soul-shaping (moral and psychological) effect of this legal regime and the new legal and civic sensibility (a civil-criminal hybrid) that advances under its auspices. These characteristics of the law begin to make plain, at the very least, that the effort to fight discrimination follows its own path and not that of traditional liberalism.

Penetrating Aims:
Regulating Society and Individual Behavior, Speech, and Thought

Discrimination appears in many places and the impulse of anti-discrimination law is always, naturally, to try to root it out wherever it may be found. As a direct result of this, the first essential attribute of anti-discrimination law is its aim (successful so far) to regulate in a direct way many important areas of what liberalism calls private life. This was signaled at the outset in a simple way, Title VII reaching into the private sector of business and Title II regulating one important site of communal or social life, public accommodations. But it is necessary to press the point beyond this formal level of the law's basic terms. Anti-discrimination regulates and seeks to regulate in a general way society, interpersonal interactions, sexual relations, speech, and thought—that is to say, it regulates culture, life. This might sound like libertarian (or Gramscian) hyperbole, and so it is necessary to make some brief demonstrations by proof-at-law.

Anti-discrimination law undeniably attempts to regulate what we call society. The workplace is already an important social site, of course, but anti-discrimination's regulation of society does not stop there. The role played by anti-discrimination law in our neighborhoods (housing laws), as well as in all the different areas we deem public accommodations, cannot be accounted for in any other terms. This was always the meaning of "desegregation." Segregation is a social phenomenon and not primarily (though it may be accidentally) an economic one. The terms of Title II of the 1964 Act, which takes aim at segregation most directly, provide in a very direct way for the regulation of social relations, penalizing and protecting at the level of individual "persons"—not institutions or economic entities. "No *person* shall withhold, deny, or attempt to withhold or deny, or deprive or attempt to deprive, any *person* of any right or privilege secured."[23] Laws desegregating private clubs and associations likewise reach into private social life in a straightforward and obvious way.[24] Finally, efforts undertaken to desegregate *education*, public and private, are among the most important of our attempts to affect the social relations of Americans (deploying the "contact hypothesis" was precisely an experiment in *social* contact). Liberalism's separation of state and society has not stood in the way of these developments, and it is no surprise that the old line drawn by liberalism between political equality and social equality, which, as we saw in chapter 2, was common even among civil rights advocates before 1964, has entirely disappeared.

But anti-discrimination law also reaches into our social interactions in a more direct and forceful way. Anti-discrimination law began by regulating the formal or official actions of institutions (hiring and firing of employees, admittance or nonadmittance of students) but has evolved into a scheme of regulation that involves itself in the one-on-one interpersonal interactions of individuals. Regulating harassment-as-hostile-environment must take as its object the most ordinary forms of human contact and seeks to govern what one individual may deem insulting or demeaning treatment by another.[25] This is the regulation of how we treat one another; to that end, anti-discrimination more than implicitly upholds a *standard* of interpersonal treatment—a very basic standard, in other words, of morality or justice. This may not be the call to love your neighbor as yourself, but it is surely something more than liberal notions of toleration or live and let live. Justice Scalia underestimated Title VII when he insisted that anti-harassment law would not amount to a "civility code."[26] It is that and much more.

The very special case of sex discrimination in particular demands that the law seek to reshape at least to some degree the most intimate regions of our social relations. In its regulation of sexual desire and related personal interactions, anti-discrimination's reach into private life reminds one of the efforts of *religion* in the past—to different ends, of course—but certainly not of liberalism. This is in a way obvious and does not need to be belabored, but it is one important part of the whole that has a general effect on the rest. As Carole Pateman has famously said, "the dichotomy between private and public . . . is, ultimately, what the feminist movement is about"

(1983, 281). Today, we are still trying to figure out what it means to say that sex and gender stereotypes are wrong, for example. Indeed, this penetrating dimension of anti-discrimination law has not yet run its course. In another great expansion of Title VII, the term "discrimination because of sex" was extended by the Supreme Court to include discrimination based on sexual orientation and gender identity (in its 2020 *Bostock* decision, one more vitally important expansion of the law penned by a conservative Justice).[27] Now the very meaning of gender, of man and woman, come under legal scrutiny, calling into question, in the name of the law, important and long-standing assumptions about life that are deeply and unavoidably personal.

It is restrictions on *speech*, perceived by many to encroach improperly upon personal liberties, that for a long time now have received the most attention in the debates that swirl around the anti-discrimination revolution. But defenders of freedom of speech do not typically see the reach of the law in what troubles them about the new censorship. Recent battles over free speech tend to highlight "private" sphere efforts, and not so much the efforts of government—on college campuses, countering microaggressions and "dog whistles," creating safe spaces, and insisting upon trigger warnings and diversity statements; in the online environment, censorship by corporations that own search, content, and social media platforms. But here, too, it is crucial to see just how deeply entrenched these limitations of speech are in the law (what law professor Jack Balkin has called, approvingly, "collateral censorship" [1999]). By far the most important of these restrictions derive from the anti-stereotype and anti-harassment measures of Title VII (and their extension through Title IX) summarized above. Not only do institutions necessarily lay down speech restrictions as a result, but they back them with coercive force (corrective firing and the like). But this development, as important as it is, is only one element in a broader regulatory scheme reaching speech. There are in fact at least a dozen other kinds of anti-discrimination policies that similarly restrict speech—to include FCC regulations, housing and other laws that restrict advertising, public accommodations laws, policies calling for old monuments to be pulled down, anti-bullying efforts, hate speech ordinances, and hate crimes laws.[28] One result of the intense debate over these issues has been the development of what is by now a fairly robust body of work by lawyers and social and political theorists who advance to much fanfare an attack on the idea of free speech as such, as well as the recent establishment of new institutions dedicated to defending free speech with suddenly necessary vigor.[29] The Supreme Court's contribution to the large question of the relationship between anti-discrimination and freedom of speech in all of these controversies has mainly been to ignore it or, at best, to take firm stands (in unanimous or near-unanimous decisions) on both sides of the question (on balance it has sided mostly with anti-discrimination).[30]

But anti-discrimination law does not stop at speech and also seeks very directly to alter the thought, the mind, of citizens. This is built into the law in a very direct and explicit way, which is and must be concerned with intent and motive, stereotypes, offensive conduct, and offensive statements. The penalties and punishments for discrimination *always* take aim at the discriminatory beliefs behind discriminatory actions. For the same reason, anti-discrimination law mandates, in many different ways, efforts to *teach* its civic lessons, and it does so without apology. "Dissemination of Policy Through Guidance, Regulations, Technical Assistance, Education, Outreach, and Publicity" is one of seven "Essential Elements of Effective Federal Civil Rights Enforcement," according to the U.S. Commission on Civil Rights.[31] I would of course emphasize multicultural education here (which has long been official policy, if at the state level), but other governmental efforts in this direction are also noteworthy. The EEOC has always held education to be one of its two main aims (the other being "law enforcement") and, from the beginning, its Education Division has provided an array of educational programming for employers to use.[32] Today, the EEOC Training Institute offers instruction to individuals from the public and private sectors alike. Similar dedicated efforts of the U.S. Commission on Civil Rights, the Department of Labor (through its Education and Training Administration and Civil Rights Center), the U.S. Office of Personnel Management, the Community Relations Service, and other federal agencies do likewise.[33] At least as important, and more visible, are diversity training efforts and the like offered throughout the domain of the workplace, public and private, and in our colleges and universities. The legal basis of diversity training is provided by the general drift of Title VII's development, but it is also directly affirmed in an important, if relatively unheralded, Supreme Court decision, *Kolstad v. American Dental Association*, where Justice

O'Connor held that "the purposes underlying Title VII are . . . advanced where employers are encouraged to . . . *educate* their personnel on Title VII's prohibitions."[34]

In all of this it is crucial to insist once again upon the obvious—namely, that it is in every instance *laws*, well-established and more or less unquestioned if not always very well-known, that achieve all of this. Conservative critics of these developments point to a variety of rival causes—cultural Marxism, radical feminism, postmodernism, the runaway freight train called higher education. But these are nothing in comparison with anti-discrimination law in terms of the power it has to govern our social interactions, censor our speech, and shape our thought. (In a kind of concession to its achievements, today we witness conservatives beginning to try to harness the instrumentalities of anti-discrimination law—treating DEI training as racial harassment, notions of reverse racism and reverse harassment in the workplace and in education, for example—to fight the perceived excesses of anti-discrimination law.)

Privatized Enforcement, Citizen-Enforcers

Like the aims they pursue, the characteristic means employed by the anti-discrimination regime similarly disrupt the received view of things under traditional liberalism. The quietest of all revolutions occurred in the late 1990s and early 2000s, when the enforcement of anti-discrimination law, now expanded to include stereotypes and harassment, was shifted to employers and universities and other such institutions, which then detailed managers, deans, HR workers—and eventually everyone within their sphere—to make it happen. It is no exaggeration to say that in every major corporation, in every college and university, in every major media outlet, in every large religious organization, in every hospital, in every military unit, in every government agency (and at all levels of government)—indeed, in every major institution in our society, public or private—there stands a small army of institutionally authorized diversity or equity or equal opportunity officers whose job it is to ensure adherence to the law and, naturally therefore, to uphold and advance its moral and political outlook. This is a massive undertaking involving individuals acting as semi-official enforcers of the regime's demands, an effort that may enlist, at least potentially, perhaps the majority of the population, insofar as coworkers and the like also share in responsibility for policing their fellows (and where sins of omission have serious consequences). This may not be quite what Barry Goldwater feared would happen—"the development of an 'informer' psychology in great areas of our national life, neighbors spying on neighbors, workers spying on workers, businessmen spying on businessmen"—but it is surely something unprecedented in liberal societies.[35]

It is important to emphasize that the EEOC and the federal courts did not simply tell employers and other institutions that they needed to take preventive and corrective measures to avoid liability for harassment and other forms of discrimination occurring in their domains, but spelled out in some detail what would be considered a good faith effort. A wide range of concrete tasks were specified that our citizen-enforcers would need to take on—of course, diversity training, but also formulating and publicizing various internal policies; assessing the status or climate of the workplace or educational institution; monitoring bias-reporting systems; fielding discrimination and harassment claims; conducting investigations; meting out corrective consequences; keeping records.[36] The same legal framework likewise created a demand for a host of new (nongovernmental) officers (Equal Opportunity officers, Title IX officers, the Chief Diversity Officer, etc.), officially designated institutions (Diversity Task Forces, Equity Teams, Bias Incident Response Teams, Workplace Responsibility Committees), and offices (the Office of Diversity, Equity, and Inclusion or the campus Multicultural Student Center).

We lack terms to name properly this dimension of the effort so that we can see it and comes to terms with it. Like Christopher Caldwell, I think it sensible to lean on the liberal tradition when trying to come to grips with "the great . . . innovation of the civil rights era—the proxy exercise by private institutions of government power" (2020, 273). There is much of illuminating force in speaking of this development as the privatization of anti-discrimination enforcement, the rise of the citizen-enforcer. Legal scholars on the Left who study the phenomenon also struggle to devise a new terminology to capture it: "the legalization of the workplace"; "the managerialization of law"; "institutional citizenship"; "legal endogeneity."[37] None of these latter terms has gained wide currency, but they all capture something useful precisely in their indifference to, their blurring of, the public-private divide. Indeed, by ignoring liberalism's framing of the issue, these latter terms all, in a way, better conform to the logic of anti-discrimination. But privatized enforcement is not only noteworthy from the point of view of liberalism; equally important is the contribution that it has made to the success of the anti-discrimination revolution. The test for this claim is a thought experiment in which we imagine a special federal government agency or police force doing all the enforcement work now undertaken by our fellow citizens. It is hard to believe that such a thing could exist—or, if it did, that it would have proved as effective as the current order.

Corrective Firing and Cancel Culture: The Hidden Fist of Anti-Discrimination Law

But the single most important fact about contemporary anti-discrimination law, causal and descriptive, is the coercive punitive force that is brought to bear upon the individual by our citizen-enforcers in the law's penetrating regulation of so many intimate aspects of life. (By now we surely see that to insist legalistically that anti-discrimination law does not reach the individual—because Title VII only applies to employers with fifteen employees, or something like that—would be a grave distortion.) This aspect of anti-discrimination law—the fact that people lose their jobs and are silenced, shamed, and otherwise punished in terms that affect their ability to earn a living—is in a way well-known but also somehow obscure; it is at any rate not immediately thought to be something achieved by the law. Most citizens today would begin in their thinking about the fight against discrimination by considering it to be a matter of public *morality* (something obviously right), first and foremost. But the role of coercion and the threat of coercion, and the effect they have on the tenor of anti-discrimination morality itself, must not be underestimated.

In order that my claims for the law here do not appear exaggerated, it is necessary to make explicit the more or less hidden legal basis of this, the regime's most coercive instrumentality. It is true that the EEOC guidance statements initially mandating these developments are obscure, and even more than obscure, in a legalistic sense. But the legal web created by those mandates, enforced by the courts and then obeyed and implemented by employers, are today as powerful as any statute. The basic terms of the original

EEOC documents certainly leave nothing to the imagination. "Disciplinary action against the offending supervisor or employee, ranging from reprimand to discharge, may be necessary" (U.S. EEOC 1990). "Examples of Measures to Stop Harassment and Ensure that it Does Not Recur [include] oral or written warning or reprimand; transfer or reassignment; demotion; reduction of wages; suspension; discharge; training or counseling of harasser to ensure that s/he understands why his or her conduct violated the employer's anti-harassment policy; and monitoring of harasser to ensure that harassment stops."[38] Such measures are among those to which the Supreme Court quietly gave its blessing in its *Ellerth-Faragher* liability test, where employers were called upon to demonstrate that they had "exercised reasonable care to *prevent and correct promptly* any . . . harassing behavior."[39]

Demotion, loss of pay, and outright loss of employment—as well as expulsion and other related consequences in the education context—are strong medicines in a bourgeois society, where people not only depend upon their income but often define themselves by what they do in the world of work. The range of activities for which individuals have been sanctioned is revealing. At one extreme are infamous cases of harassment and, in the case of sexual harassment on campus in particular, this extends to sexual assault as well. But at the other extreme are people deemed innocent, or who suffer penalties merely for their beliefs (there is a small literature here—essays in *Time*, the *Atlantic*, and the *Federalist*, e.g.: "Stop Firing the Innocent"; "We Can't Have 'National Dialogues' If People Get Fired for Talking Honestly"; "Can You Be Fired for Being a Racist?" "Is Being a White Supremacist Grounds for Firing?").[40] But in between there is a wide range of activities punished under the new order: offensive statements in the workplace; offensive statements outside the workplace (posted on social media or sent by private email but somehow discovered by others); actions or words *interpreted* to be offensive or discriminatory (using an "OK" hand sign, e.g.); similar actions in the remote past (photos of offensive Halloween costumes, e.g.); forwarding or "retweeting" the offensive statements of others; statements structured in neutral terms (otherwise legal), like the language of modern science, that convey a message deemed nevertheless to be offensive (Harvard president Larry Summers and Google's James Damore on gender disparities in science and tech, e.g.); failing to report or to take action against the discriminatory actions done by others; lackluster efforts to uphold the cause of anti-discrimination (especially in universities or corporations caught up in some kind of discrimination controversy or lawsuit, and especially for those in leadership positions); expressing (perfectly legal) criticism of politically controversial phenomena relating to anti-discrimination politics (gay marriage laws, abortion, the Black Lives Matter movement); criticizing, or refusing to take part in, diversity training and the like; raising criticisms against the means by which an institution enforces its perceived anti-discrimination mandates; criticizing the alleged hypersensitivity to discrimination of others (students, coworkers). Finally, in all of this, actions (and inaction) count against the accused for as long as employers and other relevant parties may learn of them—which means, of course, that one instance of apparent discrimination can be a career-ending event.

These cases are veiled in secrecy (employee privacy rights; non-disclosure agreements) and both the employee and the employer have good reasons to want to keep them quiet. Any person terminated in this way will find it difficult to object effectively; anyone in this position wanting to find a job elsewhere without a tainted record will have a major incentive to acquiesce even when feeling that the outcome is unfair. At any rate there is often little or no recourse for those fired or demoted or otherwise disciplined in the workplace. This is partly because of one added step in the legal story, the law of "at will employment" in the United States. As one textbook on employment discrimination law puts it, "'employment at will' means that an employer can hire, fire, promote, or transfer an employee for good reason, bad reason, or no reason at all" (Secunda, Hirsch, and Seiner 2018, 6).

In what we call cancel culture, the silencing of speech also takes a coercive form and is in a way part of or akin to corrective firing in its intent and effect. Cancellation, deplatforming, demonetization, and compelled speech (required diversity statements for job or school applicants and the like) all likewise have an effect on the targeted individual's ability to earn a living or to receive an education. Because most of these more coercive or forceful forms of censorship are undertaken by nongovernmental institutions or individuals, they are not generally subject to the free speech protections of the First Amendment.[41] Largely as a result of the way anti-discrimination enforcement has been structured by the law, we arrive at the point described by John McWhorter: "millions of innocent people scared to pieces of winding up in the sights of a zealous brand of inquisition that seems to hover over almost any statement, ambition, or achievement in modern society" (2021, 5).

A New Civic Sensibility:
Blurring the Line Between Civil and Criminal Law

Here is another place where we lack the terminology to describe what is going on. In its punitive or coercive aspect, anti-discrimination law is effectively creating a new *kind* of law, a hybrid of civil and criminal law. In the workplace and in the universities, charges must be laid, investigations must be undertaken, preventive and corrective actions must follow, and records must be kept. All this looks and feels more like the criminal law than like civil lawsuits. Two anti-discrimination policies—hate crimes statutes and rules governing sexual assault/sexual harassment on college campuses—in fact explicitly overlap with the criminal law. Anti-discrimination law's fixation with intent and motive (central to Title VII disparate treatment law) matches criminal law, not torts, as does its tendency to use the language of victims and offenders. Governmental weaponization of official investigations (by the EEOC, the DOJ, or DOE) to publicize and thereby shame the accused is another matter of deliberate policy that looks and feels more like the prosecutorial dimension of criminal law than civil law.[42] Some, like law professor Catharine MacKinnon, would go even further in this direction, calling for harassment lawsuits against *individuals*, for example. "Being able to sue individual perpetrators and their enablers, jointly with institutions, could shift perceived incentives for this behavior" (2018).

One could even say that anti-discrimination law goes further than the criminal law, but in the same direction. Anti-discrimination law penalizes with powerful sanctions behavior that the criminal law does not. If the criminal law may be said to be a kind of regulation of interpersonal behavior, anti-discrimination amounts to something both more exacting and more intimate in its reach, a kind of very Western, secular, and up-to-date alternative to a Ministry for the Propagation of Virtue and the Prevention of Vice. Such considerations make all the more striking the fact that, because anti-discrimination law is technically or officially categorized as civil law, individuals are deprived of the extensive due process guarantees granted criminal defendants under long-standing constitutional norms. Governing our personal interactions, speech, and beliefs with punitive sanction is far from anything in the liberal tradition—indeed, one might say that it was resistance to something like this that originally inspired the liberal impulse in the first place.

Anti-discrimination law is also akin to the criminal law in its power to shape the moral sensibilities of those living under its forceful admonitions. As multicultural education will help us to see, anti-discrimination's greatest claim, as well as its greatest source of persuasive power, is and has always been a compelling moral one. Coercion and force must play a role, however, because (as in the criminal law) moral claims and exhortations by themselves sometimes prove inadequate to the task. But then force and punishment in turn carry with them contributions of their own to the substance and shape of the morality of anti-discrimination that is taking hold of the public mind. Here is the most penetrating, the most intimate, effect of anti-discrimination law, in its shaping of a new civic moral outlook and a new sense of what it means to be a democratic citizen. Liberalism may try to say that morality should not be affected by politics, that opinion cannot and should not be affected by force; anti-discrimination teaches us differently.

How has the democratic personality been altered by the anti-discrimination regime and the striking character of its laws? We are manifestly in need of a new rendering of political psychology (the new Left outlook's unapologetic ties to law will presumably require a reconsideration of the old Frankfurt School condemnation of deference to authority). Some preliminary suggestions may be made on the basis of the citizen's relation to the law. The most obvious fact is that the law creates a new and more penetrating sense of personal moral responsibility for resisting discrimination. For the decent citizen who has internalized the civic and moral meaning of the law, discrimination is and must be an individual failing, a personal defect of character, a source of guilt and shame. But under the law we are also our brothers' and our sisters' keepers, responsible for *their* actions and beliefs too. Under the law we will in any event be *held* responsible for our own actions and for the actions of others by agents acting with powerful sanctions if we fail to live up to what is said to be our duty. Lying behind all of this, it is necessary to add, is a pervasive and deep sense of anxiety that begins with institutions (fear of lawsuits, fear of toxic reputation) but is then passed along to the managers, employees, teachers, and students under their charge (a corresponding fear of loss of employment, educational opportunities, and reputational harm). How much of this is simply fear or shame and how much of it is more genuinely moral sentiment (true remorse, guilt) will depend on the individual. Clarifying the contributions of the moral and the merely psychological here, and distinguishing the human types operating under the regime's influence, will require some delicate parsing. But the spirit of anti-discrimination morality operates in the opposite direction as well, generating more vigorous moral and psychological effects, and not merely those associated with the passivity of fear. Again, the criminal law is our guide, for righteous indignation and moral outrage naturally characterize the decent citizen's response to unjust discrimination. Anti-discrimination morality is necessarily a morality of blame and punishment as much as it is a morality of guilt.

We need to identify the range of human types arising out of the rule of anti-discrimination law. The extremes—zealous true believers and embittered resisters—are easy to identify (even if the latter are presumably not easy to find or uncover). More interesting are those in the middle. Individuals with more complicated motives for taking up the cause (self-interest, ordinary ambition, and other drives), in addition to or instead of the rightness of the cause, will see personal opportunities that are not simply identical to the ends of the new order. Similarly, how many of those seemingly committed to doing what is right are in fact only passive, fearful followers of the fashion of the moment? Indeed, does not the history of racism itself, the evidence we see of its widespread hold upon the past, teach us to be skeptical of the purity of the morals of the average anti-discriminatory citizen today—even if he or she may seem to be entirely given over to the new order? Also in the middle we confront the question of determining the range of *mixed* feelings about the fight against discrimination among those subject to its mandates—even among those charged most directly with enforcing them.

Affirmative Action (Or: Disparity-as-Discrimination)

Until now I have deliberately omitted discussion of affirmative action and related matters because preoccupation with them, especially for conservatives, often works to distort the overall picture of civil rights law. Conservatives' passionate opposition to affirmative action often has the odd consequence that much of the rest of the civil rights regime is effectively overlooked and taken for granted—a view that our survey to this point calls into question. Very much related to this, fixating on affirmative action also leads to an unthinking assumption that anti-discrimination law per se is somehow consistent with the liberal tradition while affirmative action is not (the standard interpretation I mentioned in chapter 1). We are prepared by now to see that this is bad legal-political interpretive line drawing that obscures (politically) a proper understanding of the anti-discrimination effort taken as a whole.[43]

But of course affirmative action and related policies form a vital part of the broad effort that is anti-discrimination law. There are in fact three different sets of questions that can get jumbled together under the heading of affirmative action. The first, and the starting point for all, is that for some anti-discrimination groups, manifest inequalities ("disparities") do obviously exist, touching on a wide variety of important areas of life—education, wealth, housing, incarceration, health, and so on. Second is a claim (made on the Left, denied generally by the Right) that those inequalities *are* discrimination (or ought to be treated as such). Under Title VII, this is the legalistic distinction between disparate *treatment* claims (where group inequalities don't usually play a role) and disparate *impact* claims (where they are central). Disparate impact is thus yet another very important, seventh or first, expansion of Title VII, marked officially by the Supreme Court in a unanimous 1971 opinion written by Chief Justice Burger, *Griggs v. Duke Power Co.*, and in subsequent decisions.[44] Affirmative action enters, finally, as only one among several different kinds of *remedies* for these inequalities. Despite some appearances to the contrary (especially a few misleading US Supreme Court cases), both the disparity-as-discrimination legal point of view and affirmative action policy are alive and well in America.[45] The importance of this understanding of discrimination is significantly magnified because of the effect of its logic on *voting rights* in particular in the United States—what Abigail Thernstrom (political scientist and later vice chair of the Civil Rights Commission) called "affirmative action in the electoral sphere" (1987, 27). Here, too, there are famous decisions of the Supreme Court that appear to limit the reach of this logic in the voting domain, but the reality is mostly to the contrary. The Supreme Court permits, and the Department of Justice at times requires, the deliberate creation of racially defined "majority-minority" ("max-Black" and "max-Hispanic" being the legal terms of art) electoral districts.[46]

Like stereotypes and harassment plus employer liability as matters of law, disparity-as-discrimination considerably enlarges or magnifies the commitment to fighting discrimination. There is, indeed, a whole separate terminology and logic—legal, moral, sociological, psychological—associated with the disparity-as-discrimination point of view. No longer in the realm of overt and obvious (individual, intentional, identifiable) acts of discrimination, here it is institutions, social norms, and cultural practices that are, according to this view, blamed for the inequalities in question. The causal link here may involve "hidden" bias or "unconscious" bias—but it need not do so to be considered unjust discrimination covered by the law. This tricky point is made in an oft-quoted passage from a lower court decision of the 1970s: "Effect, and not motivation, is the touchstone, in part because clever men may easily conceal their motivations, but more importantly because . . . we now recognize that the arbitrary quality of thoughtlessness can be as disastrous and unfair . . . as the perversity of a willful scheme."[47] Disparity-as-discrimination is, as we say, discrimination that is *systemic* or *structural* or *societal*, a terminology that usefully blurs or obscures the causal-moral claim ultimately at the bottom of things. Those better off in one way or another may not have intentionally harmed or discriminated against those with a lesser portion, but what they have is illegitimate nonetheless—unearned *privilege*, in our current usage. The standard by which we are to judge successful remediation is group *proportionality*, though this may not be stated too plainly or openly without political cost.

Disparity-as-discrimination and affirmative action are not so much opposed to liberalism as to the middle-class way of life. Treating disparities as discrimination means abandoning or rejecting anything that may be said to lead to group inequalities. That includes a number of important standards of behavior guiding many modern practices: hiring screening processes that assess educational attainment and employment history; criminal record and other similar background checks; other employment requirements emphasizing ability or training (certification and licensing requirements, skills tests); the criminal law in general and drug laws in particular; credit check requirements in matters pertaining to lending, homeownership, and landlord-tenant relations; a host of educational practices—grading, tracking, school discipline, truancy policies (precisely the list Banks will target in his "equity pedagogy"[48]). Disparity-as-discrimination likewise renders suspect the powerful moral notions of the bourgeois ethos—merit, personal responsibility, accountability—dismissed now as privilege or, worse, as mere pretexts for racism, sexism, and the like.

Opposition to affirmative action, but not to the rest of the anti-discrimination effort, common on the Right, is explained partly by the fact that the latter seems perhaps not to tax us so much, requiring only the bending of our minds and not our pocketbooks. But it is also explained by how strange, nigh-impossible, it would be to consider opposing both together. At any rate, generally speaking, the advance of one supports the advance of the other. Privatized enforcement of discrimination at the individual level (anti-stereotype, anti-harassment, etc.) makes us more sensitive to anything that might look like discrimination and thus prepares us to see group inequalities too as discrimination or as evidence of discrimination; group inequalities, in turn, seem to provide some important evidence that our society has failed to address discrimination in an effective way, justifying ever-more stringent efforts to combat discrimination at the individual level.

A Note on Constitutional Law

In a way, constitutional law is the worst place to look to see the meaning of the anti-discrimination revolution. This should not be surprising since the Constitution represents the old order of liberal democratic politics and its public-private divide. Statute, not the Constitution, has made the anti-discrimination regime and the liberal Constitution's key civil rights provision, the Fourteenth Amendment's Equal Protection Clause, does not reach the private sector. Moreover, the Supreme Court may be viewed (not entirely accurately) as tending conservative on at least some important constitutional civil rights questions in a way that distorts the overall picture by suggesting that the anti-discrimination regime is hemmed in when it is not (the classic cases here are pronouncements on free speech, affirmative action, and voting rights mentioned above). When it comes to Title VII, on the other hand, it is Supreme Court justices (and often conservatives) who have done some of the most important work to expand the anti-discrimination regime's legal architecture.[49] Most problematic, as we saw most clearly in the case of free speech, the Supreme Court seems never to face squarely the many legal tensions between the old order and the new, and is in fact supremely adept at helping to obscure them.

Nevertheless, because such tensions are too big to hide, they necessarily make an appearance in constitutional law debates. These conflicts are in fact relatively easy to see if one but looks and they help to illuminate some of the differences between the old order and the new in arresting ways. The most visible—concerning free speech—we have discussed. The point in constitutional thought where liberalism's public-private divide is most explicitly articulated and defended, the Supreme Court's state action doctrine, was challenged from the very first by the 1964 Act's regulation of domains deemed private (in Titles II and VII).[50] Controversies over the exclusion of racial minorities, women, gays and lesbians and others by private clubs and groups raise additional questions about First Amendment freedom of association doctrine.[51] First Amendment religion clause jurisprudence has been reworked to mimic Fourteenth Amendment Equal Protection clause jurisprudence, in different ways, on behalf of both religious minorities and the Christian majority alike, altering how we think about the separation of church and state and the free exercise of religion.[52] Efforts, especially on college campuses, to police sexual assault under the new legal framework connected to anti-harassment have led to concerns about the watering down of traditional due process protections (the right to know and to confront one's accuser, the right to an attorney, the right to evidentiary discovery, the right to trial by jury).[53] An individualistic (one person, one vote) understanding of representation is challenged on the Court by a new understanding that champions the rights of racial minorities when it comes to drawing electoral boundary lines.[54] Debates over desegregation and busing not only broke new doctrinal ground but also compelled the federal court system to raise fundamental questions about its own institutional role as guarantor or enforcer of civil rights law.[55] Taken altogether, these conflicts suggest that a considerable portion of American constitutional debate may be viewed as an effort to sort out the conflicts between the demands of anti-discrimination and the features of the Constitution that represent its traditionally liberal democratic core. It is no accident that one of the great intellectual or scholarly achievements of the civil rights revolution was the amassing of a great literature critical of the public-private divide (and of its legalistic cousin, the state action doctrine).[56]

But just as striking are constitutional debates where the dividing line is not that between anti-discrimination and liberalism but between two competing interpretations of the meaning of anti-discrimination itself. Here we deal with efforts—above all, affirmative action/disparate impact law—that, in tackling group *inequalities*, may be said to take the commitment to fighting discrimination to a higher level of effort. What is revealing in these debates is that the Supreme Court cannot, and does not attempt to, settle the issues raised by reference to anything in the traditional liberal democratic understanding of politics.[57] Here Left and Right can have no recourse other than to competing interpretations of what the fight against discrimination requires and justifies—that is, to some sense of what anti-discrimination by itself means. This raises the question of the constitutional status of anti-discrimination law itself. Is anti-discrimination law the "law that ate the Constitution," in Angelo Codevilla's arresting formula (2016)—or does it represent a new law of constitutional stature? While all of what we today know as anti-discrimination law is not enshrined explicitly in the Constitution (as it is in Canada, for example), one could certainly argue that some understanding—whether Left or Right or some compromise mixture—of this basic commitment has now become so essential to American politics that we may need to rethink our notion of what constitutes our fundamental law in order to accommodate it.[58]

Anti-Discrimination Politics is Architectonic: What Multiculturalism Can Teach Us

By now the claim that anti-discrimination law is shaping modern democratic life with great force, and in ways that are important, ought to be uncontroversial. An enormous amount of work has been done by academics on the Left over the past couple decades to demonstrate the *weakness* and even the injustice (from the point of view of the fight against discrimination) of anti-discrimination law—part of an even bigger "critique of rights" literature that goes back to the 1970s.[59] Such a scholarly point of view, astonishing to me, is itself evidence of the power of the anti-discrimination regime to alter life, in this case intellectual life, in its direction—not the last occasion we will have for this observation.

If we step back just a little from all the twists and turns of the law, it is impossible not to be impressed by the scope and scale of the effort in the United States to try to vanquish discrimination. One could add other kinds of evidence of the power of anti-discrimination to reformulate other areas of policy besides those governed by Title VII and Title IX—in criminal law, the regulation of broadcasting and the internet, environmental protection, public health and mental health, adoption, immigration, foreign policy.

I would also make a claim for a basic alteration of our political party system as a result of the anti-discrimination revolution. There is a large literature on the role that race has played in reorganizing the logic of American party politics since the 1950s, and a few political scientists have even begun to speak of a wider "civil rights realignment."[60] By becoming the party of anti-discrimination, the Democratic Party has alienated much of its old working-class/labor constituency, and this has helped to create the enduring tie or stalemate between Democrats and Republicans that has been predominant since the end of the 1960s (largely economic alignments having been enduringly disrupted by new kinds of moral-political claims and groups and social cleavages that have been made forceful by the politics of anti-discrimination).

But the law's effect on other areas of policy or the broader political system is not the most important evidence of the regime's power. The true test is whether and how this new political project alters what liberalism calls private life. To begin to assess this question, a more difficult and more delicate task for political science, is the main purpose of the rest of this study.

It is tempting here to try to catalogue in advance some of the general evidence of the anti-discrimination regime's effect on the thought and moral opinions and life of democratic citizens today. In my view, anyone who would take the time to study any of the fields of the social sciences and humanities—or contemporary literature, art, popular culture, and religion—would find plenty of evidence for anti-discrimination's cultural impact.[61] The effect of the anti-discrimination regime on family and sexuality—or sexual life, or sexual identity, or gender identity, or however we are now to call it—is among the most important of its consequences, and another place where we probably still lack terms even to describe the nature of the changes under way. Likewise, within the different affected groups, the experience that people have of life, how they view themselves and the world, as well as what they think they can expect or demand from others, are all fundamentally altered by passing through the filter or lens of the fight against discrimination as a widely embraced political enterprise. Here, too, is change at the level of the self-understanding of individuals and individual moral opinion.

We will focus our attention on what multicultural education can teach us along these lines. Our study of multiculturalism and multicultural education will not exclude the question of the role of the law, especially in its early years (we turn to this in the next chapter). But the study of multicultural education illuminates the shaping power of the anti-discrimination revolution in American *life* in numerous ways. As an academic enterprise undertaken by sophisticated people, multicultural education begins to help us to see how anti-discrimination politics shapes academia and democratic intellectuals. A set of pedagogical teachings and insights, it brings to light a political reworking of the meaning and purpose and substance of public education. As an account of the nature of groups and of group politics, it offers a reformulation of our ideas or imaginings of democratic pluralism. More important are the lessons it teaches to the American people. As a civic education it offers a new political understanding, a new vision of political psychology, and a new democratic morality. In offering this new account of things it works without apology to shape the modern heart and mind. In doing so, it also provides a template that will help us to reflect on the *logic* of the law—on the anti-discrimination's regime's expectations, hopes, dreams, and demands. If the anti-discrimination regime has taken hold at a deep level in modern democratic life (and our survey of the law suggests, to say the least, that it has many powerful means at its disposal to do so), then we are in need of the opportunity to think about the articulation of its overarching civic vision or outlook that multiculturalism provides because, politics being what it is, we will increasingly need to understand it in order to understand ourselves.

Chapter 4
A BRIEF (POLITICAL) HISTORY OF AMERICAN MULTICULTURAL EDUCATION

> The Civil Rights Act of 1964 protects my right to speak my language and continue to identify with my culture.
> —U.S. Department of Health, Education and Welfare poster[1]

Exploring the facts of multiculturalism's history is useful because it establishes in a simple and convincing way the essential connection between the idea of multiculturalism and the politics of anti-discrimination.[2] This is partly a story about the law and the effects of the law, but it is also one involving the independent efforts of citizens inspired by the promise of the law. As we shall see, an important role for law in the life of multicultural education was present from the beginning and continues to the present day. But the history of multicultural education also demonstrates in very direct terms the effect of the civil rights revolution on a distinct subset of American intellectuals who, in turn, as activist-leaders, succeeded in establishing in one narrow but important domain of American life—teacher education—a set of social institutions and norms (a socio-political infrastructure) designed to advance the aspirations and demands of the new political order. These social institution-builders were encouraged and supported by the law but they also undertook initiatives that extended the spirit of the anti-discrimination regime to efforts going beyond the reach of the law. While their success, which is undeniable in the most simple terms, may not be measured precisely, what they achieved has altered the world within which they exerted their energies.

The first emergence of the idea of multiculturalism in the United States may be traced fairly precisely to the period of the late 1960s and early 1970s. It is hard to say which came first, multicultural education as an academic discipline or the sanction of the idea by civil rights education policy. The first direct federal government support came in the 1968 Bilingual Education Act, supplemented by efforts of two other federal laws passed in 1972. Already by 1970, enough scholarly work existed to fill out a bibliography of "multicultural education" materials (Mathieson and Tatis 1970). The first survey of multicultural teacher education programs was published in 1971, and doctoral dissertations on multicultural education in the U.S. were completed as early as 1972.[3] Also in 1972, in a crucially important step, the teacher education establishment weighed in, when multicultural education was formally endorsed by its main professional body, the American Association of Colleges for Teacher Education (AACTE) (AACTE 1973). At the state level, following earlier tentative efforts in Minnesota and Illinois in 1971 and 1972, Iowa was the first to adopt a comprehensive "Multicultural and Nonsexist Education Policy" in 1975. Two years later, multicultural education became cemented into the world of American teacher education in another powerful way when the main teacher education accrediting body (the National Council for the Accreditation of Teacher Education [NCATE]) formally added multicultural education to its accreditation standards. "Standard: The institution gives evidence of planning for multicultural education in its teacher education curricula including both the general and professional studies component" (NCATE 1977, 7).

Before turning to the details of the manifestly political outlines of this history, it is worth noting that multicultural education scholars themselves trace their roots, universally and without hesitation or apology, to the struggle for civil rights reform. They reject any ties to the liberal tradition or to liberal pluralism—including liberal "cultural pluralism." Horace Kallen's brief for cultural pluralism (a term he coined in the first decades of the twentieth century) was framed emphatically in terms of liberty and was essentially an extension of the logic of individualism, and the outlook of liberal *religious* pluralism in particular, now applied to a wide range of different kinds of ethnic, social, and cultural groups or associations. While Banks admits that efforts by Kallen (and others arguing along similar lines) contributed to the well-being of minorities in America, it is plain that he does not frame multiculturalism in such terms. Indeed, at points Banks explicitly rejects cultural pluralism, precisely because it is inadequate to the needs of American life under the new dispensation. "Racism, sexism, and dehumanization," he says, "are aspects of human cultures which can be justified with the cultural pluralism argument."[4] As a matter of genealogical connection, Banks and other multicultural education writers insist that old-style liberal cultural pluralism was only a vaguely related pluralist forerunner but not in any way "a root" of multicultural education in the United States.[5]

As I say, multicultural educators themselves see their history as beginning with the anti-discrimination revolution. "In the United States multicultural education emerged from the civil rights and other protest movements of the 1960s and 1970s. . . . It is usually considered by both its advocates and critics as a metaphor for equal educational opportunities for victimized cultural, gender and ethnic groups. Consequently, to oppose multicultural education in the United States would most likely be perceived as support for racism, sexism and social class inequality."[6] Multicultural education was, as Carl Grant put it in 1977, a reflection of the fact that a "recent realignment of political power in the United States has . . . forced us to recognize that we are not a homogenous nation" (1977a, 29). Many of multicultural education's leading theorists and advocates got their start in the late 1960s and early 1970s as academics in education departments of American universities, scrutinizing textbooks (especially in history and social studies) and instructional methods with a view to correcting discriminatory assumptions and practices.[7] Geneva Gay, an early advocate of multicultural education who has written extensively on the subject of its history, emphasizes the protest efforts of "student activists, abetted by the efforts of textbook analysts," as marking the first steps on the road to multiculturalism. "They employed many of the strategies pioneered by the first civil rights activists. They, too, marched, boycotted, sat-in, locked-out, and issued lists of demands. Instead of demanding direct social change, however, they demanded that educational institutions stop their racist, oppressive practices of ignoring and distorting the cultural heritages and contributions to society of ethnic minorities" (Gay 1983, 561). Such an understanding of American multiculturalism's origins, which is the unchallenged view among multicultural education writers who discuss its history, is amply vindicated by a more detailed examination of multicultural education's earliest years.[8]

From Cultural Deprivation to Cultural Difference to Multiculturalism

Two aspects of its initial development show clearly the extent to which multicultural education, as it took shape at the outset, was always defined by the civil rights revolution. One, already indicated, is the role of official policy, a somewhat complicated story to which we shall return in a moment. But equally revealing is the manner in which "multicultural education" first came to appear as a term of American public discourse, the direct product of an education debate of the 1960s connected to school desegregation efforts. When, in 1967, Native American educator Jack Forbes first employed the term in its contemporary meaning, he was using it to stake out a position on the question of educational inequalities in the name of victims of discrimination.

In addition to mandating the desegregation of education, Title IV of the 1964 Civil Rights Act also directed the Commissioner of Civil Rights to conduct a survey "concerning the lack of availability of equal educational opportunities for individuals by reason of race, color, religion, or national origin in public educational institutions at all levels in the United States" (U.S. House of Representatives 1970, 21). The study, conducted by a team of social scientists led by James S. Coleman and commonly referred to as the "Coleman Report," compiled data on the different levels of educational resources distributed among various groups and correlated those results with variations in educational achievement (Coleman 1966). The results were surprising:

> James Coleman and his associates failed to find what they expected to find, direct evidence of large inequalities in educational facilities in schools attended by children from different majority and minority groups. The study set out to document the fact that for children from minority groups school facilities are sharply unequal and that this inequality is related to student achievement. The data did not support either conclusion. What small differences in school facilities did exist had little or no discernible relationship to the level of student achievement. (Lesser and Stodolsky 1969, 126–27).

According to Daniel Patrick Moynihan, Coleman's findings "caused not consternation but something near to alarm" in the Office of Education (Moynihan 1969, 26). Equally controversial was Coleman's *explanation* of the unequal educational achievement of Blacks and other minorities. Following a line of argument similar to that of "The Negro Family: The Case for National Action," Moynihan's famous report initially published in 1965, Coleman argued that "the analysis showed what had already been well-known: the powerful relation of the child's own family background characteristics to his [educational] achievement, a relation stronger than that of any school factor."[9]

Confronted with unequal outcomes that were nonetheless noticeable and persistent, the first response of civil rights reformers was to call for "compensatory education" for minority students, toward which the $1 billion expenditure in Title I of the 1965 Elementary and Secondary Education Act was an important beginning (see Bloom, Davis, and Hess 1965, 6). But if the Coleman Report's findings were correct, then a justification for a program of compensatory education would have to be found in something other than inequalities in educational resources. Many of the defenders of compensatory education, progressive social scientists and education reformers, came to advance the view that educational inequalities arose instead from the "cultural deprivation" of minority groups, a position akin to that of the "Moynihan Report." Compensatory education thus came to be framed largely as a remedy for group inequalities tied to one particular explanation of those inequalities—namely, what multicultural education writers later came to call the "cultural deprivation paradigm." As one social scientist put it in the late 1960s, "The disadvantages of culturally deprived children stem from their social status in American society and their isolation and insulation from the main cultural milieu. . . . Skillful teaching geared to the needs of culturally deprived children is called for, including remedial programs, pre-school programs, and community-wide programs."[10]

But to many minority advocates, "the use of such terms as 'culturally deprived' in referring to mainly minority populations reflects a kind of colonial stance" (Fantini 1972, 16). To say that members of minority groups were culturally deprived was to explain educational inequalities by reference to some shortcoming or defect in those groups themselves. This was, to cite the title of an influential book of the time, "blaming the victim" (Ryan

1971). Along similar lines, multicultural education theorists came to question the basic idea of "compensatory education" as well. "Use of the word compensatory tended to imply that different cultures are inferior" (Grant and Grant 1975, 66).

The alternative to the cultural deprivation outlook that emerged almost immediately and that represented a sharp political contrast was an interpretation of educational inequalities from the point of view of "cultural difference."[11] The cultural difference perspective sought ultimately to overthrow the moral basis of the earlier explanation. What is needed is "a reorientation from our present 'student-fault' to a stronger 'system fault' position" (Fantini 1972, 17). "Cultural difference theorists believe that the school, rather than the cultures of minority students, is primarily responsible for the low academic achievement of minority students" (Banks 1994a, 49). Most fundamentally, the cultural difference outlook addresses the question of educational inequalities that exist between groups associated with past discrimination and the rest of American society by reframing them in accordance with a clear political-moral logic. "The cultural difference paradigm maintains that ethnic minority youths often do not achieve well in school not because they have a deprived culture, but because their cultures are different from the culture of the school. The school should therefore modify the educational environment in order to make it more consistent with the cultures of ethnic minority youths."[12]

The logic here is essentially identical to what eventually became a central pillar of the Left interpretation of civil rights politics in America, attributing group inequalities to systemic or societal policies and practices (as opposed to overt/intentional acts) and in fact defining discrimination itself in these terms (the basic difference between "disparate impact" and "disparate treatment" we saw in chapter 3).[13] Describing the emergence of the cultural difference line of interpretation in 1969, Nathan Glazer pointed out the importance of persisting educational inequalities as its central cause.[14] He would later go so far as to say that "were it not for the pattern of poor achievement among blacks in the schools, the multicultural movement would lose much of its force" (1991, 19). The question of who is to blame for inequalities among specific ethnic and racial groups and the rest of America—the Left blaming racism at a systemic level, the Right blaming 1960s reforms and, more controversially, various aspects of the cultures of discrimination victim groups themselves—provides the subterranean moral outline of much of American civil rights debate.

The cultural difference paradigm is thus an attempt at a fairly straightforward moral-political inversion arising more or less immediately from the demands of anti-discrimination politics: what the cultural deprivation paradigm held to be problematic (the "cultural milieu" of minority students) is rendered beyond criticism by the cultural difference perspective. While the general logic of anti-discrimination policy does not necessarily entail adopting a "system fault" stance, it surely renders problematic a "student fault" view of things. Civil rights reform had made educational inequalities an inescapable concern of public policy; as a result, the explanation of those inequalities (by cultural deprivation or by cultural difference) became an important site of the battle over how those inequalities would be understood and remedied. (I cannot resist adding that the appeal to "difference" here has nothing at all to do with postmodernist theory's later obsession with that word.)

It almost goes without saying that in the context of post-1960s education debates the "cultural difference" label has always referred to anti-discrimination groups—and not literally to cultural difference in the abstract. As we shall see, the specific perspectives (or groups) covered under the heading of cultural difference in practice came to bear a striking resemblance to the list of racial and ethnic groups (and other categories—like gender, age, and disability—that do not obviously denote "cultures") protected under civil rights law. But that in no way diminishes the ambition of the cultural difference paradigm. Especially as it came to encompass a much broader argument advanced by multicultural education theorists, putting cultural difference at the heart of American education came to mean putting anti-discrimination groups at the heart of a new understanding of America.

When Jack Forbes deployed the multicultural education term in his 1967 essay "The Education of the Culturally Different, A Multi-Cultural Approach" (the first use of the phrase in its current meaning of which I am aware), he did so in the context of this academic debate as a way to state more capaciously the cultural difference position.[15] Forbes sought to address "the problems of culturally different minority populations as they relate to formal educational processes," as well as "to distinguish the concept of the culturally different pupil from that of the 'culturally disadvantaged' and to explore the manner in which the mono-cultural orientation of schools has perhaps needlessly created educational disadvantages for all pupils" (1967, i). Citing "a maze of new programs of an educational nature funded through the Office of Education" that recognize "the importance of providing better educational opportunities for the culturally different and the poor," Forbes proposed the "multi-cultural . . . school" and a "multi-cultural approach to education" as a general "remedy" to the problem of educational inequalities (1967, i, 4). He rejected the cultural deprivation approach out of hand, judging it in stark terms according to a clear political criterion: "'Cultural deprivation' is not a new concept. For at least a century it has been an expression of Anglo-American racism, chauvinism, and superiority" (1967, 9). Warning of the "'social dynamite' represented by dissident, undereducated groups [that] can explode . . . to harm the interests of even the powerful and the affluent," Forbes insisted that "Anglo-American educators . . . can no longer afford to ignore the demands of the culturally different" (1967, 21). According to Gwendolyn Baker, who wrote one of the first doctoral dissertations in the field of multicultural education in 1972, "Jack Forbes can be credited as being one of the pioneers in the usage of the term 'multicultural education.'" For Baker, "his 1969 publication [a slightly revised reprinting of his 1967 work] entitled *The Education of the Culturally Different: A Multicultural Approach* . . . was recognized as one of the most explicit contributions to the concept."[16] While it would be left to later theorists like Banks to work out in greater detail the full logic of multicultural education, here at the outset the defining role of civil rights politics is fairly plain.

Multicultural Education as Civil Rights Policy: Federal Efforts

Although it is not immediately obvious, multicultural education is policy in the United States—and it always has been, more or less since its inception. While it is true that the United States has never had anything like Canada's well-known national commitment to multiculturalism—no "American Multiculturalism Act" exists as of yet—it is nevertheless true that multicultural *education* has drawn crucial support from official government policy at every turn. Indeed, it seems fair to say that multicultural education would not exist in anything like its current state without the considerable backing it has received from federal and state law over the years. Generally speaking, one could say that the initiatives of the federal government led the way at the start while state policies gave multicultural education sanction and sustenance for the longer term. The quasi-legal authority of accreditation standards and teacher certification policies governing the world of teacher education played a vital role as well.

Reform of public education was among the most vigorous, and certainly among the most visible, of the civil rights efforts of the federal government.[17] Today we recognize the massive role that Title IX plays in the domain of education, but that is just the most obvious point of reference in a broad and deep legal architecture affecting American education. Like every other area of American life, education and teacher education had been deeply implicated in America's history of race discrimination. Not only were America's schools and universities formally segregated; the teaching profession itself was as well. White teachers of White students were represented by the National Education Association (NEA), while teachers (Black and White) of Black students were represented by the American Teachers Association (ATA). The ATA and NEA did not merge until 1966, two years after the 1964 Act and twelve years after *Brown v. Board of Education* (Scott 2004, 80). Long the domain of state and local government, education has become increasingly subject to federal government oversight mainly because of the civil rights revolution. *Brown* may have set forth a standard of equality for public education potentially affecting every American city, town, and neighborhood, but for more than a decade it had very little effect on schools in the American South. Only the 1964 Civil Rights Act began to tackle the problem with adequate energy. While Title IV of the Act forbade racial segregation in public education, the denial of federal funds in Title VI to those engaging in discriminatory practices provided at least the threat of effective enforcement. The federal courts' controversial busing decisions seemed to show that school desegregation would not be established by decree alone. Crucially, in 1965 Congress took the step of giving the 1964 Act's framework compelling force by creating a sizeable pool of federal funds that states would receive only if compliant with the desegregation mandate (Title I of the 1965 Elementary and Secondary Education Act (ESEA)—$1 Billion in 1966, more than $15 Billion today).[18]

But the general federal campaign to bring civil rights reform to education went well beyond desegregation efforts and included, crucially, programs to affect the substance of American public education in line with the commitment to fighting discrimination. It is here that official sanction and support for multicultural education comes into play. The scale of this extensive governmental initiative is suggested by its bureaucratic outline. Prior to 2000, two of the Education Department's seven main divisions were devoted almost entirely to civil rights programs (the Office for Civil Rights and the Office of Bilingual Education and Minority Languages Affairs). Two others made important contributions: the Office of Educational Research and Improvement funded multicultural and bilingual education research; the Office of Elementary and Secondary Education supervised regional Equity Assistance Centers. These and other related activities have been enlarged and made more complex as anti-discrimination law has been expanded to include a variety of different affected groups. Moving beyond the originally defining case of race, a number of major educational initiatives were launched by federal statutes designed to fight discrimination on the basis of language, sex, ethnicity, disability, and age.[19] Taken together, reform of American elementary and secondary education in the name of fighting discrimination amounts to a powerful matrix in light of which more focused efforts to support multicultural education in particular must be viewed.

Early on, three federal laws stand out as contributing directly to the future development of multicultural education. The first to provide support for the cultural difference paradigm was the Bilingual Education Act of 1968.[20] This became explicit in the law's 1988 reauthorization, the text of which recognizes "that many such [minority] children have a cultural heritage which differs from that of English-speaking persons; [and] that a primary means by which a child learns is through the use of such child's language and cultural heritage."[21] In its final reauthorization in 1994, the law would go so far as to speak of "developing bilingual skills and multicultural understanding."[22] In addition to the funding made available through federal bilingual education programs, two 1972 statutes provided direct support for what was by that point emerging as the academic subdiscipline of multicultural education: the Ethnic Heritage Studies Program (Title IX of the ESEA reauthorization) and Title VII of the Emergency School Aid Act (ESAA). The latter of these provided extra funding to aid a variety of voluntary desegregation efforts, including what one scholar writing in 1983 characterized as "ESAA-funded multicultural education."[23] The better known statute establishing the Ethnic Heritage Studies Program, signed by Richard Nixon, offered funds to study "the differing and unique contributions to the national heritage made by each ethnic group," holding out the hope that "in a multiethnic society a greater understanding of the contributions of one's own heritage and those of one's own fellow citizens can contribute to a more harmonious, patriotic, and committed populace."[24] Ethnic Heritage Studies funds helped to establish a "Multi-Ethnic Heritage Institute" for the National Education Association and the New Jersey Education Association and an "Ethnic Heritage Center for Teacher Education" for the AACTE, supporting a range of multicultural education projects.[25] Grants from the program also funded early bibliographical surveys, advocacy pieces, and summaries of the "state of the scene" of multicultural education undertaken in the 1970s by the AACTE and the National Commission on the Social Sciences.[26]

At least as important as these specific statutes, the broader effort of the federal government to desegregate education in America likewise provided direct support for the initial emergence of multicultural education. Provisions of Title IV of the 1964 Civil Rights Act guaranteeing educational "technical assistance," "training institutes," and grants (sections 403, 404, and 405) created a bureaucratic infrastructure providing at least some support to multiculturalism for the long term. The institutions funded by the federal government to assist in the planning and implementation of school desegregation were initially dubbed "General Assistance Centers" but their later nomenclature bears the unmistakable imprint of its political source, becoming in turn "Desegregation Assistance Centers" and eventually "Equity Assistance Centers" (see Scott 1999). Crucially, "as second-generation problems of within-school segregation and tracked curricula emerged, the centers expanded their assistance to include program planning and *curriculum development* within schools."[27] Examples of services provided by the Equity Assistance Center (EAC) housed at the University of Michigan in the 1990s included, for example, "Untracking curriculum and instruction," "Multicultural, gender-fair curriculum," "Cross-cultural communication," "Diversity awareness training," and an "Anti-Bias Curriculum Program."[28] Over time, the mission of the EACs would expand beyond questions of race to embrace anti-discrimination efforts pertaining to women, the disabled, and other minorities as well.[29] At points (though not routinely so far as I can tell) federal government efforts even skirted the edge of *requiring* multicultural education as a mandatory curriculum correction. For example, in every school district having enough minority language students to trigger the federal bilingual education requirements, multicultural education was indeed mandated, at least in principle.[30] Similarly, at points, federal courts referenced multicultural education as part of desegregation orders.[31]

Multicultural Education Policy in the States

But it was the widespread adoption of multicultural education policies at the state level, beginning in the early 1970s, that ultimately made multicultural education a force to be reckoned with in America. Even if it is true that, as two early multicultural education pioneers put it, "state provisions related to the cultural diversity of school settings and society have generally followed the lead of the federal government," nevertheless, state control of education policy, as a practical matter, was much more important for the long haul than the initial endorsements and inducements at the federal level (Giles and Gollnick 1977, 156). State government control over the curriculum and textbook selection, and, above all, state regulation of teacher education, secured a place for the academic field of multicultural education by backing it with the mandates and stimulus of law. Iowa's comprehensive "Multicultural and Nonsexist Education policy" adopted in 1975 (on the heels of less ambitious and less clearly articulated efforts in Minnesota and Illinois), was clearly informed by the commitment to fighting discrimination, as the policy's title already suggests.[32] "The educational program shall be characterized by practices which provide equal opportunity for all participants regardless of race, color, age, national origin, religion, or handicap."[33] Surveys conducted in 1977 and 1978 by multicultural education scholars and the AACTE indicated that roughly half of America's fifty states had adopted, in some form or another, policies or guidelines mandating "some aspects of multicultural education."[34] By the mid-1990s, multicultural education writer Donna Gollnick (later President of the AACTE) undertook a national survey on the basis of which she would go so far as to say that forty-five out of the forty-seven states that responded "had at least minimal requirements related to multicultural education" (1995, 49). Later surveys of the states found something similar.[35] It is safe to say, at a minimum, that every state has formally embraced multicultural education in some fashion, at some point, at least to some degree.

Government support at the state level was deemed by multicultural education's advocates themselves to be crucial for the obvious reason that it brought with it all the inducements of formal political life, negative and positive, to affect compliance to the new order. State government efforts to regulate the curriculum are effective because "they [can] either *mandate* the inclusion of instruction and/or materials which accurately portray the cultural and racial diversity of society . . . or *prohibit* instruction and materials which adversely reflect upon persons because of their race, sex, color, creed, national origin or ancestry" (Giles and Gollnick 1977, 139; emphasis in the original). As Gollnick's description of the initiatives undertaken in Iowa suggests, government sanction of multicultural education mandates could be a wide-ranging and powerful warrant.

> In 1978 Iowa passed a law requiring each school board in the state to adopt a plan for multicultural, nonsexist education that addressed issues of race, ethnicity, gender, religion, and age. The plans had to include goals and objectives with timelines and specific provisions for implementation as well as staff development activities and a process for evaluating the plan. The members of the advisory committee in each school district had to reflect cultural diversity and include persons with disabilities. Schools were required to keep their plans on file. . . . Beginning in 1985, staff from different departments of the state education agency conducted regular, on-site visits to schools as part of an equity-monitoring system. These visiting teams checked adherence to federal and state laws related to equity and multicultural education. (Gollnick 1995, 53)

Multicultural education programs lacking governmental endorsement were in danger of not being taken seriously. "The most effective approach was [state] legislation that required the development of plans to be monitored or assessed on a regular schedule. . . . Without the legislative leverage, guidelines were soon ignored and staff development not supported" (Gollnick 1995, 62). Above all, the power of state governments to deny teacher certification was crucial. "We must use the [state] legislatures, where we can, because of the effects they may have on the state educational certification offices" (Baptiste 1984, 105). (Local school districts could also be used to achieve something similar through hiring requirements [see Baker 1979, 258].) "Teacher certification standards that include a multicultural component seem to be an effective means for forcing teacher education institutions to train all preservice trainees for working in and teaching about the multicultural society" (Giles and Gollnick 1977, 148).

In at least one instance (in 2005), the compelling force of state multicultural education mandates helped to prompt, and then later to justify, the expulsion of a teacher education student from a graduate program (at Le Moyne College in New York). The graduate student had written a paper for a class titled "Planning, Assessing, and Managing Inclusive Classrooms" in which he said that multicultural education had no "philosophical place or standing in an American classroom." After the paper was shared with his department chair, the student received a letter notifying him that he "would not be permitted to register for any additional courses." The letter cited "the mismatch between [his] personal beliefs regarding teaching and learning and the Le Moyne College program goals." In the lawsuit that followed, the school's provost defended the decision by arguing from precisely the authority of the law. "We have a responsibility as an accrediting body for teachers, to be confident that these individuals when they go out and teach, are going to obey the laws of New York state and in this [instance] . . . , we could not be confident that this individual would abide by the laws of New York state." Although the student eventually won the lawsuit and was reinstated, the case usefully illustrates how laws supporting multiculturalism are viewed as providing prescriptive and obligatory guidance by college administrators.[36]

One final, crucial, piece of multicultural education's legal architecture took the form of the quasi-public/quasi-private requirement of teacher education accreditation standards. In 1977, this became formalized when the National Council for the Accreditation of Teacher Education (NCATE) mandated multicultural education. The accreditation process is a powerful instrument (failure to be accredited has severe consequences) and in the years since 1977 teacher education programs in American colleges and universities have been governed continuously by a series of different multicultural education or diversity standards, all enunciating a robust commitment to civil rights reform. When, in 1987, two other, more specialized national accrediting bodies formed—the Interstate New Teacher Assessment and Support Consortium and the National Board of Professional Teaching Standards—they followed NCATE's lead, making diversity a requirement of their teacher review processes.[37] NCATE's own multicultural education mandate later advanced under the label of "diversity," and diversity remained one of its six main accreditation criteria until 2012, when NCATE merged with a rival accrediting body.[38] NCATE's successor, the Council for the Accreditation of Educator Preparation (CAEP), despite being labeled conservative by some multicultural education advocates, has crafted its diversity norm as a kind of metastandard, ensuring that concern for it infuses the rest of the teacher education experience and curriculum (an accounting of diversity initiatives must be given for every one of CAEP's other accreditation standards).[39] Similarly, the Association for Advancing Quality in Educator Preparation (AAQEP), yet another national teacher education accrediting body launched in 2017, includes specific, diversity-related subcriteria within three of its four general accreditation standards.[40]

Institutionalizing Civil Rights Reform in the Domain of Teacher Education

By emphasizing the broad causal role of law and policy, I do not mean to deny the contribution of educators on the ground who did the work to develop multicultural education into a successful academic enterprise. It is true that education laws and accreditation requirements played a very direct practical role; at a minimum, those legal and quasi-legal mandates created significant demand for college courses and textbooks and thus for research and scholars. But it is also obviously true that it was the efforts of literally thousands of educators and teacher educators—led by dedicated reformers, some of whom we have encountered here—who not only wrote and pushed for those policies but also succeeded, generally speaking, in making American teacher education an important site of civil rights reform. Multicultural education reformers and theorists developed the educational content that was now needed and served as leaders within the world of teacher education. As a result, eventually American teacher education taken as a whole became one important site in which the anti-discrimination revolution was institutionalized, not by law simply (though law was obviously important) but by the norms, practices, and expectations of a profession exerting considerable influence over an important domain of life. This general phenomenon (activist-led social institution-building) has played a major role in the expansion of the anti-discrimination regime, especially in the world of education and academia, but also in other professions and anyplace where life is somewhat formally structured and organized—what conservatives are now beginning to call (borrowing from the neo-Marxists) "the long march through the institutions" (see Gonzalez 2021). Accounts of the influence of anti-discrimination politics in Hollywood and in the worlds of medicine and journalism, for example, help to map out this territory; and there is by now a large literature on "woke capitalism" and the vitally important part in the anti-discrimination revolution played by the personnel management profession.[41]

Certainly the teacher education establishment has been solidly behind multicultural education ever since the AACTE endorsed it in 1972. In the 1970s, other leading educational associations—the National Council for the Social Studies (where James Banks played a leading role), the National Council of Teachers of English, the Association for Supervision and Curriculum Development, and the Council for Exceptional Children—likewise followed suit and endorsed the idea of multicultural education in clear terms.[42] Already in the 1970s multicultural education had become a distinct scholarly enterprise with a notable presence in the world of teacher education. Articles began to appear on the topic in *Phi Delta Kappan*, *Educational Leadership*, the *Journal of Negro Education*, and in many other education journals on a regular basis. The leading scholarly outlet for multicultural education early on was the AACTE's journal, the *Journal of Teacher Education*, and scholarly publication on the topic was very visible in its pages through the 1990s (it remains an important site of multicultural education advocacy to the present day).[43]

By the 1980s at the latest, one could say that the discipline of multicultural education had arrived. The first multicultural education textbook appeared in 1979 and another appeared in 1981, written by Banks; others by a variety of authors soon followed.[44] Christine Sleeter and Carl Grant's 1987 comprehensive survey and categorization of the multicultural education literature published in the *Harvard Educational Review* (later expanded into a book that has been reissued in several subsequent editions) announced unmistakably that multicultural education had become part of the education establishment.[45] A number of academic journals dedicated to multicultural education were launched in the 1990s, with several academic book series (edited by Banks, Sleeter, and Sonia Nieto) on topics in the field appearing shortly thereafter.[46] In 1990, scholars formed a professional association, the National Association for Multicultural Education (NAME).[47] I cannot resist noting here two illuminating signs of the connection between multicultural education and the initial legal support it received from the federal government in elementary facts of NAME's own history and structure: not only did two of NAME's first six presidents serve in federal Equity Assistance Centers (EAC), but NAME's ten geographic regions were originally identical in composition to the federal EAC system's ten regional divisions.[48]

Why Multiculturalism's Political History Matters

The word "multiculturalism" may later have taken on other meanings, but at the outset, in the United States, its obvious connection to civil rights politics is uncontroversial and not open to doubt. It is this meaning that was also at the heart of the national debate over multiculturalism that commenced in the early 1990s, more than two decades after American multicultural education first emerged. Clear markers at the commencement of that debate are prominent critical responses to multiculturalism by historian Arthur Schlesinger and by education history scholar (later Assistant Secretary of Education) Diane Ravitch. Both had been provoked as a result of their participation in the battle over adoption of a multicultural education curriculum in New York State.[49] Similar debates in Texas and California about multiculturalism also centered on multicultural education.[50] If the debates that followed made things more complicated—layers of distortion introduced both by its critics and by new rival theories of multiculturalism—it is important to insist upon the simple and clear political meaning that defined the idea at the moment the concept was first used and at the moment it entered the American political lexicon.

To repeat, the basic claim being made here is *not* a causal one about the effect of multicultural education on American political culture, however important that may be (indeed, most multicultural education advocates themselves worry that it has not been causally important enough).[51] The causal work that matters here is that done by anti-discrimination politics. In addition to demonstrating the latter, by showing the effect of the civil rights revolution on American educators as a class of American intellectuals, the main point of presenting this merely historical evidence is to banish all doubt, by reference to facts that are not controversial, about the proposition that the word "multiculturalism" is and has always been tied at some level to the fight against discrimination in the United States. Multiculturalism in America does not originate in postmodernism, or in the liberal pluralist tradition, or in Canada. It is not mainly the product of "social science" (its opponent, the "cultural deprivation paradigm" being equally the product of social science). Later, it is true, in the debate over multiculturalism, especially among academics, the original idea became covered up to some degree by competing theories, interpretations, and misinterpretations.[52] The question of whether the original meaning is superior to the alternatives that came along after can only be addressed by engaging the idea of multiculturalism directly. We turn now to that more fundamental task.

PART 2.
THE IDEA OF MULTICULTURALISM IN AMERICA

Chapter 5
THE "MULTICULTURAL IDEOLOGY" OF JAMES A. BANKS

> That the legislator must, therefore, make the education of the young his object above all would be disputed by no one. Where this does not happen in cities it hurts the regimes. One should educate with a view to each sort, for the character that is proper to each sort of regime both customarily safeguards the regime and establishes it at the beginning.
> —Aristotle, *Politics*[1]

The main task of this chapter is to set forth in a serviceable way the inner logic of anti-discrimination politics as it is comes to sight in the thought of American multicultural education's foremost non-postmodernist theorist, James A. Banks. For the purposes we have in mind, Banks proves an excellent resource and dialectical partner. As an educational theorist and fashioner of a new civic education for a new age, Banks is the contemporary equivalent of Noah Webster, the great education reformer of the American founding period. But Banks's attempt "to re-envision, rethink, and reconceptualize America" is at the same time an effort to advance a new form of democratic pluralism, something comparable in the liberal pluralist tradition to Kallen's theory of cultural pluralism or Locke's original argument for religious pluralism.[2] He is also the relatively sober, temperate—and for that reason very influential—advocate of what is ultimately a fairly radical understanding of democratic politics. By way of analogy, one might say that Banks is the more moderate "Locke" to his more openly radical (and more controversial) "Hobbesian" or "Spinozist" associates (postmodernist or otherwise). In part 3 the question of how his account of multiculturalism differs from liberal pluralism will be taken up in detail. For Banks, however, the question of the liberal tradition is in fact at best a secondary concern, and so we will touch on it here briefly only at the very end. The main goal for now is simply to spell out his vision of multiculturalism—a vision of civil rights politics—in the clearest possible terms.

In reconstructing Banks's thought I have tried at every point to be true to what he thinks and to make no claims for him that are not adequately supported by statements he himself has made. That being said, Banks is an education scholar and does not try to set forth a work of political theory. This means that I have had to supply an outline for his thought emphasizing its political content that he does not himself provide and, at points, to make connections among ideas that he might not make. The outline I utilize is partly dictated by the subject matter that appears in his work, but it is also admittedly shaped by my desire to make use of Banks's pedagogical prescriptions to figure out the inner logic of the anti-discrimination regime.[3] That I do not do violence to Banks's thought in holding anti-discrimination politics to be its animating source will be demonstrated in due course, but for anyone doubting that starting point there are places in his work where the evidence for it is provided in clear terms.[4] As our analysis will make plain, the disparate elements of Banks's body of work are informed by the same civic impulse, and I proceed by assuming that the best way to understand his thought is by approaching it in that light—as a coherent, unified whole.

Banks is a great teacher of the meaning of our contemporary democratic world. If we take him at his word, what Banks offers is a new vision of political life made necessary by the anti-discrimination revolution. If we are to do justice to his account of multiculturalism, it is necessary to take seriously his claim that multicultural education is "*largely a way of viewing reality and a way of thinking, and not just content about various cultures and groups*" (1992c, 90; emphasis in the original). Not for nothing does Banks speak in terms of a "multicultural ideology," an "ideal type" designed to provide a general framework for discussing multicultural education's basic goals.[5] Indeed, Banks goes so far as to say that multicultural education is engaged in "an ideological struggle . . . , one might even say an ideological war" (1996b, 28). That this struggle is political in the most ordinary sense is established in a clear way by the "conservatives," "neoconservatives," and "Western traditionalists" who mount a "strenuous and well-orchestrated challenge" to multicultural education, one that "will be fierce, and will at times become ugly and pernicious."[6]

Banks's brief for multicultural education proposes, as I say, a new democratic civic education, a "civic education that reflects cultural democracy" (1997a, 136). Banks has been presenting multicultural education by reference to the language of civic education since 1983 (at the latest), and he makes the case for such a view of his project at greatest length in his 1997 book *Educating Citizens in a Multicultural Society*.[7] We will explore the positive substance of this new program of civic education in detail but the main point—its defining connection to civil rights politics—may be stated in general terms now: "Citizenship education in a multicultural society must have as an important goal helping all students, including white mainstream students, to develop the knowledge, attitudes, and skills needed not only to participate in, but also to help transform and reconstruct society. Problems such as racism, sexism, poverty, and inequality are widespread within U.S. society."[8] "Discrimination against groups based on race, class, language, gender, or sexual orientation constitutes barriers to social justice and participatory democracy. Citizenship education that seeks to cultivate democratic values in students should provide them with the opportunity to think deeply about racism and other forms of inequality" (Banks et al. 2005, 21). Today we take it for granted that steps must be taken to halt discrimination; Banks helps us to see that this must be a central task of civic life, a broad, citizen-making project.

Banks also makes plain that this entails a fairly dramatic break with the past that challenges the previously reigning civic order.

> Citizenship education for the twenty-first century must . . . help students to understand and to deal reflectively with the contradictions that result from the ideals within American society (such as those that make up the American Creed, that is, liberty, justice, and equality) and the racial discrimination that they will experience or observe in history, current affairs, and the wider society or in the school community. . . . Some people of color, both children and adults, feel a modicum of resentment and betrayal when they are required to say these words in the *Pledge of Allegiance*, "With liberty and justice for all." Schools must recognize that such ambivalent feelings are caused by the institutionalized racism

and discrimination that people of color have experienced historically and still experience today.[9]

Perceived failures of the past and present make necessary "the construction of a national civic culture that embodies and exemplifies democratic values" (1999b, 54). This is what Banks has in mind when he says that "citizenship education must be *changed* in substantial ways to prepare citizens to function effectively in the twenty-first century" (1999b, 54; emphasis added).

Why Banks?

Banks saw from the very beginning that his efforts would be political and transformative and that they would entail a rethinking of the received categories of American life. He seems always to have had a suitably ambitious sense of his own general purpose. What he said in 1973—referring, in this instance, to Black studies—would seem to apply to his work as a whole:

> The social studies curriculum which I advocate could possibly prevent chaos and destructive instability within our society, while at the same time providing means and methods whereby oppressed groups and new generations can shape their own destinies, use those aspects of traditional society which are consistent with their needs, and create new, legitimate life-styles and values when it is necessary to do so. *What is legitimate, normative and valued is subject to reconstruction in each new generation.*" (1973b, 154; emphasis in the original)

Already in the 1970s, Banks saw his task to be that of "develop[ing] a philosophy and theoretical framework for a movement which already exists, with the hope that we may be able to influence what it might become in the future" (1976a, 33). An African American, Banks had been affected by the "African American teachers [he had] in elementary school" and by "growing up Black in the segregated South" (2006c, 3). He "came of age during the Civil Rights Movement of the 1960s and 1970s," commencing graduate school at Michigan State University in 1966 (2006c, 1–3). Extending the basic objectives of civil rights reform in the world of education has shaped his entire academic career.

The "Multicultural Ideology" of James A. Banks

The leading member of its founding generation, Banks is American multiculturalism's advocate, theorist, movement unifier (and sometimes disciplinarian), and political strategist. One could look as well to other early prominent non-postmodernist multicultural education theorists or, alternatively, one could approach the vast multicultural education literature by reference to the surveys and typologies that attempt to summarize and navigate it.[10] The fact that there is no single, readily identifiable intellectual "founder," no sole theorist, of American multiculturalism reflects its general political origin. But one could insist on the choice of Banks if only by reference to the relative effect he has had on American multicultural education as an academic discipline. The author of more than one hundred articles, and the author or editor of some twenty books, Banks has written more, and is cited more frequently, than any other writer in the field.[11] Present at the beginning, Banks contributed to the development of multicultural education on many levels, and his leading role has been recognized in a variety of ways.[12] Just as important, as an author of popular multicultural education textbooks, Banks has had a wide influence on a couple generations of American teacher educators and teachers.[13]

But the most important reason to investigate Banks is the considerable reach and range of his thought. As a theorist of multicultural education, Banks looks consistently to the long-term aspirations of what he has termed the "multicultural movement," keeping in view the broad context of American politics, history, and intellectual life within which multicultural education is situated.[14]

> The ultimate fate of multicultural education as a discipline will to a large extent be determined by the kind of vision we develop and implement in the field. . . . We must act now to set and pursue a rigorous scholarly and research agenda, develop a cadre of strong academic leaders who will shepherd the field in the future, . . . and take vigorous steps to assure that multicultural education . . . [is] consistent with a transformative tradition that promotes justice, equality, and human dignity." (1997a, 121)

Not joining other multicultural education writers who embrace postmodernism, Banks negotiates a settlement between postmodernist claims about the construction of knowledge and social science approaches to similar questions.[15] It is important to insist, however, that in making multicultural theory a sophisticated enterprise, Banks never subordinates his primary (political) aims to any merely intellectual trend or school of academic thought. Indeed, what allows him to try to bring social science and postmodernism together, for example, is ultimately the political perspective from which he views both of them. Rejecting a lax "conceptual democracy," Banks insists that multicultural education must "attain some level of conceptual consensus" if it is to be taken seriously.[16] "If the multicultural education movement is to spearhead effective educational change, concepts such as racism, sexism, culture and ethnicity must be clearly delineated and educational reforms must be precisely targeted" (1979b, 237–38). Attempts to unify and systematize the substance of multicultural education abound in his writings, as do summary accounts of both the ends and means of the discipline.[17]

Politically, Banks self-consciously presents himself primarily as a reformer; but this, as we shall see, is always with a view to what are in fact fairly radical objectives and aspirations. This means that Banks is alive to the need for rhetorical deftness and, where necessary, effective, if perhaps temporary, compromise. As Banks puts it, "multicultural educators must live with the contradiction that they are trying to promote democratic and humane reforms within schools that often reflect and perpetuate anti-democratic values within the wider society" (1984b, 62). The political situation of American multiculturalism makes necessary overtures to that "wider society" that will simultaneously appeal to it and change it. At the same time, Banks advocates "reformist approaches" to multicultural education, explicitly rejecting "radical proposals for the reconstruction of American society and schools" (1984b, 63). For Banks, this is partly a question of rhetorical strategy. "Movements that appear to threaten the nation's democratic ideals, such as neo-marxist notions of school reform, are likely to be summarily rejected by most American educators without serious analysis or consideration" (1984b, 63). But his criticism also evinces a certain frustration with the utopian idealism of his more radical allies and colleagues. "The radical critics can maintain their innocence because many of them are professors in educational policy studies foundations and departments. Consequently, they have the luxury to write, talk, and dream about schools without having to confront directly the challenges that teachers, student teachers, and students must experience each day" (1992a, 283). But, to repeat, this reformist *stance* adopted by Banks is taken as a way to advance what is in fact a profoundly revolutionary outlook, and this combination, evidently successful, is reflected in the wide sway he holds within the field of multicultural education—among, it is important to emphasize, more and less radical theorists alike.[18]

Analyzing in detail the substance of the new ideology, the new civic education, and the new pluralism that Banks offers us is the task of the rest of this chapter. To do justice to his thought, it is useful to organize the discussion according to its major elements. Banks provides a complex and sophisticated elaboration of a view of democratic life that begins with the fight against discrimination and an account of its moral necessity. He then sets forth in detail a variety of strategies for educating citizens to its requirements. But his pedagogical theorizing necessarily entails more general reflections on the relationship between individuals and the social order. The new civic education Banks has in mind is not simply a set of individual classroom strategies. Ultimately, it rests upon a sophisticated account of political or social psychology; it employs a new public morality; and it advances a new understanding of group politics. Framing all these aspects of his theory in turn are illuminating reflections on the requirements of the task of fighting discrimination.

"Change the Center"

Perhaps the most important thing to see about Banks's thought at the outset is the far-reaching character of its bold aspirations. What Banks hopes to achieve is nothing less than to establish in the minds of the young citizens shaped by multicultural education a new understanding of the "center" of modern democratic life. Multicultural education aspires to convey a new account of "the common culture," of "the mainstream"—the "*unum*" in "*e pluribus unum*"—and offers a "new metanarrative," a "new story," that may do justice to the transformative requirements of the civil rights revolution.[19]

> We can create an inclusive, democratic, and civic national community only when we change the center to make it more inclusive and reflective of our nation's diversity. This action will

require bringing people and groups on the margins of society into the center. When groups on the margins of society begin to participate in the center, the center must change in fundamental ways. One important change is that groups with power must share it; equal-status relationships must be established between powerful and marginalized groups. (1999b, 56–57)

Banks does not seek to reject the "mainstream" of modern American life so much as to transform it. "The mainstream must be reconstructed to reflect the diverse cultural, ethnic, and language groups within it" (1999b, 58). Likewise, contrary to superficial appearances, multiculturalism does not mean renouncing the idea of a common culture but instead calls us to "*redefine what the common culture actually is*" (1976d, 103; emphasis in the original). Banks emphasizes the *political* nature of this redefinition when he says elsewhere that the new "common culture" is indeed to be a new "common *civic* culture": "The reformulation must also involve power sharing and participation by people from many different cultures who must reach beyond their cultural and ethnic borders in order to create a common civic culture that reflects and contributes to the well-being of all. This common civic culture will extend beyond the cultural borders of any single group and constitute a civic 'borderland' culture" (1993d, 24).

This also means, to begin with, rethinking the meaning of "America." "One of the goals of ethnic studies," Banks says, "should be to change the basic assumptions about what *American* means and to present students with new ways of viewing and interpreting American history and culture. Any goals which are less ambitious, while important, will not result in the substantial and radical curricular reform which I consider imperative" (1976b, 79; emphasis in the original). "The multiculturalists view *e pluribus unum* as an appropriate national goal, but they believe that the *unum* must be negotiated, discussed, and restructured to reflect the nation's ethnic and cultural diversity. The reformulation of what it means to be united must be a process that involves the participation of diverse groups within the nation, such as people of color, women, straights, gays, the powerful, the powerless, the young, and the old. The reformulation must also involve power sharing and participation by people from many different cultures."[20] The new account of what is now to unite America is conceived by Banks in the broadest possible terms: "We have to construct a new metanarrative, we have to construct a new story of America that's inclusive" (1998a).

But the reach of the new multiculturalism metanarrative extends further still, embracing "the West" as well. Reckoning with the injustices of the past can lead to a new view of the West emphasizing the commitments of the civil rights revolution. "Although multicultural education is not opposed to the West," Banks argues, "its advocates do demand that the truth about the West be told, that its debt to people of color and women be recognized and included in the curriculum, and that the discrepancies between the ideals of freedom and equality and the realities of racism and sexism be taught to students" (1993d, 23). For Banks, "multicultural education itself is a product of the West. It grew out of a struggle guided by Western ideals for human dignity, equality, and freedom. Multicultural education is a child of the civil rights movement led by African Americans that was designed to eliminate discrimination in housing, public accommodation, and other areas."[21] Starting from this crucial point, Banks's main concern is to "deconstruct the myth that the West is homogeneous, that it owes few debts to other world civilizations, and that only privileged and upper-status Europeans and European-American males have been its key actors" (1991a, 34).[22]

The implications of this reformulation are usefully illuminated in Banks's sometime characterization of multiculturalism in the language of "globalism" and "global education."[23] As Banks says, "it is . . . important for students to develop the ability to view concepts, problems, events and situations from the points of view of ethnic groups within other nations."[24] Looking at things from the perspective of not just other nations but "ethnic groups within other nations" reflects the fact that globalism is ultimately informed by the logic of anti-discrimination. As Banks says, an individual with "global competency" has "internalized the *universalistic* ethical values and principles of humankind" (2001b, 137; emphasis added). Banks's rethinking of the meaning of the West is connected to this. "The concepts, paradigms, and projects that facilitated the rise and triumph of the West between the sixteenth and the twentieth centuries are ineffective in the changed world of the twenty-first century. Citizenship education in the United States—as well as within other Western nations—must be reinvented so that it will enable students to see their fates as intimately tied to that of people throughout the world" (2006b, 210). This is for Banks not simply a theoretical but a practical imperative as well, one reflecting domestic American politics in a very straightforward way. "There is emerging evidence that the role of the Western world will be considerably different in the future than it is today. In the world society of the future, nonwhites will play an increasingly important role in making social, economic, and political decisions that will affect us all. . . . The white race is a world minority."[25] Moreover, because of immigration and international norms, this trend will likely continue to gather speed. "National boundaries are also becoming more porous because of international human rights that are codified in the Universal Declaration of Human Rights (1948) and by the European Union. . . . Serious tensions exist between the conceptions of international human rights and national sovereignty" (2008a, 132).

But perhaps the most ambitious expression of what he is after is to be found in Banks's new understanding of "democracy." Multicultural education is, to repeat, a "civic education that reflects cultural democracy" and this means, to begin with, "help[ing] students from diverse cultures develop a commitment to national values and concerns by respecting, acknowledging, and understanding their diverse cultures" (1997a, 136). "I think the argument ought to be for the sake of democracy," Banks says, "for the sake of giving all students and cultures a voice" (1996b, 27). As we shall more clearly when we explore his argument in detail, this new understanding of democracy puts front and center the need to combat the injustices of discrimination; indeed, Banks articulates the failings of American politics precisely in terms of "the gap between American democratic ideals and American racism" (1990, 213). "Pedagogies that merely prepare students to fit into society and to experience social class mobility within existing structures—which are characterized by pernicious class divisions and racial, ethnic, and gender stratification—are not helpful in building a democratic and just society."[26] Just as many have come simply to equate "democracy" with the doctrines and practices of *liberal* democracy, so Banks seems to equate democracy with a new form, anti-discrimination democracy—or, as he puts it, "cultural democracy."

Whether multiculturalism can deliver on such a promise, on its claim to offer a new ideology and a new civic education—and a new vision of America, the West, global society, and democracy—on the basis of the commitment to fighting discrimination, must remain for now an open question. But what Banks makes clear is that someone who begins from the commitments of the civil rights revolution and really takes them seriously may well be inspired to try to remake the world on their basis. Banks does not exaggerate when he says that multiculturalism is a "way of viewing reality and a way of thinking."

The Fight Against Discrimination: Generalizing the Particular

The aim and starting point, the end and the beginning, of multicultural education is the task of resisting and overcoming discrimination. That effort is a necessarily and essentially negative one and while, as we shall see, Banks offers many strategies for recasting it in positive terms, this crucial fact about multicultural education must never be forgotten. "Racism has been a decisive force in our nation since its beginning and is still a major force in America today" (1984c, 90). A "major goal of multicultural education is to reduce the pain and discrimination that members of some ethnic and racial groups experience because of their unique racial, physical, and cultural characteristics" (1999a, 3). Although some gains have been made as a result of the civil rights revolution, the problems it addressed have by no means been solved: "Even though many laws have been enacted to ban discrimination in all areas of American life, and even though much progress has been made in eradicating it, discrimination is institutionalized in the United States" (1984c, 63). The nature of the task means that multiculturalism will necessarily proceed politically, in the face of resistance and opposition. "A reform movement such as multicultural education, which deals with highly controversial and politicized problems and issues such as racism and inequality, is especially likely to be harshly criticized during its formative stages because it deals with problems in society, and appears to many individuals and groups to challenge established institutions, norms, and values. It is also likely to evoke strong emotions, feelings, and highly polarized opinions" (1984b, 59).

But the commitment to fighting discrimination at the core of Banks's vision of multiculturalism is complex, pointing in two different directions at the same time. Reflecting the nature of the fight against discrimination itself, again and again we will see a recurring juxtaposition of anti-discrimination's narrow negative starting point (in the realities of discrimination and the particular interests of its victims), on the one hand, and aspirations that are positive, general (even universal), and ultimately moral, on the other. As Banks says, "the aim of citizenship education should be to attain a delicate balance between education for unity and nationhood and educating citizens to recognize, confront, and help resolve inequality manifested in forms such as racism, sexism, and classism."[27]

It is both the promise and the peril of politics that its aim must be at some point to generalize, authoritatively, some particular point of view. The generalizing tendency of politics has become incredibly sophisticated, and extremely influential, in modern times with the advent of comprehensive theories of political life ("ideologies") that expound and then extrapolate from some universal account of things (arguing from human nature, from history). But it is also true that political life has always worked this way, reflected most simply in the fact that no law fails to speak generally. If Banks's "multicultural ideology" is not as famous as the ideologies of liberalism or Marxism, its aspirations are no less ambitious. The first lesson of political science is or ought to be that every political order always points in these two different directions simultaneously, a lesson that Banks and anti-discrimination may help citizens of a liberal democratic order (who incline always and everywhere to the universalistic side of the divide) to rediscover.

Multicultural education is thus political in one sense because it advances the interests of specific groups, those whose members are victims (or potential victims) of discrimination. But multicultural education is also political in another sense in that it makes its case generally (in the language of civic education or morality or pluralism or "ideology") and, in doing so, seeks to embrace the collective interest of the entire community. Because of the first task, Banks's multicultural ideology must at points speak to different groups differently. But the ideology also articulates, simultaneously, a vision of civic life meant to have universal appeal. This duality marks out his account of multiculturalism as a complex expression of broad and ambitious political reform and it shapes Banks's account of multiculturalism throughout.

In a 1974 essay titled "Curricular Models for an Open Society," Banks indicates with striking clarity the narrow or particular political requirements and claims of the specific groups from which multiculturalism begins, and the corresponding precisely tailored strategy it must follow to advance the interests of those groups in the face of discrimination. Banks proposes in this essay what one may term a "group-differentiated" approach to the education of young Americans.[28] What is needed for those groups suffering or likely to suffer discrimination is a "Curriculum for Oppressed Groups" (the "Shared Power Model"). For members of the majority, on the other hand, agents (or possible agents, at least in the past) of discrimination, what is appropriate is a "Curriculum for Dominant Groups" (the "Enlightening Powerful Groups Model"). Although he uses the very general language of the "dominant" and the "oppressed" here, Banks clearly has in mind the fairly specific problem of discrimination and, above all, American racial discrimination. Tactics to be employed on behalf of discrimination's victims include the following: rejecting "the definitions of themselves which are perpetuated by dominant groups"; debunking the myths arising from "a conspiracy to make them believe that they are less than human"; and "studying about the ways in which they have been psychologically and physically exploited and dehumanized." Members of "oppressed groups" must also be helped to "gain *power* and shape public policy" in a way that will "ensure their existence as a group [with] essential societal cohesion."[29] The "primary goal" of the Enlightening Powerful Groups Model, on the other hand, is "to help whites develop more positive attitudes toward oppressed peoples and a willingness to share power" (1974, 49). As Banks puts it elsewhere, multicultural education works to counteract the "sense of false superiority in white students" and to overcome their tendency "to believe, as many do today, that they are the only humans on earth" (1971a, 821). This approach seeks "to 'enlighten' dominant groups by changing their attitudes toward excluded groups" (1974, 57).

If the starting point and ever-present orienting aim of multiculturalism is the fight against discrimination, how does Banks understand discrimination itself? In brief, he embraces the Left interpretation. His view that discrimination is rooted in systemic social forces pervading American life is basic to his outlook: "When discrimination based on race becomes institutionalized within a society and the dominant group has the power to implement its racial ideology within these institutions, institutional racism exists."[30] While Banks does think that prejudice and discrimination are explained partly by the "attitudes and personality" of individuals, he holds that no explanation can ignore its basis in the wider "social structure": "*An adequate theory of prejudice must take into account both personality variables and the social structure.* Explaining prejudice and discrimination as totally a product of a disorganized personality ignores the facts that human beings are social beings and that their reactions in a social setting reflect not only their individual idiosyncrasies and biases but also the prevailing norms and expectations" (1994b, 241; emphasis in the original). "African Americans do not enjoy full citizenship rights in the United States primarily because of institutionalized racism and discrimination. . . . Regardless of their social class, race still remains an intractable barrier. The racial microaggressions that many middle-class and upper-middle-class African Americans experience indicate that social class mobility reduces but does not eliminate racial categorization and stigmatization" (2017, 6; citations omitted). By insisting that discrimination is a societal, systemic, and institutional problem, Banks rejects the view, common among conservatives and predominant in US Supreme Court interpretations of the Fourteenth Amendment, that the state need only concern itself with instances of the deliberate discriminatory actions of identifiable individuals or organizations. His rejection of the "color-blind constitution" ideal is very direct. "Colorblindness was used to justify inaction and the perpetuation of institutionalized discrimination within the school. Colorblindness is part of the 'racial text' of teacher education which . . . teachers and teacher educators must 'unlearn'" (2001a, 12; citing Cochran-Smith 2000). While Banks says little in his multicultural education writings about many controversial civil rights policies—like affirmative action, busing, hate speech codes, voter redistricting representational schemes, reparations—or other positions taken up on the Left in public debate about civil rights politics, he does embrace the essential premises of the Left's understanding of the problem and nature of discrimination.[31]

Starting from this more pessimistic view of what discrimination is, Banks holds that the fight against it will not be easy, to say the least. "The final phase of ethnic revitalization is a process that does not end until diverse ethnic and racial groups experience structural inclusion and equality within the nation-state. . . . Even when ethnic groups attain *inclusion* into institutions, they do not necessarily experience *equality*" (1994b, 34; emphasis in the original). Discrimination has not gone away just because the law has changed but has instead become "much more subtle and less blatant than it was prior to the Civil Rights Movement of the 1960s and 1970s" (1999a, 60). Stated positively, the goal for Banks is thus, as he says, "structural inclusion."[32] "Failed citizenship occurs when the social, cultural, economic, and political systems within a nation-state prevent marginalized groups from attaining full structural inclusion into the nation" (2015, 152).

But if the narrow beginnings of anti-discrimination politics and the negative orientation associated with resisting discrimination are central to Banks's starting point, it is also important not to overstate the extent to which they predominate, or to exclude more positive dimensions of the argument. Banks appeals at least as often to an affirmative and generally applicable vision of the political aspiration of multiculturalism. This is true of the 1974 article mentioned above, in which Banks lays out an explicitly group-differentiated political account of multicultural education; that essay begins from and finally returns to an appeal to the political community as a whole and, for the most part, Banks stays on that broader and more positive plane to some considerable extent in all his writings (1974, 43, 63). This dimension of Banks's presentation of multiculturalism will be the focus of our attention in most of what follows, and we have seen some important evidence for it already, in Banks's appeal to a new vision of America—a new center, a new *unum*—and a new vision of democracy. The positive general formulations of multiculturalism deserve our attention because they help us to see how politics (and the politics of anti-discrimination in particular) works causally to shape how we see the world. The positive general face of anti-discrimination politics is both more important and more interesting than the narrow particular interests or concerns from which it originates, even if those interests or concerns are never entirely out of view.

Civic Education as Political Pedagogy

Education is a crucial site of reform in the fight against discrimination. "The school . . . may be the only institution within our society which can spearhead the changes essential . . . [to] eliminating ethnic hostility and conflict in America" (1972a, 267). The connection between other forms of political change and the educational effort Banks has in mind is complex. "Schools alone cannot eliminate racism and inequality in the wider society [although] they can reinforce democratic social and political movements beyond the school walls and thus contribute in important ways to the elimination of institutional racism and structural inequality" (1984b, 61). At a minimum, education can play a vital supporting role in a more comprehensive political transformation. "We will either have to redistribute power so that groups with different ethnic and cultural characteristics will control entry to various social, economic, and political institutions; or we will have to modify the attitudes and actions of individuals who will control future institutions" (1974, 45).

Indeed, for Banks education is not merely incidental to the task of fighting discrimination, because the problem centers in the socially constructed mind of the citizen. Moreover, the education of the past has contributed in significant ways to it. "The school is usually viewed by the victimized ethnic group not only as an important vehicle that can help it to attain equality but also as an institution that contributes to the group's exclusion because it reinforces the dominant anti-egalitarian ideologies and values of the nation-state. Since the school is viewed by ethnic reformers as an important institution in their oppression, they attempt to reform it because they believe that it can be a pivotal vehicle in their liberation."[33] Banks recognizes the difficulty of the challenge. While "changing the racial attitudes of adults is a cumbersome task," still, "the research suggests rather conclusively that children's racial attitudes can be modified by experiences in the school designed specifically for that purpose."[34] The effort "to modify children's racial attitudes" must be *deliberate*" and "structured for that purpose in the earliest grades," and it must "be *sustained* over a long period of time" (1974, 60; emphasis in the original). As Banks says, "if the twig is going to be straightened, we must start as early as possible" (1991b, 467). But discrimination is also unpredictable and tenacious. "When we approach the realization of [democratic] ideals for particular groups, other groups become victimized by racism, sexism, and discrimination. Consequently, within a democratic, pluralistic society multicultural education is a continuing process that never ends" (1997a, 68).

The first and most obvious task of multicultural education is the simple and direct one of teaching young people that they should not discriminate against one another. Banks identifies "prejudice reduction" as a central component of multicultural education.[35] Although this is a more pressing concern for members of groups that are likely to be, or that have in the past been, agents of discrimination, it is typically presented as a generally applicable teaching. In comprehensive surveys of the multicultural education literature, Banks assesses several different prejudice reduction strategies. Some approaches call for straightforward "antiracist teaching" or "curriculum interventions" (multicultural topics, readers, etc.). Likewise, students may be taught "to differentiate the faces of [those in] out-group[s]" in order to reduce prejudice against them; or teachers may reinforce positive associations with the colors black and brown. Other approaches—"increased positive racial contact," role playing, or "cooperative learning" strategies, for example—rely more on incorporating direct interpersonal engagement.[36] But whatever the means, the end of prejudice reduction is to "help students develop positive racial attitudes and perceptions," to "develop democratic racial attitudes," "to learn democracy" (2006b, 206–7).

If Banks's thought is characterized by a tension between reformist and radical impulses, at points this comes to sight in teachings at the more radical end of the spectrum. Pedagogical prescriptions aligned with the fight against discrimination thus include preparing students for political participation and political activism. "We would try to equip exploited people with the strategies which will enable them to attain power, while preventing their extermination and maintaining an essential degree of societal cohesion" (1974, 49). Sometimes this is presented in a general way as a lesson for all. "Citizenship education in a multicultural society must [help] all students, including white mainstream students . . . not only to participate in, but also to help transform and reconstruct society" (1990, 211). This is indicated, for example, when Banks embraces the "social action approach" over and above three other curricular reform models (the "additive," "contributions," and "transformation" approaches) (1999a, 30–32). Teaching the ways and means to major political transformation is a necessary part of multicultural education because the latter's essential aim is the same as that of the "black civil rights movement that emerged in the 1960s [that] stimulated the rise of ethnic revival movements" in the United States and elsewhere—namely, "to change the social, economic, and political systems so that structurally excluded and powerless ethnic groups would attain social and economic mobility and educational equality" (1987, 531). In this context, likewise, "the teacher [is] an agent of change and a cultural mediator. Such a teacher interprets ethnic and majority cultures for mainstream and minority students and helps them to see why social change is essential."[37]

At points Banks goes so far as to say that multicultural education must undertake the task of "radicalizing" students from groups who suffer discrimination. "We must radicalize oppressed students so that they will continually challenge the position of those in power. We must train them so that they will develop the skills and knowledge to obtain power and use it to build institutions which they will control. Until oppressed people obtain power and independent institutions, they will be victims of the ruling elite."[38] Imparting the "skills and knowledge to obtain power" ensures that multicultural education's lessons will not be merely theoretical or academic:

> Ethnic youths must be taught how they have been victimized by institutionalized racism. They must become involved in social action projects which will teach them how to influence and change social and political institutions. One of the major goals of ethnic studies should be to help ethnic minority students become effective and rational political activists. We must provide opportunities for them to participate in social action projects so that they can become adept in influencing public policy which affects their lives. (1972a, 267)

When he characterizes multicultural education as a new form of civic education, Banks employs what is probably the most important positive, general formulation of what he is trying to do. But if the basic idea of civic education appeals to some notion of a common community, and even to ideals of patriotism and devotion to country, it is necessary to emphasize the radical character of the concept as Banks employs it. This is visible most simply in his rejection of the civic education of the past (an issue we noted earlier). The first problem with the old civic education is that it was used to marginalize those now protected by the civil rights regime.

> In the past, citizenship education embraced an assimilationist ideology. Its aim was to educate students so they would fit into a mythical Anglo-Saxon Protestant conception of the "good citizen." Conformity was the goal of this conception. One of its

aims was to eradicate the cultures and languages of students from diverse ethnic, cultural, racial, and language groups. . . . Minorities often became marginal members of their cultural communities as well as marginal citizens, because they could function effectively neither within their cultural communities nor within the national civic culture. Even when they acquired the language and culture of the mainstream, they were denied structural inclusion and full participation in the civic culture due to their racial characteristics. . . . Only when the national civic culture is transformed in ways that reflect and give voice to diverse ethnic, racial, and language communities will it be viewed as legitimate by all its citizens.[39]

The second problem with traditional civic education is that it undermines the political activism and radicalism Banks holds to be vital.

> Political education within the United States has traditionally fostered political passivity rather than political action. . . . Students are taught to vote and to participate in the political systems in ways that will not significantly reform US society. Newmann writes, "By teaching that the constitutional system of the U.S. guarantees a benevolent government serving the needs of all, the schools have fostered massive public apathy. . . ." Rarely do we deliberately educate students for social change. . . . To participate effectively in social change, students must be taught social criticism and be helped to understand the inconsistency between our ideals and social realities.[40]

As Banks put it in the 1970s, multicultural education began precisely as "a strong reaction to the traditional approach to citizenship education."[41]

One of the most interesting and illuminating of Banks's positive, general formulations of the aspirations of multicultural education is his account of what he terms the five "stages of ethnicity" or the "stages of cultural identity." Banks presents this "typology" as a merely descriptive and explanatory framework for understanding the role of ethnic or cultural identity in the lives of individuals. But it is also, and more fundamentally, an account of progress—

political and moral—from less to more ideal stages of civic development. The first two stages describe a situation in which discrimination reigns, where some internalize "negative ideologies and beliefs about [their] ethnic group" (stage 1: "ethnic psychological captivity") while others believe in their ethnic superiority (stage 2: "ethnic encapsulation"). The next three stages mark off a progression, first to self-acceptance (stage 3: "ethnic identity clarification"), and then to "biethnicity," and, finally, to "multiethnicity" (or, in a later formulation, "multiculturalism") (stages 4 and 5).[42]

It is stage 5 that Banks believes "describes the idealized goal for citizenship identity within an ethnically pluralistic nation" (1980, 121). "The Stage 5 individual has clarified, reflective, and positive personal, cultural, and national identities; has positive attitudes toward other cultural, ethnic and racial groups; and is self-actualized" (2001b, 136). The Stage 5 individual may lay a claim to attaining both justice and self-fulfillment. "Such multicultural perspectives and feelings, I hypothesize, help the individual live a more enriched and fulfilling life. . . . Individuals within this stage have a commitment to their cultural group, an empathy and concern for other cultural groups, and a strong but *reflective* commitment and allegiance to the nation-state and its idealized values, such as human dignity and justice" (2001b, 137; emphasis in the original). The Stage 5 individual may thus be said to represent Banks's ideal of the good citizen, the well-instructed student of the regime, which suggests, moreover, that the good citizen is also (as "self-actualized," as able to "live a more enriched and fulfilling life") a good human being.[43] Although couched to some degree in the quasi-clinical and seemingly apolitical language of social science, Banks's account of the Stage 5 individual provides another useful indication of the great civic ambition of multicultural education—in the suggestion that anti-racism and anti-discrimination provide a measure that might or ought to shape the life aspirations of individuals.

Another of Banks's pedagogical prescriptions that might not seem immediately to have anything to do with politics is the idea of "cross-cultural competency." There is here a suggestion that "multiculturalism" could be taught in a kind of simple, literal sense, as a skill for communicating and operating in a complex culturally diverse world. "Cross-cultural competency consists of the skills, attitudes and abilities needed to function within a range of cultural and ethnic groups and the ability to interact effectively with individuals who belong to diverse racial and ethnic groups" (1980,

113). That students ought to be taught "to view and interpret concepts, events and issues from diverse ethnic perspectives," is not a stance immediately suggesting any overt political meaning.[44] Every American youth a Herodotean, an inquisitive traveler to distant lands and times. But here multiculturalism's starting point defines the substance of the effort in a way that discloses fairly clearly its narrow and even rigid political orientation. For cross-cultural competency works, above all, to overcome what Banks terms the "Anglo-American Centric Model," according to which "many teachers assume that *American* means the same thing as *Anglo American*" (1980, 116; emphasis in the original). A crucial dimension of cross-cultural competency is thus effectively a call to view somewhat suspiciously any skill or "competency" students might already have for navigating what used to be the dominant culture, a culture now condemned by its association with discrimination. "In the past, Americans have tried to reach [unity] by eradicating diversity and forcing all citizens into a White Anglo-Saxon Protestant culture" (1994d, 4). Cross-cultural competency is therefore not a neutral teaching; it requires that different cultures be treated differently from a fairly clear political and moral point of view.

Perhaps the most important lesson of multicultural education, at least in terms of its practical implications, is its rethinking of the *history* of America and the West (part of the project to "reconceptualize" America and the West we encountered earlier). The new history is one that will takes its bearings entirely from the fight against discrimination. Once again, Banks's account of it makes plain the dependence of the generalizing aspiration of multiculturalism on its group-differentiated beginning point: "The point which I am trying to emphasize is that the study of America must be seen through the eyes of the vanquished, since students now study it primarily from the viewpoint of the victors."[45]

> To understand fully the nature of American society and the role that ethnicity plays within it, teachers will have to reconceptualize their views of America. For example, the United States is usually studied as an extension of European social and political institutions. However, American Indians were in America centuries before Columbus. To view America merely as an extension of European institutions ignores American Indian

institutions and cultures. Ethnic studies demands that teachers and students reconceptualize their views of the winning of the West, the meaning of slavery, the purpose of American expansion in the late 1800s, and the nature of democracy as it is practiced in contemporary American society. (1984c, 424–25)

It is above all in "social studies" and in the retelling of history that multicultural education can achieve most directly its fundamental reinterpretation—and revaluation—of what was once taken for granted as the American tradition. "Students can be asked to think of words that might have been used by the Lakota Sioux to describe the same people that a textbook might label *settlers* and *pioneers*. Such terms as *invaders*, *conquerors*, and *foreigners* may come to their minds" (1991c, 139; emphasis in the original). Banks almost agrees—but not quite—with E. D. Hirsch's call for "cultural literacy." "I agree with Hirsch that there is a need for all US citizens to have a common core of knowledge. However, the important questions are: *Who will participate in the formulations of that knowledge?* and *Whose interests will it serve?*" (1999a, 29–30; emphasis in the original). Banks, who began his career examining how Blacks were characterized in American history textbooks, places himself in a new tradition of historians and social scientists who challenge mainstream interpretations of American life that fail to come to terms with America's legacy of discrimination.[46]

Banks's pedagogical prescriptions remind us that any robust civic education entails the more or less direct shaping of hearts and minds with a view to unmistakable political aspirations. This is something that liberal democracy does not feel comfortable with and does only stealthily and paradoxically: a civic education that teaches freedom and the toleration of differences might seem not to impose any moral teaching at all (even if the result is that its citizens just so happen to embrace a morality of freedom and toleration). It is true that the narrow, partial beginning point of multicultural education, advancing the interests of discrimination victim groups, is readily visible if one looks for it. But it is also necessary not to exaggerate that side of things. The general, universal face of political life is at least as important, and it is certainly more interesting. In turning more deliberately to those elements of Banks's argument that serve to appeal to the community as a whole and that are intended to appeal presumably to anyone and everyone—in the language of political or social psychology, in a new set of moral terms, and in a new account of pluralism—the narrow, particular starting point from which antidiscrimination politics begins will not be left entirely behind. But because the categories of the positive, general face of politics, if internalized, shape our perspectives, our minds, indeed, our lives (old-fashioned people would say our "souls") as citizens, it is necessary to pay attention to what Banks says his education is trying to achieve on that level. This will be our focus for the remainder of the chapter.

The "Psychological Project"

"Identity" is a crucial concern for Banks, the central concept informing what must be termed multiculturalism's political psychology. Identity has of course also become an increasingly important concept in our wider democratic discourse in recent years—and I believe it is largely for the same (political) reason. While the concept of identity plays a role in modern epistemology and psychology and sociology, Banks uses it in a new, politically relevant way; in doing so, he only follows the necessary reasoning of the fight against discrimination. That Banks can help us understand how and why we increasingly find it necessary to make use of the language of identity is one more indication of the utility of his thought. In Banks's work, identity plays a role similar to the psychological assumptions that ground Madison's famous formulation of liberal pluralism in *Federalist* 10, for example. There Madison tries to show why some degree of intergroup conflict is unavoidable, arguing from certain irreducible facts of the human situation or human nature (unavoidable differences of opinion and interest, the ambition of leaders, etc.), and then proposing to build on that foundation a solution that does not try to evade or wish away inescapable problems but instead deals with them on their own terms. The arc of Banks's account of identity follows a similar path (from pessimistic beginnings to melioristic prescriptions), although both its psychological assumptions and policy implications differ markedly.

For Banks the language of identity is necessary because, first of all, it pinpoints in psychological terms both the site of the harm done by discrimination and also the seriousness of that harm. "Racism," he argues, "frequently causes ethnic group members to have confused racial identities, and negative attitudes toward self, and to strive to attain impossible racial and ethnic identities" (1976c, 540). (Although most of Banks's reflections on this question were worked out by him in reference to racism and racial identity, his discussion is applicable to other forms of discrimination and identity as well.) In an early essay devoted to the topic, "Racial Prejudice and the Black Self-Concept" (in a 1972 book he coedited titled *Black Self-Concept*), Banks spells out how living in a world where discrimination is prevalent negatively affects the identity formation of its victims.

> A person in our society validates his identity through the evaluations of "significant others." However, the average black American has never been able to establish social or self-identity that is comparable in terms of social valuation to that of the white majority. . . . In his attempt to shape a new identity and to gain control of those factors which most profoundly affect his life and destiny, the black man confronts an immense hurdle—a system of white institutional racism which perpetuates racial myths to justify the oppression of the black man.[47]

This dynamic forms the basis of Banks's claim that discrimination's victims confront a situation of "psychological captivity."[48]

A more general account of the role of identity in human life, which Banks takes from theorists of social psychology, provides a framework for gauging the depth of discrimination's harmful effects on individuals. "A person's sense of 'identity' and 'peoplehood' is essential for his psychological health"; identity answers "personal, moral, spiritual and psychological needs."[49] Group identity also provides individuals with "notions of what is right and wrong," "ideas about the sacred and the secular," and "fundamental beliefs about the world in which they live."[50] The obvious implication here is that, by adversely affecting identity, discrimination warps the fabric of life.

Banks thus helps us to see how the logic of anti-discrimination politics on its own tells us why discrimination is wrong or unjust. Liberalism, of course, has its own answer to that question (when discrimination denies the universal equality of human beings as rights holders and the like), but an argument from identity offers a very different kind of starting point.

As important as identity is, at the same time the very process by which it is formed within a social context seems, almost inescapably, to be itself one of the great causes of discrimination. Banks, following the view of Henri Tajfel and other social psychology theorists, sketches a pessimistic account of how identity-formation occurs:

> Social psychological research . . . indicates that whenever in-groups and out-groups form, stereotypes, prejudice, and discrimination develop. It also indicates that when mere categorization develops, individuals favor the in-group over the out-group and discriminate against the out-group. This is the case even though the in-group and out-group may have had no prior history of animosity and conflict. The basis for the in-group/out-group distinctions can by quite arbitrary and contrived.[51]

The language of in-groups and out-groups reflects the dynamic of group discrimination and no other important social phenomenon; this terminology is, of course, still very much in use today, a stock teaching of social psychology. The state of affairs described here represents a basic problem: a sound identity is a requisite of psychic health and proper "notions of what is right and wrong," but the very nature of identity formation is a chief cause of group-based prejudice—and hence, a source of discrimination, warped identities, psychological ill health, and distorted notions of morality. Escaping this trap is one of the challenging tasks of multicultural education.

The solution to the problematic relation between identity and discrimination begins to emerge from the great malleability of human identity itself. Banks's thought in this respect also reflects his political starting point: the realm of identity with which he is concerned is one where "ascriptive" (given) identity characteristics are enmeshed in "socially constructed" interpretations of those characteristics. On the one hand, "members of an ethnic minority group possess unique physical and/or cultural characteristics enabling members of other groups easily to identify its members, usually for the purposes of discrimination."[52] On the other hand, group identity is also something "we acquire . . . from other human beings."[53] "Even though one's sex is determined primarily by physical characteristics . . . , gender is a social construction created and shaped by the society in which individuals and groups function" (1993c, 17). Without some intervention, the situation that prevails ordinarily is one in which groups necessarily struggle and compete to capture the levers of social construction for themselves, to advance a view of their identity that affirms their place in society and, all too often, their superiority over others. Banks's goal is to interrupt the ordinary flow of group-based identity-formation, to channel the course of identity-construction precisely for the purpose of halting discrimination. If identity itself can be defined or constructed around anti-discrimination, perhaps the social cycle of group-based identity discrimination may be broken. If Locke and some of the liberal pluralists started from something like human nature (or "natural right"), Banks begins from a view of human identity that emphasizes its great malleability.[54] Optimistic about what may be achieved through politics, the proposed effort suggested here is also very ambitious: to fight discrimination, multicultural education must advance a direct, explicit, and fully self-conscious (and state-sanctioned) campaign of the identity formation of citizens.

Banks's project of identity construction follows a now-familiar pattern, combining strategies that are both particular or group-differentiated, on the one hand, and general or universal, on the other.

The first task of reworking the American identity is to deal with aspects of it that foster discrimination: "There is a movement among ethnic minority groups to reject their old identities, shaped largely by white society, and to create new ones, shaped by themselves. The calls for black, red, brown, and yellow power are rallying cries of these movements" (1972a, 267). Multicultural education "must facilitate the quest by minority group students to shape new identities and to rediscover their unique culture elements which have been lost and stolen" (1971b, 116). At the same time, Banks holds that the "very difficult psychological project" of "reconstructing White identity and deconstructing the current one"—necessary because "much of White identity is invested in the United States as it has been mythologized"—is a central component of "the project to reform the curriculum in the nation's schools."[55] Reworking the American identity is likewise central to "prejudice reduction" which is either an effort to help minority students "to augment their self-concepts [and] to feel more positively toward their own cultures" or, as a teaching for all students, a matter of "develop[ing] positive attitudes toward different racial, ethnic, and cultural groups."[56]

For Banks, promoting a more positive vision of identity for minorities is emphatically *not* the same as promoting minority "self-esteem" as a means of improving minority educational performance. "I'd like to deconstruct the established notion of compensatory [education] and have us think about it in a new way.... The usual way of thinking of it as compensatory is thinking of it as doing something to bolster the self-concept of African American and Mexican American students.... The claim that multicultural content will affect student achievement is not an argument I find very convincing."[57] In public debate, conservative opponents of multicultural education have emphasized in their criticisms perceived arguments from self-esteem promotion.[58] The real issue, Banks maintains, is how the very self-understanding or identity of minority students is affected by living in a society that discriminates against them and theirs, something very different from a strategy for enhancing student self-esteem. Banks's discussion of identity insists that much more is at stake than the critics of self-esteem education suggest.[59]

Where prejudice reduction and other group-differentiated teachings of multicultural education serve to rework identity according to the most immediate requirements of anti-discrimination, Banks also advances a new general and positive account of "citizenship identity," the core of which is something like diversity or multiculturalism in their simplest, most literal meanings. Multiculturalism, the highest stage in Banks's typology of the "stages of ethnic identification" detailed above (and embraced by the Stage 5 individual), is to be understood as precisely the "idealized goal for *citizenship identity* within a culturally diverse nation."[60] This peak of Banks's psychological project is ultimately the same as the new multicultural understanding of "the American identity," an outlook according to which those who have suffered discrimination in the past can "demand that their visions be reflected in a transformed America" (1993d, 28). The content of the new American identity is also identical to Banks's account of the new "center," the new "*unum*," which we encountered earlier. Here, too, the new understanding of our history—"seen through the eyes of the vanquished, since students now study it primarily from the viewpoint of the victors"—is also in play. Whether, in articulating such a vision, Banks ever fully escapes anti-discrimination's negative starting point is a good question, but the importance of these teachings cannot be overstated, since this new vision of our community and of our history is to be internalized and taken to heart at the level of the citizens' very identities. Yet again we see that, to the extent that this aspect of Banks's project is successful, multicultural education serves truly to bring about a new "way of viewing reality and a way of thinking."

Banks's thoughtful deployment of the newly relevant and, indeed, central language of identity is especially important because his use of it shows how a variety of complex issues are drawn together and interrelated according to a psychological logic that has its ultimate root in a fairly straightforward political orientation. It almost goes without saying that in none of this does Banks rely in any way upon the traditional liberal understanding of politics.

Moral Education

Banks's use of the language of identity is not properly understood if it is confined to the realm of social or political psychology. Indeed, I would venture to say that identity is one of the central terms in the new *moral* logic of anti-discrimination politics. In a way I indicated this earlier when I noted that identity helps us to see how or why discrimination is unjust. This may be stated more positively as well. Multiculturalism must be able to point to some important value that is denied or put in jeopardy by discrimination, in the name of which discrimination is to be resisted; it is identity that supplies this crucial moral premise. The human good at the bottom of anti-discrimination cannot refer to the universally applicable claims associated with traditional liberalism, such as liberty or natural right or Kantian human dignity, because these do not capture what is denied to individuals in their *particularity*, as members of specific groups, when they suffer discrimination. But a general concern with identity, as Banks presents it, captures this perfectly. In addition, identity might also be said to try to complete—that is, to attempt to provide a compelling or persuasive ground for—a new constellation of other moral concerns (inclusion, respect, recognition, equity, a new equality) that express positively the political aspirations of the anti-discrimination ideal. I would go so far as to say that identity is the "good" called forth or necessitated by anti-discriminatory justice, playing a role similar to the concept of *freedom* in liberalism.

Identity's moral meaning and its connections to other important principles and ideals suggest the necessity of examining directly the moral dimension of Banks's thought. Banks makes use of a new moral vocabulary all the time but he does not do so in the spirit of academic analytical philosophers parsing each term's substance under a logical microscope. Instead, he employs the new moral logic spontaneously and naturally, simply in the course of giving expression to his varied concerns. Like much else associated with anti-discrimination politics, this moral language is novel and yet also somehow familiar, and Banks's unhesitating use of it provides us with an opportunity to see these newly relevant terms in action and to begin to understand each part in relation to the others and to a (political) whole.

For Banks, moral education is central to multicultural education: "Knowledge construction clearly has to be related not only to students' cognitive development but to their moral development."[61] The necessity of moral education follows immediately from the nature of the problem multiculturalism is designed to address. That discrimination is an injustice, above all the injustice of racism and the "chronic and agonizing malady" of "white racism" in particular, is one of the fundamental assumptions underlying all of Banks writings (1972b, 5). For American minorities, "justice" is a "deferred and shattered dream." "Because of their salient physical and cultural traits, non-European peoples in America have been denied both the symbols and substance of justice" (1973e, 641, 639). Discrimination itself is understood partly in moral (and not merely psychological) terms by Banks, as comprising the use of power by some to "oppress and dehumanize another group" (1984c, 65). Banks encourages Americans to view discrimination from the perspective of their core commitments and to address the "contradictions" between the ideals of "the American Creed—i.e., liberty, justice and equality," on the one hand, and the facts of discrimination in American life, on the other (1997a, 16). When Banks speaks of "rethinking and reimaging the United States," the point is to do so "in ways that will make it more just and equitable," an effort that "will enrich us all" (1999b, 60).

Long before "equity" had become a general stand-in for a firm commitment to anti-discrimination politics, Banks had gone so far as to characterize multicultural education as an "equity pedagogy," this indeed being an "essential component" of the whole.[62] Equity pedagogy helps students to acquire "the knowledge, skills and attitudes needed to function effectively within," as well as to "create and perpetuate, a just, humane, and democratic society," but this "cannot occur within a social and political context embedded with racism, sexism, and inequality." As any serious moral education must do, multicultural education seeks genuine inner transformation, an effort of individuals that entails "reflective self-analysis." "Reflective self-analysis," in turn, "requires teachers to identify, examine, and reflect on their attitudes toward different ethnic, racial, gender, and social-class groups. Many teachers are unaware of the extent to which they embrace racist and sexist attitudes. . . . Reflective self-analysis cannot be a one-time event. Multicultural awareness can result only from in-depth work on self." If successful, the result of equity pedagogy is a citizen who readily sees that "the nature of U.S. society must be interrogated and reconstructed" (Banks and Banks 1995, 151–53, 156). Banks also proposes what he terms the "Banks value inquiry model," a framework designed to help students not only to clarify their values but also "to develop democratic values" and "to act on their moral decisions."[63]

If Banks does seem at points to show some hesitation about directly teaching morality through a new public education, such old-fashioned (liberal democratic or social scientific) hesitations are easily overcome in the face of the injustice of discrimination. "I feel strongly that American schools cannot take a value-free position on issues related to racism and institutional discrimination" (1977b, 697). While Banks insists that "standards that guide a person's life must be freely chosen from alternatives after thoughtful consideration of their consequences," he nonetheless also maintains that "many ethnic and racial problems within our society are rooted in value confusion," and that the schools should help students "to make moral choices intelligently." "All values are not equally valid. Some values, such as inequality, racism, and oppression, are clearly inconsistent with human dignity and other American creed values" (1984c, 96, 98). While Banks holds that students must be able to express their "beliefs freely and openly," they are to do so with a specific purpose in mind. "Beliefs which are unexpressed cannot be rationally examined. While we must eliminate racism in America in order to survive the challenges of the 21st century, students must be able to reflectively analyze racism and its effects before they can develop a commitment to eliminate it" (1973b, 170). Similarly, Banks holds that "we can't teach democratic values with a stick and coercion," but he does see the need for appeals to the conscience and sense of guilt of those who discriminate (1999a, 89). While not entirely confident about the possibility of "Enlightening Powerful Groups" through moral suasion, this approach nevertheless "assumes that people with power feel guilty about the ways in which exploited groups are treated, or can be made to feel guilty" (1974, 49–50). The role of the victims of discrimination in this moral drama is vital. "Cultural and ethnic communities need to be respected . . . because they serve as a conscience for the nation-state. These communities take action to force the nation to live up to its democratic ideals when they are most seriously violated. . . . People and groups in the margins have been the conscience of the United States" (2001a, 7).

Because it begins from the injustice of discrimination and resistance to it, multicultural morality is in part a fighting morality, and it contains an important element of corrective justice. This spirit is especially clear in Banks's earliest writings. Although already in 1977 he could reflect that "emotions have cooled, perspective has been gained, and ethnic minorities are now engaging in serious introspection and policy formation," just a few years earlier he characterized himself and a group of colleagues collaborating on an ethnic studies book as "a group of fighters who have an unrelenting commitment to social justice."[64] Standing up to perceived injustice is indeed normally associated with, and presumably greatly aided by, the energy supplied by moral or righteous indignation. "Multicultural content is inherently emotive, personal, conflictual, and involving. Consequently, it is essential that students be given ample opportunities to express their feelings and emotions, to interact with their peers and classmates, and to express rage or pride when multicultural issues are discussed" (1994a, 96). In a provocative formulation, Banks goes so far as to cast the entire project in such terms. "The challenge is herculean. The odds are against us. The hour is late. However, what is at stake is priceless: the liberation of the hearts and minds of all American youth. Thus, we must, like Don Quixote, dream the impossible dream, reach for the unreachable star, and act decisively to right the unrightable wrong."[65] The possibility intimated here, that righting the past wrongs of discrimination offers modern democracy a positive goal of great worth, an "unreachable star," captures very helpfully the complicated combination of moral motives—fashioning a new common good from a perpetual struggle against injustice that cannot therefore dispense with corrective justice—that informs Banks's effort.

The Substance of the New Morality

To repeat, much of the characteristic moral content of multicultural education is not simply or even primarily negative, rooted though it is in reaction to the injustices of discrimination. "Multicultural education can help us live together in a civic moral community" (1994e, 13). First and most simply, Banks offers a new view of the American common good. Rejecting attempts of multiculturalism's opponents to "define their own interests as universal and in the public good and the interests of women and people of color as *special interests*," Banks articulates what he holds to be a more expansive or inclusive notion of the common good (1994a, 22; emphasis in the original). "To create civic, moral, and just communities that promote the common good," multicultural education must teach above all what is necessary "to work with people from diverse groups" (Banks and Banks 1997, 185).

The substance of the new morality, moreover, works to enunciate the claims of anti-discrimination politics in a series of different appeals to general, positive ideals and principles. We have seen this already in Banks's employment of the identity term. Other new terms, interrelated with identity and one another, articulate in a compelling way the complex (and relatively coherent and internally consistent) whole that is the morality of anti-discrimination politics. Mapping out how exactly all the terms of this new morality have arisen in relation to a new political determination, as well as the question of which is cause and which is effect, would be a project of considerable complexity (but presumably an important one for political scientists). While Banks does not offer any direct discussion of this aspect of his understanding of things, his thought does allow us to see it as a fully realized fact. Examining the new moral terms at work in his account of multiculturalism offers an extremely useful starting point for investigating this fascinating phenomenon.

Perhaps the most *visible* shift in our moral language associated with anti-discrimination politics is a new standard of "respect" that stands opposed to the old liberal ideal of toleration. The call for respect announces a new measure of correct interpersonal treatment and while Banks sometimes makes reference to the traditional liberal ideal, he more typically employs the new term.[66] Banks goes so far as to say that "the major goal of multicultural education is to change the total educational environment so that it promotes a respect for a wide range of cultural groups and enables all cultural groups to experience equal educational opportunity" (1984c, 21). "The school curriculum," for example, "should respect the ethnicity of the child and make use of it in positive ways" (1976d, 105). Banks enunciates the same standard in an early position statement he coauthored for the National Council for the Social Studies (NCSS): "Simply admitting the existence of ethnic diversity is not enough. Acceptance of and respect for differences in ethnic values, traditions, and behavior are called for."[67] Harms going *beyond* the denial of respect are of course part of the reality of group-on-group discrimination, but anti-discrimination must be concerned with respect both because the denial of respect is a harm in itself (the harm of indignity or insult) and because that psychological harm stands as a marker of, and often a prelude to, more tangible forms of mistreatment. Anti-discrimination law can address the more concrete harms but it is education, especially, that can attempt directly to teach citizens to respect members of groups who are or have been discrimination's victims.

Sometimes, the ideal of respect is expressed as the need to overcome and undo the "negative" portrayals of minorities and, at the same time, to create a new "positive" view of them. While this dichotomy is sometimes presented as serving students' strictly educational needs, its political/moral meaning is also obvious. "Many of the messages ethnic minority youths receive from significant individuals and institutions within American society regarding their ethnic groups are negative and dehumanizing" (1984c, 68). The problem is especially acute in teaching materials—above all, in American history textbooks.

> The histories of minority groups have been written largely by members of the mainstream groups. They usually write histories of ethnic minorities that legitimize the dominant social and economic structure and that often depict minorities negatively. Anglo-American mainstream writers and social scientists often

invent myths and stereotypes about ethnic minorities to explain why they "deserve" the low status in society to which they are most often assigned. Such stereotypes and myths are rampant within our society. (1984c, 71)

Banks's reform at this level is meant to pervade every aspect of the educational system: "Another appropriate goal of multiethnic education is to change the total educational environment so that it will respond to ethnic students more positively and enable them to experience educational equality" (1979b, 240). This informs the basic idea of prejudice reduction as well, an aim of which is "to help students develop positive attitudes toward different racial, ethnic, and cultural groups" (1997b, 22).

Major goals of these [educational] interventions should be to help students of all racial, ethnic, and cultural groups to develop more positive connotations for brown and other nonwhite colors; to have positive vicarious experiences with people from a variety of racial and ethnic groups; . . . and, where possible, to have positive cross-racial interactions with children from different ethnic groups that are characterized by cooperation, equal status, and shared goals. (1997a, 97)

Promoting positive "attitudes" about certain groups enlists the seemingly apolitical language of social science to express the new moral imperative of respect.

Another central dimension of multiculturalism's moral reasoning we have by now seen Banks employ many times is a complex account of equality—or "equity." In fact, two *different* ideals of equality are at work in Banks's thought, capturing different aspects of anti-discrimination politics. One has to do with attaining equal *outcomes* in tangible, material terms. This is, of course, familiar from the affirmative action debate, although Banks does not usually use the language of "equality of results," and his case for this form of equality is largely confined to equality in the *educational* domain. More interesting is a second important ideal that emphasizes social "status," a notion of equality that does not yet have a name. While Banks also (and, in a way, more commonly) uses the term "equality" in a general sense, as well as the language of "equality of opportunity" (the latter associated simultaneously with liberalism and civil rights politics), it is these first two formulations that go to the heart of things in his moral understanding.[68]

It is helpful to treat each of these two different egalitarian positions (briefly) in isolation. The novel, and even somewhat awkward or at least unfamiliar, egalitarianism to which Banks gives voice—seeking equal *status situations* for groups—marks off the moral claims of the fight against discrimination in a way that reflects its necessary concern for matters of respect and identity. "Multicultural theory," Banks says, "reveals that equity may not always mean treating different groups the same. It may sometimes be necessary to treat different groups differently in order to create equal-status situations for marginalized students."[69] "The total environment and culture of the school must also be transformed so that students from diverse groups will experience equal status in the culture and life of the school" (2006b, 10). Banks uses the term to express a broad claim extending well beyond the domain of education. "One important change," he says, "is that groups with power must share it; equal-status relationships must be established between powerful and marginalized groups. Racial and ethnic harmony will not occur unless equal-status relationships are established and power is shared" (1995b, 57). Banks derives this ideal of equal status situations from social scientists of the 1950s and 1960s who wielded it as a merely descriptive term (a condition for successful integration efforts), but then deploys it, more clear-sightedly in my view, in a moralized way, as a new *standard* of equality—a new "must."[70] "Diverse racial, ethnic, cultural, social-class, and gender groups within the nation-state . . . must experience—or believe that they can experience—equal status within the nation-state."[71] Although it is not a well-known formulation, it names a powerful ideal because it captures a moral claim underlying all anti-discrimination politics—the notion of equality implied when we say that Blacks are equal to Whites or that women are equal to men, and the like. Banks is not the only person to have made use of this formulation, but his emphatic use of it helpfully clarifies its meaning and importance.[72] Such a claim is something more than what is promised by equality before the law or equality of opportunity (which is also a way to say liberty), and something less than equality of results.

But at points Banks does go all the way, roughly, to equality of results or equal outcomes. Banks's understanding of inequality as it pertains to race (connected to his view that discrimination is institutional and systemic, mentioned earlier) is that it is "structural" (see 1984b, 61–62). While he does not often weigh in on the wider affirmative action debate (presumably because linking multicultural education to that debate would draw unnecessary negative attention), he does embrace the basic principle that—at least in the field of *education*—a presumption of equal achievement or outcomes ought to be made. Banks goes so far as to define multicultural education in terms of "help[ing] children from diverse groups to experience educational equality" (1984b, 58). Banks is very clear that practices standing in the way of equal educational outcomes, practices contributing to group *inequalities*—"grouping and labeling practices," for example—are to be rethought (1993c, 22). Equity pedagogy "requires the dismantling of existing school structures that foster inequality," and it essentially reframes teaching accordingly—everything from grading policies and teaching methods to "the traditional power relationship between teachers and students" (Banks and Banks 1995, 153). "Equity pedagogy has important implications for assessment. Educators who embrace it must interrogate traditional tests and letter grades" (Banks and Banks 1995, 155). Stated positively, equity pedagogy means using "techniques and teaching methods that facilitate the academic achievement of students from diverse racial, ethnic, and social-class groups" (1999a, 16–17). Generally speaking, something like a standard of group proportionality in education renders suspect "disproportionality in achievement, disproportionality in enrollment in gifted and special education programs" (1993c, 22). Banks goes so far as to state this as a standard to be applied to all educational outcomes: "A norm will have to be institutionalized within the school that states that all students *can and will learn*, regardless of their home situations, race, social class, or ethnic group" (1994a, 38; emphasis added). This takes us back to the very origins of multicultural education and to the cultural deprivation-difference debate—to the idea that we must take a "system-fault" and not a "student-fault" view of educational inequalities.

These two ideals of equality are connected to one another, Banks's equality of status situations formula providing a kind of (more politically powerful or persuasive) ground for claims of equal outcomes. If we say that all groups are equal in deserving status or respect, then how are inequalities among them to be explained such that we do not call into question the respect we have for all groups? Not only does the cultural difference paradigm insist that unequal educational outcomes should not be made attributable to characteristics of the groups involved, but it provides a justification for this precisely from matters pertaining to the status or worth of minority groups. "Educational programs that spring from the idea of cultural deprivation show disrespect for students' home culture" (1983b, 585). This connection between these two equality ideals perhaps explains Banks's use of the word "equity" to refer to *both* of them (without, to my knowledge, defining that term as a distinguishable third ideal). Banks thus helps us to see that if equity has any *precise* meaning (as something more than a general indication of support for civil rights), it is to be found here, in its (usefully) ambiguous relation to the different (more and less controversial) equality claims made in anti-discrimination politics.

At times, Banks also uses the language of "recognition," a term made famous or inescapable by Charles Taylor's brief for a "politics of recognition" and by the recognition-redistribution debate centered on the work of Axel Honneth.[73] But it is worth emphasizing that when Banks uses the language of recognition, such formulations are almost always coupled in a suggestive way with some other term that supplies a needed moral additive. Above all, recognition is tied to "respect." Number one among "four premises" of an account of "ethnic pluralism" is the claim that "ethnic diversity should be recognized and respected at individual, group, and societal levels" (Banks et al. 1976, 9). Schools and teachers must "respect and/or recognize the cultures of students."[74] Recognition is connected to other moral categories in related formulae: "recognition and acceptance"; "cultural recognition and rights"; "be recognized and included"; "recognize and legitimize."[75] Similarly, Banks sometimes uses the language of "status," but, when he does use it prescriptively, the term is almost always paired, as we have seen, with the word "equal" ("equal status situations"). Just as Banks distanced himself from simple notions of "self-esteem" education, so his apparent reluctance to embrace the recognition term without qualification reflects an insistence that the claims of discrimination victim groups retain their proper *moral* meaning and not be trivialized in any way.[76]

Finally, at the more explicitly political end of the moral spectrum, Banks employs something like a new ideal of representation expressed in the language of "inclusion" and "voice." The traditional, individualistic (one person, one vote) view of representation is challenged by a new standard according to which (previously marginalized) voices must truly be heard in order to be considered fully part of the political community: "People of color, women, and other marginalized groups are demanding that their voices, visions, and perspectives be included" (1991a, 33). This means, to begin with, that we must truly hear these voices in order to draw upon them as resources of our collective self-understanding. But this cannot mean merely to recognize the "contributions" of minority groups.[77] "Giving all students and cultures a voice" must ultimately entail a project of including those voices in a redefinition of our common culture and national identity (1996b, 27). "Only when the national civic culture is transformed in ways that reflect and give voice to diverse ethnic, racial, and language communities will it be viewed as legitimate by all its citizens" (1999b, 55). "The American identity is being reshaped, as groups on the margins of society begin to participate in the mainstream and to demand that their visions be reflected in a transformed America."[78] Such a teaching about the (new) meaning of our collective cultural identity, advanced as we have seen already by Banks in a number of arresting formulations, is properly within the reach of the field of education in particular. But such a new vision of things is only part of what Banks means by inclusion. What the previously excluded and marginalized require is also *structural* inclusion, which indicates a more straightforwardly political notion: minorities have been "denied structural inclusion and full participation in the civic culture due to their racial characteristics" (1999b, 55). "Ethnic revitalization," therefore, "is a process that does not end until diverse ethnic and racial groups experience structural inclusion and equality within the nation-state."[79]

 Banks helps us to see how all these distinctive moral terms, which are familiar to anyone living in contemporary democratic society, work together in a coherent scheme. Even if Banks is not concerned with systematizing these concepts like an analytical philosopher might be, his consistent and fluent use of them permits us to think about them and their connection to the requirements of anti-discrimination politics. To fight the injustice of discrimination is to seek to protect the very identity of individuals as well as to stand against the denial of respect (and recognition or status) and other related harms that follow if such injustice is left unanswered. Confronting injustice is not easy and it will perhaps necessarily require making use of the spirited dimension of the desire for justice. The moral aspiration of anti-discrimination politics may be stated positively as a standard of interpersonal treatment insisting on respect for those who are or have been the victims of discrimination and as a standard of representation that insists on their inclusion. It advances a corresponding notion of equality (or equity), the equal status of members of all groups—which in turn renders problematic unequal outcomes for groups. The new moral outlook redefines the common good and democracy and America (and the West) by putting the fight against discrimination at their center. All this together may be said to offer an account of what Banks and others associated with the anti-discrimination revolution refer to as "social justice," a phrase that is not strictly speaking novel but that has a clear and relatively precise meaning today if we begin with the commitment to fighting discrimination. "The goal of multicultural education is to teach students to know, to care, and to act to promote democracy and social justice."[80]

Multiculturalism's (and anti-discrimination's) internally consistent set of interrelated moral claims should help to answer those who would suggest that "the intellectual premise of multiculturalism is cultural relativism" (D'Souza 1995, 18). Banks is very clear on this point. "Our critics misinterpret multiculturalism by claiming we are cultural relativists. Nowhere in my writing, or in the writing of other multicultural educators, do we advocate cultural relativism. Rather, we make a strong, unequivocal commitment to democracy, to basic American values of justice and equality. And that means that values that contradict justice and equality are not acceptable."[81] This may be an exaggerated claim when it is made on behalf of *all* multicultural educators (as we shall see in our discussion of postmodernist multiculturalism), but Banks's effortless deployment of moral argumentation confirms our sense, immediately apparent on the surface of things, that anti-discrimination politics expresses itself first and foremost, and unapologetically, in the language of justice.

We will return to this most important plane of the outlook associated with the civil rights revolution, devoting two chapters (9 and 10) to exploring the new morality in detail, to contrast it with the old, and to reflect on what it augurs for the citizens who embrace it. There we will examine a host of social and political theorists laboring to advance the new terms as they try to figure out what they mean. We can see now how Banks provides us with an invaluable starting point for engaging the wider debate over the import and status of these new ideals. By showing how their essential meaning originates always in the imperatives of the fight against discrimination, Banks makes plain how the new morality is the product of an obvious political development, not any complicated story from academic theory or intellectual history. Unafraid to challenge Americans' hesitations about "legislating morality," and offering indeed a new system of moral categories, multiculturalism challenges both the form and the substance of the liberal democratic understanding of things in a very direct way. Here, more than anywhere else in Banks's thinking, the full meaning of civic education, its mind- and heart-shaping power, is brought home with full force.

Multiculturalism as a Form of Pluralism

We are now in a position to restate Banks's argument in the language of pluralism. In part 3 I will provide an extended comparative analysis of the differences between multiculturalism and the liberal democratic pluralist tradition and, to avoid unnecessary repetition, my remarks here will be condensed. But it is useful to see now how multiculturalism works as a form of "group politics," and the exploration of Banks to this point provides us with the materials to sketch the main outlines of this new democratic pluralism. Banks himself often frames his treatment of multiculturalism in terms of general questions raised by group politics, and "pluralism" is a central theme in many of his writings.[82] But Banks is also very clear that pluralism takes a new form in multiculturalism, one not beholden to earlier models or to any tradition of pluralism in America (and not to liberal "cultural pluralism," in particular).[83]

The "group" is for Banks never a mere abstraction of sociological theory but is defined at every step by the realities of discrimination. Banks is neither simply for nor against groups (or cultures) as such; everything depends on where groups are located within a framework of group-on-group discrimination. Groups may of course be sources of prejudice, bigotry, and discrimination, and Banks is well aware of the need to resist this aspect of group life. "Helping students to develop reflective, clarified, and positive identifications with their cultural groups does not mean that we should teach cultural hero worship, group ethnocentrism, and cultural myths and fantasies. Too much of traditional American history teaching commits these sins" (1997a, 127). The problem here is a deep one. "Whenever groups with different racial, ethnic, and cultural characteristics interact, ethnocentrism, discrimination, and racism develop."[84] Indeed, as we saw earlier, Banks follows the social psychology literature, which holds that prejudice and discrimination arise "whenever in-groups and out-groups form" (1997a, 88). But, at the same time, "the ethnic community . . . serves as a supportive environment for the individual and helps to protect him or her from the harshness and discrimination which he or she might experience in the wider society" (1976d, 100).

> Individuals more successfully attain goals through the political system when working in groups than when working alone. Important examples are the political, cultural, and educational gains that African Americans won through their participation in the Civil Rights Movement during the 1960s and 1970s, as well as the momentous changes that the movement initiated in U.S. society as a whole, with significant benefits for other racial, ethnic, and language groups, women, and people with disabilities. (2008a, 131)

To the extent that they protect individuals against discrimination, groups are good, but to the extent that they are the source of discrimination, they are a force to be checked.

At points, groups are more or less defined by Banks in a general way in terms of their relation to discrimination. "Multicultural education suggests a type of education which is concerned with the cultural groups within American society that are the victims of discrimination and assaults because of their unique cultural characteristics. . . . Multicultural education . . . rests upon the assumption that concepts such as prejudice, discrimination, identity conflicts, and alienation are common to these diverse groups" (1977a, 74–75). Elsewhere, Banks distinguishes two different kinds of groups depending on whether they are on the giving or receiving end of discrimination's injustices: "While presently *excluded groups* must learn to value their own cultures, try to attain power, and develop group solidarity and identity in order to participate fully in this society, they must also learn that . . . even though *dominant groups* treat them in dehumanizing ways, it would not be to their advantage to treat other groups similarly if they attained power positions" (1974, 55; emphasis added).

Starting here, Banks's view of the relations *among* groups is, of course, already fundamentally pessimistic. In- and out-groups forming wherever groups appear, group-on-group discrimination and oppression would seem to be unavoidable dimensions of group life as such. Because the consequences of discrimination for individuals are so profound, the relationship between individuals and the groups into which they fall is a powerful one. Identity markers of anti-discrimination groups being often ascriptive or given, the individual cannot easily opt out of his or her group situation; group identity and status being the product of social construction, individuals have every incentive to identify with their group's struggle to resist constructions that are hostile to their aspirations. This does not, of course, take place in the abstract. Discrimination does not happen behind a veil of ignorance, and the identities of past (and perhaps future) perpetrators and victims of discrimination are often well-known; multiculturalism thus necessarily takes sides in thinking about actual groups in American life.

Affected groups must also seek allies—especially, other anti-discrimination victim groups—and they must never forget that they have real enemies:

> Perhaps an important goal of multicultural education should be to help students who are members of particular victimized groups better understand how their fates are tied to those of other powerless groups and the significant benefits that can result from multicultural political coalitions. These coalitions could be cogent vehicles for social change and reform. Jesse Jackson's attempt to form what he called a Rainbow Coalition . . . had as one of its major goals the formulation of an effective political coalition made up of people from both gender groups and from different racial, ethnic, cultural, and social-class groups. (1993c, 7)

Finally, this pluralism places new demands on the political order. The problem of discrimination being intractable, the fight against it means a much more interventionist, hands-on form of the management of intergroup relations by government and through the law. But this is not simply a matter of expanding the role of "the state" in terms of new bureaucratic agencies or the like, though that is of course part of the picture. As multicultural education itself attests, lessons of the new pluralism must be taught in a fairly direct way by the political order itself, especially to young people through its schools. This is partly a matter of group-differentiated lessons tailored to the needs of perpetrators and victims of discrimination (the victims of discrimination, especially, must be steeled to vigilant self-protection, encouraged to seek allies, and tutored in political activism). But it also entails a new teaching intended for everyone, a civic education program for the community as a whole that advances a new reading of American and Western history, a new moral sensibility, and a new democratic self-understanding or identity.

The Unanswered Question: Multiculturalism and the Liberal Tradition

Banks's account of multiculturalism signals unmistakably the emergence of a new understanding of American democracy that does not fit easily into the traditionally received forms of the liberal tradition and that indeed seems to break with them at crucial points. Since the core of his multiculturalism is the fight against discrimination, we are compelled to confront the broader question of the relationship between the civil rights revolution and liberalism, the subject of part 3 of this study.

Banks himself does address it, albeit briefly and somewhat indirectly, and what he has to say is instructive. At points Banks does take some pains to emphasize lines of continuity between multiculturalism and the broad political tradition out of which the civil rights revolution emerged. "Multicultural education is a child of the civil rights movement. The leaders of the civil rights movement . . . internalized the American democratic ideal stated in such important United States documents as the Declaration of Independence, the Constitution, and the Bill of Rights."[85] Although the question of liberalism is not a prominent theme for him, Banks does go out of his way at points to present multicultural education as precisely a "Liberation Curriculum" and an "Education for Freedom" (1991a, 1994a, ch.6).

But Banks's overtures in this direction must be put together with obvious evidence that cuts the other way, not the least of which is to be found in the novelty of his basic claims and categories. Moreover, to repeat, Banks advances his vision of multiculturalism without *any* reliance upon the tradition of liberal pluralism, explicitly rejecting any debt to Kallen's notion of "cultural pluralism" in particular. Banks also expresses a certain wariness of the American founders and other iconic figures associated with the liberal tradition (Lincoln, e.g.) from the point of view of anti-discrimination politics.[86] Similarly, his appeals to the meaning of America and the legacy of the West are more notable for their reinterpretation of the tradition than they are for any suggestion of continuity between the old and the new.

Banks comes near to a genuine reckoning with liberal pluralism in a brief (two-page) discussion of what he terms "*assimilationist, liberal,* and *universal* conceptions of citizenship education"—a position that, he says, "should be interrogated" (2008a, 129; emphasis in the original). In his summary of the liberal position, Banks emphasizes the tendency of "the liberal assimilationist ideology" to make "the rights of the individual . . . paramount" and to view "group identities and rights [as] inconsistent with and inimical to the rights of the individual." According to Banks's summary of the liberal view, group attachments are problematic because they "lead to conflicts and harmful divisions within society" and, if managed properly "within a modernized pluralistic democratic society," "group attachments will die of their own weight." But Banks joins with "social scientists and political philosophers to raise serious questions about the liberal analysis and expectations for identity groups." Above all, Banks rejects the liberal view because it diminishes the claims of "many racial, ethnic, and language groups." "Group differences are not included in a universal conception of citizenship" and, moreover, many groups in modern democratic life face "structural exclusion and discrimination," problems that are not adequately recognized in the liberal account of group politics. Citing his own work at this point, Banks states the ultimate standpoint of his disagreement with the liberal tradition: among the "factors" causing the social scientists and political theorists to question the liberal standard is "the rise of the ethnic revitalization movements since the 1960s and 1970s, which demand recognition of group rights as well as individual rights by the nation state." Banks makes what is already here a fairly direct conflict even clearer:

> Liberal assimilationist notions of citizenship assume that individuals from different groups have to give up their home and community cultures and languages to attain inclusion and to participate effectively in the national civic culture. According to these conceptions of citizenship, the rights of groups are detrimental to the rights of the individual. In contrast, using the Civil Rights Movement of the 1960s and 1970s as an example, I argue that groups can help individuals to actualize their rights and opportunities.[87]

I would quibble with Banks when he terms the civil rights movement merely "an example" in his analysis, but otherwise this is an important and revealing statement of a basic opposition between liberal group politics and "civil rights" group politics. One wishes that Banks would say much more about all of this. At the very least, what he does say does not call into question the idea that a good way to think about the anti-discrimination revolution is to contrast it with the liberal tradition.

At least as interesting and suggestive are Banks's attempts to express the aspirations of multiculturalism in the language of liberty. The main result is a revealing effort to rework or redefine that fundamental ideal to fit the new political outlook. In his article titled "A Liberation Curriculum," Banks frames liberty precisely in terms of liberation from "oppression" at the level of human identity. To reach the "deflation of the self-concepts of oppressed groups," liberty must be understood, above all, as "psychological liberation." "A liberation curriculum for blacks and other oppressed groups must not only recognize their feelings toward self, but must help them clarify their feelings to free them from this kind of psychological captivity, and to convince them of their value."[88] Similarly, when Banks presents multicultural education as "an Education for Freedom," a novel meaning of freedom is in play. Banks here suggests "three important senses" in which multicultural education embraces that ideal. By providing students, first, with "the freedom to function beyond their ethnic and cultural boundaries," multiculturalism might begin to sound traditionally liberal. But the other two meanings—enabling "students to freely affirm their ethnic, racial, and cultural identities" and helping "students to develop the commitment and skills needed to participate in personal, social, and civic action"—bear the unmistakable imprint of the fight against discrimination.[89]

Both Banks's attempt to articulate multiculturalism in traditional liberal terms and the difficulty he has in doing so point to a very broad question. Anti-discrimination and liberalism between them provide the moral polestars of the contemporary American political order; if these are related to one another in terms of a fundamental tension then one must say that American democracy is defined very generally and at the highest level by a basic contradiction. This is an unsettling possibility. It is, after all, not only the conservative opponents of multiculturalism who embrace the liberal understanding of politics; and it is not only progressives who believe in the fundamental justice of the fight against racism, sexism, and other forms of discrimination.

―――――――――――――――――――

In summarizing Banks's account of multiculturalism I have, of course, presented things in a particular order, as seems sensible to me. But the way I have chosen to organize all the parts is much less important than the fact that, taken together, they form a coherent and interrelated political whole. That much I hope will be granted, even if one might raise objections regarding some of the details of my presentation or see better ways to weave together the different strands of his argument. Certainly Banks's thought provides an answer to David Hollinger's claim that multiculturalism's "unifying principles have proved too vague to enable its adherents to sort out their own agreements and disagreements" (Hollinger 1995, 2).

We are confronted today with a new and sometimes perplexing way of talking about important aspects of our political life. More than anyone I know, Banks helps us to see where it comes from, what it means, and how it works. I have tried to present Banks's position as powerfully as I could so that the weight of the many claims he makes on behalf of the civil rights revolution may be fully felt. While Banks surely advances the Left vision of anti-discrimination politics, he does so in a series of deft appeals to the community as a whole that cannot but have some persuasive power in a time where everyone—Left and Right—admits the necessity of the fight against discrimination. Indeed, he is so effective, it seems to me, in large measure because he is not afraid to express the aspirations of the civil rights revolution in the new moral language that is so important to it. At any rate, because of the range and depth of his thought, Banks's account of multiculturalism provides us with an extremely helpful point of departure for seeing many different kinds of questions pertaining to our new political situation as they are thought through all at the same time, where a more piecemeal rendering of the myriad issues he takes up might obscure their common source and unified meaning. Banks did not set out to provide a general account of what the commitment to fighting discrimination means for modern democracy as such, but until someone else comes along to give us such an accounting in equally direct and forthright terms, his thought will prove an indispensable measure and guide.

Chapter 6
POSTMODERNIST MULTICULTURALISM: WHEN THEORY AND POLITICS RADICALIZE ONE ANOTHER

Anyone wanting to understand civil rights politics today or in the future will also, more or less immediately, be confronted by "postmodernist" theory, a collection of startling assertions expressed in a sophisticated jargon. This theoretical stance will still appear alien to most Americans, but its perplexing terms have become unavoidable because they are now being used widely to set forth the demands of the new politics that we have been examining.[1] The radical philosophical position that is postmodernist theory—rejecting all claims that human beings can know the world—has become important for us today mainly because this species of anti-rationalism appears as a mouthpiece of the civil rights revolution. "Postmodernist multiculturalism," our focus in this chapter, first appeared in the world of teacher education in the late 1980s. But postmodernist multiculturalism is only one of a host of related efforts by American intellectuals to put radical postmodernist epistemology together with anti-discrimination politics (to include critical race theory, critical feminist theory, and the "politics of difference," to name just the best known specimens). Intellectuals in America (and in the West generally), heirs of the Enlightenment, today turn their backs on reason and in their despair try to find salvation in politics instead.

It would be a dereliction of duty not to say at the outset that this general movement of modern political thought has been unfortunate. For one thing, in the theoretico-political combination that has emerged, it is noisy radical "theory" that gets most of the attention—when, as we shall see, it is politics that is the true heart of things. Postmodernist theory is thus largely a *distraction* that can point us in the wrong direction (especially conservatives, I have to say, never fail to take the bait) and one more reason we do not recognize how revolutionary anti-discrimination politics by itself has been. That anti-discrimination politics has been joined to postmodernist ideas is also unfortunate because, when the two are combined, each radicalizes the other in a dynamic that makes both worse. I am less interested in how postmodernism is affected in this process, but the deleterious effects on anti-discrimination politics—now made paranoid, combative, hypercritical, and explicitly radical—are not trivial.

Even if we learn much more from someone like Banks, we have no choice but to grapple as well with postmodernist theory if we want to understand anti-discrimination politics. For decades now critics have been dismissing postmodernism as a passing intellectual fad, dead in its home country of France, for example; its connection to the civil rights revolution, however, guarantees it a place in American life for the foreseeable future. To those who might (perhaps sensibly) protest about the prospect of having to examine radical theory to understand civil rights, I would say that educated Americans in the past used to see that civic literacy in the context of the Cold War demanded at least some understanding of the twists and turns of Marxist theory, for example. But it is certainly true that "the theoretical pirouettes of the postmodern left" are often bewildering—radical, perplexing, hard to understand (McLaren 1997b, 288). To the uninitiated, theory can be off-putting, to say the least. Theory's deployment of convoluted jargon and its many complicated obfuscations seem, indeed, to be part of a deliberate strategy of intellectual intimidation that lends postmodernism some significant portion of its authority.

Our task of understanding postmodernist theory in its relationship to anti-discrimination will be greatly aided if we begin from the *political* side of the ledger. As I will argue, politics is, in fact, the senior partner in this merger, and so starting there will best illuminate the whole. Moreover, emphasizing the political dimension immediately exposes the massive *contradiction* that defines postmodernist multiculturalism, critical race theory, and other manifestations of this general development. This contradiction is suggested by the puzzling spectacle of a social movement that was characterized at the outset by great moral seriousness and dignity now turning itself over to the care of radical anti-rationalism. But it is no less strange to see such a loudly self-proclaimed theoretical radicalism become the enthusiastic servant of a powerful and well-established, even revered, civic project. Postmodernist multiculturalism attacks all knowledge claims—and then turns around and wants to tell everybody what they ought to think and how they ought to behave. If we start from these obvious perplexities, we will be freed at the outset from some of the intimidation that may accompany theory's uninviting and unappealing first appearances. Sharply distinguishing theory and politics will also help; what we need to know will remain hidden if we leave these as we find them, typically jumbled together in a complicated muddle. We must *disentangle* postmodernist theory and the civil rights impulse when they are put together. Our task must be to see each part in relation to the other, to identify what each needs or wants from the other, and to track how each is then affected or altered when they are joined. Above all, what we hope to learn here is something about the nature of anti-discrimination politics as that is revealed by its intermingling with radical theory.

One important preliminary point must be made now. There is a very simple answer to any claim that postmodernist theory is intrinsically or necessarily bound to a politics of difference or diversity or any such thing. This is to be found in the politically embarrassing historical roots of postmodernism in the thought of Martin Heidegger, who spoke of the "inner truth and greatness of National Socialism," even after World War II (1959, 199). It is also demonstrated today in the existence of White supremacist postmodernists. "Heideggerian freedom has a racial imperative." "The terrifying darkness now descending on the white world speaks to the question of Being."[2] Postmodernist theory may indeed be inclined to some kind of radical politics, but there is no reason for insisting that it is more suited to the radical Left than to the radical Right.

The discussion that follows begins with a brief recounting of the coming together of postmodernism and anti-discrimination politics focusing on the world of teacher education—what two participants in the merger termed "the precipitous theoretical and political convergence of critical pedagogy and multicultural education" ("critical pedagogy" being the postmodernist branch of teacher education) (Sleeter and McLaren 1995a, 8). We narrow our discussion in this way partly because it follows from our examination of multiculturalism thus far. But doing so is also useful because the conjoining of theory and politics in postmodernist multiculturalism highlights in a very clear way the *difference* between the two sides of the merger: this is the joining of two independent academic subdisciplines, neither of which owed anything to the other prior to their coming together. But, to repeat, the tie between postmodernist theory and civil rights politics in teacher education is only a small part of a much wider development, visible today in every area of intellectual life. What we can see by examining postmodernist multiculturalism in detail has broader implications. After providing a brief summary of postmodernist theory's main philosophical tenets and claims, we will explore in detail how that theoretical perspective has become intertwined with Left anti-discrimination politics. As I have said, politics is the dominant partner here, but, when joined to postmodernist theory, the character and tone of the fight against discrimination are altered in alarming ways. It is not a matter of interpretation to say that postmodernist multiculturalism is fundamentally negative and destructive. Postmodernism's skepticism is aggressively imperialistic and comes to sight in open, loud, and uncompromising assaults on every *authoritative* claim made about our world. Its effect on civil rights discourse, in particular, has been to set its acidly critical spirit (if in a partial, one-sided way) upon anything standing in the path of all but the most radical commitment to revolutionary change. The postmodernist outlook exaggerates what is at stake in civil rights politics and encourages a spirit of permanent rebellion tempered only, at points, by radical (theoretical) doubts and (political) despair. More disturbing still, postmodernist multiculturalism's most noteworthy concrete contribution to civil rights politics has been the development of "Whiteness" theory, an attempt, not altogether unsuccessful, to deliberately recast civil rights discourse in raw racial terms, as an explicit and self-conscious critique of Whiteness and Whites. Banks's non-postmodernist alternative, however radical it may be on its own terms, proves an infinitely better guide to thinking about our situation, both theoretically and civically.

Emphasizing the *political* dimension of postmodernist multiculturalism and related phenomena will put us on a collision course with some powerful opinions on the Left and the Right. On the Left, when theorists call for a new "politics of difference" or insist upon the importance of "intersectionality," it is not immediately obvious that what they are expressing is only the logic of good old civil rights politics—although that is in fact what they are doing. Indeed, the writers who have famously advanced these two terms in particular, political theorist Iris Marion Young and law professor Kimberlé Crenshaw, both go so far as to *disavow* anti-discrimination law. This might suggest that my attempt to put anti-discrimination politics at the heart of their ideas underestimates the role of theory on its own. Is Jacques Derrida right to suggest the primacy of theory when he says that "there is nothing fortuitous about the fact that the critique of ethnocentrism [is] systematically and historically contemporaneous with the destruction of the history of metaphysics" (Derrida 1978, 282)? As we shall see, exaggerating the role of ideas and underestimating the force of anti-discrimination politics is a mistake.[3]

But it is a mistake made by conservative *critics* of postmodernist multiculturalism as well. Conservatives prefer to attribute what bothers them in the battles over political correctness, identity politics, wokeness, and so on, to alien, and therefore easy-to-dismiss and criticize, causes—and to anything but the civil rights revolution. In the 1990s this was a tendency simply to equate multiculturalism with relativism, as in Dinesh D'Souza's claim that "the intellectual premise of multiculturalism is cultural relativism," or sociologist Alvin Schmidt's view that "multiculturalism is really the marriage of cultural relativism and postmodernism."[4] D'Souza went so far as to suggest that "the civil rights movement developed as a direct outgrowth of cultural relativism"—a claim Richard Rorty rightly regarded as "startling" and "weird."[5] Today, this is the discovery by conservatives of the political vulnerability of critical race theory. A related claim is the idea that critical race theory and related phenomena (to include critical pedagogy) are reducible to neo-Marxism (the Frankfurt School "with a dollop of Nietzschean relativism") or "cultural Marxism" (as opposed to economic/class-based materialist Marxism) or even "race Marxism."[6] (While Marxism and neo-Marxism are surely part of the story of postmodernist theory of the past fifty years, the influence of the former was much more important before the collapse of communism in 1989. Indeed, the legacy of Marxism has now become a large and very obvious *problem* for postmodernists who since that time have clearly become aligned with the politics of anti-discrimination.[7])

Emphasizing intellectual history (or Marxism) may seem reassuring to conservatives, because such interpretations allow them to focus on enemies already defeated or so outside the mainstream as to appear nonthreatening. But the effect of such an interpretation is to obscure the role of the civil rights revolution in the development of claims and arguments in public life that now seem revolutionary or troubling. Certainly to ignore anti-discrimination politics or to suggest, even rhetorically, that it plays no role in the development of phenomena like critical race theory (as in one podcast: "NO! Critical Race Theory Does NOT Continue the Civil Rights Movement") is obviously misleading.[8] No one who started from the political history and substance of multicultural education, and its eventual merging with postmodernist theory, would suggest something along those lines.

As I said at the outset of this study, the fight against discrimination, the anti-discrimination regime, is simultaneously a moral cause, a set of "groups," a host of laws, and the work of institution-building reformers—but it is also a wide-ranging set of *ideas* elaborating a complex view of social life and of the individuals and groups within it. In an echo of liberalism's origins, to be an advocate of anti-discrimination today is somehow also to be a kind of *intellectual*. Not to know the latest terms to describe discrimination in all its apparently infinite complexity (the emerging vocabulary around gender identity at the moment, for example) is to prove oneself morally or politically dubious—but also *unsophisticated*. Banks proves that many of these ideas are *not* dependent upon postmodernist theory for their origin or for their expression, but that does not dispense with our need to grapple with what postmodernist theory contributes to the mix. Knowing in advance that we need to distinguish the political from the theoretical will, however, help us to make progress when we confront them in combination.

The Merging of Politics and Theory in the Late 1980s and Early 1990s: The "Nietzscheanization of the Left," Continued

As a matter of historical fact, the union of American multicultural education and postmodernist theory is straightforward, plainly visible in a deliberate joining of academic forces. Critical pedagogy is a separate field within teacher education, seeking to overhaul the American education system in the name of postmodernist theory.[9] The combination, commencing in the late 1980s, is marked out in clear terms by the appearance of multicultural education writings influenced by postmodernist theory—most notably, early on, in the work of Christine Sleeter and Carl Grant (both later presidents of the National Association for Multicultural Education).[10] Several prominent multicultural education writers (to include Sleeter, Grant, Geneva Gay, and Sonia Nieto) explicitly mapped out in some detail the lines of theoretical and political convergence between multicultural education and critical pedagogy.[11] Deliberate collaborative efforts in the 1990s between leading multicultural education and critical pedagogy theorists (among the latter, most notably Henry Giroux and Peter McLaren) likewise show how the coming together of these two groups of theorists was a matter of explicit and self-conscious choice.[12] By 1995, multicultural education pioneer Gay could say, "multicultural education and critical pedagogy are mirror images of each other" (1995, 156). The second and third generations of multicultural education academics (Banks's descendants) have by now almost entirely gone over to postmodernism. As a perusal of contemporary multicultural education journals would immediately attest, the influence of postmodernism in the field is predominant and has become more or less normalized; figures like Banks, who mainly steered clear of postmodernist theory, are today the exception.[13]

As I said at the outset, the combination of postmodernist theory with anti-discrimination politics is, of course, a very widespread phenomenon. Although neither theory nor politics, strictly speaking, requires the other, this political and philosophical mix frames how educated Americans on the Left think today to such a degree that one must assume there are some very powerful forces driving them together. This is explicit in a number of academic disciplines that were (decades ago, now) effectively created by the civil rights revolution. Those subfields make clear the subsequent influence of postmodernism in a crude way by their very terms: "critical," "theory," and "studies" replacing older terms rooted in some notion of social science. Today, the most famous—and deeply controversial—of these is, of course, critical race theory, a central target of attacks by conservatives (banned from the federal government by Donald Trump and restored by Joe Biden).[14] Critical (or "third wave") feminism, too, has been very influential, but there is a long list of others: critical Latin American and Latinx studies, Native American critical theory, critical Asian studies, Queer theory, critical Trans studies, critical Disability theory, critical Whiteness studies, and the like.[15] "Cultural studies," the fledgling contender for a place among the social sciences advancing in the shadow of the decline of old-fashioned ("scientific") anthropology, might be said to offer something like a disciplinary base of operations for all the disparate elements of diversity studies.[16] One prominent group of cultural studies theorists indeed came close to deeming "critical multiculturalism" a synonym for cultural studies.[17] The 1990s also saw broader, all-encompassing efforts to put together general accounts of a postmodernist "politics of difference" or something along those lines—advanced most prominently by Iris Marion Young but also in one form or another by Judith Butler, Drucilla Cornell, bell hooks, Martha Minow, and Cornel West.[18]

I would go further and claim that, for some time now, the merger of Left anti-discrimination politics with postmodernist theory has been a central feature of democratic intellectual and cultural life in the West. This is in a way only a new instance of what Allan Bloom described as the "Nietzscheanization of the Left and vice versa," the older combination of Marxism and existentialism now replaced or supplanted by new accounts of postmodernist multiculturalism and the like (Bloom 1987, 217–26). In the universities, where one finds postmodernist treatments of English literature, classics, modern languages, theology, political science, history, international relations, or geography—indeed, in any field of the humanities and the social sciences—one will almost always find that the specific subject matter under study also concerns questions of race, gender, sexuality, disability, and the like. The direct and immediate influence of politicized postmodernism is felt mainly among the educated; but, in a world descended from the Enlightenment, to say this is hardly to state a *limit* to its influence.

What is Postmodernist Multiculturalism?

The essential center of postmodernist theory is a rejection of all claims to genuine "knowledge," a denial of the possibility of truth or objectivity. There is no true or real world behind our partial and particular beliefs, or at least none to which we can claim genuine or unfiltered access. As leading American postmodernist theorist Stanley Fish puts it, "there is no hope of getting at what is *really*—apart from any dimension of assessment, way of describing, paradigm, or vocabulary—true."[19] At least four arguments are given for such a claim: the givenness or inescapability of our fundamental commitments; the *diversity* of our cultural and moral starting points (or commitments); the socially constructed and historical character of all claims to knowledge; and difficulties rooted in the limitations of human language.[20] Postmodernism thus combines several different species of *relativism*—cultural relativism, moral relativism, historicism, and subjectivism. On some such basis, postmodernists show an amazing confidence that they may draw sweeping conclusions dethroning all general knowledge claims. Now, it would seem necessary that the union of postmodernism and the fight against discrimination must have some *other* center besides this (only one half of the whole), but, at points, postmodernist multiculturalists themselves more or less define their stance, seemingly nonpolitically, in terms of epistemology—as "avoiding essentialism" or as "anti-essentialism" (essentialism being the view that things as they are, in their essences, may be known).[21] If human reason depends upon our ability to know the world, then postmodernist theory is very much a form of anti-rationalism. An array of postmodernist claims and insights—not only anti-essentialism, but also deconstruction, decentering, treating knowledge-claims as the products of (mere) "discourses" or "discourse communities"—all come together at this point.

As we shall see, the true center of postmodernist *multiculturalism* is located finally in the political and moral commitments of the fight against discrimination. To be sure, this causes many obvious problems for radical theory. But in order to see why, it will be helpful to postpone briefly our discussion of the political dimension and to explore the outlines of the theoretical side of things for a moment more.

The *implications* of postmodernism's radical skepticism (its anti-epistemology, its denigration of knowledge and reason) are at least as radical and breathtaking as the basic claims themselves. For, on the basis of its allegations about the weakness of reason and knowledge, postmodernist theory questions all the authorities—political, legal, economic, cultural, moral, artistic, religious—who dare to speak in the language of general claims about the world. The "grand metanarratives of legitimation" of social and political life are presumed to be questionable, mere assertions of the dominant order, myths advanced to shape our world on behalf of its narrow interests or purposes. "Postmodernism presents itself as a critique of all forms of representations and meanings that claim transcendental and transhistorical status. It rejects universal reason as a foundation for human affairs and poses, as an alternative, forms of knowing that are partial, historical, and social in nature" (Giroux 1991a, 69). Knowledge is power but that means (as in Foucault's analysis of "power/knowledge") that (false) claims to knowledge (merely) serve as agents of the powerful. The mind is the site of fundamental political struggle; language and knowledge claims are weapons of a mental and cultural war with concrete consequences. This takes on a very practical meaning in critical pedagogy. "Schooling always involves power relationships and the privileging of certain forms of knowledge. Invariably, these forms of knowledge serve to reproduce social inequalities. . . . Critical pedagogy involves recognising how existing curriculum, resources and approaches to teaching offer students a perspective on the world that serves to marginalise certain voices and ways of life" (Morgan 2000, 274). Suspicion of broad knowledge claims, the bigger the more worrisome, becomes the credo of postmodernism: "Simplifying to the extreme, I define *postmodern* as incredulity toward metanarratives" (Lyotard 1984, xxiv; emphasis in the original). The central authoritative claims of modern Western life—Enlightenment rationality, liberal natural rights theory, constitutional government, modern science, capitalism, sometimes Marxism and socialism, too—are all subject to probing postmodernist critical scrutiny.

The implications of the postmodernist outlook for our ordinary *moral* understanding are fairly obvious and are admitted more or less frankly by its theorists. Because of their universal form, "impartiality, the general good, and community" are suspect (Young 1990, 7). Likewise, "justice, fairness, and human dignity" are "rhetorical structures" (Fish 1994, 222). Postmodernism works to "erase . . . the picture of an ahistorical, natural center, the locus of human dignity, surrounded by an adventitious and inessential periphery" (Rorty 1991c, 176). This is not to say that history itself provides any solid anchor to guide human life: "History is a strong myth, perhaps . . . the last great myth" (Baudrillard 1994, 47). Jacques Derrida extends such a critique of morality quite far:

> [A] deconstructive interrogation that starts . . . by destabilizing, complicating, or bringing out the paradoxes of values like those of the proper and of property in all their registers, of the subject, and so of the responsible subject, of the subject of the law (*droit*) and the subject of morality, of the juridical or moral person, of intentionality, etc., and of all that follows from these, such a deconstructive line of questioning is through and through a

> problematization of law and justice. A problematization of the
> foundations of law, morality and politics. (1990, 929–31)

The attack on moral (and political) ideas here may be formal (or abstract, a critique of concepts in general and not directly engaging the substance of particular claims) but what it lacks in depth, it makes up for in breadth.[22]

Two other insights developed by postmodernist theorists are especially relevant to the study of postmodernist multiculturalism. The first is a new understanding of and appreciation for "politics." "The political—the inescapability of partisan, angled seeing—is what always and already grasps us" (Fish 1994, 38). Precisely because there exists a diversity of opposed worlds, historical change and the social construction of reality take place within an inescapable background of antagonism and conflict; when one worldview predominates, it does so in part by employing coercion (force and violence), which is somehow found to be (morally) acceptable by members of the political community, even those made subordinate within it. Postmodernists emphasize especially the role that ideas and beliefs (to include moral beliefs) play in this dynamic, beliefs that people may unthinkingly accept to the benefit of the powerful. Thus, much is made of Marxist Antonio Gramsci's flexible *hegemony* concept and its focus on the world of ideas and culture (and not just "class") as a crucial, somewhat subterranean or undetected, arena of struggle and domination (1971). Political conflict, on the one hand, and the influence of established political orders, on the other, characterize the creation and perpetuation of the worlds that govern human understanding. (Postmodernist social construction theory would thus be more aptly named political construction theory.)[23] In a way, postmodernists might be said to agree with Aristotle that politics is "architectonic," though its shaping power is now viewed in a more or less entirely *negative* light. The seemingly general and universal language of politics—and especially the language of moral principle associated with politics—is perhaps only the most obvious target of postmodernism's reduction of knowledge claims to assertions of power, the claim that the human understanding of the world is the work of a dominant political perspective.[24] "Every act of naming is in some sense an act of violence that makes something the object of knowledge" (Sleeter and McLaren 1995a, 19). Against Aristotle's apparently respectful treatment, the science of social life on this view can be no more than "a theory of the forms of domination," as Nietzsche says (1968, 255). Its crucial formative influence in no way redeems politics on the postmodernist view. Even if politics is the ground of morality and, indeed, of our very being, it is not for that reason worthy of our loyalty or devotion. The diversity of competing, contradictory political orders alone raises doubts about our reliance upon or trust in any of them. As one postmodernist multiculturalist puts it, politics, like history, is blind— "a logic without design" (McLaren 1995, 53).

Second, and perhaps following from such an understanding of political life, whenever postmodernist theory appears on the scene, it is almost always already engaged in some *critical* undertaking. This is obvious on the surface of things, as we have seen, where the word "critical" appears as the first term designating any number of new academic enterprises tied to postmodernism (critical race theory being only the most famous). It is important to see that postmodernism's critical efforts serve, or may serve, both epistemological and straightforwardly political ends. Because we *can* know that our world is a partial and delimiting one and, simultaneously, because we know that it is decisively formative of what we see, progress in *understanding* might seem to require lines of questioning or interrogation to liberate us from its grip. Alternatively, ordinary *political* aspirations might seem to anyone armed with the claims of postmodernist theory to demand that he or she weaken the false general claims of the ruling order to the extent that they stand in the way of what he or she deems political progress. Now, obviously, the idea of "progress"—either in understanding or in politics—would seem to be impossible on postmodernist terms; any idea of progress presupposes some transhistorical, permanent standard of judgment. This is a conundrum because the critical dimension of postmodernism (which is pervasive) cannot itself be explained without hope for *some* such end, whether theoretical or political in substance. In any event, however the tendency to criticism is explained, it takes a variety of forms: the logical dissections of Stanley Fish; Derrida's method of deconstruction and decentering; the "genealogical" inquiries of Nietzsche or Foucault.[25]

All this means that postmodernist theory is also—perhaps always or necessarily—humanly incomplete. There can be no positive program of action or way of life that claims to be *the* postmodernist way because to assert such a thing would necessarily entail adopting precisely the sort of general or neutral or universal stance against which postmodernism is defined. Fish, indeed, denies the possibility of *any* postmodernist "program." Postmodernist theory ("pragmatism" for Fish) may be of use in describing and challenging existing reality claims but it cannot prescribe. "A pragmatist *program* asks the question 'what follows from the pragmatist account?' and then gives an answer, but by giving an answer pragmatism is unfaithful to its own first principle (which is to have none) and turns unwittingly into the foundationalism and essentialism it rejects" (1994, 209; emphasis in the original). Postmodernist theory provides powerful criticisms of every important authoritative moral and political claim but it seems, therefore, to be constitutionally incapable of generating a positive account of life on its own. While this does not necessarily amount to a theoretical problem for postmodernism, it does pose an obvious human problem, especially because the chief targets of postmodernism are precisely the most common and practically important answers we give to the question of how to live, the beliefs at the core of social and political life. Some of the most prominent figures associated with postmodernism themselves call attention to the human implications of such a view when they admit that "Only a god can save us."[26] Fish's insistence that "nothing" follows from postmodernist theoretical presuppositions is bracing in its clarity and candor and perhaps admirable for its stance of Protagorean courage but it can be satisfying only from a very rarified point of view.[27]

Politics at the Center

Today the incompleteness of the postmodernist theoretical outlook is filled in almost exclusively by the moral and political commitments of the fight against discrimination. This is clearly the case for postmodernist multiculturalism but, as I have indicated, the coming together of theory and politics here is also a much broader phenomenon. It would seem that the civil rights revolution was the revelation postmodernism was waiting for. History, too, abhors a vacuum. The idea that such a sophisticated, radical, and ostentatious theoretical stance is mainly, in practice, the servant of a political program—indeed, a widely respected one that is well-established through the law—is so far from the pretensions of the theory's basic propositions that it will seem doubtful. Making plain the supremacy of politics in the combination is thus a key first step in understanding postmodernist multiculturalism not only because it gets at the truth of the matter but also because, if we do not see it, radical theory will continue to mislead us by occupying the center of our attention.

The supremacy of politics to theory is almost never explicitly *admitted* by our postmodernist multiculturalists, but there is abundant evidence that this is where matters stand. The predominance of politics is suggested, to begin with, by the fact that politics provides *direction* for theory, postmodernism being essentially aimless if left to itself. The issue may also be tested by the question: which one bows? Certainly not anti-discrimination politics in its Left interpretation. To my knowledge, postmodernist multiculturalists do not advance even constructive criticism of their political master, the Left view of the civil rights revolution (though attacks on the Right interpretation are routine).[28] Indeed, whenever the civil rights movement, or its heroes and leaders, are mentioned, suddenly postmodernist subversive radicalism and insubordination give way to the hushed tones of abject reverence.[29] It is always anti-discrimination politics that defines, and severely limits, the meaning and uses of theory.[30] "Central to postmodernism and poststructuralism is the investigation of power and how power relations are played out among various groups, whether they be gender, ethnic, cultural, or sexual identities."[31] It is true that there is an extensive literature devoted to the postmodernist critique of identity and the politics of identity (as essentialist, etc.), which does touch a nerve.[32] But when the radical critique of identity is perceived to come at the expense of anti-discrimination groups, that becomes a reason to back away from the critical claims of theory.[33]

Other proofs of the supremacy of politics over theory in postmodernist multiculturalism are provided in the deference displayed when postmodernist theory's distinctive terms are reworked, or censored, by a very simple and sure political disciplining. Anti-essentialism—in a way, the defining general aim of postmodernist theory—becomes amazingly narrowed to a fixation with "neo-essentialist racist discourse," "white racist essentialism," and related concerns: "a legacy in which blacks, Latinos, and other groups are essentialized as either biologically or culturally deficient and treated as a species of outsiders," the attempt "to create anti-essentialist race consciousness [placing] discussions of political equity at the center of debate."[34] Politics rules proposed educational efforts, the substance of critical pedagogy's work, which now take on a very untheoretical aim: "the critical perspective allows us to scrutinize schooling more insistently in terms of race, class, power, and gender" (McLaren 1989a, 163). What is needed is "an education that empowers students to resist and transform racist practices."[35] Critical take-downs of "the discourse of modernism," the West, and the like are similarly confined by a political, not a theoretical, imperative. "From the postmodernist perspective, modernism's claim to authority, on the one hand, privileges Western patriarchal culture and, on the other hand, simultaneously represses those voices deemed subordinate or oppressed because of their color, class, ethnicity, race, or cultural and social capital."[36] Postmodernist multiculturalists sometimes cast their efforts as "postmodern notions of emancipation" or "liberatory education."[37] But what they mean by that is not some freeing of the mind by way of theory's power to lift the veil of ignorance: "Within the parameters of multicultural education, postmodern notions of emancipation mean being free of the psychological stress and intellectual doubts resulting from impositions of racial and cultural inferiority"; "teachers are better empowered to implement liberatory education if they . . . are racially, ethnically, and culturally unbiased" (Gay and Hart 2000, 183).

Similar evidence of the political reworking of postmodernism's distinctive vocabulary is plentiful. Derridean deconstruction (binaries and signifiers and signifieds), naming, counter-histories, de-centering, re-centering, the border, and postmodernist politics (empowerment, resistance, and struggle)—all predictably rotate around one political center, theory subordinated entirely and always to the fight against discrimination.[38] Let us not fail to note here that theory's terms are in many instances distorted when they are so taken over by politics. Not every use of theory falls as flat as Iris Marion Young's odd claim about anti-discrimination groups—that they share "the character of what Martin Heidegger calls 'thrownness:' one *finds oneself* as a member of a group, which one experiences as always already having been" (Young 1990, 46; emphasis in the original). The spirit of postmodernist multiculturalism's deployment of theory is one of conformity to political discipline; politics, not theory, directs the show.

The supremacy of politics here may be hard to see at first, partly as I have said because the theory on offer is so arresting and noticeable, a radical challenge to our common sense view of things. But we are also inclined today, for good reasons, to credit the power of ideas. It is hard to disagree with Allan Bloom's view that "philosophy and science took over as rulers in modernity and purely theoretical problems have decisive political effects" (Bloom 1987, 197). Nevertheless, not every important modern idea has a purely theoretical basis, and postmodernist multiculturalism proves that even in modernity political regimes still exercise their architectonic power. Sometimes it is necessary to look at the high in light of the low—ideas in light of politics.

Defined By Contradiction

It almost goes without saying that postmodernist multiculturalism is defined, as I said at the outset, by a set of basic and fairly massive contradictions. Theory is skeptical and calls everything into doubt, except when it comes to civil rights, where political claims are put forward with vigorous certitude. Postmodernism rejects truth and the general language of morality and political reform, but the fight against discrimination must deploy these all the time and as a matter of course. Theory presents itself as rejecting all authority, but postmodernist multiculturalism is defined by its service to authority.

Very plain evidence that this simple and large problem matters is visible in a disagreement within the world of postmodern theory between theoretical *purists* (a tiny minority) and those who do not hesitate to employ theory for political purposes. From the perspective of our clearly political postmodernist multiculturalists, this is a divide between political and insufficiently serious, "ludic" (ludicrous, playful), postmodernists, the latter rejected as "a kind of left mandarin terrorism."[39]

> Much of the discourse of postmodernism has been criticized for betraying a dry cynicism in which irony and pastiche become politics' last recourse at social change. It often reveals an uncompromising distaste for the masses, adopts a form of highbrow, antibourgeois posing, and occasionally assumes the role of a self-congratulatory vanguardism which resonates dutifully with the "high seriousness" of the academy, at times appearing as dressed-up restatements of Nietzsche and Heidegger.[40]

Against this view, as we have seen, at least one non-multiculturalist postmodernist, Stanley Fish, serves as a kind of postmodernist policeman of all attempts to apply its theoretical insights to concrete political projects. Indeed, Fish takes direct aim at critical pedagogy in particular, criticizing its attempt to sketch out a general politics of difference (his immediate target is McLaren): "Just where is heterogeneity to be located? Whose heterogeneity (read 'difference') is it? If it is located somewhere, then it is not heterogeneity. If it is located everywhere, then it is universalist liberalism all over again, and the supposed enemy has been embraced." [41]

Other evidence of the internal incoherence of postmodernist multiculturalism is visible in several different strategies that those in this position use to try to handle the competing and contradictory demands of theory and politics. One clear indication of a certain wariness of engaging in simple politics, despite the fact that this is central to the effort, is a concern to distinguish "politicizing education" (bad) from "political education" (good) or, alternatively, "political pedagogy" (bad) from "radical pedagogy" (good).[42] We will explore briefly other striking evidence along these lines: postmodernist multiculturalism's opposition to "totalizing" projects, combined with a recognition of the need for some "totalizing vision"; its inability to speak the language of morality while seeing the necessity of doing so; its veering back and forth between utopian hopes and political despair.

Viewed from the perspective of pure theory, it is hard to see how the merger with politics does not mean abandoning something fairly essential. Applying anti-foundationalism's insights in a one-sided political way and only to the categories employed by one's political enemies—ever the loyal political servant—is not, to say the least, something that follows immediately or necessarily from the tenets of such an avowedly radical theory. That smacks of politics and everything that makes politics seem dubious (liberalism has its reasons for trying to evade or transcend "the political").

Radical Theory Unbound

But there is at least one way in which its alliance with politics might seem to allow postmodernist *theory* to come into its own, to blossom fully into what it really seems to want to be. While I am primarily concerned with the effect that the postmodernist-multiculturalism merger has on civil rights politics, the result from theory's point of view is worth briefly noting. The main thing is a very simple *practical* consequence of its joining with anti-discrimination politics—namely, the opportunity afforded critical pedagogy not only to gain a wider audience but to entertain in a serious way the idea that its task is to teach everyone, or at least all American teachers and schoolchildren, its radical lessons. For it is only the respectability of its political partner (and its seemingly unassailable moral claims) that allows critical pedagogists to think that they will be given a respectable hearing and that permits them to venture out from under the hiding places in academia to which they would be otherwise be consigned. (This can be demonstrated by the following thought experiment: imagine critical pedagogy's status if it were radically critical of both the Left and the Right, and in equal measure.) Because it is shielded in part by the civic role it has taken on, it becomes possible to think that critical pedagogy might actually offer its radical critical teachings—anti-political, anti-legal, anti-social, anti-moral, and anti-rationalist—as a strange new kind of civic-minded anti-civic education. This is the most radical of all radical "enlightenments" (or anti-enlightenments) ever proposed or imagined, an education in radical unreason attacking all authoritative claims proposed in all seriousness as a national public teaching (though we are not told precisely in what grade instruction is to begin).

In a word, critical pedagogy ("the instructional formation of postmodernist ideology") is *empowered* by its alliance with civil rights politics to be a greater force in the world, a more ambitious version of itself (Gay and Hart 2000, 170). Critical pedagogy always began by seeking to wake people up, to teach them to free themselves from the shackles of their culturally reproduced minds. Existing schools are "disciplinary sites" and places of "educational oppression," "camps for ideological internment, factories for domestication."[43] If only we take them at their word, we see that what they propose in all earnestness is an astonishingly radical education undertaking an uncompromising attack on almost everything. The task is "to strip away the unexamined reality that hides behind the objectivism and fetishism of 'facts' in positivist pedagogy. In doing so, the fixed essences, the invariant structures, and the commonsense knowledge that provide the foundation for much of existing public school pedagogy can be shown for what they are" (Giroux 1979, 280). "Critical pedagogy teaches students how to interrogate master narratives so that the fallacy of objective reality, universal truth, and knowledge as transcendent of culture, social context, time, and intentionality can be unveiled and transformed" (Gay and Hart 2000, 177). Not far behind is an open attack on the basic claims to authority of our political and moral categories. "Multicultural education and critical pedagogy bring into the arena of schooling insurgent, resistant, and insurrectional modes of interpretation and classroom practices which set out to imperil the familiar, to contest the legitimating norms of mainstream cultural life, and to render problematic the common discursive frames and regimes upon which 'proper' behavior, comportment, and social interaction are premised" (Sleeter and McLaren 1995a, 7).

In a way, the opportunity thus afforded critical pedagogy to hawk its wares to an unsuspecting public has an obviously comedic aspect. Indeed, were reading, writing, and radical epistemology the only lessons of postmodernist multiculturalism, to be preached up in all earnestness by our teachers to the country's schoolchildren, we could rely on American comedians to do justice to it. But the main reason postmodernist multiculturalism matters today is that, politically, the fight against discrimination increasingly comes armed with the terms and spirit of postmodernist theory—and, as we shall see, there is nothing funny about that.

Politics Radicalized by Theory and Vice Versa: "Critical Rather Than Merely Good Citizens"

Postmodernist multiculturalism's radicalism is visible on the surface of things. It is radical in two senses of the word "radical," advocating an *extreme* account of the fight against discrimination and, in doing so, taking a stance of maximum *disruption and opposition* to the existing order. Its confrontational style is immediately apparent, manifest in the very terms by which the effort is named—labels like "insurgent multiculturalism," "critical multiculturalism"—or "resistance," "transformative," "transgressive," "social reconstructionist," or "revolutionary" multiculturalism.[44] One simple confirmation of this aspect of the overall result is available in a crude political measure: postmodernist multiculturalism is so radical that when its basic claims are exposed to public scrutiny they become a liability to Left civil rights politics (witness today the political price paid for any association with critical race theory). This tendency to radicalism is partly the result of the character of postmodernist theory. But it is also partly owing to the innate radicalism—in the sense of its great ambition at the very least—of anti-discrimination politics.

The sum total is that, when combined, each radicalizes the other in a mutually reinforcing dialectic. This is especially clear in postmodernist multiculturalism's *critical* mode: while theory makes such a stance necessary, anti-discrimination politics makes criticism urgent and energetic. Postmodern theory, on its own, naturally inclines already to critical projects of deconstruction, decentering, boundary-crossing, and the like: "Radical pedagogy does not simply bracket reality, but radically restructures it, dismantling secured beliefs and interrogating social practices and the constituents of experience while foregrounding and rendering visible the power/knowledge relation between the teacher and the student."[45] But when such efforts are undertaken to expose the racism, sexism, and homophobia of our cultural and political authorities, past and present, criticism becomes a vigorous moral imperative: "Theory becomes posited as a form of resistance. . . . The subject of knowledge in this case is always theoretically positioned in the context of class, race, and gender relations."[46] "The critical perspective allows us to scrutinize schooling more insistently in terms of race, class, power, and gender" (McLaren 1989a, 163). The critical work of theory now becomes characterized by a more energetic political spirit. "As pedagogies of difference, resistance, hope, and possibility, multicultural education and critical pedagogy are inherently revolutionary and transformative" (Gay 1995, 181). The enemies of multiculturalism must be confronted with a "discourse of irruption," a "discourse of disruption and subversion," and an effort "to reauthor the discourses of oppression in politically subversive ways."[47] As Giroux puts it in an arresting formula, "critical pedagogy equates learning with the creation of critical rather than merely good citizens" (Giroux 1991a, 72).

The most important targets of all its radical critical dismantling are the most obvious, the broadest and most respected, metanarratives of our world, wide claims (to repeat) made on behalf of Western civilization, the Enlightenment, the modern project, and America's European heritage. But now the assault on these pillars of our world is to be undertaken as an urgent, and spiritedly moral, requirement of the fight against discrimination.

Only through postmodernism's embrace of anti-discrimination politics does the critical task of theory become an insistence that we "interrogate," "deterritorialize," and "break down" the "master narrative of Eurocentrism."[48]

It is worth pausing briefly to note two of these critical interrogations in particular (a third, the attempt to reframe the question of American race discrimination politics as an attack on "Whiteness," will be taken up at the end). The first is a vigorous attack made against "the false promises of neoliberalism and the false hopes of liberal democracy" (McLaren 1997b, 300). Liberal pluralism's appeal to some idea of diversity is rejected as a cynical myth: "When liberal humanists maintain . . . that all groups are serially situated in variegated contexts that together constitute a shared community of values . . . they paint a false picture of a society whose hegemonizing drive and sovereign narratives of desire help to sift the best ideas from the worst in order to regulate and accommodate the social in the interests of all."[49] The effort "to tie multiculturalism to the idea of diversity and liberal democracy" is "an exceedingly problematic—even dangerous—venture" (McLaren 1997b, 294). Critical assaults on specific liberal teachings that stand in the way of the Left interpretation of anti-discrimination politics—color-blindness, equal opportunity, individualism and individual rights, the public-private divide, toleration, even (liberal) pluralism—likewise depict liberalism ("the Terror of Neo-liberalism") in such a way as to equate it with discrimination in uncompromisingly critical terms of condemnation.[50] Where Banks is careful and seeks to incorporate multiculturalism into what is best about the West, or reconsiders the meaning of freedom to make room in it for the moral commitments of anti-discrimination politics, postmodernist multiculturalism aims simply to tear it all down.

Another critical assault of postmodernist multiculturalism, against arguments from nature and human nature (categories of Enlightenment rationality, e.g., or modern science), is particularly illuminating: "Any definition of human nature is dangerous because it threatens to devalue or exclude some acceptable individual desires, cultural characteristics, or ways of life" (Young 1990, 36). The problem with arguments from nature in the context of anti-discrimination politics is visible at the origins of multicultural education (in the cultural deprivation-difference debate). Central to that debate was the question of how to explain group inequalities in educational achievement and in that context nature *could* be said to offer one potential answer. "The members of some social groups . . . come to believe that their educational failure, rather than coming from their lowly esteemed social or cultural status, results from their natural inability: their lack of giftedness" (Corson 1998, 10). But politically, the idea that group inequalities (in education and beyond) may derive from natural differences cannot be sustained or permitted because if it were, anti-discrimination policy would be contrary to nature, contrary to the natural human situation—and, as such, anti-discrimination policy would itself be open to powerful moral criticisms. Today, arguments from the natural differences among the races, or among or between other anti-discrimination groups, are of course politically more or less out of bounds, grounds for corrective firing and the like. Postmodernism supports the assumptions of anti-discrimination politics here in a powerful way when it denies, along with all general claims, any suggestion that there exists a permanent, fixed, and necessary natural order to which we have access (the basic assumption of modern science).[51] If reality (or our knowledge of it) is only socially constructed, then appeals to "nature" are no more than narratives about which we should be incredulous. Postmodernists also go further, suggesting that science, like everything else, is an instrument of the dominant political powers. As Giroux puts it, the "culture of [scientific] positivism" reflects a "logic . . . situated in a structure of dominance [that] exists to meet the most fundamental needs of the existing power relations and their corresponding social formations." What is needed is "to delegitimize the culture of positivism and the socio-economic structure it supports."[52] But one might say that the politics of anti-discrimination is already inclined to go further than postmodernist theory in this direction: where the latter doubts our ability to understand nature, the former at crucial points insists (without any room for doubt) that nature cannot and must not be said to explain inequalities among groups, or at least inequalities involving groups covered by anti-discrimination law.[53]

The character of postmodernist multiculturalism's critical spirit, radical for both theoretical and political reasons, helps to make sense of the otherwise puzzling claims made by some theorists in this camp to the effect that they *reject* the "anti-discrimination" ideal and, more commonly, the perceived limitations of anti-discrimination law. This is a position taken occasionally by postmodernist multiculturalists but more commonly by others who share their outlook in political theory and law—like the two writers I mentioned earlier, Iris Marion Young and Kimberlé Crenshaw.[54] Critical of everything in sight, these theorists, we should perhaps not be surprised to see, turn even on anti-discrimination. But in fact any such criticism is really only of existing anti-discrimination *law* (or its Right interpretation) and always in the name of nothing but a radicalized Left version of anti-discrimination *politics*. If one considers Young's seemingly ambitious new general theory of "oppression," for example, one will find hiding under its somewhat complicated terms nothing other than a new way of characterizing "discrimination"; similarly, while Crenshaw's famous idea of intersectionality certainly might *sound* postmodernist, it originates in the logic of civil rights politics and nothing but civil rights politics.[55]

Everything Exaggerated and Negative

In rethinking civil rights politics, postmodernist multiculturalism dramatically expands or inflates the problem of discrimination by seeing it as a fundamental assumption of our basic worldview, our collective cultural or historical horizon. The main work of postmodernist multiculturalism is on the cultural or mental or imaginative plane; it *reimagines* modern democracy and American life from the point of view of a radicalized notion of the fight against discrimination. Under theory's influence, discrimination must be understood as one important site of a struggle for mind and world creation. This tendency is coupled with an aggressively negative vision of the basic situation of the past, present, and future of civil rights politics. The view that discrimination is a common evil reasonably opposed by decent people of good will is challenged by a much more paranoid vision of deep and broad cultural oppression. Wariness becomes principled dissatisfaction and mistrust of everything short of similarly deep and broad cultural transformation. But here the *political* impulse of postmodernist multiculturalism makes its characteristic contribution: once again, what might begin as a theoretical critique of the metanarratives of our world takes the tone of severe moral condemnation. Hopes of progress on behalf of civil rights become radical inflated demands that, since they cannot be met, work to suggest, in the end, that nothing can be done. All that is left to us is mapping the contours of an unjust world with the help of theory and to dream of revolution. This overall situation is made worse by the fact, as we shall see, postmodernists are constitutionally predisposed to be *bad* at generating even the most simple cultural or political solutions (which require one to speak generally). Driven to hope for great change, postmodernist multiculturalism is ultimately beset by grave disappointment.

For Banks, we recall, the problem of discrimination is serious enough, harming individuals in significant ways and emerging necessarily out of the very nature of group life—intractable and tenacious. But for the postmodernists the problem becomes something much bigger and worse, an all-pervasive cultural hegemony that hides its manipulations and domination under a veil of powerful and authoritative but also largely concealed cultural and moral claims. The postmodernist view of the role that politics (and its force and violence) plays in social life greatly amplifies our sense of what is at stake in the fight against discrimination, now a struggle for the general terms—knowledge claims, metanarratives, the terms of morality—that create our vision of life and the world. In a way, literally everything is at stake here. Where the problem of fighting racism, sexism, homophobia, transphobia, and the like might be viewed as a matter of relatively simple—and manifestly very narrow—moral instruction and correction, supported as needed by the law and its reinforcements, now it becomes a project to remake the entire culture, the entire collective mind: "Postmodernism redraws and retheorizes the objects and experiences of politics by extending the reach of power and meaning to spheres of the everyday that are often excluded from the realm of political analysis. . . . The field of political contestation is not restricted to the state and the workplace, but also includes the family, mass and popular culture, the sphere of sexuality, and the terrain of the refused and forgotten" (Giroux 1991b, 227). Unlike liberal skepticism, which preaches humility about what we know, and therefore toleration, the postmodernist outlook teaches that there is nothing but conviction or commitment at the bottom of things. On this view, we are locked in a zero-sum battle over the mental or cultural landscape and we have no choice but to assert our claims lest we lose out against others who will assert theirs. This is readily admitted by Giroux: "it is precisely because of the possibility of rewriting dominant cultural narratives and social relations that multiculturalism appears so threatening to conservatives and liberals" (1997a, 239).

This exaggerated view of our situation informs postmodernist multiculturalism's understanding of the character of discrimination. Differences and conflicts among anti-discrimination groups are not to be accounted for by reference to mere "prejudices" that may be overcome somehow by responsible reform; they reflect, as Giroux (following Homi Bhabha) says, "*incommensurable* meanings and identities."[56] Discrimination must now be viewed as a pervasive, inescapable, world-shaping phenomenon: "People don't discriminate against groups because they are different but rather the act of discrimination constructs categories of difference that hierarchically locates people as 'superior' or 'inferior' and then universalizes and naturalizes such differences" (McLaren and Torres 1999, 55). Giroux criticizes some on the Left precisely for their "refusal to locate cultural differences in a *broader* examination of how the boundaries of ethnicity, race and power make visible how whiteness functions as a historical and social construction" (1992, 117; emphasis added).

In an extended discussion of what he terms "the new cultural racism," Giroux provides a very clear illustration of how postmodernism tries to frame our thinking about discrimination and anti-discrimination in a relentlessly pessimistic way.[57] What is "cultural racism"? In brief, it is Giroux's term for the Right's approach to civil rights politics, the "hegemonic politics of race and representation practiced by conservatives" (1993a, 102). In Giroux's mind, whatever arguments conservatives make about race are discredited in advance; anything they say is a product of their effort to dominate the social space through their preferred terms of discourse. Indeed, for postmodernist multiculturalists there never can be any point in addressing the substance of arguments made by one's political opponents. Civil debate and collective deliberation are myths; everyone has a metanarrative and he or she is sticking to it. Cultural racism, a "new racial politics of containment" is just a replacement for the "old racism" from the years before the civil rights revolution (1993a, 95, 99–100). (Giroux here almost admits that the civil rights revolution happened, conceding a "shift in the 'dominant regimes of representation' around race and multiculturalism" [1993a, 101]). While "the New Right" may have abandoned overtly racist categories, now it advances "a powerful new strategy . . . that equates the nation, citizenship, and patriotism with a racially exclusive notion of difference," a strategy that allows conservatives to frame the claims of racial minorities as "a threat to national unity" (1993a, 98, 102). Giroux lists other related strategies of the Right, to include asserting "that whites are the victims of racial inequality" or using "coded" racial terms ("quotas, busing, welfare, and multiculturalism") "to mobilize white fears." Other coded messages are deployed by Republican politicians and the media to characterize "the Los Angeles uprising" of 1992. "The dominant press repeatedly labeled the uprising as a riot, and consistently referred to the events that took place as acts of lawlessness" (1993a, 102). All of this is presented as part of the "hegemonic project" of conservatives to remake precisely civil rights politics to serve their own purposes in battles with the Left: "difference is . . . firmly established as a cultural construct only to be reworked within a hegemonic project that connects race and nation against the elimination of structural and cultural inequality" (1993a, 95).

But cultural racism is not the preserve of conservatives alone. In the same discussion, Giroux applies this bitterly critical and hyper-suspicious outlook to what could be viewed as a generally hopeful tale of interracial friendship set forth in the 1991 film, *Grand Canyon*. The possibility of a positive racial future for America (the film is informed in a loose way by progressive sensibilities on race and racism) rubs our radical postmodernist multiculturalist the wrong way. He has no time for a story in which "the immensity of the racial, cultural, political, economic, and social differences that separate these [Black and White] families are erased in a New Age notion of unity and spirituality" (1993a, 111). The film must be deplored because it fails to "acknowledg[e] the wider grid of social relations marked by existing systems of inequality and discrimination" (1993a, 109). In Giroux's bleak interpretation the spirit of radical political condemnation blots out every other human impulse. In the film, a Black tow truck driver comes to the aid of a White immigration lawyer whose car has broken down in a dangerous neighborhood. The lives of the two men, and their families, eventually become intertwined in a story showing, among other things, Blacks and Whites sharing life on friendly terms. Giroux will have none of it. The main Black character, clearly a decent man, is dismissed as a product of White hegemony, "trapped within the limits imposed by poverty, racism, and the culture of survival, [maintaining] a view of society that allows him to go on with his life but undercuts his own sense of individuality and collective agency" (1993a, 110). More troubling to Giroux, the main White character is not portrayed "through the evocation of a critical reading of history, an invocation of dangerous memory, or an understanding of how social relations that evoke privileges and power must be unlearned and transformed" (1993a, 111). One can imagine Giroux's alternative telling of this story (the ostensible purpose of his interpretation of the film is to propose "a critical pedagogy of representation" that will teach students how to "interrogate" and "demystify" such works [1993a, 115]). A positive story of Blacks and Whites is out of the question; only a poisonous political drama of empowerment and disempowerment, of blame and righteous indignation and guilt and remorse, of fundamental mistrust and antagonism, may be used to depict race relations in America.

Postmodernist multiculturalists' view of the vital role of *education* in engaging the task of cultural reimagination called for by the fight against discrimination bears witness to similar exaggerations and distortions. The current education system must be viewed as offering no more than a "form of cultural reproduction which endorses, models, and transmits Eurocentric cultural values and ignores or denigrates other cultural heritages" (Gay 1995, 165). As McLaren says, "for too many minorities, schools have become cathedrals of death."[58] The curriculum becomes "a battleground over whose forms of knowledge, history, visions, language, culture, and authority will prevail" (Giroux 1987, 178). Under the guidance of theory, the task of education in the service of the fight against discrimination must now entail an effort to remake the entire world against efforts of a thought-controlling juggernaut that would frustrate it at every turn: "An education that empowers students to resist and transform racist practices uncovers the deeply ingrained ideological, historical, economic, cultural, and political factors in society which generate, embody, and perpetuate racism" (Gay 1995, 178). "Both teachers and students [should] examine the nature and effects of hegemony, especially as it relates to the educational experience of various cultural groups, whether these be based on race, gender, religion, sexuality, or whatever" (Grant and Sachs 1995, 101). On such a view, education is at the forefront of an all-or-nothing, hegemonic, world-creating struggle.

The Question Concerning "Moral Technology"

One place where theory *stifles* the imagination is in the domain of the moral claims that are so central to political life. This is not to say that postmodernist multiculturalists are not driven fundamentally by moral impulses (they are) or that they do not ever use the language of "social justice" or "ethics" (they do). But, under the influence of theory, morality is also a large *problem* to be wrestled with. Postmodernist theory is inclined against all moral claims because they are general and because they aim to be authoritative. Morality makes postmodernists nervous and this is apparent in the way they talk about it—a wariness concerning "moral and social regulation," or "political and moral regulation intimately connected with technologies of power," or in such circumlocutions as "moral technology."[59] This hesitation of theory becomes outright condemnation of morality when morality is found to be on the side of those deemed guilty of discrimination. "Postmodernism exhibits a profound cynicism—if not sustained intellectual contempt—towards what it regards as the Eurocentric Enlightenment project of human progress, equality, justice, rationality, and truth, a project built upon patriarchal master narratives."[60]

But the postmodernist anxiety concerning morality, and a consequent awkwardness or ineptitude in relation to moral matters, comes at a price, as Giroux and McLaren themselves admit: "Radical educational theorists as a group have eschewed trying to develop a theory of ethics. . . . We have been unable to move from a posture of criticism to one of substantive vision. . . . We have rarely discussed what the moral referents might be for defending particular social and cultural practices."[61] Here, once again, the contrast with Banks is stark. Radical in its own way, his account of multiculturalism is nevertheless always an appeal to the community as a whole that is not afraid to speak in the language of our commonsense notions of morality.

Because claims of morality and justice are so obviously central and essential to civil rights politics, postmodernist multiculturalism unavoidably makes use of its terms, however unartfully. The first of Gay and Hart's seven "postmodern education principles," for example, is "community," the "normative center" of their vision of multicultural education and "a value to be practiced habitually" (Gay and Hart 2000, 172). But this is, as a I say, mainly a problem for postmodernist multiculturalists. The challenge for the moralizing postmodernist becomes apparent in an extended discussion by McLaren of "The Struggle for the Ethical Self" (McLaren 1997b, 284–90). McLaren does not in the end find a way to bridge the divide between the universalizing tendencies of morality and postmodernism's suspicion of such claims; his discussion simply goes back and forth between them. Offering an account of "ethical selves [who] die for the dignity of other human beings and their well-being," McLaren at one point seems to go so far as to want to resist the morality-undermining force of postmodern thought, to "refuse to allow postmodern culture to domesticate the people, to render them useless" (McLaren 1997b, 284). In this vein, quoting theorist Enrique Dussel, he seems even to call for embracing the legacy of the Enlightenment and its rationalism: "We do not deny the rational kernel of the universalist rationalism of the Enlightenment. . . . We do not negate reason . . . , but the irrationality of the violence generated by the myth of modernity."[62] This is, of course, a startling suggestion from the point of pure theory; is *this*, perhaps, "the sacrifice of critical pedagogy" of which McLaren speaks at the beginning of this essay (McLaren 1997b, 285)?

At the same time, and more predominantly, postmodernist hesitations and anxiety concerning universal moral programs are too essential to be tossed aside. McLaren quotes another theorist, Ella Shohat, to outline the postmodernist problematic, the need "to avoid either falling into essentialist traps or being politically paralyzed by deconstructionist formulations."[63] In the end, McLaren's moralizing is always informed by theoretical doubts:

> We must identify a common ground of struggle in which a universality of rights and the common good passes into particular social struggles and then is reinitiated dialectically at a higher level of universality, and so on, without final closure. I am pointing to a nonabsolutist form of cultural politics, one that is never quite free from historically given languages, cultural codes, positionings of time and space. . . . The new political subject that will emerge will be constituted by deessentializing forms of agency. (1997b, 289)

This is not a statement of how the basic problem of postmodernist moralizing may be overcome, but merely a recitation of formulations embodying that problem.

McLaren and Hammer at one point go so far as to insist that "critical pedagogy must become a means of counter-hegemony."[64] That is a stark admission, for counter-hegemony is still, of course, hegemony. To say that is to suggest that Left anti-discrimination politics is nothing more than a new, alternative system of domination—and therefore no more just than what it condemns. This difficulty is sometimes noted—the obvious and significant danger that counter-hegemony will "simply invert relations of power [so that] the oppressed, newly freed from their bondage, would inevitably recuperate the logic of the oppressor"—but never satisfactorily resolved (McLaren 1997b, 288).

Another attempt to address postmodernism's problematic relationship to morality is "strategic essentializing"—the deliberate telling of lies, advancing (general) moral or ideological claims known to be false so as not to deprive oneself of the powerful terms of ordinary political and moral language.[65] The polemical appeal of this surprising solution, very dubious from a moral point of view, is easy enough to see. The general claims of morality, of principle, of ideology, of law—must postmodernists give up all that to fight for their cherished political cause? Not if they can learn to speak in two modes—one, a serious (critical or theoretical) mode, always suspicious of general claims, and another more practical (or "strategic") way of speaking that employs the same (general) terms used by everybody else in the political arena. This is the old distinction between inner and outer, esoteric and exoteric, but now the point is entirely to ensure that the work of politics is not hampered by theoretical insight (yet another sign of the supremacy of the former in this merger). As we shall see, the harsh and openly aggressive strategy of Whiteness-talk that postmodernist multiculturalists champion betrays a certain lack of skill in this department—as does their failure thus far to advance a successful moral doctrine. Strategic essentializing is evidently hard to do.

One related consequence of postmodernist multiculturalism's difficulty with ordinary moral usage is a certain loss of the *restraint* that often accompanies appeals to morality. The limitations imposed by appeals to the common good and to the wider political community—to say nothing of civic peace or social order—are more or less rejected by postmodernist multiculturalism out of hand. Beginning from a view of all-or-nothing political contestation, compromise must be viewed as making concessions to some unjust hegemon's totalizing oppression. The moral impulse of postmodernist multiculturalism is thus not moderated by the potential effect that morality can have to soften the blunt edges of political life. It does retain the morality of opposition and conflict, of demand and accusation, of corrective justice and political struggle, but without transcending that lower moral domain in the direction of an appeal to the community taken as a whole. Its moral spirit is also, as a consequence, intransigently and radically uncompromising in its combativeness and commitment to total change. "A revolutionary multiculturalism must begin with . . . revolutionary praxis rather than melioristic reforms" (McLaren 1997b, 289). "Revolutionary multiculturalism . . . is not about reforming capitalist democracy but rather transforming it by cutting at its joints and then rebuilding the social order from the vantage point of the oppressed" (McLaren 1997b, 287). Never embracing the common good means that an attempt must be made, instead, to use morality (of a certain sort) as a weapon to advance some of the partial claims of Left anti-discrimination politics. There is much talk of the "commitment to marginalized others in the service of justice and freedom" and the need for "solidarity with the oppressed and an identification with past and present struggles against imperialism, against racism, against sexism, against homophobia, against all those practices of unfreedom associated with living in a white supremacist capitalist society"—but there is no account of what this amounts to as a positive moral vision for the community taken as a whole (McLaren 1997b, 289, 288). Unimpeded by the restraining ties of ordinary morality, postmodernist multiculturalism instead energizes by moralizing in a radical way what are ultimately no more than the most ordinary, narrow, and partial political claims.

The uncompromising character of postmodernist multiculturalism is made explicit when its theorists commonly express disdain for and denunciations of what they deem tepid, soft, or otherwise insufficiently aggressive forms of multiculturalism: "Multicultural education has been partially incorporated within neoconservative and neoliberal discourses in ways that currently block its fuller democratic potential. . . . In an ironic and contradictory way, multicultural education typically has been institutionalized within the curriculum and within public schools in ways that affirm the boundaries between the center and the margins of the curriculum."[66] The National Association for Multicultural Education is said (incredibly, in my view) to advocate mere "liberal multiculturalism," "a 'feel good' approach in which diversity is achieved through a humanistic agenda that promotes tolerance and acceptance but pays little attention to the dominant culture in preventing equality and excellence for all" (Lee 2005, 73). A similarly dubious and surprising claim is extended as well to Banks, who is characterized as insufficiently radical and likewise deemed merely a "liberal" (Giroux 1996, 197). Starting here, "changing" and "troubling" the rest of multicultural education as it is currently constituted is a recurring theme.[67]

"Oppositional Utopia"—or Doubt and Despair?

Postmodernist multiculturalism's intransigently insurgent, critical, and combative sensibility is, at points, presented almost as the end or aim of the whole. Eschewing as inadequate all compromise, aiming for total transformation, and lacking a concrete intermediate agenda, postmodernist multiculturalism sometimes comes to sight as advocating in a general way for conflict, antagonism, resistance, and (eternal?) struggle, almost for its own sake. Such a notion, which might perhaps be said to follow from the understanding of social and political life advanced by postmodernist theory, is embraced by Gay and Hart as a commitment to "Resistance and Struggle" (another of their "seven postmodern education principles"): "Postmodern and multicultural visions are not easily or quickly accomplished, nor is the journey toward them always harmonious and consensual. Overcoming racism, political imperialism, economic inequities, psychological abuse, academic underachievement, and cultural hegemony often are not conducive to gentle and congenial remedies" (2000, 184). At one point Giroux goes so far as to try to characterize something like this in positive terms, as "oppositional utopianism." "Combining the discourse of critique with that of hope is crucial in order to affirm that critical activity offers the possibility for social change. In this way, democracy is viewed as a project and task, as an ideal type that is never finalized."[68] The idea is likewise visible in Sleeter's account of the postmodernist rejection of authority that is then made into a positive ideal of "resistance" by which multicultural education is reconceived as a very general program of "resistance to oppression."[69] Such a view of social life is suggested as well by like-minded political theorists—in Chantal Mouffe's account of democratic politics as "agonistic pluralism," for example.[70]

While the radical impulse of their overall vision may not *consistently* lead postmodernist multiculturalists to a call for endless conflict and strife, the ultimate aim of their project is nevertheless always problematic. The stated goal takes various forms that reflect the effects of its mutually radicalizing—theoretical and political—starting point, veering from grand hopes to political despair. This is basically the same problem we saw with postmodernist multiculturalism's encounter with morality—needing to deploy it but incapable of doing so well or without a guilty conscience. Giroux's "oppositional utopianism" is one of "educated hope," but his outlook is also betrayed by nagging postmodernist doubts: "the often overlooked tension between being politically committed and pedagogically wrong," the need for "a politics which is simultaneously utopian but always distrustful of itself."[71] Postmodernist multiculturalism embraces a "border pedagogy . . . that insists on an open-endedness, an incompleteness, and an uncertainty about the politics of one's own location."[72] Similarly, McLaren and Lankshear call for "social dreaming," "an arch of social dreaming [that] gives shape, coherence, and protection to the unity of our collective struggles. It means attaining a vision of what the total transformation of society might mean" (1993, 411). But this is, of course, also a problem from the point of view of theory. "We need to struggle towards a critical multiculturalism which can speak to the universal values of freedom and justice without such values becoming totalizing."[73] The solution on offer, such as it is, is one informed by doubt and hesitation: "When we refer to a totalizing vision, . . . it must be clear that we intend what Laclau calls 'the search for the universal in the contingent' as well as the 'contingency of all universality.'"[74]

A tendency to self-doubt is thus at work in postmodernist utopianism, but it is also perhaps owing to the unrealizable—precisely because so radical—*political* aims of postmodernist multiculturalism. Seeking not only to empower victims of discrimination but also to tear down, recenter, and rewrite the false worldview of the hegemony that frames modern life, while lacking any positive vision other than opposition to discrimination, postmodern multiculturalism seems to aim for something not of this world. As a result, there are also important notes of resignation and despair in the postmodernist multiculturalism outlook, as a passage from the epilogue to McLaren's book *Revolutionary Multiculturalism* indicates:

> The smell of blood lingers in the air. A regime of madmen watch from the darkness that is preparing to descend. It is a

> darkness brought by the false promises of neoliberalism and the false hopes of liberal democracy. As hope moves into full retreat throughout the globe, the postmodernists stumble about like weekend drunks, trying to reinvent catharsis in a world where abjection has replaced interpretation, where the signifier has replaced meaning, where spectators have replaced participants. . . . The only option available is the creation of new fictions of identity cut loose from history. The challenge that we face in the approaching millennium cannot be met in this arena of American spectacles. . . . The night descends and it is business as usual in Los Angeles. (1997b, 300–301)

At another point McLaren strikes a more hopeful attitude, but to do so he suggestively embraces the language of religious or spiritual longing: "The present historical moment is populated by memories that are surfacing at the margins of our culture. . . . Here saints and Iwa walk together and the Orishas speak to us. . . . Within such borderlands our pedagogies of liberation can be invested once again with the passion of mystery and the reason of commitment."[75]

We should not be surprised if the teachings and strategies of postmodernist multiculturalism, a radical stance torn perpetually between competing theoretical and political impulses, point in different directions at the same time. Anti-rationalism is not necessarily the same thing as irrationalism, but we do see here clear evidence of some of the consequences for civil rights politics in embracing a teaching that rejects reason.

"Naming Whiteness": Postmodernist Multiculturalism's Contribution to Civil Rights Discourse

The most striking and, in a way, characteristic, contribution of postmodernist multiculturalism to contemporary civil rights discourse is an effort to turn it away from generalities (like "civil rights") toward a more direct engagement with the politics of race and racial grievance, in a new emphasis on "the study and teaching of whiteness" and even a "pedagogy of whiteness" that begins from the idea that contemporary life is dominated by "White Terror."[76] "Naming whiteness and white people in this sense helps dislodge the claims of both to rightful dominance" (Frankenberg 1993, 234). Here is the effectual truth of the mutually radicalizing effects of theory and anti-discrimination politics. Radical theory having made impossible or nearly impossible any general political and moral discourse, now the claims of civil rights—made radical and unrestrained in spirit partly by the goading of theory—are lowered to the level of insulting racial reductionism. Whiteness talk is not a theory of anything; there is no sophisticated "critique" of any significant "idea" here. Theory is revealed as abetting the diminishing of political discourse in the direction of name-calling. Worst of all, the result is disastrous *politically* since now something calling itself anti-racism is made into a kind of racial goading—something very close, to use the terms of the law, to racial harassment as a broad cultural strategy.

It is no coincidence that the postmodernist critique of Whiteness (a development involving theorists in many academic disciplines) occurred in the early 1990s, at the very moment of the postmodernist-multiculturalism merger.[77] Today Ibram X. Kendi and Robin DiAngelo make headlines for drawing attention to White supremacy and White fragility claims, but such a move was worked out in great detail several decades ago.[78] Only the mutually radicalizing effects of theory and politics that we have been describing could suggest or justify or permit such a move. It would be a mistake to think that Whiteness-talk is a product mainly of epistemology or *theory* here (an idea that Whiteness-talk "gains particularity while losing universality," or something along those lines) (Nakayama and Krizek 1995, 294). As the advocates of Whiteness-talk themselves are quick to insist, Whiteness is an "essentialism," the meaning of which is politically contested, a category to be critically taken down by theory.[79] Here as elsewhere it is instead a radicalized political understanding of the fight against discrimination—narrowed severely now to take the form of allegations of White racism and White domination—that suggests such a strategy. The call to recenter public discourse around an attack on Whiteness ("the central political implication arising from the insight that race is socially constructed is the specific need to attack *whiteness*") is a very aggressive effort to transform radically the rhetorical plane on which American civil rights debate takes place (Roediger 1994, 3; emphasis in the original).

It is necessary to say that in attempting to do this both theory and politics are debased, goaded by one another into the lowest kind of mischief.

One is tempted to add a kind of trigger warning here since Whiteness-talk seeks to re-racialize public discussion of matters that are treated infinitely better on the plane of general principles and common aims. By doing so, wittingly or unwittingly, postmodernist multiculturalism encourages all groups to think in terms of what divides them; at points, "Whiteness theory" sounds very much like the kind of sweeping condemnation of one race that the fight against discrimination ought to have rendered beneath contempt and out of bounds. Its defenders will say that this is done in the name of anti-racism, but such protestations are woefully insufficient. At least in this instance we must agree with Sleeter and McLaren when they say that "naming is in some sense an act of violence" (1995a, 19).

The center of Whiteness-talk is a very simple moral-political judgment condemning the White race for its past sins. Giroux expresses this "assumption" in no uncertain terms:

> Heavily indebted to the assumption that "whiteness" is *synonymous with domination, oppression and privilege*, the critical project that largely informs the new scholarship on "whiteness" rests on a singular assumption. Its primary aim is to unveil the rhetorical, political, cultural and social mechanisms through which "whiteness" is both invented and used to mask its power and privilege. The political thrust of such work seeks to abolish "whiteness" as a racial category and marker of identity.[80]

Other Whiteness theorists enunciate a similar starting point: "It is not merely that whiteness is oppressive and false; it is that whiteness is *nothing but* oppressive and false" (Roediger 1994, 13; emphasis in the original). McLaren and Torres put the point in equally stark terms: "we argue against celebrating whiteness in any form."[81] (Here, at last, postmodernist multiculturalists prove capable of articulating something like a general principle!) Critical reflection on non-White racial groups, on the other hand, is out of bounds. Social scientists and others who suggest that there is a connection between the cultural traits of Black Americans and their socio-economic situation, for example, are dismissed as representatives of "the new racism" (Giroux 1997b, 377–80).

The rest of the logic of Whiteness-talk, such as it is, revolves always around the simple political center already stated ("oriented around the deconstruction of white supremacy") and may be summarized quickly (Sleeter and McLaren 1995a, 22). The first aim of Whiteness theory is to "expose," "unveil," "deterritorialize," "denaturalize" Whiteness, "interrogating the culture of whiteness," tasks that must be undertaken because in American life Whiteness is the "invisible center," "an oppressive hidden norm" that surreptitiously benefits Whites while harming racial minorities.[82] "The supposed neutrality of white culture enables it to commodify blackness to its own advantage and ends. It allows it to manipulate the other but not see this otherness as a white tool of exploitation" (McLaren 1995, 50). Not only are "whites . . . taken as the norm," but "whiteness represents itself as a universal marker for being civilized"; in doing so it "posits the Other within the language of pathology, fear, madness, and degeneration."[83] "The white privilege of universalizing its characteristics as the 'proper ways to be' has continuously undermined the efforts of non-whites in a variety of spheres" (Kincheloe and Steinberg 1997, 208). Naming Whiteness serves to disrupt and loosen the hold of "the dominant discourses and representations that secure 'whiteness' as a universalizing norm" (Giroux 1993a, 101).

Other aspects of the rhetoric of Whiteness aim not so much to expose the purportedly silent normalizing power of Whiteness as to demonstrate the connections between White culture and White privilege, White supremacy, and White racism. "Even though no one at this point really knows what whiteness is, most observers agree that it is intimately involved with issues of power and power differences between white and non-white people" (Kincheloe and Steinberg 1997, 207). Evidence is offered to demonstrate the centrality of White racism in European colonialism, the American founding, and through much of American history—the whole modern development now presented racially as the problematic doings of Whites: "Postmodernism . . . recognizes that inherent in the modernist paradigm are falsely perceived constructions that disease humanity and have a sole purpose to sustain and ensure the supremacy of the group defined as 'White'."[84] Similar claims are made for contemporary American political developments as well (extending from Right anti-discrimination politics deemed part of the "new racism" to the "white racist essentialism" of someone like David Duke).[85] But the connection between Whiteness and racism is also made more simply and more sweepingly: "Racism in America . . . is a phenomenon constructed by Americans socially defined as 'White,' and . . . its primary role is to ensure that group's primacy to the exclusion of all others at whatever cost" (Akintunde 1999, 2).

From the claim that Whites should be seen first and foremost from the point of view of their racism, it is a short step to condemning Whites for other sins as well. American Whiteness "can be seen historically in widespread acts of imperialism and genocide and linked to an erotic economy of 'excess'" (McLaren 1997a, 9). "[Whiteness] is the empty and therefore terrifying attempt to build an identity based on what one isn't and on whom one can hold back" (Roediger 1994, 13). "White Culture . . . is the kind that is cold, the kind that laughs at feelings while demanding that all surplus libido, energy, and capital be handed over to it" (MacCannell 1992, 130). McLaren goes so far as to discuss the question under the heading "Whiteness: The Invisible Culture of Terror" (1995, 49). Such criticisms of Whites are more or less clearly tied to the main criticism (their alleged racism) and they may not amount to a deliberate campaign to demonize the White race. But it is not easy to distinguish this impulse to characterize a whole race of people (politically "essentializing" race in the most outrageous way) in a relentlessly critical spirit from the sort of discriminatory attitudes and opinions that first launched the civil rights revolution. As one oft-cited Whiteness-talk historian puts it, the project must go beyond "exposing [and] demystifying" to also "*demeaning* the particular ideology of Whiteness" (Roediger 1994, 12; emphasis added).

On this critical foundation Whiteness scholarship proposes strategies of "subversion," "dismantling whiteness," and "re-imagining 'whiteness.'"[86] "White people must learn to listen to non-whites' and indigenous people's criticism of them and the cultural norms they have established and imposed on non-European and lower socio-economic class peoples" (Kincheloe and Steinberg 1997, 101). "Educated Whites [must] work toward racial justice. In part this involves learning to . . . step aside and take a back seat" (Sleeter and McLaren 1995a, 22). (Racial justice means teaching members of one race to take a "back seat"?) Whiteness theorists offer arresting formulas like encouraging Whites to "choose . . . not to be white," committing "race treason," even the "abolition of whiteness."[87] "What is needed, to get rid of such oppressive identities is, in a sense, to encourage the widespread suicide of privileged identity-infused selves" (Jungkunz 2011, 3). Taking such steps would be "an act of transgression," but one that is always justified in the name of anti-racism—"a traitorous act that reveals a fidelity to the struggle for justice."[88]

Much is made in the Whiteness literature about the "silences" and "evasions" of White people who seem disinclined to absorb these lessons. Whiteness "resists, sometimes violently, any extensive characterization that would allow for the mapping of its contours" (Nakayama and Krizek 1995, 291). "Whites evade a discourse on White racism to protect [their] own interests. . . . To open up a discussion of White racism challenges the legitimacy of White peoples' very lives."[89] Postmodernist multiculturalists sometimes admit a kind of problem here—namely, that of "engag[ing] white people in an understanding of their white privilege in a way that would not simply anger them to the point they shut down conversation."[90] Such questions are, however, "exceedingly difficult to answer, since the very nature of whiteness scholarship is designed to undermine practices and ways of seeing that work to protect white privilege."[91]

It is very important to emphasize how "whiteness scholarship" follows from and seeks to advance the cause of the Left interpretation of American anti-discrimination law and politics by recharacterizing its *Right* interpretation as merely the outlook of Whites.[92] The logic of the color-blind Constitution, equal opportunity, merit, and a critical attitude toward disparity-as-discrimination ("disparate treatment," yes, "disparate impact," no) are, on this view, no more than tools of Whites, a collection of "disguises, euphemisms, silences, and avoidances"—the "bag of tricks"—of White hegemony.[93] "Current legal definitions of race embrace the norm of color blindness [in which] blackness and whiteness are seen as neutral and apolitical descriptions . . . unrelated to social conditions of domination and subordination." [94] The "view that reduces racism to individual, intentional acts" becomes a "power-evasive" move of Whiteness.[95] "Racism . . . for most whites . . . ignores the societal, systemic, institutional, and political institutions [that] protect white privilege. When racism is regarded in this way, it . . . helps whites to erect defense mechanisms to ignore its direct implication and involvement in the maintenance of white racism, white privilege, and the construction of 'other' [*sic*]" (Akintunde 1999, 2). Whites are held to ignore disparities among the races and to defend practices that sustain them as a matter of deliberate strategy. "Tests required for teacher certification, although not necessarily measuring good teaching itself, contribute to keeping the teaching profession disproportionately White. . . . Research studies find teacher testing to reinforce White dominance."[96]

Recasting the Right interpretation of anti-discrimination politics as White surely works to discredit and undermine it.[97] Doing that may indeed be the main purpose of Whiteness theory:

> As whites, white students in particular, come to see themselves through the eyes of blacks, Latinos, Asians and indigenous peoples, they begin to move away from the conservative constructions of the dominant culture. Such an encounter with minority perspectives moves many white individuals to rethink their tendency to dismiss the continued existence of racism and embrace the belief that racial inequality results from unequal abilities among racial groups. (Kincheloe and Steinberg 1997, 208)

To characterize the Right interpretation as White is already a significant rhetorical achievement; it is also a step on the way to defining conservativism as racist. Such rhetorical maneuvers of misdirection set the terms of debate in a way that is meant to confound any opposition to the Left interpretation of anti-discrimination. Anyone compelled to begin by answering such charges as "what you are saying reflects your Whiteness" or "you are a racist" is not likely to be very successful in conveying his or her own vision of what is or ought to be entailed by civil rights politics.

Nothing is spared. Even reason is subjected to this political rough treatment, becoming "white reason: the colonial power of whiteness" and characterized as merely a weapon of political domination and exploitation. Western rationalism, the Enlightenment, and "science" are now reduced to being not just "White" but the tools of White privilege, White supremacy, and White racism.

> We believe that a dominant impulse of whiteness took shape around the European Enlightenment's notion of rationality, with its privileged construction of a transcendental white, male, rational subject. . . . In this context whiteness was naturalized as a universal entity. . . . Reason in this historical configuration is whitened and human nature itself is grounded upon this

reasoning capacity. Lost in the defining process is the socially constructed nature of reason itself, not to mention its emergence as a signifier of whiteness. Thus, in its rationalistic womb whiteness begins to establish itself as a norm that represents an authoritative, delimited and hierarchical mode of thought. In the emerging colonial contexts in which whites would increasingly find themselves in the decades and centuries following the Enlightenment, the encounter with non-whiteness would be framed in rationalistic terms—whiteness representing orderliness, rationality and self-control, and non-whiteness as chaos, irrationality, violence and the breakdown of self-regulation. Rationality emerged as the conceptual base around which civilization and savagery could be delineated. This rationalistic modernist whiteness is shaped and confirmed by its close association with science. (Kincheloe and Steinberg 1997, 208–9)

"White reason," on this view, is said explicitly to serve "white power": "White reason with its white epistemology reproduces linear, capital-driven knowledge forms that in their removal of analysis from a humanized context reinforce the naturalization of white power. Indeed, white power patrols its boundaries, on the lookout for threats to its supremacy." [98]

Whiteness-talk is one way to view the ultimate meaning of the supposedly sophisticated postmodernist takedown of reason. Twenty-five centuries of reflection and thought and debate about the meaning, status, and reach of human knowledge and rationality now reduced to a unitary racial mindset, the low doings of "White power." This is the kind of thing that discredits *political* life, and it surely discredits any "theory" associated with it. What would civil rights politics be like if it were to go further in following the lead of the kind of crude political reductionism that postmodernist Whiteness theory represents?

Benefits of the Merger—and Costs

It is easy to see how theory benefits in its merger with civil rights politics, acquiring a powerful political patron of unquestioned respectability. Constitutionally incomplete and rudderless, postmodernism gains moral seriousness and purpose that it cannot generate on its own. The costs to theory (political obedience and deference, massive contradiction and incoherence) are readily borne, apparently—ignored or sublimated.

The costs to civil rights politics are not so easily repressed or wished away. This is the fight against discrimination made into an unlovely project, a very harsh version of itself. There is, indeed, a kind of outline of anti-discrimination politics provided here—or at least an outline of its most aggressive and combative features. Guided by postmodernist theory, civil rights politics becomes neurotic. Claims and grievances are exaggerated but at the same time undermined by doubt. Already negative and wary, under the influence of postmodernism anti-discrimination politics becomes suspicious and pessimistic about social life to the point of paranoia. Where anti-discrimination politics is transformative and disruptive, postmodernist theory encourages it to be recklessly so, heedless of the civilizational consequences of its critical destructive work. The politics of friends and enemies that anti-discrimination may well engender becomes, through theory, the view that social life is constituted by all-or-nothing political conflict or strife. Where anti-discrimination politics is already ambitious in remaking much of modern democratic life, postmodernism's claim that political struggle literally makes the whole world—the world we see in our mind's eye—distorts the debate over civil rights by magnifying what is at stake to an extraordinary degree. Everything about ordinary civil rights politics that might seem to require the moderating guidance of statesmanship is radically inflated or exaggerated and made intransigent and destructive by postmodernism. What postmodernist multiculturalism reveals to us about anti-discrimination politics is that under the influence of irresponsible parties it has the capacity to do harm to the political order and to those it would serve. It is in need of steady guidance of some kind. Up to this point, one of the most important cultural resources serving this purpose has, of course, been the influence of the liberal tradition—one of the chief targets of postmodernism's ire.

Because postmodernist theory is simply incompatible with the general moral commitments normally associated with civil rights politics—and the claim that they are *true*—it is possible that someday this may be the cause of postmodernist multiculturalism's undoing. For it is above all the energy, assumptions, and aims derived from its claims about justice that most drive multiculturalism and the civil rights revolution. In this (formal) respect, the anti-discrimination regime is just like liberalism (and every other established political order); to speak authoritatively and in the language of morality (or law) is to speak generally. Can multiculturalism really even entertain the notion that the determination to stand up to racism is, like everything else, just one more rhetorical fiction of one more historically contingent interpretive community seeking to impose its will on everybody else? It does not take a lot of thought or imagination to apply the lessons of postmodernism to the anti-discrimination political project—and, indeed, that is done by some (though not of course by postmodernist multiculturalists).[99] The fight for civil rights has always been torn between general or universal aspirations, on the one hand, and the particular concerns of discrimination victim groups, on the other. Postmodernist theory introduces a principled refusal to admit general propositions, common solutions. Through its influence, the spirit of compromise and civic good will is perceived to be weakness and betrayal. By way of theory the moral certainty of the fight against discrimination is reduced to moral indignation and intransigent combativeness, a radically politicized remnant of the original.

It is such difficulties, it seems to me, that explains Banks's reservations concerning postmodernist theory and his apparent decision early on (in the 1990s) to keep his distance from it.[100] Banks rejects relativism (which "can be used to justify racism") and embraces the supremacy of "democratic values," the view that "one value is not as good as the other."[101] His aim is "to create an education that will help foster a just and inclusive pluralistic national society that *all* students and groups will perceive as legitimate."[102] His account of multicultural education is meant to be "more truthful" as well as more "inclusive" (1991c, 138). Indeed, a commitment to its truth means that "accuracy is [multicultural education's] first and most important goal" (1996b, 27). While it might go too far to say that Banks embraces some kind of rationalism (he never does so explicitly), he evidently senses the dangers inherent in the explicit alliance with anti-rationalism that has become so common among those who champion anti-discrimination politics.

Its extreme and incoherent radicalism also explains why postmodernist multiculturalism and similar efforts (critical race theory is again the obvious example) have such a problematic and politically costly reputation, as

Sleeter more or less openly concedes: "Those of us who work in multicultural education find ourselves walking a tightrope between naming issues accurately and antagonizing potential supporters. The left would have the field develop a much more explicit critique of White racism, capitalism, and patriarchy, a position with which I agree. . . . Yet it is difficult to work on naming social justice issues squarely in the context of the right's characterization of the field as un-American and dangerous" (1995a, 92). For Sleeter, this dilemma requires deft handling and the use of workable rhetorical strategies—and perhaps a bit of strategic essentializing.

> One cannot assume that advocates of multicultural education spell out their entire agenda in print and that one can infer all they are thinking or doing by reading the multicultural education literature. . . . The politics of bringing about change has necessitated frequently couching arguments for school reform in language that white educators would attend to. . . . The strategy of appealing to whites through relatively benign language sometimes has been more effective than many recognize. . . . Many activists who are working to make changes in education work with whatever points of entrée they can gain in whatever fashion is acceptable to others with whom they work. (Sleeter 1996, 8–9)

This is revealing, but it is also an admission of the price anti-discrimination politics must pay to team up with radical theory.

What, then, are the perceived benefits to anti-discrimination politics that would explain the broad movement of so many of its devotees to embrace radical theory? The critical ferocity of the latter might seem politically useful, though that, of course, is a double-edged sword. There is also, perhaps, some benefit to be gained in this "community of struggle" that makes "the voice of reform more commanding and the possibility of being 'heard' more likely" (Gay 1995, 183). Multiculturalism does derive the benefits (real or perceived) of a complex and seemingly sophisticated theoretical outlook, as well as whatever reputation it has with which to engage in a public debate that is often led by intellectuals. Nor is the prevalence in American life of a soft version of something like the postmodernist outlook—in modern skepticism, in liberal toleration, in moral and cultural relativism—an infertile soil for this more radical extension of those prior tendencies. But it is hard to believe that the apparent theoretical sophistication of postmodernism is the main attraction.

A better explanation is that there is at least some element of the civil rights effort and its quest for justice that inclines necessarily in a radical, even utopian, direction. Does the fight against discrimination see something in radical theory that it needs? Anti-discrimination reform seems always to some degree *limited*, even today, by powerful constraints—liberalism, bourgeois morality, nature, history, the Right interpretation of anti-discrimination law—and radical theory offers strategies and energy with which to go on the offensive against such powerful and authoritative hindrances. If the price to be paid is theory's rejection of *reason*, too, even that may seem to be justified by the spirit of the new effort. The great ambition of civil rights reform, which comes to sight also as extraordinary moral hope or moral demand, may be said to point in such a direction because of the difficulty, and indeed perhaps the impossibility, of the task that the anti-discrimination project sets for itself. Progress on one front (overt racism and sexism) is coupled with retrenchment on others (persistent inequalities, the discovery of new kinds or ever subtler manifestations of discrimination). Recurring questions about the role of what some would deem natural differences (in debates about inequalities associated with gender, sexual preference, age, and disability, for example) may make the postmodernist critique of reason—and hence, of an intelligible nature—seem not only attractive, but indispensable. Where a purely postmodernist moral and political program may be impossible *in theory*, the full realization of the anti-discrimination program may well be impossible *in practice*. Even Banks says that "multicultural education is a continuing process that never ends," that its aim may be an "impossible dream," an "unreachable star."[103] For such a project, something like postmodernism may well fit a real need.

Even so, we are led by the toxic results of the merging of anti-discrimination with postmodernism to see Banks's unwillingness to embrace the latter as a sign of his superior political or civic wisdom. Postmodernist theory debases public discourse and it surely has debased civil rights discourse. Postmodernism tells all sides that what they fight for is nothing less than the ground of their very being; that they are opposed by enemies with whom they have no hope of finding common cause; that their enemies indeed seek to wield the terms of political and moral discourse against them as powerful instruments of oppression; and that the necessary task for all is an unending "agonistic" struggle to control the language or terms of discourse by which the world is governed. Not the state of nature but instead so-called "civilized" life is a state of war. In a debate over civil rights framed in these terms, each side must begin by denying to the other the use of any and all general terms (in morality or the law) with the result that the discussion is explicitly and deliberately and without irony reduced to the level of "Whites" and "Blacks" and so forth. Postmodernists help to remind us that the general language of morality and political reform, by reference to which American civil rights debate has always taken place and still takes place, usefully blunts many sharp edges. Seeing those sharp edges may or may not be theoretically enlightening, but in practice the power of "glittering generalities," which call upon all to speak of and by and for all, is not to be underestimated.[104] A debate between racial, ethnic, and other group antagonists armed with nothing but the cultural anxiety and powerful critical tools of postmodernism is already here; its further development would not be a pretty sight. Fortunately, the overwhelming majority of Americans—Black and White, women and men, gay and straight, Christian, Jewish, Muslim, and atheist—do not yet see civil rights debate entirely through the eyes of postmodernism. We can only hope that democratic common sense will continue to resist the latest radical tide of democratic theory.

PART 3.
THE CHALLENGE TO LIBERAL PLURALISM

Chapter 7
THE LIBERAL PLURALIST TRADITION

By now we have confronted several times the general question of the relationship between the anti-discrimination regime and liberal democratic politics. The issue has been part of the picture from the very start, in the story of liberalism's inability adequately to address the problem of discrimination and in the basic facts of the anti-discrimination regime's legal and political history. Banks's delicate maneuvering around the question of multiculturalism's relation to liberty (mostly in silence, but at points also in a provocative effort to *reinterpret* the meaning of liberty) is another sign, as is the open and emphatic rejection of liberalism by postmodernist multiculturalists.

Part 3 of this work (this chapter and the next three) takes up the contrast between these two political frameworks, viewed as two different kinds of pluralism and two different moral schema, in a deliberate way. This chapter begins by providing a brief summary of the outlines of liberal pluralism with a view to distinguishing it from contemporary multiculturalism. Chapter 8 then explores how the two different accounts of democratic pluralism express the essential aspirations of contemporary political life in the language of groups, and in competing accounts of the relations of groups to individuals, to other groups, and to the state. Doing that allows us to begin to see the spirit of each and prepares us to see, further, the most important general alterations of the democratic outlook brought on by the anti-discrimination revolution. For by this point we will have enough evidence to say that anti-discrimination politics introduces a new view of the relationship between politics and morality as well as a new view of the content or substance of democratic morality (the subject of chapters 9 and 10).

I will not repeat everything I said in the introduction to defend the simple method I employ here, comparing and contrasting multiculturalism/anti-discrimination with liberal pluralism. The relationship between anti-discrimination and liberalism is or ought to be a question for us and we need to engage it—carefully, respectfully, but also critically and directly. To examine the question we will not need to have recourse to any terms other than those—political, moral, psychological—given to us by the arguments for multiculturalism, on the one hand, and for liberal pluralism, on the other. It may be true that some of the tensions between the two suggest that common sense cannot be the last word here. Nevertheless, the clarification and refinement of common sense is the surest path out of its limitations.

The Structure of Liberal Pluralism

The task of much of the rest of the book requires some attempt to sum up the liberal pluralist tradition. Doing that also provides us with an opportunity to assess and to acknowledge the view of political life that multiculturalism now challenges and, to the extent that the new pluralism has been successful, erodes. The great and undeniable practical achievement of liberal pluralism to this point in history, which the case of religion alone ought to establish in a rough way, suggests that we ought to consider its structure and aim with care. Liberal pluralism has a complex history, but at its core is a set of ideas that has withstood the test of time.

It is true that, like liberalism itself, liberal pluralism has been rethought and reconceived many times in many ways—in American political thought, arguments for religious pluralism, Madison's treatment of "faction" in *Federalist* 10, Horace Kallen's "cultural pluralism," liberal social science's interest group pluralism, more recent accounts of "values" (or moral) pluralism, and John Rawls's brief for "political liberalism" provide a crowded roster of alternatives.[1] But, as is true elsewhere in political discussions of diversity, appearances of multiplicity, even in the forms taken by pluralism, can be deceptive. In fact, there is a remarkable consistency in the outlook that animates all these disparate liberal accounts of pluralism. None of them, to begin with, is merely a recognition of the existence of diversity or some simple "neutral" response to it. Instead, they all represent merely variants within a common political or ideological frame. Liberal pluralism, in its many guises, takes a distinctive approach to the question of social diversity from a clearly identifiable moral, philosophical, and practical perspective.

The several varieties of liberal pluralism represent one very specific and readily recognizable outlook, one that differs markedly from multiculturalism.

Every argument for liberal pluralism is grounded in three clearly identifiable general premises—moral and epistemological—and culminates in a familiar set of distinctively liberal political or institutional strategies for dealing with groups, as well as in a characteristically liberal view of the "group." All the different forms of liberal pluralism share these main elements of a common outlook and, in the end, their seemingly great variety reflects only differences of emphasis in how those elements are ordered and ranked. The first crucial premise is moral; or rather, it is a cluster of related moral commitments (freedom, voluntarism, toleration, consent) which frames what we may hope for and demand of groups, individuals, and their interactions. A second characteristic feature of liberal pluralism is a soft skepticism, a view of human reason and knowledge that makes one less certain about the truth of one's own views (especially our views about morality) and thus, presumably, more amenable to compromise. Another is an emphasis on the benefits of social stability and a perspective on groups that begins from the challenge they pose to civic peace. Mixtures of these three—a realism coupled with idealism, a moderate idealism not rooted in claims of justice but in the logic of freedom, an idealism tempered further by skepticism—inform all the different accounts of liberal pluralism, uniting them in a consistent pattern. Characteristic prescriptions that follow from these foundational starting points, concerning the (limited) role of government and a set of assumptions about group politics (group-to-group, group-to-individual, group-to-state), are, in a way, defined in advance by them. Even if this outline of the logic of liberal pluralism does not contain every aspect of every variety of these arguments (I would maintain that it captures everything essential), it is more than enough to serve the purposes of drawing comparisons with contemporary American multiculturalism.

To summarize and explore the mindset that our different versions of liberal pluralism all share, it will prove very useful to begin by examining the outline of the basic argument provided in John Locke's foundational treatment of *religious* pluralism in *A Letter Concerning Toleration* (even if he did not ever use the word pluralism to characterize it). One of the remarkable features of liberal pluralism is how little has been added to or subtracted from Locke's rendering of the basic idea. Since all the important elements of the liberal pluralist perspective are put together here, all at once and at the beginning, Locke provides a useful point of reference, to say nothing of the depth, thoughtfulness, and persuasive force of his original formulation.

It may be objected by some that to begin from Locke and thus "classical" liberalism is to distort liberal pluralism and hence to set up an exaggerated statement of the differences between liberal pluralism and contemporary multiculturalism. But there is nothing in the pluralistic arguments made by Locke, in his writings on religion, that tie them to his stances on property, acquisition, and "comfortable self-preservation," or other topics that might seem politically controversial. The pluralist dimension of Locke's thought does not depend on anything like a libertarian view of economic life. Locke's view of the politics of religion and the separation of church and state (which today is embraced more passionately by the Left than the Right) cannot, for example, be reduced to a simple view of the need to *limit government*, for limiting society (or at least religion) is also very important. At any rate, the reason to start with Locke is that all the key features of his outline of the argument are to be found in subsequent accounts of liberal pluralism, most of which have been associated with the American Left.[2] Everything of importance in Locke's position is prominently on display, for example, in John Rawls's rendering of the pluralist outlook in *Political Liberalism* (1993). That later accounts of liberal pluralism follow a pattern visible in Locke's writings, regardless of whether the later writers would repudiate other elements of Lockean liberalism, is a striking fact suggesting these are enduring concerns at the heart of the liberal outlook. It is not necessary to assume that Locke's thought is the direct or main cause of the shape of later accounts of liberal pluralism to say that to begin with him is a natural step. Indeed, not to begin with Locke would be arbitrary and unwise.

The Outline of Liberal Pluralism in Locke's *Letter Concerning Toleration*

It is a measure of the importance of pluralism in the liberal lexicon that one could wonder whether it or "individualism" is the "-ism" most closely associated with the politics of freedom. Like individualism, pluralism is one way of expressing positively the liberal democratic command *not* to impose authority, without the consent of the governed, on any individual or group of individuals. Although Locke does not ever use the term "pluralism" in *A Letter Concerning Toleration*, the question of toleration is one that necessarily addresses some situation of social diversity that has become politically problematic. "It is not the diversity of opinions (which cannot be avoided), but the refusal of toleration to those that are of different opinions (which might have been granted), that has produced all the bustles and wars that have been in the Christian world upon account of religion" (Locke 1963, 53).[3] It is Locke's answer to the question of diversity, especially religious diversity, that helps us to see the contours of what later came to be called liberal pluralism.

Most prominent on the surface of Locke's treatment is a distinctive set of moral principles, derived from the morality of the social contract, extended to the group (in this first instance, the religious group). "Toleration" is most immediately visible—and indeed, Locke presents the "duty of toleration"—as a virtue of good Christians and citizens alike (1963, 5, 16–23). But it is the freedom of the individual that provides the truly central animating moral principle of the *Letter*. Individuals have "supreme and absolute authority" in matters of faith; "liberty of conscience is every man's natural right" (1963, 41, 47–48). The religious group, the "church," is also understood by Locke according to the morality of freedom, as a "voluntary society of men, joining themselves together of their own accord" (1963, 13). Members "joining together . . . is absolutely free and spontaneous" and a church's authority extends only "to those whom the society by common consent has authorized thereunto" (1963, 14). (Some might think to emphasize more than I do the role of "natural right" in considering the moral appeal of Locke's treatment of religious diversity; I do not, partly because this is not a principle most *later* liberal pluralists rely upon, but also because I do not think it central to the argument for toleration in the *Letter*.[4]) The distinctive moral language of liberty, individualism, voluntarism, consent, and toleration is pervasive in Locke's presentation and, as we shall see, works to define the groups under consideration.

But Locke's liberal moralism is informed and qualified by a soft skepticism that is at least as important as the language of liberty and toleration. In the *Letter* this skepticism helps to lay the ground for insisting that belief may never be "imposed" (a word he uses repeatedly)—certainly not by government.[5] Locke's starting point—the view that, to repeat, "the diversity of opinions . . . cannot be avoided"—is at the heart of what is simultaneously a philosophical, theological, and political stance (1963, 53). This step in the argument is mostly framed theologically in the *Letter*, although it has implications for other kinds of opinions and for social life: "Every church is orthodox to itself" and each necessarily pronounces all the other churches to be in error. Worse yet, the dispute between contending beliefs "is on both sides equal," since there is no authoritative judge of this dispute in this world, "either at Constantinople or elsewhere upon earth" (1963, 18–19; see 39–40). Beginning here, liberal pluralism can insist that those who would impose their beliefs on others act merely in a "spirit of persecution" (1963, 9). Above all, from this perspective, the state is never justified in coercing belief. "Speculative opinions . . . and articles of faith . . . cannot be imposed on any church by the law of the land" (1963, 39). In his *Essay Concerning Human Understanding* Locke develops this skeptical stance at length. There it extends beyond religious opinion to a great deal of what human beings claim to know. Moreover, the *political* purpose of the epistemological outlook that is presupposed in the *Letter* is explained in the *Essay*: "It would, methinks, become all Men to maintain Peace, and the common Offices of Humanity, and Friendship, in the diversity of Opinions, since we cannot reasonably expect that any one should readily and obsequiously quit his own Opinion, and embrace ours, with a blind resignation to an Authority which the Understanding of Man acknowledges not."[6] Finally, this stance is connected to a claim that Locke makes about the extent or limit of the law's authority as well: "But the business of the laws is not to provide for the truth of opinions, but for the safety and security of the commonwealth and of every particular man's goods and person" (1963, 40). Overall, the skepticism adumbrated here is as I say a soft one; these arguments have the effect of loosening (or undermining) some of our moral and political convictions without rendering us incapable of drawing important moral and political conclusions. Locke does not shy away from calling his a "doctrine of toleration," for example, and there seems to be no doubt about the ends of politics ("safety and security") or the human (or "natural") ground of political authority in the brief summary of the social contract teaching that appears in the *Letter* (1963, 47).

That the business of government is "the safety and security of the commonwealth" brings us to the third pillar of liberal pluralism, its spirit of down-to-earth realism. As Locke's mention of "all the bustles and wars that have been in the Christian world upon account of religion" reminds us, Locke cares about "peace and security" at least as much as he does about freedom and toleration (1963, 20). Much of the rhetorical force of the *Letter* comes from Locke's condemnation of those who deny religious liberty and toleration from this practical perspective: "how pernicious a seed of discord and war, how powerful a provocation to endless hatreds, rapines, and slaughters they thereby furnish unto mankind" (1963, 20). Locke goes so far as to speak of "this doctrine of toleration and peace," a formulation that captures perfectly the combination of realism and idealism in play (1963, 21).

Consistent with his concern for (mere) peace and security, Locke's account of the causes of religious conflict, as well as his proposed solution, are certainly presented in pragmatic, worldly terms. Religious diversity cannot be avoided because the "diversity of opinions" cannot be avoided. This situation is made worse by the "avarice and insatiable desire of dominion" of religious leaders, "the immoderate ambition of magistrates," and "the credulous superstition of the giddy multitude" (1963, 53). Religious and political leaders perceiving some advantage in religious divisions counsel oppression. Oppressed groups, in turn, rebel "from the common disposition of all mankind, who when they groan under any heavy burthen endeavour naturally to shake off the yoke that galls their necks" (1963, 49). Liberal pluralist political psychology is thus not simply dependent on liberal morality. Indeed, in the *Letter*, Locke refers to religion several times in the language of "faction" (1963, 36, 47, 52). (In the *Second Treatise*, Locke refers more generally to the problem of faction: "I grant, that the pride, ambition, and turbulency of private men have sometimes caused great disorders in commonwealths, and factions have been fatal to states and kingdoms" [1988, 418; see 328–29].)

While Locke's official solution to the problem of religious diversity may seem to be a moral one—advocating toleration and a view of religious groups stressing individualism, voluntarism, and freedom—he proposes another that depends on nothing but the self-interest of religious groups:

> Those [of other sects] that are averse to the religion of the magistrate will think themselves so much the more bound to maintain the peace of the commonwealth as their condition is better in that place than elsewhere; and all the several separate congregations, like so many guardians of the public peace, will watch one another, that nothing may be innovated or changed in the form of the government, because they can hope for nothing better than what they already enjoy—that is, an equal condition with their fellow-subjects under a just and moderate government. (1963, 50)

Regardless of whether Madison's *Federalist* 10 borrows explicitly from Locke's *Letter*, the realism of the argument for pluralism is as vigorous in the latter as it is in the former.[7]

The down-to-earth quality of Locke's reasoning helps to explain his repeated use of the language of "interest" to sketch what is at issue for all concerned—whether "the interest of religion," "the interest of the commonwealth," or "civil interests" ("life, liberty, health, and indolency of body; and the possession of outward things, such as money, lands, houses, furniture, and the like") (1963, 20, 34, 10). In the *Second Treatise*, Locke uses this language to describe the very general problem of "the variety of opinions and contrariety of interests, which unavoidably happen in all collections of men"—the starting place, likewise, for Madison's account of interest group politics in *Federalist* 10 (Locke 1988, 333). By tending in the direction of reducing political life to a contest among mere interests, liberal pluralism works to remove or to minimize the role of morality in politics and to lower the stakes for groups, in a way that is consistent with the aims of safeguarding "peace and security." Interest means above all self-interest. It is the coin of barter, of compromise and peace. It is principle—justice—that is the language of intractable strife. One critic of liberal toleration and pluralism admits at least this one strength of the liberal framework: "It is much easier to accept a compromise between competing interests . . . than between opposed principles which purport to be objectively valid. The genius of American politics is its ability to treat even matters of principle as though they were conflicts of interest" (Wolff 1965, 21). The tendency of liberalism to de-moralize political life is also, perhaps paradoxically, consistent with the liberal morality of freedom and toleration. This lends some support to those who argue that liberal morality may well be, in the last analysis, the servant of a more fundamental regime of peace and security (or at least that it was originally).[8]

All these different elements of liberal pluralism reinforce one other. At the very least, the morality of freedom and toleration is surely consistent with the mundane concerns of peace, security, and collective self-interest. Toleration is essentially the virtue of peaceable agreeableness. In a politics of individual freedom the contentious and divisive questions of "justice"—who "deserves" to rule, and in the name of what high purpose—are removed or at least diminished. Indeed, under the politics of freedom the idea of rule itself seems almost to disappear. Liberal pluralism's idealism moves in the same direction as its realism. Both are bolstered by the soft skepticism that makes political compromise and agreeableness seem not only sound policy and morally right but also the product of a deep appreciation of the limitations of human reason.

These essential core premises of the liberal pluralist outlook lead, in turn, to the familiar liberal political solution of the social contract arrangement: freedom for individuals, an account of the separation between the spheres of public and private life, and various limits upon government. In the *Letter*, Locke "esteem[s] it above all things necessary to distinguish exactly the business of civil government from that of religion," the two being "in their original, end, business, and in every thing, perfectly distinct, and infinitely different from each other" (1963, 9, 21). The separation of church and state comes to sight, to begin with, as a limitation on the state. Above all, arguing from theology as well as from a strictly secular logic, Locke insists that the state must refrain from attempting to coerce faith, since "the care of the salvation of men's souls cannot belong to the magistrate" (1963, 12). The liberal state does not legislate religion. Elsewhere, in an unpublished work, Locke would press the point further: liberal politics, like liberal pluralism, ought not, as we say, to legislate morality either. "However strange it may seem, . . . the law-maker hath nothing to do with moral virtues and vices, nor ought to enjoin the duties of the second table any otherwise than barely as they are subservient to the good and preservation of mankind under government" (Locke 1993, 194–95). The idea of limited government is part of a complex and in a way bold strategy to remake political life on a new basis: "The soul of the modern development, one may say, is a peculiar realism, consisting in the notion that moral principles and the appeal to moral principles—preaching, sermonizing—are ineffectual, and therefore that one has to seek a substitute for moral principles which would be much more efficacious than ineffectual preaching. Such substitutes were found, for example, in institutions or economics" (Strauss 1989, 242). In a world of freedom, where government is limited and made separate from private society, where the state keeps out of private matters of religious and moral belief, older notions of regimes, deserved rule, and rule itself seem not just antiquated, but wrong.[9]

Finally, another general result of this account of pluralism is a specific view of the nature of the "groups" (in the *Letter*, "churches") that have been shaped according to its requirements. Consistent with the principles of the liberal social contract, only the individual and the state have official status in liberal pluralism—and on this view groups are necessarily subordinate to both. Liberal voluntarism and individualism weaken the authority of groups from below. In liberalism, "individualism" is thus more fundamental than "pluralism" and at the same time shapes it: the authority of mere groups over individuals is in a way morally suspect. Liberalized groups are, as Locke terms them, "voluntary associations" and no more. Religious groups "stand as it were in the same relation to each other as private persons among themselves" (1963, 18). At the same time, not only are groups deprived of any official status in relation to the state (to say nothing of the use of force or compulsion), but the state is supreme in all clashes between itself and the group. Groups such as these accord with both liberal idealism and liberal realism: framed in this way, they are less likely either to be intolerant or to disturb the peace because they have been deprived, in advance, of the power to do so effectively.[10] Liberal pluralism is about limiting groups at least as much as it is about limited government. "Where they have not the power to carry on persecution and to become masters, there they desire to live upon fair terms and preach up toleration."[11]

The Liberal Pluralist Tradition in America: Variations on Essential Themes

Different versions of liberal pluralism appearing in American political thought have taken this basic argument in different directions, but while each may emphasize some one aspect of the pattern appearing in Locke's account—liberal moralism, epistemological skepticism, political realism, and a view of government's role and of the groups arising therefrom—none adds anything essential to the argument that is new.[12] They all continue to combine the central elements in the same basic mix, differing only as to which receives the greatest emphasis. While many later pluralists might repudiate other aspects of Locke's thinking that point to something like capitalism, they abandon nothing essential of his rendering of the pluralist perspective as it appears in his treatment of religion. The striking similarity of all the several different versions of the argument suggests a deep connection between liberal *pluralism* and the heart of the liberal perspective generally.

That Locke's thinking on these matters is clearly visible in the workings of American religious pluralism in particular is perhaps unsurprising, since this is one place where his influence is more or less direct and not easily doubted. This is true in a general way in US Supreme Court First Amendment doctrine, for example, which begins in reflections on individual liberty, takes very seriously the threat to peace that religious conflict poses, and enforces the basic liberal political solution. Even more clearly, the writings of Jefferson and Madison on religion (whom the Court has looked to for authoritative guidance at crucial moments) follow the outline of Locke's thinking fairly directly at almost every step.[13] If Jefferson and Madison differ from Locke it is only by pushing religious pluralism's realist bent farther than Locke does himself (being less deferential to religion and taking a harder line on "separation"). This is visible in *Federalist* 10, where religion is treated no differently from any other group or "faction" in Madison's account of the "regulation of these various and interfering interests" (Madison 1961, 79). A similar sentiment, and one that suggests a telling valuation of religious "diversity," is presented even more forcefully in Jefferson's *Notes on the State of Virginia*: "They [sects] flourish infinitely. Religion is well-supported; of various kinds, indeed, but all good enough; all sufficient to preserve peace and order" (1944b, 276). The role of realism in their stance should not be overstated, however. Madison and Jefferson also clearly argue from the morality of liberty and both rely repeatedly upon a soft skepticism to minimize the claims being made in religious matters.[14] If, in their works, the subordination of liberal morality and its soft skepticism to liberal pluralism's concern for peace and security is somewhat clearer than in Locke's account, it is nevertheless true that the overall form and substance of the argument are the same.

Another obvious point of comparison is to be found in Madison's broader argument in *Federalist* 10. There, liberal pluralism is framed in somewhat harsher terms as a general theory of "factions." Although Locke had already used this language, Madison is said to have followed David Hume to develop this aspect of the argument.[15] (Hamilton's related argument in *Federalist* 9 explicitly follows Montesquieu [Hamilton 1961, 71–76].) Hume also combines all the key elements of the basic pattern—skepticism (soft or hard), a morality of liberty, a concern for peace—in his political thinking. What becomes more pronounced in his discussion of religion is the use of the pejorative language of "faction" to describe groups, and the language of "interest" as the main term to describe what is at stake for groups. In his essay "Of Parties in General," Hume insists that "factions . . . from interest" are "of all factions, . . . the most reasonable," while factions "from principle" (especially religious principle) "seem to have been the origin of all religious wars and divisions" (1889, 130–31). This helps to make explicit something that is only implied in Locke's use of the language of interest. Because moral principle is an important source of political conflict (political conflict that is held to be largely unjustified and hence unnecessary, from the point of view of liberalism's soft skepticism), recasting group politics in the language of interests can help to tame and pacify political life. What later becomes commonplace in liberal accounts of "interest groups" and interest group politics was thus initially a deliberate Enlightenment maneuver arising out of a concern for peace and security. "A landed interest, a manufacturing interest, a mercantile interest, a moneyed interest, with many lesser interests, grow up of necessity in civilized nations, and divide them into different classes. The regulation of these various and interfering interests forms the principal task of modern legislation, and involves the spirit of party and faction in the necessary and ordinary operations of government" (Madison 1961, 78). This step also prepares the way for the unsentimental *solution* proposed in *Federalist* 10 (also prefigured in Hume and, as we have seen, in Locke)—namely, that of allowing a multitude of factions to dissipate their potentially dangerous energies under free institutions.

But while *Federalist* 10 is best known for its tough realism, beginning as it does from the problem of "the violence of faction" and "the instability, injustice, and confusion introduced [by them] into the public councils," it is important not to overlook the ways in which this account of group politics likewise retains the other elements of the liberal pluralist argument (Madison 1961, 77). Madison's assumptions about the weakness of knowledge and the human mind buttress his seemingly pessimistic view of groups and their doings. "The latent causes of faction are . . . sown in the nature of man. . . . As long as the reason of man continues fallible, and he is at liberty to exercise it, different opinions will be formed."[16] Madison also argues, and emphatically so, from fundamental liberal moral principle. To remedy the disease of faction "by destroying [that] liberty . . . , by giving to every citizen the same opinions, the same passions, and the same interests," is for him "worse than the disease" (1961, 78). Madison's liberal prudence is consistent with his liberal principle.

As we move forward in time from Madison, the varieties of liberal pluralism distinguish themselves by emphasizing one or another element of the original, each retaining nonetheless the outline of the whole.

In the first half of the twentieth century, immigrants facing "Americanization" and the pressure to assimilate turned to liberal pluralism as a way to defend themselves on the basis of something quintessentially American. Horace Kallen's "cultural pluralism," arguably the form of liberal pluralism most immediately connected to the question of contemporary multiculturalism, is the best known of these efforts and one that emphasizes liberal pluralism's idealist strand.[17] A leading student of William James, and a contemporary of and collaborator with John Dewey, Kallen might be thought to begin first and foremost from a skepticism that takes the form of James's pragmatist philosophical or ontological or metaphysical pluralism (rejecting all theoretical "absolutist" or "monist" reductionisms). But while Kallen's pragmatist skepticism is very much in evidence, it is the moral framework of liberal democracy—freedom, individualism, toleration, and consent—that predominates in his brief for pluralism.[18] In emphasizing the moral basis of liberal pluralism, Kallen does not forget its realistic aspect but he does press liberal moralism to new extremes.[19]

It would be impossible to exaggerate the extent to which Kallen frames cultural pluralism in terms of the moral postulates of the liberal democratic theory of politics.[20] As a pragmatist, Kallen explicitly makes liberalism his "faith," and he espouses a vision of cultural pluralism that is nothing other than an elaboration of his understanding of "the American Idea" and the principles of the Declaration.[21] "Cultural Pluralism, while not identical with 'good old traditional Americanism,' has to be a growth of that original seed, and is actually one of its truest exfoliations" (1956, 183). Kallen, who held Tom Paine to be "a sober thinker in a new environment," interpreted liberty in a particularly idealistic way, reducing every freedom (including, for example, Roosevelt's four freedoms) to one, that of thought and belief (1924, 52). Freedom of thought and belief, in turn, is likewise conceived of in a very high-minded way: "The civil liberties are initiated in the creative freedom of the artist. The latter is prior because it is primal; it is not freedom in the arts which result from democracy, but democracy which results from freedom in the arts."[22] Kallen (author of a book titled *Secularism is the Will of God* [1954]) sometimes derives cultural pluralism directly from the logic of religious pluralism, though here, too, he emphasizes its moral underpinnings: "The first freedom is the freedom of choice, and its first field cannot be anything other than the inward field of belief and thought and expression. . . . What follows from it in religion indicates its consequence in every other institution of cultural economy" (1956, 74).

Groups for Kallen are understood first and foremost through this moral lens, but such a starting point leads nevertheless to a dramatically realistic appraisal of their status. "The members of organizations can exist without them, can join them and leave them at will. . . . Membership in them is voluntary" (1924, 197). Kallen's commitment to a fairly radical individualism is developed in *Individualism: An American Way of Life*, the central argument of which he simply equates with cultural pluralism (1933, 12). Kallen takes to new heights Locke's view that every "individual decides for himself . . . to join this society or leave that": for Kallen even the individual's "relation to his family . . . is a function of this commitment" (1956, 23). Kallen does not leave it at saying that "cultural pluralism is possible only in a democratic society whose institutions encourage individuality in groups"; his liberal principles indeed require him to admit to a wholly unsentimental view of what the shaping power of liberal pluralism will mean for groups (1924, 43). "The record" suggests that "equal liberty for different individuals" serves "not . . . to abolish or nullify the diversity of groupings, but to alter their associative structure; to change from isolationist, authoritarian, hierarchical configurations to intercommunicative, democratic and congregational ones."²³ Paradoxically, the liberalization of groups does not violate freedom but is for Kallen the meaning of freedom.

A different camp of pluralists, associated with political science in the United States, veer in the opposite direction and emphasize liberal pluralism's realist side. The leading lights of social science pluralism, who became prominent in the 1950s and 1960s, might reject the view that theirs should be counted within the "liberal" pluralist tradition at all. Indeed, at first glance, social science pluralism and the realist outlook that characterizes it appear to originate in a commitment to modern science and scientific method, which might seem to make unlikely any deep moral or ideological commitment to liberalism. When it first appeared—in Arthur Bentley's *The Process of Government* (1908)—this was a description of political life emphasizing groups and "social pressures" in the name of empiricism, a new approach rejecting legal formalism and a rigid focus on government institutions as superficial. Like Bentley, David Truman (whose *Governmental Process* explicitly followed Bentley in important respects) and Robert Dahl (like Truman, a president of the American Political Science Association in the 1960s) understood pluralism to be part of the "attempt to improve our understanding of politics by seeking to explain the empirical aspects of political life by means of methods, theories, and criteria of proof that are acceptable according to the canons, conventions, and assumptions of modern empirical science."²⁴ "Groups," for example, are not to be defined in the terms of liberal morality, as "voluntary associations," and both Bentley and Truman reject accounts of groups that insist on any reductionist individualism.²⁵ Moreover, if social science pluralists emphasize the study of "interests," this is not explicitly tied to the liberal project's deliberate attempt to defuse and de-moralize political life. As Bentley puts it, "the interest I put forward is a specific group interest in some definite course of conduct or activity. It is first, last and all the time strictly empirical."²⁶ Dahl's pluralism in particular begins from an explicit rejection of "Madisonian democracy," especially its reliance on natural right ("the assumptions that made the idea of natural rights intellectually defensible have tended to dissolve in modern times") (1956, 45, 4–33). Likewise, political scientist Nelson Polsby explicitly distinguishes social science pluralism from accounts of pluralism connected to the "intellectual tradition that has some strength in American political theory," one that includes "Madison, Tocqueville, Montesquieu, and Locke" (1980, 153–57).

But social science pluralism fits within the liberal pluralist tradition more than it stands apart from it. This is to some degree plain on the surface, most obviously in its reliance on the language of "interest." Moreover, precisely its realism reflects something more than a scientific impulse. For Dahl, pluralism not only attempts to describe American political reality but is a "relatively efficient system for reinforcing agreement, encouraging moderation, and maintaining peace in a restless and immoderate people" (1956, 151). As its critics on the Left were quick to point out, social scientific pluralism's satisfaction with mere "process equilibrium" and social peace (and its rejection of any notion of a "common" interest) rendered it a conservative political stance in the face of Marxism and other political challenges (including the civil rights revolution).[27] Social science pluralism's anti-utopianism derives from a specifically liberal spirit, not simply a scientific one. Similarly, social science pluralism's connections to pragmatism, and hence to liberalism's soft skepticism, are fairly clear. Bentley coauthored with John Dewey *Knowing and the Known*, which was an extension and clarification of Dewey's general epistemological stance, and Bentley's conception of politics as a loose "process" reflects, in particular, his (and later Truman's) acknowledged debts to pragmatism.[28]

Even on the subject of its moral content, which might at first glance seem to distinguish this version sharply from the other variants of the liberal pluralist tradition, there is remarkable consistency. Its scientific protestations of objectivity and value-neutrality aside, social science pluralism seems to presuppose the importance of individual liberty. Dahl went so far as to claim that it was "not [his] purpose . . . to make a case for polyarchy" (his account of the liberal political arrangement), and he in fact boasted (or joked) that his scientific rendering of polyarchy could benefit its opponents just as well as its supporters.[29] But liberal moral and political aspirations inform the social science pluralism of Dahl through and through, removing any doubts about its inclusion in the liberal pluralist pantheon. While David Truman was honest enough to make his embrace of liberal morality fairly clear, a similar reliance is visible in Dahl's work as well.[30] Despite his explicit rejection of "natural right," Dahl does not hesitate to enlist (in only partly concealed terms) the morality of freedom and equality.[31] Indeed, in the end Dahl became a democratic political theorist and moralist.[32]

A moral commitment to individual freedom would seem in fact to provide one crucial source of social science pluralism's brand of soft skepticism. In a debate over the use of "interest" as a point of departure (from a Left critic who had insisted on a distinction between true and false interests), Polsby claims that "there is no method for determining when analysts [like the critic] are choosing better than actors in the actors' behalf and when they are not" (1980, 224). For Polsby this is ultimately a moral rather than an epistemological stance since he denies "that observers [like the objector] are *entitled* to assert what conduct and what choices are in the interests of actors, regardless of the actors' own choice behaviour" (1980, 222; emphasis added).

More generally, social science pluralism is misunderstood if it is not seen first, politically, as a defense of liberal democratic politics presented in scientific and nonideological terms. In the context of the Cold War, and Marxist and other critiques of American democracy from the Left, the view that political power was distributed pluralistically, and not controlled by powerful "elites," served to advance the cause of liberal politics under the guise of claims of mere empirical or scientific accuracy. Social science pluralist descriptive accounts—like Dahl's polyarchy or Truman's "governmental process"—are in the end no more than a translation of liberal democracy into purportedly neutral terms that strain but nevertheless fail to avoid the pattern of liberal thinking. "Behavioralism was at its core an affirmation of liberalism, . . . a commitment to liberalism qua pluralism" (Gunnell 2004, 221).

A more recent incarnation of liberal pluralism in America (and beyond) takes the form of what William Galston calls the "values pluralism movement in contemporary moral philosophy," a movement that is one site of a vast swirling conversation about pluralism and diversity among political theorists that has been ongoing since the late 1980s. Ultimately, values pluralists may be said to place something akin to Locke's soft skepticism and his claim that "the diversity of opinions . . . cannot be avoided" at the heart of liberal pluralism.[33] Like Kallen, values pluralists are "idealistic," but their idealism is perhaps less naïve or open than Kallen's embrace of the "American Idea." These are in the main logic-chopping analytical philosophers, and their questions are precisely the clarification and ordering of different kinds of moral claims that compete with one another (values pluralism is sometimes termed moral or ethical pluralism).[34] The problem confronted in values pluralism is not merely the diversity of opinions but, in Isaiah Berlin's formulation, "a plurality of values, equally genuine, equally ultimate, above all equally objective; incapable therefore of being ordered in a timeless hierarchy, or judged in terms of some one absolute standard" (1991, 79). Values pluralists differ as to *why* disagreement about vital matters is inescapable (a debate about the limits of skepticism, relativism, absolutism), but they agree that it is the first fact for political reflection. Michael Walzer states the connection of the moral and the epistemological at work here: "You have to look at the world in a receptive and generous way to see a pluralism of Berlin's sort, i.e., a pluralism that encompasses a variety of genuine but incommensurable values. And you also have to look at the world in a skeptical way. . . . And receptivity, generosity, and skepticism are, if not liberal values, then qualities of mind that make it possible to accept liberal values" (1995a, 31).

Values pluralists also agree, by and large, about the basic outlines of liberal pluralism and liberal politics in practice; where they disagree is over *which* liberal moral principle—freedom, equality, toleration—provides the superior ground for the overall argument. But their focus on questions of values or morality does not make them any less realistic; indeed, the central practical conclusion drawn by values pluralists is the quintessentially liberal one about the impropriety of moral intransigence. As Berlin puts it, "values clash," and "if these ultimate values by which we live are to be pursued, then compromises, trade-offs, arrangements have to be made if the worst is not to happen"—a stance he embraces despite the fact that it may appear "too tame, too reasonable, too bourgeois."[35] Those who make *liberal* morality their business, even or especially with a heavy dose of skepticism, seem inescapably to be in the business of promoting social peace.

Limited Government and "Political Liberalism"

Now to this point I have focused on what I take to be the three core premises of liberal pluralism, but I have said less about the standard conclusions drawn from them in the liberal political arrangement, the idea of the public-private divide and some concept of "limited" government. I have postponed this question to avoid having to debate it more than once. One could certainly object that, at least since the New Deal, *this* aspect of liberal pluralism has come under fire. Even if we pass over for now the impact of the civil rights revolution (since this is what we are examining), legal reforms concerning organized labor and changes in interest group politics that accompanied the rise of the welfare/regulatory state already challenge this aspect of liberal pluralism in important ways. Is it sensible today to consider "limited government" an important element of liberal pluralism?

The substantive meaning of "limited government" and the location of the dividing line between public and private have undoubtedly shifted over the past century, but these defining ideas have remained no less important to liberal pluralism later than they ever were earlier. All the more recent advocates of the liberal pluralist argument, beginning with Kallen (who was an outspoken defender of the New Deal), take for granted that what they are doing is expressing the extent of the diversity that should be protected in the private sphere. To be sure, the most important meaning of the private sector no longer has to do with the free market or private property. But other interpretations of the private liberty protected by liberalism today fill the void created by the (relative) decline of the ideal of private enterprise. The result has been the emergence of two competing (Left and Right) interpretations of freedom or limited government. Despite disagreements over where to draw various lines, religious liberty and the separation of church and state are certainly alive and well in the United States. Freedom of speech, "due process" protections of individuals in their dealings with the police and the courts, and the discovery of a general principle of "privacy" (or personal liberty) are all central features of the development of American constitutional law in the past century. The very terms of "cultural" and "values" pluralism, staking out the private domains liberal politics is to protect, correspond perfectly with this wider tendency. Kallen's statement of the issue, from the point of view both of the state and of the group/individual, still holds. On the one side, "the function of the law remains 'to render unto everyone his right' according to the American Idea, to keep the ways of life equally open to the enterprise of whoever in good faith chooses to seek his spiritual or material fortune upon them" (1956, 74). On the other side, liberal pluralism does not exist if groups and individuals are not free to participate in the "free commerce in thoughts and things with all mankind" (1956, 100). If economic and regulatory reforms from the New

Deal onward have altered how we understand the private sphere, they have by no means rendered the idea of the private sphere a nullity for liberal pluralism. (It should also be said that the ideas reflecting the older view—the idea of private enterprise and the language of interest group pluralism—are not exactly dead in America either.)

Even John Rawls, the most prominent liberal theorist of the past half century, whose liberalism is so deeply opposed to Lockean liberalism on the question of equality and government's role in attaining it, nevertheless seems compelled in the end to embrace fully *every* important element of Locke's pluralism. Rawls's later work *Political Liberalism* is precisely a recasting of his earlier *A Theory of Justice* to make it compatible with the practical challenges posed by pluralism (1993; 1971). This is *not* because, writing in 1993, Rawls felt that he had not previously gone far enough to deal with questions raised by the civil rights movement. Instead, he returned emphatically to the essential core of traditional liberal pluralism and readily conceded that his discussion of diversity does not extend to questions of "race, ethnicity, and gender," saying that his "emphasis on the Reformation and the long controversy about toleration as the origin of liberalism" may seem "dated."[36] It is no surprise that Rawls has been criticized by feminists and others connected more closely with civil rights politics.[37]

Rawls's famous earlier book, *A Theory of Justice*, provided an egalitarian interpretation of liberal moral principle. This is already something of a shift from the traditional emphasis on liberty (and one that many of the values pluralists also adopt), but it is far from a wholesale abandonment of the morality of liberty. Rawls clearly presents himself as a champion of certain freedoms—freedom of speech and association and, most importantly from the point of view of liberal pluralism, "liberty of conscience."[38] More to the point, later, in *Political Liberalism*, Rawls revises *A Theory of Justice* to add two things: a heavy and explicit reliance on liberal skepticism, on the one hand, and a new emphasis on "stability," on the other. One could not ask for a clearer illustration of the power of the pluralist framework to order the minds of those who embrace and wish to speak authoritatively on behalf of liberalism. Rawls's emphatic reliance on liberalism's soft skepticism, announced in a much heralded article titled "Justice as Fairness: Political Not Metaphysical" shapes the argument for political liberalism decisively.[39] "We try, so far as we can, neither to assert nor to deny any particular comprehensive religious, philosophical, or moral view, or its associated theory of truth and the status of values."[40] But for Rawls, the correction most emphasized is to his earlier "account of stability" in *A Theory of Justice*—which was "unrealistic and must be recast" (1993 xvi–xvii). "Now the problem is this. A modern democratic society is characterized not simply by a pluralism of comprehensive religious, philosophical, and moral doctrines but by a pluralism of *incompatible* yet reasonable comprehensive doctrines" (1993, xvi; emphasis added). Reframing liberalism as "political not metaphysical" is one way Rawls addresses the problem. Another is by reference to what he calls the "overlapping consensus," a practical device that looks a lot like traditional liberal pluralism, to make agreement more likely in the face of the many (potentially contentious) "comprehensive doctrines" that populate modern democracies.[41] Such concerns come in for Rawls only at "stage two" of his project, since moral concerns come first, but they are nonetheless important enough to justify an overhaul of the original (1993, 140–41). Rawls's "political liberalism," then, is an account of liberal moralism joined with liberal skepticism and liberal realism that together address the "serious problem" of pluralism.

A Worldly Wise Pluralism?

To repeat, in all these more recent accounts of liberal pluralism nothing essential is new. Liberal pluralism's soft skepticism may take different forms (the pragmatism of Kallen, the positions debated among the values pluralists), but it is never seriously challenged. Social scientific pluralists claim "scientific" objectivity and method as the basis of their realist appraisal of interest groups, but this does not ultimately stop them from coming down on the side of liberty. Some advance liberal pluralism under a different name ("political liberalism"). Different advocates may emphasize different parts but none abandons any essential component of the basic amalgamation.

Liberal pluralism is not the sum total of liberal political theory (it is not *directly* bound up with arguments about natural right, for example, and it says very little or nothing about equality, property, representation, or institutional arrangements) but it does carry with it a considerable portion of the liberal sensibility. What do the consistently recurring principles and concerns of liberal pluralism contribute to or reveal about the liberal democratic outlook more generally? It is, to begin with, a combination that is fraught with tensions. Do not liberty and toleration sometimes ask us to make sacrifices inconsistent with the realistic spirit that makes a politics of peace and security our guide? If we are seriously committed to either liberal morality or liberal realism, do we not violate at some point even the soft skepticism of liberal pluralism?

But whatever the ultimate questions that may be raised about it, this ingenious human contrivance, which has long endured through centuries of fluctuating group and political wranglings, was no "logic without design." The perspective of liberal pluralism is a moral one that aims above all at finding social peace among people with contradictory viewpoints and conflicting interests. It is a tough political realism that confronts deep disagreement without ever abandoning basic moral commitments of restraint (freedom, toleration, keep the peace). Its appeal includes the fact that those who adopt its outlook may think themselves simultaneously tough, intellectually sophisticated, morally serious, yet also reasonably accommodating and tolerant of their fellows—an apparently powerful combination. Moreover, in its skepticism, as well as in other ways, liberal pluralism provides a distant and, in a way, condescending view of actual political life from a perspective that understands itself to be both morally and intellectually superior to, but also somehow responsible for, its stresses and strains. If the original core of liberal democratic modernity is a Promethean conquest of nature, the enduring spirit of its political understanding as revealed by pluralism is a paradoxical one of detached devotion to managing a world of intractable human conflict that borders on chaos but that may in fact be contained with wise or prudent care. Liberal statesmanship is a knowing and somewhat resigned, perhaps tragic, quest for peace and toleration amid largely blind and potentially dangerous confusion. "Among so many who are not good," a decent, public-spirited, person must take the world as it is. Such a view may not ultimately be unproblematic, and it is not clear that its most thoughtful progenitors (Locke, e.g.) thought of it simply or entirely in such terms, but the source of its enduring appeal to the intellectuals who have advanced it ever since would seem to be located here.

It would be an amazing coincidence if the success of liberal pluralism—a position reinvigorated and reiterated in a variety of different guises over the course of several hundred years—were not in some way connected to some wisdom of its design. If liberal pluralism aims at peace, we must say that it has succeeded at least on that level (again, I would point, above all, to religion). One could say (and contemporary multiculturalism will say) that in aiming at peace, it aims too low. But in politics one should not scoff at success of even the most basic kind. If the end is peace (or "security," as Locke and Montesquieu say), then that means skepticism—and even liberty—are above all means to peace (means more or less within the reach of intellectuals willing to engage politically with the weapons of ideas, we might add). Skepticism weakens every claim of groups, especially moral (and religious) claims. Liberty (or individualism or voluntarism or toleration) works, morally, to supplant other moral claims, especially those high claims of virtue and justice that incline people to get angry and to fight. On the basis of this understanding of things, liberalism's practical institutional framework—limited government, separation of public and private—may be set forth without apology. The view of groups associated with liberal pluralism that is the overall result of this end and these means is one of weakened, domesticated groups, groups of some obvious importance but whose ultimate status is made less exalted and more worldly (we should never forget that the original target of liberal pluralism was religion). Sober, restrained, and moderate, liberal pluralism, we may say, goes some distance to check the worst tendencies of political life. Liberalism surely complicates the rule of those who, in advancing their own interests, are certain they know what is best for everyone else and welcome the opportunity to use force and the political order to impose their will—which, the historical record shows, is often no better than aggressive blind stupidity armed. Contemporary political science (even the social science pluralists) may perhaps not be permitted, in the name of scientific value-neutrality, to endorse liberal pluralism, but an older view of political science reminds us to be impressed by any scheme that makes politics less harsh and oppressive than it otherwise is inclined to be. From that point of view the value of what liberal pluralism has achieved is hard to deny. This does not settle the question of whether peace or justice ought to be the aim of democratic pluralism, but it does require us not to ignore the genuine contributions of liberal pluralism.

At the very least, we may say that in the following discussion we are not wrong to assume that the liberal pluralist tradition has an identifiable and more or less consistent logic that has endured over time. The more than family resemblance among the many different versions of liberal pluralism in that tradition makes all the more striking contemporary multiculturalism's clear departures from it.

Chapter 8

THE NEW PLURALISM AND THE OLD

Every pluralism is a mental construct, an attempt to simplify social life as it is or as we think it ought to be by reference to somewhat abstract generalizations about "groups." As such, it is partly a product of the tendency to "theorize," and hence to universalize, social description in a world where both ideology and social science are powerful forces. There are important limitations to this way of looking at things, not the least of which is a tendency to obscure the (always partial) political dimension of social life. Nevertheless, the manifest differences between Banks's multiculturalism and the outlines of the liberal pluralist tradition suggest that the examination of politics at the level of accounts of pluralism can usefully illuminate major changes in political life that are otherwise surprisingly obscured from those who live in and through them. Pluralism's use of broad generalities and abstractions, and its employment of moral argumentation, may soften hard political edges, but when these elements themselves change significantly—or when we witness the emergence of a new and different general moral-descriptive language of pluralism—then we are compelled to look beneath the surface for the deeper political explanation of such a transformative development. Pluralist frameworks helpfully draw together and sum up many different aspects of social life, but in so doing they do not simply, or always successfully, hide the political logic that is at work.

In this chapter, I will contrast our two pluralisms, sometimes from the point of view of multiculturalism, at other times from the point of view of liberal pluralism. (The next two chapters explore in detail the moral dimension of this comparison, although we will unavoidably touch upon it here as well.) I rely upon Banks's thinking as a key point of departure for this task, considering postmodernist multiculturalism only occasionally, where appropriate. As I said at the outset, to emphasize the differences between liberalism and postmodernist multiculturalism would skew the overall result and obscure the important things that Banks's unadulterated connection to anti-discrimination politics can teach us. Indeed, the opposition between postmodernist multiculturalism and liberalism is so stark—the former openly rejecting the latter as a false and oppressive metanarrative (along with Eurocentrism, the Enlightenment, etc.)—that such a contrast would not be very revealing or helpful. More attached to radical criticism, postmodernist multiculturalists seem not to have given much thought to what liberalism represents or to the heritage they would so cavalierly toss aside. The fact that Banks largely sidesteps liberal pluralism is already an interesting fact inviting our attention, but in sketching in detail an *alternative* to it, he makes possible an investigation that illuminates both.

While my primary purpose here originates in a certain view of political science, in an attempt to understand from that point of view both group politics and the character of the American regime at present, I emphatically do not approach the task with any hope of contributing to some universal account of group politics as such. This study was written partly to show the limitations of the purportedly neutral and scientifically general accounts attempted by rational choice theorists like Mancur Olson (1965) or, earlier, by pluralists like Bentley and Truman and their interest group theory imitators (the same goes for "social movement theory" as well). The examination of multiculturalism suggests the need to remain close to the plane of common sense of actual political life, to seek out the inner logic of a given pluralism by following its lead, by taking it as it comes, and not by imposing any nonpolitical "scientific" framework (e.g., the psychological assumptions of contemporary rational choice method or theories of identity) upon it. When we let these pluralisms speak for themselves, the utility of operating at the level of the regime, of the political order, as the cause of our view of the world, becomes apparent.[1] It would undoubtedly be possible to study multiculturalism from the perspective of any number of general explanatory accounts of how human groups function in the abstract; and while such approaches do wish to be empirical in their focus on the causes internal to groups (beginning with the empirical facts of individuals and their interests, or groups and their identities, e.g.), their inattention to the regime as the formal cause of the whole is a decisive limitation. For the formative power of the political order is also an undeniable, indeed obvious, empirical fact of the greatest importance; groups and the individuals within those groups are decisively shaped by the political order in advance, especially by its moral terms and limitations.

If this starting point does not accord with the common practices of contemporary social science, failing to proceed in this way leads the so-called scientific approaches into serious difficulties. Most relevant to us, theories of groups and group politics that do not begin from the political order as a whole are blind to the obviously central defining terms of both multiculturalism and traditional liberal pluralism, terms that purportedly scientific, general renderings of group politics simply build into their systems without reflection. As we have already begun to see, even the terms "individual," "interest," "group," and "identity" are not without political meaning and importance. In the end, social scientific accounts of interest group pluralism, or the shift from them to new theories of social movements, are ultimately best understood as *evidence* of the political order's power to shape the way we think about social groups, to include even the very terms of social scientific description: "The 'political' nuclei, which are meant [in political science] to supply explanations for the political things proper, are already molded, nay constituted by the political order or the regime within which they occur: an American small group is not a [Soviet] Russian small group" (Strauss 1962, 312).

Multiculturalism and Liberal Pluralism Compared

Both multiculturalism and liberal pluralism try to describe all at once many different features of social and political life; comparing them reveals a number of fairly sharp contrasts. Revealed in these differences are at least some nontrivial attributes of anti-discrimination politics. Our two forms of pluralism begin from different views of the problem of social diversity and, correspondingly, hold different views of how to try to manage it. Both are pessimistic about groups and group politics, and both are wary of groups, but for different reasons. Each speaks a distinctive moral language; each uses different terms of social description; and each is informed throughout by a different spirit or sensibility. The two pluralisms also define and see groups—and their relations to one another, to government, and to individuals—in different terms. These many differences often take the form of important disagreements and where multiculturalism's logic does not directly contradict that of liberal pluralism, it often competes with it.

That liberal pluralism is not identical with the pluralism arising out of anti-discrimination politics is established by several elementary but noteworthy facts we have already confronted in the preceding discussion. Kallen's 1915 account of cultural pluralism had perhaps taken liberalism as far as it could go in answering the challenges not just of anti-immigrant xenophobia but also of anti-Semitism and racism. But civil rights reforms of the 1960s began by rejecting the limitations imposed by the liberal legal and political framework. Even as late as the mid-1950s, reflecting back on the cultural pluralism idea he had first developed forty years earlier, Kallen did not indicate that the problem of discrimination (against Blacks or any other group) had properly registered as a fundamental question for him. This is a failing for which he has been widely criticized (somewhat unjustly, in my view) in the post-civil rights world.[2] For Locke and Jefferson and Madison, it almost goes without saying, the question of discrimination in the private sector barely even comes up.[3] Banks's explicit disavowal of liberal cultural pluralism as an inadequate "antecedent" to multiculturalism, and in no way its cause, as well as his reworking of the meaning of freedom whenever he appeals to it, both point to the same disconnect between the old and the new. But to say that liberalism did not reach the shore of anti-discrimination is only a thought-provoking first step to considering the substantial differences between them.

Both multiculturalism and liberal pluralism may be said to begin negatively, from somewhat pessimistic assumptions about the *problem* posed by groups to healthy political life. On the traditional liberal view, this is a more or less general wariness concerning groups ("factions") and their tendency to conflict and strife, their threat to political stability, to civic peace, and to the security and freedom of the individual that it is liberalism's job to secure under the basic terms of the social contract. Multiculturalism's prime concern is much more precisely located in the specific concrete harm of discrimination, a sign in turn of a broader intergroup dynamic in which a struggle for social domination is central. Multiculturalism is the more pessimistic of the two because its view of the basic problem suggests a darker view of human nature. Where liberal pluralism holds group competition and conflict to be the inescapable byproduct of human self-interest, human diversity, and the inevitability of human error and disagreement over matters high and low, multiculturalism claims that there is something in human beings that inclines them to group together and then, as groups, to seek to dominate others outside their group for no reason other than the twisted satisfaction that comes from being on top—and often on grounds (race, etc.) that ought not to matter. This is a problem that will not go away, since discrimination seems to arise "whenever groups with different racial, ethnic and cultural characteristics interact" (Banks 1999a, 59). The problem to be remedied also looms larger in the here and now, is more vital and real, and is thus more urgently in need of confrontation, in multiculturalism than in liberal pluralism. Discrimination is for some a lived experience of the present and a painful memory of the past that makes some solution to it an immediate necessity, whereas the factional strife that is liberalism's concern—even religious strife—may seem in the United States (though not, to be sure, in many other places) an ancient memory, more a theoretical possibility than a pressing reality. Moreover, in the liberal perspective, the danger posed by groups is only something to be dispensed with on the way to a bigger political project; groups themselves are not taken seriously except insofar as they fit into or are a threat to the larger aim of guaranteeing security, liberty, and prosperity. With anti-discrimination, protecting some groups from other groups is the whole point. A full appreciation of the problem of discrimination is, in addition, one that liberalism is not inclined to confront fully because of the limitations imposed by the public-private divide. Liberalism is willing to permit or entertain a certain amount of ugliness in private life—a certain amount of "private injustice," as Justice Waite put it—as part of the give and take of democratic life. Thus for multiculturalism, liberalism itself is part of the problem that must be addressed.

Another way of stating the starting points of multiculturalism and liberal pluralism is by reference to what is at stake for each. For multiculturalism what must be confronted is to begin with the felt harm, and the personal indignity and insult suffered, by victims of racism, sexism, and other forms of discrimination. But the harm of discrimination is not merely a matter of "recognition"; unchecked it is a threat to every conceivable good, including material well-being and even life itself. As civil rights lawyer and legal scholar Paul Brest put it, "because acts of discrimination tend to occur in pervasive patterns, their victims suffer especially frustrating, cumulative and debilitating injuries" (Brest 1976, 8). In addition, multiculturalism holds that group-on-group discrimination affects individuals at the fundamental level of their identities, with all that is thereby implied in terms of human well-being and fulfillment. (Postmodernist multiculturalists would go even further at this point, to say that discrimination is part of a struggle for the plane on which the very cultural or mental depiction of reality that we use to navigate life is constructed.) The stakes are made higher still by the fact that the dangers associated with discrimination are faced collectively by members of groups bound together by their shared suffering or vulnerability. Self-interest there surely is here, but the commonality of interest among members of discrimination groups means that when we think of the threat of discrimination, we ordinarily think of others to whom we are tied—and thus necessarily invoke the language of justice and injustice.

What is at stake for liberal pluralism is not so much the specific concerns of groups but the threat they pose to the good order of the body politic. Every account of what is at stake for groups themselves seems aimed precisely at minimizing their claims. Above all, the emphasis on the *interests* of groups points in this direction—where interest is not obviously anything more than the *self*-interest of individuals or the collective self-interest of groups. This reductionism is embraced explicitly and without apology in liberal pluralism, and it is intended precisely to lower the stakes of group politics. Political life so conceived becomes a less morally charged matter of presiding over competition among groups, whose squabbling is or ought to be readily amenable to compromise. People are more likely to fight if their political disagreements concern religion, fundamental justice, the greatest good, or the highest things; the history of liberal democracy, on the other hand, seems to prove that they can be made content with bargaining for their piece of the pie. The spirit—and the remarkable achievement—of liberal politics is well summarized in Jefferson's formulation: "It does me no injury for my neighbor to say there are twenty gods, or no God. It neither picks my pocket nor breaks my leg" (1944b, 275). Interests are not negligible, but neither does their invocation tend to rouse the spirit so vigorously as do anti-discrimination's more intensely personal and openly moral claims. It is on such a basis as this that liberal pluralism can become in practice mainly a framework for thinking about generally peaceful intergroup competition (for Kallen, a "fellowship of freedom and cooperation").

Now, one might insist that this understates what is at stake in liberal pluralism. Is not the chief goal securing *liberty*, and do not people feel as strongly about liberty as they do about justice? There is something to this, but it is important to see how the morality of liberty also works, paradoxically, to de-moralize politics—and thus to minimize the kinds of claims made by groups. Liberty is a moral claim that has the effect, at least to some degree, of shaking off the yoke of other, potentially stronger, moral claims. Moreover, liberty is above all for *individuals* and its guarantee thus comes at the expense of groups. What is at stake for voluntary associations, liberal groups defined by liberty, is not unimportant, but the claims they make are more likely to be flexible, and made in an accommodating spirit.

These different starting points give each of our two pluralisms its own sensibility or feel. Liberalism views the world of groups (and hence pluralism) as, at best, a second-order concern, as the source of potential obstacles to more important things (like building a stable, prosperous, enlightened society). As a result, liberal pluralism is somewhat detached about the doings of the groups under its sway—aloof, philosophical, and somewhat condescending in its attitude toward their wranglings. This is very far from the basic sentiment of multiculturalism, which is respectfully attuned to victim groups and committed to their protection. Because so much is at stake in anti-discrimination politics, and because legally proscribed discrimination is held not to be justified by any human impulse that will bear scrutiny, multiculturalism sees the need for, and does not hesitate to insist upon, elementary norms of correct interpersonal treatment. Multiculturalism's most immediate or primary response to the problem of discrimination is thus a moral response, a demand of basic justice. Its political instinct is also different. Confronting group life directly—defending those under threat, resisting those who threaten—is the vital and urgent business of anti-discrimination and multiculturalism from start to finish. The spirit of the anti-discrimination effort is characterized by the high moral seriousness of the protection of the innocent from injustice; its watchword is vigilance; it is characterized by a sense of constant urgency and a willingness to do whatever it takes to make justice a reality. The fight against discrimination and its pressing urgency means that multiculturalism cannot but be, as Banks says, "inherently emotive, personal, conflictual, and involving" (1994a, 96).

Viewing the problems of political life that appear at the level of groups differently, multiculturalism and liberal pluralism naturally propose different approaches or schemes to address them. If we begin from the terms of liberal theory, the question may be stated provisionally as that of the role of the "state." For liberalism, the main strategy is to structure things so that groups are *deprived* of any power to do harm—above all, in the division of the world into public and private realms, the idea of the "separation" of groups and the state. In this context it is crucial to see that, in the pattern-setting and quintessentially liberal approach worked out in the case of religious groups ("groups" that had, of course, made significant political claims in the past), the separation of church and state means, above all, denying to the former the power and resources of the latter: the beginning point of the liberal politics of religion is that every law must have a (merely) secular purpose. Once groups are deprived of all overt and direct political power, the policy of the state toward them is to be one of "laissez-faire," leaving them alone to seek their own destinies. To repeat Kallen's formula, "the function of the law remains . . . to keep the ways of life equally open to the enterprise of whoever in good faith chooses to seek his spiritual or material fortune upon them" (1956, 74). To be sure, groups thus conceived may have influence reflected through representative institutions, but this is indirect and not recognized in an official way. Indeed, when interest groups have too much power (captive bureaucracies, "iron triangles"), this is thought to be a violation of the liberal ideal. "Corporatism" is still a liberal term of abuse. In theory, the state's only job is to remain "neutral" among the different groups operating in the private sphere. Stated in terms of liberal pluralism's realist strand, a relatively passive state sets the stage for the sort of intergroup competition within a complex modern society that is to render "factious combinations less to be dreaded," in a counterbalancing of their harmful effects that weakens all groups and lessens the political danger posed by any one of them. Moreover, while the public-private divide and "separation" may seem a passive policy, leaving groups to pursue their own interests, it is also a scheme designed to keep group designs in bounds.

Applied to race and ethnicity, the logic of neutrality and separation becomes the ideal of "color-blind constitutionalism." Will Kymlicka disparages this position as a policy of "benign neglect," but for libertarian political theorist Chandran Kukathas a "politics of indifference" is precisely what is called for.[4] "The liberal state is indifferent to these matters. . . . From a liberal point of view, it does not matter what happens to the identities of particular groups or to the identities of individuals" (Kukathas 2003, 250).

The contrast with multiculturalism on this level is especially clear. For multiculturalism and anti-discrimination, the liberal laissez-faire solution for groups is plainly inadequate, marked off most decisively in traditional liberalism's constitutional incapacity even to notice private sector discrimination and its past history of not doing anything about it. The reality of discrimination means that overbearing groups have *already* succeeded in dominating others in practices that ignore liberalism's division of the world into public and private realms. In response to that now-unacceptable possibility, a much more vigorous harnessing of the legal and political order to intervene directly in group politics and to attempt to manage it more closely is thought to be unavoidable. Whether my neighbor believes in twenty gods or no god is one thing, whether he or she is a racist, sexist, or homophobe is evidently quite another. Anti-discrimination policy is the effort made in a world where state (public sector) "non-discrimination" has clearly failed. The fight against discrimination requires a much more hands-on approach to intergroup relations. The complex and ambitious effort launched by the 1964 Civil Rights Act begins by harnessing the considerable resources of government to regulate the domains of public and private life in the name of a new and explicitly moral standard of behavior. But, as we saw in chapter 3, the legal framework that began with that essential mandate has expanded considerably according to a new set of powerful internal imperatives. In a relatively short period of time, anti-discrimination efforts became an effective campaign extending from the public sector of government to the economic sphere and the workplace, to every institution of public and private education, to relations among individuals in "society" (neighborhoods, schools, places of recreation and leisure), and to various kinds of private speech and thought. This new legal-political arrangement has, moreover, turned the public-private divide on its head, making privatized enforcement of legal requirements a more pervasive and forceful instrument of the new political order than any strictly governmental effort could have been. Our examination of multicultural education in particular has given us many reasons to think that anti-discrimination politics is far from reluctant to employ not only government but also the educational establishment (public and private) and, of course, individual educators trained up under the new order for the purpose of remaking society and its individuals according to its imperatives. Indeed, education—civic, political, moral—has always been an indispensable tool of the anti-discrimination effort and one backed with the force of law in many ways. This much already renders inadequate any account of civil rights that takes its bearings from some view of the proper limitations of the role of the public sector or "the state."

Tamed Groups, Politicized Groups

To this point we have focused our attention on how multiculturalism and liberal pluralism assess the challenge or problem of pluralism and their corresponding responses to it at the most general level of the political order taken as a whole. What is the result of all this for groups and for the dynamic of group politics that follows in each case?

If liberal pluralism is a deliberate strategy to domesticate or tame groups by diminishing them and limiting their claims, we should not be surprised if success has had a corresponding effect on groups. Deprived of political authority in advance by "separation," liberal pluralism's groups are also weakened by liberalism's commitment to individualism and freedom, which deny them any authority over their members. Groups thus conceived are *no more* than "voluntary associations." Liberal individualism guarantees what political theorists today term a "right of exit," which is of course a right to exit one's group. The predominance of individualism cannot but come at the expense of groups shaped by it. The overall result is a world where, as Kallen puts it, "modes of association develop and pass away; it is individuality, entering and leaving them, which endures" (1933, 14). "The stability of . . . 'ethnoid group patterns' seems to me to be continually subject to battering from competing organizations of interest, and to depend for its continuity on how far the members who are its life feel that it assures them freedom, fellowship and fulfillment" (1956, 200). The claims that may be made by liberal pluralism's groups are, as we have seen, deliberately de-moralized: these groups not only lack any special state sanction but must be viewed as somewhat *dubious* interest groups or factions. To the extent that liberal groups are understood morally—in the morality of liberty, individualism, and voluntarism—that logic serves to protect individuals *from* groups and to deprive groups direct access to the political domain ("separation"). Even or especially liberal morality thus further depoliticizes and deflates the claims of liberalized groups. Liberal pluralism's skepticism about the claims made on behalf of groups has a similar diminishing effect. One may say that liberal pluralism intentionally *liberalizes* groups, seeking, as Kallen readily admits, to "alter their associative structure; to change [them] from isolationist, authoritarian, hierarchical configurations to intercommunicative, democratic and congregational ones" (1956, 180). Something like this also follows generally from the most formal terms of the liberal political outlook, where the only relationship that counts is that between individuals as rights bearers and the state. The upshot is that groups in the liberal scheme are undercut from above and below, subordinated both to the state and to the individual. A policy of laissez-faire for groups can be imagined on the liberal pluralist view only because it deals with groups that have been liberalized in this way, groups made much less likely to assert themselves politically or to cause trouble.

By contrast, multiculturalism's groups are defined fairly precisely by the political situation in which those experiencing discrimination ordinarily find themselves. In the terms of political psychology employed by Banks that have by now become commonplace, members of anti-discrimination groups see themselves as sharing identities that are, at least partly, ascriptive or given, and partly the product of social construction. But it is crucial not to leave it at this somewhat arid level of social scientific description, for these identities are forged above all by a collective experience of perceived injustice. "Multicultural education suggests a type of education which is concerned with the cultural groups within American society that are the victims of discrimination and assaults because of their unique cultural characteristics" (Banks 1977a, 74). These are not groups framed in terms of liberal individualism, voluntarism, and freedom; anti-discrimination groups are literally victim groups of a specific kind. This context, as well as the mix of ascription and social construction in the identities of these groups, orients them naturally in the direction of political engagement. If there is choice or freedom for such groups, it is not to be found in the discrimination they suffer from outside (which is linked in some cases in obvious ways to their shared unchosen characteristics). But crucially, the relative status of ascriptive identity for different groups is not set in stone. According to multiculturalism, some reworking of a group's identity, to elevate its social status, *can* be made a matter of social or political construction, if the machinery of politics is properly set to make that happen. To that end, anti-discrimination victim groups necessarily try to renegotiate the terms of their identity politically in the direction of some new and better version of the place or standing of their group. The social or political construction of group identity is both the disease and the cure. If group discrimination is one's starting point, "freedom" or laissez-faire looks like passive acquiescence to the rule of somebody else and to the possibility that others will construct my group identity for me in ways that are harmful to me and mine. On such a view it would not be possible, obviously, to accept a solution extending only to the public but not to the private sector.

It must also be said that multicultural groups are more than "interest" groups, that their claims are ones that the political order must attend to with greater solicitude. While it is true that discrimination affects the interests of its victims (in a way, all interests all at the same time), to speak in such terms does not capture the moral dimension—the challenge to dignity, the palpable sense of injustice of group-based subordination—characterizing the politics of anti-discrimination. The claims of anti-discrimination groups are first and foremost moral claims, and the language of "interest" (or even "recognition") does not fully capture what is at stake.

The relationship between groups and their individual *members* likewise differs in each of these accounts of pluralism. In liberalism, the individual is supreme; a crucial guarantee of liberal pluralism is that no group has authority over any of its members. It is true that anti-discrimination groups do not attempt to exert any overt authority over individuals within them. Nevertheless, from at least one side of multiculturalism's group-differentiated perspective, victims of discrimination may be said to be bound more tightly to the groups that are thus singled out for negative treatment. This is so first because individuals are held to have little or no choice in the matter and second because a collective experience of victimization and oppression provides a stronger bond than the ties of most voluntary associations. Because the multicultural group "serves as a supportive environment for the individual and helps to protect him or her from the harshness and discrimination which he or she might experience in the wider society," the multicultural understanding of the relationship between individuals and groups makes room for "group solidarity and identity" that do not register in liberal pluralism.[5] These are bonds of "solidarity as unity among members of an oppressed group, in a context of marginalization and struggle" and, as such, they have a kind of moral substance—in a shared sense of injustice and at points a call to personal sacrifice on behalf of others—not routinely part of the experience or self-understanding of most liberalized groups (Sleeter and Soriano 2012, 9). As in the title of a prominent book on identity politics, anti-discrimination politics is "not only for myself" (Minow 1997). (Religion under the old liberal framework is of course an exception to this rule, but it is a very special one.)[6]

Generally speaking, a great deal follows from the fact that where liberalism seeks to depoliticize groups, anti-discrimination would politicize and reinvigorate them (or at least some of them). This important divergence in turn explains other important differences: in the way groups view one another; in the interactions among groups; and in the character and extent of groups' expectations and aspirations.

Multiculturalism's politicization of group life means, to begin with, taking steps to awaken and to stir up victims (or potential victims) of discrimination. As one multicultural education writer put it, "multicultural education confronts the fact that this is a racist society with a history of White supremacy. . . . Its aim is to reduce the ignorance that breeds racism and to develop the understandings and actions people need to become antiracists" (Bennett 1986, 55–56). In sharp contrast to liberalism's many different strategies designed to minimize the claims and aspirations of groups, anti-discrimination politics aims deliberately to make individuals more aware of their situation as members of groups and, for victims, of their shared precarious group fate and struggle. In the name of protecting groups from similar harms now and in the future, anti-discrimination politics must ensure that the injustices of the past are not forgotten; it must make members of affected groups more sensitive to discrimination; and it must encourage them to remain wary and vigilant.

Anti-discrimination's more openly political engagement in the affairs of groups must also break with liberalism's purported standard of "neutral" or "color-blind" equal treatment: given the nature of the problem it confronts, multiculturalism must be color-sensitive (or difference-sensitive) and inclined to *take sides* with those who suffer at the hands of others. By treating all groups alike by reference to the ordinary concerns they share (interests), liberalism works to play down the differences among groups. Anti-discrimination politics must be in some important sense a politics of difference, but it is crucial to see that "difference" does not mean diversity or cultural diversity in the abstract so much as it means the difference between victims and perpetrators of discrimination. In this way, and in this way only, is multiculturalism concerned with the particularities of groups and their specific (political) histories. Liberalism can speak of unity and union without apology; anti-discrimination begins by separating the world into groups defined morally by their connection to past injustices done by some to others. It is no exaggeration to say that liberalism strains to unite where anti-discrimination is morally constrained to divide. (Postmodernist multiculturalism's heightened attention to "Whiteness," undertaken without hesitation and in a severely critical mode, is only the most vivid and extreme sign of this feature of the whole.) While law usually speaks generally, not all anti-discrimination policy does, in fact; and, as we have seen more than once, multicultural education does not hesitate to name names.[7] This is a political world constituted by friends and enemies—not that of liberalism's interest-based competitors or voluntary associations floating and jostling in a sea of freedom. But anti-discrimination does more than simply heighten divisions in the abstract; it also works to bring victim groups together and to unite them against potential oppressors ("allyship" being a new term denoting the tie among anti-discrimination coalitions). As Banks says, "multicultural political coalitions" provide "significant benefits" and can be "cogent vehicles for social change and reform" (1993c, 7). As multicultural education theorists point out, the multicultural political coalition is precisely the coalition of those groups similarly situated as historical or likely victims of discrimination. "In contexts of political struggle, we can consider building two related forms of allies: those who share marginalization on the basis of one form of difference (such as gender) but not another (such as race), and those who do not share marginalization but choose to work alongside a marginalized group anyway" (Sleeter and Soriano 2012, 10).

Politicizing groups and the relations among them means that groups are expected and encouraged to engage in political life in the most basic way. Anti-discrimination groups must seek *power*, multicultural education teaches, a large goal to be pursued along converging avenues of approach. "The most important factor in understanding racism is that the majority group has power over the minority group. This power has been used to prevent people of color from securing the prestige, power, and privilege held by whites. Racism is also practiced by some whites and their institutions to maintain a dominant-subordinate relationship with nonwhite groups" (Gollnick and Chinn 1990, 93). For Banks, we will recall, multicultural education must teach members of "oppressed groups" how to "gain power and shape public policy," "how to obtain and exercise political power in order for them to liberate themselves from physical and psychological captivity." [8] At the same time, efforts must be made "to help whites develop more positive attitudes toward oppressed peoples and a willingness to share power" (Banks 1974, 49). More broadly, multiculturalism aims also "to help transform and reconstruct society"—which either means taking steps to "redistribute power so that groups with different ethnic and cultural characteristics will control entry to various social, economic, and political institutions" or, perhaps only second best, it means taking the indirect route available to multicultural education and modifying "the attitudes and actions of individuals who will control future institutions."[9] Multiculturalism thus also teaches groups to see the state and the law as indispensable instruments of self-defense, and it provides them with justifications and incentives to seek to harness the political order and its many instrumentalities (not the least of which is public education) as a matter of course.

Encouraging groups to engage in power politics in this way, the pluralism associated with anti-discrimination is characterized by fairly profound and perhaps inescapable and enduring group *struggle*, which, because it cannot be avoided, must be faced squarely: "Whether through policies, programs, effects, or personal experience, encounters between victim and victimizer are inherently conflictual. . . . The most public of these struggles occur as champions of the status quo trying to protect their position of privilege collide with forces of social transformation" (Gay and Hart 2000, 185). "The main idea behind resistance theory is that those who are oppressed should not just sit back and take it" (Sleeter and Grant 1988, 181). Some multicultural education writers borrow from Marxist strains of social science, in sociological "conflict theory," to capture the character of intergroup relations in a world where discrimination is unavoidable. "Conflict theories see society organized in groups which struggle with each other for resources and in which dominant groups structure social institutions in ways that maintain or increase their advantage. People, consciously or not, resist oppression. . . . Conflict theories argue that the structures dominant groups use to perpetuate their advantages must be changed and that people need to be taught how to do this."[10] Consistent with such an understanding of the task of political life, multicultural education holds as well that it is necessary to "radicalize oppressed students so that they will continually challenge the position of those in power" (Banks 1973a, 405). A view of politics emphasizing its struggles is taken further by postmodernist multiculturalists, who seem almost to embrace the harsh facts of group conflict in semi-programmatic terms—as "oppositional utopia" or agonistic democracy.

While not unconcerned, like liberal pluralism, with political stability and civic peace, multiculturalism cannot afford to make them a top priority. Although anti-discrimination *is* a framework for halting group oppression, and is thus a tool intended to manage group conflict, it operates in a way that does not hope (as liberal interest group pluralism seems to) that group antagonisms will simply cancel one another out or, more optimistically, that the "free commerce in thoughts and things with all mankind" will be characterized by "the harmonies of this commerce at home and abroad" (Kallen 1956, 100). Anti-discrimination must protect some groups from others and in that spirit it is not optimistic about the amicable mixing of groups left to their own devices. Moreover, Banks would insist, it is discrimination, and not the effort to *fight* discrimination, that is the original source of political discord. Admitting that "ethnic polarization is highly dysfunctional in a pluralistic democratic society," Banks nevertheless holds that "ethnic discrimination and prejudice" themselves "contribute to polarization and hostility" (1977b, 696). To trust hopefully or optimistically in some common future would require giving up the hard lessons of the past. "Integration," once the byword of American civil rights reform, is not an important term of reference for American multiculturalism.

Table 1. Contrasting multiculturalism and traditional liberal pluralism as different accounts of the logic of "group politics."

	Traditional liberal pluralism	Multiculturalism
Assumptions about group-on-group relations	Assume group competition and conflict owing to natural human differences and conflicts of interest and opinion	Assume group competition and conflict due to tendency of individuals to discriminate and of groups to vie for social dominance
Goal of inter-group regulation	Social peace, overcome conflict	Resist/counteract proscribed discrimination; remedy effects of past discrimination
Groups defined descriptively	"Voluntary associations" and/or "interest" groups	Groups of identifiable victims of discrimination specified by law; groups linked by often ascriptive characteristics that are important to socially constructed identities
Actual groups championed (in practice)	Religious groups; immigrant groups; interest groups; lobby groups	Victims of discrimination—race, gender, disability, age, sexual orientation, etc. (also religion)
What is at stake for individuals and groups	Interest, freedom	Interest, recognition, identity, justice
Group-individual relationship	Individualism and "voluntarism"; groups have no authority over individuals; right of exit	Mutual protection against discrimination; solidarity and identification and sacrifice; group membership given, not usually "chosen"
Group-state relations	Separation of public and private (church-state model); indirect influence ("lobby group" model); "laissez-faire"; "benign neglect"	Direct political effort to halt discrimination and protect its victims blurring public-private, to include moral education and citizen identity-construction
Character of group interaction	Fluid, peaceful competition and/or cooperation (typical); outright factional strife (rare and to be combated)	Resistance against discrimination by victims; partnership with other victim groups ("allies"); wary politics of friends and enemies
Resulting group politics dynamic	Groups and intergroup relations tamed, depoliticized	Groups energized and put on guard, intergroup relations politicized

Where Multiculturalism and Liberal Pluralism Agree: Anti-Assimilation, Diversity, and Epistemology

To this point we have surveyed the many important differences between our two pluralisms (see table 1). But there are ways in which liberal pluralism and multiculturalism are alike as well. First, formally, because they are species of pluralism, they both firmly oppose *assimilation*, on the one hand, and champion *diversity*, on the other. Second, perhaps because both have been the work of intellectuals, they find an important place for epistemological (ultimately, skeptical) appeals and arguments. These areas of agreement are worth exploring, but in every case politics retains its supreme hold on all aspects of the arguments being made. Even these seeming similarities confirm our sense that the two are related in terms of a basic political divergence.

Liberal pluralism's opposition to assimilation in the name of individual freedom is easy enough to understand. For Kallen, assimilation—above all, the idea of America as a "melting pot"—is to be rejected precisely as a form of cultural coercion and an assault on individual liberty: "When those producers [of culture] undertake to force their products on me, to compel me to consume them and to support and participate in their production, when they pursue totalitarian ends by authoritarian means, they are using their products to wage war against my freedom" (1956, 193). In an arresting and puzzling formula, Kallen maintains that "democracy is anti-assimilationist" because the only acceptable conformity is "conformity to the right not to conform, that is conformity to freedom" (1956, 204). Multicultural education's hostility to assimilation is no less emphatic.[11] "The widely held assumption . . . in the United States that American society should be a homogenized melting pot has destructive results. This assumption works to . . . deny acceptance of diversity" (Gay 1994, 7). Now this stance might seem to suggest a deeper connection to liberalism, as when Banks emphasizes the "nonvoluntary . . . *forced assimilation*" of some groups in American life (1984c, 60; emphasis in the original). But multiculturalism's more fundamental objection to assimilation is rooted in the concerns of the civil rights revolution. Banks rejects what he terms the "assimilationist ideology" as precisely "a racist ideology that justified damaging school and societal practices that victimized minority group children."[12] For Gay, the real problem with assimilation is that it "demean[s] some segments of society" (1994, 7).

Liberalism and anti-discrimination thus ultimately reject assimilation for different (political) reasons. But this points to a general problem with *all* political arguments against assimilation. Every such stance must be a kind of mirage—or a species of deliberately misleading rhetoric—because every *political* argument against assimilation serves a political outlook that is itself unavoidably a powerful source of assimilation. Anyone doubting this need only ponder the broad assimilating effects of liberalism, on the one hand, and of anti-discrimination, on the other; surely neither brooks serious opposition to its political supremacy.[13] Perhaps because anti-discrimination has grown up partly in opposition to the liberal tradition, it seems to be more alive to this fact, or at least more willing to own up to it. For Banks, "the assimilationist conception is not so much wrong as it is flawed and incomplete." The point is to "make sure that the view of the American common culture which is perpetuated in the schools is not racist."[14] Assimilation to anti-discrimination is not only permissible but is in a way the whole point of multiculturalism.

The same basic problem applies equally to the rhetoric of *diversity* shared by our two pluralisms. Diversity is more important for anti-discrimination and has been central to the rhetoric of civil rights reform since at least the famous 1978 affirmative action decision, *Regents of the University of California v. Bakke*.[15] We recall, too, that multicultural education originated in the "cultural difference paradigm" and, today, advances primarily under the banner of teacher education accreditation "diversity" standards.[16] But, as one political scientist has aptly put it, "the arguments for and against cultural diversity are a kind of false front hiding other aspects of multiculturalism. Nothing is more important for understanding it than seeing through this false front without losing sight of its importance" (Forbes 1991, 24–25). "Diversity"—the diversity of groups and of individual characters and types and inclinations—may well capture the essence of humanity, but it does not capture the essential nature of any kind of politics. Every political order must, through the authoritative commandments of the law and everything that goes with citizen-making, impose some limit upon the diversity of wishes and aspirations of the individuals under its sway. That limitation may be more or less justified, more or less humane, but it is inescapable. The proof of this is already visible in the different *forms* that diversity itself takes in liberal pluralism and multiculturalism and in the way each characterizes the "groups" it is devoted to protecting. Despite its obvious pretensions to championing a genuine diversity of *cultures*, multiculturalism is in reality concerned with just a handful of racial groups (Blacks, Latinos, Native Americans, and Asians) plus an array of other groups (women, the disabled, the elderly, religious groups, gays and lesbians, and others), all identified by law entirely because they are held to need protection against discrimination—and not because they are cultures.[17] (In fact, early on, some multicultural education writers explicitly called for *limiting* their focus to race; this disregard for the full range of protected classes was then corrected by others in the discipline who insisted on including all the other kinds of groups covered under anti-discrimination law as well.[18]) Liberal pluralism, by contrast, sees diversity through the lens of voluntary interest groups—and, especially for twentieth-century cultural pluralism, the diversity that counted was either narrower (in practice, usually religious groups and immigrant ethnic groups) or broader (all interest or lobby groups). Each can plausibly accuse the other of exclusion, liberal pluralism being blind to many discrimination victim groups and multiculturalism narrowing the range of religious, ethnic, and immigrant groups by focusing on race (and treating many groups of concern in the older pluralism under one heading, as "European" or "White").[19]

The rhetoric of diversity and anti-assimilation thus yields to an analysis that suggests, yet again, that the political difference between liberal pluralism and multiculturalism is the heart of the matter. But the practical *utility* of this apparent overlap for multiculturalism should not be underestimated. By speaking the language of diversity and in opposing assimilation, multiculturalism can plausibly seem to continue a long-standing tradition of pluralist thinking in American politics; indeed, it may even appear to do so in the name of the older logic of individual freedom. It is mainly on this basis that many assume, however problematically, that multiculturalism is an offshoot of the liberal pluralist tradition.[20]

At least as striking are the political differences exposed by the shared reliance of liberal pluralism and multiculturalism upon arguments from forms of epistemological *skepticism*. For liberal pluralism, skepticism limits the certainty with which *all* groups press their claims, setting the stage for toleration and peaceful coexistence with others who see the world differently. One might even say that liberal pluralism's skepticism is a kind of general or universal suspicion of *every* received cultural identity. Multiculturalism's employment of skeptical argumentation is more selective, postmodernists wielding their critical apparatus to expose and undermine the dominant general or universal claims of institutions, arguments, and principles that are said to sustain regimes of discrimination and inequality. Where liberalism's soft skepticism works to moderate the demands of all parties, multiculturalism's view of knowledge construction is much more clearly a group-differentiated tool or weapon to be used by some (the marginalized, victims of discrimination) to resist and overcome the general terms of cultural discourse authored by those in power. The interpretation of history and the terms of social analysis must be retaken and restated, as Banks says, through the "eyes of the vanquished" (1974, 61). Even more striking, when it takes the form of postmodernist multiculturalism, the critical spirit appears as a kind of mind-altering rebellion against hegemony, as well as a steeling of those under its sway to bold and decisive political action. Where liberal skepticism sought to weaken conviction in order to temper political struggle, postmodernist multiculturalism reduces all thought to nothing but conviction and tells us that only political struggle will settle things. It does not go too far to say that the political use of skeptical argumentation in multiculturalism is the *opposite* of that in liberal pluralism.

Return of the Political

Anti-discrimination's tendency to stir up the groups under its purview is part of a wider repoliticization of social life that is visible wherever its shaping force is felt. This is one place where postmodernist multiculturalists do *not* exaggerate—when they speak of "the return of the political."[21] Fighting discrimination means a much more open, direct, and vigorous application of the political order (to include, obviously, the power of government, although the political order is more than that) to social relations and a much more direct engagement with social groups in what is viewed as a basic struggle over vital interests and social status. Names must be named; inequalities must be detected and measured; injustices must be confronted and rectified. Such matters become the focus of a significant portion of political and social or cultural life under the anti-discrimination regime. Anti-discrimination and multiculturalism thus move in the direction of restoring what we are tempted to call the natural understanding of political life according to which politics crucially shapes not only the social world and "groups" but also the individual (as "citizen") in its own image. It is no accident that education is a central requirement and concern of anti-discrimination policy. Because of the power and visibility of anti-discrimination in our world, it becomes harder and harder to deny that politics is a great formative general cause of private life—to include, as we shall see in the next chapters, especially private moral opinion. In this way, anti-discrimination helps to make it possible to understand Aristotle's claim that politics is "architectonic."

What we witness here is something like the reemergence of the kinds of regime claims taken up in book 3 of Aristotle's *Politics*, though in a kind of democratic moral inversion. A new affirmation of the group has begun to make necessary a new and stronger understanding of politics. If today our debates are not about who—which group or class—ought to *rule* over all the others and why, they are debates about, as we say, claims of "inclusion." But in a democracy, to call for inclusion is to insist upon one's place at the political table, and this is at the very least a claim to participate in rule. And insofar as the newly included exert their new fuller share in rule at the expense of—delimiting and depleting the power and status of—those who may be said to have predominated previously (and who must acquiesce to this reversal), this is a kind of contestation in which inherently controversial assertions are necessarily made. At a minimum, such claims are often accompanied by the moral condemnation of groups that in the past acted in overtly discriminatory ways or that, today, benefit from present and past inequalities held to be tied to such discrimination ("privilege"). In turn, the groups asked to relinquish power do not always do so with relish. At the very least, we may say that this new democratic agonistic dynamic is contentious, much like the old battle among the regimes described by Aristotle.

All of this is everything that liberal pluralism wanted to avoid. Indeed, liberal pluralism's many strategies to weaken groups and to tame group politics are only among the more successful of liberalism's many efforts to subdue politics as such. From start to finish liberalism is oriented against any kind of politics in a strong sense, any notion of regime or any ideal of rule or of who ought to rule. Questions that begin *there* are bound to divide and to stoke conflict. Instead, offering a comprehensive *theory*, liberalism offers a universal account of how social or political life works and how it ought to work. A system of seemingly anodyne generalizations, liberalism begins from abstractions about individuals (individual rights and freedoms, individual interests) and ends in a view of government as neutral apparatus (the rule of law, impersonal legal proceduralism, mechanisms of representation, institutional arrangements) in which politics in a strong sense all but disappears. At most, "all" in the liberal scheme, equally free and equally represented, are said to rule "all." Politics does not entirely disappear on this view, but it is greatly diminished, reduced to truncated claims about the freedom of individuals in their relations with the state (formalized in the public-private divide); or interests that everyone is said to share; or institutional and legal arrangements and what is held to be proper or improper within them. It may well be true that this view of things obscures the fundamental reality of political life and the kinds of demands and obligations arising from it—a protestation anti-discrimination politics has no choice but to make if its aspirations are to have purchase. Indeed, it is tempting to say that liberalism's many universalizing tendencies all aim precisely at overcoming or obscuring the world of regimes, of political orders, of politics in a strong sense, in a deliberate way. What justifies the attempt by liberalism to replace the struggle among regime claims with a universal theory that works to stifle or suppress or hide the plane of ordinary political contestation? Liberal realism, skepticism, and morality all answer in a similar vein at least to this extent: they all at least implicitly *reject* the moral claims of regimes or political orders, the idea that there might be some group or class or individual *deserving* to rule. Liberalism must presuppose that such claims are problematic—not true, to begin with, but also dangerous and oppressive. This ultimately radical claim about politics lies at the heart of liberalism, a claim liberalism does not announce with fanfare but that is implied by everything about it.

For the same reason that anti-discrimination cannot accept liberalism's attempt to diminish the place of groups, it must likewise break with liberalism's efforts to depoliticize the world. The repoliticization of groups must go together with a broader repoliticization of democratic life. In anti-discrimination the *kinds* of people participating in political life—particular kinds of groups with specific histories—gain prominence and their claims take on a less general or less abstract character. A more direct and energetic grappling with the social order—and the individuals comprising it—must be undertaken in order to guarantee that the ambitious aims of anti-discrimination politics become a reality. Conflict and contention, signs on the liberal view that something has gone wrong, cannot be avoided if discrimination is to be fought effectively. Liberalism's effort to overcome and to obscure the political character of life must be rejected because it entails an understanding of things that would evade or obscure the plane on which discrimination takes place and on which it must be opposed.

The new understanding of politics that arises from the anti-discrimination revolution is not without its own evasions (its appeals to diversity and anti-assimilation, its own desire to speak universally), and it does not proceed without some perceived cost in a world informed by the liberal perspective. But, for good or ill, there can be no doubt that this aspect of the fight against discrimination takes aim at something at the very heart of liberalism.

Chapter 9

POLITICS AND MORALITY: A TASK FOR POLITICAL SCIENCE

> We can understand—without rancor or hatred—how this all happened. But it cannot continue. Our Constitution, the foundation of our Republic, forbids it. The principles of our freedom forbid it. Morality forbids it. And the law I will sign tonight forbids it.
> —Lyndon Johnson, "Radio and Television Remarks Upon Signing the Civil Rights Bill" (July 2, 1964).[1]

The emergence of new moral categories, a relatively rare phenomenon, is obvious and powerful evidence of basic political change; it also suggests the reach and importance of such change. Many times to this point it has been impossible not to notice the many differences, large and small, between the moral logic of anti-discrimination and the moral logic of liberalism. We must acknowledge again our debt to Banks, which is greater here than at any other point. His deft employment of our new moral terms—identity, inclusion, recognition, respect, equity, a new equality—helps us to understand their meaning and to appreciate their interrelationship and their connection to the wider political impulse that is their ultimate source or cause. (It almost goes without saying that postmodernist multiculturalism's awkwardness with regard to morality renders it more or less completely useless to us at precisely this crucial point.) We turn now to address head-on and in a general way the broad and vitally important question of the place and substance of morality in liberalism and anti-discrimination.[2]

If anti-discrimination politics teaches us anew the formative power of politics and citizen-making generally speaking, it also teaches us the power of every political order or regime to generate a morality specific to it. Here, too, we may claim to follow Aristotle: his treatment of regimes is famous for focusing precisely on the claims to rule—claims of deserving and of justice, moral claims—of each of the different regimes. Again, ours must be a kind of democratic inversion of Aristotle's procedure, and one that emphasizes elements of corrective justice at points: disputes about who has suffered unjustly and how much—who is to blame for having made others suffer, and what ought to be done to remedy injustices done—take the place of disputes about who deserves to rule. But these are for us still very much disputes about deserving and justice, disputes about morality, that have today become vital to democratic life. More loosely, we may say that the language of morality pervades civil rights discourse, as Banks makes abundantly clear. Any treatment of the anti-discrimination revolution that does not address its moral claims and its moral reasoning with care will avoid the most important facts about it.

The expression of political aspirations in the language of morality is the ultimate generalization or universalization of particular demands. Here is the ground of the dignity of law, which in its generality likewise seems always to presuppose and bespeak some fundamental ideal of fairness, some concern for society as a whole, some common good. The authoritative character of political life, the fact that, at the most basic level, no political order ever brooks genuine opposition, means that the vital judgments of good and bad, right and wrong, noble and base, are necessary concerns of the political order. Every politics has its own morality and too much is at stake for the political order not to seek to insist with all the force at its disposal on the rightness of its terms. Alternatively, one may say that because human aspirations are ultimately expressed through the medium of morality, individuals and groups will not be able to rest until their moral point of view (their view of justice, their view of the good or of the good or deserving human being) predominates politically. Politics powerfully influences morality also because willing citizens of a particular regime place its moral vision somewhere very close to the center of their lives. And most human beings, most of the time, are what we would term decent citizens.[3] The relationship here is of course complex and necessarily results in continual variation—and not a little conflict or disagreement. But it is not necessary to adopt a cynical postmodernist view of the process by which (partial) political perspectives become translated into morality to take the questions posed here seriously. Indeed, it is because so much is at stake in these moral claims—the shaping of citizens' hearts and minds, as well as the future outlines of what is thought possible or permissible in political and social life—that such transformative moments in the life of a community must be treated with the utmost seriousness. (I cannot resist adding that because of its dramatic shaping effect on the mind, this must be the first study, as a kind of ground clearing, of political science, and for the individual political scientist.) To interrogate the differences between liberalism and anti-discrimination on this level, on the plane of morality, may also be said to be the most respectful approach available to us, treating the most serious claims made by each in the most serious way.

There are two different kinds of questions that must be addressed to reckon adequately with the morality of anti-discrimination, especially as it comes to sight in the contrast with liberal morality. The first concerns the general relationship between politics and morality. In a way one could say that anti-discrimination offers a kind of innocent or naïve view of this relationship: of course, justice must guide political life. This must be a question for us—something we have to stop and think about—primarily because liberalism has tried so hard, with amazing success, to render such a view problematic. While the terms—even, we may say, the moral terms—of liberal pluralism work to de-moralize and to tame group politics, in civil rights politics the assertion of vigorous and spirited moral claims is a necessary and highly visible task. The manifest tensions between liberalism and anti-discrimination on this crucial point compel us to confront in a straightforward way a very basic question of politics and of life that no serious person can ignore.

The second question or set of questions we must address (taken up in the next chapter) concerns the *substance* of the new morality of anti-discrimination politics, usefully clarified once again through many contrasts with liberalism's moral categories—the newly irrepressible language of identity, inclusion, respect, recognition, equity, and other terms. What do these terms mean? How or why are they associated with anti-discrimination politics? What is their relation to liberalism and to the morality of liberalism? On this plane, it will be unavoidable for us to take further steps than we have already to think in a more dialectical mode.[4] The new morality comes to sight already bound up in debate with the old morality, and in assessing the arguments between them we cannot but consider the merits of the claims made on both sides, especially because so much is at stake for us as citizens.

Legislating Morality

Liberal democracy is the only political system known to us in which "legislating morality" is said to be the height of immorality. In the fight against discrimination, however, harnessing the political order in the name of justice to change not just the power relations among groups, but also to shape in a deliberate way the opinions and moral opinions of citizens, are obvious steps. That repoliticizing the world means remoralizing the world has by now been indicated in many ways. What citizens feel they can expect or demand from democratic politics and from their fellows has shifted on a fundamental level. If it means breaking with the traditional liberal reluctance to use politics or government to intrude on individual or private morality, this is something advocates of multiculturalism are willing to face: "Those who would equate a stand against racism with preaching values can be told that it is un-American and antihuman to be racist" (Bennett 1986, 169).

There are few things more important to the liberal democratic outlook than the view that morality and politics should be kept separate. Without this principle, liberal individualism, the separation of church and state, freedom of speech, and the very idea of limited government all lose their coherence. In a maneuver now familiar to us, removing contentious moral (and religious) opinions into a sphere deemed private, where they are less powerful and less likely to cause trouble, lowers the stakes of political life. All the schools of liberal pluralism agree here, their moral terms (freedom, individualism, voluntarism, consent) as well as their realism and skepticism all tending in the same direction. With the exception of the criminal law, fundamental questions of morality are, as we say, private matters of personal freedom removed from the public agenda. "Our obligation is to define the liberty of all, not to mandate our own moral code"—so said the United States Supreme Court in a prominent abortion case (a quotation repeated in a famous LGBT rights case striking down American anti-sodomy laws).[5] On this view, the idea that politics is or ought to be about who deserves to rule, and to what moral end, is rejected out of hand. Just how far the anti-moralistic tendency of liberalism may go is well-captured in social theorist Alan Wolfe's "moral freedom" ideal, holding that the "final freedom" of modern societies is precisely the freedom of individuals to "decide what is right and wrong."[6] It is unnecessary to determine whether this makes sense (liberal anti-moralism being a kind of morality) in order to show that the anti-discrimination regime's open embrace of the language of morality breaks with it.[7]

Perhaps the most important thing about the anti-discrimination revolution is that it puts matters of basic justice at the heart of modern democratic life. That anti-discrimination makes the connection between politics and morality plain was, from the very first, a worry to many who saw the importance of the change. Even Martin Luther King Jr. was apologetic and clung to the liberal belief-conduct distinction (the logic of the First Amendment) when the issue was raised: "Now, people say, 'You can't legislate morals.' Well that may be true. Even though morality may not be legislated, behavior can be regulated" (1986, 213). But if King, perhaps for tactical reasons, did not want to draw attention to the full extent of the change underway, Paul Freund, who wrote the Kennedy administration's brief on the constitutionality of the 1964 Act, was more willing to face the question squarely: "Is the role of law then simply an amoral manipulation of behavior? Certainly not, because the moral quality of law is itself a force toward compliance and the change of attitudes. A feeling of guilt upon violation of law becomes a feeling of shame if the law is felt to be morally right, and shame reflects one's innermost nature."[8] This (seemingly illiberal) view could be applied, of course, to any law, but it holds for anti-discrimination policy in an especially powerful way because the core of that reform is a new standard of the just treatment of one's fellow citizens, a standard widely felt to be, as Freund puts it, "morally right." Robert Bork opposed the 1964 Act precisely for this reason: "The principle of such legislation is that if I find your behavior ugly by my standards, moral or aesthetic, and if you prove stubborn about adopting my view of the situation, I am justified in having the state coerce you into more righteous paths. That is itself a principle of unsurpassed ugliness" (1963, 22). Anti-discrimination theorist and law professor Andrew Koppelman states the issue in terms of a general duty toward those mistreated by discrimination.

> [Once] overt racism has been stigmatized and largely eliminated from political and legal decision making . . . our remaining obligations to the groups that those like us [members of the majority] have traditionally oppressed and whose oppression continues to benefit us [include a commitment to] chang[ing] our very patterns of cultural expression and unconscious thinking. . . . And this project of cultural transformation is one in which the state is appropriately enlisted where it can be helpful.[9]

If there are questions one might raise about the insistence of liberalism that private morality and politics ought to be separated, the demands of anti-discrimination policy force them out into the open. To regulate with penalties and rewards the private interpersonal "behavior" of citizens cannot but be accompanied by a public justification of such a stance, and the names for that are justice and morality.

A Spirited Morality

Not only does anti-discrimination put morality and politics together again, but the task this political order undertakes demands a vigorous, spirited morality, a fighting morality. Anti-discrimination responds immediately to what is perceived to be the felt experience of a basic injustice. Too much is at stake for the language of justice not to be invoked. Discrimination begins with unequal treatment affecting one's status (segregation) but points to the possibility of other injustices and material harms as well (economic loss, physical hurt, violence). Moreover, what is held to be at stake is also the threat of negative distortions of the very identity or self-understanding of members of victim groups. Because the injury suffered here is in a way collective, the claim of justice is never for the individual alone but includes an entire community similarly vulnerable with a shared memory of injustice. Because they aim to address past and present wrongs, the claims of justice made are naturally vigorous, informed by the spirit of corrective justice and a vigilant determination to stand up to discrimination in the future. More positively, anti-discrimination law establishes a standard for judging our interactions with others. That is how President Kennedy framed the issue in a 1963 speech regarding the "moral crisis" America faced on the subject of civil rights: "We are confronted primarily with a moral issue. . . . The heart of the question is whether . . . we are going to treat our fellow Americans as we want to be treated" (1967a, 65). In contrast with liberalism's emphatically realistic appeal to a scheme of collective self-interest, the civil rights regime attempts to make us more aware of our fellow citizens in order to make us more responsive to their moral claims and demands. Anti-discrimination policy obviously does not express the whole of justice, but its aspirations are solidly rooted in a moral appeal that has no obvious counterpart in the liberal tradition.[10]

Anti-discrimination may be said also to begin from a moralized place, and to gain its distinctive moral spirit, as a result of the *kind* of harm that is discrimination. Anti-discrimination does not accidentally make questions of status and recognition—and worth—a central concern of our political life. Anti-discrimination is partly about concrete harms (income, education, housing, etc.), but it is also a response to the insult, the disrespect, the demeaning implications of discrimination. We oppose segregation not primarily because it means lost "opportunities" but, rather, because it denies the dignity or honor or status of affected individuals and groups. The main problem with being told to sit at the back of the bus is not that the good seats are up front. Race discrimination was, as President Kennedy put it, "an arbitrary indignity that no American in 1963 should have to endure" (1967b, 249). The Supreme Court concurred, affirming Congress's finding that "the fundamental object of Title II [of the 1964 Act] was to vindicate 'the deprivation of personal dignity that surely accompanies denials of equal access to public establishments'."[11] The Supreme Court's judicial scrutiny of discrimination is concerned precisely with cases of "invidious"—insulting—discrimination.[12] Questions of insult, honor, status, dignity, and worth are manifestly questions of justice, and anti-discrimination law makes these a necessary part of our public life. Attempting to regulate the distribution of honors, even in the crude mechanisms of desegregation and anti-discrimination and anti-harassment policies, contributes in an elementary way to anti-discrimination's tendency to assume the necessity of engaging the social world morally. As we have seen, such matters are prominent in multicultural education, where achieving or creating "equal status situations" for groups is in a way the orienting goal and where the rewriting of history is largely about reassigning the praise and blame accorded to the groups that fall under the purview of anti-discrimination law.

These considerations also help to explain why the regulation of speech is not an accidental but an essential and vital part of the whole. All the many different strategies that anti-discrimination law pursues to regulate speech may be said to be necessary because they tackle in a direct way an immediate source of the insult and indignity and disrespect that form a core harm of discrimination.[13]

But anti-discrimination's regulation of speech, as controversial as that is from the point of view of liberalism, is much less important than the fairly direct moral education of citizens that is vital to the anti-discrimination effort. We have of course focused our attention on multicultural education here but, as we saw in chapter 3, educational or training efforts are pervasively important as part of the enforcement machinery of anti-discrimination law (most visible in efforts associated with Title VII and Title IX, but not only there). Here the law directly requires public teachings about how one ought to view one's fellow citizens and how one ought to treat them. Multicultural education helpfully makes explicit what the law already implies—namely, that these are efforts of *moral* education. Multicultural education is an "equity pedagogy"; Banks puts his own "value inquiry model" forward precisely to help students "to identify and clarify their values and to make reflective moral choices" (1994a, 77). "All values are not equally valid. Some values, such as inequality, racism, and oppression, are clearly inconsistent with human dignity and other American creed values" (1984c, 98–99). Multicultural education seeks "to modify the attitudes and actions of individuals who will control future institutions" and necessarily includes a "strong affective component." This must be, as Banks says, "a *deliberate* program of instruction," one devoted to "modify[ing] children's racial attitudes" that "must be structured for that purpose in the earliest grades [and] *sustained* over a long period of time."[14] This education teaches in a very direct way basic moral lessons of the new regime like "prejudice reduction" and "reflective self-analysis" but also offers a broad new interpretation of our history, a politically reimagined account of America and of Western Civilization that reverses old moral categories of judgment.[15] This moral education may be said to culminate in multicultural education's project of the deliberate reshaping of the identities of citizens, eliminating unhealthy and immoral aspects of identity for some, promoting stronger identities for others, and advancing at the same time a novel "citizenship identity" for all that puts the justice of the fight against discrimination at the very center of things (Banks 1980, 121).

While anti-discrimination's explicit moralization of politics raises questions from the perspective of traditional liberalism, this new public emphasis on ethical matters also helps to explain much of the appeal of the new dispensation, even to those who are not themselves immediately protected under it. "The civil rights movement is the great morality tale of modern America. The nation faced a choice between right and wrong" (Schmidt 2016a, 179). Anti-discrimination's emphatic moralism is often a cause for celebration, as in Richard Rorty's claim that the civil rights movement was "the great, inspiring moral event of our lifetime, the moment at which our country showed that it was still capable of moral progress and of a national moral identity"—a view that many would embrace, and not just on the Left (1995a, 9). The great success of liberal democracy in America has no doubt been due in large measure to the hard-headed realism built into it, but this has always gone together with its somewhat uninspiring lack of moral ambition.[16] By asking citizens to be more attentive to their treatment of others, anti-discrimination puts forward a more demanding standard of citizenship and may thus seem to ennoble our public life in ways that liberalism cannot. As one advocate of multicultural education says, it offers "a new vision of the good life; a vision based on equality and community rather than upon vulgar, simplistic materialist comforts" (Adams 1985, 87). In contrast with the liberal inducements to let one another alone, anti-discrimination provides a more prominent place for justice in our lives, offering new opportunities for moral courage and sacrifice going beyond liberalism's deliberately de-moralized view of politics. At the same time, while anti-discrimination may be more exacting than liberalism, it seems not to tax us too much, requiring mainly the bending of our minds and not our pocketbooks. While anti-discrimination insists upon a certain kind of interpersonal treatment and a certain attitude toward others, it does not demand outright material equality (at least not absolutely or immediately), and this makes it possible for Americans to feel ennobled without having to abandon entirely the individualism and competitive acquisitiveness associated with the economic side of traditional liberalism. (Woke billionaires are well-explained here, as is the common stance of opposition to affirmative action but not to anti-discrimination.)

But liberalism had its reasons for attempting to rein in the moralism of political life. As one law professor has put it, the moral appeal of anti-discrimination politics may be a mixed blessing: "At its best, the civil rights movement harnessed the energy of moral outrage to pragmatic legal and policy reform. . . . [However,] when moralism overwhelms pragmatism, we often go to extremes, adopting punitive . . . measures that make matters worse" (Ford 2011, 21). At the very least, we must say that anti-discrimination politics today pays a (political) price for its attempts to moralize. "Virtue-signaling" and "political correctness" are still terms of abuse, not praise, that echo our liberal sensibilities. As multicultural education theorist Sonia Nieto concedes, presenting multicultural education as a form of "values education" is not always or immediately an advantage, since "students sensed that they were being manipulated and resented it."[17] But these may prove to be quibbles, a sign for now of liberalism's lingering hold on the public mind. The longer that anti-discrimination succeeds in shaping our world, the more its education in the language of public justice and morality will alter our general view of things at the expense of the traditional liberal understanding.

A Task for Political Science

We seem to be living through a genuine transvaluation of values, perhaps total and enduring, perhaps not. But regardless of the final result, I can imagine no higher task for contemporary political science than to study it. The new categories in play—identity, inclusion, recognition, respect, equity, and the like—were not used in their present sense, and were certainly not used together in a systematic way, when the 1964 Civil Rights Act passed.[18] But there is by now a new moral vocabulary associated with anti-discrimination politics that differs from and at many points challenges the received moral categories of liberalism and this is something that can be indicated in fairly simple terms. The contrasting schemes of moral terminology can indeed be reduced to a table (table 2).

Table 2. Contrasting moral concerns:
Anti-discrimination versus traditional liberalism.

	Traditional liberalism	Anti-discrimination
Underlying justifying "good"	Freedom (individual)	Identity (group-based)
Standard of interpersonal treatment	Toleration	Respect
What is at stake stated non-morally	Interests	Recognition (also identity)
Equality interpretation	1. Equality before the law (public) 2. Equal opportunity (public and private, mainly private)	1. Equal status situations for members of discrimination victim groups (public-private) ("equity") 2. Equal outcomes (pub-priv) (proportionality) ("equity")
Representational ideal	One person, one vote (social contractarian, rights-based individualism); representation schemes cut across lines of group division for the sake of civic unity	Proportional group representation ("inclusion" of marginalized groups or voices); schemes remedy relative under-representation of elected officials for groups recognized under anti-discrimination law
Morality/politics relation	Morality a "private" matter; avoid "legislating morality"	Politics encompasses justice; requires the open and direct moral education of citizens
Fundamental moral spirit	Skeptical of passionate moral claims; compromise; keep the peace	Confront and resist injustice of discrimination; remedy past injustices; mistrust and vigilance; compensatory, corrective justice

Here is work for our political scientists and students of "civic culture." Generally speaking, there is perhaps no better way to approach the anti-discrimination regime than by operating on the level of its highest claims and examining them with the seriousness such claims make upon us. But only political science can do justice to this task, for the crucial questions to be posed are all ones that only a political analysis will illuminate adequately. We are perhaps somewhat behindhand in taking up these questions in such a scientific spirit, but it is not too late to track the emergence and usage of these terms, and to weigh the relative frequency of their employment against their equivalent terms under the older morality.

We need to engage our new civic moral understanding as a political scientist would; in saying this, however, I do not mean that we should pin our hopes on modern scientific method. Following the prejudices of social science would mean attempting to erect some explanatory hypothesis for what we see when what we really need is a direct but clear-sighted engagement with the new morality on its own terms. The methods of contemporary social and political science too often work to reduce the opinions in question to something overly simple or, worse, to something *else* (some explanatory framework, like "rational choice" or "recognition," e.g., imposed upon the phenomena under examination). Such approaches are removed from the plane of common sense on which any effective study of morality must operate. Coding categories, polling data, and content analysis will not reveal fully what we need to know unless a proper preparation at the level of common sense is undertaken first. A penetrating investigation of the moral dimension of the anti-discrimination revolution will need to engage the new ideals in play both more thoughtfully and more simply. What is needed, to begin with, is an attempt to wrestle with the citizen perspective using the terms it employs. Here again we see our debt to Banks: although Banks is an academic and a theorist, the civic-political task he has taken up always inclines him, it seems to me, to speak ultimately in the language of our common sense (even as he has tried to help usher in a new common sense). But, at the same time, our quest for a scientific or rational engagement with the new morality means that we cannot simply bow to common sense as a kind of authority. Here the contested character of the new morality, locked in a debate with an older rival, contributes to our understanding by providing a rich context in which to analyze in detail and in depth the meaning of all the different controversial new terms (a step reductionist scientific method would be likely to skip or cut short). More importantly, the debate also to some degree frees us to examine the new moral principles (as well as the old) with a critical eye, a task that modern science would not even think of attempting but that any truly rational enterprise would deem indispensable.

Exploring the new morality in its differences from the old is admittedly a big undertaking and I propose here only a kind of preliminary reconnaissance of the territory. For this task, we are in luck to have at our disposal not only the work of someone like Banks, who helps us to see the big picture, but also a lot of sophisticated reflection on all the different terms of the new moral language. This is to be found in hundreds of scholarly books and essays devoted to defining, weighing, and systematizing the new terminology, in a literature of our contemporary social and political *theorists* (academics advancing one concept or another, theorists mostly of the analytical philosophy school, but also postmodernists, feminists, critical race theorists, etc.). It is interesting to note that the disagreements we uncover here among our intellectuals over the meaning and relative ranking of identity, inclusion, recognition, respect, equity, and related terms, by now a fairly massive literature, does not really emerge until the 1990s—fully a quarter century after the civil rights revolution began in earnest. Wading into what the theorists have written proves a useful way to clarify the new moral terrain and to think about the new logic in amazing detail. One can easily compile a long list of academics who have adumbrated whole theories along these lines—the "politics of" recognition or identity or inclusion or difference or diversity or social equality—over the past thirty years.[19] Were political scientists to approach this literature in the way of a field excavation, treating these writers and their work as *evidence* of a broad political and moral transformation caused by the anti-discrimination revolution, and looking to it in order to learn how the new understanding works in detail and how it contrasts with that of the past, much light could be shed on the inner logic of contemporary democratic life. Crucially, these writers, though sophisticated academics, nevertheless operate more or less, or to some significant degree, on the ordinary citizen plane. They are trying to figure out what these ideas mean for us, how they relate to one another, and which of them is most important, in large part because they feel they have an obligation to do so. While I believe there are limitations to the work of these theorists (limitations that a proper understanding of political science must try to remedy), the existence of this large academic literature is a useful starting point for anyone who wants to assess the moral dimension of our new political situation carefully and in detail.

But there are, as I say, some important limitations to the moral-intellectual labors undertaken by our social and political theorists that must be noted in advance. First and foremost among their shortcomings is the fact that there is no general or sharp and clear awareness that the newly important terms under discussion represent one thing, that they are the *products* of a single source, a single political change. This is perhaps understandable: to admit that, the theorists would have to see themselves as soldiers in a cause, moralists laboring on behalf of a new political order. The theorists simply do not fully *see* the anti-discrimination revolution, even as they both inhabit it and are inhabited by it. Our theorists are thus perhaps too beholden to the new morality to think about it as freely as they might. This problem is compounded by the distorting influence of a prejudice in favor of intellectual over political history shared by our professional political and social theorists. Reading the large literature that maps out the new morality without considering the relatively recent political developments that made it possible or necessary, one might be led to think that it is the academic theorists themselves who invented the language of identity and inclusion and equity and the like. Nor is it very helpful to go rooting around in the history of these ideas, as many of these theorists are wont to do, tracing out their earlier use by famous thinkers for whom the anti-discrimination revolution was not even a distant dream.

All these problems are made significantly worse by the methodology of analytical philosophy, in particular. The approach of this school is to try to systematize and order moral and political concepts in accordance with some sense of their "best" arrangement; to the extent that ideas are related one to another, it is in the direction of a kind of moral system-building enterprise. As a consequence of this, there is even an element of what one must term turf fighting among the theorists of these newly important concepts. One can launch an academic career by laying out (or even simply marching behind) a theory championing one or another of these principles as supreme among all the rest (defenders of the identity concept pitted against theorists of recognition, etc.). Much more problematic is a tendency to disregard the question of the truth of the foundations of the edifices they are constructing, perhaps partly because the theorists have invested so much in their projects of moral theory building, but mainly because they think that the truth of the premises of moral argumentation is not reachable by human thought.[20]

Banks's honest and forthright labor on behalf of the political cause he defends is invaluable because it permits him to articulate the new moral and political logic in all its complexity without these encumbrances and shortcomings. Above all, unlike the academic theorists, his thought makes more than plain the simple political source and aim of the new moral categories. Following Banks on this crucial point, and not the professional moral theorists, is very important. But while Banks thus *makes use* of the new morality—and thus allows us to see it as an interconnected whole, a system in operation and up and running—he provides neither an extensive discussion of each of the new moral terms nor an account of their relationship to one another or to liberalism. The wide-ranging discussion among our academic theorists, on the other hand, does help to undertake those tasks. If we begin from the big-picture point of view that Banks's use of these terms makes possible, we can benefit from the more detailed, concept-scrutinizing work of the academic theorists without being misled by their limitations—above all, their strange lack of political self-awareness.

One way to correct for the shortcomings of our academic theorists is to approach the study of them and the new morality, to repeat, in the way of political scientists. This is not to say that we are to treat our subjects like triangles or fish. We, too, are citizens and we must begin from the common sense of our world. The emphasis must be placed on the "political" in political science; we must proceed with a full appreciation of the power of politics to shape human life. Concretely, in the study of anti-discrimination this means three things. First, tutored by Banks, it means that we will be on the lookout for ties between the new morality and the broad political effort with which it is so obviously associated. How, generally, is the political impulse of the fight against discrimination the cause of the new moral terms? What (political) purposes do they serve? Likewise, at the same time, what do its moral claims reveal about the *nature* of this political effort? Second, a proper study of the new morality will not ignore the contested nature of its concepts and claims. This exploration appropriately, necessarily, examines mainly the thought of the contemporary Left (and sometimes its conservative critics). The wide contest between liberalism and anti-discrimination lying behind much of the discussion must never be forgotten and illuminates a great deal. Here it will be necessary to combat another limitation of at least some of our theorists, namely, the more defensible but equally distorting tendency to labor to *reconcile* the new morality and the old: to show how toleration leads to respect, how identity and freedom might be brought into harmony, and the like. While we should not of course simply and blindly reject evidence where we see that the new and the old do indeed merge or overlap, precisely our beginning point in an appreciation of the broad political backdrop will make us wary of efforts of synthesis that, though perhaps civically salutary, obscure what we most want to know. This also means that precisely because our social and political theorists usefully operate within the citizen perspective, some attempt at attaining a critical distance on what they are saying must be made. Here the third element of the political science viewpoint comes to sight. This is already suggested in, and in a way made necessary by, the fact that the new morality competes with and contradicts the older morality. We have no choice but to "question authority" to some degree, admittedly a delicate task, assessing the validity of the terms of the new moral order that is taking hold in the modern world. The novelty of our situation suggests it; the gravity of the change under way demands it; the existence of a competing morality out of and against which the new order emerged makes it possible (which means, of course, that we must not fail to examine critically the old morality as well). A sober political science begins with common sense (and not scientific abstractions), but common sense alone cannot do all the work that must be done.

These are questions for political science because they presuppose the supreme shaping influence of the political order upon morality and because they are guided by an objective that is not necessarily provided, or at least not simply provided, by either the new morality or the old. If today political science does not seem particularly well-suited to taking up these questions, perhaps the spectacle of the anti-discrimination revolution's introduction of a new morality for democratic life will inspire and embolden the discipline to try.

Chapter 10
THE NEW MORALITY AND THE OLD

To grapple directly with the moral claims of multiculturalism and anti-discrimination is to attempt to come to terms with the political order at the level of principle. To speak in the language of morality and justice is to appeal to what may be said to be the highest of human things. To engage political life in this way holds out the promise that we will perhaps be freed from some of its less attractive aspects. Thinking about, without prejudice and without preconception, the morality of anti-discrimination, even if in part critically, offers a kind of respite from some of the heat and passion of ordinary polemical debate that so characterizes anti-discrimination politics, its friends and its enemies. To take seriously the task of exploring questions of morality is to take a truly "privileged" stance toward political life.

To sketch the contours of what an exploration of the new morality on its own terms and in relation to liberalism might look like, I take up the contrast between the new and the old by reference to five important categories of the new: identity, respect, equity, inclusion, and recognition. One could make the case for exploring a range of other related moral concepts—"social" justice, solidarity/allyship, dignity, marginality, privilege, supremacy—that likewise have their originating impulses in the anti-discrimination revolution (one important set of terms—diversity and anti-assimilation—we have treated already).[1] It is not yet possible to know which of these concepts will eventually take pride of place in the anti-discriminatory moral cosmos and my choice of five is determined in part by the guidance Banks provides. My treatment of the issues is also limited because I reduce the relation of the new and the old to simple oppositions (identity versus liberty, respect versus toleration, etc.) when of course the full picture could be made more complicated than that (relating identity to toleration as well, respect to liberty, and the like).[2] The arrangement I follow is useful, however, because it allows for a relatively brief treatment, appropriate to a preliminary survey of the issues, and because it helps to draw attention, once again, to obvious lines of tension between liberalism and anti-discrimination, now on the plane of morality.

Identity versus Liberty

Banks helps us to see why identity is a central category of anti-discrimination politics, and a moral category as well—locating the site of discrimination's harms, justifying the exertions of anti-discrimination efforts. To repeat our formula, group identity is the *good* of anti-discrimination politics that is equivalent to individual freedom under liberalism. Since the 1990s there has been an explosion of interest in the concept of identity. Whole theories of the "politics of" identity, along with separate critical discussions of the concept by analytical and postmodernist philosophy professionals, compete for attention alongside a movement within the *social sciences* to develop new theories of identity as an explanatory variable. This broad development follows mainly from the role that the identity concept plays in the logic of anti-discrimination, but that political origin is not usually emphasized by those deploying the term (once again, Banks is very helpful here). In fifty years I suspect that a simple political explanation will seem obvious to intellectual historians of the turn to identity; today, the sheer scale of this scholarly upheaval works to muddy the picture and to suggest instead that, somehow, a new and invaluable conceptual insight has broken upon the world.[3] It is important to recall that for Banks it is not only that identity is a vitally important term, but also that what is needed is the regulation and reformulation of identity in the name of anti-discrimination—a campaign of "reconstructing White identity and deconstructing the current one" (admittedly a "very difficult psychological project").[4] This latter effort immediately suggests an obvious and powerful challenge to the liberal understanding of things: liberalism cannot countenance putting something as intimate as identity—even mere group identity—under the management of the political order. But this is only the most glaring point of contradiction between the new and the old. Indeed, generally speaking, it is hard to imagine a more profound moral opposition than the one between liberty and identity. Efforts to lump them together (to rethink identity as a kind of liberal individualism or something like that) are doomed in advance and point us away from the most important things that we have to learn from their interrelationship.[5]

One significant liberal objection to identity is straightforwardly political. Representative government may be said to depend upon the freedom to criticize those in power, the right of political opposition. Protecting robust political debate is usually said to be the most important justification for freedom of speech.[6] But as political theorist Will Kymlicka points out, identity is or can be a powerful threat to the give and take of republican self-government:

> To say that a particular cultural practice is part of my 'identity' is sometimes a way of inviting others to consider and debate its value and significance. But in other contexts, this claim is invoked as a way of foreclosing that debate, by implying that any questioning of that practice will be interpreted as a sign of disrespect for me as a person. Where identity claims are presented in this way as non-negotiable trumps, the result is to erode the potential for democratic dialogue. (2007, 102)

Identity politics becomes, as one law professor puts it, "pathological insofar as it is perverted to stifle . . . the openness of democratic political conflict" (Parker 2005, 55).

But a much more fundamental opposition between liberty and identity comes to sight in how each relates to the human *good*.[7] Both freedom and identity are incomplete and point to some specific and more substantial *content*. Freedom itself cannot be the core of—nor can it sustain—a life; freedom must always be freedom for something in particular. Nor does anybody live for the sake of identity in the abstract, as an end in itself. Neither liberty nor identity is the good; the good is more fundamental than both liberty and identity. Higher things—virtue, justice, happiness, other claims of human fulfillment—stand in judgment of what we do with our freedom and tell us the value of every particular identity.

But in their incompleteness, freedom and identity point in very different directions. Freedom makes each individual responsible for his or her choice of the good. What freedom gives is an opportunity to choose a good life—the rest is up to us. There is, of course, considerable potential for error here, and some people are undoubtedly misled into thinking that freedom *is* the good; but the politics of freedom is, in an obvious way, a kind of indirect politics of the good.[8] Identity, on the other hand, orients around what we *already* are, and that necessarily means severely narrowing the range of the goods we are free to consider and take seriously. Identity is to be valued precisely because it is something we may take for granted, something we cherish regardless of whether—and perhaps even especially when—*others* challenge or raise questions about it. Freedom throws us back on ourselves and bids us to take more seriously our choices in life; identity reminds us of our ties to others and of our obligations to take them seriously. The opposition here is profound, and made sharper by the fact that freedom also means the freedom to *question*, precisely in the name of the good, every received opinion, every assumption about who we are. Liberalism means not only freedom of speech, but also freedom of religion and freedom of the mind—important not only for republican self-government, but also, if we make use of them, for us as individuals. Here the challenge to identity from liberty is at its most pointed. We want to live good lives, worthy lives, and liberty can be our ally in permitting us to *think* about what that means. Identity, on the other hand, always already offers an answer, and a powerful one, that must unavoidably treat questions about it as challenges to it, as threats. Freedom in the highest sense is precisely freedom to question identity; to take our identity seriously is partly to safeguard it from such questioning. That identity ought to bow where the freedom to question it succeeds in raising compelling objections is easily proved. Could anyone really take a particular identity seriously were it shown *not* to be good for him or her? We know in advance that there are bad and unhealthy and immoral identities (anti-discrimination would be the first to agree). Both freedom and identity must bow to the good, but where freedom may readily be made a servant to the good and necessarily yields to it, identity is always inclined in advance to buck and balk.[9]

Even more problematic is the elevation of identity under anti-discrimination politics, since there only one very limited dimension of identity—*group* identity—matters. It is far from obvious, at least without looking into particulars, that one's membership in an anti-discrimination group should be given greater weight, for its own sake, than other aspects of one's identity, or that such group membership should be preferred to goods lying *beyond* identity. Indeed, if group identity makes powerful claims upon us, as Banks shows it does, do we not have all the more reason to examine it critically? For liberal theorist George Kateb, to take too seriously one's group identity is indeed to indulge the vices of "complacent confusion," "wishful thinking," and "plain dishonesty" (1994, 524–29). Is it not in fact highly likely that the claims of cultural identity are laden with precisely the sorts of potential errors we are most in need of questioning? Indeed, do we not know, and precisely from the fact of cultural *diversity*, that there must be errors to be found here—since diverse communal identities can and often do contradict one another on important questions (e.g., on moral and religious matters)? More generally, is not unquestioned identity, love of what is one's own simply because it is one's own, precisely *the* enemy of serious reflection about life for any individual seeking his or her own true fulfilment?

Liberalism's criticisms of something like Banks's proposed project of deconstructing and reconstructing our civic identity are even easier to see. Unless we can say that we know absolutely how to do this successfully and well, is it wise even to entertain such a task? Is Banks's Stage 5 individual, for example, truly the good citizen, the good human being?

Now, in defense of Banks here, one could say that his program of identity regulation is simply an honest—indeed, amazingly frank—admission of all that politics is and does and hopes to do. If we really want to fight racism and other forms of discrimination, how can we not, for example, deplore the idea of letting people retain their racist, sexist, homophobic, and transexclusionary identities (even if they do not act on them)? Recalling the efforts that have been undertaken to date—lessons in schools and the workplace, the rewriting of our history, the fate of an older generation's heroes, the tearing down of monuments, and the like, most of these by now matters of policy—one might say that a broad program of identity reconstruction has in fact already proved to be fairly successful. Even so, the challenge to individual freedom posed by this kind of cultural or political engineering reminds us that Banks himself does not ever abandon the promise of freedom. (Even the postmodernist multiculturalists do not go that far.)

At this point, we recall as well that Banks has serious reservations about identity, group identity being in a way the chief cause of discrimination.

Indeed, one could say that anti-discrimination politics does not really care about identity in the abstract at all, that its employment of the concept of identity is politically selective and politically partial: identity is neither good nor bad but discrimination makes it so. (The attempt to fashion a general theory around "ascriptive" identity as the ground of anti-discrimination claims has faltered for similar reasons.)[10] Nobody needs or even really wants a universal theory of identity, and to think that we do is to pursue intellectual precision where it is probably neither welcome nor useful. Such considerations suggest that the anti-discriminatory good is not ultimately identity, but justice. Likewise, the project of citizen identity reconstruction is saved, if it is saved, by its justice—and so we must turn then to the elements of anti-discrimination morality that assert more emphatically its justice—which is especially clear in demands for respect and the language of equity.

Respect versus Toleration

The heart of the debate between respect and toleration is the very simple fact that toleration may be said to be consistent with discrimination. Thus, the first of the "paradoxes of toleration" listed in the Stanford Encyclopedia of Philosophy entry for toleration is "the paradox of the tolerant racist" (Forst 2017). The Southern Poverty Law Center changed the name of its curriculum development arm from "Teaching Tolerance" to "Learning for Justice": "The fact is, tolerance is not justice. It isn't a sufficient description of the work we do or of the world we want" (Dunn 2021). The critique of toleration from this point of view is a teaching of both multicultural education and contemporary political theory.[11] To point out that there is a liberal tradition of thinkers—George Washington, William James, and Horace Kallen, for example—who see in toleration a pointer to something *higher* would probably sound like special pleading today.[12]

But one must insist, at the very least, that nothing in toleration encourages or requires discrimination—and even if it is true that, strictly speaking, toleration *permits* discrimination, this does not amount to any direct criticism of the original arguments made for toleration. The liberal ideal of toleration, which is rooted in humility about our claims to know that we are right and is suspicious of those who would use force to assert such claims on the rest of us, especially in the name of the claims of their *group* or in the name of idealistic zeal, calls out the dangers of moral and political (and, of course, religious) intransigence. The insights of our Enlightenment forebears about politics informing the ideal of toleration have not been proved false by events, even if a new political program says they are not good enough, morally.

At any rate, surely the new standard of respect is not above question. Liberal realism will wonder whether a standard insisting that citizens from different groups literally respect one another will be successful. If not, its foreordained failure seems certain to undermine intergroup trust, goodwill—and peace. How well, for example, do anti-discrimination politics and the standard of respect help to manage religious groups (the original concern of liberalism) in their relations with other protected classes (LGBT groups being the most obvious point of opposition at the moment)? More fundamentally, the question must be asked: why should anti-discrimination groups and their members be respected? What is the standard by which we are to deem them worthy of respect? Theorists on the Left would insist that respect is not to depend upon "merit."[13] But can an ideal of respect really be cut off from all notions of merit or deserving? Does the new standard of respect for groups contain some *alternative* foundation for such a judgment—and if so, what is it? It cannot be identity for the reasons given. It cannot be the injustices of the past because respect is a positive claim, not a negative, compensatory, one. And what would a mere demand for intergroup respect, devoid of some basis in merit or deserving or some other claim, really amount to? Would it be anything more than a kind of democratic, group-based lèse-majesté?

Equity and the New Equalities

We are still in need of a moral anchor for the whole. Does equality—or equity—provide it? Banks helps us to see that equality has two different but related meanings in the logic of anti-discrimination. We have seen Banks make use of the standard Left ideal of equal outcomes or equal results in the material realm (jobs, wealth, education, etc.); however, this is joined in his thinking by another formulation that is less familiar but also much less controversial. The latter notion is the idea that "diverse racial, ethnic, cultural, social-class, and gender groups within the nation-state . . . must experience—or believe that they can experience—equal status within the nation-state."[14] This second ideal—equal group status or worth—is less prominent (something like it does show up in the work of some political theorists),[15] but it expresses a vitally important moral intuition of contemporary democratic life. Equal group status or worth is a helpful way of stating generally what must be granted when we say that Blacks are equal to Whites, women are equal to men, and so on.[16] Alongside these two equalities connected with anti-discrimination are others long associated with civil rights reform but stamped with the logic of the liberal tradition: equality of rights (public), equal protection of the law (public), and equal opportunity (mainly private).

Politically, none of these several different forms of equality is simply predominant; this reflects the fact that there are important problems with all of them. Liberal public sector equality—equal rights and equality before the law—fails to reach private sector discrimination and, in its individualism, offers nothing to groups beside a promise they will be ignored—neither harmed nor helped (color-blind constitutionalism, benign neglect). Equality of opportunity does extend to the private sector, but anti-discrimination politics is clearly about more than opportunity. It is true that discrimination hampers human opportunity in general and economic and educational opportunities in particular. But these do not summarize the totality of the harms of discrimination according to its victims. Opportunity does not speak to the characteristic concerns of anti-discrimination politics in the way that identity, respect, recognition, and related terms do—while the standard of "equal status situations" for groups addresses those concerns in a fairly precise way. The usual opposition between equality of opportunity and equality of results is unsettled by the fact that equality of group status stands *between* them. Moreover, if we admit that equal group status has a claim upon us, we will also be inclined to grant that it points to the need for something even more, something along the lines of equal outcomes or results. It does so by compelling us to grant that, yes, all anti-discrimination groups are all equal in some important sense that goes beyond opportunity (when we say Blacks are equal to Whites, women are equal to men, we are thinking about something more than just opportunity). But if that is true, then what do we say about the manifest tangible inequalities (unequal outcomes, unequal results) that we cannot but notice? Have we not admitted in advance, if we accept something like the idea of equal status situations for groups, a presumption of suspicion at least for any significant material inequality affecting anti-discrimination groups? As Daniel Patrick Moynihan put it in 1964, "it may be that without unequal [favorable] treatment in the immediate future there is no way for [American Blacks] to achieve anything like equal status in the long run."[17]

But, at the same time, a full and open embrace of equal group outcomes in contemporary democratic life is a political nonstarter. The idea of equal outcomes as a matter of policy—affirmative action and disparate impact law—remains deeply controversial; this is one area where conservatives are free to attack openly a plank of the anti-discrimination platform, and an area where such attacks hit home with effective force, politically. Nobody actually proposes a comprehensive theory of simple, total, group equality as a matter of principle that would include equality for groups in wealth, education, and other material goods (the closest thing to it are arguments for "group rights," the least successful of all arguments pertaining to civil rights questions to emerge in the past several decades).[18] Here the anti-discrimination Left does seem to reach a hard limit.

Even the ideal of equal group status or worth, impossible to deny as a practical matter today, is not without difficulties. True, our intuition that Blacks are equal to Whites, that women are equal to men, does have significant purchase in contemporary life. But, like the claim of "respect," without something more, how is it not merely an assertion or demand? It is certainly not obvious that all social groups are or ought to be equal in status or worth—and anti-discrimination does not even make such a general or universal claim, limiting the reach of this equality to a select few groupings (those named by the law). Surely anti-discrimination cannot hold, for example, that discriminatory individuals or groups are equal, morally, to anti-discriminatory individuals or groups. Alternatively, why is this standard of equality so unequally applied? We must accuse this equality by reference to itself: why are so many unequal in group status (so many kinds of human unfairness and misfortune) excluded by it? And why is the equal status of all *within* groups never an issue? This appeal to a morality of group equality surely has persuasive power today, but lacking a clear ground and limit, its ultimate status remains elusive.

These difficulties help to explain why "equity," so usefully ambiguous, has become such an important and visible term. Today equity increasingly signifies primarily the Left interpretation, equality of results—but without quite owning up to the fact. But it also seems to suggest equality or fairness in general; moreover, as in Banks's use of it, equity may also refer to anti-discrimination's other equality claim, equal group status or worth. Those who use the term equity to advance anti-discrimination politics can thus appeal simultaneously to a vague sense of fairness, and to some unspecified sense of the justice of the fight against discrimination in particular, while advancing a claim for equal outcomes without having to defend—or even to specify—that latter, deeply controversial stance.[19]

Given the serious difficulties, political or otherwise, in all of these interrelated conceptions of equality, it is necessary to look further afield for the true source of our sense that anti-discrimination groups ought to be accorded some kind of equality (leaving aside mere demands for equality, which may be politically important but do not withstand moral or theoretical scrutiny). Here we are aided by the views of theorists of *representation* like Melissa Williams, who emphasize the injustice of *past* discrimination, and thus some notion of compensatory or corrective justice, in their moral reasoning: "The groups that merit representation . . . are characterized by two attributes: their contemporary inequality as compared to other social groups *and* a history of discrimination and oppression. Because of the connection between contemporary inequality and past discrimination, considerations of justice provide the strongest grounds for the special recognition of certain social groups."[20] Our sense that discrimination against groups in the past was morally wrong provides a powerful reason to insist that, going forward, we must treat those groups better—and, at the very least, that we will treat them as equals. It seems to me that this is a very important moral basis of contemporary anti-discrimination claims, not only for equal outcomes claims, but also for equal group status claims as well.[21]

But it is also telling that no full-throated explicit theory of corrective or compensatory equality for the victims of discrimination plays any prominent role in contemporary political debate. Many problems with such a view have been raised in debates over affirmative action and reparations.[22] Who deserves to be compensated and on what grounds; above all, who pays or deserves to pay? Shall injustices of the past committed by people now dead be compensated by their descendants? How is that not a kind of corruption of blood? As Supreme Court justices have pointed out, compensating for historical group injustices has "no logical stopping point." "Remedying the effects of 'societal discrimination [is] an amorphous concept of injury that may be ageless in its reach into the past."[23] How will such claims and debates over them, formed in part by a logic of corrective or punitive justice, not descend into a bitter spiral of group recrimination fixating public life on the injustices of the past and not a common future? The call for reparations, in particular, is, like critical race theory, a political liability for the Left today; even if reparations proposals are taken seriously, as they are in some places, they are highly polarizing and not supported by anything like a majority of the American people (see Blazina and Cox 2022). Moreover, as Banks helps us to see, this dimension of the logic at work (which may be very important, ultimately) contradicts the usual inclination or aspiration of the anti-discrimination ideal itself, which mainly strives to speak to and for the community as a whole, deploying the language of higher, more positive, moral principles. Arguments from corrective or compensatory justice therefore cannot be made explicit (and no equality ideal can openly operate solely by reference to them) because of the high aspirations of the anti-discrimination ideal itself. Resting the morality of the project entirely upon injustices of the past would be fundamentally negative, whereas the civil rights regime wishes to be positive, to advance some common good. It would also mean that anti-discrimination would remain narrow and *partial* (focused on particular harms to particular groups) where it wishes very much to be general or universal.

Inclusion and Group Representation

The concept of inclusion (defined in an obvious way against the *exclusions* of discrimination) demonstrates the real-world importance of the claims of the new morality.[24] Sometimes inclusion is an ideal for reimagining our world and its history. Banks states this as a kind of principle—"people of color, women, and other marginalized groups are demanding that their voices, visions, and perspectives be included"—and it forms the basis of his efforts to redefine "the center," the "common culture," the American "*unum*."[25] But this new ideal also has a more practical political application that may prove just as far-reaching, in new theories of "inclusive" *representation*. Here the most basic mechanism of modern democratic politics is being reshaped according to the logic of anti-discrimination. Theorists of inclusive representation advance their cause under a number of connected designations: "descriptive" or "mirror" or "pictorial" or "substantive" representation—or "positive discrimination" representation or "fair group representation for marginalized groups."[26] The standard of representation put forward by these theorists is basically equal group *outcomes* in the electoral field, an ideal of proportionality. As representation theorist Williams argues, "the design of the electoral system should itself be subject to a standard of *equity* as well as a standard of *equality*. . . . At a minimum, . . . equity in the electoral sphere would seem to require some degree of proportionality."[27]

Group representation schemes are alive and well in America as a practical matter. As we saw in chapter 3, "max-Black" and "max-Hispanic" voting districts are championed by the Department of Justice and largely acceded to by the courts.[28] Indeed, as in the affirmative action debate that this one mirrors, in a way they fare better in practice than in theory (ever since Lani Guinier's brief for group representation led President Bill Clinton to abandon her nomination as Assistant Attorney General for Civil Rights, nobody is permitted openly to favor election "quotas"). Opposition to racial gerrymandering is in fact weak *politically* because it is perceived to benefit both parties (Abigail Thernstrom rejects Republican pretensions of opposition to the practice as "pure myth") [2009, 112].) The Democratic Party openly embraces proportional representation schemes for internal purposes. Its 2020 convention rules specified "affirmative action programs" for "African Americans, Hispanics, Native Americans, Asian Americans and Pacific Islanders and women" in its national delegate selection process (and similar lesser efforts for "members of the LGBTQ+ community, people with disabilities, and youth").[29] After disappearing in the 1950s, ranked-choice voting schemes, promoted today primarily for their ability to benefit anti-discrimination groups, have started to make a comeback in cities and in some states (see Zoch 2020). The exploration by political scientists of a variety of electoral and voting schemes, mainly with a view to increasing representation for members of anti-discrimination groups, has become a hot field of study.[30]

The Left's commitment to anti-discrimination group representation, in theory and in practice, demonstrates the political power of this ideal.

But, as in the affirmative action debate, there is a significant limit here, since such practices cannot be openly or readily defended in public without cost. These new representation schemes are controversial in large part because they appear to contradict the liberal democratic understanding of representation in important ways. The divide between anti-discrimination and liberalism in this domain first comes to sight in allegations that the new regime deviates from the one person, one vote, principle spelled out by the Supreme Court most famously in 1964 in *Reynolds v. Sims*. That view of the logic of representation—more or less embraced by Left and Right alike—would seem, obviously, to reflect deep ties to the liberal social contract and liberal individualism.[31] As one legal scholar put it, "the assumption that all representation is the representation of groups does not come naturally to Americans, who have always tended to view representation as the representation of individuals."[32] Even Lani Guinier felt compelled to say, "I have always believed in one person, one vote, and nothing I have ever written is inconsistent with that" (1994, 190).

Another powerful line of criticism of group representation relies on the *realist* strand of liberal thinking, emphasizing, as Justice O'Connor does in *Shaw v. Reno*, the ways in which "racial classifications with respect to voting carry particular dangers."[33] (Moreover, objections may be raised to the idea that, to be liberal, representation must be *individualistic*.)[34] The practical worry is partly that group representation will perpetuate racial classifications and racial discrimination.[35] But the main danger that critics of proportional racial representation schemes have in mind is the threat they pose to civic unity and peace—the fear that what they launch will be, in the words of Justice O'Connor, an unhealthy and perilous "politics of racial hostility," or, to use a famous phrase from the Reagan years, a "racial spoils system."[36] On this view, proportional representation schemes would take over the essential machinery of democratic self-government to institutionalize a form of group politics that openly divides groups against one another, encouraging a politics of permanent zero-sum competition, mistrust, and blame—where it should instead work to heal the wounds of the past and to promote the common good of all.[37] These concerns are held to be especially urgent now because what is being framed is the politics of *racial* or *ethnic* groups in particular—not something to be handled ineptly. Racial representation schemes help to harden or ossify group claims of the kind that liberalism always took pains to undermine and weaken. Proportional representation institutionalizes a heightened sense of group self-regard, group grievance, and even group segregation by giving elected politicians an incentive to appeal openly to insular and dubious prejudices of groups and to encourage mistrust of outsiders and of the political system more broadly.[38] As Justice Clarence Thomas put it, "our drive to segregate political districts by race can only serve to deepen racial divisions by destroying any need for voters or candidates to build bridges between racial groups or to form voting coalitions."[39] Where Williams holds out the hope that group representation will begin a "spiral of trust," critics suggest that a likelier result would be a bitter spiralling of our group politics in the opposite direction (1998, 172). Lost in this "racial 'piece-of-the-action-approach'" are more elevated aims of racial and political "integration" and notions of "common citizenship" (Thernstrom 1987, 242–43). As a demand for justice formalized in group representation schemes, inclusion means forever reliving the pain of the past and affirming group mistrust for the present and future.[40]

The main and simple retort from the Left to worries about civic unity and civic peace is to draw attention to instances of significant underrepresentation and to remind us of their alleged injustice.[41] But at the same time, to repeat, the Left's moral position is not permitted to be expressed as a simple or full-throated call for group proportionality. Claims of justice thus clearly fail to settle things in a decisive way. The question then becomes whether institutionalizing group relations along these lines works to overcome injustice or condemns us to being obsessed by it. It is not necessary to fret about outright group conflict—which, as much as American politics is polarized, remains a distant concern—to say that traditional liberal worries about social harmony and mere peace are worth taking seriously. Political trust is an important good and our laws and institutions ought not undermine it. If, in the divergence between the claims of peace and the demands of justice, we see once again the tension between liberalism and anti-discrimination politics, we also must ask how or whether contemporary democracy can now articulate an effective principle of political unity or community. We are in a strange place if inclusion means rejecting notions of union and civic harmony and racial integration as the rhetoric of oppression.

Recognition versus Interest

Recognition is another term commonly employed by political theorists and other intellectuals in contemporary debate about multiculturalism and civil rights politics.[42] Now, following Banks, I would insist that to focus on the language of recognition is to understate the *moral* dimension in anti-discrimination politics.[43] Academics like Charles Taylor and Axel Honneth, who have made the politics of recognition famous, in my view indulge in a kind of reductionist explanation of what drives or energizes the new politics instead of engaging the new logic on its own terms.[44] But, in some obvious ways, anti-discrimination *is* a politics of recognition. Crucial concepts like respect, or the idea of equal group status, are obviously related (if in a moralized way to be sure) to matters of social recognition. More important, we may say that specifying in the law the kinds of discrimination the community is to police makes everyone more sensitive to the (relative) status or recognition of the groups so singled out for official attention. We are today nothing if not obsessed by the status of women and men, Blacks and Whites, and so on.

Recognition also sheds light on the conflict between anti-discrimination politics and the liberal tradition. For in the concept of *interest*, an equivalent term of submoral or psychological meaning is used to characterize something essential in the liberal understanding of politics. Exploring the differences between a politics of interests and a politics of recognition is indeed very productive. As Aristotle teaches, to care about recognition is to hand over to someone else the basis of one's estimation of oneself. At the same time, preoccupation with recognition serves to inflate desire beyond what is actually needful or good, beyond the concrete requirements of life like wealth or health or education or virtue, in the direction of something ephemeral—as Aristotle says, something "superficial."[45] The great weakness of Taylor's famous discussion of the "politics of recognition" is his refusal to say the obvious: that the quest for recognition for its own sake (no matter how common it may be) is not something worthy of the attention of a serious person. Moreover, the situation is made worse when this problematic concern becomes central to the logic of group politics. As political scientist H. D. Forbes puts it, "social status is a 'positional good,' and status rivalry among groups is a 'zero sum game'."[46] For groups, the politics of recognition is a frustrating and fraught struggle for a problematic good. These difficulties reach a critical point when recognition is denied or is perceived to be denied—which, in the nature of things, it inevitably will be.[47] Koppelman goes so far as to locate the most important harm of discrimination here:

> Stigmatized social status and the concomitant withholding of respect are in a sense the central evil the [anti-discrimination] project seeks to remedy, since it is the source of the poison that contaminates, and renders unfair the outcomes of, public and private decision making. Stigma and insult are familiar parts of the daily experience of many in our society who are, for example, black, female, or gay. . . . The other injuries that concern the antidiscrimination project are bound up with this one.[48]

(Koppelman necessarily—and rightly—moves from the language of "status" to that of morality here.) But the characteristic responses to insults and perceived slights are generally anger and indignation. An institutionalized politics of recognition, such as anti-discrimination is, is likely to be an angry affair. As the basis of group relations, the politics of recognition in a democracy will likely devolve into a dialectic of recrimination and resentment.[49] To say the least, in practice any politics of recognition will be, as Forbes puts it, "inherently and inescapably antagonistic" (2019, 133).

All of this is the opposite of liberalism's deliberate effort to tame by lowering the stakes of political life, by replacing the language of deserving and justice with the language of interest. To repeat briefly what I said in chapter 7, the language of interest is the language of *self*-interest (whether group or individual), and this means that, under liberalism, all groups begin by conceding the (merely) selfish character of their claims. Interest politics diminishes and undermines group claims where recognition politics inflates them. When our interests conflict with similar competing claims of others, as much as we want our interests to prevail, we lack the motives and justifications that a more moralized view would offer to exaggerate ours at the expense of theirs; thinking about politics as a matter of competing interests inclines all in the direction of compromise—and peace. Conflicts on the level of recognition, on the other hand, and the sense of insult and grievance characteristic of them, are not readily resolved according to compromise.

They are more likely to result in further accusation and recrimination. To repeat Hume's formula, factions of interest are "the most reasonable factions"—unlike factions of recognition, which are in a sense made neurotic by the problematic and scarce good they pursue.

A Politics of Justice and Injustice: The Spirit of the New Morality

On the basis of this preliminary scouting of the territory, we may say that the moral logic associated with anti-discrimination politics tends to heighten our concern with "justice" where almost everything in the liberal understanding was directed to taking claims of justice off the main stage of political life. The many differences between the new moral sensibility and the old are consistent with, and confirm our sense of, the many differences between new and old at the level of group politics or pluralism that we summarized in chapter 8. Where the old morality worked to weaken the kinds of charged claims that can lead to deep conflict, the new morality works to politicize and to stir people up in a drama of moralized group self-protection and self-assertion. A politics of the liberty of individuals—and of the protection of the individual from state over-reaching—is very different from a politics that starts from the identity claims of groups enlisting the state as a matter of course. Where the logic of toleration minimizes the expectations of groups and individuals alike, demands for respect ramp them up. Where the language of interest de-moralizes group claims in a way that makes it harder to insist upon them in the public arena, claims of group identity and recognition are already defined by reference to the broader social or public world, rendering group aspirations more contentious, less flexible, and harder to manage. Conflicting or competing interests yield compromise; conflicting or competing identities do not. Where the guarantees of equal opportunity, equal rights, and equality before the law emphasize the rule of law and individual responsibility, the new understanding of equality focuses our attention on group inequalities, deems them unjust, and requires a government-led politics of remediation, redistribution, and reparation—or, at a minimum, new schemes of inclusive group representation highlighting group differences, grievances and exclusions. Liberalism's lessons about the dangers of moralistic politics, its strategies to undermine and moderate moral claims, to separate morality and the state, its easygoing morality of live and let live, are all rendered problematic. Taking justice more seriously, and raising the standard of justice higher (or at least making the claims of justice more demanding), the new morality is more ambitious than the old, asking more from both the political order and the individuals within it. Again and again, anti-discrimination's moralism runs up against liberalism's realism.

Our claim at the beginning of chapter 9 that anti-discrimination morality is a fighting morality, a spirited morality, has been vindicated several times over. Indeed, it is more accurate to say that the new morality is more preoccupied with *injustice* than it is with justice. Anti-discrimination is a moral reform effort borne of bitter, harsh experience, shaped decisively by the painful encounters with injustice and the characteristic harms (insult, indignity, and worse) of discrimination from which it begins. This is a spirited morality that reflects the psychic toll of standing up to injustice. This must be done for oneself, but it must also be done because to ignore discrimination would be to accede to its harms for others like oneself; it is a morality of protecting and defending others from mistreatment. To fight discrimination is also then to confront injustice and to confront those doing injustice, no easy task. At its most fully self-conscious, that means also finding the will to reverse the social valuations of the world in which discrimination was acceptable. It means looking at the world anew, now from the point of "the vanquished," where once it was seen from the point of view of the "victors"; it means taking a "system fault" view of our situation.[50] (These last steps are all necessary, we note, even before we add in the extreme mind-making and world-making claims of postmodernism.) This morality thus takes sides; it must chasten and challenge the unjust while defending and aiding the vulnerable in a politics of friends (allies) and enemies. Confronting injustice also means resisting injustice in the future by reckoning with the past, a manifold task. This requires a campaign affecting those who were formerly victims and perpetrators in different ways. Drawing at points on the logic of corrective or punitive justice, it is necessarily a morality that holds people accountable, parsing and dispensing blame. It also means insisting upon dignity and respect and equality for discrimination's victims and seeking compensation for harm done. It means never forgetting the pain and humiliation of bygone times, keeping alive the memories of injustice as a protective necessity. Looking ahead, for the future, its program of defense against discrimination must teach potential victims to be suspicious of those who have done injustice before now and to arm them with mistrust and wary vigilance. Indeed, this outlook assumes that discrimination and its injustices are inevitable and unavoidable, permanent features of human life. This moral spirit is in turn reflected in features of the law put in place to achieve its corrective ends.[51] Indeed, as one legal scholar put it, relying on Aristotle's analysis of kinds of justice, anti-discrimination law is more like corrective than distributive justice: the "motivating values" of anti-discrimination law "relate to correction of wrongs committed by individuals and . . . closely follows the contours of corrective justice" (Morris 1995, 200).

Anti-discrimination morality is thus not only a spirited morality but a somewhat angry morality, though its defenders would insist that it has earned the right to its anger. Anti-discrimination deals with what Koppelman deems "justified resentment"—"the justified resentment at the injustice of being insulted with impunity" (1996, 195). As Koppelman says, "those who are constantly subjected to insults . . . , [also] suffer a different kind of injury, that of resentment, tension, and anger" (1996, 62). Even when overt insults are not the issue, group inequalities can have the same effect. "The fact that some groups receive more rewards from society than other groups can be observed by the members of oppressed groups. This resentment often causes tension between ethnic groups that can lead to conflict. It is not easier to accept a subordinate status just because most individuals of the dominant group are not prejudiced or do not discriminate" (Gollnick and Chinn 1990, 93). Associated with corrective morality is also, for those deemed guilty, a sense of shame. Here is vindication for the Kennedy administration legal advisor Freund's claim, cited earlier, that "guilt upon violation of law becomes a feeling of shame if the law is felt to be morally right" (1968, 41). We recall that Banks considered (without being entirely optimistic about) approaches to multicultural education that assume "that people with power feel guilty about the ways in which exploited groups are treated, or can be made to feel guilty" (1974, 49–50).

Now I want to emphasize that, for Banks, appeals to corrective justice are not the only thing—indeed, not even the main thing. On the other hand, as we have seen, an angry tone is especially characteristic of the writing of postmodernist multiculturalists, a necessary accompaniment, perhaps, to their avowedly revolutionary and insurgent self-understanding:

"[Students] need to develop habits and skills for critiquing the presumed universality of any one canon of truth. . . . These skills are underscored by ethical outrage and moral indignation at the way the democratic imperative is routinely distorted to justify Eurocentric cultural hegemony and political dominance" (Gay 1995, 178). "The notion of critical pedagogy begins with a degree of indignation" (Giroux and Simon 1989, 252). By focusing on Banks and not the postmodernists, I may well understate the role of the punitive spirit in the new logic overall (as I have pointed out, the latter are today predominant, at least among multiculturalism theorists). But even for Banks, it is precisely "act[ing] decisively to right the unrightable wrong" that holds out the hope of an "unreachable star" and "the liberation of the hearts and minds of all American youth" (1973d, 750). The question is whether a collective commitment to corrective justice can, in fact, provide an enduring common good.

Almost everyone takes for granted the legitimacy of corrective justice in the ordinary criminal law (even those, mostly on the Left, who abjure the language of strictly "punitive" justice in that context). But it must be said that this aspect of the morality of anti-discrimination politics is troubling, especially since, unlike the criminal law, we are not dealing primarily with individuals but with groups and group transgressions. More generally, is not the punitive spirit in a way perhaps always troubling, no matter how justified it may seem, wherever it is confronted?

When Injustice Is the Center

To the extent that this accurately captures some significant portion of the morality of anti-discrimination, postmodernist political theorist Wendy Brown's arresting analysis of "politicized identity" is extremely useful. Brown's account of "the dominant political expression of the age—identity politics" applies Nietzsche's exploration of *ressentiment* (the moral indignation of the injured) to the impulse of anti-discrimination in a thought-provoking analysis.[52] Brown's inclination to make use of Nietzsche's insights is much to be preferred to the tendency of those on the Right who would blame Nietzsche and the influence of his ideas for the phenomenon she describes.[53]

> [Nietzsche's] thought is useful . . . to understand the codification of injury and powerlessness. . . . Examples of this tendency abound, but it is perhaps nowhere more evident than in the contemporary proliferation of efforts to pursue legal redress for injuries related to social subordination by marked attributes or behaviors: race, sexuality, and so forth. This effort, which strives to establish racism, sexism, and homophobia as morally heinous in the law, and to prosecute its individual perpetrators there, has many of the attributes of what Nietzsche named the politics of *ressentiment*. . . . [I am not] suggesting that what currently travels under the sign of "harassment" is not hurtful, that "hate speech" is not hateful. . . . Rather, precisely because they are hurtful, hateful, and political, because these phenomena are complex sites of political and historical deposits of discursive power, attempts to address them litigiously are worrisome. (Brown 1995, 26–27)

Brown describes a logic of suffering, blame, resentment, and retribution in order to highlight its shortcomings precisely from the point of view of the victims of discrimination whom the law now seeks to protect and aid. For Brown, politicized identity in this context is above all an "identity structured by *ressentiment*," the resentment and moral indignation of the insulted and the wounded. Brown characterizes in psychological terms the experience of moral indignation (and our sense of retributive justice) as it comes to sight in the case of "politicized identity"—as an "attempt to displace [the] suffering" of injustice (1995, 70). "Politicized identity [is] premised on exclusion and fueled by the humiliation and suffering imposed by its historically structured impotence" (1995, 70–71). "It delimits a specific site of blame for suffering. . . . In its economy of perpetrator and victim, this project seeks . . . the revenge of punishment, making the perpetrator hurt as the sufferer does."[54] Any politics that embraces and enshrines a logic of blame and a desire for retribution attempts a complex psychological (and of course largely unconscious) attempt to make something good out of something terrible.

> If the "cause" of *ressentiment* is suffering, its "creative deed" is the reworking of this pain into a negative form of action, the "imaginary

revenge" of what Nietzsche terms "natures denied the true reaction, that of deeds." This revenge is achieved through the imposition of suffering "on whatever does not feel wrath and displeasure as he does" (accomplished especially through the production of guilt), through the establishment of suffering as the measure of social virtue, and through casting strength and good fortune ("privilege," as we say today) as self-recriminating, as its own indictment in a culture of suffering.[55]

On Brown's view, *moral* claims that are made in this context are revealed to be part of the dubious psychological defense mechanism at the bottom of the desire for retribution. The "identity structured by this ethos" seeks precisely "to assuage the pain of its powerlessness through its vengeful moralizing" and "in this reaction achieves its moral superiority" (1995, 70). Brown is thus wary of attempts to use moral language to characterize such claims today—as, for example, "a righteous critique of power from the perspective of the injured"—and is generally suspicious of the "contemporary tendency to moralize in the place of political argument" (1995, 26–27).

Brown is worried about the influence of such forces in contemporary democratic politics and she provides a detailed accounting of their negative consequences. She suggests, in effect, that a politicization of corrective justice tends at points in the direction of political pathology or social neurosis—a psychological defense mechanism gone awry. The inversion that the spirit of retribution attempts takes a great toll on the ones seeking retribution themselves because they must come to *define* themselves by the one experience they would most benefit from overcoming or leaving behind. "Identity structured by *ressentiment* . . . becomes invested in its own subjection" and in "its own impotence" (1995, 70). Instead of seeking genuine inclusion, groups and individuals bound up in this dynamic can seem to find a (deleterious) value in their experience of exclusion. "Politicized identity . . . becomes attached to its own exclusion both because it is premised on this exclusion for its very existence as identity and because the formation of identity at the site of exclusion, as exclusion, augments or 'alters the direction of the suffering' entailed in subordination or marginalization by finding a site of blame for it."[56] Groups and individuals operating according to this logic also come to define themselves negatively in the process. "Politicized identity that presents itself as a self-affirmation now appears as the opposite, as predicated on and requiring its sustained rejection by a 'hostile external world'."[57] In addition, seeking illusory goods, this attempt at psychological compensation or redemption takes the place of healthier and more substantial aspirations while dissipating the energies and effort needed to make them a reality. Seeking as it does primarily "the revenge of punishment, making the perpetrator hurt as the sufferer does," "this project" does *not* seek "power or emancipation for the injured or the subordinated" in fact (1995, 27). "Politicized identity . . . is as likely to seek generalized political paralysis, to feast on generalized political impotence, as it is to seek its own or collective liberation through empowerment" (1995, 70–71; see 27). Finally, Brown's analysis suggests that, under the influence of this logic, politics would be doomed never even to hope of escaping the disturbing starting point of hateful antagonism, rooted in past oppression and injustice, from which it must forever take its bearings. The spirit of corrective justice works to lock politics into a particular point of mistrustful and resentful conflict, a point of great suffering, regardless of whether the original ill is still present or has been remedied or diminished: "Politicized identity thus enunciates itself, makes claims for itself, only by entrenching, restating, dramatizing, and inscribing its pain in politics; it can hold out no future—for itself or others—that triumphs over this pain" (1995, 74).

Applying these reflections to anti-discrimination politics as Brown suggests we do, we see that such an analysis emphasizes the harms done by politicized retribution and resentment to the victims of discrimination and to the workings of the political system as a whole. Similar considerations also apply to those the anti-discrimination regime would police in its corrective efforts. As Brown says, "a strong commitment to equality, requiring heavy state interventionism and economic redistribution, attenuates the commitment to freedom and breeds *ressentiment* expressed as neoconservative anti-statism, racism, charges of reverse racism, and so forth" (Brown 1995, 67). Generally speaking, to the extent that multiculturalism's attempt to fashion a common good out of the spirit of punitive justice succumbs to Brown's account of "politicized identity," we should not hesitate to be guided by the consideration that there is something disturbing about the punitive spirit, especially if it is meant to supply some important component of our national moral self-understanding.

The New Morality and the Old

> We Americans were able to found a government on the rights to life, liberty, and the pursuit of happiness because there was general agreement that these rights were indeed fundamental, the gift of nature's God; that, we declared, was a self-evident truth. We have also been able to enforce the various provisions of the 1964 Civil Rights Act because, again, there was a general agreement that discrimination on the basis of race or gender was simply unjust.
> —Walter Berns, *Taking the Constitution Seriously*[58]

Our duty to engage the new order on the high plane of principle, with the added hope that we may thus also be able to operate at some remove from the heat and noise of political life, is a further recommendation for attempting such a broad comparison at the level of moral opinion. Looking at liberalism and anti-discrimination from the point of view of morality also reveals things we would not otherwise see, or see as clearly. But does the debate at the level of principle elevate as much as we might wish? Three important problems come to sight here that merit further thought. We have already explored the first, namely, the inclination of the new morality in a corrective or punitive direction. Anti-discrimination seems unable fully to escape the hold of its necessarily negative starting point. There does not seem to be any important place in it for transcending the plane on which it fights against evil; there is no important place for reconciliation, for forgiveness, for integration even (a word strangely old-fashioned sounding to us now). The idea that we might at some point be able to "relax" about discrimination, or even, for example, about the discrimination of the past—to let bygones be bygones, to accept our history as flawed but not, therefore, simply to be condemned and hated—contradicts everything that the moral spirit of anti-discrimination politics teaches us. Is there not something to the idea, as Aristotle puts it, that "friendship holds cities together and . . . lawgivers are more serious about it than about justice"?[59]

A second large difficulty is the strikingly incomplete or unsettled character of the morality of anti-discrimination. There can be no doubt that anti-discrimination *aspires* to offer a vision of its claims in the general and universal language of morality. In the complexity of its moral terms we can even see a kind of *system* of interrelated moral concepts, all organized in a consistent pattern and all serving the same end. We are certainly compelled to take this new morality seriously if for no other reason than because its terms are now widely embraced and have therefore become, to some degree, authoritative for us. But there are many places where the new morality does not satisfy our expectations. First and most obvious are the places where the new morality must rely on evasions, where it cannot say what it thinks openly and must resort to rhetorical sleight of hand to press its case. This is clear in the crucial logic of equal outcomes and the call for proportional group representation that follows from it. These are arguments that can be made only with a guilty conscience in America today. That they must be hidden under the cloak of a problematic notion of "equity" only confirms our sense that something is wrong here. Another related problem is the reliance upon moral claims that are implied but not made explicit, or that are only barely stated and at the margins. This is the issue with arguments from compensatory justice. It is true that Americans think that past treatment of Blacks and other groups was unjust, but an open or official reliance upon that as a general principle is impossible because its manifest narrowness and partiality would jeopardize the aspirations to universality of the anti-discrimination regime. Other key ideas—like respect or equal group status—are compelling but manifestly incomplete, requiring some further argument or principle that is lacking. Finally, in the concept of identity, we witness an indispensable principle for the morality of anti-discrimination about which anti-discrimination itself is ambivalent. Identity is what anti-discrimination must protect, but is also an important cause of discrimination. In the end, it is hard to avoid the conclusion that in its quest for general or universal principles of morality, anti-discrimination raises as many questions as it answers.

The last question concerns the future of our two moralities. The old morality—a product of long and costly experience, formed and fitted together in the minds of world-historical figures who still hold our respect, and once the faith of progressive intellectuals across the globe—is now challenged at many points by a morality of a very different sort arising out of a political development not fully or clearly intended in many of its dimensions by those who launched it. To say the least, this is a striking spectacle to behold. The laws of moral physics would seem to require in the present instance that any increase in the new morality be accompanied by an equal reduction of the old morality. Moral opinion is not the only cause affecting this equation, of course, but it is worth noting that in the contest between liberalism and anti-discrimination it is the appeal to the justice of the latter that seems to be its greatest strength.

Chapter 11
THE NEW AMERICAN DILEMMA:
ANTI-DISCRIMINATION REGIME AND CITIZEN

> To reform a regime is no less a task than to institute one from the beginning, just as unlearning something is no less a task than learning it from the beginning.
> —Aristotle, *Politics*[1]

What is American multiculturalism? We have learned that despite some appearances to the contrary it is to begin with a coherent idea. If we look to the originators of the concept in the United States, in the multicultural education literature, we see always and everywhere the same message, originating in and expressing the impulse of the civil rights revolution. In a formula: multiculturalism is a way of saying "anti-discrimination" in a seemingly positive and capacious way. Multiculturalism is also an extremely helpful *teacher* of the radical—transformative, challenging, unsettling—character of the politics of the fight against discrimination.

By now I will presumably be permitted to insist on the following propositions: (1) that a number of nontrivial differences or disagreements between multiculturalism and liberal pluralism exist; (2) that these many differences are a reflection of the much broader development that is the anti-discrimination revolution's challenge to the liberal democratic political tradition. For the moment, the new order coexists uneasily alongside the old. That some synthesis of these two different outlooks might well serve a useful civic purpose in contemporary American life is obvious; that it would be theoretically coherent is less so. These important differences, to repeat, are evident even *before* we take up more extreme political lines of opposition (the disparate treatment versus disparate impact debate, e.g.) or more radical theoretical expressions of the new order (in postmodernist multiculturalism or critical race theory, e.g.). Further study would presumably confirm that these differences or tensions inform not only legal, educational, and theoretical debate but also shape American political culture and American life in a general way.

Underestimating the Anti-Discrimination Revolution

But if the commitment to fighting discrimination introduces a new way of thinking about democratic politics, why is this not generally admitted or recognized? When we turn to the question of the connection between liberalism and anti-discrimination proper, we are confronted by the almost universal consensus opinion that the civil rights revolution by itself does not represent anything other than some continuation, culmination, or extension of the liberal tradition. Only a few radical partisans on either side—like Richard Epstein, who has called for the repeal of the 1964 Act in the name of liberty, or Andrew Koppelman, who offers a far-reaching critique of liberalism in the name of anti-discriminatory justice—articulate the issue in these terms.[2] The power of this standard interpretation of anti-discrimination is clear also, for example, in the work of political theorists laboring to fit the terms of the new moral logic *into* the familiar categories of liberalism. The conviction that anti-discrimination is the product of, or is in some other way fundamentally consistent with, liberalism predominates not only in political and social theory but also in the disciplines of political science, law, history, and sociology; it is indeed the starting point for almost all prominent scholarly treatments (Left or Right) of American civil rights politics.[3] This mistaken general understanding of things matters because it stops us from fully coming to terms with the fight against discrimination, a central feature of our world, as a distinct entity.

That we do not see our situation in terms of a basic tension or set of tensions between liberalism and anti-discrimination is partly explained by the outline of the contemporary civil rights debate as it has been shaped by battles over policies like affirmative action that conservatives would say go *beyond* anti-discrimination. A common thread in the standard interpretation, especially but not only on the Right, holds that traditional liberalism is opposed not by anti-discrimination but only by more radical policies associated with it, such as speech codes, group representation, and, above all, affirmative action. From this perspective it is conceded that the relationship between *some* civil rights policies and America's liberal tradition is worth thinking about, but then the line of division is drawn one step removed from the commitment to fighting discrimination itself (which is assumed to be unproblematically located within liberalism). This supposition informs, for example, the analysis of leading civil rights historian Hugh Davis Graham, who says that the introduction of affirmative action served to separate "two phases of the Civil Rights Era." The distinction made by Graham, "between classic liberalism's core command against discrimination on the one hand, and [a] new theory of compensatory justice on the other" (for the latter he has in mind affirmative action), is one shared by many.[4] But this outline of the issues is insufficiently attentive to the kinds of evidence of tension surveyed here that suggest the revolutionary character of anti-discrimination policy, from the point of view of liberalism, on its own. Interpretations that divide the old and the new by focusing on affirmative action and other similarly controversial policies abstract from the massive middle ground and pivotal intermediary role represented by the basic commitment to fighting discrimination in the private as well as the public sphere.

The true relationship between anti-discrimination and liberalism in America is further obscured or distorted by two other common assumptions, one Right and one Left. The tendency of conservatives to reduce the Left's interpretation of anti-discrimination politics to postmodernism or some other alien theory of intellectuals, or to some vaguely related but less central political development, is one that we have encountered already. The Left, on the other hand, misinterprets the changes we see around us by attributing them to a cultural or social, rather than to a political, revolution. On this view, the groups themselves, the discrimination they have suffered, the struggles they have made against oppression—and not the law—are the key to understanding where we are and where we are going. Indeed, as we have seen, anti-discrimination law itself is sometimes criticized from the Left for its perceived inadequacies. This stance is partly a populist democratic mythology (the agency of the people, valorizing bottom-up struggle), partly the result of some of the prejudices of modern social science, and partly a product of the broad depoliticizing tendencies of liberalism. But mainly it is the result of the fact that the members of the anti-discrimination

Left are so defined by the anti-discrimination regime, so bound up in it, that they cannot see it as a distinct phenomenon. While it is largely true that the civil rights *movement* preceded the civil rights revolution, the struggle of only one group—Black Americans—was truly decisive at the outset. Other groups now identified with anti-discrimination politics (women, the disabled, the elderly, gays and lesbians, religious groups, transgender persons) of course existed, as a matter of crude demographic fact, prior to 1964, but some of them became politically self-conscious and publicly engaged only as a result of the possibilities that the new political framework offered them. The Right's blindness here is a form of "denial," of wishing the world were not as it is; the Left's is an incapacity to step outside that (political) world.

But the deepest explanation of our lack of attention to the anti-discrimination revolution is to be found in a kind of conspiracy of the hopes and fears of both the Left and Right. The Left, demanding even more extensive reforms, refuses to concede that anything dramatic has been achieved through anti-discrimination policy. To treat the anti-discrimination regime as a phenomenon would necessarily be to treat it as an established and authoritative one, and the Left has a great deal invested in an ideal of anti-discrimination politics as revolutionary, insurgent, and unfinished. On that view, anti-discrimination policy shows *not* that America is an astonishingly anti-racist, anti-sexist country, a country obsessed with discrimination and fighting discrimination, but instead proves that it continually falls woefully short of the mark. The Right, on the other hand, wishes to believe that the American liberal tradition is essentially unchanged by the new commitment to anti-discrimination, that there was never anything wrong with our laws and institutions in the first place that the liberal tradition could not fix. Locating the cause of trouble elsewhere, in foreign ideas or fringe radical groups, permits conservatives to minimize what has taken place. In the end, it is easier for all parties to assume that because America is somehow liberal, and since Americans universally endorse anti-discrimination, these two must somehow go together. The commitment to fighting discrimination ought at least to be a question for us, but precisely because everyone (on the Right as well as the Left) is so dedicated to it, we do not permit ourselves the detachment to see it, to see its novel and distinctive character.

Moral Reform, Political Unease

What is anti-discrimination? When we seek the meaning of the anti-discrimination regime in the many differences between multiculturalism and liberal pluralism, what stands out, above all, is a bold and wide-ranging program of moral reform. The moral in question is a simple one: discrimination is unjust, an evil heretofore tolerated but no more. But this program of moral reform is also, at the same time, a massive political project; and in the step from moral ideal to political undertaking other characteristic features of the whole come into view. In the many and vigorous challenges posed to the old by the new, it is indeed hard not to be struck by the disruptive, charged, and disquieting character of the new. If the recognition of contradiction is the beginning of the path to wisdom, the relationship between liberalism and anti-discrimination is a broad highway. We are in the middle of a sea change of a fundamental sort. Analogies to the rise of Christianity, Protestantism, the Enlightenment, modern democracy, Marxism may go too far, but then again they may not. Certainly nobody knew that this is what the civil rights revolution would mean when its main legal instruments and institutions were first put in place. It is up to us now to try to assess its logic, even or especially if its designers did not fully understand what it was they were setting in motion.

Anti-discrimination politics has been and continues to be a radical force. This is a question that we confronted in our discussion of postmodernist multiculturalism: was *its* radicalism owing to postmodernist theory or to the politics informing it? By now we have some reason to think that there is something about the fight against discrimination that makes it an intrinsically radical endeavor. Is the commitment to fighting discrimination a perfectionist project, a utopian undertaking—is it, as Banks says, an "impossible dream"? It would be unwise to turn away from its radical attributes as though they did not point to the essence of things—from moderation or civic accommodation or public-spirited meliorism, or from any other motive. Certainly one does not have to look far in the study of anti-discrimination to find its extreme or radical attributes (to include, of course, its many challenges to traditional liberalism). Indeed, I believe it can be shown fairly easily, by reference to important facts that are well-known, that what anti-discrimination asks of democratic life is extraordinary and indeed, by any measure, extreme and radical. This is a judgment that I believe even its most ardent defenders could be compelled to admit (even if they would, of course, defend the necessity of such efforts).

The most immediately obvious evidence of the extraordinary ambition of the anti-discrimination effort is indicated by the ceaseless expansion of its laws. With the exception of court-ordered busing plans for school desegregation, I am not aware of any important area of anti-discrimination law that has been significantly curtailed or rolled back. The imperial advance of anti-discrimination law, put in place by the Right and the Left both, takes many different forms: new and expansive ways of defining discrimination itself (disparate impact, stereotypes, harassment); a host of new monitoring and regulatory institutions and officials; ever-inventive, ever-evolving enforcement measures, including ones that involve all of us as citizens; increasingly important efforts of moral and civic education; group after group seeking the law's protection, adding layer after layer of more and yet more laws. In a way, this empire of laws looks mighty as it advances almost unchecked, conquering within and through the various domains in which its expansion unfolds. Or is there something about its very expansiveness that suggests the effort is forever unfinished and unfinishable, that new laws will always be found inadequate, thus spawning only further laws?

Several other undeniably radical features of anti-discrimination politics have been brought to light in our contrast with liberal pluralism. The first is that anti-discrimination politics is unavoidably an effort aiming explicitly to engage, and indeed to rework, the citizen soul, on the level of identity. One need not be a libertarian to have severe doubts about such a project. The second is the tendency of anti-discrimination to put at the center of public life in general, and group politics in particular, a spirited and, to some degree, punitive morality. The legal regime that created corrective firing and cancel culture has disrupted the balance of democratic life. Given a choice between liberalism's campaign to weaken the political passions and anti-discrimination's efforts to stir them up, it is hard not to feel some renewed appreciation for the achievements of liberal pluralism, especially when the new path is proposed as a general program (and not as a momentary, temporary reaction to some one particular set of injustices). These manifestly radical challenges to liberalism help, in turn, to clarify the ultimate meaning and importance of the more visible lines of confrontation between anti-discrimination and liberty under the Constitution—the battle over free speech, but also concerning freedom of religion and due process rights. The terms set by liberalism are in all these instances adequate to the task of describing these aspects of anti-discrimination politics and suffice to expose their troubling character.

Another radical dimension of the anti-discrimination regime that this study has highlighted is its alliance with postmodernist thought. Generally speaking, postmodernism tends to radicalize whatever it touches, and this is certainly the case with anti-discrimination politics. To say the least, postmodernism's unmooring of political deliberation from the constraints of reason does nothing to moderate anti-discrimination's radical or punitive tendencies.[5] Moreover, the anti-essentialism of postmodernist theory intensifies and encourages the fundamentally negative orientation of anti-discrimination and, in particular, the inclination to a wholesale condemnation of liberalism, the Constitution, the Enlightenment, "Western civilization," and indeed, the whole of the human past (insofar as it may be said to have been racist, sexist, homophobic, and so forth). Worse yet, it introduces, somehow in the name of theory, an explicit racialization of democratic politics and a campaign to reduce all the complexities of civil rights politics to an attack on "Whites" and "White culture" as the root of all evil. This is worse than the relativism it espouses, although that, too, is worth worrying about. While it is true that liberalism's embrace of individualism, freedom, toleration, and empiricism may indirectly suggest or imply, and hence promote, something approaching relativism, with multiculturalism, moral and cultural relativism became the official policy of the state of Iowa (Iowa DOE 1989a, 11). As a political stance, this seems to me to be merely ridiculous, but it points to broader consequences that are not trivial.

Two further features of the anti-discrimination regime that illustrate its radical character, aspects of the whole that I have either left out or understated, are worth mentioning now.

The first is the basic idea of prohibiting "sex discrimination," the source of the single most penetrating alteration of human life associated with the new order. This meant at the outset the regulation of discriminatory hiring practices but by now entails a massive effort of cultural reform and transformation calling into question our traditional notions of masculinity and femininity as well as our very understanding of human sexuality and gender. Taken as whole, this rethinking cuts in many directions at once and its effects for how we live and see ourselves have only begun to be felt. Do we know what we are doing here? The radical character of the effort is already plain in something as mundane as the law's prohibition of the use of "stereotypes," a seemingly innocuous, uncontroversial, and easily overlooked feature of anti-discrimination law.[6] As law professor Robert Post points out, to question stereotypes associated with male and female is in effect to question gender itself. "'Generalizations' and 'stereotypes' of this kind are, of course, the conventions that underwrite the social practice of gender. To eliminate all such generalizations and stereotypes would be to eliminate the practice" (2001, 24). As Post rightly says, the problem here will persist so long as "gender conventions remain salient within our culture" and "to the extent that gender remains a culturally inescapable fact" (2001, 39). While Post avoids any talk of "nature," he is nevertheless willing to go so far as to say that "sexual attraction is so firmly attached to existing gender roles that the effort to transform such roles by dislodging the 'stereotypes' presently manifested by sexual attraction seems an implausible ambition for the law" (2001, 30). Yet the prohibition on sex stereotypes is today more or less unquestioned—as I say, a settled assumption of the law. Something like this view of things has been pushed very far by the interventions of Title IX in our colleges and universities. Political scientist Shep Melnick summarizes the essential aim of Title IX as it has come to be interpreted by the Department of Education in a way that echoes Post's characterization:

> Title IX regulation is no longer primarily concerned with traditional education in the classroom, but rather with the education of both students and the general public on all matters sexual. Sexual stereotyping—which can include virtually all conventional thinking about sex and gender—must be identified, condemned, and corrected. Outmoded stereotypes about "masculinity and femininity"—based as they are on a mistaken bimodal, biological understanding of gender—should be replaced by an understanding that recognizes both the fluidity and the socially constructed nature of gender. (2018, 240)

The questioning of what used to be commonsense notions of gender and sexuality is taken further because of the extension of anti-discrimination protections to include lesbian, gay, bisexual, transgender persons, and others, an effort that is just beginning to feel its full strength in the law. Only very recently, in 2020, in the *Bostock* decision, have the powerful protections of Title VII for sex discrimination been extended to sexual orientation and gender identity in a clear legal mandate.[7] What stereotypes about human sexuality and gender have thereby become officially stigmatized and prohibited under the law? On the basis of these achievements alone we are justified in saying that anti-discrimination law undertakes a challenge to cultural norms and assumptions as radical as anything attempted in the history of human politics.

The other important radical element is the view, central to the Left interpretation, that the mere existence of significant inequalities for anti-discrimination groups *is* discrimination or is *evidence* of it—the basic idea undergirding affirmative action policy, group representation, and disparate impact law. This is the view that "smoking gun" discriminatory intent or motive need not be proved or even present in order to insist that "racism" is at work in policies and outcomes pertaining to unemployment, policing, education, housing, and so on. I have deliberately tried to avoid emphasizing this dimension of anti-discrimination politics because of its tendency to draw attention away from other, more important, and often overlooked, elements or attributes of the anti-discrimination regime, but it would be a mistake to deny its role and its significance, especially in connection with the question of anti-discrimination's tendencies to radicalism.[8]

As I said in chapter 3, the issue here is not really liberalism. The revolutionary character of this ideal is not to be found primarily in its upending of traditional legal norms (undermining as unimpressive the ideals of equal protection of the law, equal opportunity, and color-blind constitutionalism), though it does accomplish that. More important is the fact that this understanding of anti-discrimination advances a set of accusations and criticisms directed against a wide array of specific social, civic, and economic expectations and practices (any that are held to be associated with group inequalities). The disparity-as-discrimination point of view represents a rejection of all such criteria of judgment that may be thought to stand in the way of group equality (test scores, background checks, the lower reaches of the criminal law, etc.). Because there are so many of them, the cumulative effect, over time, cannot but be a general erosion of the sources of discipline that modern democratic peoples have at their disposal. For a time this might have seemed a theoretical matter—as in the critique of the morality of merit by Left intellectuals in the affirmative action debate. But by now it has been popularized and brought home to everyone by daily experience in many different areas of life (routine practices of business and education and government). In addition, the *argument* for it is no longer the province of academic theorists and appears now in a much simpler and more forceful political formulation: today, merit and personal responsibility are said to represent the language of privilege, a mask for hidden or implicit bias, a cover for racism. The lived result, where everyone sees the standards of personal responsibility being disregarded or repudiated (only for some, at first, but then eventually for everyone) cannot but have a pervasive and systemic effect—especially powerful because all of this is happening precisely in the name of *justice*. The result might make some people cynical about justice, but it will also further encourage and embolden those who already want to tear down the tangible working measures of responsibility, discipline, hierarchy, and inequality. Bourgeois life has long been bereft of defenders and derided as shallow, inauthentic, unhappy. But can modern democratic peoples really dispense with some basic education in personal responsibility?[9]

One might well object that in emphasizing these radical dimensions of the anti-discrimination project I have distorted the whole. Many elements of anti-discrimination policy are indeed utterly uncontroversial from any sane perspective. The end of public sector discrimination—the integration of the civil service and the military and non-discrimination in the provision of government services, for example—was easy to achieve and all to the good. Even an effort in the private sector like Title II of the 1964 Act, banning discrimination in the arena of public accommodations, decried at the time by defenders of traditional liberalism like Barry Goldwater, was entirely without ill effect and immediately effective (signs barring racial minorities from restaurants and the like disappeared more or less overnight) (see Wright 2013, chapter 2). Likewise, stopping overt, blatant practices of employment discrimination under Title VII (disparate treatment with smoking gun evidence) required only the threat of lawsuits to succeed in the workplace. Public opinion, public morality, have been affected in a beneficial way as well. Who today would not agree with Voltaire, that prejudice is opinion "without judgment," the error of those who "judge without reasoning, and who, being deceived, deceive others"?[10] And even if hidden or suppressed racism and sexism lurk in the recesses of some or even many modern democratic people's minds, the fact that crude prejudice and bigotry must now hide in the shadows is a salutary achievement of democratic politics.

But somehow these solid accomplishments, as manifest and as impressive as they are, do nothing to abate the demands for more, ever more, in the fight against discrimination. This, too, points to the radicalism, the utopianism or perfectionism, of the whole. Is anti-discrimination's power to unleash the force of morality in politics connected to this tendency to radicalism? Is our credo now "extremism in the defense of justice is no vice; moderation in the defense of justice is no virtue"? When it was introduced, the anti-discrimination program was strong medicine devised to remedy one particularly clear-cut case of deep and long-standing group mistreatment. The question is whether it can well serve as the permanent pattern for all of our social relations. In the face of the extreme demands that are laid upon us, it is hard not to bring to mind the doubts and worries of our Enlightenment forebears concerning all such ambitious moral reform efforts and to recall the sober modesty of their aspirations for political life.

Anti-Discrimination and the Liberal Tradition

Awakening to the tensions between anti-discrimination and liberalism is bracing, but facing our situation squarely helps us to see anti-discrimination politics as a separate phenomenon in its own right, a large shaping force at the heart of contemporary democratic life. It might be an exaggeration to say that America is shifting from a world framed in terms of liberal democracy to something like "anti-discrimination democracy," but, if so, it is a useful one. Highlighting the tensions between these two supreme moral authorities of our age may be unsettling, but the alternative would be to remain blind to a defining feature of our political situation.

It is true that the challenge to liberalism here is fundamental, extending to its basic understanding of politics, its moral categories, much of its history, and many of its heroes. The erosion of liberalism's solidity by the anti-discrimination regime is no small matter, especially when liberalism today is either undefended or poorly defended by theorists who no longer dare to claim to know what is true—and where it is more or less defenseless (because laden with a guilty conscience) on the question of discrimination. Is it possible that precisely such a powerful and uncompromising challenge to the liberal tradition, once we see it for what it is, will be the reason for a revival of the spirit of liberty? One could certainly point out the wisdom and clear-sightedness of the older liberal understanding of group politics in particular that we seem at the moment to be discarding without a full accounting or recognition of what might be lost. This was after all an attempt deliberately to guide by reason—or at least to limit and chasten— the harmful energies of politics and the doings of potentially dangerous groups by means of a reckoning with human nature and a realistic appraisal of social and political life. Are not the philosophical architects of modern liberal politics to be preferred at least to their postmodernist descendants, if only on the basis of a crude political calculation? Once more unto the Enlightenment?

But what would that look like as a strictly *political* program? It might seem to some to be tempting simply to "go back," fully and completely, to the liberal tradition, to see anti-discrimination policy as a (temporarily) necessary step that has by now been permitted to go too far or that has served its purpose. Were one inclined in this direction, the liberal framework as it applies to religion could perhaps be the model. One could argue that liberalism's failure in the case of race was a consequence of the extraordinary legacy of slavery in America, an anomaly and not a sign of some more general failing of liberalism as such. Following a necessary correction owing to extraordinary circumstances, after the intervention of more than half a century of anti-discrimination law, why could not racial and other forms of group politics be recast so as to follow the largely successful program used in the past to manage religious diversity?

For many reasons, the idea of a return to a more purely liberal past is at best doubtful. While we are reminded by the fate of Marxism to be leery of foretelling the political future, it seems very safe at the present moment to predict the continued forceful effect of the broad array of anti-discrimination policies with which we are familiar. The success of the civil rights movement is today widely viewed as being the noblest achievement of American political history. The strictly moral energy of the anti-discrimination revolution shows no signs of abating, and in my opinion this is at least as important for explaining its political power as the legal framework that underpins it or the groups who champion it. Moreover, because anti-discrimination policy emerged precisely as a response to the failures of the liberal scheme, no one, rightly or wrongly, trusts in mere liberal toleration to do the job that must be done to keep America from going back to a situation in which racism and other forms of discrimination would be permitted to reassert themselves. Even more important, for both moral and political reasons, so long as significant group inequalities persist in the United States between Blacks and Whites in particular, anti-discrimination will seem an indispensable policy.

At any rate there are other more political and practical reasons to suspect that the future is with the anti-discrimination regime. I think it is too early to begin to speak of our woke world as being, to use John McWhorter's arresting formula, "a detour in humanity's intellectual, cultural, and moral development" (2021, v). Even if racial inequalities were rectified, other ethnic groups, women, the elderly, the disabled, gays and lesbians, transgender persons, and yet still others protected by anti-discrimination law would presumably perceive themselves as having too much at stake to permit any real questioning of the new framework. As a matter of crude politics, the potential anti-discrimination coalition today includes in effect the entire population. Championing the cause of anti-discrimination is also, as a result, irresistible to elected politicians (Left and Right both) who seem ever inclined to expand its reach. Moreover, Americans have become accustomed to the protections of the law—and to a host of norms, practices, and social institutions emanating from them—in the workplace, in education, and in many other important realms of social life. So far, nobody seriously proposes rolling back, with the partial exception of affirmative action policy, the many expansions of anti-discrimination law. Anyone going so far as to call for the repeal of the 1964 Civil Rights Act is criticized even by the Right today as being out of touch with what is acceptable and unacceptable in democratic politics; almost no one contemplates a general questioning of (to say nothing of overthrowing) the anti-discrimination regime.

But neither is liberalism today simply on the verge of collapse, even if most of its theorists are somewhat weak-kneed and the anti-discrimination framework does challenge, erode, and rework its inner logic. Some uneasy coexistence of these two political frameworks will continue to define American democracy for the foreseeable future. Moreover, at least to this point, anti-discrimination has not demonstrated that it is, by itself, up to the task of replacing liberalism. As we have seen, its morality in particular remains incomplete and unsettled. The negative, critical power of anti-discrimination politics is obvious, but its positive content still remains somewhat unclear. Although Banks speaks of a "multicultural ideology," in fact the anti-discrimination framework is not broad or comprehensive enough to do all the work that liberalism has done to this point. From this perspective, too, we are indeed compelled to hope for the continued vitality of liberalism. As thoughtful civil rights advocate and economist Glenn Loury has put it, "to recognize the flaws of the liberal tradition is one thing; to replace it with something else is quite another" (2002, 120).

At the very least, our situation suggests that if we are to live happily with the commitment to fighting discrimination at the center of our democratic life, we will need to find some principle by which to regulate it, a principle that its own moral logic does not seem to provide. Is liberalism now strong enough to supply such guidance? Perhaps the many tensions between anti-discrimination and liberalism will have to suffice for this purpose—although that would mean the best we can do is a kind of state of civic indigestion in and through which our faith in liberalism seems likely, in turn, to be continually weakened.

That disconcerting prospect suggests that it is our duty to begin to think about the task of reforming and improving the anti-discrimination regime in a forthright and deliberate way. It is not immediately obvious that the liberal tradition by itself will be adequate here. Does liberalism supply reformers with the habits of mind they will need to engage anti-discrimination politics on the vitally important plane of public morality, for example? Does liberalism teach us how to think about the formative power of law? In my view, the most important starting point for reform must be a reconsideration of the nexus of (federal) laws at the center of the effort: privatized enforcement of hostile environment harassment under Title VII and Title IX, boundlessly expanded employer liability, and the characteristic measures (political training, corrective firing, censorship) we now associate with the oppressive atmosphere of America's workplaces and universities. This did not abolish the public-private divide but turned it on its head, making the private the strong arm of the public. To address this, the role of the law as the cause of things must be made *more visible* in order to make all the questions raised by the new arrangement subject to political contestation and debate, as they ought to be. Addressing that complex, tightly-drawn legal knot is a very tall order, and reform there will likely mean some *greater* role for government (in, for example, government-directed content of diversity training, limitations or clearer government guidance on corrective firing and censorship, due process rights for those sanctioned). Likewise, in my opinion, direct and open efforts to address the noticeable inequalities between Blacks and Whites (a very special case, and the single greatest source of moral energy for the entire anti-discrimination regime) ought to be on the table. This would not be reparations, but neither would it be the dishonest (universally framed but in fact racially justified) and counterproductive approaches we take now (abandoning the standards of middle-class life in the name of "equity"; expensive anti-poverty programs that often don't work). Attacking aggressively Black-White inequalities by means that encourage bourgeois aspiration—to promote education, home ownership, jobs, and small businesses for Black Americans—would require not only government action but also some rethinking of the terms of color-blind constitutionalism (there are in fact plenty of "compelling governmental interests" here). It seems to me that even the defense of liberalism now will require some reckoning with the regime and its unavoidable psychological and moral dimensions: supporting the politics of freedom today will involve showing people how their interests are affected when their souls, or the souls of their children, are shaped under the influence of the still-emerging political order. There is an opportunity to learn many things of great value from the changes we are living through that we must not forego simply because we are in the midst of them. The role of necessity in human affairs must include political necessity and the strongest necessity in political affairs is the regime.

It is true that some conservatives have begun to use the law to respond to perceived ill consequences of some aspects of anti-discrimination politics, though these efforts do not yet amount to an attempt to reform civil rights law as such. Even when what is being proposed is laudable, what we see is a pattern we have noted before: criticism along the extreme edges of anti-discrimination politics while bracketing the civil rights revolution itself. Some would use the law to ban or curtail various products of anti-discrimination policy (critical race theory, diversity statements, DEI activities in public universities); others would push back against some anti-discrimination efforts from other pre-existing legal redoubts (free speech, parental rights). These approaches are alike in that they leave more or less untouched the massive edifice of civil rights laws that gave rise to the different practices being opposed in the first place. Another, in a way more telling, conservative legal strategy is to harness the machinery of anti-discrimination law on behalf of Whites, males, Christians—all those who feel pinched under the current order. To say the least, this approach, like the others, does not serve to make the original structure of anti-discrimination law a question, and indeed suggests the power of anti-discrimination to shape now the political efforts of conservatives.

It is not the purpose of this book to enter into the question of reform in any detail. Besides, and more to the point, at present we still do not in fact even *see* the anti-discrimination regime, even if all around us we cannot help but notice many of its works and feel their unsettling effects. The obvious task for us now must be to do better to think about anti-discrimination politics and to clarify its nature or character; to name its phenomena in a way that captures everything that is at stake; and to begin to provide a critical framework for considering how to judge its merits and limitations. Some of this is already being done to an extent in the rough and tumble of political debate. But the task needs to be one of deliberate reflection and study as well; and it must be accompanied by an effort to educate the wider public in proper terms about the nature of our situation. That is not the work of a day.

Regime and Citizen:
The Case for Old-Fashioned Political Science

The main objective of this book has been to describe the civil rights regime so that we may see it and reckon with it as a distinct authoritative constitutive element of contemporary democratic life. But to describe a regime or political order is at the same time to make a broad causal claim, for what the political order is determines much of what goes on within it. We are compelled by the appearance of a new political order or, at the very least in this case, a significant change in the political order, to see that we are in need of a different approach to the study of politics.

This investigation has surely begun to show that the anti-discrimination regime is a general shaping cause of our world. As a direct result of the civil rights revolution, America (among other modern democracies) has a new moral vocabulary, a new understanding of the relationship between politics and morality, new institutions and legal orders, new constitutional doctrines, new politically relevant "groups," a new form of pluralism or "group politics," new ideologies or theories of politics (postmodernist and non-postmodernist), and, in multicultural education, a new civic education—all of them challenging their older equivalents. From the perspective of three thousand years of Western history, the changes in the political framework surveyed here amount perhaps to a variation on the theme "democracy"; but from the perspective of the American regime, and life within it, this reorientation is fundamental and dramatic.

Our examination of multiculturalism and the anti-discrimination revolution thus suggests we take seriously a very simple view of political science as the study of the regime or the political order as the most important general cause of social and cultural life and of the hearts and minds of its individual, politically-shaped citizens. Such a view, which is consistent with the original understanding of political science, has largely been abandoned in modern times—the result of the influence of modern science, on the one hand, and of liberal democracy, the politics of freedom, on the other. Social and political science in America are disinclined to see the political as general or formal cause because they have been so thoroughly shaped by that cause.

It is for this reason, too, that we lack a comprehensive, penetrating, and undeceived understanding of the anti-discrimination revolution as a great and decisive guiding influence in American life, without doubt the single most important development of American domestic politics of the past seventy-five years. Where are our social and political scientists on the subject of the anti-discrimination regime as cause? We have many studies that apply the tools and theories of social and political science to take the civil rights revolution into its many parts and to map its multitude of causal pathways to and fro. We have many more studies by scholars (and not just in the social sciences) of the different ways the goals of the anti-discrimination effort have or have not been met. The former are dominated by the logic of modern science, and in them the anti-discrimination regime itself almost disappears from view; in the latter, the logic of anti-discrimination prevails, to be sure, but this stops us from seeing anything else. What we do not have are studies of the nature and the effect of the anti-discrimination regime taken as a whole. This is a real puzzle. In the studies we do have, why is the anti-discrimination regime itself not treated as the fundamental cause of the new language of morality that reshapes the public mind, for example, or of the new dynamic of group politics that reworks social relations in America? Such questions are politically controversial from the point of view of the new regime itself because raising them would mean treating anti-discrimination as an established authority—no longer simply an aspiring or insurgent one. They are also problematic from the point of view of liberalism because to suggest that a regime is shaping life is, from a liberal perspective, to suggest that something disturbing is going on.[11]

If we follow where it leads, the anti-discrimination revolution may begin to provide us, especially those of us who call ourselves social and political scientists, with an education. The first step in the investigation of any phenomenon treated by any of the social sciences ought to be to look to the general shaping framework of the political order or regime. Political scientists ought to see themselves, in their relation with the rest of the social sciences, not only as the describers of regimes (their first task) but also as the keepers of one formative underlying cause, the political order or regime taken as a whole. On this very old-fashioned (but not for that reason conservative) view of political science, it is better to say that the world—life, culture, society, economy—is effect and that politics is cause (the "independent variable" *par excellence*) than the reverse. This will not make "measurement" easy, but that is no reason to ignore the obvious facts of life. Instead, modern social and political scientists look to politics as if it were merely one domain of the broader and more fundamental whole, "culture," and to understand the sphere or domain of political life merely as a diffuse aggregation of diverse processes and entities (some loose totality of "public" institutions, parties, movements, opinions, etc.) that are then treated as if they were simultaneously the product and the cause of other cultural or social or economic facts, and then back again. Politics, culture, society, economy as ocean—where politics is just one current or eddy among many.

Anti-discrimination, after the revolution, helps us to see that politics is not merely one part of the picture but that it may claim pride of place in human affairs. Just because political revolutions and the establishment of new regimes are rare occurrences does not mean that they can be relegated to a footnote about the background "rules of the game." For the political order is the formal cause of human life. Or, to speak as if the formal cause were an efficient cause, a political order, especially when it reigns unchallenged for an extended period of time, has "resources" and ways of shaping human beings that other areas of life do not possess, or that do not run together in the same way and to the same extent. Except where it is contested, the political order has at its disposal, in broad daylight, the use of force (or violence) and the right to punish and to impose other costs (financial, reputational, and otherwise) on individuals within society; it codifies its ruling wishes and demands and hopes formally, in laws that carry weight with anyone who accepts or lives under the reigning order; it has at its disposal money and other inducements (to include the giving and taking of jobs, the creation or redefinition of property, for example) with which to influence communal life or to benefit those it wishes to reward or persuade; it has the power to conduct investigations, to inspect whatever it wishes, to gather information to wield in public debate; it creates holidays, memorials, monuments, ceremonies, and spectacles—even "civil religion"—to enshrine the rightness of its ways; its heroes and its narrative of struggle and victory provide the substance of fashionable art, literature, and drama; it teaches in detail its own logic not only through the force of all of these instrumentalities but also in direct efforts of public and civic education.

Above all, the hopes and fears of the regime define the morality of the age. The political order and its laws and ways are certainly not, in most instances, experienced by citizens as merely the repression of their desires. The morality of the political order, its praise and blame, is internalized by citizens and, as a result, shapes the vision of life of the whole community at a deep level. It is the nature of this relationship that makes politics so centrally important in human life and, indeed, that gives political life its dignity.[12] The political order is the pervasive and authoritative framework that gives the social or cultural whole its characteristic form, that imposes order—or attempts to—on that fluid field. The political order shapes us, for good or ill, but shape us it does. The civil rights revolution demonstrates that the reigning prejudice in political science and the social sciences *against* such a view of broad political causality must be rejected. While it seems unlikely that political science will be up to the task anytime soon, it is this academic discipline that ought to lead the way to a proper understanding of the general causal power and place of the political within human life.

Anti-discrimination and multiculturalism and old-fashioned political science may be said to share at least one aim; for different reasons they both must attempt to get out from under the influence of the view of social and political life given to us by modern science and by liberalism. Even in modern democratic times, regimes and the formative shaping of citizens by regimes ought to be central to our understanding of culture, society, economics, and politics. Where liberalism insists that statecraft must not be soulcraft—that individual thought and belief must be left free, that legislating morality is to be prohibited by law as immoral—the logic of multiculturalism as the voice of the anti-discrimination revolution shows how the remaking of citizens according to a clear political imperative and its corresponding moral claims may be deemed necessary and even how it may be done. Where contemporary social and political science focus on narrow and discrete (measurable, quantifiable) causes and effects, studying multiculturalism and anti-discrimination compels us to come to terms with the general formative power of politics as the cause of broad but real phenomena such as group politics and the citizen heart and mind. This is not to deny, of course, that there is movement in both directions, the causal arrows point both ways—from the regime to the social/cultural dimension but also back again—as events leading up to the anti-discrimination revolution make plain. Regimes fail, obviously, and new ones take their place. But when this happens, the change that occurs is marked at some point by sudden and dramatic developments; social or cultural forces that the old regime failed to contain necessarily appear in new political form, while what once predominated is discarded and discredited.

Thus far, the contributions of American social and political science to the understanding of the anti-discrimination revolution have been primarily efforts in the service of the new political order. While the *American Political Science Review*, for example, said little or nothing about race and gender (and nothing of gays and lesbians, the disabled, or other anti-discrimination groups) even well into the 1960s, in the years since the revolution such topics have of course become ever more important in its pages. To the extent that political scientists take up current events pertaining to the civil rights revolution itself—in debates over various pieces of the puzzle, but never the whole—they do so mainly to further its aspirations. As we have seen in detail, many political theorists today likewise toil to elaborate, codify, and enshrine the new morality. Data gatherers in all the social sciences employ newly relevant explanatory frameworks ("identity," having become the inescapable variable) in search of mid-range empirical theories. They explore as well, and in great detail, the inequalities that persist between those groups championed by the new order and the rest of the population while interpreters of culture and political culture seek out and find subtle (hidden, unconscious) forms of prejudice.

However, the new political criterion of relevance that is obviously at work in all of this is never made explicit and is certainly never itself the object of study. This is especially clear in today's new version of anti-discriminatory "Whig history" (to be sure, a more critical, embittered, rival to that older form of political triumphalism), where the viewpoint of historians and social scientists examining America's past is identical to the outlook of the new order. Characteristically, the goal of such works is not so much to see in the past pointers to present progress as it is to illuminate in extraordinary detail the injustice of past discrimination and the political, legal, and cultural mechanisms that supported it. Along the way, liberalism is often judged by reference to this standard—sometimes as a brake on discrimination, sometimes as a covert instrument of it—and no longer stands as the unproblematic criterion of progress. Anti-discriminatory spelunkers now mark out in detail whole worlds of discrimination operating, alongside liberalism, as "constitutive" regimes or political orders of American political development, what one recent president of the American Political Science Association, for example, has termed variously an "ascriptive Americanist" or "inegalitarian ascriptive" or "'white supremacist' racial order."[13] The role of the anti-discrimination regime in making such a perspective visible or appealing or useful or persuasive from a political point of view is fairly obvious (the idea of an "ascriptive Americanist" tradition in America is essentially an inversion of the anti-discrimination regime, an inversion of "multiculturalism," now a lens for looking back at injustices of American history to which we are newly attentive). Looking *ahead*, or even to the present moment, why not be even more interested in the new political framework, taken as a whole, that manifestly shapes our contemporary world and that indeed drives so much of contemporary social and political science?

Multiculturalism and the anti-discrimination regime suggest the greater necessity of extending our historical and political studies to the world launched *after* 1964. As much as we are inclined to look back, we need to learn to look forward from the civil rights revolution as well, and with new eyes. We need to be more attentive to the new anti-discrimination regime that operates beyond liberalism's logic, one that (unlike the discriminatory regimes of the past) not only dispenses with the protective cover of liberalism's language but operates at points in defiance of liberalism's basic terms, without apology, employing a creed of its own. Even a rudimentary awareness of the novelty and distinctiveness of anti-discrimination politics today presses certain obvious questions upon social and political science. What is the anti-discrimination regime, its range and extent and limit? How did it develop out of and against liberalism and how did its originators understand and justify its break with liberalism? Why do its laws take the form that they do? Who benefits from anti-discrimination politics and why are some not benefited by it who might be? What do those falling under its protection want from it? What are the demands that the new order imposes upon citizens and upon the community as a whole? What is the new moral code that this political order calls into being, and what is its ultimate status? What have been the regime's effect on all the many different dimensions of American culture, society, and life that it touches? Above all, the fundamental question of political science must govern all these investigations: is the good citizen of the anti-discrimination regime a good human being?

BIBLIOGRAPHY

Abdelal, Rawi, Yoshiko M. Herrera, Alastair Iain Johnston, and Rose McDermott. 2006. "Identity as a Variable." *Perspectives on Politics* 4 (4): 695–711.

———, eds. 2009. *Measuring Identity: A Guide for Social Scientists*. New York: Cambridge University Press.

Abramowitz, Alan I. 2018. *The Great Alignment: Race, Party Transformation, and the Rise of Donald Trump*. New Haven, CT: Yale University Press.

Ackerman, Bruce. 2014. *We The People, Volume 3: The Civil Rights Revolution*. Cambridge, MA: Harvard University Press.

Adair, Douglas. 1957. "'That Politics May be Reduced to a Science': David Hume, James Madison, and the Tenth *Federalist*." *Huntington Library Quarterly* 20: 343–60.

Adams, Harold. 1985. "Repression and Recovery: Fight Racism Through Education." In *Multicultural Nonsexist Education: A Human Relations Approach*, edited by Nicholas Colangelo, Dick Dustin, and Cecelia Foxley. 2nd ed. Dubuque, IA: Kendall/Hunt.

Akiba, Motoko, Karen Sunday Cockrell, Juanita Cleaver Simmons, Seunghee Han, and Geetika Agarwal. 2010. "Preparing Teachers for Diversity: Examination of Teacher Certification and Program Accreditation Standards in the 50 States and Washington, DC." *Equity and Excellence in Education* 43 (4): 446–62.

Akintunde, Omowale. 1999. "White Racism, White Supremacy, White Privilege, and the Social Construction of Race: Moving from Modernist to Postmodernist Multiculturalism." *Multicultural Education* 7 (2): 2–8.

Allport, Gordon W. 1954. *The Nature of Prejudice*. Reading, MA: Addison-Wesley.

Amar, Akhil Reed. 1998. *The Bill of Rights: Creation and Reconstruction.* New Haven, CT: Yale University Press.

American Association of Colleges for Teacher Education (AACTE). 1973. "No One Model American: A Statement on Multicultural Education." Adopted November 1972 by the AACTE Board of Directors. *Journal of Teacher Education* 24 (4): 264–65.

———. 1978. *State Legislation, Provisions and Practices Related to Multicultural Education.* Washington, DC: American Association of Colleges for Teacher Education. ED 206626.

Anderson, Carol. 2003. *Eyes Off the Prize: The United Nations and the African American Struggle for Human Rights.* New York: Cambridge University Press.

Appelbaum, Peter. 2002. *Multicultural and Diversity Education: A Reference Handbook.* Santa Barbara, CA: ABC-CLIO.

Appiah, Kwame Anthony. 1994. "Race, Culture, Identity: Misunderstood Connections." *The Tanner Lectures on Human Values.* Delivered at the University of California, San Diego, San Diego, CA, October 27–28. https://www.researchgate.net/publication/266275987_Race_Culture_Identity_Misunderstood_Connections.

———. 1998. "The Limits of Pluralism." In *Multiculturalism and American Democracy*, edited by Arthur M. Melzer, Jerry Weinberger, and M. Richard Zinman. Lawrence: University Press of Kansas.

———. 2005. *The Ethics of Identity.* Princeton, NJ: Princeton University Press.

———. 2018. *The Lies That Bind: Rethinking Identity.* New York: Liveright.

Arendt, Hannah. 1959. "Reflections on Little Rock." *Dissent* 6 (1): 45–56.

Aristotle. 1984. *The Politics.* Translated by Carnes Lord. Chicago: University of Chicago Press.

———. 2011. *Nicomachean Ethics.* Translated by Robert C. Bartlett and Susan D. Collins. Chicago: University of Chicago Press.

Arkin, Marc M. 1995. "'The Intractable Principle': David Hume, James Madison, and the Tenth Federalist." *American Journal of Legal History* 39 (2): 148–76.

Bibliography

Arnesen, Sveinung, and Yvette Peters. 2017. "The Legitimacy of Representation: How Descriptive, Formal, and Responsiveness Representation Affect the Acceptability of Political Decisions." *Comparative Political Studies* 51 (7): 868–99.

Association for Advancing Quality in Educator Preparation (AAQEP). 2021. *Guide to AAQEP Accreditation.* Fairfax Station, VA: Association for Advancing Quality in Educator Preparation. https://aaqep.org/files/2021%20Guide%20to%20AAQEP%20Accreditation.pdf.

Atkeson, Lonna Rae, and Nancy Carrillo. 2007. "More is Better: The Influence of Collective Female Descriptive Representation on External Efficacy." *Politics and Gender* 3 (1): 79–101.

Atsusaka, Yuki. 2021. "A Logical Model for Predicting Minority Representation: Application to Redistricting and Voting Rights Cases." *American Political Science Review* 115 (4): 1210–25.

Bachrach, Peter, and Morton S. Baratz. 1962. "Two Faces of Power." *American Political Science Review* 56 (4): 947–52.

Bagenstos, Samuel R. 2014. "The Unrelenting Libertarian Challenge to Public Accommodations Law." *Stanford Law Review* 66 (6): 1–33.

Baker, Gwendolyn C. 1972. "The Effects of Training in Multi-ethnic Education on Preservice Teachers' Perceptions of Ethnic Groups." PhD diss., University of Michigan.

———. 1979. "Policy Issues in Multicultural Education in the United States." *Journal of Negro Education* 48 (3): 253–66.

———. 1983. *Planning and Organizing for Multicultural Instruction.* Reading, MA: Addison-Wesley.

Baker, Judith, ed. 1994. *Group Rights.* Toronto: University of Toronto Press.

Balkin, Jack M. 1999. "Free Speech and Hostile Environments." *Columbia Law Review* 99 (8): 2295–320.

Banks, Cherry A. McGee. 2005. *Improving Multicultural Education: Lessons from the Intergroup Education Movement.* New York: Teachers College Press.

Banks, James A. 1969a. "A Content Analysis of Elementary American

History Textbooks: The Treatment of the Negro in Race Relations." PhD diss., Michigan State University.

———. 1969b. "A Content Analysis of the Black American in Textbooks." *Social Education* 33 (8): 954–57, 963.

———. 1971a. "Teaching Black History with a Focus on Decision Making." *Social Education* 35 (7): 740–45, 820–21.

———. 1971b. "Teaching Ethnic Minority Studies with a Focus on Culture." *Educational Leadership* 29 (2): 113–17.

———. 1972a. "Imperatives in Ethnic Minority Education." *Phi Delta Kappan* 53 (5): 266–69.

———. 1972b. "Racial Prejudice and the Black Self-Concept." In *Black Self-Concept: Implications for Education and Social Science*, edited by James A. Banks and Jean D. Grambs. New York: McGraw Hill.

———. 1973a. "Curriculum Strategies for Black Liberation." *School Review* 81 (3): 405–14.

———. 1973b. "Teaching Black Studies for Social Change." In *Teaching Ethnic Studies: Concepts and Strategies* (43rd Yearbook), edited by James A. Banks. Washington, DC: National Council for the Social Studies.

———, ed. 1973c. *Teaching Ethnic Studies: Concepts and Strategies* (43rd yearbook). Washington, DC: National Council for the Social Studies.

———. 1973d. "Teaching for Ethnic Literacy: A Comparative Approach." *Social Education* 37 (8): 738–50.

———. 1973e. "Teaching Strategies for Discussion of Justice in America: Fact or Fiction?" *Social Education* 37 (7): 639–42.

———. 1974. "Curricular Models for an Open Society." In *Education for an Open Society*, edited by Delmo Della-Dora and James E. House. Washington, DC: Association for Supervision and Curriculum Development.

———. 1975a. "Teaching Ethnic Studies: Key Issues and Concepts." *Social Studies* 66 (3): 107–13.

———. 1975b. *Teaching Strategies for Ethnic Studies*. Boston: Allyn and Bacon.

———. 1975c. "The Implications of Ethnicity for Curriculum Reform." *Educational Leadership* 33 (3): 168–72.

———. 1976a. "Cultural Pluralism and Contemporary Schools." *Integrated Education* 14 (1): 32–36.

———. 1976b. "Ethnic Studies as a Process of Curriculum Reform." *Social Education* 40 (2): 76–80.

———. 1976c. "Evaluating the Multiethnic Components of the Social Studies." *Social Education* 40 (7): 538–41.

———. 1976d. "Pluralism, Ideology, and Curriculum Reform." *Social Studies* 67 (3): 99–106.

———. 1977a. "Pluralism and Educational Concepts: A Clarification." *Peabody Journal of Education* 54 (2): 73–78.

———. 1977b. "A Response to Philip Freedman." *Phi Delta Kappan* 58 (9): 695–97.

———. 1978a. "Multiethnic Education across Cultures: United States, Mexico, Puerto Rico, France, and Great Britain." *Social Education* 42 (3): 177–85.

———. 1978b. "Teaching About Ethnicity: Canadian Perspectives." Paper presented at the Meeting of the Social Studies Council, Alberta's Teacher's Association, Calgary, Alberta, May 25.

———. 1979a. "Ethnicity: Implications for Curriculum Reform." *Social Studies* 70 (1): 3–10.

———. 1979b. "Shaping the Future of Multicultural Education." *Journal of Negro Education* 48 (3): 237–52.

———. 1980. "Developing Cross-Cultural Competency in the Social Studies." *Journal of Research and Development in Education* 13 (2): 113–22.

———. 1981. *Multiethnic Education: Theory and Practice.* Boston: Allyn and Bacon.

———. 1982a. "Educating Minority Youths: An Inventory of Current Theory." *Education and Urban Society* 15 (1): 88–103.

———. 1982b. "The Future and the American Dream." *Social Education* 46 (5): 388–89.

———. 1983a. "Cultural Democracy, Citizenship Education, and the American Dream." 1982 Presidential Address, National Council for the Social Studies. *Social Education* 47 (3): 178–79, 223–32.

———. 1983b. "Multiethnic Education and the Quest for Equality." *Phi Beta Kappan* 64 (8): 582–85.

———. 1984a. "Ethnic Revitalization Movements and Education." Paper presented at the Second National Conference on Multicultural and Intercultural Education. Sponsored by the Canadian Council for Multicultural and Intercultural Education, Toronto, Ontario, November 7–10.

———. 1984b. "Multicultural Education and its Critics: Britain and the United States." *New Era* 65 (3): 58–65.

———. 1984c. *Teaching Strategies for Ethnic Studies*. 3rd ed. Boston: Allyn and Bacon.

———. 1986a. "Ethnic Diversity and Education: Challenges and Opportunities." Paper presented at conference, Facing the Multicultural Reality: Tools for Educators, sponsored by Manitoba Education, Winnipeg, Manitoba, March.

———. 1986b. "Multicultural Education: Developments, Paradigms and Goals." In *Multicultural Education in Western Societies*, edited by James A. Banks and James Lynch. New York: Praeger.

———. 1986c. "Multiethnic Education and Its Critics: Britain and the United States." In *Multicultural Education: The Interminable Debate*, edited by Sohan Modgil, Gajendra K. Verma, Kanka Mallick, and Celia Modgil. London: Falmer Press.

———. 1986d. "Race, Ethnicity and Schooling in the United States: Past, Present and Future." In *Multicultural Education in Western Societies*, edited by James A. Banks and James Lynch. New York: Praeger.

———. 1987. "The Social Studies, Ethnic Diversity, and Social Change." *Elementary School Journal* 87 (5): 531–43.

———. 1990. "Citizenship Education for a Pluralistic Democratic Society." *Social Studies* 81 (5): 210–14.

———. 1991a. "Multicultural Education: For Freedom's Sake." *Educational Leadership* 49 (4): 32–36.

———. 1991b. "Multicultural Education: Its Effects on Students' Racial and Gender Role Attitudes." In *Handbook of Research on Social Studies*

Teaching and Learning, edited by James P. Shaver. New York: Macmillan.

———. 1991c. "Multicultural Literacy and Curriculum Reform." *Educational Horizons* 69 (3): 135–40.

———. 1992a. "African American Scholarship and the Evolution of Multicultural Education." *Journal of Negro Education* 61 (3): 273–86.

———. 1992b. "Banks Replies to Grinter." In *Multiethnic Education: Theory and Practice*, edited by James Lynch, Celia Modgil, and Sohan Modgil. London: Falmer Press.

———. 1992c. "Multicultural Education: Approaches, Developments and Dimensions." In *Cultural Diversity and the Schools*. Vol. 1, *Education for Cultural Diversity Convergence and Divergence*, edited by James Lynch, Celia Modgil, and Sohan Modgil. London: Falmer Press.

———. 1993a. "Approaches to Multicultural Curriculum Reform." In *Multicultural Education: Issues and Perspectives*, edited by James A. Banks and Cherry A. McGee Banks. 2nd ed. Boston: Allyn and Bacon.

———. 1993b. "The Canon Debate, Knowledge Construction, and Multicultural Education." *Educational Researcher* 22 (5): 4–14.

———. 1993c. "Multicultural Education: Characteristics and Goals." In *Multicultural Education: Issues and Perspectives*, edited by James A. Banks and Cherry A. McGee Banks. 2nd ed. Boston: Allyn and Bacon.

———. 1993d. "Multicultural Education: Development, Dimensions, and Challenges." *Phi Delta Kappan* 75 (1): 22–28.

———. 1993e. "Multicultural Education for Young Children: Racial and Ethnic Attitudes and their Modification." In *Handbook of Research on the Education of Young Children*, edited by Bernard Spodek. New York: Macmillan.

———. 1993f. "Multicultural Education: Historical Development, Dimensions, and Practice." In *Review of Research in Education* 19, edited by Linda Darling-Hammond. Washington, DC: American Educational Research Association.

———. 1994a. *An Introduction to Multicultural Education*. Boston: Allyn and Bacon.

———. 1994b. *Multiethnic Education: Theory and Practice.* 3rd ed. Boston: Allyn and Bacon.

———. 1994c. "On Educating for Diversity: A Conversation with James A. Banks." Interview by Ron Brandt. *Educational Leadership* 51 (8): 28–31.

———. 1994d. "Transforming the Mainstream Curriculum." *Educational Leadership* 51 (8): 4–8.

———. 1994e. "Whose Unum?" Interview by Anne Turnbaugh Lockwood. *Focus in Change* 16: 12–14.

———. 1995a. "Multicultural Education and Curriculum Transformation." The 1995 Charles H. Thompson Lecture—Colloquium Keynote Address. *Journal of Negro Education* 64 (4): 390–400.

———. 1995b. "Transformational Challenges to the Social Science Disciplines: Implications for Social Studies Teaching and Learning." *Theory and Research in Social Education* 23 (1): 2–20.

———. 1996a. "The African American Roots of Multicultural Education." In *Multicultural Education, Transformative Knowledge, and Action: Historical and Contemporary Perspectives,* edited by James A. Banks. New York: Teachers College Press.

———. 1996b. "An Interview with James A. Banks." Interview by Margaret Smith Crocco. *Social Science Record, Journal of the New York Council for the Social Studies* 33 (2): 27–34.

———. 1996c. "Transformative Knowledge, Curriculum Reform, and Action." In *Multicultural Education, Transformative Knowledge, and Action: Historical and Contemporary Perspectives,* edited by James A. Banks. New York: Teachers College Press.

———. 1997a. *Educating Citizens in a Multicultural Society.* New York: Teachers College Press.

———. 1997b. "Multicultural Education: Characteristics and Goals." In *Multicultural Education: Issues and Perspectives,* edited by James A. Banks and Cherry A. McGee Banks. 3rd ed. Boston: Allyn and Bacon.

———. 1998a. "Multiculturalism's Five Dimensions." Interview with Michelle Tucker. *NEA Today Online.* https://www.learner.org/wp-content/uploads/2019/02/3.Multiculturalism.pdf.

———. 1998b. "The Lives and Values of Researchers: Implications for Educating Citizens in a Multicultural Society." *Educational Researcher* 27 (7): 4–17.

———. 1999a. *An Introduction to Multicultural Education.* 2nd ed. Boston: Allyn and Bacon.

———. 1999b. "Multicultural Citizenship Education." In *Teaching and Learning in the New Millennium,* edited by Barbara D. Day. Indianapolis: Kappa Delta Pi.

———. 2001a. "Citizenship Education and Diversity: Implications for Teacher Education." *Journal of Teacher Education* 52 (1): 5–16.

———. 2001b. *Cultural Diversity and Education: Foundations, Curriculum, and Teaching.* 4th ed. Boston: Allyn and Bacon.

———. 2003a. "Series Foreword." In *Educating Teachers for Diversity: Seeing with a Cultural Eye,* by Jacqueline Jordan Irvine. New York: Teachers College Press.

———. 2003b. "Teaching for Multicultural Literacy, Global Citizenship, and Social Justice." *The 2003 Charles Fowler Colloquium on Innovation in Arts Education.* College Park: University of Maryland.

———. 2003c. *Teaching Strategies for Ethnic Studies.* 7th ed. Boston: Allyn and Bacon.

———. 2004a. "Introduction." In *Handbook of Research on Multicultural Education,* edited by James A. Banks and Cherry A. McGee Banks. 2nd ed. San Francisco: Jossey-Bass.

———. 2004b. "Multicultural Education: Historical Development, Dimensions, and Practice." In *Handbook of Research on Multicultural Education,* edited by James A. Banks and Cherry A. McGee Banks. 2nd ed. San Francisco: Jossey-Bass.

———. 2004c. "Preface." In *Diversity and Citizenship Education: Global Perspectives,* edited by James A. Banks. San Francisco: Jossey-Bass.

———. 2004d. "Race, Knowledge Construction, and Education in the United States: Lessons from History." In *Handbook of Research on Multicultural Education,* edited by James A. Banks and Cherry A. McGee Banks. 2nd ed. San Francisco: Jossey-Bass.

———. 2006a. "Acknowledgments." In *Race, Culture, and Education: The Selected Works of James A. Banks*. New York: Routledge.

———. 2006b. "Democracy, Diversity, and Social Justice: Educating Citizens in a Global Age." In *Race, Culture, and Education: The Selected Works of James A. Banks*. New York: Routledge.

———. 2006c. "Introduction: My Epistemological Journey." In *Race, Culture, and Education: The Selected Works of James A. Banks*. New York: Routledge.

———. 2008a. "Diversity, Group Identity, and Citizenship Education in a Global Age." *Educational Researcher* 37 (3): 129–39.

———. 2008b. *Teaching Strategies for Ethnic Studies*. 8th ed. Boston: Pearson.

———. 2009. "Diversity and Citizenship Education in Multicultural Nations." *Multicultural Education Review* 1 (1): 1–28.

———. 2013. "The Construction and Historical Development of Multicultural Education, 1962–2012." *Theory Into Practice* 52: 73–82.

———. 2015. "Failed Citizenship, Civic Engagement, and Education." *Kappa Delta Pi Record* 51: 151–54.

———. 2016a. "Civic Education in the Age of Global Migration." In *Global Migration, Diversity, and Civic Education: Improving Policy and Practice*, edited by James A. Banks, Marcelo M. Suarez-Orozco, and Miriam Ben-Peretz. New York: Teachers College Press.

———. 2016b. "Expanding the Epistemological Terrain: Increasing Equity and Diversity Within the American Educational Research Association." *Educational Researcher* 45 (2): 149–58.

———. 2017. "Failed Citizenship and Transformative Civic Education." *Educational Researcher* 20 (10): 1–12.

Banks, James A., and Cherry A. McGee Banks. 1995. "Equity Pedagogy: An Essential Component of Multicultural Education." *Theory into Practice* 34 (3): 152–58.

———. 1997. "Reforming Schools in a Democratic Pluralistic Society." *Educational Policy* 11 (2): 183–93.

Banks, James A., Cherry A. McGee Banks, Carlos E. Cortés, Carole H. Hahn, Merry M. Merryfield, Kogila A. Moodley, Stephen Murphy-

Shigematsu, Audrey Osler, Caryn Park, and Walter C. Parker. 2005. *Democracy and Diversity: Principles and Concepts for Educating Citizens in a Global Age*. Seattle: University of Washington Center for Multicultural Education.

Banks, James A., Carlos E. Cortés, Geneva Gay, Ricardo L. Garcia, and Anna S. Ochoa. 1976. *Curriculum Guidelines for Multiethnic Education*. Position Statement, The NCSS Task Force on Ethnic Studies Curriculum Guidelines. Arlington, VA: National Council for the Social Studies.

Banks, James A., and Jean D. Grambs, eds. 1972. *Black Self-Concept: Implications for Education and Social Science*. New York: McGraw-Hill.

Banks, James A., M. Lucia James, Clare A. Broadhead, Delmo Della-Dora, and James E. House. 1974. "Can Educators Help Create an Open Society?" In *Education in an Open Society*, edited by Delmo Della-Dora and James E. House. Washington, DC: Association for Supervision and Curriculum Development.

Banks, James A., and William W. Joyce. 1971. *Teaching Social Studies to Culturally Different Children*. Boston: Addison-Wesley.

Baptiste, H. Prentice, Jr. 1979. *Multicultural Education: A Synopsis*. Washington, DC: University Press of America.

———. 1984. "Multicultural Education: Reflections and Promises." A Conversation with H. Prentice Baptiste, Jr. by Hazel S. Taylor. *Texas Tech Journal of Education* 11 (1): 99–107.

Baptiste, H. Prentice, Jr., Mira L. Baptiste, and Donna M. Gollnick. 1980. *Multicultural Teacher Education: Preparing Educators to Provide Educational Equity*. Vol. 1 of *Knowledge Interpretation Program: Training Educators to Provide Educational Equity*. Washington, DC: American Association of Colleges for Teacher Education.

Bardolph, Richard, ed. 1970. *The Civil Rights Record: Black Americans and the Law, 1849–1970*. New York: Thomas Y. Crowell.

Barrett, Michéle, and Anne Phillips, eds. 1992. *Destabilizing Theory: Contemporary Feminist Debates*. Stanford, CA: Stanford University Press.

Baruth, Leroy G., and M. Lee Manning. 1992. *Multicultural Education of Children and Adolescents*. Boston: Allyn and Bacon.

Baudrillard, Jean. 1994. *Simulacra and Simulation*. Translated by Sheila Faria Glaser. Ann Arbor: University of Michigan Press.

Baumeister, Andrea. 1998. "Cultural Diversity and Education: The Dilemma of Social Stability." *Political Studies* 46 (5): 919–36.

———. 2000. *Liberalism and the "Politics of Difference."* Edinburgh: Edinburgh University Press.

Belz, Herman. 1991. *Equality Transformed: A Quarter-Century of Affirmative Action*. New Brunswick, NJ: Transaction.

Benhabib, Seyla. 1992. *Situating the Self: Gender, Community and Postmodernism in Contemporary Ethics*. New York: Routledge.

Benhabib, Seyla, Judith Butler, Drucilla Cornell, and Nancy Fraser, eds. 1995. *Feminist Contentions: A Philosophical Exchange*. New York: Routledge.

Bennett, Christine I. 1986. *Comprehensive Multicultural Education*. Boston: Allyn and Bacon.

———. 1995. "Preparing Teachers for Cultural Diversity and National Standards of Academic Excellence." *Journal of Teacher Education* 46 (4): 259–65.

Bennett, David, and Terry Collits. 1991. "The Postcolonial Critic: Homi K. Bhabha Interviewed." *Arena* 96: 47–63.

Bentley, Arthur F. 1908. *The Process of Government: A Study of Social Pressures*. Chicago: University of Chicago Press.

Berelson, Bernard R., Paul F. Lazarsfeld, and William N. McPhee. 1954. *Voting: A Study of Opinion Formation in a Presidential Campaign*. Chicago: University of Chicago Press.

Berger, Morroe. 1968. *Equality by Statute: The Revolution in Civil Rights*. Rev. ed. Garden City, NY: Anchor Books.

Berlin, Isaiah. 1991. "Alleged Relativism in Eighteenth-Century European Thought." In *The Crooked Timber of Humanity*. New York: Knopf.

———. 2014. "A Message to the 21st Century." Statement read on the author's behalf at the University of Toronto, November 25, 1994. *New York Review of Books*, October 23, 2014. http://www.nybooks.com/articles/2014/10/23/message-21st-century/.

Berns, Walter. 1987. *Taking the Constitution Seriously*. New York: Simon & Schuster.

Bernstein, David E. 2003. *You Can't Say That! The Growing Threat to Civil Liberties from Antidiscrimination Law*. Washington, DC: Cato Institute Press.

———. 2010. "Context Matters: A Better Libertarian Approach to Antidiscrimination Law." *Cato Unbound*, June 16, 2010. https://www.cato-unbound.org/2010/06/16/david-e-bernstein/context-matters-better-libertarian-approach-antidiscrimination-law/.

———. 2019. "Administrative Laws and the Administrative State: A Skeptic's Look at Administrative Constitutionalism." *Notre Dame Law Review* 94 (3): 1381–1415.

Bernstein, Richard. 1994. *Dictatorship of Virtue: Multiculturalism and the Battle for America's Future*. New York: Alfred A. Knopf.

Berrey, Ellen. 2015. *The Enigma of Diversity: The Language of Race and the Limits of Racial Justice*. Chicago: University of Chicago Press.

Berrey, Ellen, Robert L. Nelson, and Laura Beth Nielsen. 2017. *Rights on Trial: How Workplace Discrimination Law Perpetuates Inequality*. Chicago: University of Chicago Press.

Bevier, Lillian R. 1978. The First Amendment and Political Speech: An Inquiry Into the Substance and Limits of Principle." *Stanford Law Review* 30 (2): 299–358.

Beyerbach, Barbara, and Thurman D. Nassoiy. 2004. "Where is Equity in the National Standards? A Critical Review of the INTASC, NCATE, and NBPTS Standards." *Scholar-Practitioner Quarterly* 2 (4): 29–42.

Blazina, Carrie, and Kiana Cox. 2022. "Black and White Americans Are Far Apart In Their View of Reparations for Slavery." Pew Research Center. November 28, 2022. https://www.pewresearch.org/fact-tank/2022/11/28/black-and-white-americans-are-far-apart-in-their-views-of-reparations-for-slavery/.

Bloom, Allan. 1987. *The Closing of the American Mind*. New York: Simon & Schuster.

Bloom, Benjamin S., Allison Davis, and Robert Hess. 1965. *Compensatory Education for Cultural Deprivation*. New York: Holt.

Bolick, Clint. 1996. *The Affirmative Action Fraud: Can We Restore the American Civil Rights Vision?* Washington, DC: Cato Institute.

Bolotin, David. 2021. "Liberal Education and Politics." *Academic Questions* 34 (4). https://www.nas.org/academic-questions/34/4/liberal-education-and-politics.

Bork, Robert. 1963. "Civil Rights—A Challenge." *New Republic* 149 (9/10): 21–24.

Boxill, Bernard R. 2003. "A Lockean Argument for Black Reparations." *Journal of Ethics* 7: 63–91.

Braeman, John. 1988. *Before the Civil Rights Revolution: The Old Court and Individual Rights.* New York: Greenwood Press.

Brandwein, Pamela. 2007. "A Judicial Abandonment of Blacks? Rethinking the 'State Action' Cases of the Waite Court." *Law and Society Review* 41 (2): 343–86.

Brake, Deborah L. 2019. "Coworker Retaliation in the #MeToo Era." *University of Baltimore Law Review* 49 (1): 1–58.

Breitbart, Andrew. 2011. *Righteous Indignation: Excuse Me While I Save the World.* New York: Grand Central.

Brest, Paul. 1976. "The Supreme Court 1975 Term. Foreword: In Defense of the Antidiscrimination Principle." *Harvard Law Review* 90 (1): 1–57.

Bronaugh, Juanita, and George E. Ayers. 1976. "Multiethnic Materials. A Selected Bibliography." Racine Unified School District 1, Wisconsin. Microfiche. ED 129957.

Brooks, David. 2006. "The Death of Multiculturalism." *New York Times*, April 27, 2006. https://www.nytimes.com/2006/04/27/opinion/the-death-of-multiculturalism.html.

Brooks-Immel, Demerris R., and Susan B. Murray. 2017. "Color-blind Contradictions and Black/White Binaries: White Academics Upholding Whiteness." *Humboldt Journal of Social Relations* 39: 315–33.

Brotz, Howard. 1980. "Multiculturalism in Canada: A Muddle." *Canadian Public Policy* 6: 41–46.

Brown, Wendy. 1995. *States of Injury: Power and Freedom in Late Modernity.* Princeton, NJ: Princeton University Press.

———. 2005. *Edgework: Critical Essays on Knowledge and Politics*. Princeton, NJ: Princeton University Press.

———. 2006. *Regulating Aversion: Tolerance in the Age of Identity and Empire*. Princeton, NJ: Princeton University Press.

Browne, Kingsley R. 1991. "Title VII as Censorship: Hostile-Environment Harassment and the First Amendment." *Ohio State Law Journal* 52 (2): 481–550.

Bruell, Christopher. 2011. "The Question of Nature and the Thought of Leo Strauss." *Kleis-Revue Philosophique* 19: 92–101.

Buchanan, Sidney G. 1997a. "A Conceptual History of the State Action Doctrine: The Search for Governmental Responsibility (Part I of II)." *Houston Law Review* 34: 333–424.

———. 1997b. "A Conceptual History of the State Action Doctrine: The Search for Governmental Responsibility (Part II of II)." *Houston Law Review* 34: 666–755.

Bumiller, Kristin. 1988. *The Civil Rights Society: The Social Construction of Victims*. Baltimore: Johns Hopkins University Press.

Butcher, Jonathan, and Mike Gonzalez. 2020. "Critical Race Theory, the New Intolerance, and Its Grip on America." *Heritage Foundation Backgrounder* 3567, December 8, 2020. https://stoplcpscrt.com/wp-content/uploads/2020/12/Heritage-Foundation-CRT-Report_12-8-2020.pdf.

Butler, Judith. 1990. *Gender Trouble: Feminism and the Subversion of Gender*. New York: Routledge.

———. 2001. "Appearances Aside." In *Prejudicial Appearances: The Logic of American Antidiscrimination Law* by Robert C. Post, with K. Anthony Appiah, Judith Butler, Thomas C. Grey, and Reva B. Siegel. Durham, NC: Duke University Press.

Butt, Daniel. 2013. "Inheriting Rights to Reparation: Compensatory Justice and the Passage of Time." *Ethical Perspectives* 20 (2): 245–69.

Cabello, Beverly, and Nancy Davis Burstein. 1995. "Examining Teachers' Beliefs about Teaching in Culturally Diverse Classrooms." *Journal of Teacher Education* 46 (4): 285–94.

Caldas, Stephen J., Carl L. Bankston III, and Judith S. Cain. 2003. "Social Capital, Academic Capital, and the 'Harm and Benefit' Thesis: Evidence from a Desegregating School District." In *The End of Desegregation?* edited by Stephen J. Caldas and Carl L. Bankston III. New York: Nova Science.

Caldwell, Christopher. 2020. *The Age of Entitlement: America Since the Sixties*. New York: Simon & Schuster.

Callan, Eamonn. 1997. *Creating Citizens: Political Education and Liberal Democracy*. Oxford: Oxford University Press.

Cardona, Miguel. 2011. "Sharpening the Focus of Political Will to Address Achievement Disparities." PhD diss., University of Connecticut.

Carlson, Dennis. 1997. *Making Progress: Education and Culture in New Times*. New York: Teachers College Press.

Carter, Stephen L. 1993. *The Culture of Disbelief: How American Law and Politics Trivialize Religious Devotion*. New York: Harper.

Celis, Karen. 2012. "On Substantive Representation, Diversity, and Responsiveness." *Politics and Gender* 8 (4): 524–29.

Center for Individual Rights. 2005. "McConnell v. Le Moyne College." August 3, 2005. https://www.cir-usa.org/cases/mcconnell-v-le-moyne-college/.

Chafe, William H. 1986. "One Struggle Ends, Another Begins." In *The Civil Rights Movement in America*, edited by Charles W. Eagles. Jackson: University of Mississippi Press.

Chaplin, Jonathan. 1993. "How Much Cultural and Religious Pluralism can Liberalism Tolerate?" In *Liberalism, Multiculturalism and Toleration*, edited by John Horton. New York: St. Martin's Press.

Chavez, Linda. 1998. "Civic Education in a Changing Society." In *Multiculturalism and American Democracy*, edited by Arthur M. Melzer, Jerry Weinberger, and M. Richard Zinman. Lawrence: University Press of Kansas.

Chemerinsky, Erwin. 1985. "Rethinking State Action." *Northwestern University Law Review* 80 (3): 503–57.

Cheung, Maria. 1997. "Social Construction Theory and the Satir Model:

Toward a Synthesis." *American Journal of Family Therapy* 25 (4): 331–43.

Chicago Cultural Studies Group. 1992. "Critical Multiculturalism." *Critical Inquiry* 18 (3): 530–55.

Clausen, Christopher. 2000. *Faded Mosaic: The Emergence of Post-Cultural America*. Chicago: Ivan R. Dee.

Clayton, Amanda, Diana Z. O'Brien, and Jennifer M. Piscipo. 2019. "All Male Panels? Representation and Democratic Legitimacy." *American Journal of Political Science* 63 (1): 113–29.

Cochran-Smith, Marilyn. 2000. "Blind Vision: Unlearning Racism in Teacher Education." *Harvard Educational Review* 72 (2): 157–90.

———. 2001. "Reforming Teacher Education: Competing Agendas." *Journal of Teacher Education* 52 (4): 263–65.

———. 2002. "Reporting on Teacher Quality: The Politics of Politics." *Journal of Teacher Education* 53 (5): 379–82.

———. 2003. "The Multiple Meanings of Multicultural Teacher Education: A Conceptual Framework." *Teacher Education Quarterly* 30 (2): 7–26.

———. 2004a. "Taking Stock in 2004: Teacher Education in Dangerous Times." *Journal of Teacher Education* 55 (1): 3–7.

———. 2004b. "The Report of the Teaching Commission: What's Really at Risk?" *Journal of Teacher Education* 55 (3): 195–200.

———. 2005. "The Politics of Teacher Education." *Journal of Teacher Education* 56 (3): 179–80.

———. 2006a. "Evidence, Efficacy, and Effectiveness." *Journal of Teacher Education* 57 (1): 3–5.

———. 2006b. "Thirty Editorials Later: Signing Off As Editor." *Journal of Teacher Education* 57 (2): 95–101.

———. 2021. "Rethinking Teacher Education: The Trouble with Accountability." *Oxford Review of Education* 47 (1): 8–24.

Codevilla, Angelo M. 2016. "After the Republic." *Claremont Review of Books*. September 16, 2016. https://claremontreviewofbooks.com/digital/after-the-republic/.

Cohen, Jean L. 1985. "Strategy or Identity: New Theoretical Paradigms and Contemporary Social Movements." *Social Research* 52 (4): 663–716.

Colangelo, Nicholas, Dick Dustin, and Cecelia Foxley, eds. 1979. *Multicultural Nonsexist Education: A Human Relations Approach*. Dubuque, IA: Kendall/Hunt.

Cole, Donna J. 1984. "Multicultural Education and Global Education: A Possible Merger." *Theory into Practice* 23 (2): 151–54.

Coleman, James S. 1966. *Equality of Educational Opportunity*. A special report prepared at the request of the Office of Education, Department of Health, Education, and Welfare. Washington, DC: Government Printing Office.

———. 1969. "A Brief Summary of the Coleman Report." In *Equal Educational Opportunity*, edited by the Editorial Board of *Harvard Educational Review*. Cambridge, MA: Harvard University Press.

Colville-Hall, Susan, Suzanne MacDonald, and Lynn Smolen. 1995. "Preparing Preservice Teachers for Diversity in Learners." *Journal of Teacher Education* 46 (4): 295–303.

Community Relations Service. 1998. *Guidelines for Effective Human Relations Commissions*. Revised September 1998. N.p.: United States Department of Justice Community Relations Service.

Congressional Quarterly Service. 1968. *Revolution in Civil Rights*. 4th ed. Washington, DC: Congressional Quarterly Service.

Connolly, William E. 1969. "The Challenge to Pluralist Theory." In *The Bias of Pluralism*, edited by William E. Connolly. New York: Atherton Press.

———. 1991. *Identity\Difference: Democratic Negotiations of Political Paradox*. Ithaca, NY: Cornell University Press.

———. 1993. "Beyond Good and Evil: The Ethical Sensibility of Michel Foucault." *Political Theory* 21 (3): 365–89.

———. 2005. *Pluralism*. Durham, NC: Duke University Press.

Cornbleth, Catherine, and Dexter Waugh. 1995. *The Great Speckled Bird: Multicultural Politics and Education Policymaking*. New York: St. Martin's Press.

Cornell, Drucilla. 1993. *Transformations: Recollective Imagination and Sexual Difference*. New York: Routledge.

———. 1995. *The Imaginary Domain: Abortion, Pornography and Sexual Harassment*. New York: Routledge.

Cornell, Drucilla, and Sara Murphy. 2002. "Anti-racism, Multiculturalism and the Ethics of Identification." *Philosophy and Social Criticism* 28 (4): 419–49.

Corson, David. 1998. *Changing Education for Diversity*. Bristol, PA: Open University Press.

Cortés, Carlos. 2002. *The Making—and Remaking—of a Multiculturalist*. New York: Teachers College Press.

Côté, James. 2006. "Identity Studies: How Close Are We to Developing a Social Science of Identity? An Appraisal of the Field." *Identity* 6 (1): 3–25.

Coté, Mark, Richard J.F. Day, and Greig de Peuter. 2007. "Introduction: What is Utopian Pedagogy." In *Utopian Pedagogy: Radical Experiments against Neoliberal Globalization*, edited by Mark Coté, Richard J.F. Day, and Greig de Peuter. Toronto: University of Toronto Press.

Council for the Accreditation of Education Preparation (CAEP). 2018. *CAEP Handbook: Initial-Level Programs 2018*. Washington, DC: CAEP. http://caepnet.org/accreditation/caep-accreditation/~/media/Files/caep/accreditation-resources/caep-initial-handbook-2018.pdf?la=en.

Crenshaw, Kimberlé. 1988. "Race, Reform, and Retrenchment: Transformation and Legitimation in Antidiscrimination Law." *Harvard Law Review* 101 (7): 1331–87.

———. 1989. "Demarginalizing the Intersection of Race and Sex: A Black Feminist Critique of Antidiscrimination Doctrine, Feminist Theory and Antiracist Politics." *University of Chicago Legal Forum* 1989: 139–67.

———. 1991. "Mapping the Margins: Intersectionality, Identity Politics, and Violence against Women of Color." *Stanford Law Review* 43 (6): 1241–99.

Creppell, Ingrid. 2003. *Toleration and Identity: Foundations in Early Modern Thought*. New York: Routledge.

Crocker, Stephen, Robert L. Crain, Morlie H. Graubard, Jackie M. Kimbrough, Nicki J. King, Margaret A. Thomas, and Frederick M. Wirt. 1976. *Title IV of the Civil Rights Act of 1964: A Review of Program Operations*. Executive Summary. Santa Monica, CA: Rand.

Crouch, Stanley. 1995. "The One-Out-of-Many-Blues." In *Reinventing the American People: Unity and Diversity Today*, edited by Robert Royal. Grand Rapids, MI: William B. Eerdmans.

Cull, John G., and Richard E. Hardy. 1975. *Problems of Disadvantaged and Deprived Youth*. Springfield, IL: Charles C. Thomas.

Dahl, Robert. 1956. *A Preface to Democratic Theory*. Chicago: University of Chicago Press.

———. 1961. "The Behavioral Approach in Political Science: Epitaph for a Monument to a Successful Protest." *American Political Science Review* 55 (4): 763–72.

———. 1967. *Pluralist Democracy in the United States: Conflict and Consent*. Chicago: Rand McNally.

———. 1970. *After the Revolution? Authority in a Good Society*. New Haven, CT: Yale University Press.

———. 1971. *Polyarchy: Participation and Opposition*. New Haven, CT: Yale University Press.

———. 1982. *Dilemmas of Pluralist Democracy*. New Haven, CT: Yale University Press.

———. 1989. *Democracy and Its Critics*. New Haven, CT: Yale University Press.

———. 1998. *On Democracy*. New Haven, CT: Yale University Press.

———. 2006. *On Political Equality*. New Haven, CT: Yale University Press.

Daniel, Teresa A. 2003. "Developing a 'Culture of Compliance' to Prevent Sexual Harassment." *Employee Relations Today* 30 (3): 33–42.

Davies, Gareth. 1996. *From Opportunity to Entitlement: The Transformation and Decline of Great Society Liberalism*. Lawrence: University Press of Kansas.

———. 2002. "The Great Society after Johnson: The Case of Bilingual Education." *Journal of American History* 8: 1405–29.

———. 2007. *See Government Grow: Education Politics from Johnson to Reagan.* Lawrence: University Press of Kansas.

Delgado, Richard. 1993. "Rodrigo's Fourth Chronicle: Neutrality and Stasis in Antidiscrimination Law." *Stanford Law Review* 45: 1133–60.

Delgado, Richard, and Jean Stefancic, eds. 1997. *Critical White Studies: Looking Behind the Mirror.* Philadelphia, PA: Temple University Press.

Della-Dora, Delmo, and James E. House. 1974. *Education for an Open Society.* Washington, DC: Association for Supervision and Curriculum Development.

Democratic National Committee. 2018. "Delegate Selection Rules for the 2020 Democratic National Convention." Adopted August 25, 2018. https://democrats.org/wp-content/uploads/2019/01/2020-Delegate-Selection-Rules-12.17.18-FINAL.pdf.

Derrida, Jacques. 1978. *Writing and Difference.* Translated by Alan Bass. Chicago: University of Chicago Press.

———. 1982. *Margins of Philosophy.* Translated by Alan Bass. Chicago: University of Chicago Press.

———. 1990. "Force of Law: The 'Mystical Foundation of Authority'." Translated by Mary Quaintance. *Cardozo Law Review* 11: 920–1045.

Dessources Figures, Kalisha, and Catherine E. Lhamon. 2021. "Approaching Policy with Equity in Mind." White House. March 29, 2021. https://www.whitehouse.gov/briefing-room/blog/2021/03/29/approaching-policy-with-equity-in-mind/.

Deutsch, Steven E. 1969. "Disadvantages of Culturally Deprived Children." In *Integration and Education*, edited by David W. Beggs and S. Kern Alexander. Chicago: Rand McNally.

Deveaux, Monique. 2000. *Cultural Pluralism and Dilemmas of Justice.* Ithaca, NY: Cornell University Press.

Dewey, John, and Arthur F. Bentley. 1949. *Knowing and the Known.* Boston: Beacon Press.

DiAngelo, Robin J. 2004. "Whiteness in Racial Dialogue: A Discourse

Analysis." PhD diss., University of Washington. https://digital.lib.washington.edu/researchworks/handle/1773/7867.

———. 2018. *White Fragility: Why It's So Hard for White People to Talk About Racism*. Boston: Beacon Press.

Dobbin, Frank. 2009. *Inventing Equal Opportunity*. Princeton, NJ: Princeton University Press.

Douglass, Frederick. 1966. "The Present and Future of the Colored Race in America." In *Negro Social and Political Thought, 1850–1920: Representative Texts*, edited by Howard Brotz. New York: Basic Books.

Dovi, Suzanne. 2007. "Theorizing Women's Representation in the United States." *Politics and Gender* 3 (3): 297–319.

Dowling, R. E. 1960. "Pressure Group Theory: Its Methodological Range." *American Political Science Review* 54 (4): 944–54.

Drachsler, Julius. 1920. *Democracy and Assimilation: The Blending of Immigrant Heritages in America*. New York: Macmillan.

Dryzek, John S. 1996. "Political Inclusion and the Dynamics of Democratization." *American Political Science Review* 90 (3): 475–87.

D'Souza, Dinesh. 1995. *The End of Racism: Principles for a Multiracial Society*. New York: Free Press.

Dudziak, Mary. 2000. *Cold War Civil Rights: Race and the Image of American Democracy*. Princeton, NJ: Princeton University Press.

Dunn, Jalayla Liles. 2021. "Our New Name: Learning for Justice." *Learning for Justice Magazine*, February 3, 2021. https://www.learningforjustice.org/magazine/our-new-name-learning-for-justice.

Dussel, Enrique. 1993. "Eurocentrism and Modernity (Introduction to the Frankfurt Lectures)." *boundary 2* 20 (3): 65–76.

Eastland, Terry. 1996. *Ending Affirmative Action: The Case for Colorblind Justice*. New York: Basic Books.

Edelman, Lauren B. 2016. *Working Law: Courts, Corporations, and Symbolic Civil Rights*. Chicago: University of Chicago Press.

Edelman, Lauren B., Sally Riggs Fuller, and Iona Mara-Drita. 2001. "Diversity Rhetoric and the Managerialization of Law." *American Journal of Sociology* 106 (6): 1589–1641.

Edelman, Lauren B., Linda H. Krieger, Scott R. Eliason, Catherine R. Albiston, and Virginia Mellema. 2011. "When Organizations Rule: Judicial Deference to Institutionalized Employment Structures." *American Journal of Sociology* 117 (3): 888–954.

Edsall, Thomas B., and Mary D. Edsall. 1991. *Chain Reaction: The Impact of Race, Rights, and Taxes on American Politics.* New York: W. W. Norton.

Edwards, Richard, Paul Armstrong, and Nod Miller. 2001. "Include Me Out: Critical Readings of Social Exclusion, Social Inclusion and Lifelong Learning." *International Journal of Lifelong Education* 20 (5): 417–28.

Egan, Patrick J. 2020. "Identity as Dependent Variable: How Americans Shift Their Identities to Align with Their Politics." *American Journal of Political Science* 64 (3): 699–716.

Eisele, J. Christopher. 1983. "Dewey's Concept of Cultural Pluralism." *Educational Theory* 33 (3 & 4): 149–56.

Eisenberg, Avigail. 1995. *Reconstructing Political Pluralism.* Albany: State University of New York Press.

Elazar, Daniel J. 1993. "How Present Conceptions of Human Rights Shape the Protection of Rights in the United States." In *Old Rights and New*, edited by Robert A. Licht. Washington, DC: AEI Press.

Epps, Edgar G. 1974. "The Schools and Cultural Pluralism." In *Cultural Pluralism*, edited by Edgar G. Epps. Berkeley, CA: McCutchan.

Epstein, Richard. 1991. "Two Conceptions of Civil Rights." In *Reassessing Civil Rights*, edited by Ellen Frankel Paul, Fred D. Miller, Jr., and Jeffrey Paul. Cambridge, MA: Blackwell.

———. 1992a. *Forbidden Grounds: The Case Against Employment Discrimination Laws.* Cambridge, MA: Harvard University Press.

———. 1992b. "Tuskegee Modern, Or Group Rights under the Constitution." *Kentucky Law Journal* 80 (4): 869–85.

Eskridge, William N. Jr., and John Ferejohn. 2001. "Super-statutes." *Duke Law Journal* 50: 1215–76.

Estrada, Fernando, and Geneva Matthews. 2016. "Perceived Culpability in Critical Multicultural Education: Understanding and Responding to Race Informed Guilt and Shame to Further Learning Outcomes Among White American College Students." *International Journal of Teaching and Learning in Higher Education* 28 (3): 314–25.

Eubanks, Eugene E. 2004. "School Desegregation Under *Brown*: The Role of Court Master, Guidelines and Experiences." *Journal of Negro Education* 73 (3): 209–17.

Evans, Elizabeth D., Carol C. Torrey, and Sherri D. Newton. 1997. "Multicultural Education Requirements in Teacher Certification: A National Survey." *Multicultural Education* 4 (3): 9–11.

Evans Case, Rhonda Leeann. 2004. "The Politics and Law of Antidiscrimination Regimes, 1945–1995." PhD diss., University of Texas at Austin.

Fantini, Mario D. 1972. "Beyond Cultural Deprivation and Compensatory Education." In *Language and Cultural Diversity in American Education*, edited by Roger D. Abrahams and Rudolph C. Troike. Englewood Cliffs, NJ: Prentice Hall.

Fearon, James D. 1999. "What is Identity (As We Now Use the Word)?" Unpublished paper. Department of Political Science, Stanford University. https://web.stanford.edu/group/fearon-research/cgi-bin/wordpress/wp-content/uploads/2013/10/What-is-Identity-as-we-now-use-the-word-.pdf.

Federal Emergency Management Agency. 2022. "Equity Action Plan Summary." https://www.whitehouse.gov/wp-content/uploads/2022/04/FEMA-EO13985-equity-summary.pdf.

Feinberg, Walter. 1998. *Common Schools / Uncommon Identities: National Unity and Cultural Difference*. New Haven, CT: Yale University Press.

Feinberg, Walter, and Kevin McDonough. 2003. "Introduction: Liberalism and the Dilemma of Public Education in Multicultural Societies." In *Citizenship and Education in Liberal-Democratic Societies: Teaching for Cosmopolitan Values and Collective Identities*, edited by Kevin McDonough and Walter Feinberg. New York: Oxford University Press.

Feinstein, Brian D., and Eric Schickler. 2008. "Platforms and Partners: The Civil Rights Realignment Reconsidered." *Studies in American Political Development* 22 (1): 1–31.

Felice, William F. 1996. *Taking Suffering Seriously: The Importance of Collective Human Rights*. Albany: State University of New York Press.

Filvaroff, David B., and Raymond E. Wolfinger. 2000. "The Origin and Enactment of the Civil Rights Act of 1964." In *Legacies of the 1964 Civil Rights Act*, edited by Bernard Grofman. Charlottesville: University of Virginia Press.

FindLaw. 2017. "Investigating the Sexual Harassment Claim." FindLaw.com. Accessed January 4, 2023. https://corporate.findlaw.com/human-resources/investigating-the-sexual-harassment-claim.html.

Finn, Chester E., Jr. 1990. "Narcissus Goes To School." *Commentary* 89 (June): 40–45.

Fish, Stanley. 1989. *Doing What Comes Naturally: Change, Rhetoric, and the Practice of Theory in Literary and Legal Studies*. Durham, NC: Duke University Press.

———. 1994. *There's No Such Thing As Free Speech: And It's a Good Thing, Too*. New York: Oxford University Press.

———. 1998. "Boutique Multiculturalism." In *Multiculturalism and American Democracy*, edited by Arthur M. Melzer, Jerry Weinberger, and M. Richard Zinman. Lawrence: University Press of Kansas.

———. 1999. "Mutual Respect as a Device of Exclusion." In *Deliberative Politics: Essays on Democracy and Disagreement*, edited by Stephen Macedo. New York: Oxford University Press.

———. 2002a. Foreword to *Justifying Belief: Stanley Fish and the Work of Rhetoric*, by Gary A. Olson. Albany: State University of New York Press.

———. 2002b. "Don't Blame Relativism: Can Postmodernists Condemn Terrorism?" *Responsive Community* 12 (3): 27–31.

———. 2007a. "A Fictional Minority." *Opinionator* (blog), *New York Times*, August 11, 2007. https://archive.nytimes.com/opinionator.blogs.nytimes.com/2007/08/11/a-fictional-minority/.

———. 2007b. "Revisiting Affirmative Action, With Help From Kant." *Opinionator* (blog), *New York Times*, January 14, 2007. https://archive.nytimes.com/opinionator.blogs.nytimes.com/2007/01/14/how-kant-might-view-affirmative-action/.

———. 2009. "Does Curiosity Kill More Than the Cat?" *Opinionator* (blog), *New York Times*, September 14, 2009. https://archive.nytimes.

com/opinionator.blogs.nytimes.com/2009/09/14/does-curiosity-kill-more-than-the-cat/.

———. 2011. "The Old Order Changeth." *Opinionator* (blog), *New York Times*, December 26, 2011. https://archive.nytimes.com/opinionator.blogs.nytimes.com/2011/12/26/the-old-order-changeth/.

Fiss, Owen M. 1976. "Groups and the Equal Protection Clause." *Philosophy and Public Affairs* 5 (2): 107–77.

Fitzmaurice, Deborah. 1993. "Autonomy as a Good: Liberalism, Autonomy and Tolerance." *Journal of Political Philosophy* 1 (1): 1–16.

Flathman, Richard E. 1994. "Liberalism: From Unicity to Plurality and on to Singularity." *Social Research* 61 (3): 671–86.

Fleischacker, Samuel. 2002. "Adam Smith's Reception among the American Founders, 1776–1790." *William and Mary Quarterly* 59 (4): 897–924.

Fong, Dennis M. 1978. "Comment: Cultural Pluralism." *Harvard Civil Rights-Civil Liberties Law Review* 13: 133–73.

Fonte, John. 2000. "Why There Is a Culture War: Gramsci and Tocqueville in America." *Policy Review* (December 2000/January 2001): 15–31.

Forbes, H. Donald. 1991. "Multiculturalism: Some Elements of an Analysis." Paper presented at the Annual Meeting of the American Political Science Association, Washington, DC.

———. 1997. *Ethnic Conflict: Commerce, Culture, and the Contact Hypothesis*. New Haven, CT: Yale University Press.

———. 2019. *Multiculturalism in Canada: Constructing a Model Multiculture with Multicultural Values*. New York: Palgrave Macmillan.

Forbes, Jack D. 1967. *The Education of the Culturally Different: A Multi-Cultural Approach. A Handbook for Educators*. Washington, DC: Office of Education (Department of Health, Education and Welfare).

———. 1969a. "A Case for Multicultural Schools." *California Elementary Administrator* 32 (4): 39–41.

———. 1969b. "Segregation and Integration: The Multi-Ethnic or Uni-Ethnic School." *Phylon* 25 (1): 34–41.

———. 1971. "The Mandate for an Innovative Educational Response to Cultural Diversity." In *Teaching Multi-Cultural Populations: Five*

Heritages, edited by James C. Stone and Donald P. De Nevi. New York: Van Nostrand Reinhold.

Ford, Richard T. 2005. *Racial Culture: A Critique*. Princeton, NJ: Princeton University Press.

———. 2011. *Rights Gone Wrong: How Law Corrupts the Struggle for Equality*. New York: Farrar, Straus and Giroux.

Forst, Rainer. 2002. "Toleration, Justice and Reason." In *The Culture of Toleration in Diverse Societies: Reasonable Tolerance*, edited by Catriona McKinnon and Dario Castiglione. New York: Manchester University Press.

———. 2017. "Toleration." In *Stanford Encyclopedia of Philosophy*. Stanford University, 1997–. Article published February 23, 2007; last modified June 12, 2017. https://plato.stanford.edu/entries/toleration/.

Foucault, Michel. 1980a. *The History of Sexuality*. Vol. 1, *An Introduction*. Translated by Robert Hurley. New York: Vintage.

———. 1980b. "Two Lectures." In *Power/Knowledge: Selected Interviews and Other Writings, 1972–1977*, edited by Colin Gordon. New York: Pantheon.

Frankenberg, Ruth. 1993. *White Women, Race Matters: The Social Construction of Whiteness*. Minneapolis: University of Minnesota Press.

Franklin, John Hope. 1956. *From Slavery to Freedom: A History of American Negroes*. 2nd ed. New York: Alfred A. Knopf.

Fraser, Nancy. 2000. "Rethinking Recognition." *New Left Review* 3 (May–June): 107–20.

———. 2013. *Fortunes of Feminism: From State-Managed Capitalism to Neoliberal Crisis*. London: Verso.

Fraser, Nancy, and Axel Honneth. 2003. *Redistribution or Recognition? A Political-Philosophical Exchange*. Translated by Joel Golb, James Ingram, and Christiane Wilke. London: Verso.

Freire, Paulo. 1970. *Pedagogy of the Oppressed*. Translated by Myra Bergman Ramos. New York: Seabury Press.

Freund, Paul A. 1968. *On Law and Justice*. Cambridge, MA: Belknap Press of Harvard University Press.

Fukuyama, Francis. 2018. *Identity: The Demand for Dignity and the Politics of Resentment.* New York: Farrar, Straus, & Giroux.

Gajanan, Mahita. 2017. "Can You Be Fired for Being a Racist?" *Time*, August 15, 2017. https://time.com/4901200/fired-racist-charlottesville-white-nationalism/.

Galeotti, Anna Elisabetta. 2002. *Toleration as Recognition.* Cambridge: Cambridge University Press.

Galston, William A. 2002. *Liberal Pluralism: The Implications of Value Pluralism for Political Theory and Practice.* Cambridge: Cambridge University Press.

Garcia, George F. 1979. "Foreword." In *Multicultural Nonsexist Education: A Human Relations Approach*, edited by Nicholas Colangelo, Dick Dustin, and Cecelia Foxley. Dubuque, IA: Kendall/Hunt.

Garcia, Ricardo L. 1982. *Teaching in a Pluralistic Society.* New York: Harper and Row.

Gardner, Peter. 1993. "Tolerance and Education." In *Liberalism, Multiculturalism and Toleration*, edited by John Horton. New York: St. Martin's Press.

Garnets, Linda D., and Douglas C. Kimmel, eds. 2003. *Psychological Perspectives on Lesbian, Gay, and Bisexual Experiences.* 2nd ed. New York: Columbia University Press.

Gavison, Ruth. 1992. "Feminism and the Public/Private Distinction." *Stanford Law Review* 45 (1): 1–45.

Gay, Geneva. 1983. "Multiethnic Education: Historical Developments and Future Prospects." *Phi Delta Kappan* 64 (8): 560–63.

———. 1990. "Achieving Educational Equality Through Curriculum Desegregation." *Phi Delta Kappan* 72 (1): 56–62.

———. 1993. "Ethnic Minorities and Educational Equality." In *Multicultural Education: Issues and Perspectives*, edited by James A. Banks and Cherry A. McGee Banks. 2nd ed. Boston: Allyn and Bacon.

———. 1994. *A Synthesis of Scholarship in Multicultural Education.* Oak Brook, IL: North Central Regional Educational Laboratory Urban Monograph Series. http://www.eric.ed.gov/PDFS/ED378287.pdf.

———. 1995. "Mirror Images on Common Issues: Parallels Between Multicultural Education and Critical Pedagogy." In *Multicultural Education, Critical Pedagogy, and the Politics of Difference*, edited by Christine E. Sleeter and Peter L. McLaren. Albany: State University of New York Press.

———. 2005. "Politics of Multicultural Education." *Journal of Teacher Education* 56 (3): 221–28.

Gay, Geneva, and Pamula Hart. 2000. "Postmodern Visions in Multicultural Education Preparation and Practice." In *Paradigm Debates in Curriculum and Supervision: Modern and Postmodern Perspectives*, edited by Jeffrey Glanz and Linda S. Behar-Horenstein. Westport, CT: Bergin and Garvey.

Gedicks, Frederick Mark. 1995. *The Rhetoric of Church and State: A Critical Analysis of Religion Clause Jurisprudence*. Durham, NC: Duke University Press.

Genovese, Eugene. 1995. *The Southern Front: History and Politics in the Cultural War*. Columbia: University of Missouri Press.

Gentilli, Veronica. 1992. "A Double Challenge for Critical Race Scholars: The Moral Context." *Southern California Law Review* 65: 2361–83.

Gergen, Kenneth J. 1994. *Realities and Relationships: Soundings in Social Construction*. Cambridge, MA: Harvard University Press.

Ghosh, Ratna. 1995. "New Perspectives on Multiculturalism in Education." *McGill Journal of Education* 30 (3): 231–38.

Gibson, Margaret Allison. 1976. "Approaches to Multicultural Education in the United States: Some Concepts and Assumptions." *Anthropology and Education Quarterly* 7 (4): 7–18.

Gibson, Sarah L., and Eric J. Follo. 1998. "The Status of Multicultural Education in Michigan." *Multicultural Education* 6 (2): 17–22.

Giles, Raymond H., and Donna M. Gollnick. 1977. "Ethnic/Cultural Diversity as Reflected in Federal and State Educational Legislation and Policies." In *Pluralism and the American Teacher: Issues and Case Studies*, edited by Frank H. Klassen and Donna M. Gollnick. N.p.: Ethnic Heritage Center for Teacher Education of the American Association of Colleges for Teacher Education.

Giroux, Henry A. 1979. "Schooling and the Culture of Positivism: Notes on the Death of History." *Educational Theory* 29 (4): 263–84.

———. 1983. *Theory and Resistance in Education: A Pedagogy for the Opposition*. Westport, CT: Bergin and Garvey.

———. 1985. "Critical Pedagogy, Cultural Politics and the Discourse of Experience." *Journal of Education* 167 (2): 22–41.

———. 1987. "Critical Literacy and Student Experience: Donald Graves' Approach to Literacy." *Language Arts* 64 (2): 175–81.

———. 1988. *Teachers As Intellectuals: Toward a Critical Pedagogy of Learning*. Granby, MA: Bergin and Garvey.

———. 1989. "Schooling as a Form of Cultural Politics: Toward a Pedagogy of and for Difference." In *Critical Pedagogy, the State, and Cultural Struggle*, edited by Henry A. Giroux and Peter L. McLaren. Albany: State University of New York Press.

———. 1991a. "Border Pedagogy and the Politics of Modernism/Postmodernism." *Journal of Architectural Education* 44 (2): 69–79.

———. 1991b. "Postmodernism as Border Pedagogy: Redefining the Boundaries of Race and Ethnicity." In *Postmodernism, Feminism, and Cultural Politics: Redrawing Educational Boundaries*, edited by Henry A. Giroux. Albany: State University of New York Press.

———. 1992. *Border Crossings: Cultural Workers and the Politics of Education*. New York: Routledge.

———. 1993a. *Living Dangerously: Multiculturalism and the Politics of Difference*. New York: Peter Lang.

———. 1993b. "Postmodernism as Border Pedagogy: Redefining the Boundaries of Race and Ethnicity." In *A Postmodern Reader*, edited by Joseph P. Natoli and Linda Hutcheon. Albany: State University of New York Press.

———. 1994a. "Insurgent Multiculturalism and the Promise of Pedagogy." In *Multiculturalism: A Critical Reader*, edited by David Theo Goldberg. Cambridge, MA: Blackwell.

———. 1994b. "Living Dangerously: Identity Politics and the New Cultural Racism." In *Between Borders*, edited by Henry A Giroux and Peter L. McLaren. New York: Routledge.

———. 1995. "The Politics of Insurgent Multiculturalism in the Era of the Los Angeles Uprising." In *Critical Multiculturalism: Uncommon Voices in a Common Struggle*, edited by Barry Kanpol and Peter McLaren. Westport, CT: Bergin and Garvey.

———. 1996. *Fugitive Cultures: Race, Violence and Youth*. New York: Routledge.

———. 1997a. *Pedagogy and the Politics of Hope: Theory, Culture, and Schooling*. Boulder, CO: Westview Press.

———. 1997b. "White Squall: Resistance and the Pedagogy of Whiteness." *Cultural Studies* 11 (3): 376–89.

———. 2005. "The Terror of Neoliberalism: Rethinking the Significance of Cultural Politics." *College Literature* 32 (1): 1–19.

———. 2007. "Utopian Thinking in Dangerous Times: Critical Pedagogy and the Project of Educated Hope." In *Utopian Pedagogy: Radical Experiments against Neoliberal Globalization*, edited by Mark Coté, Richard J.F. Day, and Greig de Peuter. Toronto: University of Toronto Press.

Giroux, Henry A., and Peter McLaren. 1992. "Writing from the Margins: Geographies of Identity, Pedagogy, and Power." *Journal of Education* 174 (1): 7–30.

Giroux, Henry A., and Roger I. Simon. 1988. "Schooling, Popular Culture, and a Pedagogy of Possibility." *Journal of Education* 170 (1): 9–26.

———. 1989. "Popular Culture and Critical Pedagogy: Everyday Life as a Basis for Curriculum Knowledge." In *Critical Pedagogy, the State and Cultural Struggle*, edited by Henry A. Giroux and Peter L. McLaren. Albany: State University of New York Press.

Gitlin, Todd. 1993. "From Universality to Difference: Notes on the Fragmentation of the Idea of the Left." *Contention: Debates in Society, Culture, and Science* 2 (2): 15–40.

———. 1995. *The Twilight of Common Dreams: Why America is Wracked by Culture Wars*. New York: Metropolitan Books.

Glazer, Nathan. 1975. *Affirmative Discrimination: Ethnic Inequality and Public Policy*. New York: Basic Books.

———. 1983. *Ethnic Dilemmas 1964–1982*. Cambridge, MA: Harvard University Press.

———. 1991. "In Defense of Multiculturalism." *New Republic* 205 (September): 18–22.

———. 1997. *We Are All Multiculturalists Now*. Cambridge, MA: Harvard University Press.

Gleason, Philip. 1992. *Speaking of Diversity: Language and Ethnicity in Twentieth-Century America*. Baltimore: Johns Hopkins University Press.

Goldberg, David Theo. 1994. "Introduction: Multicultural Conditions." In *Multiculturalism: A Critical Reader*, edited by David Theo Goldberg. Cambridge, MA: Blackwell.

Goldberg, Robert Alan. 1990. "Democracy and Justice in Aristotle's *Politics*." PhD diss., University of Toronto.

Gollnick, Donna M. 1978. *Multicultural Education in Teacher Education: The State of the Scene*. Washington, DC: American Association of Colleges for Teacher Education.

———. 1995. "National and State Initiatives for Multicultural Education." In *Handbook of Research on Multicultural Education*, edited by James A. Banks and Cherry A. McGee Banks. New York: Macmillan.

Gollnick, Donna M., and Peter C. Chinn. 1983. *Multicultural Education in a Pluralistic Society*. St. Louis: Mosby.

———. 1990. *Multicultural Education in a Pluralistic Society*. 3rd ed. New York: Maxwell Macmillan International.

Gollnick, Donna M., Frank H. Klassen, and Joost Yff. 1976. *Multicultural Education and Ethnic Studies in the United States: An Analysis and Annotated Bibliography of Selected ERIC Documents*. Washington, DC: American Association of Colleges for Teacher Education.

Gollnick, Donna M., Kobla I. M. Osayande, and Jack Levy. 1980. *Multicultural Education: Case Studies of Thirteen Programs*. Vol. 2 of *Knowledge Interpretation Program: Training Educators to Provide Educational Equity*. Washington, DC: American Association of Colleges for Teacher Education.

Gonzalez, Mike. 2021. "The Long March Through the Institutions." *Heritage Foundation Commentary*, March 26, 2021. https://www.heritage.

org/progressivism/commentary/the-long-march-through-the-corporations.

Gordon, Milton. 1964. *Assimilation in American Life*. New York: Oxford University Press.

———. 1975. "Toward a General Theory of Racial and Ethnic Group Relations." In *Ethnicity: Theory and Experience*, edited by Nathan Glazer and Daniel P. Moynihan. Cambridge, MA: Harvard University Press.

———. 1981. "Models of Pluralism: The New American Dilemma." *Annals of the American Academy of Political and Social Science* 454: 178–88.

Gorski, Paul C. 2009. "What We're Teaching Teachers: An Analysis of Multicultural Teacher Education Coursework Syllabi." *Teaching and Teacher Education* 25 (2): 309–18.

———. 2010. "Most Influential Scholars: 2010 Social Justice Teacher Educator Resources Survey." EdChange. http://www.edchange.org/survey/EdChangePoll-Scholars.pdf.

Gottfried, Paul Edward. 2002. *Multiculturalism and the Politics of Guilt: Toward a Secular Theocracy*. Columbia: University of Missouri Press.

Gould, Carol C. 2000. "Group Rights and Social Ontology." In *Groups and Group Rights*, edited by Christine Sistare, Larry May, and Leslie Francis. Lawrence: University Press of Kansas.

Graff, James A. 1994. "Human Rights, Peoples, and the Right to Self-Determination." In *Group Rights*, edited by Judith Baker. Toronto: University of Toronto Press.

Graham, Hugh Davis. 1990. *The Civil Rights Era: Origins and Development of National Policy, 1960–1972*. New York: Oxford University Press.

———. 1999. "After 1964: The Paradox of American Civil Rights Regulation." In *Taking Stock: American Government in the Twentieth Century*, edited by Morton Keller and R. Shep Melnick. New York: Cambridge University Press.

Graham, Patricia Albjerg. 1980. "Whither Equality of Educational Opportunity?" *Daedalus* 109 (3): 115–32.

Gramsci, Antonio. 1971. *Selections from the Prison Notebooks*. Translated and edited by Quintin Hoare and Geoffrey Nowell Smith. New York: International.

Grant, Carl A. 1977a. "Anthropological Foundations of Education That Is Multicultural." In *Multicultural Education: Commitments, Issues, and Applications*, edited by Carl Grant. Washington, DC: Association for Supervision and Curriculum Development.

———, ed. 1977b. *Multicultural Education: Commitments, Issues, and Applications*. Washington, DC: Association for Supervision and Curriculum Development.

———. 1985. "Education That *Is* Multicultural—Isn't That What We Mean?" In *Multicultural Nonsexist Education: A Human Relations Approach*, edited by Nicholas Colangelo, Dick Dustin, and Cecelia H. Foxley. 2nd ed. Dubuque, IA: Kendall/Hunt.

Grant, Carl A., and Gloria Grant. 1975. "Minorities and Educational Reform." In *Federal Role in School Reform from Sociological and Educational Perspectives*, edited by G. Thomas Fox Jr. Madison, WI: Teacher Corps.

Grant, Carl A., and Judyth M. Sachs. 1995. "Multicultural Education and Postmodernism: Movement Toward a Dialogue." In *Critical Multiculturalism: Uncommon Voices in a Common Struggle*, edited by Barry Kanpol and Peter McLaren. Westport, CT: Bergin and Garvey.

Grant, Carl A., and Christine Sleeter. 1986. *After the School Bell Rings*. Philadelphia: Falmer Press.

Green, Andy. 1994. "Postmodernism and State Education." *Journal of Education Policy* 9 (1): 67–83.

Griffiths, Melanie. 2015. "Identity." *Oxford Bibliographies*. Last modified June 25, 2015. https://www.oxfordbibliographies.com/view/document/obo-9780199766567/obo-9780199766567-0128.xml.

Guinier, Lani. 1994. *The Tyranny of the Majority: Fundamental Fairness in Representative Democracy*. New York: Free Press.

———. 2004. "From Racial Liberalism to Racial Literacy: *Brown v. Board of Education* and the Interest-Divergence Dilemma." *Journal of American History* 91 (1): 92–118.

Gunnell, John. 2004. *Imagining the American Polity: Political Science and the Discourse of Democracy*. University Park: Pennsylvania State University Press.

Gutmann, Amy. 1995. "Civic Education and Social Diversity." *Ethics* 105 (3): 557–79.

———. 2003. *Identity in Democracy*. Princeton, NJ: Princeton University Press.

Habermas, Jurgen. 1998. *The Inclusion of the Other*. Cambridge, MA: MIT Press.

Haddad, Daphne Warton. 1995. "Multicultural Education: The Views of Three Contemporary African American Theorists." PhD diss., University of South Carolina.

Hale, Myron Q. 1960. "The Cosmology of Arthur F. Bentley." *American Political Science Review* 54 (4): 955–61.

Hall, Stuart. 1991. "Old and New Identities, Old and New Ethnicities." In *Culture, Globalization and the World System: Contemporary Conditions for the Representation of Identity*, edited by Anthony King. London: Macmillan.

Hamilton, Alexander. 1961. In *The Federalist Papers*, by Alexander Hamilton, John Jay, and James Madison, edited by Clinton Rossiter. New York: New American Library.

Handler, Richard. 1997. "Interpreting the Predicament of Culture Theory Today." *Social Analysis* 41 (3): 72–83.

Haney-López, Ian. 1996. *White by Law: The Legal Construction of Race*. New York: New York University Press.

Hannaford, Ivan. 1996. *Race: The History of an Idea in the West*. Baltimore: Johns Hopkins University Press.

Harrington, Helen L., and Russel S. Hathaway. 1995. "Illuminating Beliefs about Diversity." *Journal of Teacher Education* 46 (4): 275–84.

Harris, Cheryl I. 1993. "Whiteness as Property." *Harvard Law Review* 106 (8): 1707–91.

Hartley, John. 2003. *A Short History of Cultural Studies*. Thousand Oaks, CA: Sage Publications.

Hartman, Andrew. 2004. "The Rise and Fall of Whiteness Studies." *Race & Class* 46 (2): 22–38.

Haubrich, Vernon. 1963. "The Culturally Different: New Context for Teacher Education." *Journal of Teacher Education* 14 (2): 163–67.

Hayat, Samuel. 2019. "Varieties of Inclusive Representation." In *Creating Political Presence: The New Politics of Democratic Representation*, edited by Dario Castiglione and Johannes Pollak. Chicago: University of Chicago Press.

Hayes, Matthew, and Matthew V. Hibbing. 2017. "The Symbolic Benefits of Descriptive and Substantive Representation." *Political Behavior* 39 (1): 31–50.

Haymes, Stephen Nathan. 1995. "White Culture and the Politics of Racial Difference: Implications for Multiculturalism." In *Multicultural Education, Critical Pedagogy, and the Politics of Difference*, edited by Christine E. Sleeter and Peter L. McLaren. Albany: State University of New York Press.

Heidegger, Martin. 1959. *An Introduction to Metaphysics*. Translated by Ralph Manheim. New Haven, CT: Yale University Press.

———. 1993. "'Only a God Can Save Us': *Der Spiegel*'s Interview with Martin Heidegger." In *The Heidegger Controversy: A Critical Reader*, edited by Richard Wolin. Cambridge, MA: MIT Press.

———. 2001. *Being and Time*. Translated by Jean Stambaugh. Revised and with a Foreword by Dennis J. Schmidt. Albany: State University of New York Press.

Hekman, Susan J. 1990. *Gender and Knowledge: Elements of a Postmodern Feminism*. Boston: Northeastern University Press.

Helfenbein, Robert J. 2003. "Troubling Multiculturalism: The New Work Order, Anti Anti-Essentialism, and a Cultural Studies Approach to Education." *Multicultural Perspectives* 5 (4): 10–16.

Herman, Judith. 1974. *The Schools and Group Identity: Educating for A New Pluralism*. N.p.: Institute on Pluralism and Group Identity of the American Jewish Committee.

Hess, Frederick M. 1998. *Spinning Wheels: The Politics of Urban School Reform*. Washington, DC: Brookings Institution.

Hess, Frederick M., and Michael J. Petrilli. 2006. *No Child Left Behind Primer*. New York: Peter Lang.

Higham, John. 1984. *Send These to Me: Immigrants in Urban America*. Rev. ed. Baltimore: Johns Hopkins University Press.

———. 1993. "Multiculturalism and Universalism: A History and Critique." *American Quarterly* 45 (2): 195–219.

Hill, Dave, Peter McLaren, Mike Cole, and Glenn Rikowski, eds. 2002. *Marxism Against Postmodernism in Educational Theory*. Lanham, MD: Lexington Books.

Hill, Herbert. 1998. "Lichtenstein's Fictions: Meany, Reuther and the 1964 Civil Rights Act." *New Politics* 7 (1): 82–107.

Hill-Jackson, Valerie, Gloria Ladson-Billings, and Cheryl J. Craig. 2021. "Teacher Education and 'Climate Change': In Navigating Multiple Pandemics, Is the Field Forever Altered?" *Journal of Teacher Education* 73 (1): 5–7.

Hillis, Michael R. 1996. "Research on Racial Attitudes: Historical Perspectives." In *Multicultural Education, Transformative Knowledge, and Action: Historical and Contemporary Perspectives*, edited by James A. Banks. New York: Teachers College Press.

Hills, Roderick M., Jr. 1997. "The Case against the Transformation of Culture Through Antidiscrimination Laws." *Michigan Law Review* 95 (6): 1588–1635.

Hollinger, David. 1995. *Postethnic America: Beyond Multiculturalism*. New York: Basic Books.

Honeck, Mischa. 2018. "The Boy Scouts of America is admitting girls. But it is not a betrayal of their values." *Washington Post*, May 15, 2018. https://www.washingtonpost.com/news/made-by-history/wp/2018/05/15/the-boy-scouts-of-america-are-admitting-girls-but-its-not-a-betrayal-of-their-values/.

Honig, Bonnie. 1995. "Toward an Agonistic Feminism: Hannah Arendt and the Politics of Identity." In *Feminist Interpretations of Hannah Arendt*, edited by Bonnie Honig. University Park: Pennsylvania State University Press.

Honneth, Axel. 1995. *The Struggle for Recognition: The Moral Grammar of Social Conflicts*. Translated by Joel Anderson. Cambridge, MA: Polity Press.

hooks, bell. 1993. "Transformative Pedagogy and Multiculturalism." In *Freedom's Plow: Teaching in the Multicultural Classroom*, edited by Theresa Perry and James W. Fraser. New York: Routledge.

———. 1994. *Teaching to Transgress: Education as the Practice of Freedom*. New York: Routledge.

Horowitz, Donald L. 1985. *Ethnic Groups in Conflict*. Berkeley: University of California Press.

Horton, Carol A. 2005. *Race and the Making of American Liberalism*. New York: Oxford University Press.

Hubble, Martha Weidman. 1972. "Multicultural Curriculum Training with Pre-Student Teachers in Language Arts." PhD diss., University of New Mexico.

Hume, David. 1889. "Of Parties in General." In *Essays Moral, Political, and Literary*, Vol. 1, edited by T.H. Green and T.H. Grose. London: Longmans, Green.

Hunter, William A. 1974. "Prologue: Antecedents to Development of and Emphasis on Multicultural Education." In *Multicultural Education Through Competency-Based Teacher Education*, edited by William A. Hunter. Washington, DC: American Association of Colleges for Teacher Education.

Huntington, Samuel P. 2004. *Who Are We? The Challenges to America's National Identity*. New York: Simon & Schuster.

Hymowitz, Kay S. 1992. "Self-Esteem and Multiculturalism in the Public Schools." *Dissent* 39: 23–29.

Ignatiev, Noel. 2022. *Treason to Whiteness Is Loyalty to Humanity*. New York: Verso.

Illinois Office of Education, Urban and Ethnic Education Section. 1975. *Title IX Ethnic Heritage Project Analysis*. Chicago: Illinois Office of Education.

———. 1978. *Ten Steps for Shared Roles in Multicultural Curriculum Development*. Chicago: Illinois Office of Education.

Bibliography

Inazu, John D. 2010. "The Strange Origins of the Constitutional Right of Association." *Tennessee Law Review* 77 (3): 485–562.

Ingram, David. 2000. *Group Rights: Reconciling Equality and Difference.* Lawrence: University Press of Kansas.

Iowa Department of Education (DOE). 1989a. *A Guide to Developing Multicultural, Nonsexist Education Across the Curriculum.* Des Moines: Iowa Department of Education.

———. 1989b. *A Model Multicultural, Nonsexist Education Plan.* Bureau of Administration and Accreditation. N.p.: Iowa Department of Education.

Iowa Department of Public Instruction (DPI). 1979. *Multicultural Nonsexist Education: Social Studies.* Des Moines: Education Equity Section.

———. 1981. *Multicultural Nonsexist Education: Math and Science.* Des Moines: Education Equity Section.

———. 1982. *Multicultural Nonsexist Education: Physical Education.* Des Moines: Education Equity Section.

———. 1983. *Multicultural Nonsexist Education: Guidance and Counseling.* Des Moines: Education Equity Section.

Iton, Richard. 2000. *Solidarity Blues: Race, Culture and the American Left.* Chapel Hill: University of North Carolina Press.

Itzkoff, Seymour W. 1969. *Cultural Pluralism and American Education.* Scranton, PA: International Textbook Company.

Jackson, Walter A. 1994. *Gunnar Myrdal and America's Conscience.* Chapel Hill: University of North Carolina Press.

Jacobs, Walter A. 2002. "Learning and Living: Difference That Makes a Difference." *Multicultural Education* 9 (4): 2–10.

Jacoby, Russell. 1994. *Dogmatic Wisdom: How the Culture Wars Divert Education and Distract America.* New York: Doubleday.

James, Richard L. 1971. *Directory of Multicultural Programs in Teacher Education.* Washington, DC: American Association of Colleges for Teacher Education and ERIC Clearinghouse on Teacher Education. https://files.eric.ed.gov/fulltext/ED055964.pdf.

James, William. 1899. "On a Certain Blindness in Human Beings." In *On Some of Life's Ideals*. New York: Henry Hold.

———. 1907. *Pragmatism: A New Name for Some Old Ways of Thinking*. New York: Longmans, Green.

———. 1909. *A Pluralistic Universe*. New York: Longmans, Green.

Jameson, Fredric. 1988. "Cognitive Mapping." In *Marxism and the Interpretation of Culture*, edited by Cary Nelson and Lawrence Grossberg. Urbana: University of Illinois Press.

Jay, Michelle. 2003. "Critical Race Theory, Multicultural Education, and the Hidden Curriculum of Hegemony." *Multicultural Perspectives* 5 (4): 3–9.

Jefferson, Thomas. 1944a. "A Bill for Establishing Religious Freedom." In *The Life and Selected Writings of Thomas Jefferson*, edited by Adrienne Koch and William Peden. New York: Modern Library.

———. 1944b. "Notes on the State of Virginia." In *The Life and Selected Writings of Thomas Jefferson*, edited by Adrienne Koch and William Peden. New York: Modern Library.

———. 1944c. "Letter to Nehemia Dodge and Others, A committee of the Danbury Baptist Association, in the State of Connecticut." In *The Life and Selected Writings of Thomas Jefferson*, edited by Adrienne Koch and William Peden. New York: Modern Library.

Jenks, Charles, James O. Lee, and Barry Kanpol. 2001. "Approaches of Multicultural Education in Preservice Teacher Education: Philosophical Frameworks and Models for Teaching." *The Urban Review* 33 (2): 87–105.

Jennings, Todd E. 1995. "Developmental Psychology and the Preparation of Teachers Who Affirm Diversity: Strategies Promoting Critical Social Consciousness in Teacher Preparation Programs." *Journal of Teacher Education* 46 (4): 243–50.

Johnson, Greg. 2016. "Notes on Heidegger and Evola." *Counter-Currents*. February 10, 2016. https://counter-currents.com/2016/02/notes-on-heidegger-and-evola/.

Johnson, Lyndon B. 1965. "Radio and Television Remarks Upon Signing the Civil Rights Bill" (July 2, 1964). In *Public Papers of the Presidents of the United States: Lyndon B. Johnson*, Vol. 2 (July 1–December 31, 1964). Washington, DC: United States Government Printing Office.

———. 1967. "Message on the 1966 Civil Rights Bill." In *The Civil Rights Reader*, edited by Leon Friedman. New York: Walker.

Johnston, Hank, Enrique Larana, and Joseph R. Gusfield, eds. 1994. *New Social Movements: From Ideology to Identity*. Philadelphia: Temple University Press.

Jolly-Ryan, Jennifer. 2006. "Teed Off about Private Club Discrimination on the Taxpayer's Dime: Tax Exemptions and Other Government Privileges to Discriminatory Private Clubs." *William and Mary Journal of Women and the Law* 13: 235–72.

Jones, Peter. 1999. "Human Rights, Group Rights, and Peoples' Rights." *Human Rights Quarterly* 21 (1): 80–107.

Jung, Courtney. 2006. "Why Liberals Should Value 'Identity Politics'." *Daedalus* 135 (4): 32–39.

Jungkunz, Vincent. 2011. "Dismantling Whiteness: Silent Yielding and the Potentiality of Political Suicide." *Contemporary Political Theory* 10 (1): 3–20.

Junn, Jane. 2004. "Diversity, Immigration, and the Politics of Civic Education." *PS: Political Science and Politics* 37 (2): 253–55.

Jura, Cristian. 2012. "Multiculturalism—A Confusing European Approach." *Journal of Politics and Law* 5 (2): 107–15. http://www.ccsenet.org/journal/index.php/jpl/article/view/17080/11624.

Kallen, Horace M. 1915. "Democracy Versus the Melting Pot." *The Nation* 100 (February): 190–94, 217–20.

———. 1924. *Culture and Democracy in the United States: Studies in the Group Psychology of the American Peoples*. New York: Boni and Liveright.

———. 1933. *Individualism: An American Way of Life*. New York: Liveright.

———. 1948. *The Liberal Spirit: Essays on Problems of Freedom in the Modern World*. Ithaca, NY: Cornell University Press.

———. 1954. *Secularism is the Will of God*. New York: Twayne.

———. 1956. *Cultural Pluralism and the American Idea: An Essay in Social Philosophy*. Philadelphia: University of Pennsylvania Press.

———. 1958. "On 'Americanizing' the American Indian." *Social Research* 25 (4): 469–73.

Kanpol, Barry. 1995. "Multiculturalism and Empathy: A Border Pedagogy of Solidarity." In *Critical Multiculturalism: Uncommon Voices in a Common Struggle*, edited by Barry Kanpol and Peter McLaren. Westport, CT: Bergin and Garvey.

———. 1997. *Issues and Trends in Critical Pedagogy*. Cresskill, NJ: Hampton Press.

———. 1999. *Critical Pedagogy: An Introduction*. 2nd ed. Westport, CT: Bergin and Garvey.

Kanpol, Barry, and Peter McLaren. 1995a. "Introduction: Resistance Multiculturalism and the Politics of Difference." In *Critical Multiculturalism: Uncommon Voices in a Common Struggle*, edited by Barry Kanpol and Peter McLaren. Westport, CT: Bergin and Garvey.

Kanpol, Barry, and Peter McLaren, eds. 1995b. *Critical Multiculturalism: Uncommon Voices in a Common Struggle*. Westport, CT: Bergin and Garvey.

Karst, Kenneth L. 1989. *Belonging to America: Equal Citizenship and the Constitution*. New Haven, CT: Yale University Press.

Kaser, Joyce S., Myra Pollack Sadker, and David Miller Sadker. 1982. "Sex Desegregation Assistance Centers (SDACs): A Survey of Their Programs and Practices." Paper Presented at the American Educational Research Association's Annual Meeting, March 22. ED 223009.

Kateb, George. 1994. "Notes on Pluralism." *Social Research* 61 (3): 511–37.

Kautz, Steven J. 1995. *Liberalism and Community*. Ithaca, NY: Cornell University Press.

Kehoe, John, and Megumi Segawa. 1995. "The Effects of Antiracist and Multicultural Curricula on Beliefs about First Nations People." In *Multiculturalism—The State of the Art. Report 2: Studies of Canadian Heritage*, edited by Keith A. McLeod. Ottawa: Canadian Association of Second Language Teachers.

Kekes, John. 1993. *The Morality of Pluralism*. Princeton, NJ: Princeton University Press.

Kellogg, Peter. 1979. "Civil Rights Consciousness of the 1940s." *Historian* 42 (1): 18–41.

Kelly, Erin, and Frank Dobbin. 1998. "How Affirmative Action Became Diversity Management: Employer Response to Antidiscrimination Law, 1961 to 1996." *American Behavioral Scientist* 41 (7): 960–84.

Kendall, Frances E. 1983. *Diversity in the Classroom*. New York: Teachers College Press.

Kendi, Ibram X. 2019a. *How To Be an Antiracist*. New York: One World.

———. 2019b. "How to Fix Inequality: Pass an Anti-Racist Constitutional Amendment." *Politico Magazine*. https://www.politico.com/interactives/2019/how-to-fix-politics-in-america/inequality/pass-an-anti-racist-constitutional-amendment/.

Kennedy, John Fitzgerald. 1967a. "Address to the Nation on Civil Rights (June 11, 1963)." In *The Civil Rights Reader*, edited by Leon Friedman. New York: Walker.

———. 1967b. "Report to Congress Outlining a Civil Rights Bill." In *The Civil Rights Reader*, edited by Leon Friedman. New York: Walker.

Kesler, Charles R. 2021. *Crisis of the Two Constitutions: The Rise, Decline, and Recovery of American Greatness*. New York: Encounter Books.

———. 2022. "Voting Rights and Wrongs: Three Generations of Voting Rights Are Enough." *Claremont Review of Books* 22 (3): 46–51.

Keynes, Edward, and Randall K. Miller. 1989. *The Courts vs. Congress: Prayer, Busing, and Abortion*. Durham, NC: Duke University Press.

Kimball, Roger. 1990. *Tenured Radicals: How Politics Has Corrupted Our Higher Education*. New York: Harper and Row.

———. 2000. *The Long March: How the Cultural Revolution of the 1960s Changed America*. San Francisco: Encounter Books.

———. 2004. *Rape of the Masters: How Political Correctness Sabotages Art*. San Francisco: Encounter Books.

Kincheloe, Joe L., and Shirley R. Steinberg. 1997. *Changing Multiculturalism*. Bristol, PA: Open University Press.

Kinder, Donald R., and Lynn M. Sanders. 1996. *Divided by Color: Racial Politics and Democratic Ideals.* Chicago: University of Chicago Press.

King, Desmond S., and Rogers M. Smith. 2005. "Racial Orders in American Political Development." *American Political Science Review* 99 (1): 75–92.

King, John B. 2008. "Bridging the Achievement Gap: Learning from Three Charter Schools." PhD diss., Teachers College, Columbia University. http://www.classsizematters.org/wp-content/uploads/2012/11/Kings-dissertationpart1.pdf.

King, Martin Luther, Jr. 1986. "The American Dream: Commencement Address at Lincoln University" (June 6, 1961). In *A Testament of Hope: The Essential Writings of Martin Luther King, Jr.*, edited by James Melvin Washington. San Francisco: Harper and Row.

King, Nicki J., Margaret A. Thomas, and Morlie H. Graubard. 1977. *Title IV of the Civil Rights Act of 1964: Expansion of Program Responsibilities.* Prepared for the U.S. Office of Education, Department of Health, Education, and Welfare. Santa Monica, CA: Rand.

King, Richard H. 1992. *Civil Rights and the Idea of Freedom.* New York: Oxford University Press.

Kipnis, Laura. 2017. *Unwanted Advances: Sexual Paranoia Comes to Campus.* New York: Harper.

Klarman, Michael J. 2004. *From Jim Crow to Civil Rights: The Supreme Court and the Struggle for Racial Equality.* New York: Oxford University Press.

Klassen, Frank H., and Donna M. Gollnick, eds. 1977. *Pluralism and the American Teacher: Issues and Case Studies.* Washington, DC: Ethnic Heritage Center for Teacher Education of the American Association of Colleges for Teacher Education.

Klinkner, Philip A., and Rogers M. Smith. 1999. *The Unsteady March: The Rise and Decline of Racial Equality in America.* Chicago: University of Chicago Press.

Knapp, Dale L. 1965. "Preparing Teachers of Disadvantaged Youth: Emerging Trends." *Journal of Teacher Education* 16 (2): 188–92.

Knopff, Rainer. 1989. *Human Rights and Social Technology: The New War on Discrimination.* Ottawa: Carleton University Press.

Konvitz, Morton R. 1949. "Discrimination and the Law." In *Discrimination and National Welfare,* edited by R. M. MacIver. New York: Institute for Religious and Social Studies.

Koontz, Daniel. 2020. "Hostile Public Accommodations Law and the First Amendment." *New York University Journal of Law and Liberty* 3 (2): 197–266. https://www.law.nyu.edu/sites/default/files/ECM_PRO_060971.pdf.

Koppelman, Andrew. 1996. *Antidiscrimination Law and Social Equality.* New Haven, CT: Yale University Press.

———. 2020. *Gay Rights vs. Religious Liberty? The Unnecessary Conflict.* New York: Oxford University Press.

Koppelman, Andrew, and Tobias Barrington Wolff. 2009. *A Right to Discriminate?: How the Case of* Boy Scouts of America v. James Dale *Warped the Law of Free Association.* New Haven, CT: Yale University Press.

Kraft, Nancy P. 2001. "Standards in Teacher Education: A Critical Analysis of NCATE, INTASC, and NBPTS." Paper presented at Annual Meeting of American Educational Research Association, Seattle, WA, April. ED 462378.

Krauthammer, Charles. 1990. "Education: Doing bad and feeling good." *Time* 135 (6): 64.

Kraynak, Robert. 1980. "John Locke: From Absolutism to Toleration." *American Political Science Review* 74 (1): 53–69.

Kukathas, Chandran. 2003. *The Liberal Archipelago: A Theory of Diversity and Freedom.* Oxford: Oxford University Press.

Kull, Andrew. 1992. *The Color-Blind Constitution.* Cambridge, MA: Harvard University Press.

Kymlicka, Will. 1989. *Liberalism, Community and Culture.* Oxford: Clarendon Press.

———. 1994. "Individual and Community Rights." In *Group Rights,* edited by Judith Baker. Toronto: University of Toronto Press.

———. 1995. *Multicultural Citizenship: A Liberal Theory of Minority Rights.* Oxford: Clarendon Press.

———. 2007. *Multicultural Odysseys: Negotiating the New International Politics of Diversity.* New York: Oxford University Press.

La Belle, Thomas J., and Christopher R. Ward. 1994. *Multiculturalism and Education: Diversity and its Impact on Schools and Society.* Albany: State University of New York Press.

Laclau, Ernesto. 1988. "Building a New Left: An Interview With Ernesto Laclau." *Strategies* 1 (Fall): 10–28.

Ladson-Billings, Gloria. 1998. "Just What is Critical Race Theory and What Is It Doing in a 'Nice' Field Like Education?" *International Journal of Qualitative Studies in Education* 11 (1): 7–24.

———. 2000. "Racialized Discourses and Ethnic Epistemologies." In *Handbook of Qualitative Research*, edited by Norman K. Denzin and Yvonna S. Lincoln. 2nd ed. Thousand Oaks, CA: Sage Publications.

———. 2004. "New Directions in Multicultural Education: Complexities, Boundaries, and Critical Race Theory." In *Handbook of Research on Multicultural Education*, edited by James A. Banks and Cherry A. McGee Banks. 2nd ed. San Francisco: Jossey-Bass.

Larmore, Charles. 1996. *The Morals of Modernity.* New York: Cambridge University Press.

Lawson, Steven F. 1986. "E Pluribus Unum: Civil Rights and National Unity." In *American Choices: Social Dilemmas and Public Policy Since 1960*, edited by Robert H. Bremner, Gary W. Reichard, and Richard J. Hopkins. Columbus: Ohio State University Press.

Lawton, Anne. 2004. "Operating in an Empirical Vacuum: The *Ellerth* and *Faragher* Affirmative Defense." *Columbia Journal of Gender and Law* 13 (2): 197–273.

Lee, Jim. 2005. "Multiculturalism in Teacher Education: Philosophical Frameworks and Teaching Models for Transformative Learning." In *The Politics of Inclusion: Preparing Education Majors for Urban Realities*, edited by Barry Kanpol. Cresskill, NJ: Hampton Press.

Lee, Kurtis. 2017. "Here is how the Boy Scouts has evolved on social issues over the years." *Los Angeles Times*, February 5, 2017. https://www.latimes.com/nation/la-na-boy-scouts-evolution-2017-story.html.

Lee, Sophia Z. 2014. *The Workplace Constitution from the New Deal to the New Right*. New York: Cambridge University Press.

Leege, David C., Kenneth D. Wald, Brian S. Krueger, and Paul D. Mueller. 2002. *The Politics of Cultural Differences: Social Change and Voter Mobilization Strategies in the Post-New Deal Period*. Princeton, NJ: Princeton University Press.

Leistyna, Pepi. 2002. *Defining and Designing Multiculturalism: One School System's Efforts*. Albany: State University of New York Press.

Lerner, Natan. 1991. *Group Rights and Discrimination in International Law*. Dordrecht: Martinus Nijhoff.

Lesser, Gerald, and Susan S. Stodolsky. 1969. "Equal Opportunity for Maximum Development." In *Equal Educational Opportunity*, edited by the Editorial Board of *Harvard Educational Review*. Cambridge, MA: Harvard University Press.

Levine, Alan, ed. 1999. *Early Modern Skepticism and the Origins of Toleration*. Lanham, MD: Lexington Books.

Levit, Nancy. 2005. "Embracing Segregation: The Jurisprudence of Choice and Diversity in Race and Sex Separatism in Schools." *University of Illinois Law Review* 2005: 455–512.

Levmore, Saul. 2004. "Privatizing Reparations." *Boston University Law Review* 84 (5): 1291–318.

Levy, Jacob T. 1997. "Classifying Cultural Rights." In *Ethnicity and Group Rights: NOMOS XXXIX*, edited by Ian Shapiro and Will Kymlicka. New York: New York University Press.

Lilla, Mark. 2017. *The Once and Future Liberal: After Identity Politics*. New York: Harper Collins.

Lim, Marvin, and Louise Melling. 2014. "Inconvenience or Indignity—Religious Exemptions to Public Accommodations Laws." *Journal of Law and Policy* 22 (2): 705–25.

Lincoln, Abraham. 1999. "Letter to H.L. Pierce and Others." In *The Life and Writings of Abraham Lincoln*, edited by Philip Van Doren Stern. New York: Modern Library.

Lindsay, James. 2021. "NO! Critical Race Theory Does NOT Continue the Civil Rights Movement." *New Discourses*, podcast, episode 22. February 15, 2021. YouTube video, 29:22. https://www.youtube.com/watch?v=c0RLQXL92Zs.

———. 2022. *Race Marxism: The Truth About Critical Race Theory and Praxis*. Orlando, FL: New Discourses, LLC.

Lipsky, Dorothy Kerzner, and Alan Gartner. 1997. *Inclusion and School Reform: Transforming America's Classrooms*. Baltimore: Paul H. Brooks.

Locke, John. 1963. "A Letter Concerning Toleration." In *The Works of John Locke,* vol 6. Glasgow: Thomas Tegg, 1823. Reprint, Aalen: Scientia Verlag.

———. 1975. *An Essay Concerning Human Understanding*, edited by Peter H. Nidditch. Oxford: Clarendon Press.

———. 1988. *Two Treatises of Government*, edited by Peter Laslett. New York: Cambridge University Press.

———. 1993. "An Essay Concerning Toleration." In *Political Writings of John Locke*, edited by David Wootton. New York: Mentor.

Loftus, John. 2020. "We Can't Have 'National Dialogues' If People Get Fired for Talking Honestly." *Federalist*. July 3, 2020. https://thefederalist.com/2020/07/03/we-cant-have-national-dialogues-if-people-get-fired-for-talking-honestly/.

London, Sheldon. 1999. *How to Comply with Federal Employee Laws: A Complete Guide for Employers Written in Plain English, 2000 Revised Edition*. Rochester, NY: VIZIA Enterprises.

Long, Elizabeth. 1997. "Introduction: Engaging Sociology and Cultural Studies: Disciplinarity and Social Change." In *From Sociology to Cultural Studies: New Perspectives*, edited by Elizabeth Long. Malden, MA: Blackwell Publishers.

Longshore, Douglas. 1983. "The Impact of the Emergency School Aid Act on Human Relations in Desegregated Elementary Schools." *Educational Evaluation and Policy Analysis* 5 (4): 415–24.

Loury, Glenn C. 2002. *The Anatomy of Racial Inequality*. Cambridge, MA: Harvard University Press.

Low-Beer, John R. 1984. "The Constitutional Imperative of Proportional Representation." *Yale Law Journal* 94 (1): 163–88.

Lowi, Theodore. 1969. *The End of Liberalism*. New York: W. W. Norton.

Lukes, Steven. 1974. *Power: A Radical View*. New York: MacMillan.

Lynch, James. 1986. *Multicultural Education: Principles and Practice*. London: Routledge and Kegan Paul.

Lyotard, Jean Francois. 1984. *The Postmodern Condition: A Report on Knowledge*. Translated by Geoff Bennington and Brian Massumi. Minneapolis: University of Minnesota Press.

Lyotard, Jean-Francois, and Jean-Loup Thébaud. 1985. *Just Gaming*. Translated by Wlad Godzich. Minneapolis: University of Minnesota Press.

MacCannell, Dean. 1992. *Empty Meeting Grounds: The Tourist Papers*. New York: Routledge.

Mac Donald, Heather. 2018. *The Diversity Delusion: How Race and Gender Pandering Corrupt the University and Undermine Our Culture*. New York: St. Martin's.

MacIver, Robert M. 1948. *The More Perfect Union: A Program for the Control of Inter-Group Discrimination in the United States*. New York: Macmillan.

MacKinnon, Catharine A. 1978. *Sexual Harassment of Working Women: A Case of Sex Discrimination*. New Haven, CT: Yale University Press.

———. 1993. *Only Words*. Cambridge, MA: Harvard University Press.

———. 2018. "#MeToo Has Done What the Law Could Not." *New York Times*, February 4, 2018. https://www.nytimes.com/2018/02/04/opinion/metoo-law-legal-system.html.

Madison, James. 1961. In *The Federalist Papers*, by Alexander Hamilton, John Jay, and James Madison, edited by Clinton Rossiter. New York: New American Library.

———. 1973. "Memorial and Remonstrance Against Religious Assessments." In *The Mind of the Founder: Sources of the Political Thought of James Madison*, edited by Marvin Meyers. Indianapolis: Bobbs-Merrill.

Malanson, Jeffrey J. 2014. "'If I Had It in His Hand-Writing I Would Burn It': Federalists and the Authorship Controversy over George Washington's Farewell Address, 1808–1859." *Journal of the Early Republic* 34 (2): 219–42.

Malbin, Michael J. 1978. *Religion and Politics: The Intentions of the Authors of the First Amendment.* Washington, DC: American Enterprise Institute for Public Policy Research.

Mansbridge, Jane. 1999. "Should Blacks Represent Blacks and Women Represent Women? A Contingent 'Yes'." *Journal of Politics* 61 (3): 628–57.

———. 2003. "Rethinking Representation." *American Political Science Review* 97 (4): 515–28.

Marcus, Richard L. 2000. "Benign Neglect Reconsidered." *University of Pennsylvania Law Review* 148: 2009–43.

Marcuse, Herbert. 1965. "Repressive Tolerance." In *A Critique of Pure Tolerance*, edited by Robert Paul Wolff, Barrington Moore, Jr., and Herbert Marcuse. Boston: Beacon Press.

Markell, Patchen. 2003. *Bound by Recognition.* Princeton, NJ: Princeton University Press.

Mathieson, Moira B., and Rita M. Tatis. 1970. *Multicultural Education: A Selected Annotated Bibliography.* Washington, DC: ERIC Clearinghouse on Teacher Education. ED 043572.

Matsuda, Mari J., Charles R. Lawrence III, Richard Delgado, and Kimberle Williams Crenshaw, eds. 1993. *Words That Wound: Critical Race Theory, Assaultive Speech, and the First Amendment.* Boulder, CO: Westview Press.

May, Stephen. 1999. *Critical Multiculturalism: Rethinking Multicultural and Antiracist Education.* London: Falmer Press.

Mazie, Margery, Phyllis Palmer, Mayuris Pimental, Sharon Rogers, Stuart Ruderfer, and Melissa Sokolowski. 1993. "To Deconstruct Race, Deconstruct Whiteness." *American Quarterly* 45 (2): 281–94.

McCann, Laurie A. 2017. "The Age Discrimination in Employment Act at 50: When Will It Become a 'Real' Civil Rights Statute?" *ABA Journal of Labor and Employment* 33: 89–104.

McCarthy, Cameron. 1994. "Multicultural Discourses and Curriculum Reform: A Critical Perspective." *Educational Theory* 44 (1): 81–98.

McClain, Linda C. 1998. "Toleration, Autonomy, and Governmental Promotion of Good Lives: Beyond 'Empty' Toleration to Toleration as Respect." *Ohio State Law Journal* 59: 19–132.

McKinnon, Catriona. 2000. "Exclusion Rules and Self-Respect." *Journal of Value Inquiry* 34: 491–505.

McKinnon, Catriona, and Dario Castiglione. 2002. "Introduction: Reasonable Tolerance." In *The Culture of Toleration in Diverse Societies: Reasonable Tolerance*, edited by Catriona McKinnon and Dario Castiglione. New York: Manchester University Press.

McLaren, Peter L. 1988. "Schooling the Postmodern Body: Critical Pedagogy and the Politics of Enfleshment." *Journal of Education* 170 (3): 53–83.

———. 1989a. *Life in Schools: An Introduction to Critical Pedagogy in the Foundations of Education*. New York: Longman.

———. 1989b. "On Ideology and Education: Critical Pedagogy and the Cultural Politics of Resistance." In *Critical Pedagogy, The State, and Cultural Struggle*, edited by Henry A. Giroux and Peter L. McLaren. Albany: State University of New York Press.

———. 1993. "Multiculturalism and the Postmodern Critique: Towards a Pedagogy of Resistance and Transformation." *Cultural Studies* 7 (1): 118–46.

———. 1994a. "Multiculturalism and the Postmodern Critique: Toward a Pedagogy of Resistance and Transformation." In *Between Borders: Pedagogy and the Politics of Cultural Studies*, edited by Henry A. Giroux and Peter McLaren. New York: Routledge.

———. 1994b. "White Terror and Oppositional Agency: Toward a Critical Multiculturalism." In *Multiculturalism: A Critical Reader*, edited by David Theo Goldberg. Cambridge, MA: Blackwell.

———. 1995. "White Terror and Oppositional Agency: Toward a Critical Multiculturalism." In *Multicultural Education, Critical Pedagogy, and the Politics of Difference*, edited by Christine E. Sleeter and Peter McLaren. Albany: State University of New York Press.

———. 1997a. "Decentering Whiteness." *Multicultural Education* 5 (1): 4–11.

———. 1997b. *Revolutionary Multiculturalism: Pedagogies of Dissent for the New Millennium*. Boulder, CO: Westview Press.

———. 2000. *Che Guevara, Paulo Freire, and the Pedagogy of Revolution*. Lanham, MD: Rowman and Littlefield.

McLaren, Peter L., and Ramin Farahmandpur. 1999. "Critical Pedagogy, Postmodernism and the Retreat from Class: Towards a Contraband Pedagogy." *Theoria: A Journal of Social and Political Theory* 93: 83–115.

———. 2001a. "Class, Cultism, and Multiculturalism." *Multicultural Education* 8 (3): 2–14.

———. 2001b. "Teaching Against Globalization and the New Imperialism: Toward a Revolutionary Pedagogy." *Journal of Teacher Education* 52 (2): 136–50.

McLaren, Peter L., and Henry A. Giroux. 1997. "Writing from the Margins: Geographies of Identity, Pedagogy, and Power." In *Revolutionary Multiculturalism: Pedagogies of Dissent for the New Millennium*, by Peter McLaren. Boulder, CO: Westview Press.

McLaren, Peter, and Rhonda Hammer. 1989. "Critical Pedagogy and the Postmodern Challenge: Toward a Critical Postmodernist Pedagogy of Liberation." *Educational Foundations* 3 (3): 29–62.

McLaren, Peter L., and Colin Lankshear. 1993. "Critical Literacy and the Postmodern Turn." In *Critical Literacy: Politics, Praxis, and the Postmodern*, edited by Colin Lankshear and Peter L. McLaren. Albany: State University of New York Press.

McLaren, Peter L., and Rodolfo Torres. 1999. "Racism and Multicultural Education: Rethinking 'Race' and 'Whiteness' in Late Capitalism." In *Critical Multiculturalism: Rethinking Multicultural and Antiracist Education*, edited by Stephen May. London: Falmer Press.

McWhorter, John. 2021. *Woke Racism: How a New Religion Has Betrayed Black America*. New York: Portfolio/Penguin.

Meier, Kenneth J., and Joseph Stewart. 1991. *The Politics of Hispanic Education: Un paso pa'lante y dos pa'tras*. Albany: State University of New York Press.

Bibliography

Melnick, R. Shep. 2018. *The Transformation of Title IX: Regulating Gender Equality in Education.* Washington, DC: Brookings Institution Press.

Melucci, Alberto. 1995. "The Process of Collective Identity." In *Social Movements and Culture,* edited by Hank Johnston and Bert Klandermans. Minneapolis: University of Minnesota Press.

Merton, Robert K. 1949. "Discrimination and the American Creed." In *Discrimination and National Welfare,* edited by R. M. MacIver. New York: Institute for Religious and Social Studies.

Michaels, Walter Benn. 2006. *The Trouble with Diversity: How We Learned to Love Identity and Ignore Equality.* New York: Metropolitan Books.

———. 2016. "A Universe of Exploitation." *The Nation,* December 16, 2016. https://www.thenation.com/article/archive/what-is-the-left-without-identity-politics/.

Milikh, Arthur. 2020. *'Hate Speech' and the New Tyranny over the Mind.* Heritage Foundation. May 19, 2020. https://www.heritage.org/civil-society/report/hate-speech-and-the-new-tyranny-over-the-mind.

Miller, Maurice, Roberta Strosnider, and Elizabeth Dooley. 2000. "States' Requirements for Teachers' Preparation for Diversity." *Multicultural Education* 8 (2): 15–18.

Mills, Charles W. 2008. "Racial Liberalism." *PMLA* 123 (5): 1380–97.

Minnesota Department of Education. 1974. *Human Relations Guide I: Inter and Intracultural Education.* St. Paul: Department of Education.

Minow, Martha. 1990. *Making All the Difference: Inclusion, Exclusion, and American Law.* Ithaca, NY: Cornell University Press.

———. 1997. *Not Only for Myself: Identity, Politics, and the Law.* New York: New Press.

Mitchell, Bruce M., and Robert E. Salsbury. 2000. *Multicultural Education in the U.S.A.: Guide to Policies and Programs in the 50 States.* Westport, CT: Greenwood Press.

Mitchell, Joshua. 2020. *American Awakening: Identity Politics and Other Afflictions of Our Time.* New York: Encounter Books.

Mitchell, Mark T. 2020. *Power and Purity: The Unholy Marriage That Spawned America's Social Justice Warriors.* Washington, DC: Regnery Gateway.

Montalto, Nicholas V. 1982. *A History of the Intercultural Education Movement, 1924–1941*. New York: Garland.

Morgan, Edmund S. 1986. "Safety in Numbers: Madison, Hume and the Tenth Federalist." *Huntington Library Quarterly* 49: 95–112.

Morgan, John. 2000. "Critical Pedagogy: The Spaces that Make the Difference." *Pedagogy, Culture and Society* 8 (3): 273–89.

Morris, Andrew J. 1995. "On the Normative Foundations of Indirect Discrimination Law: Understanding the Competing Models of Discrimination Law as Aristotelian Forms of Justice." *Oxford Journal of Legal Studies* 15 (2): 199–228.

Moses, Michele S. 1997. "Multicultural Education as Fostering Individual Autonomy." *Studies in Philosophy and Education* 16: 373–88.

Mouffe, Chantal. 1993. *The Return of the Political*. New York: Verso.

———. 1994. "Political Liberalism, Neutrality and the Political." *Ratio-Juris* 7 (3): 314–24.

———. 1999. "Deliberative Democracy or Agonistic Pluralism?" *Social Research* 66 (3): 745–58.

———. 2005. *On the Political*. New York: Routledge.

Mouffe, Chantal, and Paul Holdengräber. 1989. "Radical Democracy: Modern or Postmodern?" *Social Text* 21: 31–45.

Mounk, Yascha. 2020. "Stop Firing the Innocent." *Atlantic*, June 27, 2020. https://www.theatlantic.com/ideas/archive/2020/06/stopfiring-innocent/613615/.

Moynihan, Daniel Patrick. 1967. "The Moynihan Report: The Case for National Action." In *The Moynihan Report and the Politics of Controversy*, edited by Lee Rainwater and William L. Yancey. Cambridge, MA: MIT Press.

———. 1969. "Sources of Resistance to the Coleman Report." In *Equal Educational Opportunity*, edited by the Editorial Board of *Harvard Educational Review*. Cambridge, MA: Harvard University Press.

Myers, Leah C. 2003. "Disability Harassment: How Far Should the ADA Follow in the Footsteps of Title VII." *BYU Journal of Public Law* 17 (2): 265–96.

Myers, Peter C. 2008. *Frederick Douglass: Race and the Rebirth of American Liberalism.* Lawrence: University Press of Kansas.

———. 2019. "The Case for Color-Blindness." *Heritage Foundation First Principles Report* 75. https://www.heritage.org/sites/default/files/2019-09/FP-75.pdf.

Myrdal, Gunnar. 1944. *An American Dilemma.* New York: Harper and Row.

Nagel, Thomas. 1973. "Equal Treatment and Compensatory Discrimination." *Philosophy and Public Affairs* 2 (4): 348–63.

Nakayama, Thomas K., and Robert L. Krizek. 1995. "Whiteness: A Strategic Rhetoric." *Quarterly Journal of Speech* 81 (3): 291–309.

National Association for Multicultural Education (NAME). 2003. "Multicultural Education" (Definition). Resolutions and Position Papers. February 1, 2003. http://www.nameorg.org/docs/Deifnitions-MCE-updated-2013.doc.

———. 2008. "Beyond Celebrating Diversity: ReACTivating the Equity and Social Justice Roots of Multicultural Education." Program of the Eighteenth Annual International Conference. New Orleans, LA, November 12–16, 2008. https://services.spalding.edu/ncate/files/2011/02/2008-NAME_CONF_v6.pdf.

———. 2023a. "NAME History, Founding Members and Past Presidents." Accessed January 4, 2023. https://www.nameorg.org/name_history_founding_members.php.

———. 2023b. "NAME Regions, States, Chapter organizing info." Accessed January 4, 2023. https://www.nameorg.org/name_regions_states_chapter.php.

National Council for the Accreditation of Teacher Education (NCATE). 1977. *Standards for the Accreditation of Teacher Education.* Washington, DC: National Council for the Accreditation of Teacher Education.

———. 2008. "Professional Standards for the Accreditation of Teacher Preparation Institutions." Washington, DC: National Council for the Accreditation of Teacher Education. Accessed January 4, 2023. https://files.eric.ed.gov/fulltext/ED502043.pdf.

National Council for the Social Studies (NCSS), Task Force on Ethnic Studies Curriculum Guidelines. 1976. *Curriculum Guidelines for Multiethnic Education.* Arlington, VA: National Council for the Social Studies.

National Council of Teachers of English (NCTE). 1974. *Students' Right to Their Own Language.* Urbana, IL: National Council of Teachers of English.

National Endowment for the Arts. 2022. "Equity Action Plan of the National Endowment for the Arts." https://www.arts.gov/sites/default/files/EquityActionPlan_041422.pdf.

National Endowment for the Humanities. 2022. "Equity Action Plan." https://assets.performance.gov/cx/equity-action-plans/2022/EO%2013985_NEH_Equity%20Action%20Plan_2022.pdf.

National Science Foundation. 2022. "Equity Action Plan Summary: National Science Foundation." https://www.whitehouse.gov/wp-content/uploads/2022/04/NSF-EO13985-equity-summary.pdf.

Nedelsky, Jennifer. 1990. *Private Property and the Limits of American Constitutionalism: The Madisonian Framework and Its Legacy.* Chicago: University of Chicago Press.

Nerken, Ira. 1977. "A New Deal for the Protection of Fourteenth Amendment Rights: Challenging the Doctrinal Bases of the *Civil Rights Cases* and State Action Theory." *Harvard Civil Rights-Civil Liberties Law Review* 12: 297–360.

New York State Education Department. 1991. *One Nation, Many Peoples: A Declaration of Cultural Interdependence*, Report of the New York State Social Studies Review and Development Committee, June 1991. Albany: New York State Education Department.

Newey, Glen. 1998. "Value-Pluralism in Contemporary Pluralism." *Dialogue* 37: 493–522.

Newmann, Fred M. 1968. "Discussion: Political Socialization in the Schools." *Harvard Educational Review* 38: 536–45.

———. 1975. *Education for Citizen Action: Challenge for Secondary Curriculum.* Berkeley, CA: McCutchan.

Nicholson, Linda J., ed. 1990a. *Feminism/Postmodernism*. New York: Routledge.

———. 1990b. "Introduction." In *Feminism/Postmodernism*, edited by Linda J. Nicholson. New York: Routledge.

Nickel, James W. 1972. "Discrimination and Morally Relevant Characteristics." *Analysis* 32 (4): 113–14.

———. 1997. "Group Agency and Group Rights." In *Ethnicity and Group Rights: NOMOS XXXIX*, edited by Ian Shapiro and Will Kymlicka. New York: New York University Press.

Nieman, Donald G. 1991. *Promises to Keep: African Americans and the Constitutional Order, 1776 to the Present*. New York: Alfred A. Knopp.

Nieto, Sonia. 1992. *Affirming Diversity: The Sociopolitical Context of Multicultural Education*. New York: Longman.

———. 1994. "Affirmation, Solidarity, and Critique: Moving Beyond Toleration in Multicultural Education." *Multicultural Education* 1 (4): 9–12, 35–38.

———. 1997. "School Reform and Student Achievement: A Multicultural Perspective." In *Multicultural Education: Issues and Perspectives*, edited by James A. Banks and Cherry A. McGee Banks. 3rd ed. Boston: Allyn and Bacon.

———. 1999. "Critical Multicultural Education and Students' Perspectives." In *Critical Multiculturalism: Rethinking Multicultural and Antiracist Education*, edited by Stephen May. London: Falmer Press.

Nietzsche, Friedrich. 1954. *Thus Spake Zarathustra*. Translated by Walter Kaufmann. In *The Portable Nietzsche*, edited by Walter Kaufmann. New York: Viking Press.

———. 1967. *On the Genealogy of Morals*. Translated by W. Kaufmann and R.J. Hollingdale. New York: Random House.

———. 1968. *The Will to Power*. Translated by Walter Kaufmann and R.J. Hollingdale. New York: Vintage Books.

———. 1989. *Beyond Good and Evil*. Translated by Walter Kaufmann. New York: Vintage Books.

Noel, Hans. 2012. "The Coalition Merchants: The Ideological Roots of the Civil Rights Realignment." *Journal of Politics* 74 (1): 156–73.

Noel, Jana R. 1995. "Multicultural Teacher Education: From Awareness Through Emotions to Action." *Journal of Teacher Education* 46 (4): 267–73.

Norby-Jahrer, KrisAnn. 2009. "Minor Online Sexual Harassment and the CDA Sec. 230 Defense: New Directions for Internet Service Provider Liability." *Hamline Law Review* 32 (1): 207–64.

Norris, Pippa. 1997. "Equality Strategies and Political Representation." In *Sex Equality Policy in Western Europe*, edited by Frances Gardiner. New York: Routledge.

Norton, Anne. 1988. *Reflections on Political Identity*. Baltimore, MD: Johns Hopkins University Press.

Office of Science and Technology Policy. 2022. "OSTP Equity Action Plan in Response to EO 13985." https://assets.performance.gov/cx/equity-action-plans/2022/EO%2013985_OSTP_Equity%20Action%20Plan_2022.pdf.

Ogletree, Earl J., ed. 1973. *The Socially Disadvantaged: Physiological and Psychological Aspects of Deprivation*. New York: MSS Information Corporation.

O'Gorman, Daniel P. 2007. "Paying for the Sins of Their Clients: The EEOC's Position That Staffing Firms Can Be Liable When Their Clients Terminate an Assigned Employee for a Discriminatory Reason." *Penn State Law Review* 112 (2): 425–70.

Okin, Susan Moller. 2005. "Forty Acres and a Mule for Women: Rawls and Feminism." *Politics, Philosophy, Economics* 4 (2): 233–48.

Oleske, James M., Jr. 2015. "Doric Columns Are Not Falling: Wedding Cakes, the Ministerial Exception, and the Public-Private Distinction." *Maryland Law Review* 75 (1): 142–62.

Olneck, Michael R. 1990. "The Recurring Dream: Symbolism and Ideology in Intercultural and Multicultural Education." *American Journal of Education* 98 (2): 147–74.

Olson, Mancur. 1965. *The Logic of Collective Action: Public Goods and the Theory of Groups*. Cambridge, MA: Harvard University Press.

O'Meara, Michael. 2006. "Freedom's Racial Imperative: A Heideggerian Argument for the Self-Assertion of Peoples of European Descent." *Occidental Quarterly* 6 (3): 43–61.

Omi, Michael, and Howard Winant. 1994. *Racial Formation in the United States*. 2nd ed. New York: Routledge.

O'Reilly, Kenneth. 1989. *"Racial Matters": The FBI's Secret File on Black America, 1960–1972*. New York: Free Press.

Orwin, Clifford. 1991. "Civility." *American Scholar* 60: 553–64.

Osgood, Robert L. 2005. *The History of Inclusion in the United States*. Washington, DC: Gallaudet University Press.

O'Sullivan, John. 1994. "Nationhood: An American Activity." *National Review* 46 (3): 36–45.

———. 1995. "Reinventing the American People?" In *Reinventing the American People: Unity and Diversity Today*, edited by Robert Royal. Grand Rapids, MI: William B. Eerdmans.

Owen, J. Judd. 2001. *Religion and the Demise of Liberal Rationalism: The Foundational Crisis of the Separation of Church and State*. Chicago: University of Chicago Press.

———. 2005. "The Tolerant Leviathan: Hobbes and the Paradox of Liberalism." *Polity* 37 (1): 130–48.

Pangle, Thomas L. 1988. *The Spirit of Modern Republicanism: The Moral Vision of the American Founders and the Philosophy of Locke*. Chicago: University of Chicago Press.

———. 1992. *The Ennobling of Democracy: The Challenge of the Postmodern Age*. Chicago: University of Chicago Press.

———. 2010. "How and Why the West Has Lost Confidence in Its Foundational Political Principles." In *Religion, the Enlightenment, and the New Global Order*, edited by John M. Owen and J. Judd Owen. New York: Columbia University Press.

Parens, Joshua. 1994. "Multiculturalism and the Problem of Particularism." *American Political Science Review* 88 (1): 169–81.

Parker, Richard D. 2005. "Five Theses on Identity Politics." *Harvard Journal of Law and Public Policy* 29 (1): 53–59.

Pateman, Carole. 1983. "Feminist Critiques of the Public/Private Dichotomy." In *Public and Private in Social Life*, edited by Stanley I. Benn and Gerald F. Gaus. New York: St. Martin's Press.

Patten, Alan. 2014. *Equal Recognition: The Moral Foundations of Minority Rights*. Princeton, NJ: Princeton University Press.

Pearson, Lowell. 2010. "How to Reduce Your Risk of Sexual Harassment Claims and Litigation." *Missouri Medicine* 107 (6): 361–64.

Peters, Michael. 1995. "Radical Democracy, the Politics of Difference, and Education." In *Critical Multiculturalism: Uncommon Voices in a Common Struggle*, edited by Barry Kanpol and Peter McLaren. Westport, CT: Bergin and Garvey.

Peterson, Paul E. 1983. "Background Paper." In *Making the Grade: Report of the Twentieth Century Fund Task Force on Federal Elementary and Secondary Education Policy*. New York: Twentieth Century Fund.

Peterson, Paul E., Michael Henderson, and Martin R. West. 2014. *Teachers versus the Public: What Americans Think about Schools and How to Fix Them*. Washington, DC: Brookings Institution Press.

Phillips, Anne. 1993. *Democracy and Difference*. University Park: Pennsylvania State University Press.

———. 1995. *The Politics of Presence*. Oxford: Clarendon Press.

———. 1998. "Democracy and Representation: Or, Why Should It Matter Who Our Representatives Are?" In *Feminism and Politics*, edited by Anne Phillips. New York: Oxford University Press.

Pluckrose, Helen, and James A. Lindsay. 2020. *Cynical Theories: How Activist Scholarship Made Everything about Race, Gender, and Identity—and Why This Harms Everybody*. Durham, NC: Pitchstone.

Polsby, Nelson. 1980. *Community Power and Political Theory*. 2nd ed. New Haven, CT: Yale University Press.

Posner, Eric A., and Adrian Vermeule. 2003. "Reparations for Slavery and Other Historical Injustices." *Columbia Law Review* 103 (3): 689–748.

Post, Robert C. 2001. "Prejudicial Appearances: The Logic of American Antidiscrimination Law." In *Prejudicial Appearances: The Logic of American Antidiscrimination Law*, by Robert C. Post, with K. Anthony Appiah, Judith Butler, Thomas C. Grey, and Reva B. Siegel. Durham, NC: Duke University Press.

Powell, James Henry. 1971. "The Concept of Cultural Pluralism in

American Social Thought, 1915–1965." PhD diss., University of Notre Dame.

Powell, Tia, Sophia Shapiro, and Ed Stein. 2016. "Transgender Rights as Human Rights." *AMA Journal of Ethics* 18 (11): 1126–31.

Powers, Thomas F. 1999. "Multiculturalism in America and the Rise of Anti-Discrimination Democracy." PhD diss., University of Toronto.

———. 2002. "Postmodernism and James A. Banks' Multiculturalism: The Limits of Intellectual History." *Educational Theory* 52 (2): 209–21.

———. 2005. "From the Separation of Church and State to Equal Protection for Religion: Supreme Court Doctrine (and Beyond)." Paper presented at the Annual Meeting of the American Political Science Association, Washington, DC, September 2.

———. 2007. "The Act/Belief Doctrine and the Limits of Lockean Religious Liberty." *Perspectives on Political Science* 36 (2): 73–83.

———. 2015a. "Canadian Multiculturalism is Anti-Discrimination Politics (and not anything more)." Paper presented at the Annual Meeting of the New England Political Science Association, New Haven, CT, April 24.

———. 2015b. "Multiculturalism by Law?" Paper presented at Annual Meeting of the Wisconsin Political Science Association, Oshkosh, WI, October 30.

———. 2015c. "The Precise (Political) Origins of American Multiculturalism." Paper presented at the Annual Meeting of the Illinois Political Science Association, Chicago, IL, November 7.

———. 2020. "The Civil Rights Regime is Architectonic." *American Mind*, June 19, 2020. https://americanmind.org/features/the-menace-of-hate-speech-regulation/the-civil-rights-regime-is-architectonic/.

———. 2022. "The Expanding Center: Title VII of the 1964 Civil Rights Act." Paper presented at Annual Meeting of the Midwest Political Science Association, Chicago, IL, April 9.

PS Symposium. 1996. "Political Scientists Examine Civic Standards." *PS: Political Science and Politics* 29 (1): 47–62.

———. 2003. "Nurturing Civic Lives: Developmental Perspectives on Civic Education." *PS: Political Science and Politics* 36 (2): 253–92.

———. 2004. "The Politics of Civic Education." *PS: Political Science and Politics* 37 (2): 231–66.

Ramaswamy, Vivek. 2021. *Woke, Inc.: Inside Corporate America's Social Justice Scam*. New York: Center Street.

Ramírez, Manuel, III, and Alfredo Castañeda. 1974. *Cultural Democracy, Bicognitive Development, and Education*. New York: Academic Press.

Ravitch, Diane. 1990. "Multiculturalism: E Pluribus Plures." *American Scholar* 59 (3): 337–54.

Ravitch, Diane, and Chester E. Finn. 1987. *What Do Our 17-Year-Olds Know? A Report on the First National Assessment of History and Literature*. New York: Harper and Row.

Rawls, John. 1971. *A Theory of Justice*. Cambridge, MA: Harvard University Press.

———. 1985. "Justice as Fairness: Political not Metaphysical." *Philosophy and Public Affairs* 14 (3): 223–51.

———. 1993. *Political Liberalism*. New York: Columbia University Press.

Raz, Joseph. 1986. *The Morality of Freedom*. Oxford: Clarendon Press.

Reich, Rob. 2002. *Bridging Liberalism and Multiculturalism in American Education*. Chicago: University of Chicago Press.

Reynolds, William Bradford. 1989. "The Reagan Administration's Civil Rights Policy: The Challenge for the Future." *Vanderbilt Law Review* 42 (4): 993–1002.

Riessman, Frank. 1962. *The Culturally Deprived Child*. New York: Harper and Row.

Roberts, Paul Craig, and Lawrence M. Stratton. 1995. *The New Color Line: How Quotas and Privilege Destroy Democracy*. Washington, DC: Regnery.

Robinson, Jerry W., Jr., and James D. Preston. 1976. "Equal Status Contact and Modification of Racial Prejudice: A Reexamination of the Contact Hypothesis." *Social Forces* 54 (4): 911–24.

Rodriguez, Fred. 1983. *Mainstreaming A Multicultural Concept Into Teacher*

Education—Guidelines for Teacher Trainers. Saratoga, CA: R and E Publishers.

Roediger, David. 1994. *Towards the Abolition of Whiteness: Essays on Race, Politics, and Working Class History.* New York: Verso.

Rogers, John, and Jeannie Oakes. 2005. "John Dewey Speaks to *Brown*: Research, Democratic Social Movement Strategies, and the Struggle for Education on Equal Terms." *Teachers College Record* 107 (9): 2178–203.

Roithmayr, Daria. 1998. "Deconstructing the Distinction Between Bias and Merit." *Berkeley La Raza Law Journal* 10 (1): 363–421.

Rorty, Richard. 1991a. "Feminism and Pragmatism." *Michigan Quarterly Review* 30 (2): 231–58.

———. 1991b. "Intellectuals in Politics." *Dissent* 38 (Fall): 483–90.

———. 1991c. *Objectivity, Relativism, and Truth.* Vol. 1 of *Philosophical Papers.* Cambridge: Cambridge University Press.

———. 1992. "A Pragmatist View of Rationality and Cultural Difference." *Philosophy East and West* 42 (4): 581–96.

———. 1993. "Feminism, Ideology, and Deconstruction: A Pragmatist View." *Hypatia* 8 (2): 96–103.

———. 1995a. "Color Blind in the Marketplace." *New York Times Book Review*, September 24, 1995.

———. 1995b. "The Demonization of Multiculturalism." *Journal of Blacks in Higher Education* 7 (Spring): 74–75.

———. 1997. "Back to Class Politics." *Dissent* 44 (1): 31–34.

———. 1998. *Achieving Our Country: Leftist Thought in Twentieth-Century America.* Cambridge, MA: Harvard University Press.

———. 2000. "Is 'Cultural Recognition' a Useful Concept for Leftist Politics?" *Critical Horizons* 1 (1): 7–20.

Rosenblum, Nancy L. 1998. "Compelled Association: Public Standing, Self-Respect, and the Dynamic of Exclusion." In *Freedom of Association*, edited by Amy Gutmann. Princeton, NJ: Princeton University Press.

Rufo, Christopher F. 2021. "What Critical Race Theory Is Really About." *New York Post*, May 6, 2021. https://nypost.com/2021/05/06/what-critical-race-theory-is-really-about/.

Rutherglen, George. 2014. "Title VII as Precedent: Past as Prologue for Future Legislation." *Stanford Journal of Civil Rights and Civil Liberties* 10 (2): 159–90.

Ryan, William. 1971. *Blaming the Victim*. New York: Pantheon.

Sandler, S. Gerald. 1960. "Lockean Ideas in Thomas Jefferson's 'Bill for Establishing Religious Freedom.'" *Journal of the History of Ideas* 21 (1): 110–16.

Satel, Sally. 2000. *PC, M.D.: How Political Correctness is Corrupting Medicine*. New York: Basic Books.

Scheingold, Stuart A. 2004. *The Politics of Rights: Lawyers, Public Policy, and Political Change*. 2nd ed. Ann Arbor: University of Michigan Press.

Schickler, Eric. 2016. *Racial Realignment: The Transformation of American Liberalism, 1932–1965*. Princeton, NJ: Princeton University Press.

Schlesinger, Arthur M., Jr. 1992. *The Disuniting of America*. New York: W.W. Norton.

Schmidt, Alvin J. 1997. *The Menace of Multiculturalism: Trojan Horse in America*. Westport, CT: Praeger.

Schmidt, Christopher W. 2016a. "Beyond Backlash: Conservatism and the Civil Rights Movement." *American Journal of Legal History* 56 (1): 179–94.

———. 2016b. "On Doctrinal Confusion: The Case of the State Action Doctrine." *BYU Law Review* 2016 (2): 575–628.

———. 2021. *Civil Rights in American History*. New York: Cambridge University Press.

Schmidt, Sarah Leff. 1974. "Horace M. Kallen and the Americanization of Zionism." PhD diss., University of Maryland.

Schnall, Lisa. 2005. "Party Parity: A Defense of the Democratic Party Equal Division Rule." *American University Journal of Gender, Social Policy and the Law* 13 (2): 381–414.

Schuck, Peter H. 2003. *Diversity in America: Keeping Government at a Safe Distance*. Cambridge, MA: Harvard University Press.

Schwartz, Bernard, ed. 1970. *Statutory History of the United States: Civil Rights, Part II*. New York: Chelsea House.

Scott, Bradley. 1999. "From 'DAC' to 'EAC'—The Expanding Role of the Equity Assistance Center." *IDRA Newsletter* 26 (2): 5, 8.

Scott, Daryl Michael. 1997. *Contempt and Pity: Social Policy and the Image of the Damaged Black Psyche, 1880–1996*. Chapel Hill: University of North Carolina Press.

———. 2004. "Postwar Pluralism, *Brown v. Board of Education*, and the Origins of Multicultural Education." *Journal of American History* 91 (1): 69–82.

Secunda, Paul M., Jeffrey M. Hirsch, and Joseph A. Seiner. 2018. *Mastering Employment Discrimination Law*. 2nd ed. Durham, NC: Carolina Academic Press.

Seelye, H. Ned, and Jacqueline H. Wasilewski. 1979. "Historical Development of Multicultural Education." In *Multicultural Education: A Cross Cultural Training Approach*, edited by Margaret D. Pusch. LaGrange Park, IL: Intercultural Press.

Seidman, Steven. 1997. "Relativizing Sociology: The Challenge of Cultural Studies." In *From Sociology to Cultural Studies: New Perspectives*, edited by Elizabeth Long. Malden, MA: Blackwell.

Shapiro, Ian, and Will Kymlicka, eds. 1997a. *Ethnicity and Group Rights: NOMOS XXXIX*. New York: New York University Press.

———. 1997b. "Introduction." In *Ethnicity and Group Rights: NOMOS XXXIX*, edited by Ian Shapiro and Will Kymlicka. New York: New York University Press.

Shapiro, Svi. 1995. "Educational Change and the Crisis of the Left: Toward a Postmodern Educational Discourse." In *Critical Multiculturalism: Uncommon Voices in a Common Struggle*, edited by Barry Kanpol and Peter McLaren. Westport, CT: Bergin and Garvey.

Shklar, Judith. 1991. *American Citizenship: The Quest for Inclusion*. Cambridge, MA: Harvard University Press.

Shohat, Ella. 1995. "The Struggle Over Representation: Casting, Coalitions, and the Politics of Identification." In *Late Imperial Culture*, edited by Román de la Campa, E. Ann Kaplan, and Michael Sprinker. New York: Verso.

Siegel, Fred. 1991. "The Multicultural Cult." *New Republic* 204 (7): 34–36.

Siegel, Reva. 1997. "Why Equal Protection No Longer Protects: The Evolving Forms of Status-Enforcing State Action." *Stanford Law Review* 49 (5): 1111–48.

Sigler, Jay. 1983. *Minority Rights: A Comparative Analysis*. Westport, CT: Greenwood Press.

Sistare, Christine, Larry May, and Leslie Francis, eds. 2000. *Groups and Group Rights*. Lawrence: University Press of Kansas.

Skrentny, John D. 2002. *The Minority Rights Revolution*. Cambridge, MA: Belknap Press of Harvard University Press.

———. 2014. "Have We Moved Beyond the Civil Rights Revolution?" *Yale Law Journal* 123 (8): 3002–34.

Sleeter, Christine E. 1986. "Learning Disabilities: The Social Construction of a Special Educational Category." *Exceptional Children* 53 (1): 46–54.

———. 1989. "Multiculturalism as a Form of Resistance to Oppression." *Journal of Education* 171 (3): 51–71.

———. 1993. "Advancing a White Discourse: A Response to Scheurich." *Educational Researcher* 22 (8): 13–15.

———. 1995a. "An Analysis of the Critiques of Multicultural Education." In *Handbook of Research on Multicultural Education*, edited by James A. Banks and Cherry A. McGee Banks. New York: Macmillan.

———. 1995b. "Reflections on My Use of Multicultural and Critical Pedagogy When Students Are White." In *Multicultural Education, Critical Pedagogy, and the Politics of Difference*, edited by Christine E. Sleeter and Peter L. McLaren. Albany: State University of New York Press.

———. 1996. *Multicultural Education as Social Activism*. Albany: State University of New York Press.

———. 1997. "Mathematics, Multicultural Education and Professional Development." *Journal for Research in Mathematics Education* 28 (6): 680–96.

———. 2001. "Preparing Teachers for Culturally Diverse Schools:

Research and the Overwhelming Presence of Whiteness." *Journal of Teacher Education* 52 (2): 94–106.

———. 2015. "Multicultural Education vs. Factory Model Schooling." In *Multicultural Education: A Renewed Paradigm of Transformation and Call To Action,*" edited by H. Prentice Baptiste, Ashley Ryan, Blanca Artaujo, and Rose Duhon-Sells. San Francisco: Caddo Gap Press.

———. 2017. "Critical Race Theory and the Whiteness of Teacher Education." *Urban Education* 52 (2): 155–69.

Sleeter, Christine E., and Dolores Delgado Bernal. 2004. "Critical Pedagogy, Critical Race Theory, and Antiracist Education: Implications for Multicultural Education." In *Handbook of Research on Multicultural Education*, edited by James A. Banks and Cherry A. McGee Banks. 2nd ed. San Francisco: Jossey Bass.

Sleeter, Christine E., and Carl A. Grant. 1987. "An Analysis of Multicultural Education in the United States." *Harvard Educational Review* 57 (4): 421–44.

———. 1988. *Making Choices for Multicultural Education: Five Approaches to Race, Class, and Gender.* Columbus, OH: Merrill.

———. 1994. *Making Choices for Multicultural Education: Five Approaches to Race, Class, and Gender.* 2nd ed. New York: Merrill.

Sleeter, Christine E., and Peter L. McLaren. 1995a. "Introduction: Exploring Connections to Build a Critical Multiculturalism." In *Multicultural Education, Critical Pedagogy, and the Politics of Difference*, edited by Christine E. Sleeter and Peter L. McLaren. Albany: State University of New York Press.

Sleeter, Christine E., and Peter L. McLaren, eds. 1995b. *Multicultural Education, Critical Pedagogy, and the Politics of Difference.* Albany: State University of New York Press.

Sleeter, Christine E., and Encarnación Soriano. 2012. "Introduction." In *Creating Solidarity Across Diverse Communities*, edited by Christine E. Sleeter and Encarnación Soriano. New York: Teachers College Press.

Smith, Adam. 1937. *An Inquiry Into the Nature and Causes of the Wealth of Nations.* New York: Modern Library.

Smith, David G. 1964. "Pragmatism and the Group Theory of Politics." *American Political Science Review* 58 (3): 600–610.

Smith, Donald Hugh, and Nancy Levi Arnez. 1969. "Inner City Studies: Graduate Training for Teachers of the Disadvantaged." *Journal of Teacher Education* 20 (3): 347–50.

Smith, Rogers M. 1993. "Beyond Tocqueville, Myrdal, and Hartz: The Multiple Traditions in America." *American Political Science Review* 87 (3): 549–66.

———. 1995. "Beyond Tocqueville, Please!" *American Political Science Review* 89 (4): 987–95.

———. 1997. *Civic Ideals: Conflicting Visions of Citizenship in U.S. History*. New Haven, CT: Yale University Press.

———. 2003. "Grasping the 'Invisible Hand': Race and Political Theory Today." In *Racial Liberalism and the Politics of Urban America*, edited by Curtus Stokes and Theresa Meléndez. East Lansing: Michigan State University Press.

———. 2004. "Identities, Interests, and the Future of Political Science." *Perspectives on Politics* 2 (2): 301–12.

———. 2007. "Studies in American Racial Development: An Interim Report." *Perspectives on Politics* 5 (2): 325–33.

Sniderman, Paul M., and Thomas Leonard Piazza. 1993. *The Scar of Race*. Cambridge, MA: Belknap Press of Harvard University Press.

Sokhi-Bulley, Bal. 2011. "Government(ality) by Experts: Human Rights as Governance." *Law Critique* 22: 251–71.

Sollors, Werner. 1986. "A Critique of Pure Pluralism." In *Reconstructing American Literary History*, edited by Sacvan Bercovitch. Cambridge, MA: Harvard University Press.

———. 1998. "The Multiculturalism Debate as Cultural Text." In *Beyond Pluralism: Essays on the Conception of Groups and Group Identity in America*, edited by Wendy F. Katkin, Ned Landsman, and Andrea Tyree. Champaign: University of Illinois Press.

Solomon, R. Patrick. 1995. "Beyond Prescriptive Pedagogy: Teacher Inservice Education for Cultural Diversity." *Journal of Teacher Education* 46 (4): 251–58.

Soukup, Stephen R. 2021. *The Dictatorship of Woke Capital: How Political Correctness Captured Big Business.* New York: Encounter Books.

Sowell, Thomas. 1984. *Civil Rights: Rhetoric or Reality?* New York: William Morrow.

Spencer, Mark G. 2002. "Hume and Madison on Faction." *William and Mary Quarterly* 59 (4): 869–98.

Spiecker, Ben, and Jan Steutel. 1996. "Moral Identity and Education in a Multicultural Society." *Studies in Philosophy and Education* 15: 159–65.

Spinner, Jeff. 1994. *The Boundaries of Citizenship: Race, Ethnicity, and Nationality in the Liberal State.* Baltimore, MD: Johns Hopkins University Press.

Stears, Marc. 2007. "The Liberal Tradition and the Politics of Exclusion." *Annual Review of Political Science* 10: 85–101.

Steinberg, Shirley R. 1995. "Critical Multiculturalism and Democratic Schooling: An Interview with Peter McLaren and Joe Kincheloe." In *Multicultural Education, Critical Pedagogy, and the Politics of Difference*, edited by Christine E. Sleeter and Peter McLaren. Albany: State University of New York Press.

Stent, Madelon D., William R. Hazard, and Harry N. Rivlin, eds. 1973. *Cultural Pluralism in Education: A Mandate for Change.* New York: Meredith.

Stokes, Curtis, and Theresa A. Meléndez, eds. 2003. *Racial Liberalism and the Politics of Urban America.* East Lansing: Michigan State University Press.

Stone, Allison. 2004. "Essentialism and Anti-Essentialism in Feminist Philosophy." *Journal of Moral Philosophy* 1 (2): 135–53.

Strauss, Leo. 1953. *Natural Right and History.* Chicago: University of Chicago Press.

———. 1962. "An Epilogue." In *Essays on the Scientific Study of Politics*, edited by Herbert J. Storing. New York: Holt, Rinehart and Winston.

———. 1965. "Preface to the English Translation." In *Spinoza's Critique of Religion.* New York: Schocken Books.

———. 1989. "Progress or Return?" In *The Rebirth of Classical Political Rationalism: An Introduction to the Thought of Leo Strauss*, edited by Thomas L. Pangle. Chicago: University of Chicago Press.

Sturm, Susan. 2006. "The Architecture of Inclusion: Advancing Workplace Equity in Higher Education." *Harvard Journal of Law & Gender* 29 (2): 247–334.

Suk, Julie Chi-Hye. 2006. "Antidiscrimination Law in the Administrative State." *University of Illinois Law Review* 2006 (2): 405–74.

Sunstein, Cass R. 1990. *After the Rights Revolution: Reconceiving the Regulatory State*. Cambridge, MA: Harvard University Press.

———. 1991. "The Limits of Compensatory Justice." In *Compensatory Justice: NOMOS XXXIII*, edited by John W. Chapman. New York: New York University Press.

Sutton, John R., Frank Dobbin, John W. Meyer, and W. Richard Scott. 1994. "The Legalization of the Workplace." *American Journal of Sociology* 99 (4): 944–71.

Tajfel, Henri. 1970. "Experiments in Intergroup Discrimination." *Scientific American* 223 (5): 96–102.

Tamir, Yael. 1999. "Against Collective Rights." In *Multicultural Questions*, edited by Christian Joppke and Steven Lukes. New York: Oxford University Press.

Tarcov, Nathan. 1999. "John Locke and the Foundations of Toleration." In *Early Modern Skepticism and the Origins of Toleration*, edited by Alan Levine. Lanham, MD: Lexington Books.

Task Force on Civic Education (TFCE), American Political Science Association. 1997. "Articulation Statement: A Call for Reactions and Contributions." *PS: Political Science and Politics* 30 (4): 745.

Taylor, Charles. 1989. *Sources of the Self: The Making of the Modern Identity*. Cambridge, MA: Harvard University Press.

———. 1991. *The Ethics of Authenticity*. Cambridge, MA: Harvard University Press.

———. 1992. "The Politics of Recognition." In *Multiculturalism and 'The Politics of Recognition'*, edited by Amy Gutmann. Princeton, NJ: Princeton University Press.

———. 1993. *Reconciling the Solitudes: Essays on Canadian Federalism and Nationalism.* Montreal: McGill-Queen's University Press.

———. 1998. "The Dynamics of Democratic Exclusion." *Journal of Democracy* 9 (4): 143–56.

Taylor, Lisa M. Durham. 2007. "Adding Subjective Fuel to the Vague-Standard Fire: A Proposal for Congressional Intervention after *Burlington Northern & Santa Fe Railway Co. v. White.*" *University of Pennsylvania Journal of Labor and Employment Law* 9 (3): 533–602.

Taylor, Paul. W. 1973. "Reverse Discrimination and Compensatory Justice." *Analysis* 33 (6): 177–82.

Tesconi, Charles A., Jr. 1990. "Multiculturalism in Education: The Importance of Meaning." In *Adult Education in a Multicultural Society*, edited by Beverly Cassara. London: Routledge.

Thernstrom, Abigail. 1987. *Whose Votes Count? Affirmative Action and Minority Voting Rights.* Cambridge, MA: Harvard University Press.

———. 2009. *Voting Rights and Wrongs: The Elusive Quest for Racially Fair Elections.* Washington, DC: AEI Press.

Thernstrom, Stephan, and Abigail Thernstrom. 1997. *America in Black and White: One Nation, Indivisible.* New York: Simon & Schuster.

Thomas, Laurence L. 1983. "Self-Respect: Theory and Practice." In *Philosophy Born of Struggle: Anthology of Afro-American Philosophy from 1917*, edited by Leonard Harris. Dubuque, IA: Kendall Hunt.

Thurber, Timothy. 2006. "Racial Liberalism, Affirmative Action, and the Troubled History of the President's Committee on Government Contracts." *Journal of Policy History* 18 (4): 446–76.

Toto, Christian. 2022. *Virtue Bombs: How Hollywood Got Woke and Lost Its Soul.* New York: Bombardier Books.

Tremblay, Manon. 2019. "Uncovering the Gendered Effects of Voting Systems: A Few Thoughts About Representation of Women and LGBT People." In *Gender Innovation in Political Science: New Norms, New Knowledge*, edited by Marian Sawer and Kerryn Baker. Cham, Switzerland: Palgrave Macmillan.

Trueman, Carl R. 2020. *The Rise and Triumph of the Modern Self: Cultural*

Amnesia, Expressive Individualism, and the Road to Sexual Revolution. Wheaton, IL: Crossway.

———. 2022. *Strange New World: How Thinkers and Activists Redefined Identity and Sparked the Sexual Revolution.* Wheaton, IL: Crossway.

Truman, David B. 1951. *The Governmental Process: Political Interests and Public Opinion.* New York: Alfred A. Knopf.

———. 1959. "The American System in Crisis." *Political Science Quarterly* 74 (4): 481–97.

———. 1965. "Disillusion and Regeneration: The Quest for a Discipline." *American Political Science Review* 59 (4): 865–73.

Trumbull, Elise, and Maria Pacheco. 2005. *Leading With Diversity: Cultural Competencies for Teacher Preparation and Professional Development.* Providence, RI: Brown University and Pacific Resources for Education and Learning. https://files.eric.ed.gov/fulltext/ED494221.pdf.

Tully, James. 1995. *Strange Multiplicity: Constitutionalism in an Age of Diversity.* Cambridge: Cambridge University Press.

———. 2004. "Recognition as Dialogue: The Emergence of a New Field." *Critical Review of International Social and Political Philosophy* 7 (3): 84–106.

Ungar-Sargon, Batya. 2021. *Bad News: How Woke Media Is Undermining Democracy.* New York: Encounter Books.

Unger, Roberto Mangabeira. 1976. *Knowledge and Politics.* New York: Free Press.

U.S. Commission on Civil Rights. 2002. "Final Rule: Operations, Functions, and Structure of Civil Rights Commission Part II" (November 22). 67 FR 70428. https://www.usccr.gov/files/about/pdfs/Commission-on-Civil-Rights-Regulations.pdf.

———. 2005. "Federal Procurement After *Adarand*." Washington, DC: U.S. Commission on Civil Rights. https://www.usccr.gov/pubs/docs/080505_fedprocadarand.pdf.

———. 2019. *Are Rights a Reality? Evaluating Federal Civil Rights Enforcement.* November 2019 Statutory Report. Washington, DC: US. Commission on Civil Rights. https://www.usccr.gov/files/pubs/2019/11-21-Are-Rights-a-Reality.pdf.

Bibliography

U.S. Department of Commerce. 2022. "Equity Action Plan Summary." https://www.whitehouse.gov/wp-content/uploads/2022/04/DOC-EO13985-equity-summary.pdf.

U.S. Department of Education. 1994. Educational Resources Information Center. "Varieties of Multicultural Education: An Introduction." Accessed January 4, 2023. https://files.eric.ed.gov/fulltext/ED372146.pdf.

———. 2005. "Office of Elementary and Secondary Education; Overview Information; Training and Advisory Services (Equity Assistance Center Program); Notice Inviting Applications for New Awards for Fiscal Year (FY) 2005." *Federal Register* 70 (39): 9932–36.

———. 2019. *U.S. Department of Education Fiscal Year 2020 Budget Summary.* https://www2.ed.gov/about/overview/budget/budget20/summary/20summary.pdf.

———. 2022. "Applications for New Awards: Equity Assistance Centers." *Federal Register* 87 (31): 8564–70.

U.S. Department of Health and Human Services. 2022. "Equity Action Plan Summary." https://www.whitehouse.gov/wp-content/uploads/2022/04/HHS-EO13985-equity-summary.pdf.

U.S. Department of Homeland Security. 2022. "Equity Action Plan Summary." https://www.whitehouse.gov/wp-content/uploads/2022/04/DHS-EO13985-equity-summary.pdf.

U.S. Department of Housing and Urban Development. 2022. "Equity Action Plan Summary." https://www.whitehouse.gov/wp-content/uploads/2022/04/HUD-EO13985-equity-summary.pdf.

U.S. Department of Justice. n.d. *Title VI Legal Manual.* Accessed January 4, 2023. https://www.justice.gov/crt/book/file/1364106/download.

U.S. Department of Labor. n.d. "Guide to Using the Anti-Harassment Training Program For Registered Apprenticeship Program Sponsors" (Office of Apprenticeship). Accessed January 4, 2023. https://www.apprenticeship.gov/sites/default/files/guide-to-using-anti-harassment-training-program-guide.pdf.

U.S. Department of Transportation. 2022. "Equity Action Plan Summary." https://www.whitehouse.gov/wp-content/uploads/2022/04/DOT-EO13985-equity-summary.pdf.

U.S. Equal Employment Opportunity Commission (EEOC). 1980. "Guidelines on Discrimination Because of Sex." *Federal Register* 45 (219): 74675–77.

———. 1990. "Policy Guidance on Current Issues of Sexual Harassment." March 19, 1990. https://www.eeoc.gov/laws/guidance/policy-guidance-current-issues-sexual-harassment.

———. 1997. "Enforcement Guidance: Application of EEO Laws to Contingent Workers Placed by Temporary Employment Agencies and Other Staffing Firms." December 3, 1997. https://www.eeoc.gov/laws/guidance/enforcement-guidance-application-eeo-laws-contingent-workers-placed-temporary.

———. 1998. *Best Practices of Private Sector Employers.* Washington, DC: Equal Employment Opportunity Commission. https://www.eeoc.gov/best-practices-private-sector-employers.

———. 1999. "Enforcement Guidance: Vicarious Liability for Unlawful Harassment by Supervisors." June 18, 1999. https://www.eeoc.gov/laws/guidance/enforcement-guidance-vicarious-liability-unlawful-harassment-supervisors.

U.S. House of Representatives. 1970. Committee on the Judiciary. *Civil Rights Acts of 1957, 1960, 1964, 1968; Voting Rights Act of 1965; and Voting Rights Act Amendments of 1970.* 91st Cong., 2nd sess. Committee Print.

U.S. Office of Personnel Management. 2011. *Guidance for Agency-Specific Diversity and Inclusion Strategic Plans.* Washington, DC: U.S. Office of Personnel Management. https://www.opm.gov/policy-data-oversight/diversity-and-inclusion/reports/diagencyspecificstrategicplanguidance.pdf.

University of Michigan Desegregation Assistance Center (DAC). 1997a. "Programs for Educational Opportunity." Last modified March 17, 1997. http://www.umich.edu/~eqtynet/dac.html (site discontinued; author has copy).

———. 1997b. "Staff Profiles." Last modified January 27, 1997. http://www.umich.edu/~eqtynet/staff.html (site discontinued; author has copy).

Van Dyke, Vernon. 1977. "The Individual, the State, and Ethnic Communities in Political Theory." *World Politics* 29 (3): 343–69.

———. 1982. "Collective Rights and Moral Rights: Problems in Liberal-Democratic Thought." *Journal of Politics* 44 (1): 21–40.

Vavrus, Michael. 2002. *Transforming the Multicultural Education of Teachers: Theory, Research, and Practice*. New York: Teachers College Press.

Volokh, Eugene. 1992. "Freedom of Speech and Workplace Harassment." *UCLA Law Review* 39 (6): 1791–872.

Voltaire. 1901. "Prejudice." In *The Works of Voltaire, A Contemporary Version*, Vol. 8, *A Philosophical Dictionary*. Translated by W.F. Fleming. New York: E.R. DuMont.

Von Eschen, Penny M. 1997. *Race Against Empire: Black Americans and Anticolonialism 1937–1957*. Ithaca, NY: Cornell University Press.

Waldron, Jeremy. 1992. "Superseding Historic Injustice." *Ethics* 103 (1): 4–28.

———. 2012. *The Harm in Hate Speech*. Cambridge, MA: Harvard University Press.

Walker, Samuel. 1998. *The Rights Revolution: Rights and Community in Modern America*. New York: Oxford University Press.

Wallace, George. 1992. "Inaugural Address" (January 14, 1963). In *Documentary History of the Modern Civil Rights Movement*, edited by Peter B. Levy. New York: Greenwood Press.

Walsh, John E. 1973. *Intercultural Education in the Community of Man*. Honolulu: University Press of Hawaii.

Walzer, Michael. 1995a. "Are There Limits to Liberalism?" *New York Review of Books* 42 (16): 28–31.

———. 1995b. "Education, Democratic Citizenship and Multiculturalism." In *Democratic Education in a Multicultural State*, edited by Yael Tamir. Oxford: Blackwell.

Washington, Booker T. 1974. *The Booker T. Washington Papers*. Vol. 3, edited by Louis R. Harlan and Raymond Smock. Urbana: University of Illinois Press.

Washington, George. 1997a. "Farewell Address." In *Washington: Writings*, edited by John H. Rhodehamel. New York: Library of America.

———. 1997b. "Letter to the Hebrew Congregation in Newport, Rhode Island, August 18, 1790." In *Washington: Writings*, edited by John H. Rhodehamel. New York: Library of America.

Wasserman, Dale. 2003. *The Impossible Musical: The* Man of La Mancha *Story*. New York: Applause Theatre and Cinema Books.

Watkins, Geneva F., and David G. Imig. 1974. *Utilizing Competency Based Teacher Education as a Means for Facilitating Cultural Pluralism in American Schools*. Washington, DC: American Association of Colleges for Teacher Education.

Watkins, William H. 1994. "Multicultural Education: Toward a Historical and Political Inquiry." *Educational Theory* 44 (1): 99–117.

Webster, Yehudi O. 1997. *Against the Multicultural Agenda: A Critical Thinking Alternative*. Westport, CT: Praeger.

Wegierski, Mark. 2005. "Prophets of Rootedness: Sam Francis and Friedrich Nietzsche." *Occidental Quarterly* 5 (2). https://www.toqonline.com/archives/v5n2/TOQv5n2Wegierski.pdf.

Weigert, Andrew J., J. Smith Teitge, and Dennis W. Teitge. 1986. *Society and Identity: Toward a Sociological Psychology*. Cambridge: Cambridge University Press.

Weinrich, Peter. 2003. "Identity Structure Analysis." In *Analysing Identity: Cross-cultural, Societal and Clinical Contexts*, edited by Peter Weinreich and Wendy Saunderson. New York: Routledge.

West, Cornel. 1988. "Colloquy: CLS and a Liberal Critic." *Yale Law Journal* 97: 757–72.

———. 1990. "The New Cultural Politics of Difference." *October* 53 (Summer): 93–109.

West, Cornel, and Bill Brown. 1993. "Beyond Eurocentrism and Multiculturalism." *Modern Philology* 90, Supplement (May): S142–S166.

Whisman, Vera. 1996. *Queer by Choice: Lesbians, Gay Men, and the Politics of Identity*. New York: Routledge.

White, Gillian B. 2017. "Is Being a White Supremacist Grounds for Firing?" *Atlantic*, August 14, 2017. https://www.theatlantic.com/business/archive/2017/08/charlottesvilleemployment/536838/.

Williams, Jenny. 1979. "Perspectives on the Multicultural Curriculum." *Social Science Teacher* 8 (4): 126–33.

Williams, Melissa S. 1998. *Voice, Trust, and Memory: Marginalized Groups and the Failings of Liberal Representation*. Princeton, NJ: Princeton University Press.

Williams, Patricia. 1989. "The Obliging Shell: An Informal Essay on Formal Equal Opportunity." *Michigan Law Review* 87: 2128–51.

Wilson, John. 1992. "Moral Education, Values Education and Prejudice Reduction." In *Cultural Diversity and the Schools*. Vol. 2, *Prejudice, Polemic or Progress?* edited by James Lynch, Celia Modgil, and Sohan Modgil. London: Falmer Press.

Wink, Joan. 2000. *Critical Pedagogy: Notes from the Real World*. 2nd ed. New York: Longman.

Wisconsin Democratic Party. 2020. "Wisconsin Delegate Selection Plan for the 2020 Democratic National Convention." https://wisdems.org/e186d21f8c7946a19faed23c3da2f0da/fcc4f1c94aa9414eaa887852bac4f180/files/2020-National-Convention/2020-Delegate-Selection-Plan_FINAL.pdf.

Wissot, Jay. 1975. "John Dewey, Horace Meyer Kallen, and Cultural Pluralism." *Educational Theory* 25 (2): 186–96.

Wolfe, Alan. 2001a. *Moral Freedom: The Search for Virtue in a World of Choice*. New York: W. W. Norton.

———. 2001b. "The Final Freedom." *New York Times Magazine*, March 18, 48–51.

Wolff, Robert Paul. 1965. "Beyond Tolerance." In *A Critique of Pure Tolerance*, edited by Robert Paul Wolff, Barrington Moore, Jr., and Herbert Marcuse. Boston: Beacon Press.

Wong, Sandra Leslie. 2001. *Managing Diversity: Institutions and the Politics of Educational Change*. Lanham, MD: Rowman and Littlefield.

Wood, Peter. 2003. *Diversity: The Invention of a Concept*. San Francisco: Encounter Books.

Wright, Gavin. 2013. *Sharing the Prize: The Economics of the Civil Rights Revolution in the American South*. Cambridge, MA: Harvard University Press.

Yack, Bernard. 1999. "Putting Injustice First: An Alternative Approach to Liberal Pluralism." *Social Research* 66 (4): 1103–20.

Yan, Jerrett. 2013. "Rousing the Sleeping Giant: Administrative Enforcement of Title VI and New Routes to Equity in Transit Planning." *California Law Review* 101 (4): 1131–90.

Yenor, Scott, and Anna K. Miller. 2020. *Social Justice Ideology in Idaho Higher Education*. Boise: Idaho Freedom Foundation. Accessed January 4, 2023. https://idahofreedom.org/social-justice-ideology-in-idaho-higher-education/.

York, Michelle. 2006. "Back in Class After Expulsion Over Paper." *New York Times*, February 28, 2006. https://www.nytimes.com/2006/02/28/nyregion/back-in-class-after-expulsion-over-paper.html.

Young, Iris Marion. 1989. "Polity and Group Difference: A Critique of the Ideal of Universal Citizenship." *Ethics* 99 (2): 250–74.

———. 1990. *Justice and the Politics of Difference*. Princeton, NJ: Princeton University Press.

———. 1995. "Rawls' *Political Liberalism*." *Journal of Philosophy* 3 (2): 181–90.

———. 1997. "Deferring Group Representation." In *Ethnicity and Group Rights: NOMOS XXXIX*, edited by Ian Shapiro and Will Kymlicka. New York: New York University Press.

———. 2000. *Inclusion and Democracy*. New York: Oxford University Press.

———. 2006. "Taking the Basic Structure Seriously." *Perspectives on Politics* 4 (1): 91–97.

Zavarzadeh, Mas'ud. 1989. "Theory as Resistance." *Rethinking Marxism* 2 (1): 50–70.

Zaveri, Mihir. 2020. "Boy Scouts Announce Diversity Merit Badge and Support for Black Lives Matter." *New York Times*, June 17, 2020. https://www.nytimes.com/2020/06/17/us/boy-scouts-diversity-inclusion-eagle.html.

Zeichner, Kenneth M., and Daniel P. Liston. 1990. "Traditions of Reform in U.S. Teacher Education." *Journal of Teacher Education* 41 (2): 3–20.

Zintz, Miles V. 1960a. *The Indian Research Study: The Adjustment of Indian and Non-Indian Children in the Public Schools of New Mexico. Final Report, Part 1*. A special report prepared at the request of the United States Office of Education. Albuquerque: College of Education, University of New Mexico.

———. 1960b. *The Indian Research Study: The Adjustment of Indian and Non-Indian Children in the Public Schools of New Mexico. Final Report, Part 2*. A special report prepared at the request of the United States Office of Education. Albuquerque: College of Education, University of New Mexico.

———. 1963. *Educating Across Cultures*. Dubuque, IA: Wm. C. Brown.

Zintz, Miles V, Mari L. Ulibarri, and Dolores Gonzales. 1971. *The Implications of Bilingual Education for Developing Multicultural Sensitivity Through Teacher Education*. Washington, DC: ERIC Clearinghouse on Teacher Education.

Zoch, Amanda. 2020. "The Rise of Ranked-Choice Voting." *National Conference of State Legislatures* 28 (34). https://www.ncsl.org/research/elections-and-campaigns/the-rise-of-ranked-choice-voting.aspx.

ENDNOTES

Chapter 1

1. See note 4. Wesley Yang, who coined the successor ideology term (posted on Twitter and discussed subsequently in various podcast episodes with interviewers), describes anti-discrimination democracy but for some reason prefers to retain the ambiguity of his usefully provocative label.
2. For this latter general formulation I am indebted to Thomas Pangle.
3. For a list of many such theories, see chapter 9 note 19; see also the many theorists cited in chapter 10.
4. See chapter 6, notes 54 and 55 and accompanying text. As guides to the anti-discrimination revolution, for me there is only one close contender to multicultural education (and Banks): Andrew Koppelman's book *Antidiscrimination Law and Social Equality* (1996). Rooted in the twists and turns of the law and the moralizing of other political theorists, it presents a moving target that would limit its utility. It is also partly a work of analysis, as well as one of advocacy and positive theorizing, and in this way, too, it is less illuminating in some ways than multicultural education (the latter being so much more fully the *effect* of political change). Koppelman also appears to have had some second thoughts; his later work on religion and anti-discrimination seeks a way to avoid the conflict between the old and the new that muddies the waters (see esp. 2020). But Koppelman is not a postmodernist; his view of anti-discrimination as "an increasingly ambitious project of cultural transformation" is breathtaking; and his analysis is fully alive to the question of liberalism (1996, 2; see esp. chapter 5). Another possibility is Catharine MacKinnon, who has been at the heart of things (helping to usher in expansions of Title VII we discuss in chapter 3). She does offer a (non-postmodernist) general theory (in *Toward a Feminist Theory of the State* [1989]), but its basic starting point renders it much less useful than one would hope. Her theory is narrowly confined to sexism in particular and her first question is how anti-sexism ought to be related to "Marxism." This will be grist for the mill for those who want to see neo-Marxism at work in all things civil rights but in that way and in others her theorizing *obscures* the anti-discrimination impulse more than it illuminates it.

5   I treat postmodernist multiculturalism in chapter 6. Another theory of multiculturalism influential among academics, especially political theorists, was developed by Canadian Will Kymlicka (indeed, a swarm of theories of multiculturalism emerged in response to his argument, first put forward in 1989; see note 12 below for a brief discussion and an explanation of why I do not take it up). Several common *mis*interpretations of multiculturalism also clutter discussion of the real issues. Perhaps most prominent are those who would trace multiculturalism and related phenomena to intellectual history (see note 10 below and accompanying text). Others see in the idea a continuation or radicalization of the tradition of liberal pluralism (see, e.g., Glazer 1997, 97; Higham 1993, 209; Hollinger 1995, 98–100; Jacoby 1994, 138–59; Olneck 1990; Watkins 1994). Lastly, another view holds multiculturalism to be a subpolitical phenomenon—a response to the mere "facts" of cultural or ethnic diversity or other related "group" developments like Afrocentricity or feminism or immigration (see, e.g., Crouch 1995, 64; Fish 1998; Higham 1993; Hollinger 1995, 11–12; New York 1991, 6; O'Sullivan 1994, 38; 1995, 283; Schlesinger 1992, 102, 124–26, chapter 3; Webster 1997, 26–32, 74–79). All of these are equally answered and rendered problematic by multicultural education and its clear political substance—which is, after all, the original and only actual source of arguments for multiculturalism in the United States (if we leave aside the Kymlicka debate among academic philosophers mentioned above). A clear and massive *political* cause, not any intellectual or cultural or other subpolitical source, is primary. We must also resist those who would reject multiculturalism because they think it a fundamentally incoherent idea (see, e.g., Appiah 1998, 46; Brotz 1980; Fish 1998; Hollinger 1995, 2). This claim is usually made by taking the word in its literal meaning. But multicultural education's employment of the term always means "anti-discrimination" and that idea is not incoherent—and so these critics (who do not, of course, oppose anti-discrimination) take aim at a straw man. Likewise, those who would say that the multiculturalism idea is "dead" (most famously, European leaders David Cameron, Nicolas Sarkozy, and Angela Merkel, e.g.) would presumably not say the same of anti-discrimination (see Brooks 2006; Fish 2011; Jura 2012).

6   Glazer 1997, 8; see, e.g., Clausen 2000, 60–62; Sollors 1998, 64.
7   Banks 1992a, 274. See chapter 4, note 5. See also Kallen 1915, 1924.
8   See chapter 4.
9   See the doctoral dissertations of both John B. King, second education secretary under Barack Obama, and Miguel Cardona, secretary of education under Joe Biden (Cardona 2011; King 2008).
10 Different versions of such a stance include Breitbart 2011, 124; Fukuyama 2018; Taylor 1991, 1992 (see also Taylor 1989); Trueman 2020, 2022. See also chapter 6, note 4 and chapter 10, note 44. For those who would

emphasize Marxism or Neo-Marxism in particular, see chapter 6, notes 6–8; chapter 8, note 21. Gottfried (2002), Joshua Mitchell (2020, 104–32), and Mark T. Mitchell (2020) would emphasize, in addition to intellectual history, the influence of the ideas of liberal Protestantism or Puritanism or Christianity (now distorted) in American life. This book taken as a whole is my general answer to all these claims; but the discussion of postmodernism in chapter 6, especially, provides plenty of evidence of the subordination of ideas to politics under the anti-discrimination regime, and chapters 2 and 3 state the obvious alternative (political) origin story. This is not to deny the role of intellectual history as it pertains to *other* broad social phenomena. Modernity and liberalism, astonishing projects of intellectuals, surely present plenty of evidence of the world-transformative power of ideas. But (mere) political orders, too, have great causal power, and anti-discrimination politics teaches us that we need to learn how to see better than we do that causal mechanism doing its work.

11 DiAngelo 2004, 2018.

12 The neglect is perhaps understandable in the case of Kymlicka, who begins more or less from Canadian multiculturalism, but it is surprising in the case of the academic debate's many American authors (see Baumeister 1998; Feinberg 1998; Feinberg and McDonough 2003; Ford 2005; Gutmann 1995; Ingram 2000, chapter 10; Spiecker and Steutel 1996; Walzer 1995b). For multicultural education as unsophisticated, see Moses 1997, 373–74; as morally insufficient, see Reich 2002, 177–84; as both, see Callan 1997, 207, 239n4.

I do not take up Kymlicka's theory of multiculturalism in this study mainly because he explicitly rejects what he takes to be a "pernicious" American preoccupation with anti-discrimination politics (1989, 257). Addressing his theory, which focuses on more ambitious ethnic diversity claims (to include, at the extreme, self-government and secession claims for ethnic minorities), would take us too far afield. (See, generally, Kymlicka 1989, 1995, 2007.) I do believe that Kymlicka could learn much from Banks. Despite his protestations to the contrary, it seems to me that Kymlicka's entire theory is a reflection of the upheaval (intellectual, moral, and political) brought about by the anti-discrimination revolution. The main evidence for this claim is that a central principle of his position—cultural identity—does not arise out of the liberal tradition as the other key principles outlining his theory (liberty and equality) do. Liberty/equality, plus group identity, does not necessarily add up to something "liberal." Indeed, identity can be considered a vital principle or moral intuition today only because of the civil rights revolution, something Banks helps us to see. (That someone highly attentive to anti-discrimination politics who begins from Kymlicka's understanding of things can be misled as a result—on multiculturalism and liberalism and the relationship between them—is especially clear in Ford 2005, 5–11.) For a fuller discussion of Kymlicka in the context of Canadian multiculturalism policy (which, since the 1990s, has become almost entirely focused on anti-racism politics and not the kinds of questions raised in his theory), see Powers 2015a.

13 See Task Force on Civic Education (TFCE) 1997. Multicultural education is never mentioned in the several dozen articles that have been written on the topics of civic education, civic education and political science, and service learning in *PS: Political Science and Politics*. The tendency is most clear in three symposia in that journal on the subject of civic education (see *PS* Symposium 1996, 2003, 2004). One of the 2004 essays does use the term, and even calls for "constructing a civic and multicultural education," but it does so without any reference to the already-existing world of multicultural education (Junn 2004, 253, 255).

14 Epstein 1992; Koppelman 1996; see note 4 above and chapter 11, note 2.

15 Such practices are enshrined in the American constitution and in American institutions, laws, and political culture: individuals are said to have rights and liberties, and the state is said to exist to protect them; the writers of the nation's laws accede to the will of the people through elections (reflecting the people's consent) and institutions of representation; some form of religious freedom and toleration prevails, but law is secular in its purposes; freedom of speech and of the press are guaranteed; institutions of the state are designed and arranged with a view to limiting abuses of government's power; various procedural rights for individuals (limiting the power of police and courts) are guaranteed; military force is subordinate to civilian control; to some important degree private property is protected and free enterprise promoted as the basis of prosperity (however much they may be regulated by the state in the public interest). Some or another of these practices or ideas may be challenged by intellectuals or political extremists on the Left or Right, but none is significantly challenged in fact in the day-to-day life of American politics.

16 Graham 1990, 456. See chapter 11, note 3. As noted above, there are a few exceptions to this rule (see chapter 11, note 2).

17 Glazer 1997, 12; see Schlesinger 1992, 102, 124–26, chapter 3; see also Higham 1993.

18 Those social scientists who do address these issues in a broad way do so too beholden to the insights of their discipline—as if 1,001 explanatory theories about *other* dimensions of political life will tell us what the civil rights regime is and means. This is best represented by John Skrentny's widely cited book, *The Minority Rights Revolution* (2002) and is a fly in the ointment of Melnick's otherwise extremely helpful book on Title IX (2018).

Chapter 2

1 What I term here the traditional liberal democratic approach to race discrimination should not be confused with the term "racial liberalism" that is used by some scholars. See especially Scott 1997, xiii–xiv; and Guinier 2004; Jackson 1994; Mills 2008; Schickler 2016; Stokes and Meléndez 2003; Thurber 2006. Here "liberalism" is used to refer to Left or Democratic Party politics from the New Deal on. Different authors use racial liberalism differently to describe a range of civil rights stances, beginning with, but generally going beyond, public sector non-discrimination—and sometimes including not only anti-discrimination but also affirmative action policy. Obviously, such a flexible view of the place of "liberalism" denies the importance of the decisive break achieved by the anti-discrimination revolution that I think is so important. Scholars who employ the term often use it in a somewhat pejorative sense, calling for a more ambitious program of action going beyond mere anti-discrimination (a position similar to that of postmodernist multiculturalists we will encounter in chapter 6 and very common in the affirmative action debate).

2 Genovese 1995, 280–81. For an extended alternative account of the problem, see Jeff Spinner-Halev's chapter-long discussion, "Race and the Failure of Liberal Citizenship" (Spinner 1994, 10–12, 113–39). Although Spinner-Halev's view of these questions is framed from the point of view of the Left's interpretation of anti-discrimination, his account says surprisingly little about the role the public-private divide played in this story; it thus has the effect of understating significantly the nature of the problem. Indeed, Spinner-Halev embraces the Left's critique of the public-private divide (see Spinner 1994, 5–6, 37–38) up to a point, before ultimately defending it (57–58). See also note 18 below.

3 *Civil Rights Cases* 109 U.S. 3 (1883).

4 *Civil Rights Cases* 109 U.S. 3, 24–25 (1883).

5 *Civil Rights Cases* 109 U.S. 3, 17 (1883). The state action doctrine worked in tandem with Supreme Court federalism doctrine to do its work, permitting state governments great latitude to determine the limit of civil rights protections. See *Slaughterhouse Cases* 83 U.S. 36 (1873); *United States v. Cruickshank* 92 U.S. 542 (1876); *United States v. Reese* 92 U.S. 214 (1876); cf. *Civil Rights Cases* 109 U.S. 3, 17 (1883). For a useful discussion of the *Civil Rights Cases* (as leaving "intact federal power to protect black physical security and voting"), see Brandwein 2007.

6 See Bardolph 1970; Braeman 1988; Franklin 1956; Nieman 1991.

7 The regime of racial discrimination was aided as well by a Court inclined to call things private that were clearly public and to turn a blind eye even to manifest public inequality (in the name of states' rights). In areas of life where the

common law had traditionally seen a public "duty to serve" (so-called public accommodations like hotels, restaurants, and common carriers), the postbellum courts had no trouble deeming them private and thus untouchable by federal government efforts. Justice Harlan, dissenting in the *Civil Rights Cases*, relied on the older common law view: "railroad corporations, keepers of inns, and managers of places of public amusement are agents and instrumentalities of the State, because they are charged with duties to the public and are amenable . . . to government regulation" (*Civil Rights Cases* 109 U.S. 3, 58–59; see Evans Case 2004). Other problems with the public-private divide in the case of race are visible in other important areas of legal controversy. In one line of cases, the Supreme Court upheld racial "restrictive covenants," real estate contract provisions designed to exclude Blacks permanently from White neighborhoods. The fact that courts had to uphold the contracts was not thought to mean the involvement of "state action" and so restrictive covenants were viewed simply as "contracts entered into by private individuals" (*Corrigan v. Buckley* 271 U.S. 323, 331 [1926]). "[Private] covenants replaced ordinances, turning state action into a game of 'cat and mouse' in which private individuals and corporations could avoid constitutional sanctions by subterfuges designed to avoid the appearance of state involvement, which nevertheless was ever-present" (Nerken 1977, 335). When the right of contract, explicitly affirmed in the 1866 Civil Rights Act, became a means for Blacks to resist White conspiracies to intimidate them in the workplace, the Supreme Court held that Congress had gone too far in claiming this as a matter of federal, and not state, power (*Hodges v. United States* 203 U.S. 1 [1906]). In all these cases, the private became a domain in which Blacks were denied the laws' protections; in other cases it was a sphere in which White "private individuals" were kept free from the same laws' clear prohibitions. Criminal sanctions in the 1870 Civil Rights Act (the first Ku Klux Klan Act) aimed at counteracting violence and other harms against Blacks were struck down because they were "directed exclusively against the action of private persons" and not state actors (*United States v. Harris* 101 U.S. 629, 640 [1883]). In the context of voting rights the Court made a dubious distinction between laws (clearly public) and the deeds of government officials carrying out those laws (deemed private) in order to turn a blind eye to Black disenfranchisement—the Civil War Amendments being read here again as not reaching mere "wrongful individual acts" (*James v. Bowman* 190 U.S. 127, 136 [1903]). For the legal history here I am indebted to Amar 1998; Braeman 1988; Klarman 2004.

8 When it came to public matters, sometimes the Court simply could not make up its mind: at points all-White juries indicated a manifest failing of public equality, at others they did not (*Strauder v. West Virginia* 100 U.S. 303 [1880]; *Virginia v Rives* 100 U.S. 313 [1880]; *Neal v. Delaware* 103 U.S. 370 [1881]).

Most famously, political equality came to include public segregation in the "separate but equal" doctrine. Equally problematic, from the point of view of the coherence of the public-private divide, were cases where plainly public policies and actions of state and local government officials were deemed private in order to shield discriminatory outcomes from federal government interference. Perhaps the most blatant of these was a decision upholding as "private" the all-White primary election of the Texas Democratic Party (*Grovey v. Townsend* 295 U.S. 45 [1935]). Other efforts effectively excluding Blacks from the vote—like literacy tests or poll taxes—were likewise found not to violate the Fourteenth Amendment's equal protection standard (*Williams v. Mississippi* 170 U.S. 213 [1898]; *Breedlove v. Suttles* 302 U.S. 277 [1937]). More important in practical terms was the tendency—announced in *United States v. Reese* 92 U.S. 214 (1876)—to defer to the states in matters pertaining to voting, despite the voting protections of the Fifteenth as well as the Fourteenth Amendments. One need not fully agree with Ira Nerken's conclusion that "the state action doctrine had eviscerated any substantive content of the fourteenth amendment" in order to say that the Court's determinations as to what was public and what was private had become captured by an obvious political intention (Nerken 1977, 338). For some of the voluminous scholarly literature critical of the public-private divide and the state action doctrine that emerged before and after the civil rights revolution, see chapter 3, notes 50 and 56.

9   *Pace v. Alabama* 106 U.S. 583 (1883).
10 *Plessy v. Ferguson* 163 U.S. 537 (1896). See the works cited in note 6.
11 Douglass 1966, 270–71; see Washington 1974, 583–87. As Myers makes plain (2008, 5–7, 28–32, 176–81, 196–97), this slogan—important as it may have been for general political consumption—is not the last word in Douglass's understanding of equality.
12 *Brown v. Board of Education* 347 U.S. 483 (1954).
13 Senator Andrews (D, Alabama) Cong. Rec., 8 Feb. 1964, 2562. See Wallace 1992, 217–20. See also Bardolph 1970, 365.
14 Quoted in Congressional Quarterly Service 1968, 50–61.
15 Bernstein 2003, 5; Graham 1990, 504n13; Schmidt 2016a, 189–92.
16 The quotation is from a letter W. C. Hushing sent to the U.S. Senate Committee on Education and Labor (quoted in Hill 1998, 85). How race and race discrimination divided and undermined organized labor in America is an interesting chapter in the story of the old regime; see Iton 2000.
17 See also Kennedy 1967b, 248–49; Johnson 1967, 273.
18 There is now a lively scholarly debate over whether, or how much, to blame liberalism for racism and other forms of discrimination prior to the 1960s, a debate triggered by the work of Rogers M. Smith (for a useful overview, see Stears 2007; see also chapter 11, notes 2 and 13 and accompanying text).

19 See Von Eschen 1997. In a discussion of multicultural education (in which he is critical of the field for having too narrow a view of the problem they address), William Watkins employs the decolonization interpretation of the civil rights revolution in a succinct formula: racism "must be located as socially constructed phenomenon historically operating as a function of colonial plunder, the unequal distribution of power, and the system of free market economics" (Watkins 1994, 115). Taken too far, attempts to interpret either multiculturalism or anti-discrimination as part of, or as subordinate to, the idea of decolonization reflect an odd European (I am tempted to say Eurocentric) imposition on American events, often indicating a Marxist or neo-Marxist academic stance. The moral meaning (and intention) of a decolonization framework of interpretation is not insignificant, since it works to undermine claims on behalf of American democratic politics to take credit for anti-discrimination reforms (see note 20).

20 Anderson 2003; Dudziak 2000; Filvaroff and Wolfinger 2000; Graham 1990; Klinkner and Smith 1999; Skrentny 2002. When some of these explanations of the success of the civil rights revolution insist on a central or dominant role for foreign policy, they go too far. It is true that appeals to foreign policy considerations (prominent in public statements by Eisenhower and Kennedy, for example) were part of the public debate. But such considerations cannot be more important than domestic ones, to include the role of moral opinion. It is worth noting here, as before (see note 19), the moral impulse that seems to be at work in explanations from foreign policy—namely, a desire to deprive 1960s America of any credit for the changes that came about (akin to explanations from the Right that trace the fall of the Soviet Union to the role of liberal leaders Margaret Thatcher and Ronald Reagan, for example). It is impossible to explain the behavior of the White majority, without which the civil rights revolution could not have succeeded, in terms excluding morality or moral opinion. It seems to me that an accurate explanation would have to include, as well, a kind of moral envy of the nobility of the cause of American Blacks, especially among young Whites, which seems to have fueled much of the radicalism of the 1960s. A usefully balanced view of the role of foreign policy, placed in a broader explanatory context that does not fail to give pride of place to domestic politics, is provided by Peter Kellogg (1979).

21 Consider, for example, the 2010 controversy over disparagement of the 1964 Civil Rights Act by libertarian Tea Party Senatorial candidate Rand Paul, a position widely repudiated by the Republican Party establishment and libertarians (see Bagenstos 2014). The recent, more or less respectful, reception of Christopher Caldwell's *The Age of Entitlement* (2020) suggests this may be changing, although Caldwell does not of course go so far as to call for the repeal of the 1964 Act.

Chapter 3

1. There is a kind of terminological difficulty here created by the liberal understanding of things that cannot be overcome but is useful to notice. It is tempting to say that the institutions now taking on this enforcement work are "nongovernmental," to distinguish them from the official civil rights apparatus (which sometimes plays only a relatively indirect role). But of course many of the employers, universities, and other institutions in question are themselves state entities.
2. For a general survey, see Rutherglen 2014; for the influence of Title VII on Title IX, see Melnick 2018, chapter 10.
3. See, e.g., McCann 2017; Myers 2003.
4. *Price Waterhouse v. Hopkins* 490 U.S. 228 (1989); *Meritor Savings Bank v. Vinson* 477 U.S. 57 (1986); *Harris v. Forklift Systems, Inc.* 510 U.S. 17 (1993). See U.S. EEOC 1980, 74677; MacKinnon 1978.
5. Hostile educational environment derives (eventually) from Title IX of the 1972 Education Amendments (see Melnick 2018, chapter 10); hostile public accommodations environment from Title II of the 1964 Act (see Koontz 2020). For hostile online environment, see Norby-Jahrer 2009.
6. See the works cited in notes 7 and 8.
7. See U.S. EEOC 1980; 1990; 1997; 1999. The term "preventive and corrective measures" appears in EEOC 1999. For EEOC and the courts, see Brake 2019; O'Gorman 2007. For general surveys, see Edelman 2016; Edelman et al. 2011; Lawton 2004.
8. *Burlington Industries, Inc. v. Ellerth* 524 U.S. 742 (1998); *Faragher v. City of Boca Raton* 524 U.S. 775 (1998). For a useful (critical) overview of the test and its use in the lower courts, see Lawton 2004.
9. See, e.g., Daniel 2003; London 1999, 98; Pearson 2010, 364; FindLaw 2017.
10. Dobbin (2009) provides a detailed, well-informed, and very useful overview of this last step in the story.
11. Melnick 2018, 183, 211, 256–57; emphasis added. I feel compelled to say that Melnick's book is not only excellent on Title IX but that it is the most helpful book on anti-discrimination law of which I am aware. I am particularly indebted to his account of the relationship between Title VII and Title IX (2018, chapter 10) and for his account of the role of "institutional leapfrogging" in the expansion of civil rights law (2010, 14–16). Another very good book examining Title IX, from the inside as it were, is Kipnis 2017.
12. In April 2022, the Biden White House announced the release of "Equity Action Plans" by many federal agencies. See the White House announcement, "Advancing Equity and Racial Justice Through the Federal Government," White House, accessed January 14, 2023, https://www.whitehouse.gov/equity/. See also "Fact Sheet: Biden-Harris Administration Releases Agency

Equity Action Plans to Advance Equity and Racial Justice Across the Federal Government," April 14, 2022, https://www.whitehouse.gov/briefing-room/statements-releases/2022/04/14/fact-sheet-biden-harris-administration-releases-agency-equity-action-plans-to-advance-equity-and-racial-justice-across-the-federal-government/. See also the documents cited in notes 16 and 17.

13 U.S. House of Representatives 1970, 17.
14 See note 20.
15 For both the mass media/internet and historical-cultural regulation efforts, see Powers 2022.
16 See, e.g., National Endowment for the Arts 2022; National Endowment for the Humanities 2022; National Science Foundation 2022; Office of Science and Technology 2022.
17 Federal Emergency Management Agency 2022, 6; U.S. Department of Transportation 2022, 2; U.S. Department of Commerce 2022, 7 (for both the Council for Inclusive Innovation and the Office of Minority Bandwidth Initiatives); U.S. Department of Health and Human Services 2022, 6; U.S. Department of Homeland Security 2022, 8; U.S. Department of Housing and Urban Development 2022, 3–4.
18 "Executive Order on Further Advancing Racial Equity and Support for Underserved Communities Through the Federal Government," February 16, 2023, https://www.whitehouse.gov/briefing-room/presidential-actions/2023/02/16/executive-order-on-further-advancing-racial-equity-and-support-for-underserved-communities-through-the-federal-government/.
19 Graham 1999, 202, quoted in Melnick 2018, 35. For the role of the OFCCP in affirmative action in particular see, e.g., Kelly and Dobbin 1998.
20 This is not offered as an exhaustive list and some of these programs may operate today under different names: in the Department of Agriculture, the Center for Minority Farmers; in Commerce, the Minority Business Development Agency; in Housing and Urban Development, the Office of Fair Housing and Equal Opportunity; in Health and Human Services, the Office of Minority Health, the Office on Women's Health, and the National Institute on Minority Health and Health Disparities; in Justice, the Community Relations Service and the Office on Violence Against Women; in Labor, the Office of Federal Contract Compliance Programs, the Women's Bureau, and the Office of Disability Employment Policy; in State, the Bureau of Democracy, Human Rights and Labor; in Treasury, the Office of Thrift Supervision (regulating lending discrimination); in Veterans Affairs, the Center for Minority Veterans. Some of these programs—like the Labor Department's Women's Bureau—may predate the civil rights revolution but have since become informed by its mandate.
21 New institutions include: Council for Inclusive Innovation in the U.S. Patent and Trade Office; Office of Minority Broadband Initiatives in the National

Telecommunications and Information Administration; Office of Climate Change and Health Equity (HHS); Domestic Violent Extremism Equity Task Force (DHS); Interagency Task Force on Property Appraisal and Valuation Equity (HUD); Advisory Committee on Transportation Equity (Transportation; re-launched by the Biden administration); Environmental Justice and Equity Task Group (GSA). New stand-alone officers include: Senior Advisor for Racial Equity (HUD); Anti-Hate Coordinator (DOJ); Counselor for Racial Equity (Treasury); and Chief Diversity Officers in federal agencies like the Small Business Administration and the Peace Corps.

22 Major laws extending the anti-discrimination regime to different groups include the Age Discrimination in Employment Act of 1967, the Bilingual Education Act of 1968, Title IX of the 1972 Education Amendments, the 1972 Ethnic Heritage Studies Act, the Rehabilitation Act of 1973, the Age Discrimination Act of 1975, the Pregnancy Discrimination Act of 1978, the Equal Access Act of 1984, the Americans with Disability Act of 1990, and the Genetic Information Nondiscrimination Act of 2008.

23 U.S. House of Representatives 1970, 18

24 See Jolly-Ryan 2006.

25 Harassment determinations depend, legalistically, upon a combined finding of "subjective" (the victim, not outsiders acting on the victim's behalf, e.g., must feel that he or she has been harassed) and "objective" (what a "reasonable observer" would say is harassment) factors. The meaning of the latter, especially, is greatly debated. See, e.g., Taylor 2007.

26 *Oncale v. Sundowner Offshore Services, Inc.* 523 U.S. 75, 80 (1998).

27 *Bostock v. Clayton County* 140 S.Ct. 1731 (2020).

28 For a detailed discussion, see Powers 2020, 2022. For useful discussions of recent developments, see Bernstein 2019; Mac Donald 2018; Milikh 2020; Yenor and Miller 2020.

29 The critical literature is sizeable. See Fish 1994; MacKinnon 1993; Matsuda, Lawrence et al. 1993; Waldron 2012. Prominent institutions closely associated with the cause of free speech in this context include the National Association of Scholars (founded 1987), the Foundation for Individual Rights and Expression (FIRE) (1998), Heterodox Academy (2015), Speech First (2018), as well as new journals like Quillette magazine (2015) and the *Journal of Free Speech Law* (2021).

30 *R.A.V. v. City of St. Paul* 505 U.S. 377 (1992) (9:0) is the most famous decision on the side of free speech, joined by one other, *Matal v. Tam* 137 S. Ct. 1744 (2017) (8:0), which rejected prohibitions on discriminatory trademarks under the First Amendment. But the anti-speech code decision of *R.A.V.* (involving a cross-burning statute) was, for all intents and purposes, cancelled out by *Virginia v. Black* 538 U.S. 343 (2003) (8:1) (and *Matal v. Tam* did not actually involve any civil rights statute). The other noteworthy cases are all on the other

side. The two major cases upholding the idea of regulating "harassment" as a form of discrimination, both unanimous, simply do not raise the question of free speech (*Meritor Savings Bank v. Vinson* and *Harris v. Forklift Systems, Inc.*). For free speech objections, raised briefly at the time, see Browne 1991; Volokh 1992. The same is true for the case staking out "stereotypes" under Title VII, *Price Waterhouse v. Hopkins*. Likewise, the unanimous decision (written by Chief Justice Rehnquist) upholding hate crimes penalties does not address the question of whether it is legitimate for the state to criminalize what could be considered a political intention (*Wisconsin v. Mitchell* 508 U.S. 476 [1993]).

31 U.S. Commission on Civil Rights 2019, 21.
32 U.S. EEOC 1998.
33 See, e.g., the six hundred-page enforcement review (U.S. Commission on Civil Rights 2019), which contains surveys of the "Education, Outreach, and Publicity" efforts undertaken by the federal cabinet departments. For the EEOC's Training Institute in particular, see p. 329 of that report. For the Civil Rights Commission (two of its five "Responsibilities" are "to serve as a national clearinghouse for information relating to discrimination" and "to prepare public service announcements and advertising campaigns to discourage discrimination"), see U.S. Commission on Civil Rights 2002, section 701.2. For Labor, see U.S. Department of Labor n.d.; U.S. Commission on Civil Rights 2019, 302. See also U.S. Office of Personnel Management 2011 (that document has no dedicated section on the topic, but training and education are mentioned throughout) and Community Relations Service 1998, 17–18 (a section titled "Promising Practices for Human Relations Commissions—Education").
34 *Kolstad v. American Dental Association* 527 U.S. 526, 545 (1999); emphasis added. See Dobbin 2009, 201–19.
35 For Goldwater's speech, see Schwartz 1970, 1401.
36 See Dobbin 2009; Powers 2022, 16–19.
37 Sutton et al. 1994, 944; Edelman, Fuller, and Mara-Drita 2001, 1589; Sturm 2006, 301–12; Edelman 2016.
38 U.S. EEOC 1999; see also U.S. EEOC 1997. These ideas were then employed and applied in the lower courts. Several such cases are cited in the 1990, 1997, and 1999 EEOC guidance documents I list. For the EEOC's reliance upon these court decisions for the authority of its own claims, see O'Gorman's (critical) discussion (2007, especially 440ff.). See also Brake 2019. In recent years, a number of scholars have studied how judges now view "compliance structures such as grievance procedures, affirmative action and diversity offices, and sexual harassment policies" to be significant evidence—relevant if a company is sued—"demonstrating attention to legal norms" (Edelman et al. 2011, 898; see Edelman 2016; Lawton 2004).
39 *Burlington Industries, Inc. v. Ellerth* 524 U.S. 742, 765 (1998); *Faragher v. City of Boca Raton* 524 U.S. 775, 807 (1998); emphasis added.

40 Mounk 2020; Loftus 2020; Gajanan 2017; White 2017.
41 A political strategy advanced by conservatives has been to pass (at the state level) speech protection statutes modeled on the rules of the First Amendment. Certainly the acts of censorship associated with anti-discrimination politics are variously sweeping (targeting individuals or groups as such, not specific works or statements), compulsory, and prohibited in advance—all of which are banned under rudimentary First Amendment free speech protections (the Supreme Court's overbreadth, compelled speech, and "prior restraint" doctrines).
42 For government publicity of discrimination charges, see Melnick 2018, 211.
43 This interpretive viewpoint is common among civil rights law and politics scholars; see chapter 11, note 4.
44 *Griggs v. Duke Power Co.* 401 U.S. 424 (1971).
45 Disparate impact is taught in Title VII textbooks as a matter of course, and it is used by the federal government in a range of programs; the Department of Justice's *Title VI Legal Manual* lists twenty-six such efforts (U.S. Department of Justice n.d., p. 5 of section VII entitled "Proving Discrimination—Disparate Impact"; see Yan 2013). These efforts have been expanded under the Biden administration's equity initiative. The main conservative limitation on disparate impact has been to deny such lawsuits under Title VII to private actors (see *Alexander v. Sandoval* 532 U.S. 275 [2001)]). Affirmative action by federal and state government, and by the private sector, either in the workplace or in higher education, has never been effectively called into question, despite a variety of rulings that confuse the issues. In higher education it is condemned in principle but permitted in practice, "diversity" serving as a legalistic fudge (*Regents of the University of California v. Bakke* 438 U.S. 265 (1978); *Grutter v. Bollinger* 539 U.S. 306 [2003]). As to affirmative action in government contracts, compare the overall message of *City of Richmond v. J.A. Croson Co.* 488 U.S. 469 (1989) and *Adarand Constructors, Inc. v. Peña* 515 U.S. 200 (1995) with what is reflected in the 185-page report issued by the Civil Rights Commission, "Federal Procurement After *Adarand*" (U.S. Commission on Civil Rights 2005). Executive Order 11246, the basis of federal affirmative action since 1965 (which has a significant effect on the private sector) has never suffered serious legal challenge.
46 The conservative position is staked out most clearly in *Shaw v. Reno* 509 U.S 630 (1993). But that position, famous mainly for being a target of Left criticism, is outweighed by the achievements of the Left —above all, the unanimous opinion *Thornburg v. Gingles* 478 U.S. 30 (1986)—and by the fact that the Supreme Court retreated from the position it staked out in *Shaw v. Reno* (see Thernstrom 2009, 153–54).
47 *United States v. City of Black Jack* 508 F.2d 1179, 1184–85 (8th Cir. 1974).
48 See the discussion of equity pedagogy in chapter 5.

49 There are several important decisions (all mentioned above) written by conservative Supreme Court justices that expand the meaning of Title VII: *Griggs* (Burger); *Meritor Savings Bank* (Rehnquist); *Harris v. Forklift Systems* (O'Connor); *Ellerth* (Kennedy); *Kolstad* (O'Connor); *Oncale* (Scalia); and *Bostock* (Gorsuch).

50 For useful reviews of the massive legal literature that is the critique of the state action doctrine, see Buchanan 1997a, 1997b; Chemerinsky 1985; Nerken 1977; Schmidt 2016b.

51 See *Boy Scouts of America v. Dale* 530 U.S. 640 (2000). What transpired after that case was decided (in which the Boy Scouts were permitted to exclude gay scoutmasters) seems to suggest that constitutional protections matter less than the broader effects of the anti-discrimination regime on American society. After prevailing at the Supreme Court, the Boy Scouts in 2015 reversed course and admitted gay scoutmasters—later admitting transgender members (in 2017) and girls (in 2018) as well. In 2020, the newly named Scouts BSA announced the creation of a new Diversity, Equity, and Inclusion Merit Badge (see Honeck 2018; Inazu 2010, 557–61; Koppelman and Wolff 2009; Lee 2017; Zaveri 2020). Although freedom of association is clearly tied to the liberal tradition (but not included in the text of the First Amendment, it is worth pointing out), it seems to me that one weakness of Caldwell's account (2020, 14–15) of the tension between anti-discrimination and liberalism is his emphasis on the right of association at the expense of other aspects of the liberal democratic outlook (were Caldwell to develop more fully his discussion of the revolutionary role of private sector enforcement of anti-discrimination law [273], for example, he would be compelled to go much beyond freedom of association).

52 See Powers 2005.

53 See Melnick 2018, 155–57, 203–4.

54 See the brief discussion in chapter 10.

55 See Keynes and Miller 1989, chapter 8.

56 See, e.g., Benhabib 1992, 12–13, chapter 3; Carter 1993; Gedicks 1995, 32–42; Koppelman 1996, 181–90, 211; Minow 1990, 279–83; Nedelsky 1990, 211–16, 223–24; Pateman 1983, 281–83; Spinner 1994, 5–6, 37–38. For a helpful review of this large literature that focuses on feminist theory, see Gavison 1992. See also notes 50 and 59.

57 The idea of a "color-blind Constitution," as worthy of defense as it surely is, does not solve all problems here. If that idea is restricted (as the Constitution is) to the public sphere, it is clearly limited in its ability to clarify the meaning and reach of contemporary anti-discrimination law. If it somehow may be rethought to extend into the private sphere and to embrace the expansions of anti-discrimination law we have surveyed (privatized enforcement, corrective firing, etc.), it is hard to see how it remains a part of the liberal democratic

tradition of political thought. For thoughtful defenses of the color-blind ideal, see Kull 1992; Myers 2019.

58 For a discussion of the 1964 Civil Rights Act as a "super-statute" and the "Constitution-bending effect of the Civil Rights Act of 1964," see Eskridge and Ferejohn 2001, 1237–42.

59 For the general critique of rights literature, see the useful long listing of relevant works in the second edition (xliii–xlvii) of Stuart Scheingold's early work (originally published in 1974), *The Politics of Rights* (Scheingold 2004). Scholars arguing along such lines who focus on perceived limitations of Title VII in particular include Berrey, Nelson and Nielsen 2017 and Edelman 2016.

60 For "civil rights realignment," see Feinstein and Schickler 2008; Noel 2012. The analysis in these and related works is often too much focused on race (there is a sizeable literature dealing with race and party politics; see, e.g., Edsall and Edsall 1991; Snider and Piazza 1993; Kinder and Sanders 1996; Schickler 2016; Abramowitz 2018). A wider perspective considering all of the different kinds of group conflicts that anti-discrimination politics attempts to manage (to include race) is needed. The simplest opposition at the level of the different kinds of general interests involved (class/economic/New Deal versus anti-discrimination) is addressed by this literature, but that needs to be supplemented by a more comprehensive treatment of the many tensions (among various kinds of groups, but not only that) resulting from anti-discrimination politics. One would need to map the party effects of alterations in relations between men and women owing to sex discrimination politics; of LGBT rights groups and of the effects (or the perceived effects) of their claims on non-LGBT persons (and religious groups in particular); of age, disability, and language discrimination politics. More broadly, what are the party effects of the many challenges to the American tradition (liberalism, constitutionalism, the Enlightenment heritage) wrought by anti-discrimination politics? These are very complicated questions, but any account of the current alignment (or dealignment) of American political parties that does not address them would exclude causal considerations of obvious importance. (For a discussion that begins from the much looser question of the party effects of "cultural differences," see Leege et al. 2002.)

61 The influence of anti-discrimination on all the disciplines of the social sciences and humanities has been profound, and a study of any of them tracing that out would not require complicated methods (academic journal tables of contents would immediately yield dramatic results). Likewise, its influence in the world of high culture would be established very quickly in a survey, for example, of the conservative journal *The New Criterion* and the several works dedicated (at least in part) to cataloging how civil rights politics has affected high culture by its editor Roger Kimball (see especially Kimball 1990, 2000, 2004). That journal tracks in great detail how, in many instances, the new political

impetus has shaped the energies of contemporary artists, poets, dramatists, novelists, architects, and musicians over the past thirty or forty years.

Chapter 4

1. Quoted in Ramírez and Castañeda 1974, 23.
2. For a more extensive treatment, see Powers 2015b and 2015c.
3. James 1971; Baker 1972; Hubble 1972. See also Gollnick, Klassen, and Yff 1976, 111; Gollnick 1978, 85.
4. Banks 1976a, 35. It is necessary to note that Banks uses the term "cultural pluralism" in two different ways. Sometimes he has in mind something like Kallen's (emphatically liberal) position, but he also refers at times to the "cultural pluralism ideology," an ideal type constructed by him and to which he opposes the "assimilationist ideology." In this usage, "cultural pluralism" becomes something rather different from Kallen's main argument, thereby suggesting a radicalized commitment to groups or diversity for its own sake—one that is only present in Kallen's fleeting (but oft-quoted) reference to a "federation or commonwealth of national cultures," an idea that is not meant to be taken literally and that is defined by (and thus contradicted by) his complete and total devotion to liberal political ideals and the modern way of life in the rest of his argument (1924, 116, 123–24; see the discussion of Kallen in chapter 7). Banks erects the radical version of the "cultural pluralist ideology" partly in order to reject it, along with the "assimilationist ideology," as too extreme (see 1975c; 1976d, 100; 1977a, 78).
5. Banks 1992a, 274; see Gollnick and Chinn 1990, 20–21; La Belle and Ward 1994, 16–25; Lynch 1986, 22; Sleeter and Grant 1988, 77–78. "Cultural pluralism, as envisioned by Kallen, [Julius] Drachsler, and other writers in the 1920s, was destined to fail in the United States" (Banks 1981, 183; see Drachsler 1920). Cf. Banks 2008a, 130. It is true that something called the "intercultural" or "intergroup" education movement, an effort of the 1930s and 1940s based loosely on liberal principles like those informing Kallen's cultural pluralism (with no necessary connection, however, to Kallen's argument in particular), likewise predates multicultural education. But here, too, multicultural education owes nothing to that earlier pluralist stance. Multicultural educators look to the intergroup education movement to learn from its failures, since "when the civil rights movement began, the intergroup education movement had quietly died without a requiem" (Banks 1993f, 17; see C. A. M. Banks 2005; Montalto 1982; Powell 1971). More to the point, "intergroup educators did not directly address structural and institutional racism, empowerment, poverty, and societal inequities" (C. A. M. Banks 2005, 143). Some terminological confusion may arise here, since "cultural pluralism" and

"multiculturalism" are not always so clearly distinguishable as they are in the difference between Kallen and Banks. There are, for example, some advocates of straight, old-fashioned liberal cultural pluralism in the post-civil rights movement world of American education (see Itzkoff 1969; Walsh 1973). Sometimes such writers even use the term "multiculturalism" to refer to their position (see Cole 1984; Tesconi 1990). Still others advocate something like Banks's view of multiculturalism but refer to it using the term "cultural pluralism" (see Epps 1974; Stent, Hazard, and Rivlin 1973).

6   Banks 1992b, 113–14; see Banks 1981, 14–15, 19–22; 1986d, 38–44; 1993f, 2013.
7   See, e.g., Banks 1969a, 1969b.
8   For the testimony of other multicultural educators, see Gollnick and Chinn 1990, 27–28; La Belle and Ward 1994, 21–25; Lynch 1986, 22–23; Nieto 1992, 213; Seelye and Wasilewski 1979, 49–50; Sleeter 1995a.
9   Moynihan 1967; Coleman 1969, 258; see Coleman 1966, 290–325.
10 Deutsch 1969, 42; see Cull and Hardy 1975; Ogletree 1973; Riessman 1962.
11 See, e.g., Fantini 1972; Haubrich 1963; Knapp 1965; Smith and Arnez 1969.
12 Banks 1986b, 21; see Banks 2013, 75–76. For the importance of the cultural difference paradigm in multicultural education generally, see Baruth and Manning 1992, 16–17; Gay 1983, 561; Grant 1985, 128; La Belle and Ward 1994, 101–13; Nieto 1992, chapter 7; Sleeter and Grant 1988, chapter 2.
13 It is interesting to note that the premier legal case now held to mark the emergence of the systemic discrimination point of view, *Griggs v. Duke Power Co.*, was decided in 1971, at roughly the same time as the emergence of the cultural difference paradigm (401 U.S. 424).
14 Glazer 1983, 67–68 (the work in question, "Ethnic Groups and Education," was a paper written in 1969; see Glazer 1983, 69).
15 Forbes 1967; see Forbes 1969a, 1969b, 1971.
16 Baker 1979, 254; see Baker 1972. It might be possible to trace the word "multi-cultural" in the context of American education back even further, to education writer Miles V. Zintz writing in 1960 (Zintz 1960a, 1960b). Because Zintz does not yet have in mind "multicultural education" and his use of the term is largely a descriptive one, referring to "teacher awareness of sociocultural differences in multi-cultural classrooms," it is safer to see Forbes's usage as marking the starting point (Zintz 1960a, 102; see Zintz 1963, 75). Zintz's writings are also, however, informed by the spirit of civil rights reform. See Zintz 1960b, 209; 1963, 8, 52, 99–103; Zintz, Ulibarri, and Gonzales 1971.
17 For helpful general discussions of the federal government's civil rights initiatives in education and related subsequent developments, see Davies 2007; Hess 1998; Hess and Petrilli 2006; Peterson 1983; Peterson, Henderson, and West 2014.

18 The 1966 figure was provided by Martha Jacobs, budget analyst at the U.S. Department of Education (author copy). For recent expenditures see U.S. Department of Education 2019, 10.
19 In the 1968 Bilingual Education Act, Title IX of the 1972 Education Amendments, the 1972 Ethnic Heritage Studies Act, Section 504 of the Rehabilitation Act of 1973, the 1975 Education of All Handicapped Children Act, and the Age Discrimination Act of 1975.
20 Bilingual Education Act of 1968. (P.L. 90–247), *United States Statutes at Large.* 81 Stat. 816–7. In this context it is necessary to emphasize the extent to which bilingual education policy was itself originally a product of the civil rights revolution. Anti-discrimination protection for language minorities was not the result of widespread demands of the affected groups but was the product of anti-discrimination policy's irresistible vote-getting possibilities, advanced in this case by Senator Ralph Yarborough (an Anglo Texan) (see Davies 2002, 1407–10). The Mexican-American Legal Defense and Educational Fund (MALDEF) was born in 1968 with the prompting and support of the Ford Foundation (which provided a $2.2 million grant) and was modeled on the NAACP-Legal Defense Fund (Davies 2002, 1417–18). After the Commission on Civil Rights issued its "1969 Mexican American Education Study," MALDEF and other groups complained that a disproportionate number of Mexican-American children were being wrongly categorized as intellectually disabled by the schools (Meier and Stewart 1991, 74–75). It was in this context that bilingual education began to be taken more seriously, as a question of anti-discrimination policy, from 1970 onward.
21 Bilingual Education Act, 1974 Reauthorization. (P.L. 93–380), *United States Statutes at Large.* 88 Stat. 503.
22 Bilingual Education Act, 1994 Reauthorization. (P.L. 103–382), *United States Statutes at Large.* 108 Stat. 3716.
23 Emergency School Aid Act. (P.L. 92–318), *United States Statutes at Large.* 86 Stat. 354, 359. Longshore 1983, 413n2; see, e.g., Bronaugh and Ayers 1976, iii–iv. See also Giles and Gollnick 1977, 123.
24 Education Amendments of 1972. (P.L. 92–318), *United States Statutes at Large.* 86 Stat. 346; see Fong 1978, 167.
25 Illinois 1975, 9; Gollnick, Klassen, and Yff 1976, 162.
26 Gollnick, Klassen, and Yff 1976; Gollnick 1978; Klassen and Gollnick 1977; NCSS 1976. I rely here extensively on the major cataloging efforts of Donna Gollnick, a leading early advocate of multicultural education and later senior vice president of the National Council for the Accreditation of Teacher Education (NCATE) as well as president of AACTE. Her work on behalf of AACTE and other groups to provide various bibliographical surveys and summary reports usefully tracks the development of multicultural education in its early years. In addition to the works cited above, see also Gollnick 1995;

Gollnick, Osayande, and Levy 1980; Baptiste, Baptiste, and Gollnick 1980; Giles and Gollnick 1977.

27 Rogers and Oakes 2005, 2183; emphasis added; see Scott 1999. Early on, in addition to funding the Desegregation Assistance Centers, Title IV funds supported desegregation units within state government educational agencies, the direct funding of local educational agencies, and "Training Institutes" for educators (see Crocker et al. 1976).

28 University of Michigan DAC 1997a; see also, e.g., Trumbull and Pacheco 2005.

29 King, Thomas, and Graubard 1977; Kaser, Sadker, and Sadker 1982.

30 See Glazer 1983, 132–39; Fong 1978, 154–60.

31 *United States v. City of Yonkers* (833 F. Supp. 214, 218–19 (1993); Levit 2005, 469n74. In Dallas, Texas and Rockford, Illinois, for example, desegregation orders from the federal courts put in place plans embracing multicultural education and other similar pedagogical reforms (in addition to the more typical and predominating head-counting allotment of students) (see *Tasby v. Estes* 412 F. Supp. 1192, 1203 [1976]; *Tasby v. Wright* 520 F. Supp. 683, 741 [1981]; Eubanks 2004, 2011–12). For related efforts in Lafayette, Louisiana, see Caldas, Bankston, and Cain 2003, 138. For the view of its theorists on the question of how multicultural education could or ought to be used in such a context, see Grant and Sleeter's account (1986) of attempts to introduce multicultural education reforms in a city undergoing voluntary desegregation, and Bennett's discussion (1986, 56–70) framing multicultural education in terms of its contribution to school desegregation efforts and the "contact hypothesis."

32 For the Minnesota and Illinois initiatives, see Minnesota 1974; Illinois 1975, 1978. See also Herman 1974, 59, 61.

33 Iowa DPI 1979, 2; 1981, 1982, 1983; Iowa DOE 1989a, 1989b. See also Garcia 1979, x, and Colangelo, Dustin, and Foxley 1979, a comprehensive textbook titled *Multicultural Nonsexist Education* that developed out of the experience in Iowa.

34 Giles and Gollnick 1977, 157; AACTE 1978, 82, 27, 32; Baker 1979, 260.

35 See Akiba et al. 2010; Evans, Torrey, and Newton 1997; Miller, Strosnider, and Dooley 2000; Mitchell and Salsbury 2000.

36 All of the statements quoted are taken from the plaintiff's complaint in the suit, *Scott McConnell v. Le Moyne College*, 808 N.Y.S. 2d 860 (N.Y. App. Div. 2006). The complaint is available from the website of the Center for Individual Rights, accessed January 17, 2023, https://www.cir-usa.org/legal_docs/mcconnell_v_lemoyne_cplt.pdf. In addition to the question of multicultural education, the case also dealt with the student's support for corporal punishment; it was ultimately decided on procedural grounds (whether the student, accepted into the program on a conditional basis, should have the full due

process rights afforded other students). See also Center for Individual Rights 2005; York 2006.
37 See Beyerbach and Nassoiy 2004; Kraft 2001, 5, 20–23; Akiba et al. 2010, 452.
38 See NCATE 1977; NCATE 2008, 12, 34–37. In 2012, NCATE merged with an upstart challenger, the Teacher Education Accreditation Council (TEAC, recognized in 2003 by the Department of Education), to form the Council for the Accreditation of Educator Preparation (CAEP). TEAC also always had a diversity requirement.
39 CAEP 2018, 16–17, 51–52. For the criticism of CAEP as conservative, see Cochran-Smith 2021, 16.
40 "Standard 1: Candidate/Completer Performance" includes "1c. Culturally responsive practice, including intersectionality of race, ethnicity, class, gender identity and expression, sexual identity, and the impact of language acquisition and literacy development on learning." Within "Standard 2: Completer Professional Competence and Growth" is "2b. Engage in culturally responsive educational practices with diverse learners and do so in diverse cultural and socioeconomic community contexts." Within "Standard 4: Program Engagement in System Improvement" is "4b. Seeks to meet state and local educator workforce needs and to diversify participation in the educator workforce through candidate recruitment and support" (AAQEP 2021, 11–12). That 4b calls for affirmative action is spelled out explicitly: "One persistent area of disparity in education is the underrepresentation in the educator workforce of people of color, of those from lower socioeconomic strata, and (in some certificate areas) of men, among others. AAQEP expects members to work toward more equitable representation in the educator workforce through candidate recruitment and support" (AAQEP 2021, 25). For some evidence that (Left) politics is important in the rise of AAQEP (politics in the world of accreditation bodies is often hard to see, buried under layers of nearly impenetrable bureaucratic jargon), see Cochran-Smith 2021, 15–17. (I should say that Cochran-Smith might very well object to my simple political characterization.)
41 For Hollywood, see Toto 2022; for medicine, see Satel 2000; for journalism, see Ungar-Sargon 2021. For "woke capitalism," see Ramaswamy 2021; Soukup 2021. On the history of personnel management, which laid much of the groundwork for what we today call woke capitalism, Dobbin 2009 is a very useful guide.
42 Banks 1973c; Banks et al. 1976; NCTE 1974; Della-Dora and House 1974; Grant 1977b; see Lipsky and Gartner 1997; Osgood 2005.
43 AACTE 1973; see Gollnick, Klassen, and Yff 1976, 135; Hunter 1974, 18–21; Watkins and Imig 1974, 8–9. The *Journal of Teacher Education* devoted several special volumes—four in the 1970s—to multicultural education and

related civil rights topics: a "Symposium on Multicultural Education" in 1973 (vol. 24, no. 4); an issue on "The Molding of the Nonsexist Teacher" (vol. 26, no. 4); a second issue on multicultural education in 1977 (vol. 28, no. 3); and an issue devoted to the "Educating Handicapped Individuals" in 1978 (vol. 29, no. 6). In addition, an issue on "A Federal Mandate to Change Education, 1965–1975: The Teacher Corps Exemplar" devoted a section (and seven articles) to the "major program emphasis" on multicultural education (vol. 26, no. 2). The central importance of multicultural education in this journal remained clear later as well, especially during the editorial tenure of Marilyn Cochran-Smith (when, partly because of 9/11, multiculturalism was coming under fire): more than half the articles published in the *Journal of Teacher Education* from 2000 to 2006 were devoted to questions directly related to multicultural education topics or responding to multiculturalism's critics in the context of conservative education reform efforts (see also chapter 5, note 6). More recently, in 2021, the *Journal* highlighted the contributions and leadership of prominent critical race theorist and long-time multicultural educational writer Gloria Ladson-Billings (2005 president of the American Educational Research Association), by having her coauthor an editorial offering a rousing affirmation of "respect and passion for DEI" and a rebuttal to the opponents of critical race theory in education (Hill-Jackson, Ladson-Billings and Craig 2021). See also Ladson-Billings 1998, 2000, 2004.

Other journals offered similar support to multicultural education. In 1972, *Phi Delta Kappan* devoted an issue to the subject of ethnic minority education (vol. 53, no. 5). *Educational Leadership* devoted an issue to multicultural education in 1975 (vol. 33, no. 3) and the *Journal of Research and Development in Education* and the *Journal of Negro Education* did the same in 1977 and 1979, respectively (vol. 11, no. 1; vol. 48, no. 3). Somewhat later, *Education and Society* published a "Special Supplement" on "Ideas for Multicultural Education" (vol. 1, no. 1 [1988]). *Educational Researcher, Integrated Education*, the *Journal of Educational Research, Social Education* (the journal of the NCSS), *Social Studies, Teachers College Record*, and *Urban Education* are other journals showing a continuing interest in multicultural education.

44 Colangelo, Dustin, and Foxley 1979; Banks 1981. See Baker 1983; Bennett 1986; Garcia 1982; Gollnick and Chinn 1983; Kendall 1983. One could also cite a book edited by Banks and William Joyce in 1971, *Teaching Social Studies to Culturally Different Children* (Banks and Joyce 1971), or Banks's 1975 work, *Teaching Strategies for Ethnic Studies* (1975b), as candidates for the first textbooks in the field. But while these works (the latter ending its run in its eighth edition [2008b]) advance many of the arguments appearing later in Banks's multicultural education textbooks, the focus of each is somewhat narrower.

45 Sleeter and Grant 1987, 1988.

46 Multicultural education scholarly book series have been published by Teachers

College Press, SUNY Press, and Lawrence Erlbaum Associates. Journals devoted to multicultural education include *Multicultural Education* (since 1993), *Race, Ethnicity and Education* (since 1998), *Multicultural Perspectives* (since 1999), the *Electronic Journal of Multicultural Education* (founded in 1999 and renamed *International Journal of Multicultural Education* in 2007), the *Journal of Multiculturalism in Education* (since 2002), *Journal of Language, Identity and Education* (since 2002), *Journal of Praxis in Multicultural Education* (since 2006), and *Multicultural Education and Technology Journal* (since 2007).

47   National Association for Multicultural Education 2023a.
48   Dr. William A. Howe (NAME president 2001–3) worked for the Connecticut State Department of Education, Bureau of Educational Equity, and was a consultant to the federal Equity Assistance Center at Brown University (Howe *Curriculum Vitae*, author copy). Tasha Lebow (NAME President 2005–7) served as a program manager for the Equity Assistance Center at Michigan State University (University of Michigan DAC 1997b). For the identical makeup of the ten EAC and NAME regions, cf. Department of Education 2005, 9932 and National Association for Multicultural Education 2008, 70. Later, NAME reduced the number of regions to eight (see National Association for Multicultural Education 2023b) and in 2016 the Department of Education reduced the number of EACs to four (see Department of Education 2022, 8565).
49   Schlesinger 1992; Ravitch 1990; Ravitch and Finn 1987; New York 1991. See Glazer 1997, 22–33; Wong 2001.
50   Wong 2001; Cornbleth and Waugh 1995.
51   See, e.g., Evans, Torrey, and Newton 1997, 11; Gibson and Follo 1998, 18–21; Gollnick 1995, 62; Miller, Strosnider, and Dooley 2000, 18; Mitchell and Salsbury 2000, 34, 82, 245.
52   See chapter 1, notes 5, 10, and 12.

Chapter 5

1   Aristotle 1984, 229 (1337a10–15).
2   Banks 1995a, 390. All scholarly references in this chapter are to Banks's works unless otherwise indicated.
3   Because some useful passages in Banks's work indicate more than one aspect of his overall teaching, I have been compelled at points to use some quotations more than once.
4   One good place to start is the autobiographical overview Banks himself provides in the introduction to a collection of essays published in 2006. There he spells out in detail how the civil rights revolution provided the inspiration for every step of his "epistemological and scholarly journey . . . and the quest . . . to

understand, interpret, and reduce racial inequality and advance social justice in the United States and abroad" (2006c, 3). That book, *Race, Culture, and Education: The Selected Works of James A. Banks*, is a collection of previously published essays and other works (edited by Banks), offering a useful point of entry for anyone wanting to become familiar with his writings. The book is organized in seven parts that take their main terms from what might seem to be several different areas of academic study: Black Studies, Ethnic Studies, Teaching the Social Studies, Multiethnic Education, Multicultural Education, Global Education, and Citizenship Education. But, as Banks himself makes more than plain, each of these (at the same time a stage in the development of his thinking) is the product of one single unifying civic or political source of inspiration. Banks's work in the area of Black studies was a direct outgrowth of the fact that he "came of age during the Civil Rights Movement of the 1960s and 1970s, which reinforced [his] emerging interest in Black history and social justice" (2006c, 3). Then, "Teaching Ethnic Studies" marked a "life- and career- changing" turn in Banks's thought when he "met and interacted with scholars from other racial and ethnic groups who were as committed to racial equality and social justice as [he] was" (2006c, 6). When Banks went on to develop a theory for "teaching the social studies," he did so "at a time of great social change and civil unrest in the United States. The Civil Rights Movement of the 1960s and 1970s was in full swing" (2006c, 7). Next, "Multiethnic Education" became necessary "when the Civil Rights Movement emerged in the mid-1960s [and] African Americans and other ethnic groups demanded that the schools and other institutions establish ethnic studies courses that focused on their specific ethnic groups and hire more teachers of color" (2006c, 7). "Multicultural Education" then followed multiethnic education when "the ethnic revitalization movements stimulated other groups that felt marginalized within society to begin their quests for social, economic, and political rights. The women rights movement, the movement for the rights of people with disabilities, and later, the movement for gay rights adapted some of the goals, strategies, and language of the Black Civil Rights Movement" (2006c, 9). Nor do the final stages of Banks's development listed above—"Global Education" and "Citizenship Education"—veer onto new paths but only broaden the commitment to the civil rights revolution that informs the rest (2006c, 11–13). "My intellectual journey closely parallels the evolution of the field of multicultural education. The papers in this book document my commitment to social justice and educational equality and indicate that it has been consistent through the decades, although its expression has taken different forms in various times and contexts" (2006a, xiv). (Banks indicated the same thing much earlier, holding that ethnic studies, multiethnic education, and multicultural education, for example, share the same fundamental perspective. A 1976 essay titled "Ethnic Studies as a Process of Curriculum Reform" summarizes lessons students are to learn about "the cogent role which ethnicity and ethnic conflict have played in shaping the American experience" by saying [in the same paragraph]: "This should be one of the major goals of multiethnic and multicultural education" [1976b, 77].)

Other confirmations of the centrality of civil rights politics in Banks's thought are readily available in his account of the "five dimensions" of multicultural education, a fairly influential summary accounting of the field. "I have identified five dimensions of multicultural education. They are: (1) content integration, (2) the knowledge construction process, (3) prejudice reduction, (4) an equity pedagogy, and (5) an empowering school culture and social structure" (1997a, 69; see 1992c, 1993d, 1993f, 1998a, 2004b). Each of these is defined absolutely by the task of combating discrimination, though that may not be immediately indicated by the terms themselves (see Powers 1999, 257–63). As one advocate of Banks's scheme aptly put it, "when we examine these five dimensions, they constitute an 'anti-racist education'" (Hillis 1996, 288). Other summary accounts provided by Banks indicate the same pattern. See Banks's discussion of multicultural education's three "major components" (1997a, 68); its basic goals (1994a, 16–17); the "eight characteristics of the multicultural school" (1994a, 11); and the three (or four) "approaches" taken to accomplishing multicultural education's basic objectives (1992c, 83–84; 1994a, 25).

5   1994b, 128–31. In applying this label to Banks's thought taken as a whole (in the title to this chapter), I go beyond his usage. See his discussion of using "ideal types in the Weberian sense" (1994b, 122). In that discussion the "multicultural ideology" "avoids the extremes" of the "cultural pluralist ideology" and the "assimilationist ideology" (1994b, 128, see 122–27). While Banks does not hesitate to employ the term "ideology," he is not unaware of its limitations. "An ideology is a system of ideas, beliefs, traditions, principles, and myths held by a social group or society that reflects, rationalizes, and defends its particular social, political, and economic interests" (1987, 537).

6   1993d, 28; see 1994a, 21; 1979b, 251; 1991a, 33; 1993b, 4. See also, for example, Appelbaum 2002, 112–14; Gay 2005; Sleeter 1995a. See also Marilyn Cochran-Smith's illuminating editorials in the *Journal of Teacher Education* (e.g., 2001, 2002, 2004a, 2004b, 2005, 2006a, 2006b).

7   1997a. A second edition was published in 2007. See 1983a, 1990, 1999b, 2001a, 2004c, 2008a, 2009, 2015, 2016a, 2017. Banks also led an initiative on multicultural education and civic education at the University of Washington Center for Multicultural Education, the Bellagio Diversity and Citizenship Education Project (see 2004c).

8   1990, 211; see also 1971a, 741; 1973a, 408, 410–11; 1982a, 90; 1987, 538; 1992c, 88; 1994a, 27, 39; 1996c, 345; 1997a, 27–30.

9   1990, 213; emphasis in the original. See also 1991a, 32; 1994a, 2–5; 1997a, xi.

10 Other early non-postmodernist leaders include Gwendolyn Baker, H. Prentice Baptiste, Christine Bennett, and Donna Gollnick (some early leaders, like Geneva Gay and Carl Grant, eventually embraced postmodernism). As to summary surveys, the typology developed by Sleeter and Grant (1987, 1988) is widely followed, but there are many others. See Banks 1981, 19–22; 1986b, 12–13; 1993a; 1994a, 25–27; Cochran-Smith 2003; Gay 1983, 562; Gibson 1976; Gorski 2009; Haddad 1995, 103–12; Jenks, Lee, and Kanpol 2001; La Belle and Ward 1994, 25–26, 165; Lynch 1986, 33–38; Rodriguez 1983, 2–7, 31; U.S. Department of Education 1994; Williams 1979.

11 In a survey of "multicultural or social justice" educators conducted in 2009 by EdChange (a private multicultural education training and advocacy group), Banks was found to be number one on the list of "Most Influential Scholars" (Gorski 2010). To assess Banks's scholarly influence within multicultural education I compared his publication record with that of other writers identified as pioneers and/or leaders in the field. It is possible to assemble a more or less authoritative list of early leaders. British scholar James Lynch (1986, 25) lists six: Gwendolyn Baker, James Banks, Phillip Chinn, Geneva Gay, Donna Gollnick, and Carl Grant. The state of Iowa (Iowa DOE 1989a, 5) offers a list of leaders, likewise including Baker, Banks, Chinn, and Grant, and adding Carlos Cortés and James Boyer (as well as texts by Gollnick and Chinn, Ricardo Garcia, Fred Rodriguez, and Christine Bennett). Banks offers three different listings. His shortest list (1992c, 84) of influential multicultural education textbooks lists works authored by himself and his wife, Cherry A. McGee Banks, as well as by Bennett, Grant and Christine Sleeter, Gollnick and Chinn, and Lynch. A longer list (1992a, 281–82) of "architects of the multicultural education movement" in America includes all those in Banks's list above (not counting British scholar Lynch) plus H. Prentice Baptiste, Cortés, Garcia, Hilda Hernandez, Sonia Nieto, Valerie O. Pang, and Derald Sue. Finally another list by Banks (1993f, 19) adds four prominent pioneers in the field: Boyer, Asa Hilliard III, Barbara A. Sizemore, and Jack Forbes. (See also Banks 2004b, 12.) For nineteen leaders identified from these various lists I checked the bibliographical ERIC (Educational Resources Information Center, compiled by the U.S. Department of Education) database to generate a rough number of publications (books and articles) authored or coauthored by each between 1966 (when the database begins) and November 2004. The ERIC index listed 102 records for Banks and considerably fewer for the rest (the next nine, in descending order: Asa Hilliard 64; James Lynch 56; Geneva Gay 53; Carl Grant 52; Christine Bennett 40; Carlos Cortés 39; Jack Forbes 39; Christine Sleeter 39; Sonia Nieto 34). I then counted citations in the Social Science Citation Index for the seven most prolific authors in the field (excluding three from the ERIC top ten: Lynch [who is British] and Forbes and Hilliard [scholars in other fields who have written only a few articles on

multicultural education *per se*]). Conceding both the imprecision of counting citations and the question of the meaning of such a measure, it is nevertheless the case that Banks is cited twice as often as the next most-cited authors in the field—Sleeter, Grant, and Gay. These rough measures would suggest at the very least that studying Banks is not objectionable from the standpoint of his influence in the field of multicultural education.

12 Early on, he took a leading role in writing two of the policies adopted by the National Council for the Social Studies (NCSS) endorsing multiculturalism (1973c; Banks et al. 1976). His early leadership is also reflected in his editorship of a volume of the *Phi Delta Kappan* in 1972 devoted to the subject of ethnic minority education; see *Phi Delta Kappan* 53, no. 5 (January 1972). Banks edited (with Cherry A. McGee Banks) the authoritative and widely used *Handbook of Research on Multicultural Education* (first edition published in 1995, a second in 2004) and he was editor of the four-volume *Encyclopedia of Diversity in Education* (published in 2012) as well. He was also founding director of the University of Washington, Seattle's Center for Multicultural Education. His stature and leadership are reflected in his tenure as president of two educational associations—the NCSS in 1982 and the American Educational Research Association in 1997–98.

13 At least one of his several textbooks has sold more than one hundred thousand copies (2006c, 6).

14 Banks has worked to fit multicultural education into the dominant intellectual influences of American life and to address critics on both the Left and the Right in a range of contemporary debates (see, e.g., 1984b, 1993b). As an authoritative historian of multicultural education, Banks situates the discipline in a long tradition of social scientists and other intellectuals who have borne witness to the perspective of discrimination's victims in earlier periods of American history, before the fight against discrimination had become politically predominant (1992a, 1996a, 1998b, 2004d).

15 For Banks and postmodernism, see chapter 6, notes 100–101 and accompanying text. Calling for a "new phase of sophistication," Banks sought early on to frame his efforts in terms of American social science, as a way of "help[ing] students to develop valid concepts, generalizations, and theories related to ethnicity in American life" (1977b, 696; see 1973d, 741; 1977a). All his work routinely borrows from social science terminology and research to help frame many of the issues he takes up. Later, without embracing postmodernism himself, Banks nevertheless offered a compromise between its epistemological theory and social science's goal of objectivity, a position beginning from the "*need to rethink and to reconceptualize objectivity so that it will have legitimacy for diverse groups of researchers and will incorporate their perspectives, experiences, and insights*" (1998b, 6; emphasis in the original; see 2004d, 2006c). As his attempt to bridge the gap between postmodernism and scientific method

suggests, something more fundamental than epistemological allegiances dominates Banks's vision. See Powers 2002.
16 1979b, 238; see 1976a, 32; 1977a, 73; 1994a, 16.
17 See the end of note 4 above.
18 Banks is cited as a representative figure of not one but four of the five different approaches to multicultural education in Sleeter and Grant's typology, to include their most progressive category, "education that is multicultural and social reconstructionist" (Sleeter and Grant 1988, 86–87, 114, 151, 187). Consider also Banks's work with authors (as an editor of collaborative volumes and a book series) who would certainly fall into the radical camp (see Ladson-Billings 2004; Nieto 1997, 1999, 106–10; Sleeter 2001; Vavrus 2002, 1–7).
19 1999b, 56–57; 1976d, 103; 1999b, 58; 1993d, 24; 1998a. All these quoted phrases are referenced in the cited passages appearing in the paragraphs immediately following.
20 1993d, 24; see 1994a, 90; 1994d, 4; 1996b, 33; 1997a, xii.
21 1991a, 34; see 1993d, 23; 1994a, 2–5.
22 Indeed, Banks admits that his appeals in this direction are partly governed by tactical considerations in the context of public debate that pits multiculturalism against "Western traditionalists." "When multiculturalists respond to [conservative] criticism, they often fail to describe the important ways in which the multicultural vision is consistent with the democratic ideals of the West and with the heritage of Western civilization" (1991a, 32).
23 In some of his writings Banks does more to emphasize the differences and even the tensions between multicultural education and global education (see, for example, 1994a, 17–18). But, early on as well as later, Banks makes the case for taking more seriously "the needs of a global society" (1976b, 80; see also 1982b, 389; 2003b, 2006b, 207–8; 2008a, 2009, 2016a, 2017). Eventually, "globalism and global competency" are used to stand as an extension of and close synonym for multiculturalism. See Banks's discussion of the six "stages of cultural identity" in 2001b, 134–42.
24 1980, 117; see also 1997a, 137–38.
25 1979a, 7; see also 2006b, 200–201, 209.
26 Banks and Banks 1995, 152; see Banks 1976c, 538–39; 1993b, 5.
27 1997a, 4. The mention of "class" here merits some brief discussion. While it is true that issues of poverty or "class" overlap at points in Banks's writings with the politics of anti-discrimination, the latter predominates absolutely and even works to reformulate older notions of Left democratic political reform. Banks explicitly rejects Marxist theory as "likely to be summarily rejected by most American educators" (1984b, 63). To be sure, it is true that Banks does include "class" as a category of concern to multicultural education. "A salient characteristic of the United States today is a deepening social-class

schism within as well as across ethnic and racial groups. Today the flight out of the inner-city is class as well as racial" (1999a, 39). But class and economic matters generally are a second-order set of concerns in Banks's work, taking up a relatively small portion of the whole. For example, in a discussion of "The Social Construction of Categories," Banks treats "social class" alongside three other key terms: "gender," "race," and "exceptionality" (the last dealing with the situation of the disabled) (1997b, 16–20). However, as in this example, the issue of class is typically presented from the point of view of anti-discrimination groups. "Social scientists find it difficult to agree on criteria for determining social class. . . . Social-class criteria also vary somewhat among various ethnic and racial groups. . . . The systems of social stratification that exist in the mainstream society and in various microcultures are not necessarily identical" (1997b, 18–19). "A study of data on the American economy will reveal that ethnic minorities consume millions of dollars worth of goods and services each year, but that they actually own few production industries. . . . Students should be asked to hypothesize about why this is the case" (1984c, 75–76). While poverty is treated as part of the problem of discrimination, and while Banks does at points call for "structural" societal solutions to it, his pedagogical prescriptions all address the immediate challenge of counteracting discrimination and prejudice and only rarely deal directly with broader economic inequalities or class politics. In postmodernist accounts of multicultural education, while discussion of class and even explicit links to Marxist theory are more pronounced on the surface, there is a similar tendency to subordinate matters of class to the politics of anti-discrimination (see chapter 6, note 7).

28 The phrase "group differentiated," which is very useful for discussing the politics of anti-discrimination, is used in a different sense by Kymlicka; see 1995, 26. Later, in 2008, Banks actually cites Iris Marion Young (1989) in order to advance "[a] *differentiated* conception of citizenship, rather than a universal one [which] is needed to help marginalized groups attain civic equality and recognition in multicultural democratic nations" (2008a, 131; emphasis in the original). In my view, Banks had already gotten to that insight on his own.
29 1974, 45, 52–54, 56; emphasis in the original. See 1977a; 1994a, 49.
30 1999a, 59; see 1984c, 65.
31 At one point Banks seems to suggest that affirmative action is a kind of token gesture—and is therefore not by itself adequate to the needs of combating discrimination and its effects. He says that affirmative action policies arise as one among the "symbolic concessions to ethnic groups" that are made by "nation-states [that] facilitate the movement from early to later phases of ethnic revitalization" (1994b, 33).
32 1994b, 34; see 1987, 531; 1999b, 55; 2009, 5, 12, 16; 2015, 151–52.
33 1984b, 58; see 1972a, 267.
34 1972b, 24, 21; see 1997a, 95.

35 See 1977a, 77; 1980, 122; 1991b, 460; 1993d; 1994a, 44–45; 1995a. Banks would go on to include it among the key "five dimensions" of multicultural education.
36 2004b, 16–18. For surveys of other related techniques, see 1991b, 1993e. Based on a survey of different approaches dating back to the 1940s, Banks concludes that while the benefits of such efforts "are not always consistent," they "can have a positive influence on students racial attitudes and beliefs" (1991b, 464).
37 1987, 532; see 1987, 539–41; 1992c, 88; Banks and Banks 1995, 156–57.
38 1973a, 405; see 1973b, 170–72.
39 1999b, 54–55; citing Gordon 1964.
40 1987, 538; quoting Newmann 1968, 536 and citing Newmann 1975.
41 Banks et al. 1976, 25.
42 1980, 119–20; see 1984c, 55–56; 1997a, 107–10; 2001b, 134–37 ("multi-ethnicity" becomes "multiculturalism" in the last work cited; see 2001b, 136). Sometimes Banks adds a sixth stage, "globalism," essentially a broadening of "stage 5" that does not alter the basic moral and political logic at work (see 1984c, 56; 2001b, 134–42). I believe I do not do violence to the spirit of Banks's thought by minimizing it somewhat here, as I admittedly do, in order to highlight multiculturalism as the peak (as the citations above indicate, there *are* places where it is so presented). See the discussion of "globalism" and "global competency" above, note 23 and accompanying text.
43 The movement through the stages of ethnicity parallels, roughly, Banks's sketch of the development of multicultural education as a field over time (see 2004b, 12–13) from single-group studies to multiethnic and then to multicultural education.
44 1980, 114; see 1977b, 697; 1979b, 251; 1994a, 42; 1997a, 13, 126.
45 1974, 61; see 1990, 213.
46 See 1969a, 1969b, 1998b, 2004d, 2006c.
47 1972b, 7; see 1974; 1976c, 540; Banks and Grambs 1972. Eventually Banks abandoned the "negative self-concept hypothesis" (an older position in the social psychology literature suggesting, for example, that Black identity was framed largely in terms of reactions to the dominant view of them by Whites) to adopt a more flexible view of the identity-formation process (1984c, 68–69; 1999a, 45). That shift, however, did not signal a total reorientation; the basic thrust of Banks's earlier understanding of identity persists in his later writings, especially his views about appropriate, identity-based remedies.
48 1973a, 407–8. See 1972a, 267–69; 1980, 119–20.
49 Banks et al. 1974, 192; Banks 1997a, 136.
50 1997a, 126; see, 49, 135.
51 1997a, 88; see 1973d, 740. See also Tajfel 1970.
52 1977a, 75; see 1975a, 109.

53 1972b, 6; see 1993c, 13–20.
54 For a penetrating and prescient discussion of how anti-discrimination politics relies upon or assumes an extremely malleable form of human nature, see Knopff 1989. See also chapter 7, note 4.
55 1999a, 92–93; 1996b, 32; see 1984b, chapter 6; 1997a, 107.
56 1972a, 267; 1997b, 22; see 1971b, 116–17; 1993d, 27; 1997a, 69–70, chapter 8; 2004b, 16–18.
57 1996b, 27; see 1977b, 696.
58 See, e.g., Finn 1990; Hymowitz 1992; Ravitch 1990; Schlesinger 1992, 88–93; cf. Glazer 1997, 49–56.
59 To be fair to multiculturalism's critics, Banks does at times present multicultural education in the way they suggest. See 1994a, 94; Banks and Banks 1995, 155; Banks et al. 1976, 23.
60 2003c, 65; emphasis added; see 1980, 121.
61 1996b, 29; see also 1996c, 344.
62 The importance of equity pedagogy is indicated in the title of an essay he coauthored with Cherry A. McGee Banks, "Equity Pedagogy: An Essential Component of Multicultural Education" (Banks and Banks 1995). Banks also includes this concept among multicultural education's central "five dimensions," a summative position he developed in the mid-1990s (see the end of note 4 above). By that time Banks had already been using the term "equity" for more than a decade to talk about educational equality (see 1983b, 582). See also 2016b.
63 1999a, 79, 68; see 1984c, 96–101; 1994a, 64–65, 77; 1997a, 29.
64 1977b, 696; 1973c, xi; cf. 1974.
65 1973d, 750. Banks is here quoting the lyrics of the song "The Impossible Dream," from the 1965 musical *Man of La Mancha* (see Wasserman 2003, 10, 121–22).
66 For Banks's use of toleration, see 1971b, 115; 1972a, 266; 1973d, 741; 1994c, 31.
67 Banks et al. 1976, 10; see, e.g., 1997a, 48, 129, 136, 139.
68 See the general discussion of the competing (old/new) definitions of equality in chapter 10. For Banks's use of the language of equal opportunity, see, e.g., 1984c, 73; 2004a, xi; cf. 1993c, 9–10. Banks also differentiates "equity" from equal opportunity; see 1983b, 582–83 (citing and following Graham 1980).
69 Banks and Banks 1995, 156 (citing Gay 1993).
70 Banks makes fairly plain that his use of the equal status situations formula derives from Gordon Allport's 1954 work *The Nature of Prejudice* (see Banks 1999b, 57). For Allport, however, equal status situations was a practical *social condition* of success for integration efforts (part of his discussion of the "contact hypothesis") and not a moral standard (Allport 1954, 262, 275–81). A decade later, sociologist Milton Gordon (in *Assimilation in American Life*) would

likewise argue that "equal status contact" might eventually contribute to successful "private mixed associations" (Gordon 1964, 17, see 235, 253). See also Gordon 1975, 97. For a discussion by Banks of Allport's contact hypothesis contributions, and follow-up work done by other social scientists (in which equal status situations plays a crucial causal role), see 1997a, 94–95; 2008a, 135–36. See also Robinson and Preston 1976. For the authoritative treatment of the contact hypothesis, see Forbes 1997.

71 1997a, 5–6; see 70, 86, 95; 1971b, 156; Banks et al. 1974, 190.
72 For a list of social and political theorists, as well as other multicultural education writers, who use a similar formula, see chapter 10, note 15.
73 See chapter 10, notes 42–44 and accompanying text.
74 1997a, 136; see 48, 129, 139; 1973d, 739.
75 For recognition and acceptance, see 1978a, 185; for recognition and rights, see 2006b, 209; for recognition and inclusion, see 1993d, 23; for recognition and legitimize, see 1978a, 185; 1999b, 55; 2006b, 208, 209.
76 In a later work (2017), Banks distinguishes "recognized citizenship" from "failed' and "participatory" citizenship. The former stands between the other two, as something more than failed citizenship but something less than full participatory (or "transformative" or "social justice") citizenship. For Banks "recognized citizenship [is] a status that is publicly sanctioned and acknowledged by the state" but does not "guarantee [citizens'] participation." "Some individuals who are recognized citizens are 'minimal citizens'" (2017, 4).
77 As I indicated above, Banks views the "contributions" and "additive" approaches to multicultural education to be less than ideal; see 1999a, 30–32.
78 1993d, 28; see 1991c, 138; 1994a, 12.
79 1994b, 34; see also 2015, 152–53.
80 2006b, 202; see 203, 210; 1977b, 696; 2003b; 2006c, 3, 6; 2008a, 129, 136–37.
81 1994c, 31; see 1996b, 30; cf. 1971b, 116.
82 See 1976a, 1976d, 1977a, 1990; Banks and Banks 1997.
83 See chapter 4, note 5.
84 1999a, 59 (citing Hannaford 1996; Omi and Winant 1994).
85 1991a, 34; see 1993d, 23; 1994a, 2–5.
86 See 1996b, 34; 1972a, 269.
87 2008a, 129–31, internal citations omitted. For a related but less revealing discussion of "liberal assimilationism," see 1997a, 132–35. I note that Banks in the passages I am quoting here uses the terms "group rights" and "the rights of groups," terms he does not employ elsewhere except, so far as I can see, to distance himself from them. See, e.g., 1975c, 170; 1976d, 101,104; 1994c, 31. I assume that in this instance he is not using them in any strict way.
88 1973a, 407–8; see 1991a, 35; 1997a, 26.
89 1997a, 26; see 1994a, chapter 6.

Chapter 6

1. The postmodernist label is the obvious one, though it has its detractors. "Antifoundationalism" is probably a better term, and anti-essentialism, anti-universalism, poststructuralism, constructivism, deconstructionism, social construction theory, and critical theory are others that designate related elements of the same outlook. Another connected term, "pragmatism," has a specifically American pedigree and many American thinkers—most notably, Rorty and Fish—meld pragmatist and Heideggerian insights. "Postmodernist" is, in any event, by far the most commonly used term and, as we shall see, it is also commonly embraced among writers in multicultural education and critical pedagogy.
2. O'Meara 2006, 52, 56; see Johnson 2016; Wegierski 2005.
3. For Young and Crenshaw, see notes 54 and 55 and accompanying text. Lyotard and Thébaud offer another example of the suggestion that ideas are central in their rejection of "totality" and "unity" in the name of what looks like some theoretical concern for "multiplicity" as an "idea" (and only secondarily—derivatively?—a political concern, "minority"): "The idea that I think we need today in order to make decisions in political matters cannot be the idea of a totality, or of the unity, of a body. It can only be the idea of a multiplicity or diversity. . . . [What is needed] is a politics of Ideas . . . in which justice is not placed under a rule of convergence but rather a rule of divergence. I believe that this is the theme that one finds constantly in present day writing under the name 'minority'" (Lyotard and Thébaud 1985, 94–95). (This passage provides the epigraph to chapter 6 in Young 1990.)
4. D'Souza 1995, 18; Schmidt 1997, 4. See Bernstein 1994, 226–27; Krauthammer 1990; Parens 1994; Siegel 1991.
5. D'Souza 1995, 169; Rorty 1995a, 9.
6. Butcher and Gonzalez 2020, 1; see Lindsay 2022; Pluckrose and Lindsay 2020; Rufo 2021.
7. Marxism is a problem for postmodernist multiculturalism largely because antidiscrimination politics is not reducible to economic class. Marxism must, in fact, be reworked at points in its encounter with civil rights politics (much like postmodernist theory itself). Early on in their careers, both Giroux and McLaren advanced the insights of postmodernism to raise theoretical criticisms of the many perceived failings of Marxism. "The incipient epistemological materialism of the orthodox Marxian view, according to which the objective realm independent of agency constitutes the object of social knowledge, has been refuted by numerous theorists, such as Derrida, Laclau, Mouffe, and Hirst" (McLaren 1989b, 185, 174–90; see Giroux 1983). But the bigger problem with Marxism has been political. "Postmodernists have taken Marxism to task for its perceived lack of attention to issues of race and gender" (McLaren and

Farahmandpur 1999, 90; see Giroux 1993b, 458–59). Sometimes the result is simply a mixing of Marxist and postmodernist multicultural/anti-discriminatory approaches, the "working together as self-correcting theoretical enterprises," for example, of "critical poststructuralist, neo-Marxist, and postmodern feminism discourses" (McLaren and Lankshear 1993, 402). At one point, McLaren and coauthor Ramin Farahmandpur go so far as to call for a "Marxist multiculturalism," but in their presentation of it, it is clear that this amounts to a reinterpretation of Marxism to fit the logic of civil rights politics: "Many multiculturalists see the need for a direct action politics *centered around* equality, anti-racism, and a politics of difference" (McLaren and Farahmandpur 2001a, 10; emphasis added). There is, of course, another, simpler, political problem with any attempt at a Marxist postmodernism: it is no accident that postmodernist multiculturalism emerged more or less immediately after the fall of the Berlin wall. The demise of Marxism as a going political concern means that we can expect such anxieties about its role to diminish over time. For the tensions between Marxism and postmodernist multiculturalism, and an attempt to reconcile them, see McLaren and Farahmandpur 2001b, 142–44. See also Young 1990, 50–52 and the essays (with contributions by McLaren and Giroux) in *Marxism Against Postmodernism in Educational Theory* (Hill et al. 2002). It is perhaps worth mentioning here also a similar movement of Paulo Freire from class to a consideration of questions of "race and gender" (see Sleeter and McLaren 1995a, 15). Freire, author in 1970 of *Pedagogy of the Oppressed*, and influenced by postcolonialism theorists Franz Fanon and Edward Said, was an inspiring light for American critical pedagogy writers.

8   Lindsay 2021. Contra *this* Lindsay (and the Lindsay of *Race Marxism* [2022]), I would point to the more sensible formulation of the valuable survey of postmodernist theory in Pluckrose and Lindsay 2020, 25: "Activism on behalf of women and the LGBT and, in the United States, the Civil Rights movement, were gaining broad cultural support, just as disillusionment with Marxism . . . was spreading through the political and cultural left." The problem is also clear in *Race Marxism*. The title of the book misleads, whereas the substance of the book is actually a detailed and useful account of how Left civil rights politics (in combination with postmodernist theory, focusing on critical race theory) is being marshaled against Right civil rights politics. It is one thing to say that critical race theory is a complex radical stance that includes disparate influences, to include some sympathy with Marxism and neo-Marxism. But to say that it is not fundamentally an offshoot, or a continuation, of the civil rights revolution is simply inaccurate.

9   For a general overview of critical pedagogy, see Kanpol 1997, 1999; Wink 2000.

10 See Sleeter 1986, 1989, 1996; Sleeter and Delgado Bernal 2004; Sleeter and Grant 1988; Sleeter and McLaren 1995a, 1995b; Grant and Sachs 1995. This

influence is also clear, for example, in the *Journal of Teacher Education*. Compare the first such piece (Zeichner and Liston 1990, 15) with the pervasive role of postmodernist theory in a 1995 special issue on "Preparing Teachers for Cultural Diversity." Harrington and Hathaway (1995), Jennings (1995), Noel (1995), and Solomon (1995) all rely heavily on postmodernist theory. Bennett (1995), Cabello and Burstein (1995), and Colville-Hall, MacDonald, and Smolen (1995) also cite from that literature.

11 Gay 1995; Gay and Hart 2000; Grant and Sachs 1995; Nieto 1999; Sleeter and Delgado Bernal 2004; Sleeter and McLaren 1995a. See also chapter 4, note 43 for Ladson-Billings, who came to roughly the same point by way of critical race theory.

12 Sleeter and McLaren 1995b; Kanpol and McLaren 1995b; see also May 1999.

13 For Banks's stance on postmodernism, see note 100 below and accompanying text. Like Banks, other early prominent advocates of multicultural education like Gwendolyn Baker, H. Prentice Baptiste, Christine Bennett, and Donna Gollnick, for example, show little or no trace of postmodernist influence throughout their careers. See Baker 1983; Baptiste 1979; Baptiste, Baptiste, and Gollnick 1980; Bennett 1986; Gollnick and Chinn 1983.

14 For the Trump administration policy, see Executive Order 13959, "Executive Order on Combating Race and Sex Stereotyping," September 22, 2020, https://www.federalregister.gov/documents/2020/09/28/2020-21534/combating-race-and-sex-stereotyping. See also the two memos issued in the same month by Director of the Office of Management and Budget Russell Vought: Memorandum M-20-34, "Training in the Federal Government," September 4, 2020, https://www.whitehouse.gov/wp-content/uploads/2020/09/M-20-34.pdf, and Memorandum M-20-37, "Ending Employment Trainings that Use Divisive Propaganda to Undermine the Principle of Fair and Equal Treatment for All," September 28, 2020, https://www.whitehouse.gov/wp-content/uploads/2020/09/M-20-37.pdf. These were overturned by Joe Biden's very first executive order (Executive Order 13985, signed on the first day of his presidency), "Executive Order on Advancing Racial Equity and Support for Underserved Communities Through the Federal Government," January 20, 2021, https://www.whitehouse.gov/briefing-room/presidential-actions/2021/01/20/executive-order-advancing-racial-equity-and-support-for-underserved-communities-through-the-federal-government/.

15 For helpful overviews of postmodernist feminism in particular, a vast literature, see Hekman 1990 and the essays in volumes edited by Barrett and Phillips (1992), Benhabib et al. (1995), and Nicholson (1990a). See also Judith Butler's famous book *Gender Trouble: Feminism and the Subversion of Identity* (1990). For a critical overview of several of these fields, see the extensive useful survey in Pluckrose and Lindsay 2020.

16 Hartley 2003. For the critique of old-fashioned scientific anthropology—and sociology—from the point of view of cultural studies and postmodernist

theory, see, e.g., Handler 1997, 77; Long 1997; Seidman 1997, 37. Cf. also Wendy Brown's discussion of the limitations of cultural studies in this regard, as well as her interesting account of the fate of revolutionary feminism (2005, 119, chapter 7).
17 Chicago Cultural Studies Group 1992, 530.
18 Young 1990, 2000; see Butler 1990, 2001; Cornell 1993; hooks 1993, 1994; Minow 1990; West 1990; West and Brown 1993.
19 Fish 2002a, xvi; emphasis in the original.
20 The first claim is that we are always already situated in a whole "world" full of meanings (to include moral beliefs) that shapes decisively how we view everything within it (the Heideggerian slogan: you can't get behind your thrownness) (Heidegger 2001, 272, see 365, 72–81; Fish 1994, 10). The second claim concerns the perceived *diversity* of these human (cultural) worlds and their moral claims. "Zarathustra saw many lands and many peoples: thus he discovered the good and evil of many peoples. And Zarathustra found no greater power on earth than good and evil" (Nietzsche 1954, 170). For Nietzsche, "the real problems of morality . . . emerge only when we compare many moralities" (1989, 98). Postmodernism begins from "the inescapable reality of contending agendas or of points of view or, as we would now say in a shorthand way, of 'difference'" but does not (like liberalism) seek "to contain it, to manage it" (Fish 1994, 296–97; see also 10, 214–15, 223–24). Third, connected to the first and second, is an assumption concerning "the historical and socially constructed nature of reality" (Fish 1994, 295). This last stance is actually codified today in a kind of postmodernist "theory" of knowledge, as "social construction theory" (see, e.g., Gergen 1994; Cheung 1997). Finally, claims are made about the limits of language and conceptual thought, questions long associated with the Western philosophical tradition but made prominent in Jacques Derrida's engagement with structural linguistics (there is no "transcendental signified," no "invariable center" to any given thing) (Derrida 1978, 352–33).
21 See Giroux 1995, 118; Helfenbein 2003; Jacobs 2002; Kincheloe and Steinberg 1997, 213–16; May 1999.
22 Postmodernists' epistemological critical accounts of morality almost never penetrate to the actual concrete substance of the claims being made, leaving them in effect untouched, even unexplored, and therefore ultimately undisturbed. At most, postmodernists can only say: of justice I know only that it cannot be known. (This means that justice may well exist—and that we cannot know of its nonexistence, either.) As a result, thinking about such claims, and their obvious purchase on us, is rarely attempted in a direct and penetrating way. This is the greatest failing of postmodernism: claiming to know in advance that all general moral claims are untrue, on epistemological grounds, serves to deprive the questioner of all incentive to take them seriously. Postmodernists attempt a vast flanking maneuver when many frontal assaults and

much hand-to-hand combat would be necessary to sustain their radical and disturbing rejection of morality. It is for this reason that every postmodernist is ultimately also revealed to be a moralist, despite many protestations to the contrary (a position Fish, for example, defends explicitly; see note 27).
23 A term adapted from the discussion of the "political construction" of "identity" in Smith 2004.
24 Foucault 1980a, 92–102; 1980b.
25 In *The Will to Power*, Nietzsche clarifies the relationship between genealogy and criticism: "The inquiry into the *origin of our evaluations* and tables of the good is in absolutely no way identical with a critique of them, as is so often believed: even though the insight into some *pudenda origo* [shameful origin] certainly brings with it *a feeling* of a diminution in value of the thing that originated thus and prepares the way to a critical mood and attitude toward it" (1968, 148; emphasis in the original).
26 Heidegger 1993; see Lyotard and Thébaud 1985, 16–22; Unger 1976, 293–95; cf. Pangle 1992, 29–33.
27 Fish 1994, 214–15. Fish's repeated insistence that we "already" have commitments aplenty from which to proceed (to include moral commitments), even if we are under the influence of postmodernist insights, only makes sense if "theory" is not itself a predominant authority in the worldview of the postmodernist thinker. The question certainly would seem to apply in the case of Fish himself and his life of clarifying criticism. See 1994, 41, 235–42, 295; see also, e.g., his account of his change of heart over affirmative action, driven by "arguments I have been making" in other contexts (2007b); his admission that his Milton scholarship shaped "my sense of my career and therefore . . . my sense of myself" (1994, 217); see also the last lines of Fish 2009.
28 There are some postmodernist theorists who do offer such criticisms, but they must be counted as *not* among our postmodernist multiculturalists. See the discussion of political versus "ludic" postmodernists below. See especially Fish on multiculturalism (1998) and on universalized aspects of anti-discrimination (1989, 176; 1994, 12, 74, 76–77; 1999; 2007a). See also Rorty 1991a, 1991b, 1992, 1993, 1995b, 1997, 1998, 24, 100; 2000 and the discussion of Wendy Brown's work in chapter 10. I hasten to add that Fish, Rorty, and Brown are all staunch defenders of the Left interpretation of anti-discrimination and critics of the Right interpretation. Thus, even these critics of aspects of anti-discrimination politics must ultimately be viewed as supplying evidence of the general theoretical-political linkage that I am describing.
29 See, e.g., Akintunde 1999, 8; Giroux 1991b, 219; McLaren 1997a, 5–6; Roediger 1994, 14; Sleeter 1997, 680; 2015, 114; Sleeter and McLaren 1995a, 11–12.
30 A usefully simple and general test of this claim is available in two summary statements of postmodernist multiculturalism provided by Sonia Nieto (a

six-point summary of how "critical multicultural education" overcomes what she deems to be some of the "limits" of traditional multicultural education) and Gay and Hart (their account of "seven postmodern education principles") (Nieto 1999, 206–10; Gay and Hart 2000, 171).

31 Grant and Sachs 1995, 91. For other general statements, see Akintunde 1999; Sleeter and McLaren 1995a, 8. The difficulty of getting postmodernists to say clearly which is primary is illustrated by an essay by Giroux (1991b) that sketches out in detail how "postmodernism [might] make a valuable contribution to the development of a critical pedagogy of race" (234). That formulation already suggests the subordination of theory to politics and there is other fairly direct evidence of the same kind (see esp. 226–27, 236, 239, 243, 255). But the question is not ever directly faced or addressed and, because Giroux spends most of his time talking about various insights of theory, it would be possible to read this essay (wrongly) as if the latter were predominant. Indeed, at one point, Giroux goes so far as to call attention to how "postmodern discourse provides a *theoretical* foundation for deconstructing the master-narratives of white supremacist logics" (233; emphasis added).

32 For the general postmodernist critique of identity, see, e.g., Butler 1990; Connolly 1991; Hall 1991; Minow 1997, 30–40; Peters 1995; Young 1990, 98–99. For similar reflections in the work of critical pedagogy and postmodernist multiculturalism writers, see, e.g., Akintunde 1999, 3; Giroux 1993a, 72; Goldberg 1994, 12; Kincheloe and Steinberg 1997, 91–92, 225; Leistyna 2002, 23; McCarthy 1994, 92; McLaren and Lankshear 1993, 399–400.

33 See, e.g., Kincheloe and Steinberg 1997, 92, 216; McLaren and Lankshear 1993, 390, 401–2.

34 Kincheloe and Steinberg 1997, 226, 225; McLaren and Lankshear 1993, 401–2; Jacobs 2002, 6.

35 Gay 1995, 178; see Grant and Sachs 1995, 101; Morgan 2000, 274; Sleeter and Grant 1988, 176.

36 Giroux 1991a, 69; see Akintunde 1999; Kincheloe and Steinberg 1997, 208–9; Nakayama and Krizek 1995, 300.

37 Gay and Hart 2000, 183; see Giroux and Simon 1988, 12.

38 For the anti-discriminatory meaning of Derridean deconstruction, see Ghosh 1995, 234–35; Giroux 1992, 165; Haymes 1995, 111; McLaren 1993, 120; 1995, 45–46, 51; McLaren and Lankshear 1993, 394-5; Sleeter and McLaren 1995a, 22; Young 1990, 99, 119. For binaries, see Brooks-Immel and Murray 2017; Giroux 1993a, 100, 110, 113; Haymes 1995, 111. For postmodernist notions of politics and empowerment, hegemony, resistance, and struggle, etc., see Gay 1995, 174–78; Gay and Hart 2000, 184; Grant and Sachs 1995, 91, 99, 101; Sleeter and McLaren 1995a, 22. For naming, see Sleeter and McLaren 1995a, 18–19; Nakayama and Krizek 1995. For counter-history and

counter-memory, see Gay 1995, 170–71; Kincheloe and Steinberg 1997, 219–20. For decentering, re-centering, multi-centering, and the border (and border pedagogy), see Gay 1995, 174, 177; Gay and Hart 2000, 171, 181–82; Giroux 1991a, 1991b, 1992, 1993c; Jacobs 2002, 6; Kanpol 1995, 176–81, 190–91; Kincheloe and Steinberg 1997, 101; Sleeter and McLaren 1995a, 8.

39 Sleeter and McLaren 1995a, 21; McLaren and Lankshear 1993, 393.
40 McLaren and Lankshear 1993, 383. See McLaren 1994a, 198–200; Sleeter 1996, 46–47; Sleeter and McLaren 1995a, 21; Steinberg 1995, 132.
41 Fish 1998, 85n15; see also 1994, 236–40.
42 Giroux 1996, 52–53; McLaren and Lankshear 1993, 403–4; see Zavarzadeh 1989.
43 Kincheloe and Steinberg 1997, 98; Steinberg 1995, 140.
44 See the titles of Giroux 1994a; hooks 1993, 1994; Kanpol and McLaren 1995a, 1995b; McLaren 1995, 1997b; Sleeter and McLaren 1995a, 1995b. For "social reconstructionist," see Sleeter and Grant 1988, 176.
45 McLaren and Lankshear 1993, 404, citing Zavarzadeh 1989.
46 McLaren and Lankshear 1993, 404, citing Zavarzadeh 1989.
47 Giroux 1989, 147; Giroux 1991b, 227; McLaren 1995, 54.
48 Giroux 1991a, 70; Gay 1995, 171. Such claims are pervasive in the work of Giroux and McLaren (see, e.g., McLaren 1993, 120).
49 McLaren 1997b, 297; cf. McLaren 1994b, 69. See Baumeister 2000, 15–48; Giroux 1993a, 62–67; 1994a, 328; 1997a, 237; Sleeter 1996, 42.
50 For color-blindness, see Sleeter 1996, 84; Steinberg 1995, 151; for equal opportunity, see Peters 1995, 41; McLaren and Farahmandpur 1999, 33; for merit, see Shapiro 1995, 25; for individualism, see Giroux 1997a, 243; Peters 1995, 42–46; Sleeter 1996, 37–38, 41; Shapiro 1995, 25; for individual rights, see Peters 1995, 43; Sleeter 1996, 44; for the public-private divide, see Chicago Studies Group 1992, 534; for toleration, see Goldberg 1994, 7, 26; for (liberal) pluralism, see McLaren 1995, 43–44; McLaren 1997b, 294–301; Sleeter and McLaren 1995a, 9; for the "terror of neo-liberalism," see Giroux 2005; Peters 1995, 39, see 46.
51 Postmodernist notions of a very fluid, even nonexistent, "self" provide another ground of criticism for ideas of *human* nature in particular. "How can we begin to map the more fluid boundaries of the postmodern self as constituted within new technologies and virtual realities that represent *in themselves* historically and culturally discrete systems of producing race, class, and gender relations?" (Giroux and McLaren 1992, 28; emphasis in the original).
52 Giroux 1979, 272, 282. The article from which these quotations are taken was written early in Giroux's career, and the "power relations" he has in mind involve class only, not discrimination or civil rights.
53 On the other hand, because anti-discrimination's rejection of nature is limited only to matters where inequalities affecting groups covered by anti-discrimination

law are at issue, it entails (unlike the stance of postmodernist theory) only a *partial* rejection of nature.

54 See Crenshaw 1988, 1335; 1989, 151; Delgado 1993, 1144–45; Gentilli 1992, 2363; Siegel 1997; Williams 1989; Young 1990, 195–97.

55 These two indications of the supremacy of politics over theory are illuminating and worth stating briefly. Young's discussion of the "five faces of oppression"—exploitation, marginalization, powerlessness, cultural imperialism, and violence—would seem to suggest a very general account of injustice that (with the exception of "marginalization") does not immediately indicate the primacy of the politics of anti-discrimination in particular. But even a cursory examination of the substance of her discussion (see Young 1990, 50–61), makes it clear that in almost every case what Young has in mind is the specific experience of the challenges faced by those championed in the American civil rights regime. Similarly, that intersectionality is an insight of anti-discrimination politics first, and not really postmodernist theory at all, is clear in the writings where Crenshaw introduced the idea. Compare her first discussion of it (1989), where anti-discrimination is everything and postmodernist theory is never mentioned, with an article two years later, where an effort to tie intersectionality to postmodern theory is suggested in a footnote (Crenshaw 1989, 1991, 1244–45, n. 9, 1296–99.) The titles of Crenshaw's two essays make use of the terminology of "marginalization" and "margins," and this might seem to suggest some connection to a book of Derrida titled *Margins of Philosophy* (1982). But Crenshaw never mentions that work in either essay, and the terms have a simpler obvious political meaning tied to the fight against discrimination—i.e., "marginalized" persons, etc.

56 Giroux 1995, 110; emphasis added, quoting Homi Bhabha from an interview (Bennet and Collits 1991, 50–51).

57 Giroux 1993a, 98–124; see 1994b.

58 The statement is made in an interview (Steinberg 1995, 140).

59 For moral regulation, see Giroux 1985, 23; for moral technology, see McLaren 1997b, 78. To point out that their opponents rely on moral arguments is usually meant as a criticism (see, e.g., Giroux and Simon 1988, 12, 15; Giroux 1993a, 93.).

60 McLaren and Farahmandpur 1999, 89, citing Green 1994.

61 McLaren and Giroux 1997, 19. See also Giroux 1988, 206; 1997b, 78, 284–90; Sleeter and McLaren 1995a, 25.

62 Dussel 1993, 75; quoted in McLaren 1997b, 289.

63 Shohat 1995, 177, quoted in McLaren 1997b, 287. See Giroux 1997a, 98.

64 McLaren and Hammer 1989, 50. See Giroux 1994b, 35; McLaren 1988, 57.

65 The term was coined by Gayatri Spivak. For the debate among postmodernists over the idea, see Stone 2004.

66 Carlson 1997, 65; see Giroux 1997a, 246–48; Jay 2003; McLaren 1994a,

201; 2000, 97–98. For a critical response to such accusations, see Sleeter and Grant 1988, 176, 200.
67 Changing multiculturalism is the theme of Corson 1998; Kincheloe and Steinberg 1997. For "troubling multiculturalism," see Helfenbein 2003.
68 Giroux 2007, 33–34; see 1993a, 78–81; 1995, 48–49, 54; Coté, Day, and de Peuter 2007; cf. McLaren 2000, 164–65, 191.
69 Sleeter 1996, 1–15; see 1989.
70 Mouffe 1999, 754; 2005; Connolly 1991, 178–93; 1993; Honig 1995.
71 Giroux 2007, 22–34; 1993a, 122.
72 Giroux 1995, 121 see Giroux 1989, 149; 1993a, 92–93.
73 Sleeter and McLaren 1995a, 25, see 11, 26.
74 McLaren and Lankshear 1993, 411; emphasis in the original; citing Jameson 1988, 360 and Laclau 1988, 23. See also Giroux's sketch of "a dialectical view of authority" or "emancipatory authority" (Giroux 1997a, 100–113) and the attempt of Kanpol and McLaren to articulate (following Seyla Benhabib's idea of "interactive universalism") a "common vision or common ground of understanding that weaves together many different truths or 'truth effects' that has driven us to collectively dialogue across differences" (Kanpol and McLaren 1995a, 6, citing Benhabib 1992, 228).
75 McLaren 1995, 62. Cf. Giroux 1991b, 245, where postmodernism is said to "refuse . . . forms of knowledge and pedagogy wrapped in the legitimizing discourse of the sacred and the priestly."
76 Kincheloe and Steinberg 1997, 214, 207. For "White Terror," see the title of McLaren 1995.
77 On the history, see Giroux 1997b, 376–80; Hartman 2004; Mazie et al. 1993. See, generally, the collection *Critical White Studies*, edited by Delgado and Stefancic (1997).
78 See DiAngelo 2018; Kendi 2019a.
79 The quotation from Nakayama and Krizek here might seem to suggest an exclusively or mainly theoretical move ("particularity. . . universality"). But postmodernist multiculturalists (to include Nakayama and Krizek; see 1995, 303) are unanimous in anti-essentializing Whiteness. See, e.g., Akintunde 1999, 4; Kincheloe and Steinberg 1997, 211–6; Giroux 1993a, 72; McLaren 1997a, 8; McLaren and Lankshear 1993, 399–400; McLaren and Torres 1999, 55–57.
80 Giroux 1997b, 382; emphasis added. Giroux is at least partly critical (if not very) of some of the implications of the Whiteness literature he is here summarizing. See 383–84.
81 McLaren and Torres 1999, 66. See also Frankenberg 1993, 191–92, 232; McLaren 1997b, 276.
82 Nakayama and Krizek 1995, 292; Giroux 1997b, 382; McLaren and Torres 1999, 62; McLaren 1995, 50; Kincheloe and Steinberg 1997, 220. See also

Frankenberg 1993; Giroux 1994b, 59, 61; Sleeter 1993; Roediger 1994, 12–14, 187–94.
83 Nakayama and Krizek 1995, 293; Giroux 1993a, 99.
84 Akintunde 1999, 5. This is pervasive. See, e.g., Giroux 1991b, 225–27, 233; Kincheloe and Steinberg 1997, 225; McLaren 1995, 55; McLaren and Lankshear 1993, 387; Nakayama and Krizek 1995, 300.
85 Giroux 1997b, 376–81; Kincheloe and Steinberg 1997, 225. See also McLaren 1997a, 5–8; 1997b, 251–68.
86 For "subversion," see Frankenberg 1993, 18; for "dismantling whiteness," Haney-López 1996, 136; Jungkunz 2011; for "reimagining," see Giroux 1997b, 383.
87 For choosing not to be white, see Haney-López 1996, 193; for race treason, see Ignatiev 2022; for the abolition of whiteness, see Roediger 1994. See the extensive discussion of such ideas in the Whiteness literature in McLaren and Torres 1999, 63–66 and McLaren 1997b, 271–78.
88 McLaren 1997a, 10; see McLaren and Torres 1999, 66.
89 Sleeter 1993, 14. See also Frankenberg 1993, 30–34, 142–57; McLaren 1997b, 267.
90 Kincheloe and Steinberg 1997, 228; see Sleeter 1995b, 420.
91 Kincheloe and Steinberg 1997, 228. See also Frankenberg 1993, 32; McLaren 1995, 53; Sleeter 1996, 119. Cf. Giroux's concern that "too few attempts" have been made "to develop a pedagogy of 'whiteness' that enables white students to move beyond positions of guilt or resentment" (Giroux 1997b, 383–85).
92 Kincheloe and Steinberg use the term quoted (1997, 214).
93 Kincheloe and Steinberg 1997, 222; see 208, 226.
94 McLaren 1997b, 263, see 262–64, 269–70; see Frankenberg 1993, 142.
95 Frankenberg 1993, 242, see 14.
96 Sleeter 2017, 161; see 2001.
97 For other instances of these different strategies, see Frankenberg 1993, 142–48; McLaren and Torres 1999, 54; Sleeter 1995b, 419; 1996, 84, 88. See also the commonly cited *Harvard Law Review* article "Whiteness as Property" (Harris 1993).
98 Kincheloe and Steinberg 1997, 225. See also Akintunde 1999, 3–5; Giroux 1991b, 227, 233; McLaren 1995, 55; McLaren and Lankshear 1993, 387; Nakayama and Krizek 1995, 300.
99 See, e.g., Sokhi-Bulley 2011, 252. See also note 28 above.
100 Already in the 1970s, Banks was using arguments about what postmodernists would term the social construction of knowledge, although he derived those insights from the sociology of knowledge and not from postmodernist writers. (See 1972b, 1973a, 1974, 1998b.) In the mid-1990s Banks did cite a few postmodern authors, but only for a brief span of time and with an emphatic connection to

the anti-discrimination effort: "The curriculum canons and paradigms that perpetuate racism, sexism and classism will have to be deconstructed" (Banks 1992b, 88; see 1993b, 1993d, 1993f, 1995b). Eventually, however, Banks basically dropped all mention of postmodernism. As we saw in chapter 5, while Banks makes use of various postmodernist terms—borderland, deconstruct, metanarrative, etc.—his thought is not overwhelmed by them. What might look like one possible exception to this, Banks's attempt to sketch an epistemological synthesis of postmodernism and traditional social science, does not suggest any attachment on Banks's part to the former (see 1995b, 390; 1997a, 103–5). That being said, I do not deny that there is an important tension between Banks's apparent rejection of postmodernism and his embrace of the idea of the social construction of knowledge. If he is serious about that dimension of multicultural education—whether or not he openly derives it from postmodernists—it is hard to see how his overall position would, if pressed, resist a further slide in the direction of the rest of the postmodernist outlook. It is true that his commitment to fighting discrimination is stronger than his epistemological commitments, but the difficulty here does not, for that reason, disappear. For a more extensive discussion, see Powers 2002.
101 Banks 1971b, 116; 1996b, 30.
102 Banks 1998b, 14; emphasis added; see 2003a, xi.
103 Banks 1997a, 68; 1973d, 750.
104 This phrase is associated with Abraham Lincoln (see 1999), though he did not simply embrace it.

Chapter 7

1   For further evidence of liberal pluralism's own diversity and its ability continually to be reinvented, even somehow rediscovered, and only slightly altered, again and again, see the many different versions of cultural or ethnic pluralism, social science pluralism, and values pluralism surveyed (respectively) in the exhaustive treatments provided by Powell 1971; Eisenberg 1995; Gunnell 2004; and Galston 2002. I exclude contemporary multiculturalism theorist Kymlicka from my discussion of the liberal pluralist tradition, mainly because his is a complicated case, a hybrid of liberal pluralism and strong claims on behalf of group identity (see chapter 1, note 12; Powers 2015a). Insofar as his account of pluralism is connected to the liberal tradition, however, there would be no great difficulty in demonstrating that the liberal side of his argument matches the outline I follow in this chapter, a mix of three elements: liberal moralism, realism, and soft skepticism. Kymlicka differs from some of the other liberal pluralists surveyed in this chapter mainly in emphasizing liberal moralism (in this respect he is closest to Kallen).

2   It is true that social science pluralists of the 1950s and 1960s were anti-Marxist in more ways than one, but their political allegiances within the confines of American politics at the time were generally to the left of the Republican party.

3   Unless otherwise indicated, all citations in this section are to works of Locke.

4   Most later accounts of liberal pluralism do not generally refer to natural right (as my discussion of liberal pluralists after Madison and Jefferson makes plain). For appeals to nature (among other things) in Kallen, see Powers 1999, 27. In the *Letter*, Locke does mention "natural right" twice, but in neither case does his appeal to it make any direct or important contribution to his argument for religious toleration. His first use of that phrase, already quoted ("that liberty of conscience is every man's natural right"), is a teaching Locke urges *churches* to take up. If "all churches were obliged to lay down toleration as the foundation of their own liberty; and teach that liberty of conscience is every man's natural right . . . , this one thing would take away all ground of complaints and tumults upon account of conscience" (1963, 47–48). Locke provides no argument (save perhaps the *Letter* taken as a whole, one might say) for this teaching he wishes all churches would adopt. It is true that Locke does make appeals to *nature* that support his overall position in the *Letter* ("the nature of the understanding" is such that "it cannot be compelled to the belief of any thing by outward force" [1963, 11]; church membership must be "voluntary" because "no man by nature is bound unto any particular church" [1963, 13]). But in these instances, nature supports some other aspect of his teaching (skepticism in matters of faith; the morality of voluntarism) and not "liberty of conscience" per se (unless, to repeat, indirectly). The second time Locke mentions natural right, he does so to emphasize the independence of natural right from religion: those suffering persecution will, eventually, Locke says "think it lawful for them to resist force with force, and to defend their natural rights, which are not forfeitable upon account of religion" (1964, 53–54). That Locke does not emphasize natural right in the *Letter* may have something to do with the fact that skepticism in matters of faith is so important to his overall argument for toleration. On the shifting of emphasis among the elements of Locke's thought as they appear in his different works, see Pangle 1988, 206.

5   For a very useful survey of the relationship between modern toleration and modern skepticism, see the essays in *Early Modern Skepticism and the Origins of Toleration* (Levine 1999).

6   Locke 1975, 659–60; see Tarcov 1999.

7   For the question of Madison's sources, see note 15.

8   See Kautz 1995; Pangle 1988; Strauss 1953. Some have gone so far as to note important ways in which Locke's position on religion is prefigured in Hobbes (see Flathman 1994; Kraynak 1980; Owen 2005; Strauss 1953, 221–23).

9   As liberalism's critics on the Left and the Right have long pointed out, this aspect of liberal pluralism, like the ideas of freedom and limited government,

tends to obscure certain facts of political life (see, e.g., Mouffe 2005). The difficulty is barely visible here, to begin with, in Locke's insistence (matched in practice in all liberal regimes) that "force belongs wholly to the civil magistrate" (1963, 16). Further, while the state is not to attempt to coerce faith, its authority to enforce laws regulating human actions is in no way limited by any overlapping (moral) claims of religion to regulate the behavior of the faithful. In practice, the limit of the state's authority is simply the law, and where the dictates of the law contradict the dictates of individual religious conscience, the presence of the latter is no obstacle to the enforcement of the former. "While the inventors of toleration wisely presented it as a means of getting the state off the backs of the churches, their chief concern was clearly to get the churches off the back of the state" (Orwin 1991, 557–58; see Powers 2007).

It is worth noting here briefly how the liberal outlook stands opposed to a political science that begins and ends with the regime as the underlying general or formal cause of social and individual life. Indeed, for individuals raised up under liberalism, the notion of the regime is something like science fiction. One may also say, on behalf of liberalism, that the regime can certainly appear to be an unattractive idea. For who can hold that the regime shapes the heart and mind of citizens in a profound way, to include especially morality, without wondering about the success of such efforts? Might not leaving individuals to their own devices, free to choose even if they are likely to err, be preferable to a world in which political authorities stamp everyone with a vision of life (and of their own happiness) that might be mistaken and that may in fact serve the interests of the political order as much or more than the interests of those under its care? (An explanation of why more postmodernists do not see the wisdom of liberalism, given their understanding of politics, would not be flattering to them.) However all of this may be, such considerations do not address the question of which—regime, political science, or liberalism—better describes social reality. Raising these questions is justified, if only because "pluralism" is one of liberalism's most successful strategies for hiding the regime.

10   This is not to say that the liberal theory of the group adequately describes social or political reality in the United States, especially after the rise of industrialization and the welfare/regulatory state (and, hence, of "corporations" and "iron triangles," to say nothing of "class" politics). But the political scientists who point this out are often themselves surprisingly beholden to liberal theory; see, for example, the especially clear case of Theodore Lowi's famous lament in *The End of Liberalism* (1969).

11   Locke 1963, 20. It should be noted that Locke does, in at least one place in the *Letter*, express something close to our opposition to discrimination, even to something like race discrimination: "Suppose this business of religion were let alone, and that there were some other distinction made between men and

men upon account of their different complexions, shapes, and features, so that those who have black hair (for example) or grey eyes should not enjoy the same privileges as other citizens; that they should not be permitted either to buy or sell, or live by their callings; that parents should not have the government and education of their own children; that all should either be excluded from the benefit of the laws, or meet with partial judges; can it be doubted but these persons, thus distinguished from others by the colour of their hair and eyes, and united together by one common persecution, would be as dangerous to the magistrate as any others that had associated themselves merely upon the account of religion?" (Locke 1963, 49). This follows the old logic and not the new view of things; public and private are at work in the way we expect. First, even though Locke does mention the private sector—"buy or sell"; "live by their callings"; parents/children—the point is that individuals (he terms them "citizens") would not be "permitted" to do as they like. This suggests it is above all efforts to hinder them involving force ("persecution"), and thus the role of the magistrate and law, that Locke has in mind (his other examples are public sector: the "benefit of the laws"; "partial judges"). There is also, of course, nothing in the *Letter* suggesting the kinds of vigorous efforts of regulation in the private sector (or even the public sector) that we associate with anti-discrimination politics as a matter of remedy. (It is also worth noting that Locke's "realistic" stated concern here is that persecuted groups would be "dangerous to the magistrate.") The fairly severe limitation of Locke's account of protections for minorities in the *Second Treatise*, noted by Spinner-Halev, is also worth bearing in mind. "For if [tyranny] reach no farther than some private men's cases, though they have a right to defend themselves, and to recover by force, what by unlawful force is taken from them; yet the right to do so, will not easily engage them in a contest, wherein they are sure to perish; it being impossible for one or a few oppressed men to disturb the government, where the body of people do not think themselves concerned in it" (Locke 1988, 404; see Spinner 1994, 119).

12   Of course some of the versions of pluralism surveyed here have voices outside the United States.
13   In foundational cases of both its "Free Exercise" clause and "Establishment" clause jurisprudence (*Reynolds v. United States* (98 U.S. 145 [1879]) and *Everson v. Board of Education* (330 U.S. 1 [1947]), the Supreme Court looks to the writings of Madison and Jefferson explicitly and without hesitation. In *Everson*, the court adopts Jefferson's image of a "wall of separation between church and state" as its starting point, quotes Jefferson's "Virginia Bill for Religious Liberty" at length, and includes Madison's "Memorial and Remonstrance" as an appendix (*Everson v. Board of Education*, 15–16, 12–13, 63–72). In *Reynolds*, the court goes so far as to say that Jefferson's account of the act-opinion distinction "may be accepted almost as an authoritative declaration

of the scope and effect of the [First] amendment" (*Reynolds v. United States*, 164). For the relationship between the thought of Locke and Madison and Jefferson, see Berns 1987, 143–44; Malbin 1978, 29; Sandler 1960.

14 See Jefferson 1944a; 1944b, 272–77; 1944c; Madison 1961, 78; 1973, 9, 15–16.

15 See Hume 1889. It is also possible that Madison may have been influenced by Adam Smith's discussion of religious factions in *The Wealth of Nations*, which follows Hume and Locke down the line (Smith 1937, 740–66; see Fleischacker 2002). The question of Madison's intellectual influences is much debated: see Adair 1957; Arkin 1995; Morgan 1986; Spencer 2002. George Washington's "Farewell Address" likewise frames much of his discussion in terms of "faction" (1997a, 964–65). (For the question of Hamilton's influence on the latter, see Malanson 2014.)

16 Madison 1961, 78; see 1973, 9.

17 For an exhaustive survey of the varieties of the argument, in which the tendency of all of them to appeal to the logic of liberal pluralism is plain, see Powell 1971. See also the excellent book of his teacher, Philip Gleason, *Speaking of Diversity* (1992). For a detailed discussion of Kallen's position, see Powers 1999, chapter 2.

18 Historian John Higham notes that James discussed pluralism in its philosophical sense as early as 1897 and that John Dewey also took up the idea shortly thereafter (Higham 1984, 202). That liberal moral and political conclusions are to be drawn from pragmatist philosophical or ontological pluralism is not made explicit in James's extensive philosophical treatment of the subject in *A Pluralistic Universe* and elsewhere, but it is indicated at least once by him briefly at the end of an essay titled "On a Certain Blindness in Human Beings": "And now what is the result of all these considerations and quotations? It is negative in one sense, but positive in another. It absolutely forbids us to be forward in pronouncing on the meaninglessness of forms of existence other than our own; and it commands us to tolerate, respect, and indulge those whom we see harmlessly interested and happy in their own ways, however unintelligible these may be to us" (1899, 45–46; see 1909; cf. 1907, 142). For Dewey's reaction to Kallen's cultural pluralism and for speculation about the political meaning of Dewey's pluralist stance, as well as his views on immigrants and race, see Wissot 1975; Eisele 1983.

19 For Kallen's realism, see, e.g., 1924, 309–47.

20 Somewhat surprisingly, this general interpretation of Kallen's cultural pluralism ideal as first and foremost a product of liberal idealism cuts against the grain of much recent scholarship. Looking back to Kallen in the years following the civil rights revolution, many scholars find him wanting (especially for his lack of attention to race and the plight of Blacks in America; see chapter 8, note 2). While Kallen's emphasis on liberal principle is overwhelming and

pervasive from the very first, his critics accuse him of promoting a "racialist" view of ethnic identity, based on a few statements, taken out of context, in his early writings on the subject (Kallen 1924, 93–94, 116, 122; see, e.g., Higham 1984, 205–7; Hollinger 1995, 92–94; Huntington 2004, 130; Sollors 1986). In their treatment of Kallen, scholars emphasize his intellectual training (especially his connection to William James) to explain his pluralism, but say little about his repeated and much more emphatic reliance upon liberal democratic moral principle. Even a cursory reading of the writings in question vindicates the view that Kallen's liberal ideals govern his account of pluralism absolutely, thoroughly, and from the outset. His seeming embrace of "nationality" from time to time is itself only the result of his (perhaps somewhat zealous) commitment to individualism and liberty in the first place (just as liberal religious pluralism must appear to champion the cause of religion at points, though it is not ultimately a religious stance).

21 Kallen 1956, 87; see 1924, 117–18, 191–201.
22 Kallen 1948, 159; see 1924, 198.
23 Kallen 1956, 180; see 1924, 198–99.
24 Dahl 1961, 767; see Truman 1951; 1965.
25 Bentley 1908, 389–90; Truman 1951, 14, 48; see Dowling 1960.
26 Bentley 1908, 214; see Dahl 1982, 41–43; Truman 1951, 33–34.
27 See Connolly 1969, 13; Hale 1960. Other critics decried social science pluralism's realism for its seeming indifference to the "pathologies" of interest group pluralism or various other perceived inequities implicit in the social order it described (see Lowi 1969; Bachrach and Baratz 1962; Lukes 1974).
28 Dewey and Bentley 1949; Bentley 1908, 165–72; see Truman 1951, 46–67; Smith 1964.
29 Dahl 1971, 31; see 1961, 771.
30 The desire to avoid deep reliance on "eternal principles of justice" is retained by Truman, but he concedes that liberalism needs some moral basis: "Obviously the system rests at bottom on a respect for the dignity of man" (Truman 1959, 490–91; see 487, 497). Another set of social science pluralists put these ideas together in a usefully illuminating formulation: "There are required *social* consensus and cleavage—in effect, pluralism—in politics. . . . Too much consensus would be deadening and restrictive of liberty; too much cleavage would be destructive of the society as a whole" (Berelson, Lazarsfeld, and McPhee 1954, 318; emphasis in the original).
31 Dahl 1956, 64; 1967, 22–24; 1970, 8–28; 1971, 20–32.
32 Dahl 1989, 83–131; 1998, 35–82; 2006.
33 It is worth pointing out that at least one prominent writer associated with values pluralism, Joseph Raz, rejects skepticism in strong terms, making a nonskeptical case for autonomy as liberalism's most important ground (1986, 160–61, 390–99).

34 For a useful summary of the values pluralist literature, see Galston 2002, 5. See also, in addition to other works cited here, Kekes 1993; Larmore 1996, 152–74; Newey 1998; Raz 1986.
35 Berlin 2014. Groups certainly are viewed in an unsentimental way: the "individual's right of exit from groups" is taken for granted, as are, if needed, "state protections against oppression carried out by groups against their members" (Galston 2002, 123). The realist element in the debate over values pluralism is also clear in Bernard Yack's adaptation of Judith Shklar's "liberalism of fear" to provide a starting place for thinking about deep disagreements. "Shklar's insistence on putting injustice first . . . allows her to develop a more pluralistic vision of liberal pluralism, one that does not rest on strained and implausible claims about the underlying consensus about justice" (Yack 1999, 1105).
36 Rawls 1993, xxvii. Rawls does go on to say that he believes his doctrine could be extended to such groups, though he does not spell out how in detail (1993, xxix).
37 See chapter 9, note 9.
38 Rawls 1971, 205–11; see 222–28; 328. Rawls's theory is also presented as being compatible with a certain amount of economic liberty, and he insists that it retains even the "priority of liberty" (see 1971, 243–51). Each and every one of these issues could be debated by those who would wish to deny Rawls's commitment to freedom vis-à-vis equality (or "justice"). My point is not to settle this elementary question of Rawlsian interpretation (though I do not, of course, understand him to be a libertarian). But Rawls certainly goes out of his way to present himself in the garb of liberty, and on this basis we can say that he is not outside the realm of liberal pluralism on account of his basic moral posture.
39 Rawls 1985; see 1993, xix–xx; 48–66; 150–54.
40 Rawls 1993, 150. It is interesting to note that Rawls feels compelled to reject hard skepticism (see 1993, 150–54). But this move is ultimately from the point of view of the softest of soft (I should say, tolerant) skepticisms, since Rawls's motive here is only to avoid disagreement with those who are *not* skeptical about the good. As Judd Owen puts it, Rawls's political liberalism is in a way an even "purer antifoundationalist" position than that of his postmodernist critics, since Rawls refuses "even to broach the topic of foundationalism versus antifoundationalism" (Owen 2001, 106).
41 Rawls 1993, 133–72. In a way that is reminiscent of Kallen, Rawls's moralistic bent characterizes even his realism. He insists repeatedly that political liberalism must not be "political in the wrong way" as compromise for its own sake (1993, 39–40, 142). Similarly, he rejects the idea that the "overlapping consensus" might be "a mere *modus vivendi*" (1993, 147).

Chapter 8

1   Milton Gordon came close to capturing the crucial outline of the new "pattern" of politics associated with anti-discrimination in a 1981 article titled "Models of Pluralism: The New American Dilemma." Gordon's earlier book *Assimilation in American Life* was explicitly framed in terms of Kallen's cultural pluralism argument and published in 1964; Gordon's initial success would seem to be explained by the fact that he took liberal pluralism as close to anti-discrimination as possible at the crucial moment of change. In his 1981 article Gordon went further, sketching a new "corporate pluralism" that he contrasted with traditional "liberal pluralism." Although Gordon is correct to notice the emergence of a new *kind* of pluralism in America, he fails to see that the great cause of this new form of pluralism is a broad shift in the American political order as a whole. As a result, his analysis equates "corporate pluralism" with only the radical (Left) version of arguments for policies arising out of but typically going beyond anti-discrimination (above all in the affirmative action debate). He does not notice that between "liberal pluralism" and his version of "corporate pluralism" there is a further pattern of group politics—anti-discrimination—that mediates the relationship between the two.

   In Theodore Lowi's *The End of Liberalism* (1969), it is possible to see something like an account of how New Deal reforms transformed traditional liberal (interest group) pluralism, giving rise to a new and distinctive form of pluralism. However, Lowi is not directly concerned with showing the effect of the regime on group politics and his argument is mainly civic and meliorative in its orientation. A study more strictly attentive to the shaping power of the New Deal revolution on American pluralism would presumably be fruitful.

2   Kallen 1956; see Glazer 1997, 110–11, 115; Higham 1984, 210. Criticism of Kallen on this score is the norm but it is exaggerated. Werner Sollors goes so far as to characterize Kallen's work as having a "racist component," a gross distortion (1986, 261). "Respect for ancestors, pride of race! Time was when these would have been repudiated as the enemies of democracy, the antithesis of the fundamentals of the North American Republic" (Kallen 1924, 70). Kallen was an early advocate of civil rights reform and was associated especially with the struggles of Native Americans (albeit from a traditionally liberal perspective) (see, e.g., Kallen 1924, 21; 1956, 64–86; 1958). More generally, Kallen's argument for cultural pluralism was an appeal to liberal individualism; any appeal to "nationality" in it was only an extension of that more fundamental ideological commitment (see chapter 7, note 20). Earlier, in 1956, Nathan Glazer in particular (in a letter to Kallen) expressed greater agreement. "May I say . . . that I have found your book [*Culture and Democracy in the United States*] enormously stimulating, and by far the best that exists on the

impact of immigrant groups on American culture. Returning to it . . . after some time I was amazed to discover how much that I and others had thought and written about this matter had been written by you a long time ago" (quoted in Schmidt 1974, 329).

3   For Locke in particular, see chapter 7, note 11.
4   Kymlicka 1995, 108. The controversial term, "benign neglect," was coined by Daniel Patrick Moynihan (see Marcus 2000).
5   Banks 1976d, 100; 1974, 55.
6   In a way, one could say that the main point of liberal pluralism, as it was initially conceived, was to try to *reduce* religion to the status of a mere interest group or voluntary association. This was never an easy job and if individuals retain strong ties to religion today that is not the doing of liberal pluralism.
7   This is implicit in anti-discrimination efforts, generally speaking, and it becomes explicit in policies like affirmative action and "disparate impact" analysis, where groups must not only be identified but weighed and compared. It is also clear in multicultural education's explicitly group-differentiated strategies—e.g., Banks's different teachings for "oppressed" groups, on the one hand, and for "dominant" groups, on the other.
8   Banks 1974, 52–54; emphasis omitted; 1972a, 268.
9   Banks 1990, 211; 1974, 45.
10 LaBelle and Ward 1994, 169; see Gollnick and Chinn 1990, 93–94; Nieto 1992, 228; Sleeter and Grant 1988, 178–82.
11 Opposition to assimilation in multicultural education is common. See, e.g., AACTE 1973, 264; Banks 1984c, 60; Gay 1994, 7; Sleeter and Grant 1988, 67, 100, 168, 201.
12 Banks 1981, 66; see 1984c, 60; 1994b, 127; Sleeter and Grant 1988, 64; 1994, 77.
13 A similar problem is to be found in opposition to the "melting pot" (also something of a mirage). See Gleason 1992; Powers 1999, chapter 3.
14 Banks 1987, 537. What eventually became Banks's "Multicultural Ideology" was in fact originally termed the "Pluralist-Assimilationist Ideology" (Banks 1975c, 172).
15 The US Supreme Court has declared diversity in the context of education to be a "compelling governmental interest," a step magnified in its importance because it was used to permit affirmative action policies to go forward despite seemingly important legalistic objections. See *Regents of the University of California v. Bakke* 438 U.S. 265 (1978); *Grutter v. Bollinger* 539 U.S. 306 (2003). For the impact of the *Bakke* decision on the use of the rhetoric of diversity in America, see Schuck 2003, 161–62; Wood 2003, 99–145. Both Schuck and Wood make the idea of diversity the center of their analysis of many of the same phenomena taken up in this book—in a way, the opposite of the approach I take. See also Ramaswamy 2021, 223–28.

16 See the discussion in chapter 4; see also, e.g., AACTE 1973, 264; NCATE 2008, 12. General appeals to diversity in multicultural education are ubiquitous. See, e.g., Banks 1991a, 33; 1994a, vi; 1997a, vii; U.S. Department of Education 1994, 1.

17 That the appeal to *diversity* in multicultural education is ultimately *defined*, politically, by the commitment to fighting discrimination may be seen very clearly by considering Gay's survey (1994, 2–4) of many different definitions of multicultural education and in the definitional statements of National Association for Multicultural Education 2003 and Iowa DOE 1989a, 7, 11, 14–17, 21.

18 Gay 1983, 563; see Cortés 2002, 14–16. Early on, Banks emphasized and championed multiethnic education (1976a, 33–34; see Banks 1976c, 1978a, 1981) while embracing multicultural education as well (see 1979b, 1984b). Later, he admitted that the distinction between multiethnic and multicultural education was "rarely made by other theorists and investigators" (Banks 1992a, 273; see 2013, 76–77). This parallels an earlier similar shift from Black studies to multiethnic studies; see 1973c, xii.

19 The strictly political meaning of diversity under liberal pluralism is also clear in Jefferson's praise of the diversity of *religious* groups in America (noted in chapter 7): "all good enough; all sufficient to preserve peace and order" (Jefferson 1944b, 276).

20 See chapter 1, note 5.

21 Mouffe 1993; see Mouffe 2005. The success of anti-discrimination puts radical theorists of the Left in a quandary. Generally speaking, the political is for theorists like Mouffe (and our postmodernist multiculturalists) a tool of domination or oppression by the powers that be. Because liberalism hides the political, Marxists and postmodernists were or are necessarily in the business of exposing its machinations. But anti-discrimination's success means that the political is out in the open; and drawing attention to anti-discrimination as a new instance of the political cannot but be at least politically costly. Mouffe wrestles with this problem and tries to avoid it: "No state or political order, even a liberal one, can exist without some form of exclusion, and pluralism can never be total. But it is very important to acknowledge those forms of exclusion for what they are and the violence that they may imply, instead of concealing them" (Mouffe 1994, 322). But if this means that the anti-discrimination regime is also necessarily exclusive (and implies "violence"?), it is unclear how acknowledging the fact helps either the excluded or the excluders.

I do not mean to say here that such a conception of politics, embraced by the radical Left or elsewhere, is in any sense an important *cause* of the success of the anti-discrimination regime, as some conservatives sometimes seem to imply. "All of Gramsci's most innovative ideas—for example that dominant and subordinate groups based on race, ethnicity, and gender are engaged in struggles over power; that the 'personal is political'; and that all knowledge and morality are social constructions—are assumptions at the very center of today's politics" (Fonte 2000, 18). Claims along these lines are especially common today in the conservative attack on critical race theory. "The CRT-influenced trainings that are often seen in America's workplaces and schools are little more than modern-day versions of the struggle sessions that Gramsci recommended for European workers in [the] 1920s" (Butcher and Gonzalez 2020, 26; see 5–6). The seemingly causal claims being made here between a Gramscian view of politics and anti-discrimination politics is hard to fathom. Politics in this instance has achieved all of this on its own. In fact, if the two are related it is mainly because something like Gramsci's view of hegemony is useful for describing the character of the latter (see Gramsci 1971).

Chapter 9

1 Johnson 1965, 842–43.
2 The comparative treatment of our two systems of pluralism in the preceding chapter deliberately abstracted at least to some degree from such concerns, without omitting the role of moral ideas entirely, so that we could treat them more directly now.
3 This is not to insist that morality is central, psychologically speaking, to the power of politics in human life. Fear or shame (and hence force and domination), on the one hand, and perceived self-interest are also very important. Each of these is influenced in a particular way, depending on the political regime, and each is bound up with the others, as well as with the regime's moral impulse, in a mix that it should be the job of political science to disentangle.
4 To some extent this study has already begun to raise—indeed, has been compelled to raise—critical inquiries about the anti-discrimination regime, and liberalism, along the way, in questions taking a variety of forms. At the outset it was necessary to emphasize how the anti-discrimination regime took shape precisely in response to limitations of liberalism. Highlighting multiculturalism's politics, in its history and in the logic it enunciates, was likewise a controversial step, at least from the depoliticized perspective of liberalism. Such a political orientation also compelled us to call into question multiculturalism's (and liberalism's) rhetoric of diversity and anti-assimilation. Likewise, to show that its novel political orientation challenges, erodes, and reworks the liberal moral and political framework in a number of ways is already to emphasize what is unsettling about it from the point of view of the traditional civic framework of American life (and vice versa). The various criticisms of the moral and political

visions of both liberalism and anti-discrimination that we have encountered in examining the tensions between them illuminate sometimes far-reaching questions that ought not to be disregarded simply because we discover them in the rough and tumble of political disagreement and debate.

5   *Planned Parenthood of Southeastern Pennsylvania v. Casey* 505 U.S. 833, 850 (1992); *Lawrence v. Texas* 539 U.S. 558, 571 (2003). See also the dissenting opinion (also relied upon by Kennedy in *Lawrence*) of Justice Stevens in *Bowers v. Hardwick* 478 U.S. 186, 216 (1986).

6   Wolfe 2001b; see 2001a.

7   It is of course true that the criminal law, for example, has far-reaching moral effects (and the examples here cited, i.e., prohibitions on abortion and sodomy) were once part of the criminal law. More generally, liberalism certainly asserts the moral claims of the social contract and politics based on consent. It also requires thoroughly liberal citizens who will obey the dictates of the social contract willingly, even when it is not to their own immediate advantage. Moreover, liberalism is associated with a particular way of life, the life of a commercial, technically-educated middle class. It is even perhaps legitimate to speak of liberal "virtues," as liberal values pluralist William Galston and others have insisted in recent years. But if there are virtues in liberal democracy, they are the modest or "thin" virtues—tolerance, moderation, obedience to law, self-reliance—of the social contract and the middle-class pursuit of comfortable self-preservation. Liberalism is not known for robust calls to "duty" or self-sacrifice, to justice as it has always been understood, as a commitment to putting others ahead of oneself. It may well be true that even mere obedience to the law (to say nothing of things like military service) amounts to a significant subordination of the individual to the community, a massive fact of great soul-shaping consequence; nevertheless, the question is not the reality of the situation but how the liberal theory of politics understands it.

8   Freund 1968, 41. Morroe Berger, a sociologist writing on the subject of the emerging anti-discrimination regime in the 1960s, wrestled with the same tension in revealing ways. On the one hand, Berger reflects liberal hesitations in his sense that anti-discrimination law seeks to regulate "acts while not attempting directly to affect prejudicial attitudes" (1968, 229). But his analysis focused on the question of what he held to be the likely effectiveness of anti-discrimination law in regards to a variety of different human types (following distinctions introduced by sociologist Robert Merton): "The prejudiced nondiscriminator, the unprejudiced discriminator, and those who acquire prejudice as they acquire other group values, as well as the 'indifferent equilibrium,' are all clearly susceptible to legal measures discouraging discrimination" (1968, 223; see Merton 1949). Berger thought legal policy "an effective means for reducing the discrimination or overt anti-minority conduct of the extremely prejudiced," in particular because, for the "extremely prejudiced," "one

of the few constants in their behavior is submission to the symbols of power," the law being the greatest such symbol (1968, 227). Overall, Berger went on to conclude, rightly, that "law can affect our *acts* and, through them, our *beliefs*" (1968, 237; emphasis in the original).

9   Koppelman 1996, 7, see also 197. The question of *how* this transformation in moral thinking is taking place would be an important one for political scientists to pursue.

Here we note Koppelman's effective response to anyone who would want to say that John Rawls's conception of liberalism is capacious enough to encompass all of contemporary anti-discrimination politics in an unproblematic way. As Koppelman argues, the suggestion that Rawlsian liberalism accommodates anti-discrimination policy by reference to his account of the place of the "social basis of self-esteem" is powerfully answered by reference to the question of freedom of speech and belief. Like identity and concerns of recognition or status, turning to "self-esteem," as Rawls does, would seem undeniably to move liberalism very far into what almost anybody would consider to be the realm of these "private" spheres. As Koppelman's analysis makes clear, precisely this element of Rawls's theory, which would seem to connect his version of liberalism with anti-discrimination policy, has powerfully illiberal tendencies. As Koppelman points out, Rawls's theory permits for overriding the basic rights and liberties of his scheme in certain circumstances, since, as Rawls says, "below a certain level of material *and social* well-being . . . people simply cannot take part as citizens, much less equal citizens" (Rawls 1993, 166; the emphasis is added by Koppelman). Koppelman goes on to state the implications of this fact from the perspective of his own more thoroughgoing commitment to anti-discrimination:

> Since what is most important is that every citizen have an adequate minimum of primary goods, and since "self-respect and a sure confidence in the sense of one's worth is perhaps the most important primary good," the parties in the original position should not shrink from state programs of *totalitarian reeducation* where these would enhance the self-respect of the least advantaged. For example, if the teachings of the church in a predominantly Catholic country are having the effect of damaging the self-respect of Jews or homosexuals, then the state should be entitled, and perhaps is required, to order the church to change its teachings. Can Rawls avoid this conclusion, which would destroy his theory's claim to be liberal? (1996, 197; emphasis added).

Without claiming, on the basis of the problems Koppelman brings to light, that Rawls is not a liberal, one could insist that this particular problem points to a significant and deep tension between his scheme of guaranteeing the primary goods and basic notions of freedom and the public-private divide normally associated with liberalism. Rawls elsewhere seems to try to retreat from the illiberal consequences of this aspect of his position by redefining self-esteem, but, as Koppelman shows, Rawls is not completely successful in evading the deepest implications of arguments from politicized self-esteem (see Koppelman 1996, 197–203; Rawls 1993, 318–20). Others on the civil rights Left criticize Rawls on different grounds, suggesting other tensions between his account of liberalism and the needs of the anti-discrimination impulse (see, e.g., Okin 2005; Young 1990, 1995, 2006).

10 Now one might object here that liberalism itself regulates the interpersonal relations of individuals directly and with vigor, in the criminal law and in the name of the morality of the social contract and bourgeois virtue (see note 7 above). This objection was raised in a conversation I had with Andrew Koppelman who, somewhat to my surprise (see Koppelman 1996; note 9 above; and chapter 1, note 4), wanted to deny that anti-discrimination policy breaks with liberalism as emphatically as I suggest it does.

11 *Heart of Atlanta Motel v. United States* 379 U.S. 241, 250 (1964) (quoting a report of the Senate Commerce Committee).

12 See *United States v. Carolene Products Co.* 304 U.S. 144 (1938); *McGowan v. Maryland* 366 U.S. 429 (1961); *San Antonio School District v. Rodriguez* 411 U.S. 1 (1973).

13 See the discussion of the regulation of speech in chapter 3.

14 Banks 1974, 45, 60 (emphasis in the original); 1980, 122.

15 For prejudice reduction, see chapter 5, note 35 and accompanying text. For reflective self-analysis, see Banks and Banks 1995, 151–53, 156. For the new history, see the sections "Change the Center" and "Civic Education as Political Pedagogy" in chapter 5.

16 See Bolotin 2021; Bruell 2011, 93–94. There is something to the claim that the conditions for moral revolution were set by a moral vacuum in liberal societies. Speaking politically, and in the context of liberalism's relationship with anti-discrimination politics, one would need to qualify it by reference to the moral appeal of modernity as a successful (more or less) project, the power of modern realist moralism, and the impressive victory of liberalism over its moralistic rival, communism. (The last point must, however, be tempered by the fact that against communism liberalism was allied with religion, whereas today religion has to some considerable degree accommodated itself to the anti-discrimination regime.) The fact that neither Banks nor the postmodernist multiculturalists launch an all-out assault on the morality of freedom likewise suggests that liberalism's essential moral appeal still has life. One would also need to take into account the very special circumstances of the civil rights revolution's moment of victory (in the wake of World War II and the Holocaust), liberalism's moral blind spot with respect to private-sector discrimination in particular, and the clearly illiberal legacy of slavery with which

liberalism had to contend. It is also worth noting in this context that almost all contemporary resistance to the perceived excesses of some aspects of anti-discrimination politics has been anchored in appeals to freedom of *speech*. This amounts to a significant reduction of the liberal stance; it also suggests that those we might call liberals today have to some degree forgotten how to talk about liberalism and to make use of its moral and non-moral resources, in a broad, flexible, informed, and far-seeing way. But this is not to deny the basic thrust of the claim: de-moralizing the political domain, as liberalism tries to do, comes at a price. See Pangle 2010, esp. 89.

17 Nieto 1992, 253; see Wilson 1992.
18 A useful confirmation of this is provided in "Beyond Tolerance" and "Repressive Tolerance," essays published in 1965 by Robert Paul Wolff and Herbert Marcuse. While advancing a very radical attack on toleration (for Marcuse, as precisely "protecting the already established machinery of discrimination"), these essays do not show any evidence of the workings of a distinctive moral sensibility tied to the civil rights revolution. Neither essay makes use of any of the recognizable moral terms we now associate with the latter, not even the idea of "respect" (commonly opposed today to toleration). Marcuse does refer to identity at a couple of points, and while he uses the term in a way that could be said to be headed in the direction of something like our contemporary use, his concerns nonetheless mainly reflect older influences, particularly the morality of freedom (his discussion of identity is connected to the problem of "alienation," and the question is taken up precisely in light of the "movement . . . under way against the evils of oppression and the need for being oneself") (Marcuse 1965, 115). Wolff is even more concerned than Marcuse that toleration fails from the point of view of individual freedom (see Wolff 1965, 38, 43–47).
19 Prominent among such works (some of which are partly critical) are Appiah 2005; Baumeister 2000; Connolly 1991; Creppell 2003; Deveux 2000; Fraser and Honneth 2003; Galeotti 2002; Gutmann 2003; Habermas 1998; Honneth 1995; Koppelman 1996; Markell 2003; Minow 1997; Norton 1988; Patten 2014; Phillips 1995; Shklar 1991; Taylor 1992, 1998; Williams 1998; Young 1990, 2000.
20 For a penetrating discussion of the "method" employed by political theorists of the analytical school on moral matters, see Goldberg 1990, 12–31.

Chapter 10

1 See chapter 8.
2 The one-to-one correspondence of table 2 in chapter 9 is perhaps overly clear/simple and it is offered only as a starting point; no doubt more could be

said about how different terms on either side of the divide relate to every one of the concepts on the other side of the line. For identity versus interest, for example, see Smith 2004; for identity versus toleration, see Creppell 2003.

3   Prior to the civil rights revolution, identity was a term with several different meanings—serving various purposes in philosophy, psychology, and the social sciences —that could be said to be subpolitical or at least independent of any specific political outlook. As Philip Gleason points out, "the black revolution of the 1960s and the subsequent emergence of the new ethnicity changed all that. These movements affirmed the durability of ethnic consciousness, gave it legitimacy and dignity, and forged an even more intimate bond between the concepts of ethnicity and identity" (Gleason 1992, 142). Generally speaking, as Appiah suggests, taking "identity" too seriously, in the abstract, is a mistake: "If what matters about me is my individual and authentic self, why is there so much contemporary talk of identity about large categories—race, gender, ethnicity, nationality, sexuality—that seem so far from individual?" (Appiah 1994, 122; see Griffiths 2015; Minow 1997, 30). The connection between anti-discrimination politics and the development early on of "social identity theory" is particularly clear. Banks's employment of the concept of identity as it was used in social psychology theory fits here as well (Banks relies on the work of Tajfel). (For social identity theory, see, above all, Gleason's excellent discussion, 1992, 127–43. See also Smith 2004, 303; Weigert, Teitge, and Teitge 1986, 24–26; Weinrich 2003. For the relationship between Banks and Tajfel, see Banks 1972b, 1973d, 1974; Tajfel 1970.) The formative role of anti-discrimination politics is also clear in the deployment of the concept of identity in social movement theory (see Cohen 1985; Melucci 1995; and the essays in Johnston, Larana, and Gusfield 1994) and in postmodernist social construction theory (see Gergen 1994). More broadly, it is no exaggeration to say that the identity concept has transformed both the form and substance of social science in the United States, making older analyses of "interests" or "class" or "power" or "rational actors" seem relatively unsophisticated. For useful surveys of this large literature, see also Abdelal et al. 2006, 2009; Côté 2006; Egan 2020; Fearon 1999; Smith 2004. For generally favorable accounts of, or attempts at "theories of," the *politics* of identity developed by political *theorists*, see Gutmann 2003; Minow 1997. For critical accounts of the latter, see Fukuyama 2018; Gitlin 1993; Lilla 2017; Michaels 2006. Taylor's discussion of identity (by way of a consideration of "the self" and "authenticity") offers an account of this "powerful moral ideal that has come down to us" (1991, 29; see 1989), but his emphasis on intellectual history, and his tendency to blur the difference between liberty and identity concerns, render it less useful than it might otherwise be. For the postmodernist critique of identity, see chapter 6, note 32 and accompanying text.

4   Banks 1999a, 92–93. Similarly, social theorists Chantal Mouffe and Paul Holdengräber call for "transform[ing] the identity of different groups so that

the demands of each group could be articulated with those of others according to the principle of democratic equivalence. For it is not a matter of establishing a mere alliance between given interests but of actually modifying the very identity of these forces" (Mouffe and Holdengräber 1989, 42).

5   Efforts to put liberty and identity together are common among political theorists. See Creppell 2003; Gutmann 2003; Habermas 1998; Jung 2006; Kymlicka 1989, 1995; Minow 1997; Spinner 1994; Taylor 1989, 28; Tully 1995. Appiah (2018; see also 2005) provides thoughtful reflections on the liberty-identity question.

6   See, e.g., Bevier 1978.

7   In the discussion that follows I am indebted in a general way to Kymlicka, although more for his argument from liberty than for his argument from identity (his account of multiculturalism makes the case for the importance of both without squarely facing the obvious tensions between them). For Kymlicka on liberty, see 1989, chapter 1; 1995, 75–84.

8   If we knew the good, liberty would of course be superfluous, and even possibly an obstacle to what is most important—a misleading temptation or confusion. This is one reason soft skepticism is so important in the scheme of liberal pluralism, given its practical aim of civic peace above all (and perhaps reflected in the choice of many for comfortable self-preservation, the conformity of modern bourgeois life, etc.).

9   A general identitarian critique of liberty does not really exist, so far as I know, at least not in the context of anti-discrimination politics. For an account of freedom by a political theorist that parallels Banks's discussion, see King 1992 (see also Connolly 1991, 199). King distinguishes precisely what he terms "liberal freedom" (an inadequate stance from his point of view) from three additional kinds of freedom that must be embraced to give full expression to the civil rights movement's achievements: "freedom as autonomy" (expressed in "the powerful idea(l) of 'somebodyness' and 'self-respect'"), "participatory freedom," and "freedom as collective deliverance" (King 1992, 26–28).

10 The claim that groups having ascriptive identities are more deserving of anti-discrimination's protections than those where personal choice is involved (a distinction that matches amazingly well the anti-discrimination versus liberalism dichotomy) is initially powerful. But it fails more or less immediately for the very simple political reason that it excludes some people unfairly from the protections of anti-discrimination law (those who would themselves say—as some religious people and some gays and lesbians do, for example—that their identity is, in some way, or to some degree, chosen). The solution to this problem has likewise been political: it turns out that *any* view of identity—whether ascriptive, or chosen, or something in between—is fine so long as it may be said to help protect members of a given group from discrimination. What the groups in question share, obviously, is an experience of discrimination and,

above all, the protections of the law. It must be said that today it is ultimately the law, and not any psychological or social or other fact, that defines what is or is not included in our notions of the kinds of groups or diversity that matter or ought to matter. There is a sizeable scholarly debate on this question. See, for example, the chapters on the "Debate Concerning the Extent of Choice versus No Choice in the Nature of Sexual Orientation" in Garnets and Kimmel 2003. See also, e.g., Powell, Shapiro, and Stein 2016; Whisman 1996.

11 For multicultural education, see AACTE 1973, 264; Appelbaum 2002, 135; Nieto 1994. Banks sometimes embraces the language of toleration but more commonly adopts the standard of respect; see chapter 5, note 66 and accompanying text. For the political theorists, see, e.g., Brown 2006, 10, 46–47; Galeotti 2002, 227. Some political theorists employ the new, higher standard against toleration, without necessarily noting the new political necessity for doing so: see, e.g., Chaplin 1993; Connolly 2005, 125; Deveaux 2000, 57–64; McKinnon and Castiglione 2002. I do not include here Marcuse's famous 1965 essay "Repressive Tolerance" because its criticisms of toleration are not made to any important degree from the point of view of the civil rights revolution (see chapter 9, note 18). Some theorists would try to blur the difference between toleration and respect. For "toleration as recognition," see Galeotti 2002; for "toleration as respect," see McClain 1998. See also Creppell 2003, 155; Fitzmaurice 1993; Gardner 1993; Forst 2002.

12 See Washington 1997b, 767; James 1899, 45–46; Kallen 1924, 61; 1954, 12–14.

13 For a useful survey of the Left critique of merit in the context of anti-discrimination law, see Roithmayr 1998.

14 Banks 1997a, 5–6; see chapter 5, notes 69–71 and accompanying text.

15 Writers in a variety of fields—multicultural education, law, political theory—have recourse to some version of the idea. Geneva Gay, for example, in an essay on educational equality, argues that "third generation desegregation represents a pedagogical revolution that employs . . . an ideological agenda that celebrates and promotes culturally different lifestyles, experiences, and heritages as being of equal status and worth" (Gay 1990, 61). Formulations by legal scholars like Kenneth Karst (his conception of "equal citizenship" centered on "those aspects of equality that are most closely bound to the sense of self and the sense of inclusion in a community") or Koppelman (a "right to be free from social stigma") express something similar (Karst 1989, 3; Koppelman 1996, 59). So, too, do political theorists who step back and extend the basic idea not to groups but to "cultures," as in Taylor's idea of a "presumption of equal worth" among cultures or Drucilla Cornell and Sara Murphy's "recognition of the equal dignity . . . of cultures" (Taylor 1992, 64, 72; Cornell and Murphy 2002, 441; see Cornell 1995, 200; Thomas 1983). Alan Patten's *Equal Recognition,* an extension of the Kymlicka debate, offers a

16 A telling sign of the limit of the concept of identity is that nobody proposes an ideal of equal group identity.
17 Memo, Moynihan to Secretary of Labor Willard Wirtz, April 20, 1964. Quoted in Davies 1996, 66.
18 For a helpful overview of a range of different group rights theories, see Jones 1999. The territory covered by "group rights" also appears as a variety of kinds of arguments for "collective rights," "collective human rights," "minority rights," "community rights," "corporate rights," or the "rights of oppressed groups." Useful introductions to the debate over group rights are provided by the essays in the edited volumes *Group Rights* (Baker 1994), *Ethnicity and Group Rights* (Shapiro and Kymlicka 1997a), and *Groups and Group Rights* (Sistare, May, and Francis 2000). For the other terms listed, see, e.g., Felice 1996; Gould 2000; Jones 1999; Kymlicka 1994; Lerner 1991; Sigler 1983; Van Dyke 1982 (some of these are discussed at least in part in a critical vein). Highlighting once again the difference between the new and the old, group rights are commonly criticized from the point of view of *individual* rights. See Glazer 1983, chapter 13, "Individual Rights against Group Rights"; Guinier 1994, 269n25; Jones 1999, 81–82; Shapiro and Kymlicka 1997b, 6–7. Other criticisms concern groups, their inability reliably to form an intention and act (Nickel 1997, 237–38; see Young 1990, 183–91; 1997, 369), and the inadvisability of applying the language of "rights" always and everywhere (Tamir 1999, 158). Finally, universal group rights theories must also reckon with the long history of the doings of "groups," well-known not only for violating individual rights but also, of course, for discrimination and worse. "Group rights may . . . seem to license group oppression" (Jones 1999, 94; for an extended discussion of this point, see Graff 1994).
19 One very striking example of the practical or political importance of this understanding of equity is visible in the civil rights initiatives of the Biden administration. See especially Biden's 2020 Executive Order 13985 (see chapter 6, note 14). The order specifies the goal of "closing racial gaps in wages, housing credit, lending opportunities, and access to higher education" as part of a broad "Equity Assessment" to be undertaken throughout the agencies of the federal government. See also Dessources Figures and Lhamon 2021.
20 Williams 1998, 176–77; emphasis added. See also Guinier 1994, 26, 76, 141, 194n9; Mansbridge 1999, 628.
21 There is another sizeable academic literature here. For arguments employing a principle of compensatory justice in the context of anti-discrimination questions, see, e.g., Boxill 2003; Butt 2013; Gould 2000, 51; Taylor 1973. See

also Justice Thurgood Marshall's dissenting opinion in *Richmond v. J.A. Croson Co.*, 488 U.S. 469, 552 (1989). Historian Hugh Davis Graham goes so far as to define the Left perspective in civil rights debate as "a "new theory of compensatory justice" (1990, 456). For usefully informed presentations of the arguments in the reparations debate in particular, see Levmore 2004 (for) and Posner and Vermeule 2003 (against).

22 For the arguments against compensatory justice in the context of anti-discrimination politics, see, e.g., Nagel 1973; Nickel 1972; Sunstein 1991; Waldron 1992.

23 *Richmond v. J.A. Croson Co.*, 488 U.S. 469, 498 (1989); *Regents of the University of California v. Bakke* 438 U.S. 265, 307 (1978).

24 Political theorists who embrace the banner of "inclusion" include Habermas 1998; McKinnon 2000; Minow 1990; Shklar 1991; Taylor 1998; Young 2000. Similar theories are advanced under related terms; for "voice," see, e.g., Williams 1998; for "presence," see Phillips 1995. For critical reflections on inclusion as a moral ideal, see Dryzek 1996; Edwards, Armstrong, and Miller 2001; Rosenblum 1998, 97–99; Taylor 1998.

25 Banks 1991a, 33.

26 See, generally, Celis 2012; Dovi 2007; Hayat 2019; Guinier 1994; Mansbridge 1999; 2003; Phillips 1995; Williams 1998; Young 1990, 183–91. "Descriptive" and "mirror representation" are widely used terms. For "pictorial," see Phillips 1998, 226; for "substantive," see Celis 2012; for "positive discrimination," see Norris 1997 (focusing on Europe); for the "theory of fair representation for marginalized groups," see Williams 1998, 5.

27 Williams 1998, 71; emphasis in the original. Williams (1998, 269n93) quotes also Anne Phillips's formula to the same effect; see Phillips 1993, 99. It is worth noting that Guinier called for measures going *beyond* proportionality (holding proportionality to be inadequate to the interests of American Blacks in particular [see 1994, 42–43, 54–69]). She proposed in addition more radical strategies, like a "minority veto on critical minority issues" and "cumulative voting" and "supermajority voting" in legislative bodies (1994, 108, see 16–17, 116–17, 260n119). See Kesler 2022, 51.

28 See chapter 3, note 46 and accompanying text.

29 Rules 6 and 7 of the "Delegate Selection Rules for the 2020 Democratic National Convention" (Democratic National Committee 2018, 7, 9). Similar related representational schemes are also incorporated in state Democratic Party operations (see, e.g., Wisconsin Democratic Party 2020, the section of the delegate selection document entitled "Affirmative Action Plan and Outreach and Inclusion Program"). See also Schnall 2005.

30 The works cited by Atsusaka 2021 include more than thirty published since 2010 that fit this description. See also Arnesen and Peters 2017; Atkeson and Carrillo 2007; Clayton, O'Brien, and Piscipo 2019; Hayat 2019; Hayes and Hibbing 2017; Tremblay 2019.

31 *Reynolds v. Sims* 377 U.S. 533, 558 (1964).
32 Low-Beer 1984, 177; see Williams 1998, 27–28, 57.
33 *Shaw v. Reno* 509 U.S. 630, 657 (1993).
34 The history of representation in liberal democratic countries, including the United States, finds a place for the representation of interests or concerns that have nothing to do with individualism (even if the alternative is not always readily or easily subsumed under the heading of "groups"). The main issue in the United States is the role of *states* in federal elections, especially in the US Senate and the Electoral College, which reflects something other than the one person, one vote mandate. On the tension between liberal ideals of representation and geographic districting or territorial representation, in particular, see Guinier 1994, chapter 5; Williams 1998, 37–38, 70–75. For examples of representational practices in liberal democratic countries (to include the United States) that do not follow any obviously "liberal" logic, see Levy 1997, 43; Van Dyke 1977, 350–57; 1982, 24, 27–31.
35 *Shaw v. Reno* 509 U.S. 630, 657 (1993).
36 For "politics of racial hostility, see *Richmond v. J.A. Croson Co.*, 488 U.S. 469, 493 (1989). The term "racial spoils system" was used by Assistant Attorney General for Civil Rights William Bradford Reynolds (who served under Ronald Reagan) (Reynolds 1989, 995). The strongest meaning of color-blind constitutionalism, it seems to me, lies in its realism about the dangers of racial politics, not in the moral principles ("neutrality," e.g.) that it may invoke.
37 See Glazer 1983, 272; Epstein 1992b, 884–86.
38 See Thernstrom and Thernstrom 1997, 480, 485.
39 *Holder v. Hall* 512 U.S. 874, 907 (1994).
40 See Epstein 1992b, 876. See also Justice William O. Douglas's famous statement in *Wright v. Rockefeller* 376 U.S. 52, 67 (1964).
41 Responses from the Left to conservative arguments about social disunity and conflict are not central to the former, but they are made. See, e.g., Williams 1998, 180–81, 197–98.
42 This is another large literature. See Fraser and Honneth 2003; Honneth 1995; Patten 2014; Taylor 1992; Tully 2004.
43 See also the critique of recognition from a very similar point of view (emphasizing its tendency to neglect "respect" and claims of equality) by Cornell and Murphy (2002, see esp. 422, 440–41).
44 Taylor and Honneth are surely attentive to the moral dimension of claims for recognition; but labels matter and at the very least their framing of the issues in the language of recognition *minimizes* the moral claims being made. Taylor's account of the politics of recognition, which has been especially influential in the United States, weaves together three different strands of analysis. First is a layer of general psychological reflection on the workings of recognition and group-based recognition. Second is a complicated tracing out of several different strands

of intellectual history to help us think about the origins, logic, and problems with the politics of recognition (discussing Rousseau, Kant, Herder, John Stuart Mill, and Franz Fanon; see 1992, 28–32, 44–60). Third is a proper awareness of the role of the civil rights revolution as explaining its contemporary prominence (1992, 38–39, 64–65). His analysis offers something to both defenders and critics (recognition is an undeniably important dimension of political life and so attention must be paid; recognition is not an altogether reputable dimension of political life and so one may have doubts). But it demonstrates the limitations of using the history of modern political theory to explain multiculturalism. Precisely by combining an intellectual history that can show antecedents in the West for something like a politics of recognition, Taylor's discussion serves both to weaken our sense that something novel and unprecedented is at work in multiculturalism and to obscure the extent to which it is in tension with the liberal tradition. His strictly political discussion, on the other hand, implicitly highlights the tension between the new and the old. The overall result of the incompletely digested combination of different kinds of insights on offer is to give everyone something to think about, but not in a way that ever directly confronts the most important questions that multiculturalism poses. The scholarly debate over recognition and its relation to *redistribution*, on the other hand, is an internal one for the Left that largely ignores the bigger question of the relationship between recognition politics and the liberal tradition. See, e.g., Fish 2007a; Fraser 2000, 2013; Fraser and Honneth 2003; Genovese 1995; Gitlin 1995, 236–37; Michaels 2006, 2016; Rorty 1997, 2000.

45 For Aristotle's critical reflections on recognition or honor, see *Nicomachean Ethics* (2011, 6 [1095b23–30]).
46 Forbes 2019, 133. See also Horowitz 1985, 196; Forbes 1997. Others make the same point, starting from "identity" (see Kateb 1994, 526; Kukathas 2003, 251).
47 Taylor points to this when he says, "What has come about with the modern age is not the need for recognition but the conditions in which the attempt to be recognized can fail" (1992, 35). While I agree that "failing" to be recognized is where trouble starts, I do not see why this would be a problem specific only to the "modern age." For Taylor this is the result of the fact that in modern life "inwardly derived, personal, original identity" has to "win" recognition, unlike recognition in the premodern world, where recognition is "built into" identity "based on social categories that everyone took for granted" (1992, 34). Since the politics of recognition pertains to groups, not individuals, this does not seem to me to be highly relevant. This is one of the places where Taylor's preference for intellectual history rather than political history gets him into trouble (see note 44 above).
48 Koppelman 1996, 9; see Brest 1976, 8; Lim and Melling 2014.
49 Taylor's discussion in *Reconciling the Solitudes* of what he terms a "dialectic of misunderstanding," rooted in recognition anxieties, somewhat understates the

problem (1993, 196–97), but his treatment there is more useful in my view than his essay on the politics of recognition (1992).
50 Banks 1974, 61; Fantini 1972, 17.
51 See the discussion in chapter 3.
52 Brown 1995, 74. All citations in this section are to Brown's works unless otherwise indicated. That Brown's analysis of "politicized identity" ("the dominant political expression of the age—identity politics" [1995, 74]) is an account of anti-discrimination politics is clear enough at points, as the quotation taken from pages 26–27 immediately suggests (see also 1995, 65). But Brown's ultimate position is obscured to some degree by a certain wariness and qualification. "It is important to be clear here. I am not impugning antidiscrimination law concerned with eliminating barriers to equal access to education, employment, and so forth" (1995, 27). It is also worth noting that Brown is at the same time a trenchant critic of liberalism; her book *Regulating Aversion* is a detailed critique of the liberal ideal of toleration, sometimes explicitly from the perspective of anti-discrimination politics (2006, esp. 46–47). At points, Brown diminishes the role of anti-discrimination law and seems to treat it as if it were mainly an offshoot of liberalism. There is also a strand of her argument that suggests the problem is not *ressentiment* in identity politics (her main focus) but the codification and universalization of it in the law (which might seem then to be part of her critique of liberalism) (see 1995, 27–28, 70). Were Brown to see more clearly the differences between liberalism and anti-discrimination, she might well see that it is the latter that is the main or even the sole true target of her *ressentiment* analysis. In any event, at other points Brown provides a number of other objections to anti-discrimination politics, in critiques of its universalism (1995, 64–65; 2005, 128), its inadvertent support for capitalism (1995, 61), and, in arresting Foucauldian assessments, its tendency to moralism and thought control (2006, chapter five; 1995, 133).
53 "Today's social justice warriors of the radical left embody a toxic combination of the Nietzschean will to power and Puritan moralism" (Mitchell 2020, 9).
54 Brown 1995, 27. Using statistical analysis, two Canadian academics went so far as to study the variation in the "Attribution of Blame" to be found in different (radical and less radical) approaches to multicultural education: "Students in the anti-racist group significantly increased their attribution scores compared to the other two groups (p < .05). This result indicated that students who studied the anti-racist program put more blame on government policies and other Canadians for the current situation among First Nations people" (Kehoe and Segawa 1995, 61). See also the study by two multicultural education scholars exploring how "race informed guilt and shame" can contribute to "achiev[ing] a more resolute commitment to social justice" (Estrada and Matthews 2016, 314).

55 Brown 1995, 70, quoting Nietzsche 1967, 36; 1954, 252; 1967, 123, 124.
56 Brown 1995, 73–74, quoting Nietzsche 1967, 123 ("the priest alters the direction of *ressentiment*"). See also Nietzsche 1967, 128, 134, where similar formulations are used.
57 Brown 1995, 70, quoting Nietzsche 1967, 34.
58 Berns 1987, 227.
59 Aristotle 2011, 164 [1155a23].

Chapter 11

1 Aristotle 1984, 119; 1289a4–5.
2 For the liberal side of the divide, see Bernstein 2003; 2010; 2019; Bolick 1996, chapter 3; Caldwell 2020; Davies 1996; Epstein 1991; 1992a, 3, 412; Roberts and Stratton 1995, 14. (For a critical response from the Left, see Bagenstos 2014.) Gottfried (2002) may be counted here as well (though his own position is not simply reducible to liberalism). Melnick certainly emphasizes the evidence for such an interpretation in his account of Title IX (2018, 155–58, 189–92), but he does not draw the general conclusion in a direct way. On the anti-discrimination side, see Koppelman 1996, esp. 197–203 (for an interesting discussion of the ambition of Koppelman's 1996 book, see Hills 1997). See also Loury 2002, 120–144. Postmodernist multiculturalists and postmodernist politics of difference writers may be counted alongside Koppelman, since they explicitly and indeed energetically reject liberalism and do so in the context of diversity politics (see chapter 6, notes 49 and 50). However, partly because they take anti-discrimination for granted and partly because their radicalism leads them sometimes to criticize anti-discrimination *law* (an exaggeration; see chapter 6, notes 54 and 55), they do not bring the tensions between the new and the old into focus in a helpful way.

Desmond King and Rogers Smith, advocating a "racial orders approach," do hint in the direction of a proper appreciation of the transformative power of the anti-discrimination regime when they speak of a new "transformative egalitarian racial order" or "transformative egalitarian order" operating in American politics, although this idea is narrowly focused, for the most part, on matters of race (like Banks's early narrow focus on "ethnic studies" and then "multi-ethnicity," instead of the later expansion in his work to multiculturalism) (King and Smith 2005, 75, 82–83; cf. 78; see also Smith 1997). This framework suffers, however, by substituting the ordinary language of politics with abstractions that blur the difference between traditional liberalism ("the Declaration" is at one point said to display "an incipient 'transformative egalitarian' order" [77]) and the anti-discrimination regime (82–83). In any event, this idea is not fully developed by King and Smith, who are themselves much more concerned with identifying the "ascriptive Americanist" and "white supremacist" orders of the past. See also the brief discussion at the end of this chapter. (For criticism of this position from the Left, see the overview provided in Sears 2017.) An even clearer blurring of the liberal/anti-discrimination divide is at work in Vivek Ramaswamy's very different call (following law professor Jed Rubenfeld) for a variety of expansions of anti-discrimination law, combined with borrowings from the law of free speech and religious freedom (now amplified and extended to the private sector), a scheme designed to provide Whites, males, and Christians with tools to defend themselves in the current legal environment (2021, 240–60). Some such convoluted legal arrangement may well be what the future holds: cramming more and more anti-discrimination into our laws, and legislating freedom in an aggressive way on top of that, to the point where the machinery of the regime is overwhelmed and we reach a kind of stalemate. That will not make the tension between liberalism and anti-discrimination disappear but it does mean that some effort will continue to have to be made to see it.

3 See Ackerman 2014; Belz 1991, 7–10; Berns 1987, 227; Berrey 2015; Bumiller 1988, 114–15; Chafe 1986; Chavez 1998; Dobbin 2009; Eastland 1996; Elazar 1993, 45; Fiss 1976; Glazer 1997, 12; Gordon 1981; Graham 1990, 456; Higham 1993, 195–97; Horton 2005; Karst 1989, 32–42; Kesler 2021, 161; Klinkner and Smith 1999, 287; Lawson 1986, 44; Lee 2014, 156–75; Moynihan 1967, 47; Oleske 2015; Ravitch 1990; Schlesinger 1992, 39–41; Schmidt 2021; Shklar 1991, 38; Skrentny 2002, 84; 2014; Sowell 1984, 37–39. For those deploying the concept of "racial liberalism" (which blurs the difference between liberalism and anti-discrimination in a different way), see chapter 2, note 1.

Some commentators treat anti-discrimination as part of a broader "rights revolution" that includes New Deal and welfare/regulatory state reforms, as in Bruce Ackerman's "New Deal-Civil Rights regime" formulation (Ackerman 2014; see, e.g., Lee 2014; Suk 2006; Sunstein 1990, v; Walker 1998). Others see Great Society "entitlement" politics as one key, prior, contributing force (Davies 1996; Gottfried 2002; Caldwell 2020). While such approaches may represent some improvement upon the standard interpretation, they still work to obscure the distinctive character of the anti-discrimination revolution as a separate shaping cause of American politics. The civil rights revolution is not reducible to the New Deal or the Great Society, and it goes beyond them in at least three respects: the former but not the latter engages in the deliberate, open, and unapologetic regulation of society, of speech, and of thought (to include moral opinion). (The New Deal and Great Society, like liberalism, may or may not have achieved these things in fact, but they did not endorse or openly proclaim them.)

4 Graham 1990, 456. Many of those commentators mentioned in note 3 take

this position and not only those who oppose affirmative action. See Belz 1991; Berns 1987, 227; Davies 1996; Glazer 1975; Gordon 1981; Higham 1993; Kesler 2021, 161; Skrentny 2002; Sowell 1984. See also Caldwell 2020, 29–35, 171; Ramaswamy 2021, 223–28.

5 Obviously there are exceptions like Wendy Brown and Stanley Fish, but they are not typical postmodernists.
6 See the brief discussion of the expansion of Title VII to include stereotypes in chapter 3.
7 *Bostock v. Clayton County* 140 S.Ct. 1731 (2020).
8 See note 4 above.
9 Christopher Caldwell's *The Age of Entitlement* (2020) alleges in detail that the anti-discrimination regime's war on racial inequality has challenged many such practices, and provides a sweeping (and to me, plausible) accounting of the costs: mounting national debt; the fragmenting of the family structure; the 2008 housing crisis; law enforcement challenges; immigration policy difficulties; and the rise of high-tech billionaires and the new class division they represent. See 108–19, 166, 178–83, 200–208, 243, 258–69. See 178 for the general claim.
10 Voltaire 1901, 289, 291.
11 For the tendency of social scientists to assume that anti-discrimination is liberal, see note 3 above. For political science studies of anti-discrimination politics and political parties, see chapter 3, note 60. See also note 13 below and accompanying text and chapter 1, note 18.
12 Although the idea of such a political science is simple, this does not mean that in practice the examination of politics is a simple matter. To begin with, politics is always to some degree hidden (the generality of "law" is the most important strategy it employs; liberalism provides many others). But the political order, its logic, its design, may also in some instances be to some degree unseeing; as a consequence the regime is often unclear about its aims, perhaps indeed to itself. As even Aristotle admits, "most of the usages existing among most [peoples] are, so to speak, a mere jumble, nevertheless if the laws anywhere look to one thing, it is domination that all of them aim at" (1984, 200 [1324b5–6]). A weaker way of speaking of this is by reference to certain "unintended consequences" of legal and political reform (the expansion of discrimination liability and the privatization of anti-discrimination enforcement that followed, for example, or the extension of anti-discrimination to the politics of religion).
13 Smith 1993, 558; 1995, 991; King and Smith 2005, 75; see Smith 1997, 2003, 2007.

INDEX

accreditation standards, multicultural education, 9, 69, 76, 81–82
act-belief distinction
    anti-discrimination and, 237
    liberal religion teaching, 420–21n13
activist-reformers, multicultural education and, 5–6, 68, 82–84
affirmative action, 47, 60–63
    consequences of, 62–63, 65, 283–84
    conservative overemphasis (and distorting effect), 60–61, 276–78
    limits, political, 256, 258, 261
    See also disparate treatment vs. disparate impact
age discrimination, 41, 386n22
Agency Equity Teams, 46, 47
Allport, Gordon, 405–6n70
American Association of Colleges for Teacher Education (AACTE), 69, 78, 79, 83,
American Federation of Labor, 31
American Teachers Association, 76
analytical philosophy
    criticism of, 246
    moral and political thought, approach to, 117, 201
    multiculturalism and, 15, 126
    utility of, theorists as evidence of new morality, 244–45
    See also Kymlicka; Rawls
anti-assimilation
    liberal pluralism, 18, 225

multiculturalism, 18, 225, 228, 232
anti-discrimination law, 41–49
    civil-criminal hybrid, 58–60
    constitutional stature, 65
    corrective firing and, 49, 55–57, 280, 288–89
    disparate treatment vs. disparate impact, 41, 61, 65, 73, 174, 283–84, 388n45
    domains of life regulated, 44–45
    groups (protected classes) and, 47–48. *See also* group politics: multiculturalism as harassment
    institutions of, governmental, 45–47
    interpersonal relations, regulation of, 40, 49–51
    legal center of (Title VII expansions), 41–44
    liability. *See* employer liability, expansion of (Title VII)
    limited by public-private distinction (pre-1964), 26–31, 212, 213, 380–82nn 7, 8
    "preventive and corrective measures", 42, 54, 58
    private sector regulation (post-1964) and, 30–34, 44, 48–58, 63–67, 217–18, 277, 288–89
    society, regulation of, 40, 49–51
    speech, regulation of, 20, 40, 51–53, 57, 63–64, 204, 217–18, 240, 280–81, 429–30n9, 441n3

443

anti-discrimination law (*cont'd*)
  stereotype prohibitions, 41–42, 51, 282–83
  See also anti-discrimination regime; Civil Rights Act of 1964; enforcement, anti-discrimination; *specific regulations*
Antidiscrimination Law and Social Equality (Koppelman), 376n4
anti-discrimination regime
  citizen enforcement role, 48, 53–55, 63, 217–18, 288–89
  education and: civic education, multicultural education as, 6–8, 11–12, 91, 98, 103–11, 128, 291; diversity training, 42, 52–54, 289; moral education, anti-discrimination and, 52–53, 116–20, 159, 240–42. *See also* critical pedagogy; equity pedagogy; higher education; multicultural education; "multicultural ideology" (Banks); Title IV (1964 Act); Title IX
  institutions, federal, 5, 45–47
  institutions, social (non-governmental), 5–6, 66–67, 82–84
  moral categories of, 235–36, 243, 250–74. *See also* compensatory justice; corrective justice; equality, conflicting theories of; equity; identity; recognition; representation, conflicting theories of; respect; social justice
  moral ideal primary, 5, 235, 237–38, 241
  offices/officers, 53–55
  origin of idea, 27
  party realignment theory and, 66
  punitive dimension, 55, 58–60, 119, 265–71

  radicalized by postmodernism, 136–84
  regime perspective and, 5–6, 20–22, 27, 36–37, 40–41, 108, 151, 229–32, 242–48, 279, 290–96
  theories of, 4, 245, 376n4, 431n19. *See also* "multicultural ideology" (Banks)
  See also anti-discrimination law; group politics, multiculturalism as; interpretations of anti-discrimination; legislating morality; political vs. intellectual history; public-private distinction
anti-rationalism, 143–44, 169
Arendt, Hannah, 32
Aristotle, 146, 230, 233–34, 263, 267, 272
ascription vs. choice
  defining anti-discrimination groups, inadequate for, 253, 433–34n10
  identity (Banks) and, 113, 130, 219–20
ascriptive Americanist order (Smith, R.), 295
assimilation. *See* anti-assimilation
association. *See* freedom of association; voluntary associations
Association for Advancing Quality in Educator Preparation, 82
at will employment, 57

Baker, Gwendolyn, 75, 400n10, 400n11, 409n13
Banks, Cherry A. McGee, 391n5; 400n11
Banks, James A.
  ambitions for multicultural education, 92

civil rights aim pervasive, 397–99n4
influence of, 93, 400–401n11
Marxism rejected by, 15, 94, 402–3n27
multicultural education leader, 93
postmodernism rejected by, 93–94, 178, 180
Race, Culture, and Education (Banks), 398n4
reformist vs. radical, 94
relativism, rejected by, 127
social science and, 94
See also "multicultural ideology" (Banks)
behaviorialism. See social science pluralism
benign neglect, 217, 425n4
Bentley, Arthur, 199–200, 210
Berger, Morroe, 428–29n8
Berlin, Isaiah, 202
Bernstein, David E., 440n2
bias, hidden/unconscious, 62, 284–85, 295
Bias Incident Response Teams, 54
Biden administration equity initiative, 44–47 *passim*
Biden, Joe, 99, 142
Bilingual Education Act (1968), 69, 77, 393n20
Blacks, American, 3, 26–29, 35, 72, 287, 289
Bloom, Allan, 11, 143, 151
Bolick, Clint, 440n2
Bork, Robert, 31, 237
Bostock v. Clayton County, 51, 283, 389n49
Boy Scouts of America, 389n51
Brown, Wendy, 268–71, 409–10n16, 411n28, 439n52, 442n5
Brown v. Board of Education
achievement of, 33
vs. Civil Rights Act of 1964, 33, 76
limitations of, 30–31, 33, 76
Buckley, William F., 34
bullying, anti-discrimination and, 51
Burlington Industries, Inc. v. Ellerth, 43, 56, 389n49
busing, 64, 76, 280

Caldwell, Christopher, 54, 383n21, 389n51, 440n2, 442n9
Canada, 65, 75, 85, 378–79n12
Canadian multiculturalism, 75, 378–79n12
cancel culture, 48–49, 55–58
capitalism
liberal pluralism, not tied to, 18–19, 195
postmodernism and, 145
woke, 43, 83, 395n41
Cardona, Miguel, 377n9
choice. See ascription vs. choice
Christianity, anti-discrimination and, 3, 4, 48, 64, 290, 378n10, 441n2
citizen enforcement, anti-discrimination and, 48, 53–55, 63, 217–18, 288–89
civic education, multicultural education as, 6–8, 91, 98, 103–11, 128, 291
civil-criminal law distinction, anti-discrimination blurs, 58–60
civil rights. See anti-discrimination law; anti-discrimination regime
Civil Rights Act of 1866, 27, 34, 381n7
Civil Rights Act of 1875, 27, 28, 34
Civil Rights Act of 1964
vs. *Brown v. Board of Education*, 33, 76
constitutional stature, 65
education provisions, 76, 78

445

Civil Rights Act of 1964 (cont'd)
  enactment, extraordinary circumstances of, 34–36
  expansions of, 41–43, 47–48
  importance, 33
  opposition to, 31–32
  public-private distinction and, 33, 50, 64, 217, 237–38, 284
  super-statute, 390n58
  See also anti-discrimination law; Titles II; IV; VI; VII
Civil Rights Cases, 28
Civil Rights Commission, 46, 387n33
civil rights movement
  Cold War and, 35–36, 201, 383n20
  decolonization and, 35, 383n19
  success, causes of, 35–36
civil rights realignment (parties), 66
class (economic)
  Banks's multiculturalism and, 402–3n27
  problem for postmodernist multiculturalism, 140, 407–8n7
  See also Marxism
classical liberalism, 18–19, 188
Closing of the American Mind (Bloom), 11
Cochran-Smith, Marilyn, 395–96n43
Cold War, 35–36, 201, 383n20
Coleman Report, 71–72
colleges. *See* higher education
color-blind constitutionalism
  vs. anti-discrimination, 217, 222, 256, 389–90n57
  Banks's criticisms of, 102
  liberalism and, 217, 437n36
  postmodernist multiculturalism criticisms of, 156, 174,
compensatory education, 72–73
compensatory justice
  anti-discrimination moral claim and, 255, 258, 435–36n21

  criticism of, 258–59, 273, 436n22
  representation claims and, 258
  See also corrective justice
conflict theory, 223–24
consent, 187, 189, 197, 236
conservatives
  affirmative action and, 60–61, 276–78
  anti-discrimination expansion and, 389n49
  anti-discrimination for religion, embraced by, 4, 64, 290
  critical race theory, criticism of, 15, 140–41, 408n8, 426–27n21
  legal strategies vs. Left anti-discrimination, 289–90, 388n41
  misinterpret anti-discrimination: affirmative action overemphasis, 60–61, 276–78; equate with liberalism, 19, 276; equate with Marxism, 15, 53, 140, 408n8; equate with postmodernism, 15, 53, 139, 277; equate with relativism, 140; intellectual history overemphasis, 11, 14–15, 140–41, 278
  misinterpret multiculturalism, 115, 139
  misinterpret postmodernist multiculturalism, 140–41, 408n8
constitutional law
  vs. anti-discrimination law, 64–65
  due process rights, 58–59, 64, 203, 281, 289, 379n15
  Equal Protection Clause vs. anti-discrimination, 26, 28, 63
  freedom of association 50, 64, 389n51
  freedom of religion, 64, 252, 281, 420–21n13
  freedom of speech, 51–52, 386–87n30

separate but equal, 29, 32–33, 381–82n8
state action doctrine, 28, 64–65, 380–82nn 7, 8, 389n50
voting rights, 61–62, 260–62, 388n46. *See also* representation, conflicting theories of
See also specific cases, constitutional provisions, and justices
Cornell, Drucilla, 143, 434n15
corporate culture, anti-discrimination influence, 40, 43, 53, 55–57, 395n41
corrective firing, 55–57
corrective justice
anti-discrimination and, 58–60, 234, 238, 266–71
as common good, 120
guilt and, 59–60
inequalities and, 62, 73–74
insult and indignity, central harm of discrimination, 264
multicultural education and, 117–20
postmodernist multiculturalism and, 154–81, 267–68
See also compensatory justice; punitive spirit of anti-discrimination; *ressentiment* analysis (Nietzsche)
Council for the Accreditation of Educator Preparation (CAEP). *See* accreditation standards
counter-hegemony, 164–65
counter-history, 412–13n38
Crenshaw, Kimberlé, 140, 158, 414n55
criminal-civil law distinction, anti-discrimination blurs, 58–60
criminalization of hate, 45, 51, 58, 386–87n30
criminal procedure rights, 58–59, 64, 203, 281, 289, 379n15
critical multiculturalism, 143, 154
critical pedagogy, 138, 141–42, 152–54, 164, 268, 408n9
critical race theory, 14–15
conservative criticism of, 15, 140–41, 408n8, 426–27n21
criticism of anti-discrimination law (exaggerated), 139–40, 157–58, 414n55
postmodernist multiculturalism and, 136, 137, 140–43, 147, 148, 396n43
related critical academic fields and, 142, 147
cross-cultural competency, 108–9
cultural deprivation theory, 72–75, 124–25, 156–57
cultural difference paradigm, 73–76, 125, 227, 392n12
cultural diversity. *See* diversity
cultural identity, stages of (Banks), 107–8, 402n32
cultural Marxism, 15, 53, 140, 408n8
cultural pluralism
Banks on, 69–70, 132, 211
Kallen and, 17, 197–99, 203, 226
as liberal pluralism variant, 17–18, 186–87
vs. multiculturalism, 9, 18, 69–70, 211, 391–92n5
See also liberal pluralism
cultural racism, 160–62
cultural studies, 142–43
culture, multiculturalism and, 74, 128–29, 227–28

D'Souza, Dinesh, 140
Dahl, Robert, 199–201
decentering, 144–55 *passim*, 412–13n38
Declaration of Independence, 19, 31, 131, 197–98, 440–41n2

decolonization, anti-discrimination and, 35, 383n19
deconstruction, 97, 144–55 *passim*, 407n1, 412n38
democracy
    anti-discrimination and, 1, 13, 37, 131, 285
    Banks reconceives, 98
    liberal, 2, 18, 236, 379n15
demonetization, 57
Department of Education, 43, 46, 47, 282
Department of Justice, 46, 62, 260
Department of Labor, 46, 47, 52
deplatforming, 4, 57
Derrida, Jacques, 140, 145–46, 147, 410n20, 414n55
descriptive representation. *See* representation, conflicting theories of
desegregation
    of education 31, 49–50, 280
    multicultural education and, 64, 71, 76–79, 394n31
Desegregation Assistance Centers. *See* Equity Assistance Centers
Dewey, John, 197, 200, 421n18
DiAngelo, Robin, 14, 170
disability discrimination 41, 74, 77, 180
discrimination
    Banks's account of, 99–103
    concept, expanded under Title VII, 41–44, 61–62. *See also* disparate treatment vs. disparate impact; harassment prohibitions; public-private distinction; stereotype prohibitions
    identified, individual, intentional, 62, 101–2, 174
    liberal pluralism and, 185, 212–13, 419–20n11, 424–25n2
    postmodernist multiculturalism's account of, 158–62
    reverse, 48, 53
    societal, structural, systemic, 62, 101–2, 174
    undefined by anti-discrimination law, 42
disparate treatment vs. disparate impact
    legal claims, 41, 61, 65, 73, 174, 283–84, 388n45
    moral claims, 73–74, 257, 283–84
disparity-as-discrimination, 60–63, 174, 283
diversity
    defined by politics, not demographics, 22, 377n5, 426n17, 433–34n10
    legalistic meaning (affirmative action), 388n45, 425n15
    liberal pluralism and, 195, 228
    multiculturalism and, 22, 227–28, 426n17
    as rhetoric, 22, 227–28, 388n45
Diversity, Equity, and Inclusion offices, 54
diversity officers, 47, 54
diversity statements, 51, 57, 289
diversity training, 42, 52–54, 289
Dobbin, Frank, 384n10, 395n41
due process rights, 58–59, 64, 203, 281, 289, 379n15

Edelman, Lauren, 384n7
education, anti-discrimination and
    civic education, multicultural education as, 6–8, 11–12, 91, 98, 103–11, 128, 291
    diversity training, 42, 52–54, 289
    Education and Training Administration, Dept. of Labor, 52
    EEOC Training Institute, 52
    as moral education, 52–53, 116–20, 159, 240–42

teacher education and, 6, 9–10, 68–69, 76, 79, 81–84, 138–39
  See also critical pedagogy; equity pedagogy; higher education; multicultural education; "multicultural ideology" (Banks); Title IV (1964 Act); Title IX
educational inequality, 63, 71–75, 91, 103–4, 123–24
Eisenhower, Dwight, 31, 34–35, 383n20
Elementary and Secondary Education Act (1965), 72, 76
Ellerth-Faragher liability test, 43, 56, 389n49
Emergency School Aid Act (1972), 77
employer liability, expansion of (Title VII)
  courts and executive agencies, role of, 42–43
  Ellerth-Faragher liability test, 43, 56, 389n49
  employees and third parties included, 42
  "preventive and corrective measures" and, 53–56
  privatized anti-discrimination enforcement and, 54, 288–89
enforcement, anti-discrimination
  civil-criminal hybrid, 58–60
  corrective firing, 55–57
  diversity training, 42, 52–54
  government institutions, 45–47
  non-governmental institutions, role of, 54
  privatized, 53–55, 288
  psychological effects of, 59–60, 62
Enlightenment, the
  liberal pluralism and, 196, 255, 285
  postmodernist multiculturalism and, 145, 155, 175–76
Epstein, Richard, 17, 276

Equal Employment Opportunity Act (1972), 41
Equal Employment Opportunity Commission (EEOC), 46
  enforcement power, 41
  "preventive and corrective measures", 54–56
  Title VII, role in shaping, 41–43, 387n38
  Training Institute, 52
Equal Protection Clause, Fourteenth Amendment, 26–28, 30, 63, 64. *See also* public-private distinction
equality, conflicting theories of, 243 (table 2)
  equal opportunity, 256
  equal outcomes, 122–25, 256–57, 260
  equal protection of the law, 256
  equal status situations for groups: and equal outcomes, 124–25, 127, 256–57; as moral claim (Banks), 122–23; origins in social science, 123, 405–6n70; powerful ideal, 123, 257
  equity and, 125, 257, 273
  political vs. social equality, 30–32, 50
  See also disparate treatment vs. disparate impact; disparity-as-discrimination
equity, 125, 257, 273
Equity Assistance Centers (federal), 77
  support multicultural education, 78–79, 84
  Title IV funding, 394n27
equity pedagogy, 118, 124, 240, 399n4, 405n62
essentialism, 144
ethical pluralism. *See* values pluralism
Ethnic Heritage Studies Program statute (1972), 77, 78

faction, 186, 191, 195–97, 212, 219, 265, 421n15
Faragher v. City of Boca Raton, 43, 56, 389n49
Federalist 10, 17, 111, 192, 195–97
feminism, third wave, 142
First Amendment. *See* freedom of association; freedom of religion; freedom of speech; separation of church and state
Fish, Stanley, 143, 147–48, 152, 407n1, 410–11nn 22, 27, 28, 442n5
five faces of oppression (Young), 158, 414n55
Forbes, H. Donald, 263, 264
Forbes, Jack, 71, 74–75, 400–401n11
Foucault, Michel, 144–45, 147
Foundation for Individual Rights and Expression (FIRE), 386n29
Fourteenth Amendment. *See* Equal Protection Clause
Frankfurt School, 59, 140
freedom
   Banks and, 131–34, 212
   discrimination and, 220
   group politics, effect on, 194, 215, 218–19, 230–31
   identity, contrasted with, 250–54
   individualism and, 69, 188–89, 191, 194, 197–98, 215, 218
   liberal pluralism and, 188–98, 215–19, 226, 230–31
   Locke, 189, 191–93
   Kallen, 197–98
   reinterpreted by anti-discrimination theorists, 131–34, 433n9
   security and, 191–93
   skepticism and, 193, 207
   See also anti-assimilation; legislating morality; public-private distinction

freedom of association, 31–32
   constitutional right, 64
   constrained view of liberal ideal, 389n51
   See also voluntary associations
freedom of religion, 26, 64, 203, 252, 280–81, 379n15, 420–21n13
freedom of speech
   anti-discrimination restricts, 4, 20, 40, 51–53, 57, 63–64, 204, 217–18, 240, 280–1, 429–30n9, 441n3
   conservative mandates, 388n41
   constitutional law and, 52, 386–87n30
   liberalism and, 204, 236, 251, 252, 379n15
   See also harassment prohibitions; speech regulation, anti-discrimination and
Free Exercise Clause, 64, 420–21n13. *See also* freedom of religion
free market, 19, 203. *See also* capitalism
Freire, Paulo, 407–8n7
Freund, Paul, 237, 267

Galston, William, 201, 428n7
Gay, Geneva
   anti-assimilation, 226
   diversity defined politically, 426n17
   equal status ideal, 434–35n15
   on multicultural education origins, 70
   multicultural education theorist, 400–401n11
   postmodernist, 142, 400n10
   postmodernist education principles, 163, 167, 411–12n30
gender identity discrimination, 51, 66, 282–83

Index

Giroux, Henry
  critical pedagogy, 142
  cultural racism, 160–62
  Marxism, problem of, 407–8n7
  moral maladroitness, 163, 415n74
  oppositional utopianism, 167–68
  vs. positivism, 157
  religious spirit, 169
Glazer, Nathan, 8–9, 19, 73, 424–25n2
Gleason, Philip, 421n17, 432n3
global education, 97–98, 404n42
Goldwater, Barry, 31, 36, 54, 284
Gollnick, Donna
  multicultural education theorist, 400–401nn 10, 11
  surveys of multicultural education literature, 393–94n26
  surveys of multicultural education policy, 79–80
Gordon, Milton, 405–6n70, 424n1
Gorsuch, Neil, 389n49,
Graham, Hugh Davis, 19, 44, 277, 435–36n21
Gramsci, Antonio, 146, 426–27n21. *See also* Marxism
Grand Canyon (film), 161–62
Grant, Carl
  categorization of Banks, 402n18
  multicultural education theorist, 70, 84, 400–401n11
  postmodernist, 141–42
  social reconstructionist multiculturalism, 402n18
Great Society, 441n3. *See also* New Deal
Griggs v. Duke Power Co., 61, 389n49, 392n13
group-differentiated logic of multiculturalism, 100–101, 131, 220, 223–24, 228–29, 403n28
group identity. *See* identity

group inequality. *See* cultural deprivation theory; cultural difference paradigm; disparate treatment vs. disparate impact
group politics, anti-discrimination and. *See* group politics, multiculturalism as
group politics, liberal pluralism as, 187, 188–94, 225 (table 1)
  depoliticizing effect, 192, 214–15, 218–19, 236, 264–65
  discrimination and, 185, 212–13, 419–20n11, 424–25n2
  diversity defined in, 195, 228
  group claims deliberately minimized, 194, 207, 216, 218–22
  group conflict and, 191, 196, 206, 212
  group-group relationship, 214–15, 222
  group-individual relationship, 194, 219, 220–21
  groups characterized generally, 18, 194–99, 207, 212, 218–19, 228. *See also* faction; voluntary associations
  group-state relationship, 194, 203, 216–17, 219
  individualism and, 188, 194, 198, 218
  interest claims and, 192, 196, 263–65
  limited government, and, 193–94, 202–4
  moral categories of, 189, 235–36, 243 (table 2), 250–74. *See also* consent; equality, conflicting theories of; freedom; individualism; interest claims; natural right; representation, conflicting theories of; toleration; voluntarism

451

group politics, liberal pluralism as *(cont'd)*
  multiculturalism, contrasted with, 209–32
  peace aim, 191–93, 195–96, 198, 202, 206–7, 433n8
  pessimism, 197, 211–12
  psychological dimension, 191–92, 196, 263–65. *See also* interest claims
  realism of, 191–96, 200, 205–6
  religion and, 187–96
  security aim, 190–93, 419n8
  skepticism of, 189–90, 195, 196, 197, 201–2, 204, 228–29
  success of, 206–7, 230, 235
  See also liberal pluralism
group politics, multiculturalism as, 128–31, 225 (table 1)
  discrimination and, 128–29, 213–14
  education, role of, 131, 217–18, 226–27
  group conflict and, 130, 223–24, 231
  group-differentiated logic, 100–101, 114, 131, 220, 223–24, 228–29, 403n28
  group-group relationship, 130, 222–23
  group-individual relationship, 129, 130, 220–21
  groups: characterized generally, 18, 128–30, 219–20, 227–28, 278; dangers of, 113–14, 213–14; defined by law, 47–48; excluded vs. dominant groups, 101, 129–30, 222–23. *See also* ascription vs. choice
  group-state relationship, 130–31, 217–18, 229
  in-group, out-group dynamic, 113, 130

liberal pluralism contrasted with, 209–32
moral categories of, 116–20, 235–36, 243 (table 2), 250–74. *See also* compensatory justice; corrective justice; equality, conflicting theories of; equity; identity; recognition; representation, conflicting theories of; respect; social justice
morally charged, 117–18, 215–16, 220, 229–30
peace and, 224
pessimism of, 130, 212–13
politicization of groups, 105–7, 220–24, 228–32
psychological dimension, 59–60, 62, 111–16, 250–54, 263–65, 267–71
public-private distinction inadequate for, 217–18, 220, 229–32
See also "multicultural ideology" (Banks); multiculturalism
group representation. *See* representation, conflicting theories of
group rights, 257
  Banks and, 406n87
  criticism of, 257, 435n18
groups. *See* group politics, liberal pluralism as; group politics, multiculturalism as
group theory, general social scientific, 210–11, 243–44, 419n10
Guinier, Lani, 260–61, 436n27

harassment prohibitions
  criminal-civil distinction blurred, 58–59
  discrimination concept expanded by, 42
  hostile work (educational, public accommodations, online) environment, 42, 384n5

Index

objective and subjective factors, harassment defined by, 386n25
"preventive and corrective measures" and, 54–56
regulation of social relations/society, 50–51
regulation of speech and thought, 51–53, 64, 386–87n30
Title VII and, 41–42
Harris v. Forklift Systems, 386–87n30, 389n49
hate crimes regulation, 45, 51, 58, 386–87n30
hate speech regulation, 4, 51
hegemony, 146, 159, 164, 229, 426–27n21. *See also* Gramsci
Heidegger, Martin, 11, 138, 150, 410n20
hidden bias/prejudice, 62, 284–85, 295
high culture, anti-discrimination influence, 390–91n61
higher education
  anti-discrimination and, 51–53 *passim*, 64, 288
  multicultural education and, 81–82
  postmodernism and, 143
  racial segregation of, 76
  Title IX and, 43–44, 58, 64, 282–83
Hirsch, E.D., 110
history. *See* political vs. intellectual history
Hollinger, David, 134
Honneth, Axel, 125, 263
honor. *See* recognition
hooks, bell, 143
hostile environment harassment prohibitions. *See* harassment prohibitions
Hume, David, 196, 265, 421n15

identified discrimination, 62, 73, 102

identity, 111, 250
  ascriptive characteristics, 113, 130, 254, 433–34n10
  as cause of discrimination, 113, 253–54
  criticisms of claims from, 251–54
  democratic debate limited by, 251
  freedom and, 250–54
  good, the, and, 251–52
  groups and, 113, 252–53
  harm to, from discrimination, 111–12
  in-groups/out-groups and, 113
  malleable, 113
  moral status, 111–12, 116–17, 250
  postmodernist critique of (qualified), 149, 412n32
  protection from discrimination and, 129
  socially constructed, 113–14
  social science and, 432n3
  theories of, general, 250, 432n3
  See also ascription vs. choice; "multicultural ideology" (Banks): identity; Tajfel
identity reconstruction, 253–54. *See also* "multicultural ideology" (Banks): identity reconstruction
Illinois multicultural education, 69, 79
inclusion. *See* representation, conflicting theories of
individualism, 188–91, 194, 197–98, 250, 261, 281
inequality. *See* disparity-as-discrimination
inequality, educational, 63, 71–75, 91, 103–4, 123–24
in-groups/out-groups, 113
injustice, starting point of anti-discrimination, 117–20, 258–59, 266–68

453

institutional leapfrogging, 384n11
institutions, anti-discrimination
 governmental, 45–47
 social (non-governmental), 5–6, 66–67, 82–84
insult and indignity, central harm of discrimination, 264
insurgent multiculturalism, 154
integration, 123, 224, 262, 272, 284
intellectual history and anti-discrimination. *See* political vs. intellectual history
intellectuals and anti-discrimination, 137, 141–43
intentional discrimination, 62, 73, 103
intercultural education, 391n5
interest claims, liberal pluralism and
 compromise and, 196, 264
 de-moralize group politics, 192, 196, 264
 Federalist 10 and, 196
 Hume, 196
 Locke, 192
 vs. recognition, 263–65
 social science pluralism, 199–201
interest group pluralism, 17, 186, 196–97, 211, 224, 422n27. *See also* liberal pluralism
intergroup education movement, 391n5
interpretations of anti-discrimination
 affirmative action over-emphasized, 60–61, 276–78
 as ambitious moral-political project, 279
 as *causa sui*, 27
 Cold War and, 35–36, 383n20
 decolonization and, 35, 383n19
 as liberal (standard interpretation), 19, 276, 441n3
 as Marxist/neo-Marxist, 15, 53, 140, 408n8
 as New Deal/Great Society product, 36, 202, 380n1, 390n6, 424n1, 441–42n3
 as originating in post-Civil War political necessity, 27
 as postmodernist, 15, 53, 139, 277
 as relativism, 140
 as secular religion, 377–78n10
 See also political vs. intellectual history
interpretations of multiculturalism, 377–79nn 5, 10, 12
intersectionality, 4, 139–40, 158, 414n55
invidious discrimination, 239
Iowa multicultural education, 69, 79, 80, 281

Jefferson, Thomas, 195, 212, 214, 420–21n13, 426n19
Johnson, Lyndon, 35
Journal of Teacher Education, 83, 395–96n43, 408–9n10

Kallen, Horace
 criticized as inadequately anti-racist, 212, 424–25n2
 cultural pluralism and, 17, 69, 197–99
 individualism of, 198–99
 liberal idealist, 197–98
 misinterpreted as ethno-nationalist, 421n20
 pragmatism and, 197
 realism of, 198
Kateb, George, 253
Kendi, Ibram, 45, 170
Kennedy, Anthony, 389n49,
Kennedy, John F., 34–35, 239, 383n20
Kimball, Roger, 390–91n61

King, Desmond, 440–41n2
King, John B., 377n9
King, Martin Luther, Jr., 31, 34, 237
Kipnis, Laura, 384n11
Knopff, Rainer, 405n54
Kolstad v. American Dental Association, 52–53, 389n49
Koppelman, Andrew
  anti-discrimination as cultural transformation project, 237–38
  anti-discrimination theorist, 376n4
  anti-discrimination vs. liberalism, 17, 276, 429–30n9
  criticism of Rawlsian liberalism, 429–30n9
  indignity, central harm of discrimination, 264
  justified resentment, 267
Kymlicka, Will
  Canadian multiculturalism and, 378–79n12
  influence of, 15, 377n5
  multiculturalism theory: anti-discrimination rejected as starting point, 378–79n12; identity and, 251, 378–79n12, 433n7; and liberal pluralist tradition, 417n1

legislating morality
  anti-discrimination and, 116–20, 128, 237–41, 294
  liberalism and, 110, 236–37, 241, 294
Letter Concerning Toleration (Locke), 187–94, 418n4, 419–20n11
LGBT persons, anti-discrimination and, 4, 51, 66, 236, 255, 260, 282–83, 390n60
liability. *See* employer liability, expansion of

liberalism
  characterized generally, 2, 18–19, 26, 379n15
  classical, 18, 188
  discrimination permitted in private sphere (pre-1964), 26–30, 212, 213, 380–82nn 7, 8
  regime perspective, contrasted with, 193–94, 230–32
  See also constitutional law; freedom; group politics, liberal pluralism as; legislating morality; liberal pluralism; natural right; political vs. social equality; public-private distinction; representation, conflicting theories of
liberalization, 219
liberal pluralism
  characterized generally, 186–88, 205–8
  cultural pluralism (Kallen), 17, 69, 197–99
  depoliticizing effect, 192, 214–15, 218–19, 236, 264–65
  discrimination and, 185, 212–13, 419–20n11, 424–25n2
  Federalist 10 and, 17, 111, 192, 195–97
  interest group pluralism, 17, 186, 196–97, 211, 224, 422n27
  Locke and, 187–96, 204, 418–21nn 4–15 *passim*
  moral categories of, 189, 235–36, 243 (table 2), 250–74. *See also* consent; equality, conflicting theories of; freedom; individualism; interest claims; natural right; representation, conflicting theories of; toleration; voluntarism

liberal pluralism (cont'd)
  multiculturalism, contrasted with:
    group politics, 209–32; legal
    foundations, 25–67; moral categories,
    249–74; morality-politics relation, 233–48
  peace aim, 191–93, 195–96, 198,
    202, 206–7, 433n8
  political liberalism (Rawls), 186,
    188, 204–5, 423nn 40, 41
  social science pluralism, 199–201
  values pluralism, 201–3
  See also group politics, liberal pluralism as;
    realism of liberal pluralism; religious pluralism;
    skepticism of liberal pluralism
liberty. *See* freedom
liberty of conscience, 189, 204, 418n4
limited government, 18, 26, 193–94,
  202–5, 236, 418–20nn 9, 11
Lincoln, Abraham, 132, 417n104
Lindsay, James, 141, 408n8
Locke, John, 187–96, 204, 418–21
  nn4–15 *passim*
Loury, Glenn, 288
Lowi, Theodore, 419n10, 424n1
ludic postmodernism, 151

MacIver, Robert, 34
MacKinnon, Catherine
  anti-discrimination theorist, 58,
    376n4
  harassment law architect, 41–42,
    376n4
Madison, James, 111, 186, 192, 195–
  99, 212, 420–21nn 13, 15
Marcuse, Herbert, 11, 431n18,
  434n11
Marx, Karl, 1, 11
Marxism
  Banks rejects, 15, 94, 402–3n27
  conflict theory, 224
  conservative account of anti-discrimination and, 15, 53, 140,
    408n8
  Gramsci, 146, 426–27n21
  neo-Marxism and, 83, 140, 408n8
  postmodernist multiculturalism
    and, 140, 407–8n7
McLaren, Peter
  critical pedagogy, 142
  criticized by Fish, 152
  discrimination characterized by, 160
  Marxism, problem of, 407–8n7
  religion, rejected by, 415n75
  revolutionary multiculturalism,
    166, 168–69
  social dreaming, 168
McWhorter, John, 1, 57–58, 287
Melnick, Shep
  anti-discrimination contrasted
    with liberalism, 440n11
  institutional leapfrogging, 384n11
  social science perspective, 379n18
  stereotype prohibitions, implications of, 282
  Title VII, foundation of Title IX,
    384nn 2, 11
  on Title IX, 43–44, 282, 384n11
melting pot, 226, 425n13
merit
  affirmative action and, 60–63
  critique of, 63, 174, 255, 284,
    434n13
  respect and, 255
Meritor Savings Bank v. Vinson, 386–
  87n30, 389n49
microaggressions, 4, 51, 102
Minnesota multicultural education,
  69, 79
minority groups. *See* anti-discrimination law: groups (protected
  classes); group politics, multiculturalism as

moral categories, 243 (table 2)
   of liberal pluralism, 189, 235–36, 250–74. *See also* consent; equality, conflicting theories of; freedom; individualism; interest claims; natural right; representation, conflicting theories of; toleration; voluntarism
   of multiculturalism, 116–20, 235–36, 250–74. *See also* compensatory justice; corrective justice; equality, conflicting theories of; equity; identity; recognition; representation, conflicting theories of; respect; social justice
moral education, anti-discrimination and, 52–53, 116–20, 159, 240–41
morality and politics. *See* politics and morality
moral pluralism. *See* values pluralism
Mouffe, Chantal, 167, 426–27n21, 432–33n4
Moynihan, Daniel Patrick, 19, 71–72, 256–57, 425n4
multicultural education
   academic subdiscipline, 9, 69, 82–84
   accreditation standards, 9, 69, 76, 81–82
   civic education, 6–8, 91, 98, 103–11, 128, 291
   history, 68–82
   journals, 83–84, 396–97n46. *See also Journal of Teacher Education*
   legal underpinnings: desegregation plans, 79; federal, 69, 75–79; state and local, 79–82
   origins, 69–75
   overlooked, 15–16
   postmodernism and, 141–42
   teacher education and, 68–69, 76, 79, 81–84

"multicultural ideology" (Banks)
   American identity reconceived, 95–97
   vs. Anglo-American Centric Model, 109
   anti-discrimination logic pervades, 90, 397–99n4
   civic education, 6–8, 91, 98, 103–11, 128, 291
   corrective justice, 119–20
   cross-cultural competency, 108–9
   vs. cultural pluralism, 9, 18, 69–70, 132, 211, 391–92n5
   cultural transformation and, 95–99
   Curriculum for Dominant Groups vs. Curriculum for Oppressed Groups, 100–101
   democracy reconceived, 98
   discrimination characterized, 101–2
   education, political role, 103–11
   educational inequalities, 91, 103–4, 123–4
   Enlightening Powerful Groups Model, 100–101
   equality: equal opportunity, 123, 405n68; equal outcomes, 124–25; equal status situations for groups, 123, 125, 405–6n70; equity, 125
   equity pedagogy, 63, 118, 124, 240, 399n4, 405n62
   five dimensions of, 399n4
   freedom reconceived, 131–34
   general vs. narrow political orientation, 99–103, 114
   global education, 97–98, 404n42
   group-differentiated teaching, 101, 109, 114, 131, 229, 403n28

"multicultural ideology" (Banks) (*cont'd*)
   identity: ascriptive characteristics, 113, 230; cause of discrimination, 113; harm of discrimination and, 111–12; in-groups/out-groups and, 113; moral status 111–12; protects against discrimination, 129; psychological concept, 111–12; social construction of, 113–14;
   identity reconstruction: anti-discrimination aim, 114–15; citizenship identity, 115; group differentiated (majority/minority), 114–15; optimistic, 114; solution to identity problems, 113–14; Stage 5 individual, 115, 253
   inclusion (voice), 103, 120, 125–26
   knowledge construction, 117, 399n4
   liberalism and, 131–34
   Marxism rejected, 15, 94, 402–3n27
   moral education, 116–20, 240–41
   "multicultural ideology" term, 399n5
   postmodernism rejected, 93–94, 178, 180
   power and, 100–102, 106, 123, 223–24
   prejudice reduction, 104–5, 114–15, 122, 240, 399n4
   psychological assumptions, 111–16, 250
   racial attitudes, modification of, 104–5
   radicalizing oppressed students, 106–7
   reflective self-analysis, 118, 240
   reformist vs. radical, 94–95, 105–6, 402n18
   relativism rejected, 127
   respect vs. recognition, 125
   self-esteem education rejected, 115, 405n59
   Shared Power Model, 100–101
   Stage 5 individual, 108, 115, 253
   stages of cultural identity, 107–8, 402n23
   synoptic overviews, 399n4
   systemic discrimination, 101–2
   teaching political activism, 105–7
   value inquiry model, 118, 240
   West, the, reconceived, 97
   See also Banks, James A.; group politics, multiculturalism as; multicultural education; multiculturalism

multiculturalism
   Canadian, 378–79n12
   characterized generally, 8–9, 12–13, 84–85, 275
   vs. cultural pluralism, 9, 18, 69–70, 132, 211, 391–92n5
   interpretations of, 377–79nn 5, 10, 12
   liberal pluralism, contrasted with: group politics, 209–32; legal foundations, 25–67; moral categories, 249–74; morality-politics relation, 233–48
   multicultural education and, 2–3, 6–10, 84–85
   pluralism, form of, 128–31
   See also group politics, multiculturalism as; multicultural education; "multicultural ideology" (Banks); postmodernist multiculturalism
Myrdal, Gunnar, 34

National Association for Multicultural Education (NAME), 84, 141, 166–67, 397n48, 426n17

National Council for the Accreditation of Teacher Education (NCATE)
  accreditation standards, multicultural education, 69, 81
  early role in multicultural education, 69, 81–82, 393–94n26, 395n38
National Council for the Social Studies (NCSS), 83, 121, 395–96n43, 401n12
National Education Association (NEA), 76, 78
natural right, 114, 116, 145, 189, 199–200, 205, 418n4
neo-Marxism, 83, 140, 408n8. *See also* Marxism
New Criterion, 390–91n61
New Deal, 36, 202, 380n1, 390n60, 424n1, 441–42n3
New York State anti-discrimination policy, 31, 34
Nieto, Sonia, 6, 84, 141–42, 242, 400–401n11, 411–12n30
Nietzsche, Friedrich, 11, 143, 146–47, 268–71, 410n20, 411n25
Nixon, Richard, 78

Obama, Barack, 9
O'Connor, Sandra Day, 52–53, 261, 389n49
Office of Civil Rights, Department of Education 43
Office of Federal Contract Compliance Programs (OFCCP), 46–47
Office of Small and Disadvantaged Business Utilization (OSDBU), 47
offices/officers, anti-discrimination, 53–55
Olson, Mancur, 210
originalism, multiculturalism and, 13

Owen, J. Judd, 423n40
party realignment theory, anti-discrimination and, 66
Paul, Rand, 383n21
Pedagogy of the Oppressed (Freire), 407–8n7
personnel management profession, political role of, 83, 395n41
Plessy v. Ferguson, 29, 32
pluralism
  characterized generally, 2–3, 209
  obscures politics, 2, 209, 230–31
  rhetoric, 226–28
  social science and, 210–11, 243–44, 419n10
  See also diversity; group politics, liberal pluralism as; group politics, multiculturalism as
political correctness, 4, 11, 48, 242
political education, anti-discrimination and. *See* education, anti-discrimination and
political liberalism (Rawls), 186, 188, 204–5, 423nn 40, 41
political psychology
  anti-discrimination effects on citizens, 59–60, 62, 250–54, 263–65, 267–71
  liberal pluralism and, 191–92, 196, 263–65
  multiculturalism and, 111–16, 250, 263
political science
  anti-discrimination and, 21–22, 291–96
  liberal view of politics and, 294
  Nietzsche and, 146–47
  vs. regime perspective, 210–11, 291–94
  scientific method, limitations of, 210–11, 243–44, 292–96
  See also regime perspective

political vs. intellectual history, anti-discrimination and, 10–11, 14–15, 27, 140–41, 377–78nn 5, 10, 432n3, 437–38nn 44, 47
political vs. social equality, 30–32, 50
politics. *See* regime perspective
politics and morality
    anti-discrimination and, 117–19, 233, 235, 237–38, 241–42, 245–46
    considered generally, 233–34, 243–44
    liberalism and, 235, 236–37, 242
    See also legislating morality
politics of difference (Young), 4, 136, 139–40, 143, 222, 414n55, 440n2
politics of recognition (Taylor), 4, 125, 263–64, 437–39nn 44, 47, 49
polyarchy, 200, 201
postmodernism
    anti-essentialism, 144
    characterized generally, 143–48
    critical orientation, 147, 155–58
    epistemological claims, 143–44, 410n20
    humanly incomplete, 147–48
    ludic vs. political, 151
    morality and, 144–46, 410–11n22
    politics and, 146–47
    relativism and, 143
    See also postmodernist multiculturalism
postmodernist critics of multiculturalism
    Left, 152, 268–71, 411n28
    Right, 138
postmodernist multiculturalism
    anti-discrimination law, critique of (exaggerated), 139–40, 157–58, 414n55
    combines disparate elements, 137–39, 141–43

    conservative misinterpretation of, 140–41, 408n8
    critical pedagogy and, 141–42, 155
    critical race theory and, 136, 137, 140–42, 147, 178, 396n43
    discrimination concept, magnified by, 158–62
    Enlightenment, criticism of, 145, 155, 175–76
    liberalism, criticism of, 145, 156, 413n50
    Marxism, problem of, 140–41, 407–8n7
    moral maladroitness of, 162–65
    multicultural education and, 141–42, 166–67
    nature, criticism of, 156–57, 413n51
    origins, 136, 141–43
    politics over theory, 137, 139–41, 148–51, 412n31
    politics radicalized by theory, 139, 145–48, 154–58, 165–67
    politics-theory contradiction, 151–52, 169
    punitive spirit, 267–68
    religious spirit, 169
    return of the political (Mouffe), 229, 426–27n21
    rhetoric, 170, 172, 175, 178
    self-doubting, 168–69
    theory radicalized by politics, 139, 153–54
    utopian, 167–69
    Whiteness theory, 139, 169–76
    See also postmodernism; postmodernist critics of multiculturalism
power/knowledge, 145–46
pragmatism, 148, 197–98, 200, 407n1, 421n18
prejudice, hidden/unconscious, 62, 284–85, 295

prejudice reduction, 104–5, 114–15, 122, 240, 399n4
"preventive and corrective measures", 42–43, 53–58, 384n7
Price Waterhouse v. Hopkins, 386–87n30
private sector discrimination. *See* public-private distinction
privatized enforcement of anti-discrimination, 48, 53–55, 63, 217–18, 288–89
privilege, disparity-as-discrimination and, 62–63, 230, 270
property, 27, 188, 203, 205, 293
proportional representation. *See* representation, conflicting theories of
psychological assumptions. *See* political psychology
public-private distinction
    anti-discrimination (post-1964) and, 30–33, 44, 48–58, 63–65, 67, 217–18, 277, 288–89
    critique of, 64–65, 389n56
    discrimination protected by (pre-1964), 26–30, 212–13, 256, 380–82nn 7, 8
    liberal democratic political understanding and, 26, 193–94, 202–4, 207, 216–17, 230–31, 236–37
    See also legislating morality; politics and morality; political vs. social equality; state action doctrine
punitive spirit of anti-discrimination
    corrective firing, 55–57
    legal aspect, 58–60
    moral aspect, 59–60, 117–20, 238–40, 265–68, 280
    postmodernist multiculturalism and, 154–81, 267–68

ressentiment analysis (Nietzsche), anti-discrimination and (Brown), 268–71
See also compensatory justice; corrective justice

race treason, 173
racial liberalism, 380n1
racism. *See* discrimination
radical vs. reformist multiculturalism, 94–95, 105–6, 137–39, 152–58, 402n18
Ramaswamy, Vivek, 440–41n2
rational choice theory, 210, 244
R.A.V. v. City of St. Paul, 386–87n30
Ravitch, Diane, 84
Rawls, John
    criticized by anti-discrimination Left, 429–30n9
    liberal pluralism and, 186, 188, 202–5
    moralistic realism, 204–5, 423n41
    political liberalism, 186, 188, 204–5, 423nn 40, 41
    skepticism of, 204–5, 423n41
Raz, Joseph, 422n33
realism of liberal pluralism, 187, 193–94
    interest group pluralism, 196
    Kallen, 198
    Locke, 191–93
    Madison, 195–96
    Rawls, 204–5, 423n41
    social science pluralism, 200
    values pluralism, 202, 423n35
recognition
    anti-discrimination and, 125, 263–65
    criticism of, 263
    denial of, as harm of discrimination, 438n47
    group conflict and, 263–65
    vs. interest, 263–65

recognition (*cont'd*)
　politics of (Taylor), 4, 125, 263–64, 437–39nn 44, 47, 49
　vs. redistribution, 125, 437n44
　reductionist (excludes moral claim), 125
　vs. respect, 125
redistribution vs. recognition, 125, 437n44
reformist vs. radical multiculturalism, 94–95, 105–6, 137–39, 152–58, 402n18
regime perspective
　anti-discrimination politics, and, 5–6, 20–22, 27, 36–37, 40–41, 108, 151, 229–32, 242–48, 279, 290–96
　characterized generally, 21–22, 36–37, 233–35, 290–96, 442n12
　liberalism contrasted with, 36–37, 48–49, 66–67, 178, 194, 231–32, 236–37, 288, 418–19n9, 427n3
　vs. scientific approach to politics, 210–11, 291–94
Rehnquist, William, 386–87n30, 389n49
relativism
　anti-discrimination and, 4, 29–30, 48, 64, 430n16
　Banks rejects, 127
　Iowa and, 281
　postmodernist multiculturalism and, 140, 144, 281–82
　See also skepticism of liberal pluralism
religious conservatives, anti-discrimination and, 4, 48, 64
religious diversity
　Jefferson, 228
　Locke, 189, 191–92

religious freedom, 26, 64, 203, 252, 280–81, 379n15, 420–21n13
religious pluralism
　American founders and, 195–96
　liberal pluralism and, 187–88
　Locke and, 188–94
　Supreme Court and, 420–21n13
reparations, 4, 259, 289
representation, conflicting theories of
　anti-discrimination, 125–26, 260, 436n26
　compensatory justice and, 258
　Democratic Party and, 260, 436n29
　descriptive, 260
　inclusion and, 125–26, 259–60
　liberal: limits of individualism, 437n34; one person, one vote, 261; *Reynolds v. Sims*, 261; realism of, 261–62
　mirror, 260
　proportionality, 260, 436n27
　social science interest in (recent), 260
　voice and, 125–26, 259–60
resistance multiculturalism, 154
resistance theory, 167, 224
respect
　merit and, 255
　principled foundation unclear, 255
　as toleration, 434n11
　vs. toleration, 254
ressentiment analysis (Nietzsche), anti-discrimination and (Brown), 268–71
reverse discrimination, 48, 53
revolutionary multiculturalism, 154, 166, 168–69
rhetoric
　anti-assimilation as, 226–27
　Banks and, 18, 94–95
　diversity as, 18, 227–28, 426n15

462

postmodernist multiculturalism and, 179
postmodernist Whiteness theory as, 170–75
right of association. *See* freedom of association; voluntary associations
right of exit, 218, 423n35
rights, natural, 114, 116, 145, 189, 199–200, 205, 418n4
Rorty, Richard, 140, 241, 407n1, 411n28

Scalia, Antonin, 50, 389n49
Schlesinger, Arthur, 19, 84
security
  freedom and, 193, 206
  liberal pluralism aim, 190–91, 207
self-esteem education, 115, 405n59
self-interest. *See* interest claims
separate but equal, 29, 32–33, 381–82n8
separation of church and state, 4, 26, 64, 188, 193, 203, 216, 236
sex discrimination, 22, 43–44, 50–51, 56, 58, 281–83
sexual harassment. *See* harassment prohibitions
sexual orientation discrimination, 51, 283
Shaw v. Reno, 261, 388n46
skepticism of liberal pluralism, 187
  Kallen, 197
  Locke, 189–90
  Madison, 197
  vs. postmodernist skepticism, 228–29
  Rawls, 204–5, 423n40
  social science pluralism, 200
  values pluralism, 201–2
Skrentny, John, 379n18
slavery, 32, 286, 430–31n16

Sleeter, Christine
  categorization of Banks, 401n18
  multicultural education theorist, 19–20, 84, 400–401n11
  postmodernist, 141–42, 167
  resistance theory, 167, 224
  rhetorical strategies, 179
  social reconstructionist multiculturalism 402n18
Smith, Adam, 421n15
Smith, Rogers, 295, 382n18, 440–41n2
social construction theory, 146, 407n1, 410n20, 416–17n100
social institutions, anti-discrimination (non-governmental), 5–6, 66–67, 82–84
social justice, 127, 249
social movement theory, 210, 211, 432n3
social reconstructionist multiculturalism, 154, 402n18
social science. *See* political science
social science group theory, 210–211, 243–44, 419n10
social science pluralism, 199–201
social vs. political equality, 30–32, 50
societal discrimination, 62, 73, 101–2, 392n13
speech regulation, anti-discrimination and
  cancel culture, 48–49, 55–58
  hate speech regulation, 4, 51
  hostile environment harassment regulation, 41–42, 51
  other anti-discrimination laws restricting speech, 51–52, 64, 386–87n30
  See also freedom of speech
stages of cultural identity (Banks), 107–8, 402n32

state action doctrine
  constitutional law, 28, 64–65, 380–81n7, 381–82n8
  critique of, 389n50
status. *See* equality, conflicting theories of: equal status situations for groups; recognition
stereotype prohibitions
  discrimination concept expanded by, 42
  implications, 282–83
  intimate matters, regulation of, 50–51
  social relations, speech, thought, regulation of, 51–53
  Title VII and, 41–42
strategic essentializing, 165, 179
Strauss, Leo, 29–30, 211
student fault vs. system fault, 73–74, 124
successor ideology, 1, 376n1
Supreme Court
  private-sector discrimination protected by (pre-1964), 26–30, 380–82nn 5, 7, 8
  Title VII, expanded by (post-1964), 41–43, 51, 52, 56, 61–64, 239, 389n49
  See also constitutional law; public-private distinction; state action doctrine; *specific cases, constitutional provisions, and justices*
systemic discrimination, 62, 73, 101–2, 392n13

Tajfel, Henri, 113, 432n3
teacher education, 6, 9–10, 68–69, 76, 79, 81–84, 138–39
theories of anti-discrimination, 4, 245, 376n4, 431n19. *See also* "multicultural ideology" (Banks)
Thernstrom, Abigail, 61, 260
Thomas, Clarence, 262
Thornburg v. Gingles, 388n46
Title II (1964 Act), 33, 44, 49, 239, 284
Title IV (1964 Act), 71, 76, 78, 394n27
Title VI (1964 Act), 44, 46, 76
Title VII (1964 Act)
  center of anti-discrimination law, 33, 40–41
  criminal-civil law distinction blurred, 58–60
  discrimination concept expanded under, 41–44. *See also* disparate treatment vs. disparate impact; harassment prohibitions; stereotype prohibitions
  employer liability, expansion of, 42–45, 53–54, 288–89
  "preventive and corrective measures", 42–43, 53–58
  privatized enforcement and, 48, 53–55, 63, 217–18, 288–89
  society, regulation of, 40, 49–51
  speech regulation, 41–42, 51
  See also anti-discrimination law
Title IX (Education Amendments of 1972), 9, 76
  due process and, 64
  implications, 282–83
  offices/officers, 54
  speech regulation, 51
  Title VII and, 43–44
toleration
  Banks and, 121, 405n66
  discrimination and, 254
  liberal pluralism and, 189, 190
  Locke and, 188–94
  realism of, 191–93, 194, 206
  as respect, 434n11
  vs. respect, 120–21, 254–55
transgressive multiculturalism, 154

Truman, David, 199–201, 210, 422n30
Trump, Donald, 142

unconscious bias/prejudice, 62, 284–85, 295
universities. *See* higher education

value inquiry model (Banks), 118, 240
values pluralism, 201–3
virtue signaling, 4, 242
virtues, liberal, 428n7
voice. *See* representation, conflicting theories of
Voltaire, 284
voluntarism, 189, 194
voluntary associations
    anti-discrimination, contrasted with, 215, 218, 220–22
    freedom of association (constitutional law), 50, 64, 389n51
    liberal pluralism and, 18, 26, 31–32, 199, 204, 389n51, 425n6
    Locke and, 189, 194
voting rights, 61–62, 260–62, 388n46. *See also* representation, conflicting theories of

Walzer, Michael, 202
Webster, Noah, 89
West, Cornel, 143
White reason, 175–76
Whiteness theory (postmodernist), 169–76
Williams, Melissa, 258, 260, 262
Wisconsin v. Mitchell, 386–87n30
woke capitalism, 1, 43, 83, 395n41
workplace liability. *See* employer liability, expansion of

Young, Iris Marion
    anti-discrimination law, criticism of (exaggerated), 139–40, 157–58, 414n55
    Banks and, 403n28
    politics of difference, 4, 136, 139–40, 143, 222, 414n55, 440n2

Zintz, Miles, 392n16